Canadian Democracy

An Introduction

P9-BIM-977

Canadian Democracy

An Introduction

Fourth Edition Stephen Brooks

OXFORD

UNIVERSITY PRESS

1904 ❖ 2004

100 YEARS OF
CANADIAN PUBLISHING

OXFORD
UNIVERSITY PRESS

70 Wynford Drive, Don Mills, Ontario M3C 1J9
www.oup.com/ca

Oxford University Press is a department of the University of Oxford.
It furthers the University's objective of excellence in research, scholarship,
and education by publishing worldwide in

Oxford New York
Auckland Bangkok Buenos Aires Cape Town Chennai
Dar es Salaam Delhi Hong Kong Istanbul Karachi Kolkata
Kuala Lumpur Madrid Melbourne Mexico City Mumbai Nairobi
São Paulo Shanghai Taipei Tokyo Toronto

Oxford is a trade mark of Oxford University Press
in the UK and in certain other countries

Published in Canada
by Oxford University Press

Copyright © Oxford University Press Canada 2004

The moral rights of the author have been asserted

Database right Oxford University Press (maker)

First published 2004

All rights reserved. No part of this publication may be reproduced,
stored in a retrieval system, or transmitted, in any form or by any means,
without the prior permission in writing of Oxford University Press,
or as expressly permitted by law, or under terms agreed with the appropriate
reprographics rights organization. Enquiries concerning reproduction
outside the scope of the above should be sent to the Rights Department,
Oxford University Press, at the address above.

You must not circulate this book in any other binding or cover
and you must impose this same condition on any acquirer.

National Library of Canada Cataloguing in Publication

Brooks, Stephen, 1956–
Canadian democracy : an introduction / Stephen Brooks. — 4th ed.

Includes bibliographical references and index.
ISBN 0-19-541806-9

1. Canada—Politics and government. I. Title.

JL65.1993B76 2003   320.971   C2003-903780-0

Cover and Text Design: Brett J. Miller

1 2 3 4 - 07 06 05 04
This book is printed on permanent (acid-free) paper ∞.
Printed in Canada

CONTENTS

AUGUSTANA UNIVERSITY COLLEGE LIBRARY

LIST OF FIGURES

LIST OF TABLES

PREFACE

When I began this book, about a decade and a half ago, the Progressive Conservative Party under Brian Mulroney had just been re-elected with a strong majority, the ink was still fresh on the Canada-United States Free Trade Agreement, and the Meech Lake Accord was entering its death throes. The term 'globalization' was not yet on everyone's lips, the Soviet Union was the world's other superpower, the Internet was still in its infancy, and Bill Gates was just a very rich computer nerd. Canada has changed and the world has changed.

But some things have remained the same. Canadian political scientist Donald Smiley once wrote that there were three fundamental axes around which Canadian politics turned: the division between French and English Canada, relations between Canada and the United States, and conflict between central Canada and the outlying regions. This is still a pretty good assessment of the fundamentals of Canadian political life, although newer issues and political fault lines, such as gender, the environment, and multiculturalism, have added layers of complexity to the picture.

The title of this book—*Canadian Democracy*— is not a judgement or a conclusion. It is, rather, a focus. Over the four editions of this textbook I have tried to structure my treatment of the key components of Canada's political system around such themes as equality, freedoms, rights, and access. This approach is neither an uncritical celebration of Canadian politics nor a lopsided condemnation of its shortcomings and failures. In using the complex and contested concept of democracy as my touchstone I hope to encourage readers to think about Canadian government and politics in ways that will enable them to assess fairly and realistically the performance of Canada's political system.

Canadian Democracy is organized into five parts. Part One, the first chapter, examines some basic concepts in the study of politics and government, including the central concept of democracy. Some readers will have been introduced to this material in a previous course, such as the Introduction to Politics course that is the necessary stepping stone to further political science courses at many universities. I have attempted to address these foundational concepts in ways that link them very directly to Canadian politics, so that even those students who already have taken a sort of 'Political Science 101' course can gain something useful from what might otherwise be familiar territory.

Part Two, Chapters 2–4, focuses on the broad societal context of Canadian politics. Chapter 2 looks at the ideological roots of Canadian political institutions and controversies, highlighting in particular the similarities and differences between the political values and beliefs of Canadians and Americans. Chapter 3 surveys some of the politically significant social and economic characteristics of Canadian society. In Chapter 4, which is new to this edition, the nature and political impact of regionalism are examined.

Part Three, Chapters 5–8, turns to the structures of governance. Here we examine the Constitution (Chapter 5), rights and freedoms (Chapter 6), federalism (Chapter 7), and the machinery of government (Chapter 8).

Part Four considers the main vehicles for individual and group participation in politics: Chapter 9 discusses the origins and contemporary character of Canada's political parties, their role in politics, and the nature and consequences of our electoral system; Chapter 10 looks at the characteristics and influence of interest groups; Chapter

11 examines the crucial place occupied by the mass media in modern democracies and the particular features of the media's role in Canadian politics.

Part Five, Chapters 12–14, focuses on three important issues in modern Canadian politics—language, diversity, and Canada's role in the world—that illustrate well the complex interplay of values in democratic politics. Other issues are equally deserving of attention and instructors may wish to supplement this material with an issue-oriented reader such as Christopher Dunn's *Canadian Political Debates* or a policy-oriented text like *Public Policy in Canada* (4th edition).

This fourth edition of *Canadian Democracy* represents a significant make-over of the text. Two new chapters have been added, Chapter 4 on regionalism and Chapter 14 on Canada in the world, and the earlier chapter on gender and politics has been recast to examine the broader subject of the politics of diversity. Chapter 8, on the machinery of government, has been expanded considerably from previous editions, particularly the examination of central agencies and the legislature. Every chapter has been updated, in some cases quite extensively, as in the examination of the 2000 general election in Chapter 9. Many of the tables and figures are new and those that are carried over from the last edition have been brought up to date.

As in the previous edition, this one includes review exercises at the end of each chapter. These are not conventional questions as appear in many textbooks, but are hands-on exercises requiring students to apply what they have learned and to use practical research skills. Many of these exercises are geared to the media, particularly newspapers, television, and the Internet. The review exercises have been brought up to date, with many of them being new to this edition.

Also new to this edition are the annotated bibliographies at the end of each chapter. These sources are intended to provide students with helpful leads for researching essays on topics related to the chapter material.

The glossary of key terms at the end of *Canadian Democracy* has been expanded significantly from the last edition. It is intended to provide students with a sort of one-stop shopping centre for concepts that are, in many cases, unfamiliar and perhaps a bit specialized for most laypersons, and that are important to an understanding of the material covered in this book. I assume that some instructors may also find the glossary useful for testing purposes.

Writing a book may sometimes be a solo flight. It has never been so far for me. I am indebted to a number of people who have helped pilot the various editions of this book to what I hope readers and instructors will find to be a successful landing.

My first debt is to Michael Harrison, formerly of McClelland & Stewart and now with Broadview Press. Michael encouraged me to write this book and provided valuable advice leading up to the first edition. Since then it has been my pleasure to work with several first-rate people, including Penelope Grows, formerly with McClelland & Stewart, and Phyllis Wilson, Euan White, Laura Macleod, and Mark Piel of Oxford University Press.

Anonymous reviewers for all four editions provided thoughtful comments and suggestions that I sometimes followed, and perhaps should have more often. Professors Paul Nesbitt-Larking of Huron University College and Paul Gecelovsky of the University of Windsor, both of whom have used this book, have offered helpful suggestions over the years. Richard Tallman's meticulous editing and advice on points of style and substance have transformed the manuscript for each edition of this book into a much better product. It is always a pleasure to work with him.

I am, as well, deeply indebted to Roy Peterson, award-winning cartoonist of the *Vancouver Sun*. A selection of his political cartoons is sprinkled throughout this book. I think instructors and students will agree that they add both insight and humour to an understanding of Canadian political life.

As someone who clings stubbornly to the old technology of the pen, I have much reason to be grateful to Barbara Faria of Windsor's Political Science Department. At one point or another she has typed almost every word in this book. Photographs for several of the chapters were kindly provided by Greg Vickers. It has been my good fortune to have three excellent research assistants, Stephanie Plante, Kelly Anne Smith, and Joanna Sweet, help me in updating material, preparing tables and figures, and assisting with the many small but necessary tasks that go into the preparation of a book.

Finally, I would like to thank my family, Christine, Paul, Tom, and Marianne, without whose support this book would not have been written.

Stephen Brooks
Windsor and Goderich, Ontario

PART ONE

INTRODUCTION

Competitive elections are one of the cornerstones of democracy. (Greg Vickers)

To understand politics and government, one requires a tool kit consisting of the fundamental concepts and terms that are useful in analyzing political life. This chapter aims to equip the reader with these tools by examining the following topics:

- ❏ What is politics?
- ❏ Power.
- ❏ State and government.
- ❏ Democracy.
- ❏ Consent and legitimacy.
- ❏ Political identities.
- ❏ Political fault lines: old and new.

CHAPTER ONE

AN INTRODUCTION TO POLITICAL LIFE

Politics, we all agree, is a fact of life. Some people rejoice in this, seeing in political participation and government the possibility of building a better society, or at least of fulfilling some of their personal goals. Others lament the fact, viewing politics as a corrupt and debasing activity that is largely devoid of principle and more likely to be harmful and meddlesome than socially beneficial. Then there are those who neither rejoice in nor lament the pervasiveness and character of politics, but who simply do not care one way or another. If they think about politics at all it is probably to reflect on how little difference they could make to what gets done, or how incomprehensible the whole affair seems. Retreat into indifference or ignorance, or both, is their way of 'dealing' with political life.

These three stances—the enthusiast, the cynic, and the apathetic—are obviously caricatures. Most people combine elements of each in their own political attitudes and behaviour: following politics much as they would sports (though probably less avidly); occasionally talking about the parties, their leaders, or some 'hot' issue with friends or family; voting in most elections; but maintaining a measure of cynicism about politicians and their craft. If you are like most readers of this book you probably do not follow politics very closely. A recent survey of intergenerational differences in political opinions and behaviour in Canada revealed that about six out of ten people between the ages of 18 and 27 admitted that they either did not follow politics very closely or not at all. While the vast majority of those in this age group could name the Prime Minister, only one out of five could name the Minister of Finance or the leader of the official opposition.[1]

The vast majority observe the political spectacle at some distance. But even the least interested among us must concede the modern fact of government whose tendrils wrap themselves around every important aspect of our existence. The old adage about the state being present from cradle to grave does not go far enough when technology compels governments to legislate on when life begins and on when and how it may end.

Platitudes about 'big government' do not, however, take us very far towards an understanding of politics and government. In fact, they may obscure matters by giving the impression that politics suffuses and encompasses everything. The boundaries of the political disappear, leaving the would-be student of politics with little to grasp hold of except the idea that government is somehow at the centre of it all. But politics does have boundaries, and an identification of these is an important first step towards understanding the political process.

What Is Politics?

Politics arises from the fact of scarcity. In the real world it is not possible for all people to satisfy all of their desires to the fullest extent. Limits on the stock of those things that people desire—wealth, privacy, clean air and water, and social recognition—ensure that conflicts will take place between rival claimants. These conflicts explain why politics comes about. But politics is about more than the fact of conflict. It is also about how rival claims are settled. What distinguishes politics from the conflicts, struggles, and rivalries that take place in such settings as the family, the workplace, the economic marketplace, and in social organizations like churches and labour unions is the *public nature* of political disputes and the use of public authority—embodied in the state—to deal with them. **Politics**, then, is the activity by which rival claims are settled by public authorities. The boundaries of the political are defined by the scope of the state's authority to intervene in society.

As Box 1.1 shows, this definition does not have the field all to itself. All of these contending definitions agree that politics is about the exercise of power. They disagree, however, about what power relations count as political ones. Dahl, Lasswell, Marx, and the feminist movement define politics in ways that would include the relations between bosses and workers in a corporation, between parents and children in a family, between teachers and students in schools, and between spiritual shepherd and flock in a church. And in a sense they are right. In the words of American political scientist Charles Merriam, 'obviously there is governance everywhere—government in heaven; government in hell; government and law among outlaws; government in prison.'[2] Locke and Easton both offer a more limited definition of politics, one that goes back to Aristotle's conception of the Greek *polis*. They argue that what is distinctive about politics is the association of this activity with a system of settling disputes that is both public and binding on the whole community. At the centre of this system is the state, or government, as those raised in the Anglo-American tradition are more likely to call it.

These definitions disagree in another important way. Both the Marxist and feminist definitions associate politics with a pervasive pattern of oppression—between social classes according to Marxists, and between males and females according to feminist theorists. Politics is, for them, fundamentally about how inequalities are generated and reinforced through the power relations that exist between classes/gender groups at all levels of society.

Does it matter, in the end, how we define politics? Or is this mainly a harmless diversion for academic hair-splitters? We would argue that there is a very practical reason for rejecting those definitions of politics that confer on all power relations,

---

BOX 1.1   Some Well-Known Definitions of Politics

'[A] political system can be designated as those interactions through which values are authoritatively allocated for a society.' David Easton, *A Systems Analysis of Political Life*

Politics: Who Gets What, When and How, Harold Lasswell

'Political power, then, I take to be a right of making laws with penalties of death and, consequently, all less penalties for the regulating and preserving of property, and of employing the force of the community in the execution of such laws and in the defense of the commonwealth from foreign injury; and all this only for the public good.' John Locke, *The Second Treatise of Government*

'A political system is any persistent pattern of human relationships that involves, to a significant extent, power, rule, or authority.' Robert Dahl, *Modern Political Analysis*

'Political power, properly so called, is merely the organized power of one class for oppressing another.' Karl Marx and Friedrich Engels, *The Communist Manifesto*

'The personal is political.' Slogan of the feminist movement

wherever they may be located and however limited they may be, the title 'political'. If politics is viewed as being everywhere and in all social interactions we lose the ability to see the boundary that separates the public and private realms. This boundary may not be very distinct, but it is crucial for understanding the politics of any society. Moreover, the existence of such a boundary is necessary in order to protect the freedoms that most of us believe to be important features of a democratic society. Political conflict is largely about where exactly this boundary between public and private should be drawn, what should be considered a proper matter for public life and decisions by the state, and what should remain private matters. We can agree that power relations are ubiquitous without going the next step to claim that politics, therefore, has no bounds.

Not everyone agrees. Political scientist Jill Vickers echoes many of her feminist colleagues when she argues that the public realm/private realm distinction is fundamentally sexist. It is based, she maintains, on a tradition of political thinking that accepted as natural the domination of the public realm by males and the limitation of woman to the private sphere. When women were finally admitted to the public realm it was on identical terms with men, a formal equality that failed to recognize the substantive inequalities in the typical life conditions of males and females.

But whatever sexist biases may have been embedded in the public versus private realm distinction in traditional Western political thought, is it not the case that its contemporary importance lies in the value that it assigns to individual freedom? This, too, says Vickers, is fundamentally sexist. 'The concept of *freedom*', she writes, 'has become an almost totally masculinized idea in western political thought, meaning *freedom from* constraints—an autonomy in which no dependence on another is required or recognized.'[3] According to Vickers, this is a value with little appeal to most women, who have as their goal 'interdependence among equals' rather than the freedom to act without constraint.

But there is, perhaps, another reason for adopting the more limited definition of politics that we have put forward. Only those power relations that take place in the public realm can legitimately be associated with the use of force in its most naked, punitive forms. Compulsion, punishment, and violence do of course take place in all sorts of social settings. It is clear, however, that only the public authorities—the state—have the legitimate right to back up their decisions with the full power of society. All other power relations are more limited than this. The reason for this difference is that the state is the only institution that can reasonably claim to speak and act on behalf of the entire community, and its unique function is to ensure the conditions for some degree of social order. This social order is a necessary condition for all other social activities, for without it there is no peaceful basis for reconciling conflicts in society.

POWER

Power is the ability to influence what happens. It is found in all sorts of settings, not simply political ones. When Microsoft uses its dominant market position in computer operating systems to compel PC manufacturers to integrate its Internet browser into their computers, that is power. When the Vatican issues an official proclamation on birth control or the ordination of women, elements within the Roman Catholic Church respond. The Vatican has power within the community of Roman Catholics. When a person is persuaded to give up his wallet at gunpoint, his attacker has power. Parents who are able to compel their children's obedience through the threat or fact of punishment, or through persuasive arguments, have power. A television network whose programs shape the issues that viewers are thinking about has power. And when a peaceful demonstration of citizens outside the headquarters of a corporation, or in front of the legislature, changes the behaviour of the targeted institution, that, too, is power. In each of these cases one party

...and, considering overtaxation, the devalued dollar and the brain drain, who would you vote for?

Gore...or Bush.

Recent polls have shown that only a minority of Canadians follow politics closely and most have a hard time identifying political leaders other than the Prime Minister. (Roy Peterson, *Vancouver Sun*)

affects the behaviour of another, although the reasons for compliance differ.

Social scientists like to unpack the concept of power, breaking it down into species that are distinguished from one another according to the reason why the compliant party obeys. Compliance may result from the threat or use of force (**coercion**); from the ability of A to convince B that a particular action is reasonable or otherwise in B's best interests (**influence**); or from the recognition on the part of the compliant party that the person or organization issuing a command has the right to do so and should be obeyed (**authority**). Politics involves all of these faces of power—coercion, influence, and authority—at various times and in different circumstances. Democratic politics relies primarily on the two non-coercive

species of power. But coercion is used, and no democracy is without its system of courts, police, and prisons.

How far coercion and democracy are compatible, however, is an open question. This is illustrated by a famous exchange between former Prime Minister Pierre Trudeau and CBC journalist Tim Ralfe in October 1970, a few days after the Liberal government had suspended civil liberties by invoking the War Measures Act at the time of the FLQ crisis in Quebec.

Ralfe: 'Sir, what is it with all these men with guns around here?'

Trudeau: 'Haven't you noticed?'

Ralfe: 'Yes, I've noticed them. I wondered why you people decided to have them.'

Trudeau: 'What's your worry?'

Ralfe: 'I'm not worried, but you seem to be.'

Trudeau: 'If you're not worried, I'm not worried.'

Ralfe: 'I'm worried about living in a town that's full of people with guns running around.'

Trudeau: 'Why? Have they done anything to you? Have they pushed you around or anything? . . . [T]here are a lot of bleeding hearts around who just don't like to see people with helmets and guns. All I can say is, go on and bleed, but it is more important to keep law and order in the society than to be worried about weak-kneed people. . . . I think the society must take every means at its disposal to defend itself against the emergence of a parallel power which defies the elected power in this country, and I think that goes to any distance.'

Is Trudeau right? It is one of the great ironies of democracy that, unlike other political systems, it requires that dissenting points of view and opposition to those in power be respected. Arresting people suspected of terrorist acts is, most would agree, necessary to protect democratic government. At some point, however, the protection of law and order may exact a high cost in terms of personal freedoms. In a democracy, those in power must justify their use of coercion as being necessary to maintain such values as freedom, equality, justice, and the rule of law. Inevitably, however, people will disagree over the meaning and relative importance of these values, and over how much coercion, in what circumstances, is acceptable.

The practical difficulties that can arise in an *open society*—a society in which individuals are free to speak their minds, associate with whom they wish, and move freely about without having to notify or justify their movements to the public authorities—was brought home to Canadians, and even more so to Americans, after the terrorist attacks of 11 September 2001. Access to public buildings became more restricted, border crossings became more time-consuming and stressful, air-

port security was tightened, and measures were taken to curb the rights of immigrants. Some of these changes proved to be temporary, but many—such as the new air travel security tax that all Canadian travellers have been required to pay since 2002 and the Anti-Terrorism Act, which came into force in December 2001—have become part of the new 'security' environment and will be with us for the foreseeable future. But the reflection on and debate over the appropriate balance between individual rights and national security in a democratic society that have arisen out of the events of 11 September have been and likely will continue to be the most lasting and significant impact on Canadian politics of the terrorist attacks. Some believe that Canadian co-operation with the United States in the creation and maintenance of what officialdom calls a 'common security perimeter' is necessary to protect the open society from enemies who would take advantage of the freedoms it affords to spread terror. Others see such a policy as being democracy's own 'Iron Curtain', and thus a flagrant violation of the principles that an open society is supposed to embody and uphold.

STATE AND GOVERNMENT

The existence of the state is, we argued earlier, a necessary condition for the existence of politics. But what is the 'state'? To this point we have used the terms 'state' and 'government' as though they meant the same thing. This failure to make a distinction between them is often harmless, but it can lead to serious confusion. For example, to argue that the government is corrupt or wasteful, or that its policies are undesirable, does not necessarily call into question the state's legitimacy. It does, however, challenge the authority of the particular people who control the levers of the governmental system. In an established democracy, political activity is far more likely to be directed at influencing and changing the government than at reforming the state.

Canadian political scientist Leo Panitch provides this definition of the **state**:

[The state is] a broad concept that includes government as the seat of legitimate authority in a territory but also includes bureaucracy, judiciary, the Armed Forces and internal Police, structures of legislative assemblies and administration, public corporations, regulatory boards, and ideological apparatuses such as the education establishment and publicly owned media. The distinguishing characteristic of the state is its monopoly over the use of force in a given territory.[4]

Defined this way, the state has three main characteristics. First, it involves territorial boundaries. States have borders, beyond which their legal authority is either nil or strictly limited. Second, the state consists of a complex set of institutions that wield public authority. The courts, the police, and the educational system are no less outposts of the state's authority than are the elected legislature and the bureaucracy. Third, the state is defined in terms of power; what Weber (see Box 1.2) called its 'monopoly of the legitimate use of physical force in the enforcement of its order'. For what purposes and in whose interests this power is exercised are questions left unanswered.

Some definitions of the state do, however, offer answers to these questions. The Marxist and Leninist definitions in Box 1.2 characterize the state as an instrument of class oppression. Marx argued that the end of class conflict would sound the death knell for the state. It would 'wither away', no longer having any function to perform. Contemporary Marxists, except for a few diehards, no longer predict the state's demise. Feminists view the state as a patriarchal institution, reinforcing and perpetuating the social superiority of men over women. Many political scientists, and probably most economists, would argue that the state is responsive to any group with enough political clout to persuade policy-makers that it is in their interest to meet the group's demands for public actions on private wants.

BOX 1.2   Alternative Definitions of the State

'The state is the product of the *irreconcilability* of class antagonisms. The state arises when, where and to the extent that class antagonism *cannot* be reconciled.' Vladimir Lenin, *State and Revolution*

'The executive of the modern State is but a committee for managing the common affairs of the whole bourgeoisie.' Marx and Engels, *The Communist Manifesto*

'The state is that fiction by which everyone seeks to live at the expense of everyone else.' French economist Frédéric Bastiat, *circa* 1840

'L'Etat, c'est moi.' [I am the state.]   Louis XIV of France

'[The state is that institution which] successfully upholds a claim to the monopoly of the legitimate use of physical force in the enforcement of its order . . . within a given territorial area.' Max Weber, *The Theory of Social and Economic Organization*

'All state-based political systems are patriarchal—that is, in no country in the world are women equal participants in the institutions of the state or equal beneficiaries in its distribution of power or in the norms and values sanctioned in law and enforced by those institutions.' Jill Vickers, *Reinventing Political Science*

An adequate explanation of the state must ask on whose behalf and in whose interests the state's authority is exercised. Contemporary political science offers three main answers to these questions: **pluralism**, **class analysis**, and **feminism**.

Pluralism. Those who see politics as being fundamentally a competition between different interests are likely to conclude that the state responds chiefly to the demands of those groups that are best organized, have superior financial resources, can credibly claim to speak on behalf of large numbers of voters or segments of the population that are influential for other reasons, and are successful in associating their special interests with the general interests of society. The pluralist model assumes various forms, some of which are society-centred. The *society-centred* variants emphasize the impact of groups in society on the state, while *state-centred* variants place greater emphasis on the ability of public officials to act on their own preferences and according to their own interests, rather than merely responding to the demands of voters and interest groups. Pluralist models of the state do not assume that the competition among groups takes place on a level playing field. On the contrary, many of those who work within this perspective argue that business interests occupy a privileged position within this competition.

Class analysis. Beginning with Karl Marx, class analysis has always seen the state in capitalist societies as an instrument through which the small minorities who control most of a society's wealth maintain their social and economic dominance. Precisely how this is done has been the subject of enormous debate, but the state's complicity in perpetuating inequalities that are rooted in the economic system is an article of faith shared by all variants of class analysis. Few of those who analyze politics from a class analysis perspective today would deny that the demands and interests of subordinate classes influence state decision-makers. But this influence, they argue, is sharply limited by the state's vulnerability to a decline in business confidence, the control that the dominant class has over the mass media and

popular culture, and a lack of class consciousness among even the least privileged groups in society that stems from the widespread acceptance of capitalist and individualistic values as normal.

Feminism. Feminists view the state as an inherently patriarchal institution. This means that the state, its structures, and its laws all serve to institutionalize male dominance. Increasing the representation of women in elected legislatures, the bureaucracy, and the courts, and creating governmental bodies and programs that recognize women as a group with interests and needs that are not identical to those of men can attenuate this male dominance. However, most of feminist political theory still insists that a state-centred political system will be patriarchal. 'A feminist state that is a structure of authority,' says R.W. Connell, 'a means by which some persons rule over others, is self-contradictory.'[5] It is the hierarchical nature of authority embodied in the state that makes it fundamentally patriarchal. Like Karl Marx's famous prediction that the state would 'wither away' once classes were abolished, many feminists argue that if gender discrimination is eliminated the state, *as we know it*, will disappear.

A distinction can be made between the state and government. **Government** is a term that is more usefully reserved for those who have been elected to power. It is more personal than the state, being associated with a particular group of people and, usually, with political parties. In democratic political systems governments are chosen and removed through elections. These elections—the rules and procedures by which governments are formed—are part of the state system. And like the rest of the state, they are much less likely to generate political controversy and to undergo change than are the government and its policies.

Underlying this distinction between state and government is an important practical difference in the basis on which each compels the obedience of citizens, corporations, and associations that fall within their jurisdiction. The willingness of individuals and groups to obey the decisions of government—decisions with which they may vigorously disagree, and a government for which they may not have voted—is based on their view that the state's authority is legitimate. By **legitimacy** we mean that the rules and institutions that comprise the state, and determine how governments are chosen, are accepted by most people as being reasonable. The legitimacy of the state is, therefore, based on the *consent* of those who are governed. It does not depend on an ever-present fear of the penalties that follow from disobeying the law. It rests instead on what is usually an implicit acceptance of the rules of the political game. If the state's authority, and ultimately the ability of governments to govern, depended on a sort of constant referendum of the popular will, politics would be a brittle enterprise. In reality, this popular consent is not something that people regularly (if ever!) reflect on or consciously avow (the 'Pledge of Allegiance' recited by American schoolchildren has no counterpart in most democracies, and certainly not in Canada).

Perhaps the best way to understand the importance of the state/government distinction in a democracy is to imagine what would happen if a government's ability to pass and implement laws depended on its popularity. Assume for a moment that a government's 'approval rating' sinks to 20 per cent, according to public opinion polls, and that particular actions of the government are opposed by a clear majority of citizens. Should people simply choose to disobey the law and treat this unpopular government as one that has lost its right to govern? And if polls showed that the leader of another political party was clearly preferred by most voters, would this leader have a better moral claim to govern than the discredited leader of the government?

This is a scenario for chaos and anarchy. Democracy requires some measure of stability and respect for rules, including those rules that determine who has the right to govern and how and when that right ends. A particular government or prime minister may be deeply unpopular, but people continue to obey the law and refrain from storming the legislature (although they may organize

protests and even throw some tomatoes) because of their implicit acceptance of the state's legitimacy. Government popularity and state legitimacy are not the same, at least not in a democracy.

Government may be upheld by consent or by force. In fact, it is usually upheld by both. When anti-abortion protestors defy court injunctions against demonstrating near an abortion clinic and are arrested and charged for this act of civil disobedience, they are challenging the authority of the state. When Quebec nationalists demand political independence for their province they are registering their belief that the existing boundaries of the Canadian state, and its authority in Quebec society, are not legitimate. And when striking unions ignore back-to-work legislation and thereby run the risk of being fined or having their leaders imprisoned, this also goes beyond disagreement with government policy to challenge the legitimacy of the state. The state's authority is sometimes questioned by individuals or by organized interests. When this happens the public authorities may resort to force in order to crush civil disobedience and maintain their ability to govern.

The question of when citizens may be justified in resisting the law, through either passive disobedience of public authority or violence, is an old one. Two of the world's greatest democracies, the United States and France, trace their modern origins to bloody revolutions undertaken in defence of principles that the revolutionaries believed warranted violence against the state. Some, such as the American writer and libertarian thinker Henry David Thoreau, India's Mahatma Gandhi, and the black civil rights leader Martin Luther King Jr, developed a philosophy of non-violent civil disobedience that has been influential across the world. Others, like some of the leaders of the American student movement of the 1960s, the French students whose actions paralyzed public authority in Paris and brought about the fall of the de Gaulle presidency in 1968, and Malcolm X, whose slogan 'By any means necessary' encapsulates a philosophy of justifiable resistance to unjust treatment, have acted on the premise that violent opposition to the law and those who enforce it is consistent with democracy when it targets oppression and injustice.

The debate over civil disobedience—when it is justified and what forms it may take in a democracy—has resurfaced in recent years, principally around issues associated with globalization and income inequality. Since what the media dubbed the 'Battle in Seattle', when the 1999 meetings of the World Trade Organization were disrupted by thousands of protestors and scenes of violent confrontations with the police were broadcast live around the world, organized protest has become a standard and expected part of any meeting of policy-makers from the world's wealthiest countries. This led the Chrétien government to schedule the 2002 meeting of the G-8, the world's eight largest capitalist democracies, at the isolated resort of Kananaskis in Alberta, from which protestors could be kept at a distance. The Web sites of some anti-globalization organizations provide advice and instruction on tactics for those wishing to disrupt meetings of the powerful and, crucially, to attract media attention to the anti-globalization movement.

It is, of course, perfectly lawful to provide information that one intends, in the famous words of H.L. Mencken, to bring comfort to the afflicted and afflict the comfortable. But what about advice or action that involves breaking the law? In 1999 and 2000 the Ontario Coalition Against Poverty, led by John Clarke, trashed the constituency offices of an Ontario cabinet minister and held a protest rally at that province's legislature, where firebombs and other projectiles were thrown. Clarke defended the group's actions by arguing that the violence and property damage that they caused were nothing alongside the systematic and widespread damage done to the poor by the Ontario government's policies. Some agreed, including certain opinion leaders who defended OCAP's actions as justifiable and consistent with democracy. When well-armed

Mohawk Warriors—the label they applied to themselves—set up barricades on public roads at Oka, Quebec, in 1990 and resisted the authority of the Quebec police and the Canadian military, there was no shortage of Canadians who believed that their armed resistance was a justifiable reaction to a history of oppression and a political system and justice system heavily biased against their interests. The violence that the state may inflict on groups of citizens, the argument goes, warrants self-defence on the part of victims of this violence.

Government that relies primarily on threats and violence to maintain its rule is generally unstable. Even the most repressive political authorities generally come to realize that popular consent is a firmer basis on which to govern. In some societies the popular consent that legitimizes political rule may appear to emerge more or less spontaneously from the unco-ordinated activities of the media, the schools, the family, governments: from the various social institutions that influence the ideological outlook of citizens. In other societies, the state's legitimacy is deliberately and assiduously cultivated through the organs of official propaganda. The calculated fostering of consent is a characteristic feature of totalitarian rule. **Totalitarianism** is a system of government that suppresses all dissent in the name of some supreme goal. This goal may be tied to the destiny of the 'race', as it was in Nazi Germany, or to class struggle as it was in the Soviet Union under Stalin. Distinctions between the state, government, and society lose all meaning—indeed, they are considered to be subversive—under totalitarianism.

The active mobilization of society by the state, the deliberate manipulation of public attitudes, and the ruthless suppression of dissent by the public authorities are not features that most of us associate with democracy. The way in which legitimacy is generated in political democracies is more subtle than under totalitarian rule, depending primarily on social institutions that are not part of the state system. This gives legitimacy the appearance of being based on the free choice of individuals, an appearance that some argue is an illusion. Marxist critics use the term **cultural hegemony** to signify the ability of society's dominant class to get its values and beliefs accepted as the conventional wisdom in society at large. American social critic Noam Chomsky takes this position in arguing that the privately owned mass media reinforce and perpetuate inequalities in wealth and power by presenting 'facts', images, and interpretations that either justify or gloss over these inequalities.[6] Feminists take a similar line, arguing that sexist attitudes of male superiority are pervasive in social institutions—from the bedroom to the boardroom—so that the legitimacy of patriarchal power relations is reinforced on a daily basis. For both Marxists and feminists, government by 'popular consent' is a sham that conceals the fundamentally undemocratic character of society and politics.

DEMOCRACY

When political systems as different as those of Canada, the People's Republic of China, and Iran all claim to be democracies, we may be excused for asking just what 'democracy' means. Canadian political philosopher C.B. Macpherson argued that there are in fact three different types of democracy in the modern world.[7] Only one of these, *liberal* democracy, is characterized by competition between political parties. What Macpherson calls the *developmental* and *communist* versions of democracy do not have competitive elections, and probably would not be considered democratic by most Canadians. But they both claim to attach greater importance to the social and economic equality of individuals than does liberal democracy, in addition to recognizing the formal political equality of citizens. If democracy is about equality, Macpherson argues, the developmental and communist versions are at least as democratic as the liberal version that we in the capitalist world automatically assume to be the genuine article.

If we accept Macpherson's argument that there are three types of democracy, not one, each with a legitimate claim to the title, the world looks like a very democratic place. Leaving aside personal and military dictatorships, and the odd monarchy like Saudi Arabia and the Sultanate of Brunei, most of what is left would seem to qualify. While common sense suggests that democracy is not as widespread as this, Macpherson is challenging us to reflect on what makes politics and society democratic or not. Is democracy a system of government? Or does democracy connote a type of society? Was Canada 'democratic' before the female half of the population received the federal vote in 1920, or before all Aboriginal people in Canada were finally granted the right to vote in 1960? Does the persistence of poverty and the clear evidence of large inequalities in the economic condition and social status of different groups in Canada oblige us to qualify our description of Canadian society as 'democratic'?

About the only thing that everyone can agree upon is that democracy is based on equality. Agreement breaks down over how much equality, and in what spheres of life, is necessary for a society to qualify as democratic. Majority rule, government by popular consent, one person-one vote, and competitive elections are the political institutions usually associated with democratic government. But it has long been recognized that the operation of democratic political institutions can result in oppressive government. If, for example, a majority of Quebecers agree that legislative restrictions on the language rights of non-francophones are needed to preserve the French character of Quebec, is this democratic? In order to safeguard the rights and freedoms of individuals and minorities against what Alexis de Tocqueville called 'democratic despotism', constitutional limits on the power of the state over its citizens may be set, or the political status of particular social groups may be entrenched in the formal rules and informal procedures of politics. For example, the Canadian Constitution entrenches the coequal official status of the French and

VANCOUVER SUN
Peterson

NO GAS MASKS, ROCKS OR SLINGSHOTS NEEDED. (SOME ASSEMBLY REQUIRED.)

Democracies have police forces, courts, and jails. But unlike other forms of government, they do not depend on coercion and violence and they give citizens an opportunity to choose who will govern them. (Roy Peterson, *Vancouver Sun*)

English languages at the national level, and the operation of federalism and the Canadian electoral system reinforce the political power of this country's French-speaking minority, 90 per cent of whom live in Quebec.

Perhaps even more important than constitutional guarantees and political practices are the social and cultural values of a society. Tocqueville argued that the best protection against the tyranny of the majority is the existence of multiple group identities in society. When individuals perceive themselves as being members of particular social groups—whether a religious denomination, an ethnic or language group, a regional community, or whatever the group identity happens to be—in addition to sharing with everyone else a common citizenship, the likelihood of the democratic state being turned to oppressive ends is reduced. After

all, everyone has a personal interest in the tolerance of social diversity because the rights and status of their own group depend on this.

Some twentieth-century writers have argued that cultural values represent the main bulwark against the tyranny of the majority. Democratic government, they argue, depends on popular tolerance of diversity. In *The Civic Culture*, American political scientists Gabriel Almond and Sidney Verba make the argument that democratic government is sustained by cultural attitudes.[8] According to this political culture approach, the determination of how democratic a society is must be based on an examination of the politically relevant attitudes and beliefs of the population. This, and not the mere fact of apparently democratic political institutions, is argued to be the true test of democracy.

Not everyone would agree. Socialists argue that a society in which a large number of people are preoccupied with the problem of feeding and housing themselves decently cannot be described as democratic. This preoccupation effectively excludes the poor from full participation in political life, and in this way socio-economic inequality is translated into political inequality. The formal equality of citizens that democratic government confers, and even the fact that most people— including society's disadvantaged—may subscribe to democratic values, does not alter the fundamental fact that social inequalities produce inequalities in political power. Marxists would go even further in dismissing the democratic claims of capitalist societies. They argue that inequality results from the simple fact that a very small proportion of the population—the capitalist class— controls the vast majority of the means of economic production and distribution. This inequality in property ownership, Marxists argue, far outweighs the importance of 'one person-one vote' and competitive elections in determining the real political influence of different classes in society.

Inequalities between bosses and workers, between parents and children, between men and women, between ethnic or language communities—the list could go on—are often claimed to undermine the democratic character of societies whose formal political institutions are based on the equality of citizens. Indeed, if we use any of the all-inclusive definitions of politics examined earlier in this chapter it is impossible to resist the logic of this argument. Inequalities confront us wherever we turn, and true democracy seems to be terribly elusive. Even if we define politics more narrowly to include only those activities that focus on the state, it is obvious that a small portion of all citizens actually dominates public life. This is true even in the most egalitarian societies. For most of us, participation in politics takes the form of short bursts of attention and going to the polls at election time. Is it reasonable to speak of democratic government when the levers of state power are in the hands of an elite?

The short answer is, 'It depends on what we expect from democracy.' If we expect that all citizens should have the opportunity to participate in the law-making process, we are bound to be disappointed. With some historical exceptions like the Greek *polis* and the township democracies of seventeenth- and eighteenth-century America, examples of direct government of the citizens by the citizens are scarce. Direct democracy survives in some isolated pockets, such as the Swiss *Landsgemeinde*, where citizens gather once a year on a mountain pasture in the canton of Appenzell to vote on important public questions. Modern technology, however, has created the possibility of direct democracy from people's living rooms in all advanced industrial societies. An idea of how this brave new world of participatory democracy could work was provided when an interactive soap opera called 'The Spot' appeared on the Internet in 1995. Followers of this weekly program—a sort of Internet version of *Dawson's Creek*—were given the opportunity to vote on plot development and how characters in this fictional series should behave. There is no physical or technological reason why this method of popular choice could not be adapted to political decision-making. There may, however, be other reasons for rejecting what modern technology makes possible.

Perhaps the most commonly advanced reason for rejecting direct democracy via the Internet and for being skeptical about the value of public opinion polls is that many citizens are poorly informed about important public issues much of the time, and it occasionally happens that most citizens are grossly uninformed or misinformed about public issues. What sense does it make to ask citizens what the government's policy should be on a matter about which the majority of people know either little or nothing, and where what they think they know may be factually incorrect?

Thomas Jefferson provided a famous answer to this question. 'Every government degenerates when trusted to the rulers of the people alone. The

BOX 1.3   Is Canada a Democracy?

The Canadian polity as it exists is not in fact a true democracy, even in the limited sense of representative democracy. It is an oligarchy operated by the Liberal party machine in association with central Canadian (mainly Ontarian) industrial and financial corporations—an oligarchy in which the elected representatives of the people have little real voice, since policy is established by a small inner circle of powerful ministers within the cabinet, strategy is planned and supervised by the bureaucrats and public relations experts in the Prime Minister's Office, and Parliament is regarded as an institution for formalizing the decisions of the party hierarchy, in which the opposition is seen merely as an irritant to be ignored if possible and otherwise to be bamboozled and hoodwinked by evasive and lying ministers.

George Woodcock, *Confederation Betrayed!* (1981), 16.

people themselves therefore are [democracy's] only safe depositories.'[9] Members of the public, Jefferson acknowledged, are often poorly informed or wrong in their opinions on public matters. But the democratic solution to the problem of an ill-informed public is not to exclude it from the determination of public affairs; rather, it is to educate public opinion. Jefferson placed great stress on the role of the press and public education in producing an informed citizenry.

We often hear that the information explosion generated by satellite communication, television, and the Internet has made us the best-informed generation of all time. But as Neil Postman observes, this conceit fails to comprehend why most people are unable to explain even the most basic elements of issues that have received saturation coverage in the media. This ignorance does not prevent pollsters from asking people for their opinion on matters that they may barely understand and clearly deprives the results of polls of any meaning other than the signals they send to politicians looking for waves to ride. Postman blames modern education and especially the media for this ignorance. Television, the defining medium of the last half-century, is singled out for particular blame.

What is happening here is that television is altering the meaning of 'being informed' by creating a species of information that might properly be called *disinformation*. . . . Disinformation does not mean false information. It means misleading information—misplaced, irrelevant, fragmented or superficial information—information that creates the illusion of knowing something but which in fact leads one away from knowing. . . . [W]hen news is packaged as entertainment, that is the inevitable result.[10]

The pillars that Jefferson counted on to support democratic government have rotted, according to Postman. The irony is that this has happened in an age when more information from more corners of the world is available to the average person than ever before.

All modern democracies are **representative democracies**. Government is carried out by elected legislatures that represent the people. Citizens delegate law-making authority to their representatives, holding them responsible for their actions through periodic elections. Representative democracies sometimes include decision-making processes that provide opportunities for greater and more frequent citizen participation than simply voting every few years. *Plebiscites* and *referendums*—direct votes of citizens on important public questions—frequently held elections, choosing judges and some administrative officials through election, and formal procedures for removing an elected official before the end of his or her term, as through voter petitions and 'recall' elections, are democratic institutions that appear to allow for widespread citizen participation in public affairs.

This appearance may be deceiving. In countries such as the United States and Switzerland, where referendums are a normal part of the political process, voter turnout is usually very low. Partly because of this, and partly because vested interests are quick to spend money on advertising and mobilizing their supporters, referendums may produce outcomes that do not appear to be democratic. Indeed, one of the most common criticisms levelled at referendums is that they are too easily used as tools of conservative political interests. But this is not always true. In the 1998 United States elections there were 235 referendums at the state level, about one-quarter of which were initiated by citizen petitions. Many of these had little or nothing to do with political ideology, but others, on such issues as drug liberalization, the environment, affirmative action, animal rights, and abortion, did. In contests where there was a clear ideological dimension, liberals won more often than they lost.[11]

Respect for rights and freedoms is generally considered a distinguishing feature of democratic government. Which rights and freedoms warrant protection and in what circumstances they may legitimately be limited by government are matters of dispute. Libertarians, many economists, and conservative philosophers argue that government that levies heavy taxes on citizens is undemocratic. Their reasoning is that individual choice is reduced when government, representing the collectivity, decides how a large share of people's income will be spent. Others argue that the same levels of taxation actually promote freedom by paying for policies that give less advantaged groups opportunities they would not have in a 'free' market. Even a value apparently as uncontroversial as freedom of speech often becomes embroiled in controversies over democracy. For example, some believe that any person or organization should have the right to spend money on advertising a particular political point of view during an election campaign. Others argue that unlimited freedom of speech in these circumstances is undemocratic, because some individuals and groups are better endowed than others and, therefore, the points of view of the affluent will receive the greatest exposure.

Rights and freedoms are believed by most of us to be important in democracies, but everyone except extreme libertarians believes that protecting these rights or freedoms can sometimes produce undemocratic outcomes. There is no surefire test that will tell us when democracy is promoted or impaired by protecting a right or freedom. Indeed, this is one of the greatest sources of conflict in modern democracy, sometimes portrayed as a struggle between the competing pulls of individualism (the private realm) and collectivism (the public realm). A private realm that is beyond the legitimate reach of the state is a necessary part of what is sometimes called a free society. Where this realm does not exist—where the individual's right to be protected from the state is obliterated by the state's right to impose its will on the individual—democracy does not exist. In its place one finds Tocqueville's tyranny of the majority that is able to control the levers of public authority. Individual freedoms and group rights must enjoy some respect if a society's politics is to be judged democratic.

We will argue throughout this book that formal institutions are only part of what makes a society's politics democratic or not. The activities of the media, interest groups, and political parties are at least as crucial to the quality of democracy. Likewise, the socio-economic and ideological backgrounds to democratic government have important effects on how the formal and informal features of the political system operate. Democracy, then, cannot be reduced to a simple constitutional formula or to some particular vision of social equality. Several complex elements come into play, so that defining the term 'democracy' is a perilous task. Someone is bound to disagree, either with what is included in the definition, or with what has been left out. In full recognition of these hazards, we offer the following definition. **Democracy** is a political system based on the formal political equality of all citizens, in which there is a realistic possibility that voters can replace the government, and in which certain basic rights and freedoms are protected.

POLITICAL IDENTITIES

Identities are ideas that link individuals to larger groups. They are self-definitions, such as 'I am a Canadian' or 'Je suis québécois', that help us make sense of who we are and how we fit into the world around us. An identity is a state of mind, a sense of belonging to a community defined by its language, ethnic character, religion, history, regional location, gender experiences, belief system, or some other factor.

Identities perform important psychological and emotional functions. They provide the moorings that connect us to places, beliefs, and other people. People who share an identity are more likely to feel comfortable together and understand one another than those who are not part of their identity group. Often we only become aware of their importance when we find ourselves in a very unfamiliar place or set of circumstances. Responses ranging from disorientation and longing for home—'home' understood both physically and culturally—to hostility and xenophobia are common when we become unmoored from our familiar identities.

It is in the nature of identities that they are exclusive. If, for example, I think of myself as a member of the working class I implicitly acknowledge the existence of other groups with which I do not identify. It is possible, however, to identify with a number of groups without causing a sort of multiple personality disorder. There is no reason, for example, why a person could not think of himself or herself as a Canadian and a québécois(e) at the same time. Multiple identities are common, but some will be more significant in shaping a person's ideas and behaviour than others.

A shared identity is based on a perception of having common interests. But the fact of some number of people having interests in common does not necessarily generate a shared identity. Most of us have no difficulty in recognizing that corporations in the same industry, or consumers, municipal ratepayers, or university students, have identifiable interests in common. These interests are related to the conditions that promote or impair the material well-being of the members of these groups. They become political interests when they are organized under a collective association that claims to represent the members of the group and attempts to influence the actions of the state. Organization is expected to provide the group's members with more collective influence in politics than any individual member could hope to exercise alone. The number of possible political interests is virtually without limit. Of these, only a finite number actually become organized for collective political action, and an even smaller number achieve significant political clout.

A political interest brings together individuals who might otherwise have little in common in terms of their attitudes and beliefs. What they often have in common is a material stake in how some political conflict is resolved. Wheat farmers, automotive workers, university students, east coast fishers, pulp and paper companies, and small business people are all examples of political interests. Their participation in politics as organized groups is based on considerations of material well-being. Indeed, the interests that the members of such groups have in common are primarily economic.

The desire to protect or promote one's material well-being, while an important basis for the political organization of interests, is certainly not the only one. Interest may coalesce in politics

Remember, while you're tightening your belt, our belts are tightening too...

THE DAILY SHAFT

PM, MPs GET QUIET RAISE

PM NOW PAID $270,050

MPs NOW PAID $135,000 PLUS $15,000 EXPENSES

Many Canadians are cynical about their politicians, believing them to be overpaid and hypocritical when they talk about restraint. (Roy Peterson, *Vancouver Sun*)

around ideas, issues, and values that have little or no immediate relationship to the incomes, living conditions, social status, or other self-interest of a group's members. Mothers Against Drunk Driving (MADD) is an example of a group whose political involvement is motivated by shared values rather than material self-interest. The Canadian Abortion Rights Action League and the Canadian Catholic Conference of Bishops are groups whose political involvement on the abortion issue is motivated by values—very different values in their case—rather than strictly material concerns.

Interests and identities are not inevitably political. One can be a French Canadian, an Albertan, a woman, or the member of some other social or cultural group, and be conscious of the fact, without this having any special political relevance. Identities such as these become political-

ly relevant when those who share them make demands on the state—or when the state recognizes their group identity as a reason for treating them in a particular way. Some political identities emerge spontaneously in society, while others are forged and promoted by the state. Governments in Canada have come to play an increasingly active role in defining and promoting political identities in this country, a role that has generated much controversy.

The **nation** has been a particularly crucial political identity in Canadian politics. It is probably the single most powerful political identity in the world today—although religious identity surpasses it in some societies. The meaning of the term 'nation' is hotly disputed. It is perhaps no accident that *The Canadian Encyclopedia* does not even take a stab at defining it, settling instead for a definition of 'nationalism'. 'Nationalism', Denis Smith states, 'is the doctrine or practice of promoting the collective interests of the national community or state above those of individuals, regions, special interests or other nations. . . . In the first 25 years after WWII, 66 new nations were created.'[12]

Embedded in this definition of nationalism is a claim—not universally shared—about what constitutes a nation. Most of the '66 new nations' it refers to were former colonies whose populations were divided on ethnic and linguistic lines. For example, Nigeria achieved independent statehood in 1960 and immediately had to grapple with political conflicts between its three major communities—Yoruba, Ibo, and Hausa. The members of these communities did not share a sense of belonging to the same nation. Closer to home, organizations like the Parti Québécois and the Société de St Jean Baptîste argue that French-speaking Quebec constitutes a nation that is distinct from the rest of Canadian society. They define the term 'nation' as a community united by common linguistic and historical ties. For Quebec nationalists, the concept of a single Canadian nation is nonsense (see Box 1.4).

Nationalism usually is accompanied by territorial claims. The nation is associated with some particular territory—'the homeland', 'la patrie'—which is argued to belong to the members of the nation. Quebec nationalists have asserted such claims, but so, too, have organizations representing Aboriginal Canadians, many of which are grouped together under the Assembly of First Nations. The territorial demands of organizations that claim to represent nations boil down to a demand for self-government, a demand that those making it usually justify as the democratic right of any 'people' to self-determination.

But a sense of place—a regional consciousness—may produce political demands that stop far short of independence and self-determination. A regional identity or **regionalism** may be based on a variety of cultural, economic, institutional, and historical factors that distinguish the inhabitants of one region of a country from those of other regions. This identity may influence the political behaviour of those who share it, but their political demands generally will be less sweeping than those made by nationalist groups. When regionalism enters politics, it usually takes the form of demands for fairer treatment by the national government, better representation of the region in national political institutions, or more political autonomy for regional political authorities—all of which stop short of the usual catalogue of nationalist demands.

Cultural and social identities are not inherently political. The differences that exist between religious, ethnic, language, regional, or gender groups—to name only a few of the most important social-cultural divisions in the world today—may give rise to political conflicts when they are associated with inequalities in the *economic status*, *social prestige*, and *political power* of these groups. In other words, identities acquire political consequences when the members of a group, the 'identity-bearers', believe that they experience some deprivation or injustice because of their social-cultural identity, and when a 'critical mass' of the group's membership can be persuaded to take political action based on their self-identification as women, French Canadians, westerners, or whatever the identity happens to be. Political identities may not be primarily economic, but they usually have an economic dimension. Even when the stakes appear to be mainly symbolic—for example, the long-standing political debate over special status for Quebec in Canadian federalism—material considerations generally lurk behind the demands that the representatives of a social or cultural group make on the state.

Why particular identities surface in politics, while others remain 'pre-political', is a question that can only be answered by looking at the particular circumstances of any society. The persistence of regional, ethnolinguistic, and religious identities in the modern world and the emergence of gender inequality onto the political agendas of virtually all advanced industrial societies have confounded the earlier belief of many social sci-

BOX 1.4   What Is a Nation?

'A nation is a community of persons bound together by a sense of solidarity and wishing to perpetuate this solidarity through some political means. Contributing to this solidarity are common "objective" factors such as history, territory, race, ethnicity, culture, language, religion and customs and common "subjective" factors such as the consciousness of a distinct identity, an awareness of common interests and a consequent willingness to live together. Because of the existence of such factors, there is a special relationship among members of a nation which enables them to co-operate politically more easily among themselves than with outsiders.'
Canada, *Report of the Task Force on Canadian Unity* (1979)

'A nation ... is no more and no less than the entire population of a sovereign state.'
Pierre Elliott Trudeau, 'Federalism, Nationalism, and Reason' (1965)

'Nationalism is not to be confused with patriotism. Both words are normally used in so vague a way that any definition is liable to be challenged, but one must draw a distinction between them, since two different and even opposing ideas are involved. By "patriotism" I mean devotion to a particular place and a particular way of life, which one believes to be the best in the world but has no wish to force upon other people. Patriotism is by its nature defensive, both militarily and culturally. Nationalism, on the other hand, is inseparable from the desire for power. The abiding purpose of every nationalist is to secure more power and more prestige, not for himself but for the nation or other unit in which he has chosen to sink his own individuality.'
George Orwell, 'Notes on Nationalism' (1945)

'The simplest statement that can be made about a nation is that it is a body of people who feel that they are a nation; and it may be that when all the fine-spun analysis is concluded this will be the ultimate statement as well.'
Rupert Emerson, *From Empire to Nation* (1960)

entists, and all socialists, that class divisions would come to dominate the politics of advanced capitalism. The term 'class' (like most of the concepts discussed in this chapter) means different things to different people. When used as in the labels 'upper class' or 'middle class', it refers to a social status determined by such measures as the societal prestige of a person's occupation, an individual's income, or one's lifestyle. Since Karl Marx's time, many social scientists have defined class as being primarily an economic concept. According to this usage, a person's class membership is determined by one's relationship to the means of economic production—the main divi-

sion in society being between those who control the means of production and those who must sell their labour to earn a livelihood.

No one seriously argues that modern-day capitalism is characterized by a simple division between the owners of capital—the *bourgeoisie*—and their workers—the *proletariat*—as Marx predicted would happen. Advanced industrial democracies like Canada all have very large middle-class components. Moreover, the growth of pension funds and other large institutional investors has given a significant share of the middle class a direct ownership stake in their national and other economies. Over the past century there has also been a proliferation in the number of jobs that, while they involve dependence in the sense of relying on an employer for a salary, are characterized by considerable personal freedom in terms of how work is done and even the nature of the work. These people—university professors, engineers, consultants of various sorts, physicians, and lawyers, to name a few—cannot reasonably be squeezed into a definition of the working class.

In recent years, however, the concept of class has experienced a comeback. This comeback has been linked to the phenomenon of **globalization**, which refers to the unprecedented integration of the world's economies through trade, capital flows, and internationalized production, as well as cultural integration through satellite- and computer-based information technologies. Critics argue that globalization has produced greater polarization between the affluent and the poor, both within advanced industrial democracies like Canada and between the wealthy developed countries and the poor developing countries. 'Globalization is creating, within our industrial democracies, a sort of underclass of the demoralized and impoverished', says the former United States Secretary of Labour, Robert Reich. Moreover, critics argue that the ability of governments to protect the interests of society's poorest and most vulnerable groups, and to pursue policies that are unpopular with powerful corporate interests and investors, has been diminished by globalization.

In some societies, class identity is a powerful force in politics. Political parties make calculated appeals to class interests and draw on different classes for their electoral support. This is not particularly true of Canada. The sense of belonging to a class is relatively weak in Canadian society. Other political identities, especially ethnolinguistic and regional ones, have overshadowed class in Canadian politics. Some commentators argue that this should be taken at face value—that the linguistic and regional interests of Canadians are simply more vital to them than is something as abstract as class. Others maintain that the con-

sciousness of belonging to a class whose interests are at odds with those of other classes has been suppressed in various ways by political parties and elites who have vested interests in the suppression of class awareness and action.

POLITICAL FAULT LINES, OLD AND NEW

Some of the fault lines that shape the topography of Canadian politics extend back to the early years of this country, in some cases to the colonial era of Canada's history. The rift that separates French and English Canada is the oldest, going back to the military defeat of New France by the British in 1759 and the subsequent domination of the francophone population by an English-speaking minority. The demographic balance would soon shift in favour of the anglophone population, a shift that lent even greater urgency to the fundamental issues of whether and how the language and distinct society of French Canada would be recognized and protected. These are fundamental questions, and they have not changed very much between the Conquest and the present-day possibility of Quebec separation.

A second fault line that reaches back to Canada's colonial past involves this country's relationship to the United States. The American Revolution and the victory of the Thirteen Colonies in the American War of Independence had a profound and enduring impact on Canada. At times this impact has been felt as a territorial threat from the United States. Since Confederation, however, the economic, cultural, and political influences that the United States has on Canada have replaced the fear of American troops and annexation. And over this entire period, from the Americans' Declaration of Independence in 1776 to the present, a long shadow has been cast over Canadian politics and culture by the mere, but fundamental, fact of living alongside a much more powerful neighbour that resembles us in terms of historical origins, values, and dominant language, but that, very clearly, is not us. David Bell argues that at the root of the identity dilemma in English Canada is a need—a need that goes back to 1776—to explain to ourselves who we are as Canadians and in what ways we are not Americans.

A third fault line of somewhat less ancient vintage than the French-English and Canada-United States ones involves regionalism. In a country as physically vast and diverse as Canada it was unavoidable that the economic and social characteristics of the regions would develop along very different lines. Moreover, the concentration of most of the country's population and wealth in Ontario and Quebec has led Ottawa, not surprisingly, to be more sensitive to the needs and preferences of the centre over those of the 'hinterland' regions. Interregional conflict began to acquire a sharp edge in the late nineteenth century around such issues as high tariffs and railroads. This particular fault line quickly assumed an intergovernmental character, as provincial governments became the spokespersons for aggrieved regional interests in opposition to the federal government.

These three fault lines have been called by Donald Smiley the enduring axes of Canadian politics. They are not, however, the only fault lines that scar the Canadian political landscape. Some historically prominent ones, such as religious conflict and division between agrarian-rural and urban-industrial interests, have receded in importance (in the former case because of the diminished force of religion in Canadian life, and in the second because the rural and farm populations are today vastly outnumbered by those who live in urban centres and work in non-farm sectors of the economy). But other issues, including gender equality, Aboriginal rights, environmental protection, and multiculturalism, have traced new lines in Canadian politics.

Recent years have seen the re-emergence of a political fault line that, while quite prominent in the politics of many societies, has generally assumed a rather muted form in Canada and the United States: class conflict and the politics of the distribution of wealth. It is widely believed today that the forces of globalization have widened the gap between the affluent and the poor in Canada and in other advanced industrial democracies. The conclusion of a 1998 study published by the Toronto-based Centre for Social Justice is typical. 'We're getting distanced from one another', the study warns. 'We don't have common daily experiences. We're living in a society of two different Canadas where some get to decide how the others live.'[13]

If it is true that the middle class is being squeezed by falling incomes and job insecurity and that the gap between the rich and the poor is widening, we would expect to find this increased inequality reflected politically. In other words, the class fault line should become a more prominent feature of Canada's political landscape. To this point, however, the class polarization that many argue is taking place in Canadian society has not reached very deeply into the consciousness or affected very profoundly the political behaviour of most Canadians. Political parties that appeal to voters on class issues, notably the New Democratic Party, have not experienced a surge of support. Political protest and activism by labour unions in response to issues like free trade and cutbacks to social spending probably did increase during the 1990s. It is not clear, however, that this protest and activism reflected an awakening sense of class-consciousness on the part of the general population. A more plausible argument can probably be made that the main manifestations of the new politics of class include the explosion in books, articles, and media coverage generally of globalization and class polarization, and in the prominent coverage given to the ideas and activities of labour and social activists. But if the ballot box is the litmus test of how deeply this fault line has cut into Canada's political landscape, it is safe to say that class-consciousness has not yet become central to the political behaviour of Canadians.

NOTES

1. Brenda O'Neill, *Generation Patterns in the Political Opinions and Behaviour of Canadians* (Montreal: IRPP, Oct. 2001).
2. Charles Merriam, *Public and Private Government* (New Haven: Yale University Press, 1944).
3. Jill Vickers, *Reinventing Political Science* (Halifax: Fernwood, 1997), 113–14.
4. Leo Panitch, 'State', in *The Canadian Encyclopedia*, 2nd edn (Edmonton: Hurtig, 1988), vol. 4, 2071.
5. Quoted in Vickers, *Reinventing Political Science*, 42.
6. Noam Chomsky and Edward S. Herman, *Manufacturing Consent: The Political Economy of the Mass Media* (New York: Pantheon Books, 1988).
7. C.B. Macpherson, *The Real World of Democracy* (Toronto: CBC Enterprises, 1965).
8. Gabriel A. Almond and Sidney Verba, *The Civic Culture* (Princeton, NJ: Princeton University Press, 1963).
9. Quoted in Henry Steele Commager, *Living Ideas in America* (New York: Harper, 1951), 556.
10. Neil Postman, *Amusing Ourselves to Death* (New York: Viking, 1985), 107.
11. 'The people get it right, on the whole', *The Economist*, 7 Nov. 1998, 24.
12. Denis Smith, 'Nationalism', in *The Canadian Encyclopedia*, vol. 3, 1433.
13. Quoted in Elaine Carey, 'Rich get richer as wage gap widens', *Toronto Star*, 22 Oct. 1998. Available at: <www.thestar.com/back_issues>.

SUGGESTED READINGS

Mark O. Dickerson and Thomas Flanagan, *An Introduction to Government and Politics: A Conceptual Approach*, 5th edn (Toronto: ITP Nelson, 1998). Readers who feel the need of a good introduction to political science would do well to begin with this well-written book.

Mark O. Dickerson, Thomas Flanagan, and Neil Nevitte, *Introductory Readings in Government and Politics*, 4th edn (Toronto: ITP Nelson, 1995). This collection includes many excerpts from classic treatments of fundamental concepts in the study of politics, as well as a few more recent pieces.

C.B. Macpherson, *The Real World of Democracy* (Toronto: CBC Enterprises, 1965). This somewhat dated classic—the references to the Cold War may disorient some readers—continues to perform the useful function of getting readers to think about the attributes of a democracy and whether there might be more varieties than the one we are familiar with in the West.

Jill Vickers, *Reinventing Political Science: A Feminist Approach* (Halifax: Fernwood, 1997). Vickers challenges readers to rethink conventional ways of understanding political life, viewed through a feminist lens.

Review Exercises

1. Nationalism is a powerful force in the modern world. From a Web site, a newspaper, or a magazine, find one or two stories that deal with nationalism outside of Canada. (Some Web sites that should prove helpful include the on-line *Globe and Mail* <www.globeandmail.ca> and the *National Post* <www.nationalpost.com>.) Would you say that the nationalist demands or actions in these stories are similar to or different from the nationalism you are familiar with in Canada? Why?

2. This chapter introduced some concepts and issues relevant to Canadian political life. An easy way to tell what political issues are currently troubling Canada is to look at the political cartoons included in Canadian print journalism. Find a Canadian political cartoon that relates to a political issue with which you are familiar. One of the best sources is <http://cagle.state.msn.com>. For this source, scroll down until you find 'Canada's Best Cartoons', in the right-hand column. Click on this. Or go to the 'Topics' bar and click on 'Best of Canada'. What message do you think the cartoonist is trying to communicate? Do you think the cartoonist's treatment of the subject is fair or biased? In what ways and why?

3. How does identity affect your political behaviour? If you were asked to describe who you are and what aspects of your self-image are most important to you, what would you list? When you see or hear a newsperson, a politician, or a professor do you notice his or her race, gender, signs of ethnicity, accent, or other features of the person? Do you think other people notice such traits?

PART TWO

THE SOCIETAL CONTEXT OF POLITICS

American culture casts a long shadow over Canada, as the looming towers of Detroit across the river from Windsor's Canadian Broadcasting Corporation remind us. (Stephen Brooks)

Ideas constitute an important element of political life. This chapter surveys some of the key issues pertaining to the role of ideas in Canadian politics and discusses the political ideas of Canadians. The following topics are examined:

- ❏ Ideologies, values, and institutions.
- ❏ Fragment theory.
- ❏ Formative events.
- ❏ Economic structures and political ideas.
- ❏ The political ideas of Canadians.
- ❏ The nature of Canadian–American value differences.
- ❏ Community.
- ❏ Freedom.
- ❏ Equality.
- ❏ Citizen expectations for government.

CHAPTER TWO

IDEOLOGICAL AND INSTITUTIONAL ROOTS

In 1982 Canada's best-known popular historian, Pierre Berton, wrote a book with the promising title *Why We Act Like Canadians*.[1] It was written as a series of letters to an imaginary American friend by the name of 'Sam'. The fact that Berton addressed his explanations of what he calls Canada's 'national character' to an American was no accident. Canadians—English-speaking Canadians at least—have always struggled to escape the long shadow cast by American culture. *Why We Act Like Canadians* could have easily been titled 'Why We Are Not Americans'. It is virtually impossible to discuss the political ideas and institutions of English Canada without reference to those of the United States.

The same is not true of French Canada. Language and history combine to ensure the distinctiveness of French-Canadian society. Investigations into their 'national identity' have long been as popular in French Canada as in English Canada. But they seek to explain the values and institutions of French Canadians in terms of forces that have little to do with the United States. Instead, most analyses of French-Canadian culture focus on the internal dynamics of that society and on the effects that French-English relations have had on the development of French Canada.

It is impossible to discuss questions of culture and ideas in Canada without immediately becoming ensnared in controversy. Use of the terms 'English Canada' and 'French Canada' will offend some Canadians who feel left out by these labels, or who believe that there is only one Canada, politically, culturally, and otherwise. A term like 'national character', used so confidently by Pierre Berton, is certain to bring down the wrath of most academics, who argue that it is a bogus caricature of something much more complex and diverse. Before we discuss the values and institu-

tions that characterize Canadian politics we must clarify what it is we want to explain and what concepts will help us achieve this.

IDEOLOGIES, VALUES, AND INSTITUTIONS

Ideas assume various forms in political life. When they take the form of a set of interrelated beliefs about how society is organized and how it ought to function—an interpretive map for understanding the world—this is an **ideology**. An ideology spills beyond the boundaries of politics to embrace beliefs and judgements about other social relationships, including economic ones. This holistic character of ideologies distinguishes them from more limited political value systems. The fact that most people are not aware of having ideological leanings, and might be puzzled or even startled at being labelled a 'conservative', a 'liberal', or a 'socialist', does not mean that ideology is irrelevant to their political beliefs and actions. When the politics of a society are described as 'pragmatic' and 'non-ideological', this usually indicates that a particular ideology dominates to such a degree that it has become the conventional wisdom.

Someone who regularly and consciously thinks about political matters and other social relationships in ideological terms is an ideologue, a person who is consciously committed to a particular interpretation of society. Most people are not ideological.

If ideology is the currency of the political activist, political culture is the medium of exchange favoured by the general population. A political culture consists of the characteristic values, beliefs, and behaviour of a society's members in regard to politics. The very definition of what is considered by most people to be political and an appropriate subject for government action is an aspect of political culture. The relative weight that people assign to such values as personal freedom, equality, social order, and national prestige is another aspect of political culture. The expectations that citizens tend to hold for their participation in public life, and the patterns of voter turnout, party activism, social movement activities, and other politically relevant forms of behaviour are all part of political culture, as is the pattern of knowledge about political symbols, institutions, actors, and issues. Beliefs about whether government actions tend to be benign or malign, and towards whom, are also part of political culture.

Obviously, people will not hold identical views on these matters, nor will their participation in politics conform to a single template. It is reasonable, nevertheless, to speak of a society as having certain core values or a belief system that is shared by most of its members. Political culture should be thought of as a cluster of typical orientations towards the political universe. The fact that in one society this cluster may be comparatively scattered and marked by division between different segments of society while in another it is relatively compact is, in itself, an observation about political culture.

In Canada, research on political culture has focused primarily on the differences between the politically relevant attitudes and beliefs of French and English Canadians and on the question of whether English-speaking Canada is characterized by regional political cultures. To determine whether significant and persistent differences exist, political scientists have attempted to measure such things as levels of political knowledge and participation, feelings of political efficacy (a person's sense of whether his or her participation in politics matters) and alienation (variously defined as apathy, estrangement from the political system, or the belief that politics is systematically biased against one's interests and values), attitudes towards political authority and

the different levels of government, and the sense of belonging to a particular regional or linguistic community.

A third way in which ideas are relevant for politics is through individual *personality*. One of the most often repeated claims about Canadians is that they are less likely to question and challenge authority than are Americans. Canadians, it is argued, are more deferential. We examine this claim later in the chapter. Several of the standard questions used in studies of political culture, such as those dealing with political efficacy, trust in public officials, and emotional feelings towards political authorities, tap politically relevant dimensions of personality. Much of the research on the political consequences of individual personality traits has focused on the relationship between a person's general attitudes towards authority and non-conformity, on the one hand, and, on the other, that person's political attitudes on such issues as the protection of civil liberties, toleration of political dissent, the group rights of minorities, and attitudes towards public authorities. The main conclusion of this research is that general personality traits show up in an individual's political ideas and action.

One way of categorizing political ideas—perhaps the most popular way—is to describe them as being *left wing, right wing, or centrist*. These labels are used to signify the broader ideological premises believed to lie behind an action, opinion, or statement. For example, a newspaper editorial slamming welfare fraud and calling for mandatory 'workfare' would be called right wing by some, as would a proposal to cut taxes for the affluent or to eliminate public funding for abortions. Proposals to increase the minimum wage, ban the use of replacement workers during a strike or lockout, or increase spending on assistance for developing countries are the sorts of measures likely to be described as left wing. Centrist positions, as the term suggests, fall between the right and left wings of the political spectrum. They attempt to achieve some middle ground between the arguments and principles of left and right. The centre is, virtually by definition, the mainstream of a society's politics, and those who occupy this location on the political spectrum are likely to view themselves as being non-ideological and pragmatic.

Right and left are shorthand labels for conflicting belief systems. These beliefs involve basic assumptions about how society, the economy, and politics operate, as well as ideas about how these matters *should* be arranged. Generally speaking, to be on the right in Anglo-American societies means that one subscribes to an *individualistic* belief system. Such a person is likely to believe that what one achieves in life is due principally to his or her own efforts, that the welfare of society is best promoted by allowing individuals to pursue their own interests, and that modern government is too expensive and too intrusive. To be on the left, however, is to prefer a set of beliefs that may be described as *collectivist*. This person is likely to attribute greater weight to social and economic circumstances as determinants of one's opportunities and achievements than does someone on the right. Moreover, those on the left have greater doubts about the economic efficiency and social fairness of free markets, and have greater faith in the ability of government to intervene in ways that promote the common good. Although those on the left may be critical of particular actions and institutions of government, they reject the claim that the size and scope of government need to be trimmed. Smaller government, they would argue, works to the advantage of the affluent and privileged, at the expense of the poor and disadvantaged.

In reality, the politics of left and right is more complicated than these simplified portraits suggest. For example, while opposition to abortion generally is viewed as a right-wing position, many who subscribe to all the elements of right-wing politics listed above support easy access to abortion. These people, often labelled **libertarians**, believe that individuals should be allowed the largest possible margin of freedom in all realms of life, including those that involve moral choices.

The libertarian right is, however, smaller and less of a political force than the socially conservative right. Social conservatives are distinguished by such stands as opposition to abortion, support for capital punishment and stiffer jail sentences, and rejection of forms of pluralism that they believe are corrosive of traditional values. The wellsprings of their conservatism are quite different from those of libertarianism, but their shared antipathy for the modern welfare state and their preferences for markets over state planning in economics cause libertarians and social conservatives to be grouped together on the right. The fissures in this alliance, and the limitations of the right-left categorization of political ideas, become apparent when the issue is one of personal morality (e.g., abortion, homosexuality, religious teachings in public schools).

Despite these limitations, and the fact that labels like 'right' and 'left' are more often used to dismiss and discredit one's opponents in politics than to inform in a dispassionate way, the right-left spectrum taps a crucial and enduring truth of modern politics. This involves the character of the good society and how best to achieve it. We have said that the underlying struggle is essentially one between collectivist and individualist visions of the good society. These visions differ in how they view the conditions that promote human dignity and in their conceptions of social justice. For example, it is often said that one of the cultural characteristics that distinguishes Canadians from Americans is our greater propensity to sacrifice individual self-interest for the good of the community. In this connection Canada's health-care system is invoked like a mantra whenever Canadian-American cultural differences are discussed and fears expressed by Canadian nationalists that Canada is sliding down the slope towards American values and public policies (see Box 2.1). What the watchdogs of Canadian-style health care are really saying is that the more collectivist Canadian health-care model provides greater dignity for individuals and is fairer than the more individualistic American system.

Defenders of the American health-care system often retort that Canadian health policy is a form of socialism. **Socialism** is one of a trio of ideologies that have greatly influenced the politics of Western societies since the American and French revolutions. The other two are **liberalism** and **conservatism**. The importance of these ideologies in defining the contours of political life is suggested by the fact that major and minor political parties in many Western democracies continue to use the names liberal, conservative, and socialist.

In Canada, the two parties that have dominated national politics for most of the country's history, the Liberal Party and the Progressive Conservative Party (simply the Conservative Party before the party was rechristened in 1942), have their roots in the ideological divisions of the nineteenth century. Over time, however, the labels have lost much if not all of their informative value. Today, the ideological distance between a Liberal and a Conservative is likely to be small. Indeed, already at the beginning of the twentieth century the astute French observer André Siegfried remarked that the Liberal and Conservative parties were virtually indistinguishable in terms of their ideological principles. They and their supporters shared in the dominant liberal tradition that pervaded Canada and the United States.

At the heart of this tradition was the primacy of individual freedom. *Classical liberalism*—liberalism as understood until the middle of the twentieth century—was associated with freedom of religious choice and practice, free enterprise and free trade in the realm of economics, and freedom of expression and association in politics. These liberal values constituted a sort of national ethos in the United States, where they were enshrined in the Declaration of Independence and in the American Bill of Rights. In the colonies

---

BOX 2.1   What Makes a Canadian?

What are Canadian values? Well, a few years ago, a famous Texan coined the term 'a kinder and gentler' nation. Well, that is what we in Canada are. That is what we want to remain.

Our most important values as a nation are tolerance and sharing. We know that government cannot and should not do everything. But we also know it can and must be a force for good in society. And during times of great change, government has an obligation to help people adapt.

Most important, we know that citizenship has responsibilities. Individual rights are important in Canada. Very important. . . .

But just as important are the responsibilities we have for each other and for our community. That is why health care is so important in Canada.

There is a wide consensus in our country about preserving our distinctive state-funded health care system called Medicare. Under our system, you can go to the doctor of your choice. You are admitted to a hospital if you need to be. Period. Not if you have enough money. Or the right private plan. The fact is that no one in Canada needs to worry about medical bills. It is one of our proudest achievements. Canadians want to keep Medicare. And we will.

I believe that is one thing that makes us a 'kinder, gentler' society.

Prime Minister Jean Chrétien
speaking to the American Society of Newspaper
Editors, 6 April 1995

of British North America, which would become Canada in 1867, the dominance of liberalism was somewhat more tentative than in the United States. This was due to the streak of conservatism kept alive by some of the elites in colonial society, notably the Catholic Church, the Church of England, and the British colonial authorities.

Classical conservatism was based on the importance of tradition. It accepted human inequality— social, political, and economic—as part of the natural order of things. Conservatives emphasized the importance of continuity with the past and the preservation of law and order. They were wary of innovation and opposed to such basic liberal reforms as equal political rights for all men (even liberals did not come around to the idea of equal political rights for women until the twentieth century). Unlike liberals, who located the source of all just rule in the people, conservatives maintained that God and tradition were the true founts of political authority. Consequently, they supported an established church and were strong defenders of the Crown's traditional prerogatives against the rival claims of elected legislatures.

Although no party having the label 'socialist' has ever achieved the status of even an important minor party at the national level in either Canada or the United States, socialist ideology has been influential in various ways. *Classical socialism* was based on the principle of equality of condition, a radical egalitarianism that distinguished socialist doctrine from liberalism's advocacy of equality of opportunity. Socialists supported a vastly greater role for the state in directing the economy, better working conditions and greater rights for workers vis-à-vis their employers, and reforms like public health care, unemployment insurance, income assistance for the indigent, public pensions, and universal access to public education that became the hallmarks of the twentieth-century welfare state.

The usefulness of these three 'isms' as benchmarks for reading the political map is no longer very great. First, all three of these classical ideologies, but especially liberalism and conservatism,

mean something quite different today from what they meant 100–200 years ago. For example, contemporary liberalism does not place individual freedom above all else. Instead, modern liberals are distinguished by their belief that governments can and should act to alleviate hardships experienced by the poor and the oppressed. They are more likely to worry about the problems of minority group rights than about individual freedoms, or at any rate to see the improvement of the conditions of disadvantaged minorities as a necessary step towards the achievement of real freedom for the members of these groups. Modern liberalism has also become associated with support for multiculturalism and openness towards non-traditional lifestyles and social institutions.

The doctrine of classical conservatism has disappeared from the scene in contemporary democracies, leaving what has been called the conservative outlook or 'conservative mind'.[2] Modern conservatives tend to embrace the economic beliefs that once were characteristic of liberals. And like classical liberals they defend the principle of equality of opportunity. They are more likely to place the protection of personal freedoms before the advancement of minority rights. As in earlier times conservatism is generally viewed as the ideology of the privileged in society. It is worth noting, however, that conservative politicians and political parties receive much of their support from middle-class voters whose hands are far from the levers of economic power and social influence.

Of the three classical ideologies the meaning of socialism has changed the least. There is today, however, much less confidence among socialists that state ownership of the means of economic production and distribution is desirable. Modern socialists, or *social democrats* as they often call themselves, temper their advocacy of an egalitarian society with an acceptance of capitalism and the inequalities that inevitably are generated by free-market economies. The defence of the rights of society's least-well-off elements, which has always been a characteristic of socialism, is today carried out largely under the banner of other 'isms', including feminism, multiculturalism, and environmentalism. In Canada and the United States these other collectivist-egalitarian belief systems have more of an impact on politics than does socialism.

A second reason why the traditional trio of 'isms' no longer provide a reliable guide to politics has to do with the character of political divisions in modern society. The aristocracy of land and title and the deferential social norms that nurtured classical conservatism belong to the past. They live on as the folklore of castles and estates in the once rigidly hierarchical societies of Europe, in the continuing pomp of hereditary royalty, and in Britain's House of Lords. Otherwise, classical conservatism has no legitimacy in the middle-class cultures of Western societies. In the United States the structures and values that supported classical conservatism never existed, and in Canada they achieved only a precarious and passing toehold.

The struggles of liberalism in the eighteenth and nineteenth centuries, and of socialism in the nineteenth and twentieth, have largely been won. Liberals fought for free-market reforms and the extension of political rights and freedoms, first to the new propertied classes created by the Industrial Revolution and then more widely to the (male) adult population. They fought against conservatives who dug in to protect the political privileges of a hereditary aristocracy and the economic dominance of the traditional landowning classes. Socialists fought for more government control over the economy, workers' rights like collective bargaining and limits on the hours of work, and the welfare state. They fought against both the vestiges of conservatism and liberalism's emphasis on individualism.

The classical ideologies were formed and evolved in response to one another as well as to the social and economic conditions in which they were rooted. Today, Canadians, Americans, and Western Europeans live in affluent middle-class societies that bear little resemblance to those of the nineteenth century, when Europe was a tilting ground for the rivalries between conservatism, liberalism, and socialism. As the character of Western societies has changed, so too have the ideologies that slug it out in their politics.

Does this mean, as some have argued, that the traditional ideologies are obsolete, unsuited to the realities of modern society? This is the 'end of ideology' thesis that American sociologist Daniel Bell put forward in the 1960s. 'In the western world', he argued, 'there is today, a rough consensus among intellectuals on political issues: the acceptance of a Welfare State; the desirability of decentralized power; a system of mixed economy and of political pluralism.'[3] Traditional ideological categories are rejected as unhelpful and even distorting in how they view the world and political conflict. The post-materialist thesis maintains that those who have come into adulthood since the 1960s are much less likely than previous generations to be preoccupied by material considerations—jobs, security, income—that formed the basis for conflicts between traditional ideological camps. They are more likely to be interested in matters involving the quality of life, social justice, and rights, issues that cut across the older ideological divisions and that have given rise to a new language and new ways of thinking.

It is a great mistake, however, to underestimate the continuing importance of ideology in politics. Although the traditional 'isms' now must jostle with feminism, environmentalism, multiculturalism, and other 'isms' on a more crowded playing field, and despite the changes that have taken place in the meanings of the classical ideologies, they continue to be useful, though certainly not infallible, guides to understanding political ideas. The right versus left or individualism versus collectivism dichotomy is probably the most useful. In the real world, however, we should seldom expect to find that the ideas of an individual, or those associated with a group or political party, can be neatly categorized as one or the other.

Those who would argue that the individualism/collectivism dichotomy has become obsolete, and that politics has become largely a debate about means rather than ends, underestimate the continuing vitality of the struggle between what we might call competing images of the moral order. Many of the most profoundly felt differences in contemporary public life, from abortion and euthanasia to issues of trade and taxation, are based on the different ideas that people have about what social, economic, and political arrangements are consistent with personal dignity, justice, social order, and the good society. Those on the right of the modern ideological divide are less likely than those on the left to look to state action for the advancement and protection of the moral order that they prefer. This may be seen in the ongoing debate over the consequences of globalization, a debate in which moral considerations are seldom far from the surface (see Box 2.2)

BOX 2.2 Collectivism versus Individualism: The Moral Dimensions of Globalization

In the rush to produce more and consume more it is easy to overlook the basics. What is the meaning of our lives, as individuals and as the human species? Ask these questions and you are most likely to set off a philosophical discussion, not a discussion about economics. So why, then, do we unconsciously accept that our world should be primarily defined as an economic enterprise?

Clearly there are other principles by which we govern our lives. Values such as freedom of choice (to be who I want to be) and equality of opportunity (to get a chance to be who I want to be) fundamentally underlie our way of thinking in this society. But the way we have come to define these values has separated the individual from the collective. Consequently, when we ask ourselves questions like—What are we doing with our lives? What are we here for?—they get posed as personal, not social dilemmas. . . .

Our world is rife with insecurity. As competition gets more intense, more people are economically insecure. The ground becomes fertile for racist, sexist and other forms of discrimination. This erodes people's recognition of each other as essentially equal in the eyes of creation. It dehumanizes people. The legacy of growing inequality is the crumbling of social solidarity, the sense that we share something in common.

The more that society is unequal, the greater is the number of people who are prevented from developing themselves as full human beings. This dwarfs the potential of society as a whole. As long as inequalities are growing, we are getting away from, not closer to, being the best we can be. How do we reverse the gears?

We tend to gravitate towards the option of increasing economic growth—even though it does not necessarily guarantee more equity—because in the minds of most people it is synonymous with the ability to consume more things. This, in and of itself, is considered desirable and valued. The term economic growth is also used to conjure up notions of greater freedom and greater equality of opportunity.

From *The Growing Gap*, 1998
www.socialjustice.org/gap-intro.html

Table 2.1   Liberalism, Conservatism, and Socialism: Classical and Contemporary Versions

I. CLASSICAL	Liberalism	Conservatism	Socialism
a. Characteristics of the Good Society	Individual freedom is maximized; politics and economics are free and competitive; achievements and recognition are due to personal merit and effort; a capitalist economy will produce the greatest happiness for society and maximize material welfare; personal dignity depends on the individual's own actions.	The traditional social order is preserved; individuals are members of social groups that are linked together by a web of rights and obligations; those born in privileged circumstances have an obligation to those below them on the social ladder; there is a natural social hierarchy based on inherited status; personal dignity depends on one's conformity to the norms and behaviour of one's social group.	Social and economic equality are maximized; private ownership of property is replaced by its collective ownership and management; competition is replaced by co-operation; the welfare of society is maximized through economic and social planning; personal dignity depends on work and one's solidarity with the working class.
b. Nature of Government	All just government rests on the consent of the governed; party system is competitive; the state is subordinate to society; government should be small and its scope limited; the elected legislature is the most powerful component of the state; separatism between church and state.	The rights and responsibilities of those who govern derive from God and tradition; the state's fundamental role is to preserve social order; the state is superior to society and is owed obedience by all citizens and groups; the Crown is the most powerful component of the state; the size and scope of government are small by modern standards, but are not limited by liberalism's suspicion of the state; the state recognizes an official church.	All just government rests on the consent of the governed and the principles of social and economic equality; the state should control crucial sectors of the economy; government has a responsibility to redistribute wealth from the wealthy to the less fortunate social classes; government is large and its scope wide; a socialist state is the embodiment of the will and interests of the working class; no officially recognized religion.
c. Chief Supporters	Industrialists, merchants, property-owning individuals.	Landed aristocracy, established church, military officers and agents of the Crown whose status and income depended on maintenance of the traditional social hierarchy.	Organized workers; intellectuals.
II. CONTEMPORARY	Liberalism	Conservatism	Socialism
a. Characteristics of the Good Society	Individual freedom is balanced by protection for disadvantaged elements in society and recognition of group rights; capitalism must be regulated by the state to ensure the social and economic well-	Individual freedom is more important than social equality and should not be sacrificed to the latter; state regulation of capitalism should be kept to a minimum and should not be used to promote any but	Social and economic equality are the most important values; individual rights must be subordinated to collective goals; small-scale capitalism has its place, but state economic planning and active

Table 2.1 continued

	being of the majority; social diversity should be recognized and promoted through public education, hiring, and the policies of governments; social entitlements are respected, including a certain standard of living and access to decent education, health care, and accommodation; personal dignity is based on freedom and social equality.	economic goals; social diversity is a fact, but is not something that should be actively promoted by government; individuals should be responsible for their own lives and policies that encourage dependency on the state should be avoided; personal dignity depends on one's own efforts and is undermined by collectivist policies and too much emphasis on promoting social and economic equality.	participation in the economy are still necessary to promote both economic competitiveness and social fairness; the environmental consequences of all public and private actions must be considered; systemic discrimination based on gender, race, and ethnicity is eliminated through government policies; personal dignity depends on social and economic equality.
b. Nature of Government	The state has a responsibility to protect and promote the welfare of the disadvantaged; the post-WWII welfare state is a necessary vehicle for ensuring social justice; government should reflect the diversity of society in its personnel and policies; the state should not be aligned with any religious group.	The state's primary function should be to maintain circumstances in which individuals can pursue their own goals and life plans; government should be small and the level of taxation low in order to minimize interference with individual choice; government should not remain neutral between different systems of morality, but should promote traditional values through the schools and through support for the traditional family.	The state should redistribute wealth in society and ensure the social and economic equality of its citizens; some modern socialists argue that political power should be decentralized to community-level groups as the best way to ensure democratic responsiveness and accountability; the state should reflect the society in its personnel and policies; traditional value systems are based on systemic discrimination and oppression, and government has a responsibility to eradicate these values.
c. Chief Supporters	Many middle-of-the-road advocacy groups within the feminist, environmental, and multicultural movements; public-sector workers; middle-class intellectuals in the universities and the media; the national Liberal and Progressive Conservative parties and the Bloc Québécois; think-tanks, including Canadian Policy Research Networks, the Institute for Research on Public Policy, and the Canada West Foundation.	Business groups; middle-class workers in the private sector; the Canadian Alliance party; the Alberta and Ontario Conservative parties; think-tanks, including the Fraser Institute, the Atlantic Institute for Market Studies, and the C.D. Howe Institute.	More extreme advocacy groups within the feminist, environmental, and multicultural movements; some elements in the NDP and within organized labour; think-tanks, including the Canadian Centre for Policy Alternatives, the Caledon Institute of Social Policy, and the Canadian Council on Social Development.

Not a separatist BQ MP around!
Not a St. Jean Baptiste Day leftover or
Quebec City rioter in sight! Make
it quick man!

Happy Canada Day...eh?

The long-standing division between French and English Canada has been one of the chief obstacles to the development of a confident national identity in Canada. (Roy Peterson, *Vancouver Sun*)

EXPLAINING IDEAS AND INSTITUTIONS

Explanations of Canadians' political ideas, and of the institutions that embody them, can be grouped into three main camps. They include fragment theory, the role of formative events, and economic explanations. Each of these perspectives stresses a different set of causes in explaining the origins of Canadians' political ideas and institutions, and the forces that have shaped their development down to the present.

Fragment Theory: European Parents and Cultural Genes

Canada, along with other New World societies, was founded by immigrants from Europe. Native communities already existed, of course, but the sort of society that developed in Canada had its roots and inspiration in the values and practices of European civilization. Those who chose to emigrate to the New World—or who were forced to, as was true of the convicts sent from Britain to Australia—did not represent a cross-section of the European soci-

ety from which they came. They were unrepresentative in terms of their social class (the privileged tended to stay put in Europe), their occupations, and in some cases in terms of their religion. Moreover, immigration tended to occur in waves, coinciding with particular epochs in the ideological development of Europe. New World societies were 'fragments' of the European societies that gave birth to them. They were fragment societies because they represented only a part of the socio-economic and cultural spectrum of the European society from which they originated, and also because their creation coincided with a particular ideological epoch. The timing of settlement is crucial. Along with whatever material possessions immigrants brought with them, they also brought along their 'cultural baggage': values and beliefs acquired in Europe and transplanted into the New World. As David Bell and Lorne Tepperman observe, 'the "fragment theory" sees the culture of founding groups as a kind of *genetic code* that does not determine but sets limits to later cultural developments.'[4]

But why should the ideas of the founders carry such weight that they shape the political values and beliefs of subsequent generations? Fragment theory is rather weak on this point, arguing that the fragment's ideological system 'congeals' at some point—the ideology of the founders becomes the dominant ideology—and that immigrants who arrive subsequently have little choice but to assimilate to the dominant values and beliefs already in place. The transmission of the fragment culture from generation to generation presumably depends on social structures and political institutions that date from the founding period and embody the dominant ideas of the founding immigrants.

Canada has been characterized as a two-fragment society. French Canada was founded by immigrants from France who brought with them their Catholicism and *feudal* ideas about social and political relations. Feudal society is characterized by the existence of fairly rigid social classes, connected to one another by a web of mutual rights and duties based on tradition, and by the exclusion of most people from the full right to participate in politics. According to French-Canadian historian Fernand Ouellet, this was the ideological and social condition of New France when the colony was conquered by British forces in 1759.[5] Cut off from the social and political developments unleashed by the French Revolution (1789)—emigration from France, with the exception of some priests, virtually dried up—French Canada's ideological development was shaped by its origins as a feudal fragment of pre-revolution France. Institutions, chiefly the Catholic Church, the dominant social institution in French Canada until well into the twentieth century, operated to maintain this pre-liberal inheritance.

The 'cultural genes' of English Canada are, according to fragment theory, very different. English Canada was originally populated by immigrants from the United States. These were the so-called Loyalists, those who found themselves on the losing side of the American War of Independence (1776). They migrated north to British colonies that were overwhelmingly French-speaking.[6] Their 'cultural baggage' has been the subject of much debate, but the general view seems to be that they held predominantly *liberal* political beliefs. The liberalism that emerged in the eighteenth century was built around the idea of individual freedom: in politics, in religion, and in economic relations. One of its crucial political tenets was the idea that government was based on the consent of the people. So why did the Loyalists leave the United States, a society whose political independence was founded on liberal beliefs?

The defenders of fragment theory offer different answers to this question. Some argue that the liberalism of the Loyalists was diluted by *conservative* or *Tory* political beliefs: deference towards established authority and institutions, an acceptance of inequality between classes as the natural condition of society, and a greater stress on preserving social order than on protecting individual freedoms.[7] Others reject the view that Tory values were ever a legitimate part of English Canada's political culture, arguing that this belief system had no roots in the pre-revolutionary Thirteen Colonies and therefore could not have been exported to English Canada through the Loyalist migration.[8] The Loyalists were 'anti-American Yankees' who had rejected American independence because of their loyalty to the British Empire and to the monarchy, and their dislike of republican government (or, as they were more likely to put it, 'mob rule'). Their quarrel was not with liberal ideology, as shown by the fact that they immediately clamoured for elected assemblies and the political rights they had been used to in America. Bell and Tepperman thus argue that:

> Forced to leave their country, the Tories, or Loyalists, suffered profound doubts. Expulsion kept the Loyalist from basing a fragment identity on the liberal principles of John Locke. Made to give up his real identity, the Canadian Loyalist invented a new one. As a substitute, it was not quite good enough, of course. How could it be, when he had continuously to deny its true nature, liberalism? 'The typical Canadian,' an Englishman observed a

hundred years ago, 'tells you that he is not, but he is a Yankee—a Yankee in the sense in which we use the term at home, as synonymous with everything that smacks of democracy.' The Loyalist in Canada is thereafter always a paradox, an 'anti-American Yankee.' Only one path leads out of his dilemma: creating a myth that helps him survive. In this myth, he insists that he is British.[9]

The debate over how important non-liberal values were among the Loyalists is not merely academic. Contemporary analyses of English Canada as a more deferential and conservative society than the United States often trace this alleged difference back to the original ideological mixtures of the two societies. A second reason why the debate matters involves the explanation for Canadian socialism. Some of those who contend that conservative values were an important and legitimate component of English Canada's original cultural inheritance go on to argue that the emergence of socialism in Canada was facilitated by, first, the fact that liberalism never achieved the status of an unchallenged national creed (as it did in the United States) and, second, the fact that social class was not a foreign concept in English Canada.[10] Conservatism and socialism, according to this view, are two varieties of collectivism.

Formative Events: Counter-Revolution and the Conquest

Societies, like human beings, are marked by certain major events at critical periods in their development. These events are 'formative' in the sense that they make it more probable that a society will evolve along particular lines, instead of along others. In the world of politics, these formative events are associated with both ideas and institutions. For example, the American Revolution was fought in the name of liberal values and was followed by the adoption of a constitution and structures of government that enshrined the victors' preference for dispersed political power, a weak executive, and guarantees for individual rights.

The institutions put in place after the Revolution embodied eighteenth-century liberal values of individual freedom and limited government. They shaped the subsequent pattern of American politics by promoting and legitimizing behaviour and issues that conformed to these values.

The main exponent of the formative events theory of political culture is American sociologist Seymour Martin Lipset. He first introduced it by arguing that the political development of the United States has been shaped by its revolutionary origins, while that of English Canada has been shaped by its *counter*-revolutionary origins. Lipset writes:

> Americans do not know but Canadians cannot forget that two nations, not one, came out of the American Revolution. The United States is the country of the revolution, Canada of the counter-revolution. These very different formative events set indelible marks on the two nations. One celebrates the overthrow of an oppressive state, the triumph of the people, a successful effort to create a type of government never seen before. The other commemorates a defeat and a long struggle to preserve a historical source of legitimacy: government's deriving its title-to-rule from a monarchy linked to church establishment. Government power is feared in the south; uninhibited popular sovereignty has been a concern in the north.[11]

Many of those who found themselves on the losing side of the American Revolution—the Loyalists—migrated north. They were the founders of an English-speaking society that originated in its rejection of the new American republic. This original rejection would be repeated several times: in the War of 1812; in the defeat of the American-style democratic reforms advocated by the losers in the 1837–8 rebellions in Lower and Upper Canada; in the 1867 decision to establish a new country with a system of government similar to that of Great Britain. The political history of Canada, including many of the major economic and cultural policies instituted by Canadian governments, reads largely as a series of refusals in the face of Americanizing pressures.

Is rejection of American political values and institutions proof of the greater strength of conservative values in English Canada? Some of those who agree with Lipset about the importance of formative events do not agree that counter-revolutionary gestures signify *ideological conservatism*. David Bell and Lorne Tepperman have argued that Loyalism concealed an underlying *ideological liberalism*. They acknowledge that the Loyalists were not anti-government and that Canadians ever since appear to have been more willing to use the state for social, economic, and cultural purposes than have their American neighbours. But, they argue, a fondness for government is not inconsistent with liberal values. It is only in the United States, where the Revolution was directly about the tyranny of government, that liberalism acquired a strongly anti-government character.[12]

If Loyalism was not a conservative ideology, what was it? Bell and Tepperman argue that Loyalism was essentially a self-justification for not being American. Faced with the paradox of being cast out of a society whose political values they shared, the Loyalists had a serious identity crisis. They resolved it by insisting on their Britishness and by constant criticisms of American values and institutions. This anti-Americanism is a component of Loyalism that endures even today. It explains, according to Bell and Tepperman, English Canada's centuries-old national identity puzzle.

What 1776 represents for English Canada's political development, the British Conquest of New France in 1759 represents for that of French Canada. The Conquest has always occupied a central place in French-Canadian nationalism, testifying to French Canadians' own awareness of its significance. The motto on Quebec licence plates, 'Je me souviens' ('I remember'), is in fact an oblique reference to the time before the Conquest, when French-speaking Canadians presumably were free from the oppression of Ottawa and English Canadians. Particularly under Parti Québécois governments in Quebec it has been common for the Conquest to be mentioned in official government documents on subjects ranging from language to the economy and constitutional reform.

There is no agreement as to how the Conquest has affected the ideological development of French Canada. Some, like historian Michel Brunet and sociologist Marcel Rioux, have argued that the Conquest cut off the development of a French-speaking bourgeoisie—francophones were rarely found in Canada's corporate elite until only a few decades ago—thereby depriving French Canada of that class which elsewhere was the main carrier of liberal political values. The mantle of social leadership, and the task of defining French-Canadian society, eventually fell on the Catholic Church and the ideologically conservative politicians who accepted the clerics' interpretation of that society as Catholic, French-speaking, non-liberal, and agrarian (in about that order of importance).

Others, like historian Fernand Ouellet and political scientist Louis Balthazar, maintain that there was no fledgling bourgeoisie, and therefore no catalyst for liberal political reform, in the first place. French Canada, they argue, was essentially a feudal society at the time of the Conquest. It fixated at this pre-liberal/pre-capitalist stage because of the fact that it was cut off from the future, not because French Canada was deprived of something that it once possessed.

History did not, of course, stop at the Conquest. The crushed 1837 rebellion in Lower Canada (Quebec) signalled the defeat of the politically liberal *patriotes* and consolidated the dominance of the conservative ideology in French Canada. This ideology would ultimately collapse by the end of the 1950s, finally brought down by the weight of the enormous social and economic transformations that the conservatives had ignored and even denied. Since then, conservative ideology has had little credibility in Quebec, but the memory of the Conquest continues to be a favourite starting point for Quebec nationalists.

Economic Structures and Political Ideas

From a class analysis perspective, both fragment theory and the formative events explanation are 'hopelessly idealistic'.[13] This is because they locate the sources of political values and institutions primarily in ideas—the 'cultural baggage' of fragment theory and the cultural mindset and symbols associated with the notion of formative events. An economic interpretation, by contrast, explains culture and the institutions that embody and perpetuate it as the products of class relations. These class relations are themselves rooted in the particular system of economic production and distribution—the *mode of production*, as Marxists generally call it—found in a society at any point in time. Ideas and institutions change in response to transformations in the economic system and in the class relations associated with this system. The dominant ideas and existing political arrangements of a society are not, however, merely the shadows cast by economic phenomena. But what sets this approach apart from the other two we have examined is the belief that *culture and institutions are the embodiments of power relations whose sources lie in the economic system.*

How is political culture produced? By whom? For whom? With what effects? How do political institutions embody and reinforce the power relations that characterize society? These are the questions addressed by those who approach political values and institutions in terms of economically determined class relations. They argue that the dominant ideas of a society are inevitably those of its most powerful class, i.e., those who control the system of economic production and distribution. This is due to the fact that important means of forming and disseminating ideas and information, such as the privately owned mass media, are controlled by the dominant class. Others, including the schools, mainstream religious organizations, and the state, accept and propagate the values of this class for reasons more subtle than ownership. Chief among these reasons are their support for *social order* and their rejection of tendencies and

ideas that fundamentally challenge the status quo. None of these major institutions is in the business of overturning society. They depend on a stable social order to carry out their respective activities and to satisfy their particular organizational needs. But the social order they support, and whose values they accept, embodies a particular economic system and the power relations it produces. Defence of established institutions and values is not, therefore, a class-neutral stance.

Why would the members of subordinate classes embrace values and beliefs that, according to this class perspective, are basically justifications for the self-interest of the dominant class? The answer has two parts. First, those who are not part of the dominant class—and this, by definition, would include the majority of people—may be the victims of **false consciousness**. This concept, first used by Karl Marx, involves the inability of the subordinate classes to see where their real interests lie. For example, deference to established authority and belief in a hereditary aristocracy's natural right to rule—ideas that defend the privileges of the dominant class in a feudal society—would seem to reinforce the subordinate social position of those who are not fortunate enough to be born into the ruling aristocracy. In liberal societies, the widespread belief that opportunities to move up the socio-economic ladder are relatively open to those who are willing to work hard is argued by some to reinforce the dominant position of that small minority who control the economy and who account for most of society's wealth. After all, they argue, there is abundant empirical evidence that significant barriers to socio-economic mobility exist, that a good deal of poverty is passed on from generation to generation, and that those at the top of the socio-economic pyramid constitute a largely self-perpetuating elite. And yet we learn in school, through the mass media, and in countless other ways that equality of opportunity, not systemic inequality, is a characteristic feature of our society.

The second reason why, according to this class perspective, members of subordinate classes accept the ideas of the dominant class as 'common sense' is because these ideas conform, to some significant extent, to their personal experience. Democratic claims about the fundamental equality of all persons have a false ring in societies where some people are denied a share of this equality because they are black or female, for example. But in a society in which, under the constitution, there are no second-class citizens and where everyone has the right to vote and participate in politics and enjoys equal protection under the law, claims about equality may appear to be valid. Or consider the liberal belief, discussed earlier, that opportunities to acquire wealth and social standing are relatively open. There is, in Canada and in other liberal societies, enough evidence of this mobility to make the proposition appear true. While some people never escape the socio-economic circumstances they are born into, many others do. There is enough proof that hard work and/or intelligence pays off in terms of material success to make liberalism's claim about what determines a person's socio-economic status a credible one. As Patricia Marchak observes, 'the propagation of an ideology cannot occur in a vacuum of experience; there must be a fair amount of congruence between personal experience and ideological interpretation for the propaganda [read, dominant ideology] to be successful.'[14] Where this congruence is either weak or totally absent, the dominant class must rely on force to uphold its rule.

This idea that a certain degree of congruence between the dominant values and beliefs of a society and the lived experience of most of its members must exist, otherwise the ideas of the dominant class will be exposed as pure self-interest, is important. It means that what some have called false consciousness cannot be totally false. Ideological systems that are not anchored in the social and economic realities of those subject to them are just not viable. We can understand this better by looking at the case of Quebec and the ideological changes associated with that province's 'Quiet Revolution' of the 1960s.

As recently as the 1950s, the dominant ideology in French-speaking Quebec was conservative. It was an ideology based on the concept of **la survivance** (survival): conserving the religious and linguistic heritage of French Canada in the face of assimilationist pressures. While possessing the formal structures of political democracy, Quebec's political life was dominated by autocratic politicians, rampant patronage, and social institutions—notably the Church and conservative newspapers—that encouraged submission to established authority.[15] Functions like education and social services, which in virtually all industrial democracies were already under state control, were still in the hands of the Church. Even the province's francophone labour unions were predominantly confessional, linked to a Church whose ideas about industrial relations were shaped largely by its concern for preserving social harmony. In short, the dominant ideology and the social institutions that embodied it were conservative.

This conservatism, linked as it was to the social dominance of the Church and to a sharply limited role for the provincial state, was increasingly out of step with the industrial society that had been evolving in Quebec throughout the twentieth century. Those who advocated reforms that entailed a more interventionist role for the Quebec state, such as public control over education and social assistance, and whose vision of Quebec was of a secular industrial society necessarily found themselves in conflict with the spokespersons for the conservative ideology. By the 1950s, however, as reformist elements in Quebec politics were quick to point out, the typical Québécois was a city-dweller who worked in a factory, store, or office,[16] and a new middle class of university-educated francophone professionals was gaining numerical strength in the province.[17] This new middle class was the leading force behind the expansion of the Quebec state that took place in the early to mid-1960s. Ultimately, it was the lack of 'congruence' between the values of the conservative ideology and the personal experience of most Québécois that brought about the collapse of one dominant ideology and its replacement by one more in tune with those social groups—the new middle class and the growing francophone business community—who have dominated Quebec politics since the Quiet Revolution.

THE POLITICAL IDEAS OF CANADIANS

What do Canadians believe about politics? Is it true that they value social order more, and individual freedom less, than their American counterparts? Does French Canada, and more particularly French-speaking Quebec, constitute a 'distinct society' in terms of its values and beliefs? Is it reasonable to talk about the political ideas of English-speaking Canadians, or are the regional differences in political culture too great to warrant such an approach?

There are many possible ways of approaching the subject of political culture. In the following pages we will organize our analysis under four themes: community, freedom, equality, and attitudes towards the state. These tap crucial dimensions of political culture while allowing us to explore the differences and similarities between French- and English-speaking Canadians, between different regions of the country, and between Canadians and Americans. The evidence we will use is drawn from history, survey research data on attitudes, and measures of actual behaviour—of individuals, groups, and governments—from which values can be inferred.

Community

'Canadians', someone once said, 'are the only people who regularly pull themselves up by the roots to see whether they are still growing.' This search for a national identity unites successive generations of Canadians. Indeed, as the above remark suggests, it may be that the obsessive and often insecure introspection of Canadians is itself one of the chief characteristics of the Canadian identity (in English Canada, at least).

The roots of this preoccupation with national identity go back to the Conquest and the American War of Independence. The Conquest laid the basis for a society in which two main ethnolinguistic communities would cohabit, communities whose values and aspirations would often be at cross-purposes. The American War of Independence, as explained earlier, was followed by the emigration of Loyalists from the United States to the British colonies that would become Canada. Founded by those who rejected the republican democracy to the south, English Canada would constantly compare itself to that society and seek to explain and justify its separate existence.

In more recent years these two historical pillars of Canada's identity 'crisis' have been joined by newer challenges to the political community. These have come from Aboriginal Canadians and from some ethnic minorities who object to what they argue is their marginalization within Canadian society. Lacking a confident unifying sense of national identity, Canadian society has been buffeted by identity politics and the often irreconcilable definitions of Canada—sometimes proposing the dismemberment of the country as we know it—advanced by various groups.

The term 'political community' implies, quite simply, a shared sense of belonging to a country whose national integrity is worth preserving. This is something less than nationalism, which defines a community by its language, ethnic origins, traditions, or unique history. And it is not quite the same as patriotism, which one associates with a more fervent and demonstrative love of country and its symbols than is usually considered seemly in Canada. Political community is, rather, what historian W.L. Morton once described as 'a community of political allegiance alone'.[18] National identity, in such a community, is free from cultural and racial associations. Instead, national identity is essentially political—a sense of common citizenship in a country whose members have more in common with one another than with the citizens of neighbouring states and who believe that there are good reasons for continuing to live together as a single political nation. The term 'political nationality' is used by Donald Smiley to refer to precisely this sort of non-ethnic, non-racial sense of political community.[19]

The importance of national identity and a sense of political community in politics is nowhere better illustrated than in the breakup of the former Soviet Union and Yugoslavia after the end of the Communist Party's monopoly over power. Nationalist aspirations and bitter animosities that had been kept in check under totalitarian rule were unleashed, undermining any possibility that these countries could retain their pre-reform boundaries. There was, quite simply, no popular basis for political community in these formerly Communist political systems. Once democratic institutions were in place, their breakup was inevitable.

The spectre of Canadian troops laying siege to Gatineau, or of armed barricades where the Trans-Canada Highway crosses the border between Ontario and Quebec, probably seems a lurid fantasy to most Canadians. The great national bust-up, if it comes about, would almost certainly be acrimonious. But it is unlikely that the sort of civil war unleashed by the breakup of Yugoslavia into Serbia, Croatia, and Bosnia would occur if Quebec were to declare its independence. Not everyone agrees. In public statements towards the end of 1991 Gordon Robertson, former Chief Clerk of the Privy Council under Pierre Trudeau, raised precisely the spectre of the former Yugoslavia in arguing that the breakup of Canada could very well be violent.

A more imminent possibility, perhaps, is that of another violent confrontation between Native Canadians and federal or provincial authorities, such as occurred at Oka, Quebec, during the summer and autumn of 1990. A group of Mohawk Warriors, protesting the planned expansion of a golf course on land they claimed as their own, barricaded a road leading to the golf course. The confrontation eventually escalated, resulting in the death of one Quebec police officer, a sympathy blockade by Mohawks of an important commuter bridge near Montreal and other sympathy blockades of rail lines and roads by other Indian bands in communities across the country, riots involving the white townspeople of Oka and members of the local Mohawk band, intervention by thousands of Canadian troops, and even United Nations observers.[20]

Fears of another Oka were raised in 1995 when small groups of Natives occupied land that they claimed was sacred at Lake Gustafsen, BC, and Ipperwash Provincial Park in Ontario. Violence broke out in both cases and a Native was shot dead at Ipperwash.

Outbursts of violence on the scale of Oka are not typical of Canadian politics. But they are not unknown. Indeed, Canada's sense of community has often seemed terribly fragile, threatened by French-English tensions, western grievances against Ontario and Quebec, and, most recently, conflicts between the aspirations of Native Canadians and the policies of federal and provincial governments. This apparent fragility needs to be viewed alongside evidence suggesting that the country has been relatively successful in managing (repressing, critics would say) the tensions that have threatened it. The existing Constitution dates from 1867, making it one of the oldest and most durable in the world. Moreover, the territorial integrity of the country has (so far) remained unshaken by either civil war or secession. This is not to understate the importance of the rifts in Canada's sense of community. But the problems of Canadian unity and identity should be viewed from a broader perspective.

There are four major challenges to the Canadian political community:

- French-English relations;
- Native demands for self-government;
- American influence on Canadian culture;
- regional tensions.

The first two have occasionally been associated with political violence and calls for the redrawing of territorial boundary lines. They represent clear challenges to the Canadian political community. The third challenge, that of American influence, has assumed forms that are less obviously territorial. Nevertheless, its impact on the Canadian political community has been great. We will examine American influences separately in the section on 'Independence' in Chapter 3.

The fourth challenge, regional tensions, has been an important factor in Canadian politics from the country's inception. We would argue, however, that regional grievances and conflicts have never threatened the territorial integrity of Canada. Westerners and, less stridently, eastern Canadians have long complained about policies and institutions that favour the interests of Ontario and Quebec. But their resentment has never boiled over to produce politically significant separatist movements in these regions or popular defection from the *idea* of Canada. The importance of regionalism will be discussed in Chapter 4.

For most of Canada's history, relations between the francophone and anglophone communities have not posed a threat to the political community. The differences and tensions between Canada's two major language groups have been managed through political accommodations between their political elites. This practice arguably goes back to the Quebec Act of 1774. Official protection was extended to the Catholic Church and Quebec's civil law system just when the British authorities were worried about the prospect of political rebellion in the American colonies spreading north. The tradition of deal-making between French and English Canada acquired a rather different twist in the couple of decades prior to Confederation, when the current provinces of Ontario and Quebec were united with a common legislature. The practice of dual ministries, with a leader from both Canada East (Quebec) and Canada West (Ontario), quickly developed, as did the convention that a bill needed to be passed by majorities from both East and West in order to become law. The federal division of powers that formed the basis of the 1867 Confederation continued this deal-making tradition. The assignment to the provinces of jurisdiction over education, property and civil rights, and

local matters was shaped by Quebec politicians' insistence on control over those matters involving cultural differences.

This tradition of elitist deal-making has continued throughout Canada's history at two different levels. Nationally, the federal cabinet and national political parties, particularly the Liberal Party of Canada, have been important forums where the interests of Quebec could be represented. But with the rise of a more aggressive and nationalistic Quebec state in the 1960s, the ability to represent the interests of French and English Canada within national institutions has become less important than whether compromises can be reached between the governments of Canada and Quebec.

The modus vivendi that for a couple centuries prevented French-English conflicts from exploding into challenges to the idea of a single Canada seemed to come unstitched during the 1960s. Quebec independence, which previously had been a marginal idea that surfaced only sporadically in the province's politics, became a serious proposition advocated by many French-speaking intellectuals and apparently supported by a sizable minority of Québécois. The independence option spawned a number of organized political groups during the 1960s. In 1968, most of them threw their support behind the pro-independence Parti Québécois (PQ). Since then, the debate over whether the province should remain in Canada, and if so on what terms, has been one of the chief dimensions of Quebec political life.

In attempting to understand how great a threat Quebec separatism has posed to the Canadian community, we will consider two measures, political violence and public attitudes.

Political Violence

Canadians are not accustomed to the violent resolution of political disputes. There have been only two political assassinations since Confederation, the first when D'Arcy McGee was shot down on the muddy streets of Ottawa in 1868 and the second in 1970 when Quebec's Minister of Labour,

Pierre Laporte, was strangled to death by members of the Front de liberation du Québec. *The World Handbook of Social and Political Indicators* ranks Canada well down the list of countries in terms of riots, armed political attacks, deaths from domestic political violence, and government sanctions to repress or eliminate a perceived threat to the state. Non-violent protest has occupied a more prominent place in Canadian politics, as one would expect in any genuine democracy. But even here, protest demonstrations historically have been much rarer in Canada than in most other advanced industrialized democracies.[21]

Violence has not, however, been either absent or unimportant in Canadian politics. Much of that violence has involved labour disputes or workers' protests where the police or military were called in to protect the interests of employers and the capitalist social order. The violent suppression of the Winnipeg General Strike in 1919 and the use of the Regina police in 1935 to break up the 'On to Ottawa Trek' of unemployed workers during the depth of the Depression are perhaps the two most noteworthy instances of such violence. The forcible detention of many Japanese, German, and Italian Canadians during World War II is another instance of state political violence. Indeed, in most of these cases the state decided to use violence to settle some conflict or deal with some perceived menace. The most significant instances of political violence instigated by groups or individuals against the state have been related to the French-English conflict and, more recently, the status of Canada's Native population.

The almost tribal animosities that have existed between French and English Canadians have crystallized around violent events on several occasions. The hanging of the francophone Métis leader Louis Riel in 1885, after the military defeat of his provisional government in the territory of Saskatchewan, provoked denunciations of the Conservative government and its leader, Sir John A. Macdonald, from many Francophone leaders. Although they did not sympathize with the rebel-

lion that Riel led, francophones felt that the government's unwillingness to commute Riel's execution sentence was influenced by anti-French prejudice. Violence broke out again in 1918 over the conscription issue. French Canadians believed that Canada's involvement in World War I was motivated by the colonial attachments that English Canadians still felt for Britain, and they opposed the imposition of conscription. Anti-conscription riots broke out in Quebec City during the spring of 1918, the culmination of simmering recriminations and animosities between French and English Canadians over Canada's relationship to the British Empire.

Violence flared up in the streets of Montreal in 1955 when Maurice 'Rocket' Richard was suspended by the president of the National Hockey League, Clarence Campbell. French-Canadian supporters of the Canadiens and their star player saw the suspension as more than punishment for a stick-swinging incident. They saw it as yet another example of ethnically motivated discrimination on the part of 'les maudits anglais' (the damned English).

The 1960s saw renewed violence, this time a spate of bombings and vandalism directed at symbols of the federal government's authority and anglophone domination in the province of Quebec. This was mainly the work of the FLQ, a very small group of people who achieved national prominence when they kidnapped British trade commissioner James Cross and Quebec cabinet minister Pierre Laporte in October 1970. The federal government reacted by invoking the War Measures Act, under which normal civil liberties were suspended. About 500 people were detained under the authority of the Act, although none of them were ultimately charged. Laporte's dead body was found shortly after imposition of the Act. Cross was released by the FLQ a few weeks later in exchange for safe passage out of the country for his captors.

The October Crisis, as the affair came to be called, was unique in Canada's political history. It was the only occasion when the War Measures Act has been invoked during peacetime. The government of Pierre Trudeau argued that civil order was teetering on the verge of collapse in Quebec and that there existed a state of 'apprehended insurrection'. Most commentators argue that Ottawa's reaction was excessive, even in the unfamiliar circumstances of political kidnappings and uncertainty that existed at the time. Excessive or not, the October Crisis needs to be placed in its proper perspective. The political kidnappings were the work of a tiny band of political extremists whose tactics enjoyed little support among Quebec nationalists. Although there was some sympathy for the goals of the FLQ, this evaporated after their murder of Pierre Laporte.

Perhaps the most revealing lessons to be drawn from the October Crisis involve the attitude of the Canadian public and the actions of the state when confronted with political violence. Canadians were overwhelmingly supportive of the decision to invoke the War Measures Act and both opposition parties in the House of Commons supported the government's actions. The state, faced with a challenge to its authority, reacted with its own violence, rounding up scores of Quebec nationalists, Communists, and assorted malcontents who had absolutely nothing to do with the militant FLQ. Kenneth McNaught argues that this is a recurring pattern in Canadian history, the 'stringent suppression of violence when it occurs or is threatened and lenience toward the instigators once the crisis has been weathered'.[22]

Public Attitudes

'Egalité ou indépendance!' (Equality or independence!) The sentiment is familiar to any contemporary Quebec-watcher. The slogan did not, however, originate with the PQ. *Egalité ou indépendance* was the title of a booklet written by Daniel Johnson, leader of the Union Nationale and Premier of Quebec between 1966 and 1968, and served as his party's campaign slogan in the 1966 election. But neither Johnson nor the Union Nationale was committed to separatism. With the birth of the Parti Québécois in 1968, the province acquired a political party whose leader, René Lévesque, and platform were committed to taking Quebec out of Canada. Daniel Johnson's rhetoric and René Lévesque's commitment represented and helped catalyze an important change in Quebec politics. This change involved the idea of Quebec independence. Before the mid-1960s independence was a marginal idea in the province's politics, supported by many Québécois intellectuals but not taken seriously by the main political parties or by the public. Since then, independence has attracted the support of a sizable minority of Québécois.

According to public opinion polls, the level of popular support for Quebec independence has ranged between a low of about 20 per cent to a high of nearly 60 per cent over the last few decades (see Figure 2.1). Without reading too much into the numbers, we may say that a durable core of support exists for the idea of Quebec independence. The level of support varies over time and also depending on what sort of independence is envisaged by the pollster's question. Support for 'sovereignty-association'—a term generally understood to mean a politically sovereign Quebec that would be linked to Canada through some sort of commercial union or free trade agreement—is always higher than for outright political and economic separation. It is clear that many Québécois are conditional separatists. Indeed, even among PQ supporters there has always been much less enthusiasm for complete separation than for separation plus economic association.[23]

When the PQ was first elected to office in 1976, it was clear that Quebec voters were not casting their ballots for separatism. The PQ was committed to holding a referendum on Quebec independence, so that non-separatists and those who were soft on the issue were able to vote for the party without fear that a PQ government would necessarily mean Quebec independence. Indeed, a survey conducted during the 1976 campaign revealed that only about half of those intending to vote for the PQ actually favoured independence.[24]

When the PQ sought re-election in 1981 after having lost a 1980 referendum on sovereignty-association by a 60–40 margin, it ran on its record in office rather than on its goal of Quebec independence. In fact, the PQ promised not to hold another referendum during its next term. As in 1976, the PQ's 1981 victory could not be interpreted as a vote for separatism. In 1998, three years after narrowly losing another sovereignty referendum, the PQ won re-election after a campaign in which such issues as unemployment and health-care

reform clearly overshadowed the issue of Quebec's future in or out of Canada. Premier Lucien Bouchard felt constrained to admit that the 43 per cent of votes cast for the PQ, versus 44 per cent for the Quebec Liberal Party, could in no way be viewed as a mandate for independence or even for another referendum in the near term.

The first direct challenge to the Canadian political community came in May of 1980, when the PQ government held its promised referendum on sovereignty-association. The referendum was

Figure 2.1   Support for Quebec Independence, 1978–2002

'If a referendum was held today regarding Quebec sovereignty, would you vote for or against Quebec sovereignty?'

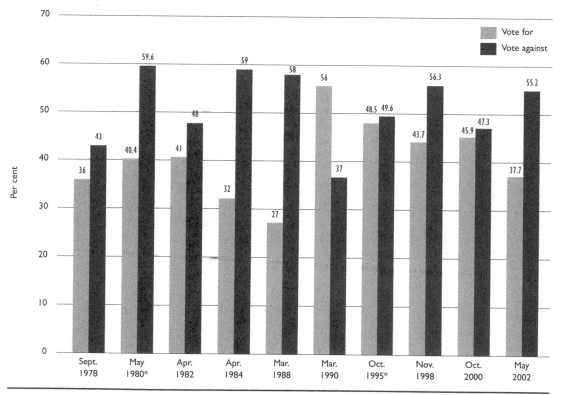

*The results for 1980 and 1995 are based on the referendum questions for each of those years.

Note: The columns for each year may not add up to 100 per cent because 'don't know' and 'no response' are not included.

Source: Adapted from Simon Langlois, *La société québécoise en tendances, 1960–1990* (Québec: Institut québécois de recherche sur la culture, 1990), 649. Percentages for 1998–2002 are based on polls conducted by Léger Marketing.

very carefully—some would say trickily—worded. It stressed that what was being proposed was not a radical break from Canada, but a negotiated political independence for Quebec that would maintain economic ties to Canada.

> The Government of Quebec has made public its proposal to negotiate a new arrangement with the rest of Canada, based on the equality of nations; this arrangement would enable Quebec to acquire the exclusive power to make its laws, administer its taxes and establish relations abroad—in other words, sovereignty—and at the same time to maintain with Canada an economic association including a common currency; no change in political status resulting from these negotiations will be effected without approval by the people through another referendum; on these terms, do you give the Government of Quebec the mandate to negotiate the proposed agreement between Quebec and Canada? Yes. No.

Despite the PQ's careful strategy, Quebec voters rejected the sovereignty-association option by a vote of 59.6 per cent ('Non') to 40.4 per cent ('Oui'). Even among francophones, a majority voted against Quebec independence.[25] Advocates of Quebec separatism were quick to point out that sovereignty-association was more popular among younger than older voters. Time, they argued, would eventually turn the tide in favour of independence. Others argued that the greater popularity of the 'oui' option among those who entered adulthood in the nationalist 1960s and early 1970s—Quebec's 'baby boomers'—reflected the exceptional politically formative experiences of this generation, and that subsequent generations, not raised in the intensely nationalist ferment that characterized the 1960s in Quebec, would find separatism less appealing.

It does not appear, however, that Quebec separation is less popular among young francophones Québécois than it was among their counterparts in the 1960s and 1970s. On the contrary, support for separatism is stronger among younger cohorts of Quebec's francophone electorate than among other voters. Support for separatism is especially strong among young, highly educated Québécois, as was also true in the 1960s. Studies of the 1995 Quebec referendum show that a solid majority of younger francophone voters, between the ages of 20 and 30, voted for independence. Separatists draw the conclusion that support for independence will grow over time, as older cohorts of the electorate are replaced by younger, pro-independence ones. Skeptics note, however, that political preferences often change as one grows older and that there is no reason to assume that the younger generation's support for Quebec sovereignty will remain firm.

Accustomed to the challenge that Quebec separatism poses to the political community, most Canadians were probably surprised when the Oka crisis revealed the existence of another challenge to the idea of a single Canada. In fact, however, the armed confrontation at Oka had several precedents. Violent confrontations between Natives and whites punctuate Canadian history, going back to the extermination of the Beothuk Indians of Newfoundland in the 1700s. Some of the major episodes of violence between Natives and whites are described in Table 2.2.

These violent clashes are linked by a common thread. It is the struggle between the traditional independence of Native communities and the authority of, first, European colonial authorities and then that of the Canadian state. Native resistance to the rule of white authorities and the efforts of those authorities to establish their rule and crush Native resistance span over three centuries of Canadian history. But the struggle between Native aspirations for autonomy and the authority of the Euro-Canadian community has only occasionally produced flashpoints of violence. Long periods of apparent peace have been more characteristic of Native-white relations. We say 'apparent peace', because even during these periods the conflict between the aspirations of many Aboriginal communities and the demands and restrictions imposed on them by the Canadian state was only dormant, waiting to be catalyzed by some issue or incident. The confrontation at Oka turned out to be just such an incident, galvanizing Native groups and throwing into sharp relief the issue of Native land claims and demands for Aboriginal self-government.

We cannot deal with these matters in any detail here.[26] The land claims issue is essentially about who has the right to control territory to which various Native communities claim a historical right. Treaties signed by Ottawa and Aboriginal groups after Confederation, which were intended by the Canadian authorities to extinguish Native claims to these territories in exchange for reserves, money, and other benefits, do not cover all of Canada. In fact, an enormous area encompassing much of the North and both the western and eastern extremities of the country were not covered by treaties. Moreover, about 40 per cent of status Indians[27] are not members

of bands that have signed treaties with Ottawa. Having never been vanquished militarily or given up their territorial rights through a treaty, they claim that the land their ancestors inhabited still belongs to them.

Land claim negotiations have progressed at a snail's pace for decades, leading most Native groups to conclude that Ottawa really has not been serious about settling these claims. The issue had only slightly intruded onto public consciousness until the Oka confrontation, when the Mohawk Warriors claimed to be an independent nation with a historical right to the land on which the local municipality planned to extend a golf course. This claim to be a sovereign nation, outside the authority of Canadian law, was more extreme than most Native demands for self-government. And it was a claim that was steadfastly rejected by the federal government. 'Native self-government', for-

Table 2.2   Major Violent Confrontations between Natives and Whites

Date	Native Group and Location	Event
1700s	Beothuk (Newfoundland)	Many were killed by Europeans.
1763	Seneca, Ojibway, and other tribes (area near Detroit)	Led by Odawa war chief, Pontiac, a confederation of tribes rebelled against British rule in several bloody confrontations.
circa 1794	Shawnee and other tribes (Ohio River Valley)	Led by Shawnee war chief Tecumseh, several Indian tribes attempted unsuccessfully to resist white settlement and control of the Ohio Valley.
1885	Métis and Plains Indians (Saskatchewan)	In the North-West Rebellion, a series of battles took place between Métis and Indian forces, on one side, and white militia volunteers and soldiers, on the other.
1869–70	Métis (Manitoba)	In the Red River Rebellion, Métis fought for provincial status and guaranteed land and cultural rights.
1990	Mohawk (Quebec)	This armed confrontation at Oka resulted in one death and riots against Natives protesting the expansion of a golf course on land that they claimed was theirs by historical right.
1995	Shuswap (British Columbia) Chippewa (Ontario)	Armed confrontations took place at Lake Gustafsen, BC, and Ipperwash Provincial Park in Ontario. In both cases a small group of Natives occupied land they claimed was sacred. A Native was shot dead at the Ipperwash standoff.
2000	Mi'kmaq (Burnt Church, NB)	Conflict between Aboriginals and non-Aboriginals over fishing rights flared up in vandalism, boat ramming, and shots fired.

mer Prime Minister Mulroney declared, 'does not now and cannot ever mean sovereign independence. Mohawk lands are part of Canadian territory, and Canadian law must and does apply.'[28] Liberal Prime Minister Jean Chrétien also rejected the claims of some Natives that they stand outside the authority of Canadian law.

Recent land claim settlements that include structures for Native self-government, notably the creation of Nunavut in the eastern Arctic and the Nisga'a Treaty in British Columbia, state explicitly that laws of general application continue to apply to those who inhabit these Native lands and that the Charter of Rights and Freedoms applies to their governments.

Freedom

'Live free or die.' So reads the motto on licence plates in the state of New Hampshire. Individual freedom is said to be part of the American political creed, symbolized in such icons as the Statue of Liberty, Philadelphia's Liberty Bell, the Bill of Rights, and the Declaration of Independence. Canadians, it is usually claimed, are more willing than Americans to limit individual freedom in pursuit of social order or group rights. Is this true?

The greater stress on individual freedom and suspicion of government control in the United States than in Canada is corroborated by many types of evidence. One of these is literature. Writers like Henry David Thoreau, Jack Kerouac, and Allan Ginsberg embody a powerfully individualistic current that runs through American culture. There is no Canadian Thoreau, whose writings about civil disobedience and the need to resist the demands of society as the price to be paid for a life of virtue and freedom have had an important influence on the libertarian tradition in American politics. Individualism and freedom are also powerful themes in American popular culture. Hollywood's portrayal of the loner who is indifferent to social conventions and the law, and whose virtue and attractiveness rest on these traits, has long been one of the most successful genres in popular film.

Marlon Brando's brooding performance in *The Wild One* and Peter Fonda in *Easy Rider* were in this tradition. Clint Eastwood, Sylvester Stallone, Charles Bronson, Harrison Ford, Bruce Willis, and Denzel Washington are among those whose film characters have embodied this against-the-grain individualism.

Americans' more passionate love affair with freedom is evident in the very different character of the gun control debate in Canada and the United States. When former Liberal Justice Minister Alan Rock introduced a law proposing tougher restrictions on gun ownership and a national registry for all firearms, opposition in Canada focused on such matters as whether the legislation would really reduce the use of guns in committing crimes and whether the legislation reflected urban Canada's insensitivity and even hostility to the values and lifestyles of hunters and rural communities. Few people argued, and not many seriously believed, that a fundamental freedom was jeopardized by this legislation.

In the United States, however, proposals to restrict the sale and ownership of firearms invariably face objections from those who see these restrictions as threatening individual freedom. It is a mistake to assume that these objections are merely the cynical ravings of National Rifle Association devotees and white supremacists who wrap themselves in the Second Amendment's guarantee of the 'right to bear arms'. Many Americans believe that gun ownership is a right, not a privilege that governments bestow on citizens. One often hears the argument that restrictions on gun ownership will leave citizens helpless to defend themselves, not simply against criminals but against the state! This argument would be met with blank stares of incomprehension in Canada. But in the United States, even many of those who do not agree that individual freedom would be placed at risk by a ban on private gun ownership at least understand the premises and beliefs that lie behind this argument.

Mistrust of the state is as old as the American War of Independence. It is woven into the American Constitution's systems of checks and balances; it was behind the adoption of a Bill of Rights before the ink had scarcely dried on that Constitution; and it was also part of the case for federalism, which, as James Madison argued in the famous *Federalist Papers*, no. 51, was expected to help check the emergence of any political majority large enough to threaten individual and minority rights. Pride in their system of government and greater patriotism than in most other democracies have coexisted in the American political culture with a mistrust of government that has its roots in both the revolutionary experience and the individualistic spirit of Americans. Thus it is that many Americans, and not just those who dress in khaki on the weekends and participate in the civilian militias that are perhaps a uniquely American phenomenon, understand the argument that government may be the problem and the enemy and that citizens have a right to defend themselves and should not have to rely on government to do it for them. Canadians are much less likely to share these views.

The state is viewed more benignly north of the Canada-United States border. As Seymour Martin Lipset observes, 'If [Canada] leans toward communitarianism—the public mobilization of resources to fulfill group objectives—the [United States] sees individualism—private endeavour— as the way an "unseen hand" produces optimum, socially beneficial results.'[29] Canadian writer Pierre Berton makes the same point when he maintains that 'We've always accepted more governmental control over our lives than . . . [Americans] have—and fewer civil liberties.'[30]

Attitudinal data also provide a basis for generalizations about the value attached to freedom in the two societies. Using questions that require people to choose between the protection of individual liberty and the defence of social order, Americans consistently give more freedom-oriented responses (see Table 2.3).

Americans' greater stress on individual freedom is often credited to their individualist culture. Canadians, on the other hand, are often portrayed as less assertive about their rights as individuals and more concerned than Americans with social order. Some object to this characterization of Americans as being more respectful of individual freedoms than Canadians because Americans' understanding of freedom as the absence of restraint on individual behaviour— what is sometimes called negative freedom— actually denies real freedom to many people. Canadians' greater willingness to permit government restrictions on individual behaviour does not mean that they value freedom less, but that they are more likely than Americans to believe that real freedom often requires that government interfere with individual property rights and economic markets and, moreover, that all citizens are entitled to such things as public education and health care in order to help equalize the opportunities available to the well-off and the less-privileged. Canadians, some argue, have what might be characterized as a positive conception of freedom, one that requires that governments act rather than get out of the way.

The somewhat weaker attachment of Canadians to what might be characterized as an individualistic notion of freedom is corroborated by the words and symbols that parties and candidates use in their attempt to win the support of voters. If we think of these words and symbols as being a sort of connective tissue between citizens and those who wish to represent them, it is clear that the key to electoral success lies in the use of ideas, images, words, and symbols that resonate positively with a large number of voters. A study of the campaign rhetoric of Canadian party leaders and the American presidential candidates in the 2000 elections held in their respective countries found that the core values and unifying themes expressed in the George W. Bush/Republican Party message were clearly more individualistic than those of any national leader and party in Canada. This simply confirms the picture that emerges from attitudinal data and other evidence from which cultural values may be inferred: the defence of

Table 2.3   Support for Liberty and Order in Canada and the United States

	Canadians			Americans
	Francophones	Anglophones	All	
a. 'It is better to live in an orderly society than to allow people so much freedom they can become disruptive.' (percentage agreeing)	77	61	65	51
b. 'The idea that everyone has a right to their own opinion is being carried too far these days.' (percentage agreeing)	45	33	37	19
c. 'Free speech is just not worth it if it means we have to put up with the danger to society of radical and extremist views.' (percentage agreeing)	38	35	36	28
d. 'Free speech ought to be allowed for all political groups even if some of the things that these groups believe in are highly insulting and threatening to particular segments of society.' (percentage agreeing)	63	47	51	60
e. 'In times of crisis, do you believe government should or should not have the power to declare a national emergency and remove all civil rights?'				

	Canada	United States
Should	48	41
Should not	49	56

Sources: Items a to d from Paul M. Sniderman et al., 'Liberty, Authority, and Community: Civil Liberties and the Canadian Political Culture' (Centre of Criminology, University of Toronto, and Survey Research Centre, University of California, Berkeley, 1988), figures 9A–9D. Item e is from the Maclean's-Decima Poll, 'Portrait of Two Nations', *Maclean's*, 3 July 1989, 32.

individual freedom can be a harder sell in Canada than in the United States (see Box 2.3).

Equality

If the Loyalists have left a Tory imprint on Canadian politics, we would expect to find that Canadians place a lower value on equality than do Americans. Tories, after all, believed that the organization of society along class lines was a natural and desirable state of affairs. They were apt to sneer at American democracy as 'mobocracy'. A long line of sociologists, political scientists, and historians, going back to Alexis de Toqueville and other Europeans who visited North America in the nineteenth century, have generally agreed that

America's political culture is more egalitarian and Canada's more hierarchical.

Whatever the historical accuracy of this characterization might have been, it is no longer obviously true. As Figure 2.2 shows, Canadians appear to value equality *more* than do Americans. They are much more likely to support public policies, such as a publicly funded health-care system and a guaranteed minimum income, intended to narrow the gap between the poor and the well-off. A comparative study of the development of the welfare state in Canada and the US corroborates this difference. Robert Kudrle and Theodore Marmor argue that ideological differences between the two societies are the main reason for the earlier enactment and more generous charac-

BOX 2.3   Should Insulting Speech Be Protected?

In the autumn of 1999 a person of what might be described as extreme religious views entered the campus of the University of Western Ontario. Situating himself in front of the student centre he began a tirade against what he believed to be the sinful behaviour, loose morals, and generally reprehensible values of the students and the society in which they lived. Some students engaged him in a shouting exchange and the campus police were called. There was no physical violence and the man at the centre of the incident at no time threatened anyone. Nonetheless, he was escorted off the campus and informed that he should not return, or at least not if he planned to do what he had done that day, which was to say publicly on the grounds of a public institution things that some people found to be highly offensive and insulting.

In the autumn of 2000 I was walking across the University of Michigan's Ann Arbor campus. A group of Christian fundamentalists, led by a very loud and articulate speaker and with a background of large signs, had attracted a crowd of at least 100 students. Many more stopped briefly or slowed their walk to hear what the speaker had to say. His was a no-holds-barred, fire-and-brimstone attack on contemporary values and what he assumed to be the beliefs and behaviours of the students listening to him. He informed the students that their sinful ways damned them to spend eternity in Hell. He spoke of abortion as an abomination and called its supporters evil. And he declared that his female listeners were whores. Some students laughed, some heckled, and others just listened. When I passed by about two hours later he was still going full force. There were no campus police in sight.

Does the very different reaction of student and campus authorities at these two universities, one in Ontario and the other three hours away in Michigan, tell us anything about differences in what are considered to be the acceptable limits of free speech in the two societies? Are Canadians more likely than Americans to believe that public utterances that some—perhaps even most—will find to be offensive, insulting, and hurtful should not be permitted? What would be the reaction on your campus?

ter of welfare state policies in Canada, observing that 'In every policy area it appears that general public as well as elite opinion . . . [has been] more supportive of state action in Canada than in the United States.'[31]

Canadians are more likely than Americans to value equality of results, whereas Americans are more likely than their northern neighbours to value equality of opportunity. Numerous cross-national attitudinal surveys confirm this observation.[32] In Canada egalitarianism has its roots in a more collectivist tradition; in the United States it draws on a more individualistic tradition. The value differences between the two societies are shaded rather than starkly contrasting, as parts 1 and 2 of Figure 2.2 show. Nevertheless, they help to explain Canadians' apparently greater tolerance—historically at any rate—for state measures targeted at disadvantaged groups and regions. Lipset's conclusion seems a fair one: 'Canadians are committed to redistribution egalitarianism, while Americans place more emphasis on meritocratic competition and equality of opportunity.'[33]

In Canada, more than in the United States, debates over equality historically have been about group rights and equality between different groups in society, not equality between individuals. This difference goes back to the founding of

Figure 2.2   Individualism: A Cross-National Comparison

A. Individuals should take more reponsibility for providing for themselves

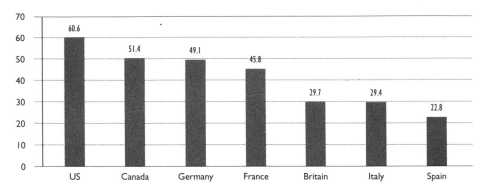

B. In the long run, hard work usually brings a better life

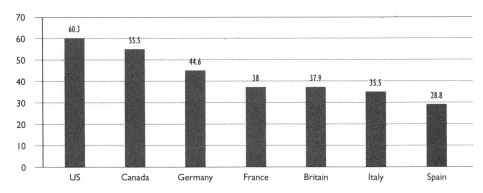

C. Private ownership of business and industry should be increased

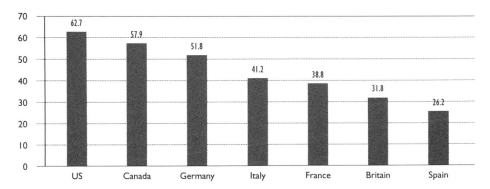

Figure 2.2 continued

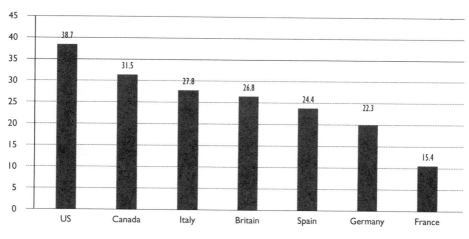

D. Why are there people who live in need? Percentage choosing 'Because of laziness and lack of will power' as their first choice

Note: This survey was taken in West Germany.

Source: Adapted from data in Tables 5–1 and 5–3 in Neil Nevitte, *The Decline of Deference: Canadian Value Change in Cross-National Perspective* (Peterborough, Ont.: Broadview Press, 1996), based on data from the 1990 World Values Survey.

the two societies. While the American Constitution made no distinction between groups of citizens, the Quebec Act of 1774 incorporated protection for religious rights, and the British North America Act of 1867 provided protections for both religious and language rights.

A by-product of Canada's long tradition of recognizing group rights, many have argued, is greater tolerance of cultural diversity than one finds in the United States. This is the familiar, if exaggerated, theme of the Canadian 'mosaic' versus the American 'melting pot'. Although there is considerable historical evidence to suggest that non-French, non-British groups have felt less pressure to abandon their language and customs in Canada than have non-English-speaking groups in the United States, rates of cultural assimilation have been high in both societies. Moreover, Canadian governments have shown themselves to be as capable as their American counterparts of discriminating

against ethnic and religious communities. For example, in both countries many people of Japanese origin were deprived of their property and kept confined to camps during World War II. The religious practices of Doukhobors, Hutterites, Mennonites, and Jehovah's Witnesses have at various times brought them into conflict with either Ottawa or provincial governments. And in both Canada and the United States immigration policy has historically discriminated against non-white, non-European peoples—although this is no longer a fair characterization of policy in either country.

Despite evidence that, in Canada, too, tolerance of cultural diversity has known limits, these limits have been less restrictive than in the United States. The treatment of Canada's Native peoples, for example, has been less harsh and less violent than that of America's Native minorities. And there is nothing in Canada's history that compares to the official discrimination and the physical violence directed against American blacks for much of that country's history. An official policy of multiculturalism has existed in Canada since 1971 and was entrenched in the Constitution in 1982.[34] Moreover, Canada's Constitution appears to provide a firmer basis for affirmative action programs and other state activities that have as their goal 'the amelioration of conditions of disadvantaged individuals or groups including those that are disadvantaged because of race, national or ethnic origin, colour, religion, sex, age or mental or physical disability'.[35] In addition, a poll published in *Maclean's* several years ago found that more Canadians (64 per cent) than Americans (33 per cent) were likely to choose 'tolerant' and 'peaceful' as the words that they felt best described the ideal citizen of their country.[36]

The thesis of the Canadian mosaic versus the American melting pot should not be pushed too hard. Despite the fact that cultural assimilation seems historically to have been part of the American ethos, to the point that it is even expressed in the national motto 'E pluribus unum' (from the many, one), a combination of government policies and court decisions in that country has steered that country away from the melting pot and towards a mosaic-type society. An extensive system of Spanish-language instruction has been created in parts of the United States, particularly California, over the last two decades. Affirmative action policies, from university admission quotas to 'minority set asides' (minority quotas in the allotment of government contracts), and boundary lines drawn to maximize the proportion of minority voters in some congressional districts began earlier and arguably have been taken further in the United States than in Canada. Universities and other schools in the United States pioneered the concept and practice of minority-oriented curricula (African-American Studies, for example), and this dimension of cultural pluralism is well established there, even while some other aspects of multicultural policy appear to be under assault. Indeed, the very intensity of controversy over multiculturalism, affirmative action, and ascription-

based policies in the United States is to some degree a reflection of just how successful the mosaic model has been in influencing public life in that society. The backlash is a tribute to the inroads it made.

We should not imagine that the idea of multiculturalism, and the programs and structures that seek to implement the mosaic model, have gone unchallenged in Canada. Neil Bissoondath's best-selling book *Selling Illusions: The Cult of Multiculturalism in Canada* (1994) and Reginald Bibby's *Mosaic Madness: The Poverty and Potential of Life in Canada* (1990) represent two of the salvoes launched against official multiculturalism (as opposed to tolerance of diversity and pluralism that is not sponsored and reinforced by the state). A 1996 study of federal multiculturalism policies, conducted for the Department of Canadian Heritage, concluded that the vast majority of Canadians supported multiculturalism, but that most people associated multiculturalism with cultural diversity rather than with government policy. Indeed, about half of the people surveyed for this study admitted to being unfamiliar with Ottawa's policy of official multiculturalism. Survey data also confirmed what one knows from following the news: public acceptance of diversity appears to decline as the visibility of the minority group increases. Tolerance is lower for Sikhs, Indo-Pakistanis, Arabs, and Muslims than it is for French, Italians, Ukrainians, and Jews.[37]

In view of how deeply the distinction between the Canadian mosaic and the American melting pot is embedded in the collective psyche of Canadians, it would seem surprising that there has been so little effort to test empirically this article of faith. But perhaps this is not so surprising. After all, the thing about articles of *faith* is that they do not require proof. They are assumed to be so self-evidently true that searching examination of the evidence on which they rest is considered a ridiculous waste of time. Moreover, there may appear to be something sacrilegious in questioning a belief that is so central to Canadians' ideas of what distinguishes their society from that of the United States.

Raymond Breton and Jeffrey Reitz risk this sacrilege in what is the most ambitious and systematic attempt to test the proposition that Canadians are more tolerant of diversity than their allegedly more assimilationist neighbours to the south. In *The Illusion of Difference* (1994) they review existing studies of the mosaic versus melting pot thesis and examine a number of comparative surveys and census data from the two countries. They conclude that the differences between Canada and the United States are 'more apparent than real'. The Canadian style, they argue, 'is more low-key than the American; moreover, Canadians have a conscious tradition of tolerance that Americans do not have.' These differences in the way multiculturalism and ethnic diversity have been thought of in the two societies 'have not produced less pressure toward conformity in Canada, or less propensity to discriminate in employment or housing.'[38] Comparing rates of language retention, ethnic group identification, participation in ethnically based social networks, and attitudes and behaviour towards racial minorities, Breton and Reitz make the case that there is almost no empirical basis for Canadians' cherished self-image of their society as being more tolerant and less assimilationist than the United States.

Perhaps in response to the public's growing sense that cultural mosaic policies have contributed to national disunity, in late 1998 the federal government proposed changes to the Immigration Act that would require prospective immigrants to Canada, other than those in the family and refugee classes, to know either French or English. This proposal was criticized by some as having the effect, if not the intention, of discriminating against prospective immigrants from countries—mainly less developed countries—where the likelihood of knowing either English or French is relatively low.

Gender equality is another dimension of group rights that has acquired prominence in recent decades. In both Canada and the United States attitudes on the appropriate roles and behaviour of men and women have changed sharply in the direction of greater equality. The visible signs of this change are everywhere, including laws on pay equity, easier access to abortion, affirmative action to increase the number of women employed in male-dominated professions, the ways in which females are portrayed by the media, and greater female participation in the political system. These are all indirect measures of attitudes towards gender equality. Although they do not provide a direct indication of cultural values, we might reasonably infer these values from the actions of governments and private organizations. Comparing Canada to the United States using such measures, we come up with a mixed scorecard. The differences between the two societies tend not to be very large, Canada being 'more equal' on some counts and the United States on others.

As in the case of the other dimensions of equality we have examined, there is no evidence to support the claim that Canadians value equality less than Americans do. Indeed, in terms of recognizing group rights, it is fair to say that Canadian governments have gone at least as far as their American counterparts. In one important respect, however, Canadians are unequivocally more committed to an egalitarian society than are Americans. This involves racial equality. Part 3(a) of Figure 2.3 confirms that racist sentiments are more pervasive in the United States than in Canada. This difference clearly has its roots in the very different histories of the two societies. Those who argue that Canadian society historically has placed greater emphasis on hierarchy and ascriptive status, and the United States on equality and achievement, forget that racial inequality was the great blind spot of American liberalism. Canadians can thank the absence of a slavery-based plantation economy in their past for the fact that racism is less ingrained in their society than in that of the United States.

Citizen Expectations for Government

Canadians, it has often been argued, are more likely than Americans to look to government to meet their needs. They are, moreover, more likely to accept state actions that they dislike, as opposed to mobilizing against such policies and the governments that institute them. Thomas Jefferson's declaration that 'That government is best which governs least' is a less accurate encapsulation of Canadian political culture than the title of a Canadian poetry anthology, *A Government Job at Last*.[39]

This view of Canadians as both more demanding of the state and more passive towards it appears

Figure 2.3   Equality in Canada and the United States

1. *Socio-economic equality*

   Do you view the following as an absolute right that can never be taken away, or as a limited right, one which in certain circumstances can be limited by government?

   a. A publicly funded health care system available to all, regardless of financial situation.

   b. A guaranteed minimum income for everyone.

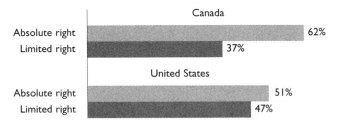

2. *Equality vs individual freedom*

   a. Too much liberalism has been producing increasingly wide differences in people's economic and social life. People should live more equally. (percentage agreeing with the statement)

   b. Certainly both freedom and equality are important, but if I were to make up my mind for one of the two, I would consider equality more important, that is, that nobody is underprivileged and that class differences are not so strong. (percentage agreeing with the statement)

Figure 2.3 continued

3. *Racial and ethnic equality*

   a. Would you be happy, indifferent or unhappy if one of your children married someone from a different racial background?

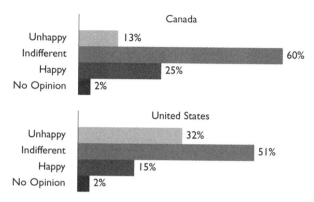

   b. What would you think is better for Canada/the United States: that new immigrants be encouraged to maintain their distinct cultures and ways, or to change their distinct culture and ways to blend with the larger society?

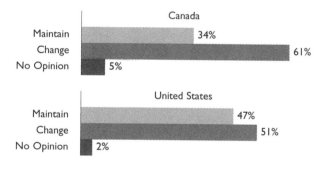

Source: Parts 1 and 3 are adapted from Maclean's-Decima Poll, 'Portrait of Two Nations', *Maclean's*, 3 July 1989, 48–9. Part 2 is based on data reported in S.M. Lipset, *Continental Divide: The Values and Institutions of the United States and Canada* (Toronto: C.D. Howe Institute, 1989), 157–8.

to be backed up by a good deal of evidence. On the expectations side, Canadian governments do more than American ones to redistribute wealth between individuals and regions of the country; their intervention in the health services sector is far more extensive than in the United States; they own corporations whose activities range from producing electricity to television broadcasting, while American governments generally content themselves with regulating privately owned businesses in these same industries; and they are much more actively involved in promoting particular cultural values, especially those associated with bilingualism, than are most governments in the United States. Overall, the state accounts for a larger share of gross national expenditure in Canada than in the United States, and by most appearances government is more intrusive in Canadian society.

AUGUSTANA UNIVERSITY COLLEGE
LIBRARY

What about the evidence for Canadians' alleged passivity in the face of government actions that they dislike? Here, the comparatively elitist nature of policy-making, including the ability of governments to pass laws that either could not get through the American legislative system or only in a much diluted form, is said to demonstrate the greater acquiescence of Canadians in the decisions of their political leaders. For example, in both countries the persistence of large public-sector deficits became an important political issue in the 1980s. But whereas a major part of the Canadian government's response was to increase taxes, which included broadening the range of taxed goods and services through the politically unpopular Goods and Services Tax, proposals for increased taxes remained non-starters in American politics. The middle-class tax revolt embodied in California's 'Proposition 13', which swept across much of the United States during the late 1970s and early 1980s, had no analogue in Canada despite generally higher levels of provincial and local taxation in this country.

To use another example, in Canada a decision of the House of Commons—actually a series of decisions[40]—eliminated capital punishment, despite widespread public support for the death penalty. In the United States, elected politicians have been more responsive to their constituents' views on this issue, and the death penalty exists in most states. Those limitations that have been placed on capital punishment, including its suspension for several years, have been due primarily to American Supreme Court decisions and not to legislative action.

Canadians' apparent greater faith in government, compared to the more skeptical attitudes of Americans, owes a good deal to a collectivist ethos that sets Canadians and their history apart from the United States. It is this ethos that Canadian nationalists invoke when they argue that Canada's public health-care system and more generous social programs reflect the 'soul' of this country, and that their dismemberment would send Canadians down the allegedly mean-spirited path of American individualism. Some of Canada's most prominent thinkers, including George Grant and Charles Taylor, have argued that the collectivist ethos and greater willingness of Canadians than Americans to use the state to achieve community goals are central to the Canadian political tradition.

In *Lament for a Nation* (1965), Grant argued that the Canadian political tradition was marked by a communitarian spirit that rejected the individualism of American-style liberalism. He traced the roots of this spirit to the influence of conservative ideas and the British connection, which helped to keep alive a benign view of government as an agent for pursuing the common good. This distinctive national character was, Grant believed, doomed to be crushed by the steamroller of American liberalism and technology, which, he maintained in later works, would ultimately flatten national cultures throughout the capitalist world.

Grant's 'lament' was in the key of what has been called **red Toryism**. Red Tories are conservatives who believe that government has a responsibility to act as an agent for the collective good and that this responsibility goes far beyond maintaining law and order. Grant and others in this tradition, for example, applaud state support for culture, as through the Canadian Broadcasting Corporation. Red Tories since Grant are comfortable with the welfare state and the principle that government *should* protect the poor and disadvantaged. Red Toryism involves, its critics would claim, a rather paternalistic philosophy of government and state-citizen relations. Defenders, however, maintain that it is compassionate and a true expression of a collectivist national ethos that distinguishes Canadians from their southern neighbours.

Charles Taylor is not a red Tory. Canada's most internationally acclaimed living philosopher is firmly on the left of the political spectrum. He agrees with Grant about the importance of collectivism in Canada's political tradition. Taylor has always been extremely critical of what he calls the 'atomism' of American liberalism, a value system that he believes cuts people off from the communal relations that nurture human dignity. Like most Canadian nationalists, he believes implicitly in the moral superiority of Canada's collectivist political tradition.

Taylor is one of the leading thinkers in the contemporary movement known as **communitarianism**. This is based on the belief that real human freedom and dignity are only possible in the context of communal relations that allow for the public recognition of group identities and that are based on equal respect for these different identity groups. Taylor argues that the key to Canadian unity lies in finding constitutional arrangements that enable different groups of Canadians to feel that they belong to Canada and are recognized as constituent elements of Canadian society. 'Nations . . . which have a strong sense of their own identity', says Taylor, 'and hence a desire to direct in some ways their common affairs, can only be induced to take part willingly in multinational states if they are in some ways recognized within them.'[41] He calls this the recognition of 'deep diversity'. The realization of deep diversity would require, at a minimum, official recognition of Quebec as a distinct society and probably constitutional acknowledgement of a Native right to self-government. To some this might sound like a recipe for dismantling whatever fragile sense of Canadian community already exists. Taylor insists, however, that one-size-fits-all notions of community do not work in the modern world.

The characterization of Canada as a deferential society, or at least one where citizens are less likely to question political and other sources of established authority than in the United States, has been challenged in recent years. In *The Canadian Revolution*, Peter C. Newman argues that the historically elitist tenor of Canadian life collapsed during the years 1985–95 under the pressure of developments in Canada and in the world at large.

Newman speaks of the rise of a 'new populism' and of what he calls the 'breakdown of trust between the governors and the governed'.[42] The growth of the underground cash economy in reaction to the GST, the breakdown of the old two-party dominance in the 1993 election, the rejection of the elite-supported Charlottetown Accord by Canada's citizens, the violent clash between Natives and Canadian authorities at Oka in 1990, and the near-victory of Quebec separatists in 1995 are, Newman argues, indications of Canadians' passage from deference to defiance. He attributes this transition to a constellation of factors, including the arrogance of politicians, the more competitive global economy, the inability of Canadian governments to continue financing the system of entitlements that Canadians came to take for granted in the 1960s and 1970s, and the decline in religious faith.

A more scientific treatment of the same phenomenon is offered by Neil Nevitte in *The Decline of Deference*.[43] Nevitte agrees that Canadians are less deferential today than in the past. He attributes this to the post-materialist values of those born in the post-World War II era. **Post-materialism** attaches comparatively greater importance to human needs for belonging, self-esteem, and personal fulfillment than does **materialism**, which places greater stress on economic security and material well-being. Such issues as employment and incomes matter most to materialists, whereas post-materialists are likely to place higher value on so-called quality-of-life issues, such as the environment, human rights, and group equality. Materialists are less likely than post-materialists to have confidence in public institutions and to trust in the judgements of elites.

Nevitte shows that Canadians' confidence in government institutions, a category that included the armed forces, the police, Parliament, and the public service, declined during the 1980s and that high levels of confidence are much less likely to be expressed by those between the ages of 25–54 than among older citizens. He also finds that Canadians are, if anything, slightly more skeptical

Figure 2.4   Trust in Politicians, 1965–1997

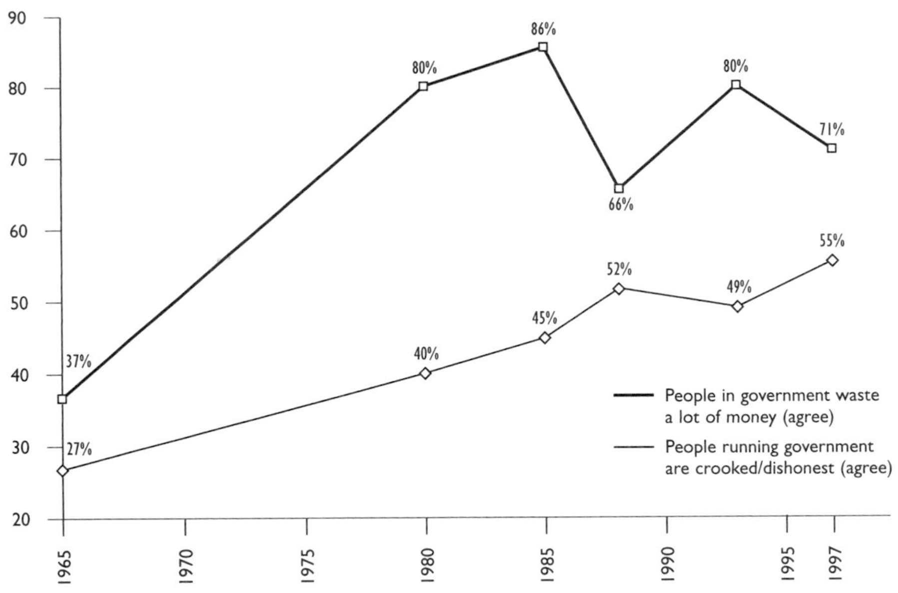

Source: Mebs Kanji, 'Political Discontent, Human Capital, and Representative Governance', in Neil Nevitte, ed., *Value Change and Governance in Canada* (Toronto: University of Toronto Press, 2002), 81.

of government institutions than are Americans—not what one would expect to find if the traditional stereotype of deferential Canadians versus defiant Americans holds true (see Figure 2.4).

Studies have long shown that Americans place much more confidence in their system of government than they do in some of the institutions that comprise it and the people who run it. The same is true in Canada. A 1995 survey found that over 6 of every 10 Canadians claimed to be either very or somewhat satisfied with the way democracy worked in their country, a level of satisfaction that was about the same as in the United States.[44] At the same time, however, about 7 out of 10 Canadians agreed that people in government waste a lot of tax money and about half agreed that those running the government are crooked or dishonest (see Fig-

ure 2.4). Only about 4 in 10 said that they had either a lot of or some confidence in the federal government and the civil service.[45] This cynicism towards public officials and certain institutions of government has increased over time. Finally, there appears to have been a sharp decline since the 1980s in the share of the population believing that politicians are responsive to the people, what political scientists call *external efficacy* (Figure 2.5).

The picture that emerges from the data is not one of a trusting citizenry, confident that public officials will do the right thing and act in the people's interest. At the same time it appears that Canadians are satisfied with their system of democracy. This paradox may be explained in a couple of ways. It may well be that many Canadians make a distinction between levels of the political system, feeling more positively towards and having more confidence in the overall rules and structures of that system than towards certain institutions and the people who run them. Or it may be that many Canadians believe that the way their democracy works, with all the flaws and shortcomings that they believe characterize it, is all that can realistically be expected.

Figure 2.5   Political Efficacy in Canada, 1965–1993

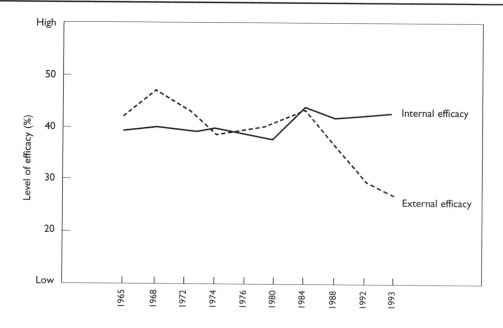

Note: The percentages reported in the figure are the average scores from the two items in the internal and external efficacy indices. Only the 'disagree' and 'strongly disagree' responses are used in the calculation of the averages. 'No opinion' responses are excluded from the analysis.

External efficacy: 1. 'Generally, those elected to Parliament soon lose touch with the people.' 2. 'I don't think the government cares much what people like me think.' (Strongly Agree, Agree, Disagree, Strongly Disagree, and No Opinion)

Internal efficacy: 1. 'Sometimes, politics and government seem so complicated that a person like me can't really understand what's going on.' 2. 'People like me don't have any say about what the government does.' (Strongly Agree, Agree, Disagree, Strongly Disagree, and No Opinion)

Source: Neil Nevitte, 'Value Change and Reorientation in Citizen-State Relations', in Nevitte, ed., *Value Change and Governance in Canada* (Toronto: University of Toronto Press, 2002), 22.

BOX 2.4   The Neighbour (Some) Canadians Love to Hate

Every country in the world is screwed up about its relationship with the US. But in Canada it is a national obsession, even a neurosis. Imagine, if you will, a homely kind of girl—well-liked but usually ignored—who lives next door to the town hunk. He is the centre of all her thoughts. She peers through the net curtains as he swaggers out for a night on the town. She reads major significance into every gesture: every time he ignores her on the street; every time he gives her an affectionate pat. She despises his unruly ways but, deep down, desperately wants to believe this is true love. He barely gives her a thought. In romantic fiction, you end up with a white wedding and happy-ever-after ending. In international diplomacy, you get the US–Canada relationship. What can Canada do? Normally, when the neighbours are this domineering and irritating, it is customary to think about moving house. It has crossed Canada's mind, in a manner of speaking. As Britain headed into what was then the common market three decades ago, Trudeau tried to push Canada into a much closer relationship with Europe too. The Canadians, with their bilingualism and consensual instincts, would absolutely love Brussels.

In practice, Canadians recognize the reality. For many everyday purposes, North America is one country: on the morning of September 11, the Canadian deputy commander was in charge at the joint air-defence headquarters at Cheyenne Mountain in Colorado. When the border was closed over the next few days and the trucks began queuing for miles, all Canadians were obliged to consider what real severance from the Americans would mean.

Matthew Engel, *The Guardian*, 16 Dec. 2002.

NOTES

1. Pierre Berton, *Why We Act Like Canadians* (Toronto: McClelland & Stewart, 1982).
2. R. Kirk, *The Conservative Mind* (London: Faber and Faber, 1953).
3. Daniel Bell, *The End of Ideology* (New York: Free Press, 1962), 402–3.
4. David Bell and Lorne Tepperman, *The Roots of Disunity* (Toronto: McClelland & Stewart, 1979), 23.
5. Fernand Ouellet, *Histoire économique et sociale du Québec, 1760–1850* (Paris: Fides, 1966).
6. Bell and Tepperman note that the estimated number of anglophones in what are now the Maritimes, Quebec, and Ontario at the time of the American Revolution was about 15,000. Between 30,000 and 60,000 Loyalists immigrated to these British colonies in the years immediately after 1776, and a steady stream of 'late Loyalists', perhaps attracted by British offers of free land, immigrated northwards to Upper Canada over the next few decades. See *The Roots of Disunity*, 45, 80–1.
7. William Christian and Colin Campbell, *Political Parties and Ideologies in Canada*, 2nd edn. (Toronto: McGraw-Hill Ryerson, 1982), 23–5; Gad Horowitz, 'Conservatism, Liberalism and Socialism in Canada: An Interpretation', *Canadian Journal of Economics and Political Science* (1966).
8. Kenneth McRae, 'The Structure of Canadian History', in Louis Hartz, ed., *The Founding of New Societies* (New York: Harcourt, Brace & World, 1964), 235.
9. Bell and Tepperman, *The Roots of Disunity*, 76–7.
10. Horowitz, 'Conservatism, Liberalism and Socialism'.

11. Seymour Martin Lipset, *Continental Divide* (Montreal: C.D. Howe Institute, 1989), 1.

12. Bell and Tepperman, *The Roots of Disunity*, 61–2.

13. Reg Whitaker, 'Images of the State in Canada', in Leo Panitch, ed., *The Canadian State* (Toronto: University of Toronto Press, 1977), 30.

14. Patricia Marchak, *Ideological Perspectives on Canada* (Toronto: McGraw-Hill Ryerson, 1975), 115.

15. Pierre Trudeau, 'Some Obstacles to Democracy in Quebec', in Trudeau, *Federalism and the French Canadians* (Toronto: Macmillan, 1968).

16. In 1951, 80 per cent of Quebec's workforce was in secondary industries (manufacturing and construction) and the service sector, a percentage that was higher than for Canada as a whole (78 per cent).

17. See Kenneth McRoberts, *Quebec: Social Change and Political Crisis*, 3rd edn (Toronto: McClelland & Stewart, 1988), 90–100.

18. W.L. Morton, 'The Dualism of Culture and the Federalism of Power', in Richard Abbott, ed., *A New Concept of Confederation*, Proceedings of the Seventh Seminar of the Canadian Union of Students (Ottawa, 1965), 121.

19. Donald Smiley, *The Canadian Political Nationality* (Toronto: Methuen, 1967).

20. See the analysis of Oka in Robert Campbell and Leslie Pal, 'Feather and Gun', *The Real Worlds of Canadian Politics*, 2nd edn (Peterborough, Ont.: Broadview Press, 1991), 267–345.

21. All of these statements are based on the rankings in Charles Lewis Taylor and David A. Jodice, *The World Handbook of Political and Social Indicators*, 3rd edn, vol. 2, *Political Protest and Government Change* (New Haven: Yale University Press, 1983); see also Judith Torrance, *Public Violence in Canada 1867–1982* (Toronto: University of Toronto Press, 1986), 57–66.

22. Kenneth McNaught, 'Violence, Political', in *The Canadian Encyclopedia*, vol. 4 (Edmonton: Hurtig, 1988), 2265.

23. McRoberts, *Quebec*, 240.

24. Ibid., 239.

25. En collaboration, *Québec: un pays incertains. Reflexions sur le Québec post-referendaire* (Montréal: Québec/Amérique, 1980), 170–2.

26. See the excellent analysis in Campbell and Pal, 'Feather and Gun'.

27. Status Indians are those registered under the Indian Act.

28. *Globe and Mail*, 26 Sept. 1990.

29. Lipset, *Continental Divide*, 136.

30. Berton, *Why We Act Like Canadians*, 16.

31. Robert Kudrle and Theodore Marmor, 'The Development of Welfare States in North America', in Peter Flora and Arnold J. Heidersheimer, eds, *The Development of Welfare States in Europe and America* (New Brunswick, NJ: Transaction Books, 1981), 110.

32. See the summary of studies in Lipset, *Continental Divide*, 155–8.

33. Ibid., 156.

34. Canada, Constitution Act, 1982, s. 27.

35. Ibid., s. 15.2.

36. Maclean's-Decima Poll, 'Portrait of Two Nations', *Maclean's*, 3 July 1989, 50.

37. Canada, Department of Canadian Heritage, *Strategic Evaluation of Multiculturalism Programs: Final Report* (Ottawa: Corporate Review Branch, Mar. 1996), 48.

38. Raymond Breton and Jeffrey Reitz, *The Illusion of Difference* (Toronto: C.D. Howe Institute, 1994), 133.

39. Tom Wayman, ed., *A Government Job at Last* (Vancouver: MacLeod Books, 1975).

40. The issue was voted on by Parliament in 1967, 1973, 1976, and 1987.

41. Charles Taylor, 'Deep Diversity and the Future of Canada', available at: <www.uni.ca/taylor.html>.

42. Peter C. Newman, *The Canadian Revolution, 1985–1995* (Toronto: Penguin Books, 1995), 12–13.

43. Neil Nevitte, *The Decline of Deference: Canadian Value Change in Cross-National Perspective* (Peterborough, Ont.: Broadview Press, 1996).

44. Richard Nadeau, 'Satisfaction with Democracy: The Canadian Paradox', in Neil Nevitte, ed., *Value Change and Governance in Canada* (Toronto: University of Toronto Press, 2002), 46.

45. Mebs Kanji, 'Political Discontent, Human Capital, and Representative Governance', in Nevitte, ed., *Value Change and Governance in Canada*, 80.

SUGGESTED READINGS

David Bell and Lorne Tepperman, *The Roots of Disunity* (Toronto: McClelland & Stewart, 1979). Bell and Tepperman present an excellent analysis of the historical roots of English Canada's long-standing identity crisis, French-English conflict, and the rise of regionalism in Canada.

Seymour Martin Lipset, *Continental Divide: the Values and Institutions of the United States and Canada* (Toronto: C.D. Howe Institute, 1989). This remains one of the best surveys of the voluminous work done on the differences and similarities in the political cultures of Canada and the United States, written by one of the most astute observers of political culture in these two countries.

Neil Nevitte, *The Decline of Deference: Canadian Value Change in Cross-National Perspective* (Peterborough, Ont.: Broadview Press, 1996). Nevitte examines the changing Canadian value system in a cross-national context that includes American and European societies.

Donald Smiley, *The Canadian Political Nationality* (Toronto: Methuen, 1967). This classic, written by one of Canada's most insightful political scientists, provides a brief history of the development of the Canadian political community in the face of the challenges of language and regional conflict.

David Thomas, ed., *Canada and the United States: Differences That Count*, 2nd edn (Peterborough, Ont.: Broadview Press, 2000). This collection includes many useful essays on differences in Canadian and American values, behaviour, institutions, and policies, ranging from health care to political reporting.

Review Exercises

1. Look at Figure 2.1, Support for Quebec Independence, 1978–2002. Can you suggest some reason(s) for the wide fluctuations in the percentage of Quebecers saying they would vote for Quebec sovereignty? Why was it so high in 1990 and 1995? Why was it comparatively low in 1984, 1988, and 2002?

2. Where would you place each of the parties represented in the federal Parliament on a political ideology scale ranging from far left to far right? Where would you place the party that governs your province? Where would you place yourself? In each case, explain why you chose a particular place on the scale for a party or yourself.

3. Choose any three organizations from the following list. From the information included in their Web sites, decide whether each organization advocates collectivist or individualistic ideas. Do you think these organizations represent the ideas of significant numbers of Canadians? Why?

   Fraser Institute: <www.fraserinstitute.ca>
   Centre for Social Justice: <www.socialjustice.org>
   Canadian Centre for Policy Alternatives: <www.policyalternatives.ca>
   Canadian Labour Congress: <www.clc-ctc.ca>
   Vanier Institute of the Family: <www.cfc-efc.ca/vif>
   C.D. Howe Institute: <www.cdhowe.org>
   National Citizens' Coalition: <www.morefreedom.org>
   Council of Canadians: <www.canadians.org>

A 2002 survey of 44 countries across the world found Canadians to be the most satisfied people in the world. This has not stopped them from worrying about poverty in their midst and the ability of their economy to remain competitive. (Roy Peterson, *Vancouver Sun*)

Politics unfolds against a backdrop of social and economic conditions. This chapter focuses on the following aspects of Canadian society.

- ❏ Material well-being.
- ❏ Equality.
- ❏ Discrimination.
- ❏ Quality of life.
- ❏ Poverty.
- ❏ Independence.

CHAPTER THREE

THE SOCIAL AND ECONOMIC SETTING

Speaking before an audience of American newspaper editors in Texas in 1995, Prime Minister Jean Chrétien referred to Canada as a 'kinder and gentler nation' (see Box 2.1). He said that Canadians' most important values were tolerance and sharing. Canada, he said, because of its bilingualism and multicultural character, 'has been referred to by some as the first "post-nationalist" country.'[1] Although he did not mention it to his American audience, he may have been tempted to crow a bit about Canada's first-place ranking at that time on the United Nations human development index (a measure that combines literacy rates, formal education levels, average longevity, and real purchasing power), a distinction that Canada has received on several occasions since the UN began to report these rankings.

Those who live in Canada are indeed fortunate. But that good fortune is not shared by all Canadians. Over four million Canadians fall below what has been called the 'poverty line', the low-income cut-offs established by Statistics Canada, although this number is expected to drop with the introduction in May 2003 of a new 'market basket measure'. More revealingly, hundreds of thousands of people use the food banks that have proliferated in Canada since the 1980s. Some of these people would probably dispute Prime Minister Chrétien's characterization of Canada as a 'kinder and gentler nation'. Within months of the Prime Minister's Texas speech violence broke out between Aboriginal Canadians and police forces in British Columbia and Ontario. And in the autumn of 1995 the Prime Minister found himself doing battle against Quebec separatists who obviously were unimpressed with his description of Canada as the 'first post-nationalist country'. It appears that not everyone shares the sunny opinion that Prime Minister Chrétien expressed to the American newspaper editors. In recent years, anti-globalization protestors, poverty activists, and spokespersons for the homeless have all been critical of conditions in Canada and the performance of government in this country.

In this chapter we will examine the social and economic setting of Canadian politics. Comparisons will be made between Canada and other countries, between regions in Canada, between various points in Canada's history, and between actual conditions and some idealized standards that have been applied to the performance of Canada's political system. Our goal in this chapter is not, however, chiefly to judge. Instead, our main purpose is to understand the societal context that influences, and is influenced by, politics and public policy. In doing so we will be selective, focusing on aspects of Canadian society and the economy that are closely associated with several general values that most Canadians consider to be important. These include the following:

- material well-being;
- equality;
- quality of life;
- independence.

Obviously, these values will be interpreted differently by different people. Disagreements aside, we have selected these values for two related reasons. First, they represent public purposes that most of us expect governments to preserve or promote. Second, political controversies are frequently about one or more of these values— disagreements over how to achieve them; over what value(s) should give way, and by how much, when they conflict; about whether they are being adequately met. It makes sense, therefore, to focus on these dimensions of the social and economic setting of Canadian politics.

Political issues and outcomes are not determined in any simplistic manner by such things as the extent and nature of inequalities in Canadian society or the level of material well-being, any more than political ideologies and institutions translate directly into political behaviour and public policy. Like ideology and institutions, the social and economic settings of politics establish boundaries to political life. They do so by determining the sorts of problems a society faces, the resources available for coping with these problems, the nature and intensity of divisions within society, and the distribution of politically valuable resources between societal interests.

MATERIAL WELL-BEING

Canada is an affluent society. This simple fact is sometimes obscured by the news of fresh layoffs, plant closings, slipping competitiveness, and pockets of poverty. For most of the last generation, the average real purchasing power of Canadians was the second highest in the world, topped only by that of Americans. In the last several years Canada has slipped a few notches, but Canadians remain firmly within the world's top 10 in terms of average real purchasing power (see Figure 3.1). Affluence affects both the opportunities and problems faced by policy-makers. The problem of poverty, for example, assumes a very different character in an affluent society like Canada from that in a poorer society like Mexico or a destitute one like Sudan. Not only does Canada's poverty problem look rather enviable from the standpoint of these other countries, but the means that governments in Canada have available to deal with this problem are far greater than those that can be deployed by the governments of poorer societies. The very definition of 'public problems' that warrant the attention of government is also influenced by a society's material conditions. Environmental pollution, a prominent issue on the public agendas of affluent societies, tends to be buried under the weight of other pressing social and economic problems in less affluent societies.

Within the elite club of affluent societies, cultural and institutional differences are probably more important as determinants of the public agenda and government response to them than are their differences in material well-being. But the particular characteristics of a national economy, factors upon which material affluence depends, are significant influences on the politics and public policies of any society. These characteristics include the sectoral and regional distribution of economic activity, the level and distribution of employment, characteristics of its labour force, the profile of its trade with the rest of the world, and so on. Despite enjoying one of the highest standards of living in the world, Canadians have seldom been complacent about their affluence. Fears that Canada's material well-being may rest on fragile footings have long been expressed. These fears have become increasingly urgent since the 1980s, as Canadians have attempted to come to grips with what global economic restructuring means for their future.

A secure job at a decent rate of pay is desired by most people. It enables one to plan for the future and achieve the goals that one has for oneself and one's family. Unemployment can be personally and socially devastating. The political importance of the employment issue is seen in the fact that it is regularly mentioned by Canadians as one of the most important issues facing the country. Governments react with rhetoric, gestures, and policies. These policies may not succeed in maintaining employment at a socially acceptable level—indeed, they may not even be expected to reduce unemployment—but no government would pass up an opportunity to express its commitment to increasing jobs and its sympathy for the unemployed.

What does Canada's employment record look like? Compared to other advanced industrialized democracies, Canada has done fairly well. The national level of unemployment has fluctuated between about 6 and 13 per cent over the last couple of decades, being about 6–9 per cent in most years. This may not impress Americans, whose unemployment rate is generally a few percentage points below Canada's. Canadians, however, are used to dismissing the superior employment record of the US as being bought with lower wages and greater income inequality than most Canadians would tolerate (the claim about lower wages is simply not true if one compares real wages and net after-tax incomes). Canada's unemployment rate has been close to the average for the more affluent OECD countries. Moreover, the economy's ability to create new jobs has been among the best. This has been important because Canada's labour force has grown more rapidly than those of most other advanced industrial democracies.

Looking at the distribution of employment across sectors of the Canadian economy, one finds that Canada closely resembles the world's other major capitalist economies. As of 2002, just under three-quarters of workers were in service industries (sales, communications, transportation, tourism, finance, public administration, etc.), about 15 per cent were employed in the manufacturing sector, roughly 4 per cent worked in primary industries like farming, fishing, forestry, and mining, and the remaining 6 per cent worked in construction. These shares are very similar to those of our major trading partner, the United States. Over time, the service sector's share of total employment has grown dramatically, from about 40 per cent in the mid-twentieth century to the current level of over 7 in 10 jobs. The shares in the primary and secondary sectors have obviously declined, more sharply in primary industries

Figure 3.1   Per Capita PPPs* (\$US) for Richest OECD Countries, 2001

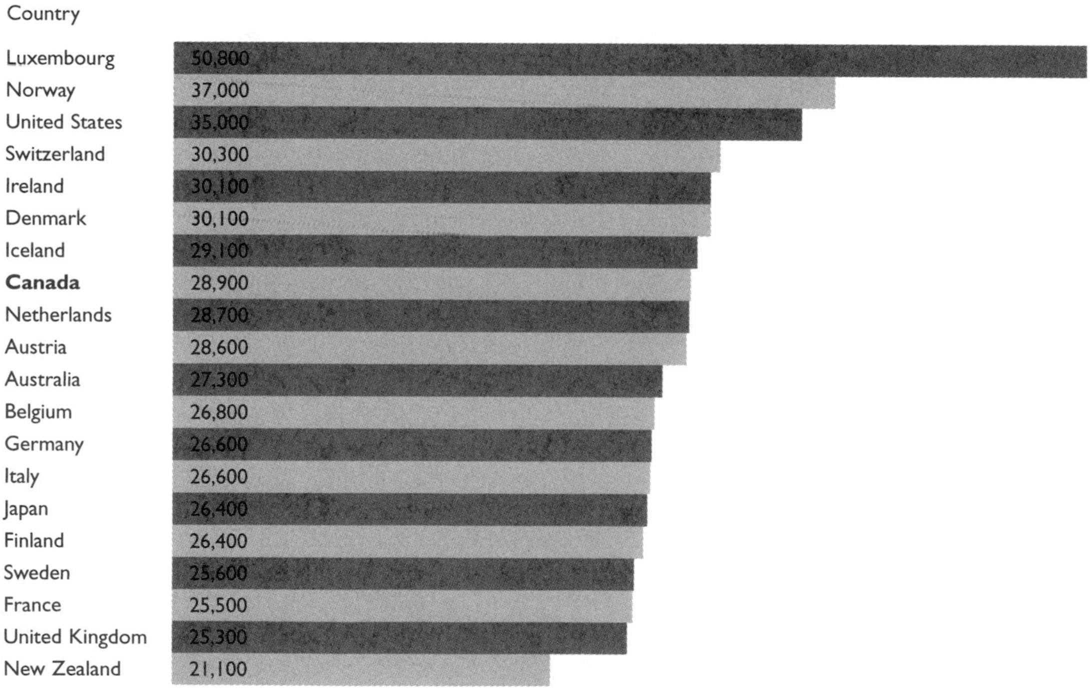

Country

Country	PPP (\$US)
Luxembourg	50,800
Norway	37,000
United States	35,000
Switzerland	30,300
Ireland	30,100
Denmark	30,100
Iceland	29,100
Canada	28,900
Netherlands	28,700
Austria	28,600
Australia	27,300
Belgium	26,800
Germany	26,600
Italy	26,600
Japan	26,400
Finland	26,400
Sweden	25,600
France	25,500
United Kingdom	25,300
New Zealand	21,100

*Purchasing power parities.

Source: Organization for Economic Co-operation and Development, www.oecd.org

than in manufacturing. These employment trends have led many to worry that the Canadian economy is 'deindustrializing'. In fact, however, these employment trends are broadly similar to those that have characterized all of the world's major capitalist economies over the last several decades.

The last two decades have seen the emergence of a politically important debate over the relative value to an economy of service versus manufacturing jobs. Some argue that service industries, particularly in regard to generating knowledge and distributing information, also produce value, and so there is no reason to worry about a shrinking manufacturing base. Others argue that the manufacturing sector is especially important, and that a point can be reached—and may already have been reached in economies like Canada's and that of the United States—where further decline of the manufacturing base undermines the overall competitiveness of the economy and drags down real incomes.[2] Much of this argument hinges on the often-heard claim that new jobs in the burgeoning service sector tend to be unskilled and low-paying—'McJobs', as they are often derisively called. These jobs, it is said, have increasingly replaced better-paying manufacturing jobs that have been exported to low-wage economies. That unskilled and low-skill manufacturing jobs have migrated to developing economies is beyond dispute. However, the belief that the new economy primarily creates McJobs is false. The new economy also creates better-paying jobs in information technology, communications, financial services, and other service industries. These jobs require education and skills, whereas McJobs do not. What has been lost in the new economy are the low-skill/high-paying manufacturing jobs that were characteristic of the factory economy of the 1950s, 1960s, and 1970s. Their disappearance has heightened the importance of education and skills as necessary qualifications for well-paying jobs. The case of a Ph.D. driving a taxi or an engineer flipping burgers will always be the one reported by the media. The reality, however, is that education and training do generally translate into higher incomes and better job security—a relationship confirmed by virtually all studies of education and income—in both developed economies like Canada's and in the developing world.

EQUALITY

One of the most persistent images that Canadians have of their society is that it has no classes. This image becomes translated into the assertion that Canadians are all relatively equal in their possessions, in the amount of money they earn, and in the opportunities which they and their children have to get on in the world. . . .

That there is neither very rich nor very poor in Canada is an important part of the image. There are no barriers to opportunity. Education is free. Therefore, making use of it is largely a question of personal ambition.[3]

This may well have been the image held by most Canadians when sociologist John Porter wrote these words in *The Vertical Mosaic* (1965). It is doubtful whether Canadians today are as confident that their society is one without serious inequalities. Stories about homelessness, food banks, poverty, and growing income inequality have become routine. Moreover, charges of discrimination made by women's groups, Native Canadians, visible minorities, gays and lesbians, and other minorities—charges that were muffled until a few decades ago—are common today. The passage of provincial human rights codes and of the Charter of Rights and Freedoms, and the proliferation of human rights officers—ombudsmen, race relations officers, equity officers, and so on—have contributed to this sharpened awareness of inequality. But these reforms were themselves inspired by a growing sense that existing policies and institutions did not adequately protect the equality of citizens and that, in some cases, laws and institutions actually perpetuated inequality.

For various reasons, then, Canadians are probably more aware of inequalities today than they were a few decades ago. But despite this heightened awareness, most Canadians still cling to the belief that their society is basically middle class. This belief—which, we hasten to add, is not totally false—springs from the dominant liberal ideology. Individualism and a belief that opportunities to get ahead in life are open to those with the energy and talent needed to take advantage of them are at the core of this liberal ideology. To say that society is basically middle class means, from this ideological perspective, that the barriers to upward mobility are relatively low for the vast majority of people. The fact that some people are extraordinarily wealthy and others are quite destitute needs to be set alongside an even more prominent fact, i.e., that most Canadians occupy a broad middle band in terms of their incomes and lifestyles.

Wealth is unevenly divided in all societies. Few people believe that the sort of levelling implied by Karl Marx's aphorism, 'From each according to his abilities, to each according to his needs', is desirable. But many people are disturbed by the jarring contrast between conspicuous luxury and destitution in their society. The gap between rich and poor is not as great in Canada as in some other industrialized democra-cies. Nevertheless, it is considerable and persistent. Moreover, some groups bear the brunt of poverty much more heavily than others.

Figure 3.2 shows that the distribution of income in Canada has remained pretty much unchanged for decades. The richest one-fifth of the population receives about 44 per cent of all income, while the poorest one-fifth accounts for just under 5 per cent. If social security benefits are left out of the picture, the inequality gap is much wider, the bottom fifth of Canadians accounting for barely 1 per cent of earned income. Compared to the distribution of income in other advanced capitalist societies, Canada's is fairly typical. The distribution of income is more equal than in some countries, such as the United States, but less equal than in others, including Japan and Sweden.

In recent years news stories and academic studies purporting to show a growing gap between the rich and the poor in Canada have contributed to a widespread belief that inequality has worsened. In fact, as the relative stability in the income shares shown in Figure 3.2 suggests, it is not entirely clear that income inequality has grown. To some degree it depends on

Figure 3.2   Distribution of Income in Canada (total money income), 1957, 2000

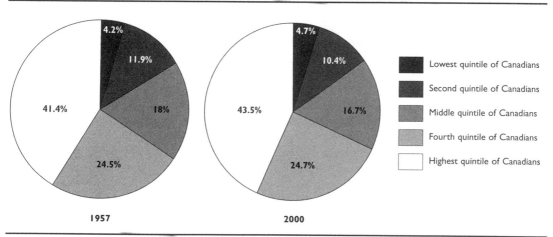

Legend:
- Lowest quintile of Canadians
- Second quintile of Canadians
- Middle quintile of Canadians
- Fourth quintile of Canadians
- Highest quintile of Canadians

1957: 4.2%, 11.9%, 18%, 24.5%, 41.4%

2000: 4.7%, 10.4%, 16.7%, 24.7%, 43.5%

Source: Statistics Canada, *Income After Tax, Distributions by Size in Canada,* catalogue no. 13–210, annual, and *Income in Canada,* catalogue no. 75–202.

decisions we make about what to measure and how to measure it. For example:

- Average family income in Canada, in 1994 dollars, was $40,516 in 1970, $52,052 in 1980, and $52,858 in 1994.[4] After plateauing in the mid-1990s, family incomes increased by about 10 per cent between 1996 and 2000.[5]
- Since the mid-1990s, years during which news stories of growing income inequality and falling incomes proliferated, the incomes of most groups in Canada's population have actually increased. These include elderly couples, married people, two-earner couples, two-parent families where both spouses work, single parents, and unattached females. The only family types to experience a decline in real after-tax income are elderly unattached males.[6]

The distribution of income is only part of the story in any assessment of equality. The other part involves the extent of poverty. 'Poverty' is to some degree a relative concept, meaning something different in an advanced industrialized society like Canada than in a developing country like Nigeria. In Canada, poverty is usually measured using Statistics Canada's definition of what constitutes an income that is so low that an individual or household lives in 'straitened circumstances'. Statistics Canada's low-income cut-off has generally been referred to by the media, academics, politicians, and others as the poverty line, most recently defined to mean that more than 55 per cent of income (20 percentage points above the national average) was spent on food, clothing, and shelter. Because the term 'poverty line' has become an established part of Canada's political vocabulary, evoking images of need and destitution in the minds of many if not most Canadians, it is important to recognize the limitations of such measures. According to a recent study of poverty lines, these limitations include the following:

- Poverty lines are relative.
- All poverty lines are arbitrary.

- Poverty lines are a research tool for measuring the incomes of *groups* of people, not a measure of *individual* need.
- Some poverty lines are better than others, but none of them is perfect.[7]

On 27 May 2003, Statistics Canada introduced a new 'market basket measure' to replace the LICOs as a measure of need. Its intent is to remove the relative and arbitrary nature of the LICOs. Its anticipated effect is that fewer people in Canada will be considered 'poor' and in need. Nonetheless, however poverty is measured, two of the groups hardest hit by poverty in Canada are Native Canadians and women. Consider the following facts:

Native Canadians
- The employment rate for Aboriginal Canadians is the lowest of any ethnic group, at about two-thirds of the national level. To put this a bit differently, the unemployment rate among Natives is usually between two and two and one-half times the national level.
- The employment rate for Natives living on reserves is only half the Canadian rate.
- About one-half of all status Indians obtain most of their income from employment, compared to roughly 70 per cent of all Canadians.
- Native incomes are about two-thirds the Canadian average.
- Close to half of Aboriginal Canadians living off reserve fall below the poverty line, a figure that is about three times greater than for the general population.

Women
- Women are more likely than men to be poor. The poverty rate for women is about one-third higher than that for men.
- Elderly women are about three times more likely than elderly men to fall below the poverty line (2001).
- Over 40 per cent of single-parent families headed by women fall below the poverty line (after-tax income), a rate several times higher than for two-

parent families and three times greater than for single-parent families headed by men.

- The poverty rate among single-parent families headed by young mothers is absolutely crushing. For mothers under 25 it is close to 70 per cent (after-tax income). Among those aged 25–44 it is roughly 40 per cent (2001).

Why are these groups particularly susceptible to poverty? The answers are too complex to be explored fully here. A few of the contributing causes may, however, be mentioned. In the case of Native Canadians, discrimination certainly plays a role in explaining their higher jobless rate and lower incomes. Lower levels of education are also a factor. But as John Price notes, these causes are considerably less important than 'cultural heritage, choice of occupation and residence far from the main centres of the economy'.[8] Likewise, poverty among women results from a complex set of causes.[9] Most of the difference in the poverty levels of women and men is due to the compara-

tively high poverty rates of single-parent mothers with children under 18 and unattached women. The lower incomes of women are chiefly due to their segregation in lower-paying occupations, as well as the greater number of women than men who work part-time.

Inequality also has an important regional dimension in Canada. Income levels and employment rates vary dramatically and persistently between provinces, as well as between regions within provinces. Personal incomes in the poorest provinces (Newfoundland, New Brunswick, and Prince Edward Island) are only two-thirds to three-quarters of the Canadian average. If transfer payments from government to individuals and households are excluded from the calculation, incomes in these poorest provinces drop to between 50 and 70 per cent of the national average. Figure 3.3 shows that interregional variation in average personal incomes has narrowed over the last few decades, although it is still quite wide. This has been due mainly to government trans-

Figure 3.3   The Gap Between the Richest and Poorest Provinces, 1954–2001

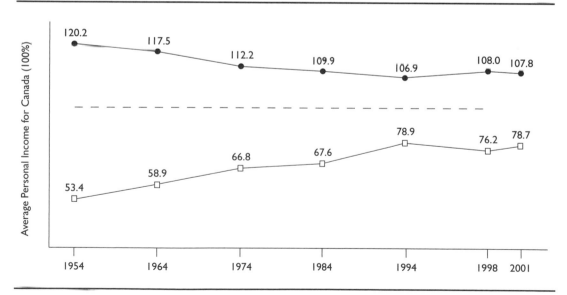

Note: The two provinces used in this comparison are Ontario and Newfoundland.
Source: Statistics Canada, *Provincial Economic Accounts*.

fers that provide greater income benefits to the residents of the poorer provinces than to those of the richer ones. On the other hand, the gap between the highest and lowest regional rates of unemployment has widened (see Figure 3.4).

One of the important dimensions of equality, and one of the chief influences on it, is socio-economic mobility. This refers to the ability of individuals, families, and groups to move from one social or economic position to another. Socio-economic mobility implies the existence of hier-

archically arranged differences in society, such as those that exist between income groups and occupations. These differences exist in all societies to a greater or lesser extent. Where socio-economic mobility is high, movement up and down the social ladder is common and the barriers to entry into high-paying occupations, prestigious status groups, or powerful elites are relatively low. This is what students of mobility call an open society. In a closed society there is relatively little inter-generational movement on the social ladder and

Figure 3.4   Regional Unemployment Rates, 1966–2001

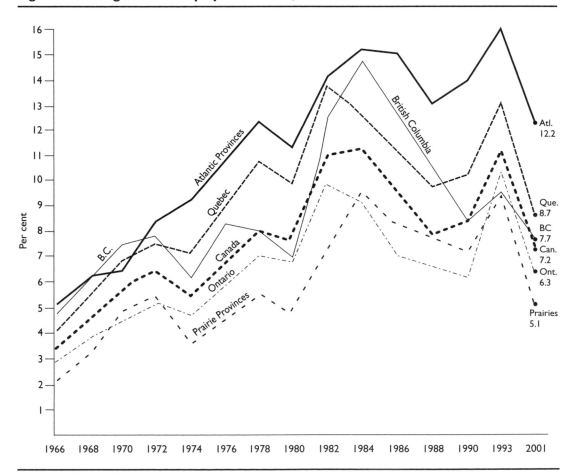

Sources: Statistics Canada, *Canadian Economic Observer*, Historical Statistical Supplement, 1994, catalogue no. 11–210; Statistics Canada, www.statcan.ca/english/econoind/indic.htm

barriers to entry into privileged social and economic groups are high.

Most Canadians believe that theirs is a relatively open society, and compared to many it is. But an enormous amount of evidence shows that social stratification in Canada remains high and real opportunities to climb the socio-economic ladder are much fewer than the conventional wisdom suggests. The 'vertical mosaic' that John Porter analyzed three decades ago has been opened up, but gender, ethnicity, race, and family background continue to exert a tremendous downward pull on mobility.

This may be demonstrated in many ways. Data from a national survey of social mobility and status achievement in Canada indicated that the socio-economic backgrounds of individuals explain about one-third of the differences between people in their level of educational attainment.[10] Educational attainment was found to be strongly related to the educational achievements of one's parents and the occupation of one's father. Education is highly correlated with income, and several years of post-secondary education are, of course, necessary to qualify for some of the most prestigious and high-paying professions in Canada. Recent studies confirm that access to these privileged professions is far from open. Glasbeek and Hasson note that law students still come 'disproportionately from the wealthier classes of societies'.[11] The sons and daughters of physicians—but especially the sons—continue to be far more likely than the children of others to enter medical schools and become physicians themselves. Looked at from the other end of the socio-economic ladder, those born into relatively poor families, where the parents' level of education and occupational status are low, are far less likely than the children of middle- and upper-class parents to achieve higher incomes and higher-status occupations as adults.

Two 1994 studies by Statistics Canada reported the following findings regarding the impact of parents' class background on their children's prospects:

- The source of the father's income is strongly associated with the adult incomes of children. The sons and daughters of self-employed fathers earned more than those whose fathers were not self-employed, and the children of fathers who received unemployment insurance (UI) benefits were likely to earn considerably less than those whose fathers never received UI.
- Fathers' incomes have greater effects on sons' than daughters' earnings.
- The affluence of the neighbourhood in which children, especially boys, spend their early teenage years is positively associated with their adult incomes.
- Sons and daughters of fathers with asset income have considerably higher incomes than those whose fathers had none.
- Children of very low-income fathers are more likely to be low-income earners themselves than to improve their position on the income ladder.
- Frequent changes of residence for children are associated with lower incomes as adults.
- About half of Canadians aged 26–35 report a higher level of education than their parents. Only 16 per cent reported less formal schooling.
- The status of a father's occupation is associated with his child's educational attainment.[12]

What about elites in Canadian society? John Porter argued that they were largely self-perpetuating, recruiting new members chiefly from those groups who already dominated them. Does this continue to be true? Academic and journalistic writing on Canada's corporate elite agrees that this group is highly unrepresentative of the general population and that access to it appears to be much greater for those from certain backgrounds than from others. The most systematic studies of the social characteristics of the corporate elite have been carried out by sociologists John Porter and Wallace Clement. Porter's study was based on data for 1951 and Clement's on data for 1972.[13] They both found that this elite (which they defined as the directors of Canada's dominant corporations) was overwhelmingly male, about a third had attended private schools such as Upper Canada College or Ridley, many had upper-class backgrounds (50 per cent in 1951 and 59.4 per cent in 1972), those with non-Anglo-Saxon ethnic origins were under-represented (comprising 13.8 per cent of Clement's 1972 group, compared to 55.3 per cent of the Canadian population), and about half (51.1 per cent in 1972) belonged to one or more of the six most prominent private clubs in Canada. The picture they sketched was one of a self-perpetuating group whose social backgrounds and adult activities set them sharply apart from the general population.

The corporate elite operates as a social network that reproduces itself largely through self-recruitment. Education at elite schools adds to what John Porter calls the 'social capital' of its members, reinforcing elite ties that are maintained in the adult world of business. Club membership provides a complement to the boardroom, a social setting that is very much part of the personal relations essential in business life. It is for this reason that the question of private club membership became a matter of political controversy during the 1980s. Women's groups especially charged that the exclusively male character of these clubs reinforced men's dominance of the business world by excluding women from its social network.

Evidence suggests that access to the corporate elite may not be more open today than in the past. Using data from 1991, Milan Korac replicated the analysis of Porter and Clement. He reported findings that are almost identical to those of these two earlier studies. For example, men constituted 92 per cent of the corporate elite; 42 per cent had attended exclusive private schools; those from non-Anglo-Saxon backgrounds were still grossly underrepresented (only 22.1 per cent of the economic elite, compared to 74.7 per cent of the population); and well over half of the economic elite belonged to one or more of the Toronto Club, the Mount Royal Club, the Rideau Club, and the St James Club.[14]

Access to the political elite is certainly more open than in the past. Traditionally, Canada's major political parties were dominated by males of either British or French ethnic origin. They still are, but the representation of females and Canadians of non-British, non-French origins has increased sharply over the last couple of decades (see Chapter 13 for data on female representation). The election of Audrey McLaughlin as NDP leader in 1989 marked the first time a woman had been chosen to lead a national political party, followed by the 1993 selection of Kim Campbell as leader of the Conservative Party and of Alexa McDonough as leader of the NDP in 1994. A handful of women have led provincial political parties and one, Catherine Callbeck of PEI, was elected premier of a province. Several of Canada's major cities have had female mayors, going back to the middle of this century. The continuing domination of Canada's political elite by males of British and French ethnic origins, albeit less strikingly than in the past, is less the result of deliberate discrimination against the members of other groups than a product of systemic discrimination.

Why do inequalities like those that we have described in the preceding pages exist? What consequences do they have for Canadian politics and society? Several factors contribute to inequality, including deliberate discrimination, systemic discrimination, choice, and politics.

Deliberate Discrimination

The prejudice that one person feels towards the members of some group or groups becomes deliberate discrimination when it is acted upon. For example, the landlord who refuses to rent to someone he suspects of being homosexual is discriminating against that person and against all members of that group. Deliberate discrimination is characterized by the intent to discriminate. The intent that underlies social prejudice and bigotry is, however, often hard to prove. While there is no doubt that this sort of discrimination is widespread in Canadian society, we would argue that it is less important in explaining inequality than the next three causes.

Systemic Discrimination

This is discrimination without conscious individual intent. It is the discrimination that inheres in traditions, customary practices, rules, and institutions that have the effect of favouring the members of one group over another. For example, in 1999 the British Columbia Human Rights Commission ruled that the section of the province's Highway Act requiring motorcyclists to wear helmets discriminated—albeit unintentionally—against male Sikhs, whose religion requires the wearing of a turban. Another example would be height and/or weight requirements for certain jobs. Because women are typically smaller than men, it could be argued that these requirements are discriminatory. Everyone recognizes, of course, that some job requirements may be reasonable and cannot be jettisoned even if they have the effect of discriminating against certain groups.

The examples mentioned above merely scratch the surface of systemic discrimination. A further example will help to demonstrate just how deeply rooted systemic discrimination may be. In our society most people learn that child-rearing is primarily a female function. This assumption is deeply embedded in our culture, in social practices, and is even reinforced through the law (why else would about 85 per cent of child custody orders in cases of separation and divorce assign sole custody to the mother?). What results is a situation where the opportunities effectively open to men and women are not equal. They may appear to be the product of individual choice, particularly where the Constitution proclaims the equality of men and women. But these individual choices are shaped by the weight of social practices and cultural values that have the effect of discriminating between males and females.

Choice

Individual choice also contributes to inequality. For example, a status Indian who decides to stay on the reserve reduces his or her opportunities of finding a job, and if one does find employment it probably will pay less than a job in the city. Native reserves are usually far from centres of population and economic activity, so that an economic cost accompanies the choice of life on the reserve. Likewise, if one decides to live in Cape Breton, northern Ontario, Newfoundland, or many other regions of Canada, there is a greater probability that one will be unemployed or earn less than someone else who went down the road to Toronto or Calgary.

We hasten to add that mobility choices like these are not always easy. A person who grows up in the poverty and deprived environment that characterize most Indian reserves may neither perceive nor have much choice about his or her future. Only by applying a rather generous meaning to the word may one conclude that someone from a second-generation welfare family has much individual choice regarding education and future career opportunities. Nevertheless, individual choice is a factor that contributes to inequality.

Politics

Although debates over equality generally draw on the rarefied language of rights and justice, this should not conceal the fact that they are essentially political struggles. How much inequality is acceptable, or, to put it differently, how much equality is enough? Are there circumstances where some forms of discrimination might be reasonable because they are necessary to protect or promote other values? What groups should be targeted for affirmative action—why, for example, do many affirmative action schemes consider Punjabis to be a visible minority, but not Chinese?

Fairness and equality are cultural notions. A century ago only a small minority of Canadians regretted the fact that women were without most of the rights that are taken for granted today. Poverty was once believed to be primarily the fault of the person suffering from it—an explanation that absolved society, the economic system, and governments from blame for the suffering of many whose greatest offence was to be born into the sort of circumstances that make a life of poverty very likely. As values and beliefs change, a society's notions of what is fair may also be transformed.

Value shifts of this sort are almost certain to be accompanied, and influenced, by political struggles. If Canadians are more conscious today of the discrimination that has been practised against the country's Aboriginal peoples it is because of the efforts of Aboriginal groups to bring these inequalities to the public's attention and influence government policy. The social policies that redistribute wealth from more affluent to less affluent Canadians did not emerge overnight: they have been built up (and, more recently, chipped away at) gradually over time in response to struggles between conflicting interests and values. Political parties, interest groups, individuals, and various parts of the state may all be participants in these struggles.

The structure of the state matters, too, affecting what sorts of inequalities are dealt with by governments and influencing the opportunities and resources available to different interests. It is likely, for example, that Canadian governments have long targeted more money at regional economic inequalities than have American governments because of the particular division of powers between Ottawa and the provinces under Canada's Constitution and the relatively greater leverage of the provincial governments than of the state governments in the United States. To use another example, the entrenchment of the Charter of Rights and Freedoms in the Canadian Constitution has had an enormous impact on the prominence of equality rights issues, the strategies that groups use to achieve their goals, and the treatment of certain groups. The interplay of interest, ideas, and institutions that is politics plays a key role in determining what inequalities get on the public agenda and how they are dealt with.

QUALITY OF LIFE

The United States, the world's wealthiest society, has one of the world's highest rates of homicide and a drug problem that costs thousands of lives and billions of dollars annually, to say nothing of the enormous misery associated with it. It also has a high rate of alcoholism, thousands of homeless people, and a high level of marriage breakup (which translates into many single-parent families, usually headed by women, and a high incidence of child poverty), to mention only a few of the social pathologies of that rich society. Racism, urban blight, and suburban sprawl are a few of the other dilemmas with which the world's richest country must cope. Canadians often take smug pride in being less afflicted by these problems. But Canada's high standard of living, like that of the United States, is also tarnished by problems that undermine the quality of life (QOL) experienced by millions. These problems often become politicized as groups demand that governments take action to deal with them. In some cases government policies are blamed for having caused or contributed to a QOL problem. For example, Native groups and those sympathetic to their demands argue that the appallingly bad quality of life experienced by many Native Canadians is due to unjust and discriminatory policies. While the QOL in Canada is comparatively high, the picture is not uniformly bright for all groups. Aboriginal Canadians, in particular, experience conditions far below what most Canadians would consider decent and acceptable in a society as wealthy as ours.

One way of measuring the QOL in a society is to ask people how satisfied they are with their lives. Pollsters have done this for decades. But the results tell us little except that most people claim to be satisfied with their lives, while a persistently large minority are not satisfied. Attitudinal data like these tell one nothing about the causes of dissatisfaction or the sorts of problems that actually undermine the QOL in a society. To get at these one must rely on objective measures that may reasonably be construed as reflections of QOL. We will look at mortality, crime, suicide, alcoholism, and destitution.

Compared to other advanced industrialized societies, Canada does relatively well on all of these measures. Its mortality rate of about 7 per 1,000 members of the population and the infant mortality rate of just under 6 per 1,000 are about average for such societies. Life expectancy is above average, at about 75 years for males and 81 years for females.

In terms of violent crime, Canada is unexceptional. Canada's current homicide rate is somewhat below 2 homicides per 100,000 population, compared to a rate of about 9 per 100,000 in the United States. Although rates vary marginally from year to year, the statistics do not support the popular assumption that murders have become more common. Canada's homicide rate has actually declined since the mid-1970s.

Statistics on other violent crimes, such as rape, domestic violence, and assault, are difficult to interpret. This is partly because of changes in reporting procedures that can produce an increase or decrease from one year to the next without there being any real change in the actual incidence of the offence. Changes to the law and public attitudes may also affect crime statistics. For example, rape charges and convictions are dramatically higher today than a couple of decades ago. This increase is mainly due to the greater willingness of victims to come forward, a willingness that results from changed social attitudes and reforms to the law on sexual assault. Interpretation problems aside, the data do not suggest that Canada is an exceptionally dangerous place to live. It certainly is much safer than the United States and it compares favourably with many other advanced industrial democracies.

Suicide and alcoholism and other drug abuse are social pathologies that are symptomatic of a low QOL. Suicide accounts for about 5 per cent of deaths among Canadians between the ages of 15 and 69, exceeded only by cancer (36 per cent),

I blame **their** generation...

The Gap

Each generation is shaped by a different set of experiences, and is likely to view politics through the lens of its own interests and values. (Roy Peterson, *Vancouver Sun*)

circulatory system malfunction (30 per cent), and accidents (10 per cent). As in other countries, the rate of successful suicide is considerably higher among men than women, at about 20 per 100,000 population for men compared to 5 per 100,000 among women. And although the rate has remained stable for females, it has increased by about 30 per cent for males since the 1960s. On the other hand, Canada's suicide rate is only about one-third that of Hungary and a little over half the Swiss rate. There is enormous international variation even when levels of national wealth are controlled for, suggesting that suicide is closely related to culture. For example, Mexico's rate is just over 1 per 100,000, Italy and the United Kingdom have rates around 8 per 100,000, while Hungary and Austria top the list at about 40 and 25, respectively. Canada's rate of about 13 per 100,000 falls in the middle.

It is conservatively estimated that about 4–5 per cent of adult drinkers in Canada, or over 600,000 people, are alcoholics.[15] This figure is based on the mortality rate from cirrhosis of the liver, national cirrhosis rates being highly correlated with alcohol consumption levels. Alcoholism in Canada is about average for Western industrialized countries. The level is dramatically lower than in such countries as Hungary, Germany, Italy, and France. Abuse of other non-medical drugs generally is not considered to be a major problem in most of Canadian society, although particular cities, including Vancouver and Toronto, and some isolated Native communities have been well-publicized exceptions. On the whole, however, the social and economic costs associated with illegal drug use in Canada are certainly much less than those produced by alcohol and tobacco consumption.

Advanced industrial societies all have in place a 'safety net' of social programs intended to protect individuals and households from destitution. Nevertheless, some people slip between the mesh. When the safety net fails to catch a significant number of those who, for one reason or another, cannot make ends meet, this is surely an indication that the QOL experienced by some people falls below acceptable standards of human decency. We would argue that homelessness and the demands placed on food banks are two indicators of holes in the social safety net.

The extent of homelessness is difficult to pin down for the obvious reason that the homeless, unlike those who have a fixed address, cannot be enumerated, telephoned, or otherwise kept track of with any accuracy. Nevertheless, there are abundant signs that homelessness is a problem experienced by thousands of Canadians and, moreover, that the number of homeless people has increased over the last several decades. Statistics Canada's first attempt to count the homeless came up with the implausibly low figure of 14,145, based on the number of people nationwide sleeping in emergency shelters on the night of 15 May 2001, a time of year when many homeless people would not be seeking shelter, not to mention that more than a small number of the homeless, for social and psychological reasons, never avail themselves of emergency shelters. The City of Toronto's Commissioner of Community and Neighbourhood Services reported that about 28,000 people used the city's emergency shelter system in 1997.[16] A study done for Human Resources Development Canada placed the number at about 26,000 for 2000. The undeniable fact of more people, including children, living on the streets led to the creation of the Mayor's Task Force on Homelessness in Toronto, whose 1999 report suggested that the true scale of the homeless problem must include the 'hidden homeless', those who live with family or friends because of their inability to pay for shelter. As Canada's largest city, with housing prices that in recent years have been surpassed only by Vancouver, Toronto probably experiences homelessness on a scale and with a visibility greater than elsewhere in Canada. It is not, however, a problem unique to Toronto. Hard numbers on the homeless and their distribution across Canada are virtually impossible to come by. In their place are various guesstimates based on emergency shelter and hostel occupancy, food bank and soup kitchen users, and impressionistic evidence ranging from 'squeegee kids' (now legally banned) in Toronto to occasional news stories of death due to hypothermia (see Box 3.1).

The number of Canadians who rely on food banks for part of their needs has also increased. The Canadian Association of Food Banks (CAFB) estimates that Canada's 615 food banks provided food to roughly 800,000 people in 2002. About three-quarters of food bank users rely on social assistance or Old Age Security as their main source of income. Refugees, the disabled, and those with no income and often no home account for another 10 per cent. Slightly more than 10 per cent of users have employment income. According to the CAFB, the number of food bank users roughly doubled since 1989.[17]

Demands on food banks are largely cyclical, increasing during periods of higher than usual unemployment. But there appears to be a more permanent component to food bank demand that has grown larger in recent years, even when the economy has been growing and the rate of unemployment has been falling. This component, many argue, is created by the gap that exists between the income that social assistance provides and the cost of paying for life's necessities. The wideness of this gap varies across the country because social assistance benefits are determined by the individual provinces and, second, because of regional variations in the cost of living. But the gap is wide in all provinces (see Figure 3.5). As social assistance benefits fail to keep pace with increases in the cost of living, the demand on food banks inevitably increases. Given the growth in the 'normal' use of food banks, an increase in the level of unemployment pushes an already strained system to the breaking point.

BOX 3.1   Death of Homeless Man Renews Call to Create More Affordable Housing

A homeless man was found dead on a heating grate yesterday, across the street from Queen's Park. The man, believed to be in his 50s or 60s, has not been identified, nor has the cause of death been determined. A police officer later retrieved his meagre possessions: a cardboard box, two sleeping bags, a blue tarp, jeans, a bottle of water, some plastic bags and an unopened can of corn.

A young woman watched reporters interviewing politicians who crossed the street from Queen's Park. She shook her head. 'I've watched a number of MPPs walk past here without even so much as glancing at homeless people living on the grates. I think sometimes they're even on their way to a meeting to discuss the problem.' Councillor Jack Layton [now the federal NDP leader] also said that 'the shelters are crowded, we don't have enough staff to help homeless people, and the result is that you end up with people staying out on the street and dying. The funding for housing that needs to be there just isn't.'

Anne Golden, who prepared the Mayor's Homeless Action Task Force report, says, 'It is so sad to think of someone dying on a grate, in a city as rich as ours. It highlights the need for swift action on the recommendations that we've put forward. We have to focus not just on the tragedy that happened, but why and how he got there, and on prevention.'

Source: *Toronto Star*, 5 Feb. 1999.

Figure 3.5   The Welfare Gap, by Province, 1999

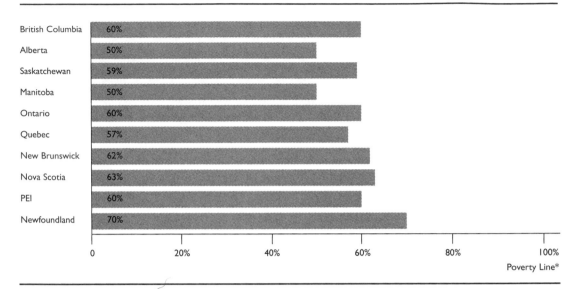

*Based on Statistics Canada's low-income cut-off line for a single parent with one child.

Note: The welfare gap is the difference between total welfare income (social assistance benefits, child tax benefits, and federal and provincial sales tax credits) and the Statistics Canada low-income cut-off line for each province. It does not take into account the value of welfare benefits such as subsidized accommodation, day care, dental care, etc.

Source: Based on data in National Council of Welfare, *Welfare Incomes 1999* (Ottawa: Minister of Public Works and Government Services Canada, 2000), Table 6.

Not everyone agrees, however, that a welfare gap exists, let alone that it is widening. We have already alluded to the limitations of measures of poverty. As an alternative to the relative approach formerly used by Statistics Canada to determine what it means to be poor, some researchers proposed measures that would be based on the actual needs of Canadians. Indeed, such research, along with the urging of some provinces for a more stringent measure, influenced the change to a 'market basket measure'. Economist Chris Sarlo of the right-wing Fraser Institute developed such measures, which he calls Basic Needs Lines. They are based on the cost of maintaining long-term physical well-being, including shelter, a nutritious diet, clothing, personal hygiene, health care, transportation, and a telephone. BNLS are considerably lower than Statistics Canada's LICOS, and they do

not automatically rise as average personal income increases. If BNLS are used to measure poverty, a very different picture emerges. Not only does the welfare gap disappear, but it is replaced by what might be called welfare surpluses for most social assistance recipients. The surplus represents the amount by which the value of all forms of income assistance, including federal and provincial tax credits and supplementary benefits whose value varies between provinces, exceeds the BNL (see Figure 3.6).

Many readers will consider absurd the conclusion that welfare benefits are in fact more generous than is necessary to meet the basic needs of many categories of recipients. It is important to keep in mind, however, that this measure of basic needs does not take into account either self-esteem or the incapacity of many people to spend efficiently on life's necessities. Whether a measure of poverty should take these factors into account is part of the ongoing debate over how poverty should be measured and how extensive it really is in Canada.

Canada is an affluent society. Its social pathologies are fairly typical of those experienced by other advanced industrial societies. The surrogate measures of the QOL that we have examined suggest that the United Nations is certainly right in rating Canada as one of the world's best countries in which to live. But the QOL is sharply lower for one group, namely, Native Canadians. Consider these facts:

- Life expectancy for status Indians is about 10 years less than for the Canadian population as a whole.
- Infant mortality rates are twice as high among Natives as among non-Natives.
- Native death, illness, and accident rates are all about three times greater than national levels. Most deaths of status Indians under 45 are caused by violence rather than illness.
- Although less than 3 per cent of the population are Aboriginal Canadians (defined to include Indians, Inuit, and Métis), about 18 per cent of those in prisons are Native. Natives also comprise almost one-fifth of all murder victims and over one-fifth of all murder suspects in Canada.

Figure 3.6   Welfare Adequacy*, Using Basic Needs Lines (BNLs), 2000

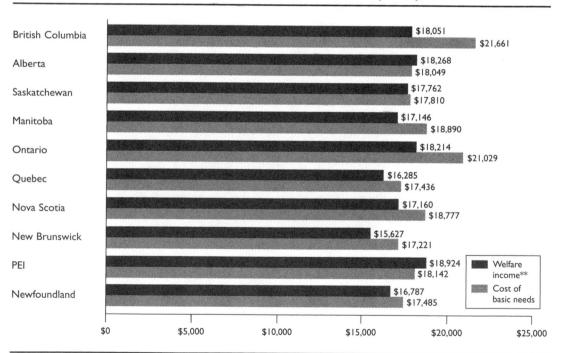

*Based on a family of four.

**This dollar figure represents the value of income assistance, consisting of general and supplementary welfare assistance, child benefits, and tax credits for each province.

Source: Adapted from www.fraserinstitute.ca, 'Measuring Poverty in Canada', and National Council of Welfare, Welfare Incomes 2000.

- The suicide rate among Natives is well over twice the Canadian rate. For the Inuit it is about six times the national rate.
- Alcoholism is much more prevalent among Natives than non-Natives. It has been estimated that 50–60 per cent of accidents and deaths among status Indians are alcohol-related.
- Many Natives live in overcrowded conditions. About one-fifth of Indian dwellings are crowded (defined as more than one person per room), the figure rising to about one-third on reserves. This is several times greater than the Canadian rate.

INDEPENDENCE

A democracy requires self-government. This means that public policies affecting the lives of citizens should be determined by people whom these same citizens have elected and who are accountable to them for their policies. The first major step towards self-government in Canada was taken in 1848 when the principle of responsible government was recognized in the colonies of Nova Scotia and the United Canadas (followed by the other British North American colonies soon afterwards). Responsible government meant that the governor, himself chosen by the British Colonial Office, was obliged to select cabinet ministers who were members of the elected legislature. A cabinet without the support of a majority in the legislature would be required to resign.

Self-government advanced another step with Confederation. The British North America Act of 1867 created a new country out of the colonies of Nova Scotia, New Brunswick, and the United Canadas, and transferred to its federal and provincial legislatures the exclusive right to make laws for Canada and its provinces. Full self-government was almost achieved. We say 'almost' because certain powers were withheld from Canadian governments and, therefore, from the voters who elected them. These included:

- *The power to enter into foreign treaties.* Under section 133 of the BNA Act this remained the responsibility of the British government. Treaty-making

power was formally tranferred to Canada in 1931 by the Statute of Westminster.
- *The power to amend the Constitution.* This also remained in the hands of the British Parliament. The BNA Act that created Canada, and which established the powers of the federal and provincial governments, was a British law. It could only be changed by passing another British law. This situation remained unchanged until 1982, when the BNA Act and all its amendments were patriated and renamed the Constitution Act, 1867. Britain's authority to pass laws applying to Canada was ended, and a procedure for amending the Constitution in Canada was established (see Chapter 5).
- *The power to interpret the Constitution.* At Confederation, the highest court for the colonies of British North America was the Judicial Committee of the Privy Council (JCPC). The JCPC was, in fact, a committee comprised of members of the British House of Lords. The BNA Act left intact the authority of the JCPC over Canada. This continued until 1949, when the Supreme Court of Canada became the final appellate court for this country and, as such, Canada's constitutional umpire.

Step by step the Canadian state achieved the full powers of self-government that it exercises today. With the passage of the Constitution Act, 1982 the last formal impediment to political sovereignty was removed. But the issue of political sovereignty has been far less controversial in the modern politics of Canada than those of economic and cultural sovereignty. The real limitations on Canadian independence, many have argued, have not come from the vestiges of colonialism that have gradually been removed from Canada's Constitution, but have been and are imposed by economic dependence on, first, Great Britain and then the United States and by the 'colonization' of Canada by American cultural industries. Formal political sovereignty, according to Canadian nationalists, is empty so long as the country's economic and cultural destinies are controlled by others.

In the real world, however, no self-governing democracy is totally independent of external influences. Trade, military alliances and animosities, and contemporary mass media are some of the chief factors that create a web of interdependence between modern societies. The question is not, therefore, whether political life in Canada or in any other country is unaffected by influences from outside. Instead, the question is whether the nature and extent of these external influences undermine the political independence of a country.

If one looks at Canada's economic relations with the rest of the world, both historically and today, there is no denying our enormous dependence on foreign sources of investment capital, imports, and markets for Canadian exports. Some of the main features of Canada's international economic relations are listed in Box 3.2.

This dependence must, however, be put into perspective. Several advanced industrial democra-

cies, including the Netherlands, Belgium, Sweden, Britain, and Germany, rely on trade for a greater share of their national income than does Canada. These countries are members of the European Union, which imposes considerably greater limitations on the policy-makers of its member states than the Canada–United States Free Trade Agreement and NAFTA impose on Canadian and American governments. What is unique about Canada is the extent to which our trading relations depend on a single partner, i.e., the United States. Among advanced industrialized economies, only Japan comes close to this level of dependence on a single trading partner (close to half of Japanese exports are purchased by the United States).

In terms of investment, Canada remains heavily dependent on foreign capital. But this dependence has weakened over the last couple of

Recent years have shown that Canada's impressive economic performance has been due largely to the country's unprecedented level of trade dependence on the United States. (Roy Peterson, Vancouver Sun)

BOX 3.2   Canada's Economic Links to the World

Past . . .
- Much of the money used to build the roads, railways, and canals of Canada's early commercial economy was borrowed from foreign, mainly British, investors.
- At Confederation, Canada was already heavily in debt to foreign investors.
- It is estimated that about 450 American companies had established subsidiaries in Canada by 1913.
- By the 1920s, the United States surpassed Britain as the major source of foreign investment in Canada.
- The level of foreign ownership in Canada peaked in 1971 at 37 per cent of corporate non-financial assets. The level was close to 60 per cent for manufacturing industries.

Present . . .
- Trade with the United States accounts for over one-third of Canadian GDP.
- Foreign investors, mainly American, control about one-fifth of corporate non-financial assets in Canada.
- Close to 60 per cent of all American investment in Canada is located in Ontario.
- As of 2001, the value of Canadian direct investment in the US was $109 billion; the value of US investment in Canada was $139 billion.[18]

decades at the same time as Canadian investment abroad—and therefore our penetration of other economies—has increased. Indeed, as a result of the increasing globalization of business and investment, Canada has come to look more and more like several other advanced industrial economies in terms of its level of foreign ownership. Again, however, Canada is rather unique in the degree to which it is dependent on a single source of foreign investment, i.e., the United States.

Culturally, Canada has always lived in the shadow of the United States. Physical proximity, a common language, and shared values have facilitated the flow of cultural products—books, magazines, films, television programs, compact discs, computer software—between the two countries. Economics has ensured that this flow has been mostly from the United States to Canada. This is because of the much greater domestic audience/readership available to American producers, which enables them to produce high-quality mass-

appeal products that are attractive to advertisers. Advertising revenue is the main or sole source of income for most privately owned media businesses (films, recorded music, and books are the chief exceptions). The Canadian dilemma was summed up succinctly by the Canadian Task Force on Broadcasting Policy, one in a long line of government inquiries into the problem of defending Canadian culture (whatever it might be) from the American onslaught. The Task Force estimated that for the $133 million that Canada's English-language private broadcasters spent on foreign programs in 1984–5, they received a production value of $3–$5 billion.[19] The unfavourable economics of television and film production in Canada has not changed.[20]

The result has been predictable. American-made films, television programs, popular music, and magazines spill over into Canada's English-language market. In fact, they dominate all of these Canadian markets. American books also do very well in the English-Canadian market, with authors like Danielle Steele, John Grisham, and Mary Higgins Clark featuring on the best-seller lists both north and south of the border. Newspapers are the main exception to the rule of American dominance. This is because of provisions in Canada's Income Tax Act that heavily favour Canadian-owned newspapers and because, for most people, newspapers are primarily sources of local information.[21]

Let us return to our initial questions. Is Canada's political independence undermined by the country's economic dependence on the United States and by the enormous influence of American mass media in English Canada? In what ways? Is the Canadian predicament so different from that faced by many other industrialized democracies in today's interdependent world?

The answer to the first question is clearly 'yes'. Canadian policy-makers, at all levels, must be sensitive to the actions and possible reactions of governments in the United States. Moreover, many of the public policy matters they deal with, from transboundary pollution to interest rates, are affected by circumstances in the United States, circumstances over which Canadians and their governments can exert little, if any, control. Canada's economic and cultural linkages with the United States affect us in too many ways to be listed here. The fact that roughly 80 per cent of our international trade is with the United States obviously means that our economy will be highly vulnerable to the state of the American economy and to changes in the exchange rate between the Canadian and American dollars. The fact that Canadians are raised on a heavy diet of Hollywood films, television, magazines, and an Internet dominated by American Web sites will certainly affect the images and ideas in their heads. To the extent that these American cultural imports erode distinctively Canadian values (whatever these may be, or might have been), one may argue that they also erode the cultural basis for a Canadian society and public policies that are different from those of the United States.

Faced with a challenge from a larger, more powerful economy and a predatory mass culture, governments typically respond with protectionist policies. They attempt to protect domestic industries or local culture through import restrictions, subsidies to domestic producers, regulations affecting business practices and cultural industries, and so on. Canadian policy-makers have resorted to all of these measures, as have policy-makers elsewhere. To cite but one example, Canadian cultural policy is determined largely by the rules that the

BOX 3.3   The Long Shadow of American Culture

- American magazines account for close to two-thirds of sales in English Canada.

- About two-thirds of television viewing time in English Canada is spent watching American programs. This increases to about 90 per cent in the case of drama and comedy viewing time.

- Canada's feature film and television production industries depend on a life-support system of government subsidies, channelled through the Income Tax Act and Telefilm Canada, and through the production activities of the Canadian Broadcasting Corporation and National Film Board. Despite this, few genuinely Canadian films reach the box office market.

- An American television series can be purchased by a Canadian broadcaster for less than 5 per cent of what it costs to produce, a mass appeal film for 1–2 per cent of its production costs.

Canadian Radio-television and Telecommunications Commission (CRTC) imposes on broadcasters. The CRTC establishes and enforces a dense thicket of regulations governing Canadian content over radio and television, regulations that have a very simple bottom line: to ensure that more Canadian music and television programming reaches the airwaves than would be the case if market forces were allowed to operate without restriction.

Finally, is the Canadian 'dilemma' really so different from that of other small and middle-sized democracies? After all, Hollywood's *Harry Potter* and *Spiderman* were the box office hits of 2002 in Western Europe, just as they were in North America. McDonald's restaurants span the globe, so much so that the standardized cost of a 'Big Mac' is used by the respected business newspaper, *The Economist*, as a measure of the cost of living in different countries. Direct broadcast satellites, the Cable News Network (CNN), international credit cards, and the multinational corporation have shrunk the globe, so that no country is free from some other's cultural or economic incursions. Is Canada really such a special case?

The answer to this question will inevitably be coloured by one's own values. How much dependence on another economy is too much? Is dependence on the world's economic colossus preferable to a more diversified trade profile with weaker or less reliable economies? Has Canada had much choice but to rely on, first, the British and then the American economies?

On the cultural front, if most Canadians prefer American films, television programs, magazines, and music over homegrown alternatives, should their governments interfere? It stretches credulity to suggest that protectionist measures like the Canadian content quotas imposed on radio stations are a response to listener demands. Obviously they are not. And anyway, what are the differences in Canadian culture that policy-makers want to preserve? Does protectionism preserve these values, or just the industries that depend on the state's cultural life-support system?

All countries are subject to external influences that limit the independence of their elected governments. Canada is not unique in this regard. Nevertheless, one may fairly say that these influences are felt somewhat more powerfully in Canada than in most other countries. We would not go as far, however, as those Canadian nationalists who claim that economic and cultural ties to the United States undermine Canadian democracy. A self-governing democracy does not require the freedom from external influence that nationalists argue would be desirable for Canada. There is almost certainly an element of anti-Americanism—a dislike of American culture, institutions, and public policies—that contributes to the Canadian nationalist critique of American influence. More importantly, however, their arguments are based on an outdated ideal of national autonomy that bears increasingly little resemblance to today's world of interdependent states.

NOTES

1. Speech by Prime Minister Jean Chrétien to the American Society of Newspaper Editors, 6 April, 1995, Dallas.

2. See, for example, Stephen Cohen and John Zysman, *Manufacturing Matters* (New York: Basic Books, 1987).

3. John Porter, *The Vertical Mosaic* (Toronto: University of Toronto Press, 1965), 3–4.

4. Statistics Canada, *Family Incomes*, Catalogue no. 13–208.

5. Statistics Canada, 'Average income after tax by economic family types', available at: <www.statcan.ca>.

6. Ibid.

7. National Council of Welfare, *A New Poverty Line: Yes, No or Maybe?* (Ottawa: Minister of Public Works and Government Services Canada, 1999), 1. Emphasis in original.

8. John A. Price, 'Native People, Economic Conditions,' *Canadian Encyclopedia*, 2nd edn (Edmonton: Hurtig, 1988), vol. 3, 1449.

9. See National Council of Welfare, *Women and Poverty Revisited* (Ottawa: Supply and Services, Summer 1990).

10. Monica Boyd et al., *Ascription and Achievement: Studies in Mobility and Status Attainment in Canada* (Ottawa: Carleton University Press, 1985).

11. Harry J. Glasbeek and R.A. Hasson, 'Some Reflections on Canadian Legal Education', *Modern Law Review* 50 (1987): 783 n.

12. Patrice de Broucker and Laval Lavallée, 'Getting Ahead in Life: Does Your Parents' Education Count?', *Canadian Social Trends* (Ottawa: Supply and Services, Summer 1998): 11–15.

13. Porter, *The Vertical Mosaic*; Wallace Clement, *The Canadian Corporate Elite* (Toronto: McClelland & Stewart, 1975).

14. Milan Korac, 'Corporate Concentration and the Canadian Corporate Elite: Change and Continuity', MA thesis (University of Windsor, 1992).

15. Addiction Research Foundation, at <www.arf.org/isd/stats/alcohol.html>.

16. City of Toronto, Commissioner of Community and Neighbourhood Services, *The Homeless Crisis in Toronto*, 29 June 1998.

17. http://www.cafb.ca/about_facts_e.cfm

18. Data from Industry Canada, available at: <http://strategis.ic.ca>.

19. Canada, House of Commons, *Report of the Task Force on Broadcasting* (Ottawa: Supply and Services, 1986).

20. This is amply demonstrated in a study produced by Coopers & Lybrand, *Canadian Television Programming: Viewing Share, Supply, Financial Return and Cost* (Toronto, 30 June 1998).

21. Canada, Royal Commission on Newspapers, *Newspapers and their Readers* (Ottawa: Supply and Services, 1981), 26, table 19; Pew Research Center, *What the World Thinks in 2002* (Washington: Pew Research Center for the People and the Press, Dec. 2002), available at: <www.people-press.org>. The Pew study found that Canadians, by a 2:1 ratio, relied on television instead of newspapers as their main source of information about national and international affairs.

SUGGESTED READINGS

Anton Allahard and James Coté, *Richer and Poorer: The Structure of Inequality in Canada* (Toronto: James Lorimer, 1998). In the tradition of John Porter and Wallace Clement, this book charts the nature and extent of systemic discrimination in Canada and the myth that Canada is a classless society.

Ernie Lightman, *Social Policy in Canada* (Toronto: Oxford University Press, 2003). Focusing on the distributional impacts of government policy, this book examines the nature and extent of poverty, the role of ideology in framing social policy discourse and shaping choices, and the ways through which social policies are financed.

Mahmoud Reza Nakhaie, ed., *Debates on Social Inequality: Class, Gender and Ethnicity in Canada* (Toronto: Harcourt Brace, 1999). This edited collection includes chapters on all major aspects of inequality in Canada and is widely used in courses on Canadian society.

Michael Ornstein and H. Michael Stevenson, *Politics and Ideology in Canada: Elite and Public Opinion in the Transformation of the Welfare State* (Montreal and Kingston: McGill-Queen's University Press, 1999). The authors examine the relationship between public and elite opinion and declining support for the welfare state in Canada.

William Watson, *Globalization and the Meaning of Canadian Life* (Toronto: University of Toronto Press, 1998). Watson argues that, contrary to the widely held view, globalization does not seriously undermine the ability of Canadian governments to pursue policies, including taxation and social policies, that are different from those of the United States.

Review Exercises

1. Look in the Yellow Pages of your telephone book under 'Social Service Organizations'. Make a list of those organizations that appear to be oriented towards helping the poor, another for those geared towards helping women, and a third list that includes those that appear to be operated by churches and religious organizations.

2. How much food bank use and how many homeless people are there in your community? How would you go about finding answers to these questions? (Suggestions: Call a member of your city or town council and ask for the names of persons or organizations that operate food banks and shelters. Alternatively, you might call your local office of the United Way or a religious organization like the Salvation Army to ask about these matters.)

3. How would you define poverty? Calculate a monthly budget for a single person—including expenditures for food, shelter, clothing, transportation, and entertainment—that you think is the minimum necessary to ensure a decent standard of living. What annual income is necessary to maintain this standard of living? Ask a friend or family member to do the same exercise (don't give him or her any hints about your own calculations).

4. Who are the most influential people in your town or city? Make a list of the 10 most influential people. Once you have put together your list, think about why you have included these particular people. Are they politicians? Business people? Journalists? Activists? Labour leaders? In each case, what is the basis for their influence and who is able to hold them accountable for their actions?

A former Prime Minister, Joe Clark, once described Canada as a 'community of communities', a characterization that often seems confirmed in the regionally fractured nature of Canadian politics. (Roy Peterson, *Vancouver Sun*)

Regionalism and regionally based conflict are enduring aspects of the Canadian political condition. This chapter looks at several important aspects of regionalism in Canadian politics, including the following topics:

❑ Predictions of the demise of regionalism.
❑ Reasons for the persistence of regionalism.
❑ The boundaries of Canada's regions.
❑ Regional political cultures.
❑ Regional grievances and western alienation.
❑ Western versus central Canadian 'visions' of the country.

CHAPTER FOUR

REGIONALISM AND CANADIAN POLITICS

'Canada has too much geography', declared the country's longest-serving Prime Minister, Mackenzie King. By this he meant that the vastness of the country and the diversity in the natural endowments and interests of its regions produced conflicts that would either not exist in a more compact country or whose resolution would be less difficult. Canadians have always accepted the truth of King's dictum, believing that the challenges of regionalism and interregional conflict are a central part of the Canadian story. Indeed, as we noted in Chapter 1, one of the most astute observers of Canadian politics, Donald Smiley, once identified regionalism as one of the three fundamental axes of Canadian politics. It was, he rightly noted, the source of major political divisions and controversies throughout Canada's history. And it continues to be one of the defining features of Canada's political landscape today.

Along with King, most Canadians have viewed regionalism as a problem. Aside from occasional patriotic celebrations of Canada's regional diversity and sheer size, as in the spate of songs that emerged around Canada's centennial year and in the speeches of politicians and after-dinner speakers, few have argued that size and regional diversity are positive attributes in political life. Students of American politics will know, however, that some of the founders of the United States believed these attributes to be positive, perhaps even necessary, characteristics of a political system respectful of freedom. In the *Federalist Papers*, James Madison argued that a larger territory encompassing a greater diversity of regional interests was more likely to provide protection for personal freedoms, group rights, and sectional interests than would a smaller, more homogeneous country. Madison reasoned that as the physical size of a country increased and the scope of its social, but especial-

ly economic interests was enlarged, the likelihood of any particular group being able to dominate others or of being able to form a coalition with other interests to achieve such domination would decline. Small countries with comparatively homogeneous populations were, he thought, incapable of maintaining respect for individual and minority rights. The majority would inevitably exercise a sort of tyranny, using their superior numbers to oppress the rights of others. This was less likely to happen in a larger, more diverse country.

Madison's argument has never resonated very positively in Canada, with the exception of some supporters in western Canada. The debates on Confederation contain no echoes of this argument for a vast republic to ensure the protection of rights. The expansion of Canada was seen by most as a necessary pre-emptive action to reduce the possibility of the vast western territories being annexed by a United States where the idea of Manifest Destiny and the fact of territorial expansion were riding high. Surprisingly, perhaps, one of the few Canadians to theorize about the consequences of regionalism in the style of Madison was Pierre Trudeau, usually thought of as being a Prime Minister with a strong preference for centralized federal power. Trudeau's thoughts on the political virtue of regionalism were, however, formulated before he entered federal politics. Aside from the early Trudeau and some disgruntled westerners, few Canadians have disagreed with Mackenzie King's assessment that regionalism has been primarily a burden on the back of Canadian politics.

THE SURPRISING (?) PERSISTENCE OF REGIONALISM

The last few decades have seen an upsurge in regionalism in Canada, a trend mirrored in many other parts of the world. The signs of this upsurge include the following:

- *The party system.* For most of Canada's history the two historically dominant parties, the Liberals and Conservatives, competed with each other across Canada. Although they did not draw equally well from all regional segments of the electorate—the Liberal Party did much better than the Conservatives in Quebec for most of the twentieth century and the Conservative Party tended to be stronger than the Liberals in the West for most of the second half of that century—both were very clearly national political parties with significant support across Canada. Since the 1993 general election, the character of Canada's party system has appeared to be more regionally than nationally based. This is most obvious in the case of the Bloc Québécois, which only fields candidates in Quebec and which elected more MPs from that province than any other party in both the 1993 and 1997 elections and ran a strong second to the Liberals in 2000. The Canadian Alliance, formerly the Reform Party, wins almost all of its seats west of Ontario and has received the greatest share of the popular vote of any party in the combined four western provinces during each of the last three federal elections. The Progressive Conservative Party, long a truly national party in terms of the regional breadth of its support, in recent years has elected more of its MPs from the Atlantic provinces than from any other part of the country. Only the Liberal Party appears capable of claiming significant support in all regions of the country, although even in the case of the Liberals their regional levels of support are very uneven. In any case, recent elections have produced party representation in Parliament that is strikingly fragmented along regional lines.
- *Western alienation.* Western grievances against Ottawa and the Ontario-Quebec axis that has dominated the national political scene have existed for as long as these provinces have been part of Canada. But in the 1970s there was a sharp upward ratcheting in the rhetoric associated with these grievances. At this point the term 'western alienation' entered the lexicon of Canadian poli-

tics. As had always been the case, economics was at the root of this discontent. Spokespersons for the western provinces argued that Ottawa treated the resources with which the West was well endowed, and which formed the basis for western prosperity, differently and less favourably than those located primarily in provinces like Ontario and Quebec. Although Albertans were the most vocal in making this case, politicians and industry leaders in British Columbia and Saskatchewan provided a supportive chorus (see Box 4.1).
- *Economic disparities.* The gap between the real prosperity of the richest and poorest provinces of Canada has not grown narrower. Indeed, if the federal government transfers intended to narrow this gap are excluded, the disparity has increased between wealthy provinces like Alberta and Ontario and less affluent provinces like New Brunswick and Newfoundland. By itself, such disparity does not necessarily mean greater interregional conflict if the central government is able to subsidize incomes and public services in the poorer regions and if taxpayers in the wealthier regions are willing to pay for this regional redistribution of wealth. These conditions have been eroded. The last two decades have shown that the political will to maintain these redistributive transfers has become weaker.
- *Intergovernmental conflict.* The pendulum of federal-provincial power has swung from Ottawa to the provinces and back again several times since Confederation. Sir John A. Macdonald's hope and expectation that the provincial governments would become little more than 'glorified municipalities', deferring to Ottawa on all matters of national importance, was stymied from the beginning by provincial politicians who had other ideas and by judges whose interpretation of the division of powers in Canada's Constitution did not accord with Macdonald's. Today, intergovernmental conflict is alive and intense on a number of fronts that include such important matters as environmental policy, health care, taxation, cities, and post-secondary education. Judging from these conflicts, regionalism continues to mark the Canadian political landscape.

BOX 4.1   Saskatchewan Speaks Out on the Unequal Treatment of Provincial Resources by Ottawa

... [W]e in the West find it passing strange that the national interest emerges only when we are talking about Western *resources* or Eastern *benefits*. If oil, why not iron ore and steel products? If natural gas, why not copper? If uranium—and we in Saskatchewan may well be Canada's biggest uranium producer in a few years—if uranium, why not nickel? And, to add insult to injury, we in the West are now being told by the Federal Minister of Transportation that the national interest demands a rail transportation policy in which the user pays the full cost. What user will pay the most under this kind of system: land-locked Saskatchewan. Air transport is subsidized. The Seaway runs monumental deficits. Our ports are all subsidized. Truck transportation is subsidized by many provincial highway systems in Canada. But in rail transport—the one on which we depend, we are told that the user must pay.[1]

The persistence and even resurgence of regionalism, in Canada and elsewhere, took many by surprise. One of the few points of agreement among most twentieth-century social and political observers was that as the conditions of people's existence became more alike their values, beliefs, and behaviour would converge. As modern transportation, mass media, public education, and consumer lifestyle habits broke down the barriers that previously separated regional communities and nurtured their distinctiveness, regionalism would become a weaker force in social and political life. Those on the left predicted that region, like religion and ethnicity, eventually would be replaced by class as the fault line in the politics of modernized societies. Indeed,

BOX 4.2   Modernization and Regionalism

The expectation ...
In ... modernizing societies, the general historical record has spelled centralization.... [T]he main reasons for this change, the major grounds of centralization and decentralization are to be found not in ...'ground rules' [the Constitution and court rulings] ... [or] in the personal, partisan or ideological preferences of officeholders, but in the new forces produced by an advanced modernity.

—Samuel Beer, 1973

The Canadian reality ...
Modernization has not led to centralization in the Canadian federal system but rather to the power, assertiveness, and competence of the provinces. Furthermore, the provinces where modernization has proceeded most rapidly are insistent about preserving and extending their autonomy.

—Donald Smiley, 1984

some went so far as to argue that only the obfuscations and manipulations of the dominant class, exercised through their control of the mass media, political parties, and such agents of cultural learning as the schools and the churches, kept alive the fiction that region, and not class, was more important in shaping the interests and identities of average people.

Contrary to these expectations, and despite the undeniable fact that in many important ways the lives of people across the rich industrialized societies of the world are more alike today than a generation or two ago, regionalism and its even more robust cousin—nationalism—continue to be important forces in political life. This certainly is true in Canada, as the signs of the vitality of regionalism listed above attest and as the persistence of a significant nationalist movement in Quebec demonstrates. Three principal factors help to explain the attraction and persistence of regionalism.

First, traditional thinking underestimated the extent to which regionally based states and elites may invest in regionalism—and regionally based nationalism, too, as in the case of Quebec—when this investment either serves their own interests or, more charitably, promotes their vision of what is in the best interests of the regional community they purport to represent. During the 1970s Canadian political scientists began to use the term **province-building** to describe the phenomenon of powerful provincial governments using the various constitutional, legal, and taxation levers available to them in order to increase their control over activities and interests within their provincial borders and, in consequence, their stature vis-à-vis Ottawa. Alberta and Quebec were the two provinces most often cited as illustrations of this drive on the part of provincial state elites to extend the scope of their authority.

But although these two provinces may have been the outstanding examples of province-building in action, the phenomenon was not limited to them. Alan Cairns argued that the strength of regionalism in Canada was, in fact, primarily due to a Constitution that gave Canada's provincial governments considerable law-making and revenue-raising powers, reinforced by what he saw as the natural tendency of those who controlled, worked for, or depended on provincial states to protect and extend their turf. We will have more to say about this later in the chapter.

A second factor that was not anticipated by those who predicted the demise of regionalism involves the failure of national institutions—political, cultural, and economic—to produce levels of national integration and identity that would overcome regionally based ways of thinking and acting in Canadian politics. To put this a bit differently, many Canadians, particularly in Quebec and in the West, have remained unconvinced that the institutions of the national government and its policies have their best interests in mind. Students of federalism have made a distinction between *inter*-state federalism, where conflict and co-operation are played out between the national and regional governments, and *intra*-state federalism, where these forces are contained within the institutions of the national state. There certainly has been no shortage of national structures and policies intended to accommodate regional interests and perspectives. A short list of these structures and policies, past and present, would include the following.

Structures

- The Senate incorporates the principle of regional representation, with Ontario, Quebec, the four western provinces, and the three Maritime provinces all being assigned the same number of seats.
- The Supreme Court Act requires that at least three of the nine justices be members of the Quebec bar. Moreover, the custom has developed over time whereby it is expected that three of the judges will be from Ontario and at least one from each of the western and eastern regions of the country.
- The federal cabinet has always been at the centre of attempts to ensure regional representation in federal decision-making. Every Prime Minister has

given careful consideration to the representation of each region and, insofar as possible, each province in putting together his or her cabinet.

- Section 36 of the Constitution Act, 1982 commits the federal government to the principle of 'making equalization payments to ensure that provincial governments have sufficient revenues to provide reasonably comparable levels of public services at reasonably comparable levels of taxation.' Although the practical significance of this constitutional commitment is far from clear, the spirit of it clearly involves a federal obligation to assist the less affluent provincial governments in paying their bills.

Policies

- For about two decades, and in response to criticism that the Canadian media and federal cultural policy were strongly biased towards central Canada, Ottawa has attempted to 'regionalize' its cultural activities in various ways. One of these involves regional programming through the Canadian Broadcasting Corporation and a conscious policy of ensuring that regional points of view are expressed in its national programming. Another involves the programs and spending activities of the Department of Canadian Heritage, which, like the CBC, has a mandate to express the diversity of Canada.
- Federal support for regional economic development has a long and much-criticized history in Canada. These activities were given an organizational focus and a major spending boost through the 1968 creation of the Department of Regional Economic Expansion, which has morphed into departments and agencies by other names over the years. Today, Ottawa's support for the economies of the less affluent provinces is channelled mainly through the Atlantic Canada Opportunities Agency and Western Economic Diversification Canada, both under the Department of Industry.
- When making decisions that have important regional spending and employment implications, from the awarding of contracts to the location of government offices, Ottawa is always sensitive to the probable reactions of citizens and their

spokespersons in regions competing for a share of the federal pie. Donald Savoie has argued that the political success of members of cabinet is, in large measure, determined by their perceived ability to win contracts, government offices, and other economic and employment benefits for their regions of the country.

Although it would be unfair to write off these structures and policies as amounting to a complete and abject failure, it is nevertheless clear that they have not succeeded in neutralizing regionalism. It is always possible, of course, that regional grievances and the acrimony that often accompanies intergovernmental relations in Canada might have been worse in the absence of these efforts at intra-state federalism.

A third factor whose importance was overlooked by those who anticipated the decline of regionalism involves the persistence of differences in the economic interests and social characteristics of regions. It is undeniably true that, in many respects, how people in Ontario and Saskatchewan live, the sorts of jobs they are likely to do, and the things they watch on television are more alike today than two generations ago. But differences persist and their political importance, often fanned by politicians or other regional spokespersons, is considerable. For example, about one-quarter of Alberta's GDP is accounted for by the petrochemical industry, a level of dependence on this particular industry that is unrivalled in Canada. Ontario's economy is far more dependent than any other province on the automobile industry, with close to 40 per cent of all provincial exports, representing about 12 per cent of Ontario's GDP, accounted for by automotive vehicles and parts. Almost all of this goes to the United States.

If we shift from economics to demography we also find some significant differences between provinces and regions. On the whole, and with one major exception, the political impact of these demographic differences tends to be considerably less than that of the different economic interests of Canada's regions. The major exception is, of course, Quebec. It is the only majority francophone province, with over 80 per cent of the provincial population claiming French as their mother tongue and a majority having French ancestry. Nunavut, where about 85 per cent of the population is Inuit, represents another case of a region whose ethnic character is dramatically different from the rest of Canada. This is not to say that there are not enormous differences in the demographic character of other provinces. British Columbia, for example, has been a magnet in recent decades for non-European immigrants, most of them from Asia, whereas in Nova Scotia the predominance of people whose ancestry is from the British Isles remains uneroded. But the political significance of these demographic differences is less than in the case of Quebec or Nunavut. The ethnic character of Nova Scotia does not get expressed in Canadian politics in the way that Quebec's francophone character does.

MAPPING REGIONALISM IN CANADA

How many regions does Canada have? The answer depends on our definition of region. A map with boundaries drawn along economic lines will look different from one drawn along lines of ethnicity or history. Some have argued that the only sensible way to conceive of regions in Canada is along provincial lines, such that each province constitutes a separate region. More commonly, however, political observers have tended to combine certain provinces into the same region, particularly the western and eastern provinces. But here, too, there are difficulties. The justification for lumping Manitoba and British Columbia into a common region designated the 'West' is not obvious. Aside from both being west of Ontario they may appear to have no more in common than Manitoba and Nova Scotia. Difficulties aside, it has been common to speak of four or five main regions in Canada: the West (or British Columbia and the Prairies), Ontario, Quebec, and the Atlantic provinces. From the point of view of both physical and cultural

geography, as well as economics, the Canadian North comprises another significant region.

There are three principal ways of determining the boundaries of regions, all of them useful. They involve economics, values, and identity.

Canada's Economic Regions

Common economic interests, often linked to physical geography, may provide a basis for classifying regions. Atlantic Canada's greater dependence on fisheries, Ontario and Quebec's greater manufacturing base, and the West's comparatively greater reliance on grain production and natural resources are economic interests that have provided a basis for thinking of these parts of Canada as constituting distinctive regions. The profile of a region's economic characteristics, including types of goods and services produced, employment, income levels, trading patterns, and investment, is referred to as the industrial structure. As Table 4.1 shows, the industrial structure of Canada's provinces varies considerably.

The regional variation that exists in Canada's industrial structure has often been at the root of major political conflicts between regions of the country and between Ottawa and the provinces. The Kyoto Protocol on limiting greenhouse gas emissions, which requires policies that would reduce the use of carbon-based fuels, has pitted Alberta against Ottawa. Albertans and their government know that the environmental gains envisaged by advocates of the Kyoto Protocol will be achieved at the expense of the industry that is central to their province's economic well-being. The federal government was able to point to public opinion polls showing that a clear majority of Canadians favoured ratification of the Kyoto agreement. It is doubtful, however, that Ottawa would have been as keen to push for major limits on greenhouse gas emissions if most of this country's oil and gas reserves were located in either Ontario or Quebec.

Historically, the federal government's major economic policies have been slanted towards the

Table 4.1   Industrial Structure, Selected Characteristics, by Province

Province	GDP per capita (2001)	Average family income (1998)	Unemployment rate (2001)	Ratio of services-producing to goods-producing employees (1999)	Most important industries	Value of mineral production as share of GDP (1999)	Value of manufacturing shipments as share of GDP (1999)	Transfers from Ottawa as share of provincial government revenue (2000)
Newfoundland	$26,060	$45,420	16.1%	3.3:1	Fishing, mining, oil and gas, newsprint	15.5%	16%	41%
PEI	$24,626	$51,072	11.9%	2.6:1	Agriculture, tourism, fishing	0.2%	31.7%	38%
Nova Scotia	$26,423	$50,460	9.7%	3.5:1	Forestry, agriculture, tourism, fishing	1.7%	33.6%	34%
New Brunswick	$26,699	$49,915	11.2%	3.1:1	Forestry, mining, agriculture	4.6%	47%	29%
Quebec	$30,839	$54,930	8.7%	2.7:1	Manufacturing, mining, hydroelectric power	1.7%	54.4%	15%
Ontario	$37,060	$69,571	6.3%	2.7:1	Motor vehicles and parts, manufacturing, finance	1.3%	66.1%	6%
Manitoba	$30,508	$55,977	5.0%	2.8:1	Manufacturing, agriculture	2.8%	32.6%	22%
Saskatchewan	$32,538	$53,468	5.8%	2.5:1	Agriculture, mining	20%	20.3%	14%
Alberta	$49,048	$65,644	4.6%	2.7:1	Oil and gas, agriculture	25%	30.3%	5%
BC	$31,835	$63,252	7.7%	2.8:1	Forestry, tourism, mining	3.7%	30.7%	8%
Canada	**$35,233**	**$62,116**	**7.2%**	**2.8:1**	—	**5.5%**	**50.5%**	—

Source: Various on-line publications of Statistics Canada, available at: <www.statcan.gc.ca> and *The Canada Year Book 2001*, published by Statistics Canada.

interests of central Canada. On occasion the discrimination against and even exploitation of other regions of the country, particularly the West, has been egregious. Examples include the following.

Tariffs. For most of Canada's history a cornerstone of economic policy was high tariffs on manufactured imports, the costs and benefits of which were distributed unequally between the country's economic regions. One study of tariff impacts prior to the Canada–United States Free Trade Agreement concluded that the per capita benefits for Ontario were about equal to the per capita costs in the West and Atlantic Canada. Quebecers were also net beneficiaries, but the decline of that province's manufacturing base by the 1980s reduced the level of these benefits from what it had been for most of the previous century.[2]

Terms of entry into Confederation. Outside of Alberta and Saskatchewan, few Canadians know that when these provinces entered Canada in 1905 they did not immediately receive all of the law-making powers held by the other provinces. Specifically, until 1930 they did not have control over natural resources within provincial borders, a power that sections 92 and 109 of the British North America Act (since renamed the Constitution Act, 1867) assigned exclusively to the provinces. The reason for this discriminatory treatment involved, quite simply, Ottawa's desire to retain control over the economic development of the Prairies, a part of the country that was being settled rapidly in the early 1900s and whose expansion was essential to the National Policy's goal of building a larger domestic market for the manufacturers of Ontario and Quebec.

Transportation policy. Throughout most of Canada's history the freight rates set by Ottawa for rail transportation—crucial to the resource-based economy of the Prairies, far from the markets for what they produced—were relatively low in the East and high in the West. Moreover, it was cheaper to transport unprocessed raw materials from the West to markets than to transport processed materials and finished products, a discriminatory policy that helped discourage manufacturing investment in the West.

The 'Crow rate', established in 1897, provided a huge public subsidy for the transportation to markets of unprocessed western grain. When it was abolished in 1982 some westerners, particularly in Saskatchewan, complained bitterly that the only part of federal transportation policy that did not work to the disadvantage of the West had been taken away.

The National Energy Policy (1981). Roughly 20 years after it was abolished by the Conservative government of Brian Mulroney in 1984, the National Energy Policy (NEP) remains vivid in the memory of Albertans. It involved, they quite reasonably believed, an enormous transfer of wealth from Alberta to the rest of Canada, and chiefly to the consumers and industries of Canada's industrial heartland, perpetrated by a Liberal government that they saw as being hostile to western, and especially Alberta's, interests. The NEP placed a limit on the price that could be charged in Canada for oil and gas from Canadian sources. This price was considerably below the going world price. Canadian producers' ability to export their petroleum at the higher world price was limited by the fact that any energy exports had to be approved by the National Energy Board. Albertans saw the NEP as a thinly disguised subsidy that their province was made to pay to central Canada.

Canada's Cultural Regions

In what is perhaps the most widely cited—and disputed—study of regional political cultures in Canada, Richard Simeon and David Elkins conclude that 'there are strong differences among the citizens of Canadian provinces and those of different language groups in some basic orientations to politics.'[3] They argue that these regional variations cannot be totally explained by demographic and socio-economic differences among Canada's regions. The sources of these differences in basic political orientations are, Simeon and Elkins admit, unclear. But their existence, they insist, is undeniable.

Other researchers have arrived at very different conclusions about the nature and extent of regional political cultures in Canada. Indeed, if there is anything approaching a consensus on this question—and it is a shaky consensus at best—it is that regional variations in basic and enduring political values and beliefs are not very great in English-speaking Canada, and while the differences between French-speaking Quebec and the rest of Canada appear to be more significant, they are not enormous.

A survey conducted in 2002 by Environics Research Group appears to support this consensus. Based on this survey of Canadians' attitudes towards the Charter of Rights and Freedoms, the study's authors note the 'lack of any significant regional differences of opinion on the Charter's legitimacy or the relationship between Parliament and the courts'.[4] (See Figure 4.1.) Moreover, they observe that there does not appear to be any difference across regions of Canada in support for such Charter principles and values as bilingualism and minority-language education rights, multiculturalism, the appropriateness of 'reasonable

limits' on freedom of expression, and the rights of the accused. The one outlier, however, was Quebec. While sharing with other Canadian regions support for the Charter and its general principles, Quebecers are considerably more likely than other Canadians to value equality over personal freedom and consistently more likely than their compatriots in other regions to support the extension of equality rights to disadvantaged groups (see Figures 4.2 and 4.3).

These findings seem to confirm the widely held view of Quebec as being a more collectivist society than other regions of Canada. Further confirmation is provided by those aspects of personal freedom for which Quebecers are more supportive than Canadians in other regions. In regard to restricting police powers and guaranteeing the legal rights of vulnerable groups, Quebecers are somewhat more likely to come down on the side of civil liberties. For example, in the 2002 Environics survey 71 per cent of Quebecers said that the police *should not* be allowed to enter and search a criminal suspect's

Figure 4.1   Opinion on the Charter and the Courts, by Region, 2002

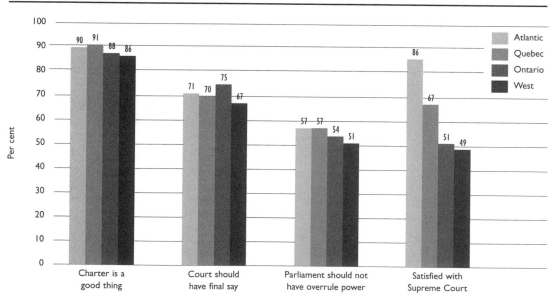

Source: Centre for Research and Information on Canada (CRIC), *The Charter: Dividing or Uniting Canadians*, Apr. 2002, 30. Available at: <www.ccu-cuc.ca>.

**Figure 4.2   Support for Freedom versus Equality, by Region, 2002
(percentage agreeing with the statement)**

A. Both freedom and equality are important. But I consider personal freedom to be more important, that is, everyone can live in freedom and develop without hindrance.

B. Both freedom and equality are important. But I consider equality to be more important, that is, nobody is under-privileged and social class differences are not so strong.

Source: Centre for Research and Information on Canada (CRIC), *The Charter: Dividing or Uniting Canadians,* Apr. 2002, adapted from Table 6, 30.

home or office without a search warrant, compared to 63 per cent in the rest of Canada. Similarly, only 61 per cent of Quebecers expressed the view that the police and courts have to spend too much time worrying about the rights of criminals, compared to 72 per cent of Canadians living outside Quebec. On the matter of the rights of refugee claimants, Quebecers were again more likely than other Canadians to support the protection of individual rights (85 per cent compared to 75 per cent).[5] Arguably, all of these issues reflect support for 'underdogs' and the vulnerable—those accused of crimes, refugees, etc.—and so Quebecers' greater support for civil liberties intended to protect those who fall into these groups may reasonably be interpreted as

consistent with the characterization of Quebec as a more collectivist society.

One of the most thorough examinations of popular ideology in Canada corroborates the conclusion that, Quebec aside, the regional variations in political culture that exist in the rest of Canada are not very great.[6] Based on a large national survey Michael Ornstein and Michael Stevenson measure Canadians' support for social programs, redistributive policies, foreign investment, labour unions, and large corporations. Their examination of the variation in the ideological profiles of the provinces reveals that the differences are, for the most part, small and that Quebec stands out as the one province that is clearly to the left of the

Figure 4.3   Attitudes on Equality, by Region, 2002

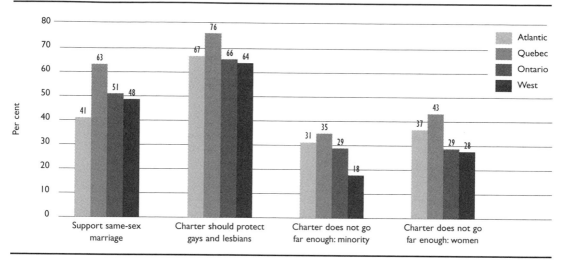

Source: CRIC, *The Charter*, 31.

others. Moreover, contrary to the findings of Simeon and Elkins 20 years earlier, Ornstein and Stevenson do not find any significant variation between the provinces, Quebec included, in levels of political efficacy or political participation. 'Not one province', they argue, 'differs significantly from the national mean for the measure of efficacy'[7] and the small provincial variations in participation do not conform to the pattern found by Simeon and Elkins.

The case for the existence of several regional political cultures in English-speaking Canada looks somewhat stronger if, instead of ideological values, one looks at how regional populations view Ottawa, its treatment of their region, and policies intended to redistribute wealth between regions of the country (see Figures 4.4–4.7). Albertans stand out as those least likely to believe that the federal government deserves their trust and confidence or that Ottawa gives them value for their tax money. They also appear to be less committed than other Canadians to the long-standing policy of equalization, whereby money is transferred by Ottawa from the richer to the poorer provinces. And they are among those least

likely to believe that their province is treated with the respect it deserves. Atlantic Canada, on the other hand, displays greater trust and confidence in the federal government than other regions of the country and is the only part of the country where citizens are more likely to name Ottawa than their provincial government as providing them with value for their money.

These findings corroborate those of Ornstein and Stevenson, who found dramatic variation between provincial populations in their responses to the question of whether the federal government treated their province fairly and whether either Ottawa or their provincial government should have more·power. For example, 64 per cent of Ontarians agreed that Ottawa treated their province fairly and only 22 per cent expressed the view that their provincial government should have more power. The percentages for PEI were almost identical. But Alberta, Saskatchewan, and Newfoundland presented an opposite view. In Newfoundland, for example, only 12 per cent agreed that Ottawa treated their province fairly and 58 per cent said that their provincial government should have more power.[8]

Regional Identities and Western Alienation

If, instead of looking for significant and enduring regional differences in fundamental political values and beliefs—the sorts of orientations that Ornstein and Stevenson look for and do not find, except in the case of Quebec—we ask whether citizens of Canada's regions view their history in different ways and hold different aspirations for their country and their region's role in it, we then find rather compelling evidence for the existence of regional political cultures. In particular, the West has long been characterized by sentiments of resentment towards and alienation from Ottawa and what westerners perceive to be the political preoccupations of central Canada, these sentiments varying in intensity across the western

provinces and also fluctuating in response to specific circumstances and events. Gibbins and Arrison argue that it is reasonable to speak of 'national visions' in the West that, in their words, 'address not simply the place of the West within the Canadian federal state, but also the nature of *Canada* as a political community.'[9] These visions are not merely reactions to citizens' sense of being unfairly treated and marginalized within Canadian politics—the resentment captured in the Reform Party's founding slogan, 'The West wants in'—but are deeply rooted in regional histories that have forged a collective consciousness and memories that are not the same as those of central and eastern Canada.

Starting in a major way in the 1950s with W.L. Morton, western Canadian historians began to react against what they saw as a narrative of

The rise and regional success of the Reform Party, now the Canadian Alliance, has been largely due to westerners' belief that Ottawa tends to ignore their interests. (Roy Peterson, *Vancouver Sun*)

Figure 4.4   Province Is Treated with the Respect It Deserves, by Region, 1998–2001

Question: In your opinion, is (name of province) treated with the respect it deserves in Canada or not?

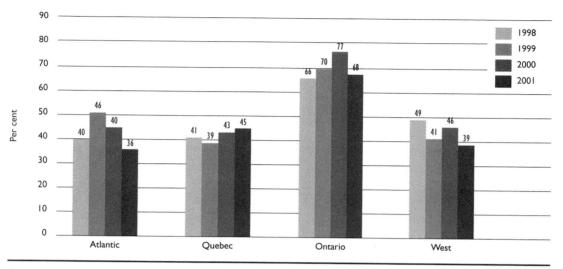

Source: CRIC, <www.ccu-cuc.ca/>.

Figure 4.5   Trust and Confidence in Federal and Provincial Governments, by Region, 2002 (percentage saying they have a great deal or a fair amount)

Question: Overall, how much trust and confidence do you have in the federal government/your provincial government to do a good job in carrying out its responsibilities?

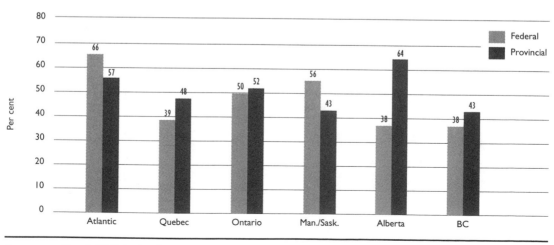

Source: CRIC, *Canada-US Federalism Survey* (Apr. 2002), at: <www.ccu-cuc.ca/>.

Figure 4.6   Level of Government That Gives You Most for Your Money, by Region, 2002

Question: From which level of government do you feel you get the most for your money? Would you say the federal, provincial, or local? (Responses for 'local government' not shown.)

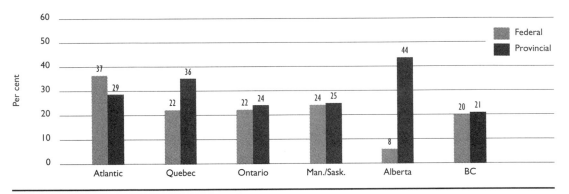

Source: CRIC, *Canada-US Federalism Survey* (Apr. 2002), at: <www.ccu-cuc.ca/>.

Figure 4.7   Support for Equalization, by Region, 2002

Question: As you may know, under the federal equalization program money is transferred from the richer provinces to the poorer ones, in order to ensure than Canadians living in every province have access to similar levels of public services. Do you strongly support, moderately support, moderately oppose, or strongly oppose the equalization program?

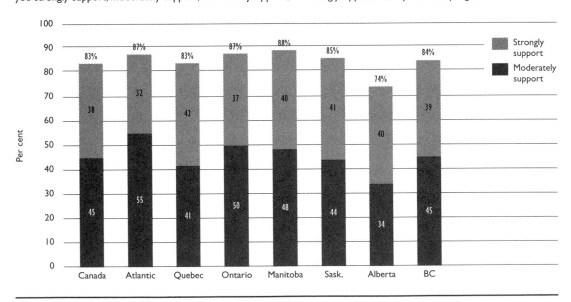

Source: CRIC, at: <www.ccu-cuc.ca>.

Canadian history told from a central Canadian perspective, with little allowance for the distinctive experiences and cultures of the West. This perspective, says Morton, 'fails to take account of regional experience and history and makes coherent Canadian history seem an "imperialist creed," an imposition on Maritime, French-Canadian, Western and British Columbian history of an interpretation which distorted local history and confirmed the feeling that union with Canada had been carried out against local sentiment and local interest.'[10] Morton and many others have attempted to counter the centralist bias of Canadian historiography, but the belief lives on that the West's stories are not given fair weight by a Canadian academic and cultural establishment whose centre of gravity is in the Toronto-Ottawa-Montreal triangle (see Box 4.3).

Writing during the height of the struggle between Pierre Trudeau, championing a bilingual vision of Canada, and René Lévesque, advocating separatism for Quebec, the writer George Woodcock fulminated about the 'betrayal' of Confederation, which he argued was based on 'the long campaign of the centralists in Ottawa to recover the power that in recent decades has rightfully flowed to the regions'.[11] Woodcock accused 'centralizers' like Pierre Trudeau of having no appreciation of or sympathy for the distinctive history and consciousness of the West.

In a broadly similar vein Barry Cooper, a Calgary-based political scientist, argues that western Canada has a distinctive political tradition, the roots of which lie in the history of that region. '[D]ualism', he observes, 'is not the political issue in the West that it is in central Canada. Moreover,

---

BOX 4.3   The West as Canada's Internal Colony

To trace the decreasing sensitivity of the national government to influences which are specifically provincial or regional would be to write the history of Canadian political institutions over more than a century.

   —Donald Smiley, 1976

Unfortunately, federal policies, the attitudes of Central Canadian governments and the biases of so-called national institutions, such as the Canadian Broadcasting Corporation, have painted regionalism with the brush of divisiveness, disunity and even treason. Influences tending to strengthen regional power are 'balkanizing,' while those working to increase the central power are 'in the national interest.' But this is true only if what is good for Central Canada is also good for Canada.

   —David Jay Bercuson, 1977

Western Canada has paid for the development of Canadian nationality, and it would appear that it must continue to pay.

   —Harold Innis, 1923

The West has never felt in control of its own destiny. None of the wealth of recent years has eased this feeling. In fact, the tremendous wealth of the region merely sharpens the contrast with the political powerlessness that exists on the national level.

   —Doug Owram, 1980

BOX 4.4   Does Ottawa's Attitude Fuel Western Alienation?

In its February 2003 throne speech, the Alberta government of Ralph Klein expressed the view that feelings of frustration and alienation were reaching the boiling point in that province. In comments to the press Klein acknowledged that groups in the province were talking seriously about separation. This led Ottawa's Minister of Intergovernmental Affairs, Stéphane Dion, to send a letter to Premier Klein, in which he called on Klein to declare his unconditional opposition to separation. Miffed by what he and many other Albertans perceived to be Dion's condescending tone and complete failure to understand western grievances and Alberta's point of view, Klein shot back with a letter to Dion's boss, Prime Minister Jean Chrétien. The following are excerpts from their exchange of letters.

Dear Premier,

I know you are a committed Canadian and how much Albertans love their country. For this reason, I am writing to address any misunderstanding that your recent comments may have created about your unwavering attachment to Canada.

I am sure you will agree that nothing justifies secession—or the threat of secession—in Canada. Nothing justifies such a threat, whether in Alberta, in Quebec or anywhere else in our great democracy.

Secession is a very grave act whereby an international border is established between fellow citizens who thus cease to be fellow citizens. There is no justification in our democracy for transforming Canadians into foreigners in relation to one another.

Nowhere in the world is the spectre of secession raised with regard to an international protocol on the environment, or a wheat board, or a firearm registry program. Albertans who oppose Kyoto, the Canadian Wheat Board or the Firearms Act are no less Canadian than other Canadians. Albertans who support those federal policies are no less Albertan than other Albertans.

Both our governments are working to develop the best policies for our country. In the process, we sometimes have disagreements, which we have to overcome as best we can. But it would be unfair to Canada to call into question its very existence simply because our governments have disagreements. Other democracies do not do so.

Stéphane Dion

Dear Prime Minister:

I am in receipt of a letter, dated February 21, from your Minister of Intergovernmental Affairs in which he seeks clarification of my position regarding the province's place in confederation. In responding to you, I seek to know whether you think it is productive for your minister to send such an inappropriate letter to a Premier.

To begin, I want to assure you and all Canadians that the Alberta government believes in a united Canada. Recent media coverage that has insinuated that my government or I have made a 'veiled separatist threat' stems from what I consider an unduly creative interpretation of a short portion of the Alberta Speech from the Throne, delivered in our Legislature on February 18.

> Separation is not the issue. What is at issue, as reflected in the throne speech, is the very real sense that on a number of matters, Albertans are not being listened to by Ottawa. I was surprised that your minister did not discuss these matters in his letter; nor did he offer any suggestions on ways that our governments could work cooperatively to allay Albertans' frustration. Instead, the focus of his letter was a misplaced emphasis on separation, which only serves to inflame the situation.
>
> It is no secret on issues such as gun control, senate reform and the appointment of *elected* Alberta senators when vacancies arise, the Canadian Wheat Board monopoly, the Kyoto Protocol, and federal funding for health, my government and many Albertans have felt that their views have been unfairly dismissed by your government. Albertans don't expect to get their way on every issue; they do expect that their views will be fairly heard and that consensus will be sought on issues in which they have a direct stake as well as a constitutional responsibility. Recently, it seems that federal-provincial policy is being shaped by federal fiat—I cite recent discussions on health funding as an example—and this quite rightly concerns Albertans. That is the issue Alberta will pursue.
>
> Your minister's letter's condescending lecture on the history of secessionism in the 20th century notwithstanding, I can assure you that my government's understanding of the consequences of separation or separatist threats is at least as comprehensive as the federal government's. It's this kind of condescension that fuels frustration with your government—frustration that could not be quelled by letters from Ottawa, but by a clear indication of a willingness to listen.
>
> Ralph Klein

multiculturalism does not mean the same thing to a third or fourth generation non-French, non-British Westerner as it does to someone from the Azores or Calabria living on College Street in Toronto.'[12] What is referred to as **western alienation**, Cooper argues, is not in fact a psychological, sociological, or economic condition experienced by those in the West. Rather, it is the awareness that the public realm—whose voices are heard and what counts as legitimate political discourse—belongs to others. These others are the citizens of central Canada and the elites who purport to speak on their behalf.

Of course, the history of the West and the political traditions that have evolved in western Canada are not disconnected from those of the rest of Canada. As Gibbins and Arrison observe, 'western visions' of the nature of the Canadian political community and their region's place in it are not restricted to the West. Gibbins and Arri-

son identify a set of core values that they believe are more solidly anchored in the West than in other regions of Canada, but the same values also find support among Canadians in other regions, including French-speaking Quebec. The difference is one of degree. Western visions of Canada are more likely to embrace the *individual* equality of all Canadians, the equal status of all provinces, and a populist style of doing political business.

Regarding the first of these values—individual equality—Gibbins and Arrison rightly note that opposition to the official recognition and even constitutionalization of multiculturalism and a group rights concept of Canada has come largely from such popular western spokespersons as John Diefenbaker, Preston Manning, and, one would add more recently, Stephen Harper. The election of ideologically conservative provincial governments, such as those of Ralph Klein in Alberta and Gordon Campbell in British Columbia, and the impressive support for Reform/Alliance in federal elections across the three westernmost provinces appear to corroborate this argument that westerners are more receptive to what might be characterized as a classically American conception of equality. This involves the equal treatment of all individuals, without taking group membership into account, and formal equality of opportunity. On the other hand, it must be said that there is little in the way of survey evidence to support the claim that westerners are significantly different from their compatriots in other regions when it comes to what they think about equality (see, especially, Figures 4.2 and 4.3). Moreover, the quite different political histories of Saskatchewan and Alberta should give pause to anyone who wishes to generalize about a *western* conception of equality. The election of CCF and NDP governments in Saskatchewan for most of the last half-century is evidence of a strong social democratic current in that province. Albertans, on the other hand, have preferred Social Credit and Conservative governments that have been much less favourably disposed towards higher taxes and social spending.

The second core value of the western vision that Gibbins and Arrison identify is provincial equality. This really has two components. One is the sense that Canadian federalism would operate more fairly if the West had more influence on decisions taken by Ottawa. The idea of an elected Senate in which each province has an equal number of senators is one that has been spearheaded by western spokespersons since the 1980s. The other component of this core value involves opposition to any arrangement that appears to treat Quebec differently from and more favourably than the western provinces. As Figure 4.8 shows, opposition to the Charlottetown Accord in the 1992 referendum was higher in each of the four western provinces than in other provinces, except Quebec. Constitutional recognition of Quebec as a distinct society and other provisions that may well have been interpreted as providing special status for Quebec were, of course, among the most controversial sections of the Charlottetown Accord. Observers of the western political scene know that westerners have often felt resentment against Quebec, believing it to be the 'spoiled child' of Confederation. The West's enthusiasm for the idea that the provinces are all equal in their rights and powers clashes with Quebecers' espousal of the 'two founding nations' thesis of Canadian Confedera-

Figure 4.8   Percentage of Voters Rejecting the Charlottetown Accord (1992), by Province

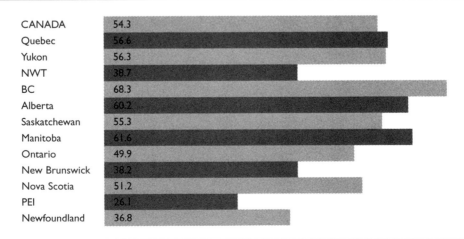

CANADA	54.3
Quebec	56.6
Yukon	56.3
NWT	38.7
BC	68.3
Alberta	60.2
Saskatchewan	55.3
Manitoba	61.6
Ontario	49.9
New Brunswick	38.2
Nova Scotia	51.2
PEI	26.1
Newfoundland	36.8

tion and their preference for a binational vision of the country in which Quebec, as the home of 90 per cent of French-speaking Canadians, and the rest of Canada are equal partners.

The third component of the western vision involves a populist style of politics. Populism arose in the American West and Midwest in the late 1800s out of the perception that economic and political elites, often far from where the people affected by their decisions lived, were too powerful and unsympathetic to the people's interests. The western Canadian version of populism was a combination of imported ideas and homegrown conditions that made the American message resonate in a farm and resource-based economy where people were constantly reminded by the railroads, the banks, the tariffs, and the grain elevator companies that they did not control their own destiny.

Populism, in its simplest form, seeks to return power to the common people. It sees elected politicians as delegates of those who elected them and therefore is hostile to party discipline and aspects of parliamentary government that reduce an elected official's ability or willingness to be a direct tribune of his or her constituents' preferences. Populists favour recall votes to remove unfaithful public officials from office, plebiscites and referendums to give people a more direct say in the decisions that affect them, short terms of office, and term limits for public officials. In what is probably the best study of referendums in Canada, Patrick Boyer shows that this favoured instrument of populist democracy has been used far more extensively in the West than in other parts of Canada.[13] The Reform Party's original platform placed a heavy emphasis on referen-

I seldom travel west of Toronto, but I know westerners are angry because they like to be angry.

Reasons for Western Alienation:#998,175,67!
THE CENTRAL CANADIAN PUNDIT

The central Canadian 'chattering class' is viewed by many westerners as out of touch with the values and interests of their region and one of the factors that fuels western alienation. (Roy Peterson, Vancouver Sun)

dums and recall votes, although this has become a less prominent feature of the Canadian Alliance platform. British Columbia passed a recall law in the 1990s—the first province to do so—and the British Columbia government of Gordon Campbell held a 2002 referendum on the highly contentious question of Native land claims and treaty negotiations in the province. All four of the western legislatures have passed laws requiring that proposals for constitutional amendment be submitted to the people in a referendum, although Canada's Constitution does not require this. There are, in short, strong indications that populist values are more solidly rooted in the West than in the rest of Canada.

CONCLUSION

It is probably true, as Michael Bliss argues in a recent essay on multiculturalism and Canadian identity,[14] that the populations of Ontario and Nova Scotia are more similar today than they were at the time of Confederation. Nonetheless, regionalism continues to cut deep grooves across Canada's political landscape, but for reasons that have far more to do with political and bureaucratic rivalries, different economic interests, and inequalities between the provinces in their political and economic clout. The importance of these factors has not diminished over time, ensuring that regional conflict remains, as Donald Smiley once described it, one of the three major axes of Canadian politics.

NOTES

1. Former Saskatchewan Premier Allan Blakeney, quoted in Roger Gibbins, *Prairie Politics and Society: Regionalism in Decline* (Toronto: Butterworth, 1980), 173–4.
2. Cited in *The Economist*, 15 Feb. 1986, special survey of Canada, 16.
3. Richard Simeon and David Elkins, 'Regional Political Cultures in Canada', *Canadian Journal of Political Science* 7, 3 (Sept. 1974): 397–437.
4. Centre for Research and Information on Canada, *The Charter: Dividing or Uniting Canadians?* (Apr. 2002), 30. Available at: <www.ccu-cuc.ca>.
5. Ibid., 31.
6. Michael Ornstein and Michael Stevenson, *Politics and Ideology in Canada* (Montreal and Kingston: McGill-Queen's University Press, 1999), ch. 5.
7. Ibid., 206.
8. Ibid., 201, Table 5–2.

9. Roger Gibbins and Sonia Arrison, *Western Visions: Perspectives on the West in Canada* (Peterborough, Ont.: Broadview Press, 1995), 45.
10. W.L. Morton, 'The Bias of Prairie Politics', *Transactions of the Royal Society of Canada* series 3, 49 (June 1955): 66.
11. George Woodcock, *Confederation Betrayed: The Case Against Trudeau's Canada* (Vancouver: Harbour Publishing, 1981).
12. Barry Cooper, 'Western Political Consciousness', in Stephen Brooks, ed., *Political Thought in Canada: Contemporary Perspectives* (Toronto: Irwin, 1984), 230.
13. Patrick Boyer, *Direct Democracy in Canada: The History and Future of Referendums* (Toronto: Dundurn Press, 1992).
14. Michael Bliss, 'The multicultural North American hotel', *National Post*, 15 Jan. 2003.

SUGGESTED READINGS

Keith Archer and Lisa Young, eds, *Regionalism and Party Politics in Canada* (Toronto: Oxford University Press, 2002). This is an excellent collection of essays on the regional nature of Canada's party system, with a particular emphasis on western Canada.

Roger Gibbins and Loleen Berdahl, *Western Visions, Western Futures* (Peterborough, Ont.: Broadview Press, 2003). This is arguably the best short survey of the special characteristics of western Canada's political value system and the roots and conse-

quences of western alienation. The authors make extensive use of attitudinal data.

Hamish Telford and Harvey Lazar, eds, *Canada: The State of the Federation 2001* (Montreal and Kingston: McGill-Queen's University Press, 2002). This is a recent volume in an annual series produced by the Institute of Intergovernmental Affairs at Queen's University. It always includes chapters on recent developments in provincial politics.

Review Exercises

1. Compare newspaper coverage in three different regions of the country. You may do this by consulting hard copies of three daily papers in three different provinces—one from the West, one from Ontario, and one from an eastern province—or their on-line editions. Check the front page, the editorial page, and letters to the editor. Do you find any indication of a different news agenda or different perspectives in different provinces?

2. Go to the Web sites of Western Economic Diversification Canada <www.wd.gc.ca> and the Atlantic Canada Opportunities Agency <www.acoa-apeca.gc.ca>. What do these organizations do? How much do they spend and on what?

3. Who were Amor de Cosmos, Henry Wise Wood, and Joseph Howe? What is the significance of each for his region of the country?

PART THREE

THE STRUCTURES OF GOVERNANCE

The Fathers of Confederation at Charlottetown. (National Archives of Canada/C733)

Constitutions are at the heart of democratic politics. This chapter examines key features of the Canadian Constitution. It includes the following topics:

- ❏ Functions of a constitution.
- ❏ Rights and freedoms.
- ❏ Parliamentary government.
- ❏ Responsible government.
- ❏ Ministerial responsibility.
- ❏ Parliamentary and constitutional supremacy.
- ❏ Judicial independence.
- ❏ The House of Commons and Senate.
- ❏ The biases of British parliamentary government.
- ❏ Changing the Constitution.
- ❏ Citizen participation in constitutional reform.
- ❏ Does Quebec have the right to separate?

CHAPTER FIVE

THE CONSTITUTION

A constitution is an essential ingredient of democratic politics. But the existence of a constitution does not by itself ensure that politics is democratic. South Africa, for example, for decades had a constitution that denied the black majority of that country rights equal to those of the white minority. The People's Republic of China has a constitution under which the violent suppression of peaceful protest and the arrest and imprisonment of people who challenge the Communist Party's monopoly on power are perfectly lawful. Closer to home, the fact that constitutional government was well established in Canada did not prevent the federal government from depriving thousands of Japanese Canadians of their rights as citizens during World War II, nor did it stop Alberta's provincial government from allowing the forced sterilization of people deemed to be mentally retarded in the 1950s. A constitution is no guarantee that human rights will be respected, that group rights will be protected, or that political opposition to those who govern will be tolerated. Without a constitution, however, the concepts of rights and limited government have no secure protection.

A **constitution** is the fundamental law of a political system. It is 'fundamental' because all other laws must conform to the constitution in terms of *how they are made* and in terms of their *substance*. A constitution is a necessary condition for democratic politics. Without it there is no civilized way of resolving conflicts and no way of predicting either the powers of government or the rights of citizens.

A constitution is expected to establish order, allowing for the peaceful settlement of differences. Early liberal thinkers such as Thomas Hobbes, John Locke, and Jean-Jacques Rousseau all used the concept of the 'state of nature' to illustrate the impulse behind constitutional government. The state of nature, wrote Hobbes, is a state of chaos in which no individual can feel secure in the possession of his property or life. It is this insecurity that leads people to demand a constitution where there is none, and to accept the necessity of a constitution even if they find it difficult to agree on its precise components.

In modern societies the alternatives to constitutional government are anarchy—the sort of chaos and civil strife that broke out in some of the newly independent republics created after the dissolution of the former Soviet Union—or totalitarianism. Where anarchy reigns, there are no generally accepted rules for resolving the differences between factions of the population. The state does not exist. Under totalitarianism the state exists. But because its powers are unlimited and all realms of social and economic life are subordinate to it, it makes no sense to talk of a constitution. If the rules of a board game can be changed at will by one of the players then it is nonsense to speak of rules. So, too, with a constitution: if its terms are purely arbitrary it ceases to be a constitution in anything other than name.

The rules that make up a constitution deal with two sets of relations. One of these involves the relationship between citizens and the state. A constitution *empowers* the state to act, to pass laws on behalf of the community. At the same time most constitutions *limit power*. They do this by identifying those individual rights, and in some cases group rights, that the state cannot violate. The other set of relations encompassed by a constitution involves the distribution of functions and powers between different parts of the state. After all, modern government is a complex mechanism. This mechanism is often analyzed under three main functional headings: the legislature (making the law); the executive (implementing the law); and the judiciary (interpreting the law). But the reality of the modern state is more complicated than this tripartite division of powers suggests. Whatever the degree of complexity, the rules that govern the relations between the various parts of the state are an important component of the constitution.

In a federal state like Canada, where the Constitution divides law-making powers between a national government and regional governments, the rules governing the relations between these two levels are also part of the Constitution. This third aspect of the Constitution has overshadowed the other two for most of Canada's history. Indeed, before 1982, when the Charter of Rights and Freedoms was entrenched in the Constitution, the relations between individuals and the state in Canada were defined by the courts mainly in terms of federal and provincial legislative powers.

A constitution, then, is a set of rules that govern political life. These rules may take three forms: written documents, the decisions of courts (called the **common law**), or unwritten conventions. **Constitutional conventions** are those practices that emerge over time and are generally accepted as binding rules of the political system. An example would be the convention that the leader of the party that captures the most House of Commons seats in a federal election is called on to form a government. In Canada the first two components of the Constitution—written documents and the common law—together comprise *constitutional law*. Conventions, while part of the Constitution, do not have the status of constitutional law, at least not in Canada. This distinction was made by the Supreme Court of Canada in a 1981 ruling (see Box 5.1). It should not be interpreted to mean that constitutional law is more important than constitutional conventions. What

---

BOX 5.1   What Is a Constitutional Convention?

. . . [M]any Canadians would perhaps be surprised to learn that important parts of the Constitution of Canada, with which they are the most familiar because they are directly involved when they exercise their right to vote at federal and provincial elections, are nowhere to be found in the law of the Constitution. For instance, it is a fundamental requirement of the Constitution that if the Opposition obtains the majority at the polls, the Government must tender its resignation forthwith. But fundamental as it is, this requirement of the Constitution does not form part of the law of the Constitution. . . .

The main purpose of constitutional conventions is to ensure that the legal framework of the Constitution will be operated in accordance with the prevailing constitutional values or principles of the period. . . .

The conventional rules of the Constitution present one striking peculiarity. In contradistinction to the laws of the Constitution, they are not enforced by the courts. . . .

It is because the sanctions of convention rest with institutions of government other than courts, such as the Governor-General or the Lieutenant-Governor, or the Houses of Parliament, or with public opinion and, ultimately, with the electorate that it is generally said that they are political.

Supreme Court of Canada,
Attorney General of Manitoba et al. v. Attorney
General of Canada et al., 28 Sept. 1981

it does mean, however, is that the rules of constitutional law are enforceable by the courts, whereas constitutional conventions are not.

CONSTITUTIONAL FUNCTIONS

A constitution does more than provide a basis for non-violent politics. It also performs several more specific functions that include the following.

Representation

All modern democracies are representative democracies, in which politicians make decisions on behalf of those who elect them. But this still leaves enormous room for variation in how the population is represented, who is represented, and how representatives are selected.

A constitution describes both the *basis* of political representation and the *method* by which representatives are chosen. The basis of democratic representation may be by population, by territory, or by group. Representation by population is based on the principle of 'one person, one vote'. Under such a system, all elected members of the legislature should represent approximately the same number of voters. This arrangement is most likely to allow the preferences of a simple majority of the population to be translated into law. Although virtually all modern democracies incorporate some form of 'rep by pop' in their constitutions, many temper majority rule by representing regions as well. For example, the American Constitution gives each state the right to two senators, despite the fact that the population of the largest state is about 50 times that of the smallest. Representation in Canada's Senate is also by region: Ontario, Quebec, the western provinces, and the Maritime provinces each have 24 seats, Newfoundland has six, and the northern territories are represented by three senators. Federalism is a form of government that embodies the principle of territorial representation. It does so by giving regional governments the exclusive right to pass laws on particular subjects.

A constitution may also accord representation to groups. New Zealand's constitution, for one, guarantees a certain number of seats in that country's legislature to representatives of the Maori minority. In Canada, suggestions for Senate reform have included proposals to guarantee seats for women and for the representatives of Aboriginal Canadians. The defeated 1992 Charlottetown Accord would have ensured that Quebec, whose share of Canada's population has been falling steadily, would maintain one-quarter of all seats in the House of Commons, which is about the province's current share. This was, one might argue, a thinly disguised guarantee for francophone group representation. Proposals like these are based on a collectivist political philosophy.

A constitution also establishes the methods by which the holders of public office are selected. Election and appointment are the two basic methods, but each allows for a wide variety of procedures that affect who is represented and how responsive public officials are to the popular will. For example, it is typical for members of the judiciary to be appointed for life, a practice that is expected to insulate them from popular passions and the transitory preferences of elected governments. An elected legislature is a standard feature of democratic political systems and, for that matter, of non-democratic ones. But many constitutions divide the legislative power between an elected chamber and an appointed one, as in Canada, the United Kingdom, and Germany.

Finally, the electoral process itself has a crucial influence on representation. As we will see in Chapter 9, the single-member constituency system used in Canada discourages political parties from directing their appeals at a narrow segment of the national electorate. Unless that segment happens to be concentrated in a particular region, such a strategy will not pay off in elected members. A system of proportional representation, whereby a party's percentage of the popular votes translates into a corresponding share of seats in the legislature, has a very different effect. It promotes a splintering of the party system and allows for the direct representation of such interests as ardent environmentalists in Germany, orthodox Jews in Israel, and virulent nationalists in Belgium. In a system like Canada's, these groups would have to rely on whatever influence they could achieve within one of the larger political parties or else turn to non-electoral political strategies.

Power

The simple fact of constitutional government means that the state is empowered to act and that its actions may be backed up by the full weight of public authority. A constitution, therefore, provides the basis for the legitimate exercise of state power. But it also *limits* and *divides* power, at least under a democratic constitution. For example, a constitutional requirement that elections periodically be held restrains state power by making those who wield it accountable to, and removable by, the electorate. The existence of separate branches of government under the constitution, or of two levels of government as in the case of federalism, divides state power between different groups of public officials. How power is divided among the various parts of the state, or between the national and regional governments, is not determined solely by the constitution. But constitutional law and conventions both affect the extent and distribution of state power.

Rights

A right is something that a person is entitled to, like the right to vote or the right not to be held against one's will without a reason being given. Constitutions vary greatly in the particular rights that they assign to individuals and to societal groups. At a minimum, a democratic constitution establishes the basic right of citizens to choose their government. But most constitutions go beyond this to guarantee—although not without limit—such rights as the individual's right to free speech, freedom of association, and freedom of religion and conscience, as well as legal rights

such as freedom from arbitrary detention and from illegal search and seizure. These are rights that limit the state's power vis-à-vis the individual either by making that power dependent on popular consent (democratic rights) or by establishing an individual's right not to be interfered with by the state (personal liberty).

Rights may also empower individuals by requiring the state to either protect or promote their interests. For example, a right to equal treatment under the law provides individuals with a constitutional remedy in cases where they have been discriminated against because of their sex, race, ethnicity, or whatever other basis of discrimination is prohibited by the constitution. The state is obliged to protect their interests. As a practical matter this may involve judicial decisions that remedy a private wrong (for example, requiring a minor hockey association to permit females to play in the same league with males). But the protection of equality may also see the state involved in more sweeping activities like affirmative action or racial desegregation on the grounds that these steps are necessary to alleviate discrimination.

Constitutions may also recognize the special status of particular groups, thereby giving special rights to their members that are not enjoyed by others. For example, Canada's Constitution declares that both French and English are official languages with 'equality of status and equal rights and privileges as to their use in all institutions of the Parliament and government of Canada'.[1] This is a *positive* right in the sense that it obliges the state to assume particular linguistic characteristics and, therefore, to protect actively the rights of French- and English-speakers—at least in matters that fall under Ottawa's jurisdiction. A constitution that recognizes the special status of particular religious denominations, as the Israeli constitution recognizes the Jewish religion, the Iranian constitution the Muslim religion, or the British constitution the Church of England, empowers the members of these religious groups to varying degrees by giving them state-protected rights that are not held by other denominations.

COMMUNITY AND IDENTITY

When Pierre Trudeau wrote that 'A nation is not more and no less than the entire population of a sovereign state',[2] he was arguing that a constitution establishes a community. And in an obvious sense it does. A constitution is the set of fundamental rules that govern political life *in a particular territory*. Its rules are operative within that territory and not elsewhere, so that it establishes a shared condition among all those who live in that territory. Individuals in Rimouski, Quebec, and in Kitimat, British Columbia, are part of the same constitutional system and share a formal political status as Canadians. Even if they perceive their differences to be more important than what they share, this does not diminish the fact that they have legal membership in the same constitutional community.

Carrying the same national passport and being eligible to vote in the same elections may seem a rather weak basis for a *sense of community*, a sentiment that transcends the cold, formal ties of common citizenship. The fact of being citizens of the Soviet Union, for example, did not erase the strongly nationalist sentiments of Ukrainians, Estonians, and other ethnic communities within that former country. For these groups the Soviet constitution and the political community it created were things to regret, not to rejoice over. Likewise in Canada, a significant minority of the population—Quebec separatists—reject the Canadian political community and would prefer to live under a different constitution creating an independent Quebec.

A constitution may, therefore, inspire negative or positive feelings among the members of a political community. Or it may leave them feeling indifferent. These feelings may be associated with the political community that a constitution creates, but they may also be associated with the particular institutions, values, and symbols embedded in a constitution. For example, the monarchy and other institutions and symbols redolent of Canada's colonial past have historically been an aspect of the Canadian Constitution

that has divided Canadians of French origin from those of British origin.

Official bilingualism and constitutional proposals that would recognize Quebec as a 'distinct society' within Canada have been two of the most divisive constitutional issues in recent years. On the other hand, some features of the Constitution unite, rather than divide, Canadians. There is, for example, overwhelming support among all regions and social groups for the Charter of Rights and Freedoms. In general, we may say that a constitution generates a shared identity among the citizens of a country to the extent that most people have positive feelings towards the political community it creates and the values it embodies. On these counts, Canada's Constitution has had a mixed record of successes and failures.

National Purpose

When the first permanent white settlement was established at what today is Quebec City, it operated under a royal charter that proclaimed the Catholic mission of the French colony. Aside from being an outpost of political and economic empire, it was to be a beachhead of Christianity, from which Catholicism would spread to the rest of the continent. The constitution of New France was therefore linked to a communal goal, to a sense of purpose and direction for society.

This is not so rare. The constitution of the People's Republic of China includes references to building a socialist society. The constitutions of the Islamic Republic of Iran and of Pakistan both declare that society should conform to Muslim religious teachings. The most controversial part of the failed Meech Lake reforms to Canada's Constitution, the recognition of Quebec as a 'distinct society', would have transformed Quebec nationalism from a political reality to a constitutionally entrenched fact. This was because the Quebec legislature and government would have been constitutionally required to 'preserve and promote' the distinct character of the province, which the distinct society proposal made clear was the French-speaking character of Quebec.

The constitutional document that created Canada, the Constitution Act, 1867, also included a number of provisions that embodied a national purpose. This purpose was the building of a new country stretching from the Atlantic to the Pacific oceans, and an integrated economy tying together this vast territory. The nation-building goal is evident in the anticipation that other parts of British North America would eventually be admitted into Canada,[3] in the prohibition of barriers to trade between provinces,[4] and even in the constitutional commitment to build the Intercolonial Railway, a project described as 'essential to the Consolidation of the Union of British North America, and to the assent thereto of Nova Scotia and New Brunswick'.[5] The Constitution Act, 1982 commits Ottawa and the provinces to the promotion of equal opportunities for Canadians and the reduction of economic disparities between regions of the country.[6] It is hard to know, however, if such declarations of national purpose are merely symbolic recognitions of current policy or whether they might someday acquire more practical significance.

CANADA'S CONSTITUTION

As constitutional documents go, Canada's is a fairly lengthy one. In fact, it is not one document but a series of laws passed between 1867 and 1982. Together they are both longer and more detailed than the United States Constitution. Even so, the written documents of Canada's Constitution provide only a fragmentary and even misleading picture of how the Constitution actually works. Many of the most basic features of the Constitution—including most of those that deal with the democratic accountability of government to the people—are nowhere to be found in these documents. On the other hand, some of what is included in the written Constitution would, if acted on, probably result in a constitutional crisis! For example, the Queen is formally the head

of state in Canada and has the constitutional authority to make decisions of fundamental importance, such as when an election will take place and who will be appointed to cabinet. No one expects, however, that she will actually make such decisions.

Canada's Constitution, like all constitutions, embodies values and principles that are central to the political life of the country. In its 1998 decision on the constitutionality of Quebec separation, the Supreme Court of Canada referred to these values and principles as the 'internal architecture' of the Constitution[7] or what, in an earlier ruling, the Court had called the 'basic constitutional structure'.[8] These basic principles, although not necessarily part of the written constitution, 'form the very foundation of the Constitution of Canada'.[9] The principles that the Supreme Court identified as making up the internal architecture of Canada's Constitution included federalism, democracy, constitutionalism and the rule of law, and respect for minority rights.

Federalism

'The principle of federalism', declares the Supreme Court, 'recognizes the diversity of the component parts of Confederation, and the autonomy of provincial governments to develop their societies within their respective spheres of jurisdiction.'[10] In other words, provinces are not constitutionally subordinate to the federal government, nor is Ottawa dependent on the provinces for the exercise of those powers assigned to it by the Constitution. The written Constitution distributes law-making and revenue-raising authority between the central and provincial governments, and this distribution reflects the underlying federal principle that some matters properly belong to provincial societies and their governments to decide, while others are national in scope and properly decided by the Parliament and government in Ottawa. We will explore more fully the nature and development of Canadian federalism in Chapter 7.

Democracy

Democracy has always been one of the fundamental, if unwritten, givens of Canada's constitutional system. A literal reading of Canada's written Constitution before the inclusion of the Charter of Rights and Freedoms in 1982 might well lead someone who knows nothing of Canada's history and culture to draw a very different conclusion. Aside from the fact that periodic elections were required under the Constitution Act, 1867, there were few other explicit indications that the Constitution adopted by the founders was democratic. On the contrary, while the authority of governments was detailed painstakingly, the written Constitution was remarkably silent when it came to the rights of citizens. Why was this so?

In explaining the silence of the pre-Charter Constitution, the Supreme Court states that to have declared explicitly that Canada was a democracy, and to have specified what that entailed, would have seemed to the founders 'redundant' and even 'silly'. 'The representative and democratic nature of our political institutions', the Court writes, 'was simply assumed.'[11] This was suggested in the preamble to the Constitution Act, 1867, which states that Canada has adopted 'a Constitution similar in Principle to that of the United Kingdom'. The very centrality of the democratic principle and the fact that it was simply taken for granted as the baseline against which government would operate explain why the framers of the written Constitution did not perceive the need to state what all assumed to be obvious.

But the precise meaning of the democracy principle, as we saw in Chapter 1, is not obvious and has evolved over time. Women did not have the vote for more than 50 years after Confederation, and only a small minority of the population found anything undemocratic in this exclusion. Even when the meaning of democracy is specified in a written constitution, as it was to a very considerable degree in the United States Constitution and the Declaration of Independence that pre-

ceded it, expectations and understandings change over time, as they have over the course of American history. What meaning is properly attributed to the democratic principle of Canada's Constitution today?

The Supreme Court's 1998 decision on the hypothetical separation of Quebec answers this question by distinguishing between process and outcomes. On the process side, the Court observed that majority rule is a basic premise of constitutional democracy in Canada. The fact that Canada has a federal constitution means, however, that 'there may be different and equally legitimate majorities in different provinces and territories and at the federal level.'[12] In other words, a nationwide majority does not trump a provincial majority if the matter in question is one that belongs constitutionally to the provinces or that requires the approval of some number of provincial legislatures (e.g., most constitutional amendments).

In a 1986 Charter decision, the Supreme Court had expressed the view that the democratic principle underlying the Charter and the rest of Canada's Constitution is also linked to substantive goals. Among these are the following:

- respect for the inherent dignity of every person;
- commitment to equality and social justice;
- social and cultural diversity, including respect for the identities of minority groups' social and political institutions that enhance the opportunities for individuals and groups to participate in society.[13]

This view was echoed in the Supreme Court's 1998 ruling. In words that were directly relevant to the issue of Quebec separation, the Court said that 'The consent of the governed is a value that is basic to our understanding of a free and democratic society.'[14] Democratic government derives its necessary legitimacy from this consent. Moreover, the legitimacy of laws passed and actions taken by a democratic government rests on 'moral values, many of which are imbedded in our constitutional structure'.[15] The Supreme Court did not expand upon these moral values.

Constitutionalism and the Rule of Law

'At its most basic level', declares the Supreme Court, 'the rule of law vouchsafes to the citizens and residents of the country a stable, predictable and ordered society in which to conduct their affairs.'[16] It guarantees, therefore, that all public authority must ultimately be exercised in accordance with the law and that there will be one law for all persons. When it comes to light that some public official has overstepped the bounds of his or her office, regardless of the office-holder's intentions, or that someone has been accorded preferred treatment under the law because of personal connections, we are often offended. The reason is that such actions violate the rule of law premise that ours is a government of laws, not of men (and women), and that everyone is entitled to equal treatment under the law.

Like the rule of law, the constitutionalism principle involves predictable governance that has its source in written rules rather than the arbitrary wills of individuals. The constitutionalism principle is expressed in s. 52 (1) of the Constitution Act, 1982, which states that the Constitution is the supreme law of the land and that all government action must be in conformity with the Constitution. Before the Charter was entrenched in the Constitution and the constitutionalism principle was expressly stated, the final authority of the Constitution was less certain. The pre-Charter era was one of parliamentary supremacy, which essentially meant that so long as one level of government did not trespass onto jurisdictional turf assigned to the other level, it was free to do as it liked. The principle of parliamentary supremacy is captured in the old saying that Parliament could do anything except change a man into a woman and a woman into a man. The constitutionalism principle, by contrast, places certain matters relating to rights and freedoms beyond the reach of any government.

Constitutionalism and the rule of law temper and modify the principle of majority rule in a democracy. They do so by ensuring that the mere fact that a majority of citizens—even an overwhelming majority—supports a particular government action does not mean that such an action will be either lawful or constitutional. Together, they constitute a sort of bulwark against what Tocqueville called the 'tyranny of the majority'.

Protection of Minorities

The recognition of group rights has a history in Canada that goes back to the beginnings of British colonial rule. The Royal Proclamation of 1763 includes considerable detail—the meaning of which is a matter of dispute—on the rights of the 'several Nations or Tribes of Indians . . . who live under our protection'. The Quebec Act of 1774 recognized the rights of Catholics in Quebec and guaranteed the overwhelmingly French-speaking population the enjoyment of their 'Property and Possessions, together with all Customs and Usages relative thereto, and all other of their Civil Rights', concessions that most historians agree were intended to ensure the support of the Catholic Church authorities in Quebec at a time when rebellion was simmering in the American colonies. Group rights were recognized again through the 'double majority principle' that operated when Canada East (Quebec) and Canada West (Ontario) were joined together through a common legislature during the period 1841–67. Under this principle any bill touching on matters of language or religion in either Canada East or Canada West had to be approved by majorities of legislators from both Canada East—mainly French and Catholic—and Canada West—mainly English and Protestant. In practice this gave a veto to each ethnolinguistic community in regard to legislation affecting minority rights.

The Constitution Act, 1867 entrenched the principle of minority rights through the section 93 guarantee of minority religious education rights and the section 133 declaration that French and English were to have official status in the Parliament of Canada, the legislature of Quebec, and courts created by either of those bodies. 'The protection of minority rights', the Supreme Court declared in its ruling on the possible secession of Quebec, 'was clearly an essential consideration in the design of our constitutional structure even at the time of Confederation.'[17] The principle acquired a new level of prominence as a result of the Charter of Rights and Freedoms. The Charter enlarges the scope of official-language minority rights, explicitly recognizes Aboriginal rights, opens the door to a multitude of group rights claims through the equality section of the Charter (s. 15), and provides a basis for a variety of minority rights claims through other sections, including the legal rights and democratic rights provisions of the Charter.

A useful way of analyzing a constitution is to approach it from the angle of each of the relationships governed by constitutional rules. As noted earlier, these relationships include: (1) those between individuals and the state; (2) those between the various institutions of government; and (3) those between the national and regional governments. The first category involves rights and freedoms, the second deals with the machinery and process of government, and the third category is about federalism. A constitution also includes a fourth category of rules that establish what procedures must be followed to bring about constitutional change. Federalism is dealt with in Chapter 7. We turn now to an examination of the other three dimensions of Canada's Constitution.

THE CHARTER OF RIGHTS AND FREEDOMS

Since 1982 Canada's Constitution has included formal distinctions between fundamental political freedoms, democratic rights, mobility rights, legal rights, equality rights, and language rights. These are the categories set down in the Charter of Rights and Freedoms. Most of the rights and freedoms enumerated in the Charter were, however, part of Canada's Constitution before 1982. In some cases they can be found in the Constitution Act, 1867. In other instances they were established principles

of the common law. The inclusion of these rights and freedoms in the Charter, however, has made an important difference in Canadian politics. Groups and individuals are far more likely today than in the pre-Charter era to reach for the judicial lever in attempting to protect their rights. Second, these rights have been more secure since the Charter's passage. This has been due to the courts' willingness to strike down laws and practices on the grounds that they contravene the Charter's guarantees of rights and freedoms.

Fundamental Freedoms

Fundamental political freedoms are guaranteed in section 2 of the Charter. These include freedom of religion, belief, expression, the media, assembly, and association. During the pre-Charter era these freedoms, or *political liberties* as they are sometimes called, were part of the common law and of Canada's British parliamentary tradition. The preamble to the Constitution Act, 1867 declares that Canada is adopting 'a Constitution similar in Principle to that of the United Kingdom'. Individual freedoms were part of the British constitution, and thus became part of Canada's. Even before the Charter, then, political freedoms occupied a place in the Canadian Constitution. Their protection by the courts, however, was rather tenuous. Except in a few instances, the courts were unwilling to rule that a freedom was beyond the interference of government. Instead, political liberties were defended using the federal division of legislative powers as the basis for striking down a particular government's interference with individual freedom.

Democratic Rights

The basic democratic right is the opportunity to vote in regular elections. This right predated Confederation. It was embodied in the Constitution Act, 1867 through those sections that establish the elective basis of representation in the House of Commons and in provincial legislatures (ss. 37

and 40), through the requirement that the legislature meet at least once a year (ss. 20 and 86), through the right of citizens to vote (s. 41), and through the five-year limit on the life of both the House of Commons and provincial legislatures, thereby guaranteeing regular elections (ss. 50 and 85). All of these sections are now 'spent', having been superseded by ss. 3-5 of the Charter.

Mobility Rights

Mobility rights were not explicitly mentioned in Canadian constitutional law before 1982. Section 121 of the Constitution Act, 1867 prohibits the provincial governments from imposing tariffs on commodities coming from other provinces, but there is no mention of restrictions on the movement of people. Such restrictions are now prohibited by section 6 of the Charter. This guarantee of individual mobility rights was prompted by Ottawa's fear that some provincial governments were undermining the idea and practice of Canadian citizenship by discriminating in favour of their own permanent residents in some occupational sectors and by imposing residency requirements as a condition for receiving some social services. The Charter does, however, permit both of these types of discrimination. It allows 'reasonable residency requirements as a qualification for the receipt of publicly provided social services'[18] and permits affirmative action programs favouring a province's residents 'if the rate of employment in that province is below the rate of employment in Canada'.[19] It is doubtful whether section 6 of the Charter has had any significant impact on provincial practices that limit the mobility of Canadians.

Legal Rights

Most rights-based litigation, both before and since the Charter's passage, has been based on individuals' and corporations' claims that their legal rights have been violated. Legal rights involve mainly procedural aspects of the law, such as the right to a fair trial, the right not to be held without a charge being laid, and the right to legal counsel. Before these rights were entrenched in the Constitution through the Charter, they were recognized principles of the common law and constitutional convention. For example, the field of administrative law was based largely on the principles of *natural justice*: hear the other side, and no one should be a judge in his own case. These were accepted parts of Canada's democratic tradition and Constitution even before they were entrenched in section 7 of the Charter. And like political freedoms, democratic rights, and equality rights, these legal rights were included in the 1960 Canadian Bill of Rights, which applied only to relations between the citizenry and the federal government. In addition, the rights of accused parties were set forth in Canada's Criminal Code. It is apparent, however, that the constitutional entrenchment of legal rights has made an important difference. The courts have been much bolder in striking down parts of laws and in overturning administrative and police procedures than they were in the pre-Charter era. For example, a successful legal challenge to Canada's abortion law only became possible when the right to 'security of the person' was explicitly recognized in section 7 of the Charter.[20] More generally, Charter decisions have expanded the legal rights of the accused, convicted criminals, and immigrants.

Equality Rights

Equality rights are entrenched in the Constitution through section 15 of the Charter. They embody the **rule of law** principle that everyone should be treated equally under the law. But the Charter extends this principle to prohibit discrimination based on race, national or ethnic origin, colour, religion, sex, age, or mental or physical disability.[21]

The particular headings in this list are important, given that Canadian courts historically have preferred to base their rulings on the precise text of laws and the Constitution. Women's groups and those representing the physically and mentally disabled clearly believed that the wording of the Charter made a difference, and both fought hard—and successfully—to have the original wording of section 15 changed. The Canadian Bill of Rights did not include age or mental/physical disability in its catalogue of equality rights.

The Charter explicitly declares that affirmative action is constitutional.[22] Thus, the equality rights section of the Canadian Constitution is designed to cut two ways. It provides individuals with grounds for redress if they believe that the law discriminates against them. But it also provides a basis for laws that treat different groups of people differently—some would say that this is the definition of discrimination—in order to improve the condition of disadvantaged individuals or groups.

Equality rights are also important features of provincial bills/charters of rights. Since 1975 every province has had such a bill. Quebec's is probably the most extensive, including even certain economic and social rights. These rights are administered and enforced by provincial human rights commissions.

Language Rights

At Confederation, the issue of language rights was dealt with in three ways. Section 133 of the Constitution Act, 1867 declares that both English and French are official languages in the Parliament of Canada and in the Quebec legislature, and in any court established by either the national or Quebec government. Section 93 of that same Act declares that rights held by denominational schools when a province became part of Canada cannot be taken away. As a practical matter, Catholic schools in Manitoba and even in Ontario at an early date were often French-speaking, and most English-language schools in Quebec were Protestant. Consequently, what were formally denominational rights in section 93 were effectively language rights as well. This did not help when it came to their protection—or non-protection (see Chapter 12). The third approach—and in practical terms the most important language

rights provision of the Constitution Act, 1867—is section 92. This assigns to the provinces jurisdiction over 'all Matters of a merely local or private Nature in the Province' (s. 92.16). Combined with exclusive provincial jurisdiction over education (s. 93), this has given provincial governments the tools to promote or deny, as the case may be, the language rights of their anglophone or francophone minorities.

The Constitution Act, 1982 extends language rights in several ways. These include the following:

- The declaration of the official equality of English and French, found in section 133 of the Constitution Act, 1867, is repeated and broadened to encompass 'their use in all institutions of the Parliament and government of Canada' (s. 161) and services to the public (s. 20).
- The New Brunswick legislature's earlier decision to declare that province officially bilingual is entrenched in the Constitution Act, 1982 (ss. 16–20).
- The right of anglophones and francophones to have their children educated in their mother tongue is entrenched, subject to there being sufficient demand to warrant the provision of such services out of public funds (s. 23).

Language rights would have been given an additional twist if the Meech Lake Accord (1987) or Charlottetown Accord (1992) had become constitutional law (see Chapter 7). The most controversial feature of both accords was the recognition of Quebec as a 'distinct society'. The wording clearly linked this distinctiveness to the predominantly French-speaking character of Quebec. The 'distinct society' clause went on to oblige the province's legislature and government to 'preserve and promote the distinct identity of Quebec'. Some critics of the 'distinct society' clause argued that it would promote the concentration of French in Quebec, with harmful consequences for the status of the French-speaking minorities in the other provinces and for the English-speaking minority in Quebec (see Box 5.2).

BOX 5.2   The End of Bilingualism? Trudeau's View of the 'Distinct Society' Clause

Those Canadians who fought for a single Canada, bilingual and multicultural, can say goodbye to their dream: we are henceforth to have two Canadas, each defined in terms of its language. And because the Meech Lake accord states in the same breath that 'Quebec constitutes, within Canada, a distinct society' and that 'the role of the Legislature and government to preserve and promote [this] distinct identity . . . is affirmed', it is easy to predict what future awaits anglophones living in Quebec and what treatment will continue to be accorded to francophones living in provinces where they are fewer in number than Canadians of Ukrainian or German origin.

Indeed, the text of the accord spells it out: In the other provinces, where bilingualism still has an enormously long way to go, the only requirement is to 'protect' the status quo, while Quebec is to 'promote' the distinct character of Quebec society.

In other words, the Government of Quebec must take measures and the Legislature must pass laws aimed at promoting the uniqueness of Quebec. And the text of the accord specifies at least one aspect of this uniqueness: 'French-speaking Canada' is 'centred' in that province. Thus Quebec acquires a new constitutional jurisdiction that the rest of Canada does not have, promoting the concentration of French in Quebec. It is easy to see the consequences for French and English minorities in the country, as well as for foreign policy, for education, for the economy, or social legislation, and so on.

Pierre Elliott Trudeau,
'Nothing left but tears for Trudeau',
Globe and Mail, 28 May 1987, A7.

Aboriginal Rights

Aboriginal rights are also included in Canada's Constitution. Their explicit recognition dates from the passage of the Charter in 1982. Section 25 declares that the rights and freedoms set forth in the Charter shall not be construed so as to 'abrogate or derogate' from whatever rights or freedoms the Aboriginal peoples of Canada have as a result of any treaty or land claim settlement. It also entrenches in the Constitution 'any rights or freedoms that have been recognized by the Royal Proclamation [of 1763]'. Section 35(1) appears to limit Aboriginal rights to the status quo that existed in 1982, stating that 'The *existing* aboriginal and treaty rights of the aboriginal peoples

of Canada are hereby recognized and affirmed' (emphasis added). In fact, however, this has been less a limit than a boost for Aboriginal rights, which have been effectively constitutionalized by the 1982 Constitution Act.

PARLIAMENTARY GOVERNMENT IN CANADA

The whole edifice of British parliamentary government is built on profound silences in constitutional law. These silences touch on the most fundamental principles of democracy and on practices that are essential to the orderly functioning of government. Such matters as the selection of the Prime Minister, which party has the right to form a government, the relationship between the Crown and the government and between the government and the legislature, the rights of the political opposition, and the role of the judicial branch of government cannot be understood from a simple reading of the constitution. Nevertheless, for all of these matters certain rules are generally agreed upon and are vital parts of the British constitution—so vital, in fact, that when they are challenged the political system faces a crisis.

British parliamentary government was exported to Canada during the colonial period. Its main features have remained largely unchanged since the middle of the nineteenth century, when the British North American colonies achieved the right to self-government in their domestic affairs. The Constitution Act, 1867 explicitly reaffirms this British parliamentary inheritance, declaring that Canada has adopted 'a Constitution similar in Principle to that of the United Kingdom'.[23] While this might appear to be a somewhat nebulous phrase, Canada's founders understood very clearly what it meant. The constitution of the United Kingdom was, and remains today, a set of political traditions rather than a series of constitutional documents. Those who founded Canada took these traditions as their starting point and grafted onto them certain institutions and procedures—particularly federalism—for which British parliamentary government provided no guide.

Parliament

The distinguishing feature of British-style parliamentary government is the relationship between the various institutions that together comprise Parliament. Parliament consists of the monarch and the legislature. The monarch, currently Queen Elizabeth II, is Canada's head of state. According to the strict letter of Canada's Constitution, the monarch wields formidable powers. These include which party will be called upon to form the government, when Parliament will be dissolved and a new election held, and the

requirement that all legislation—federal and provincial—must receive royal assent before it becomes law. In fact, however, these powers are almost entirely symbolic, and the role is primarily a ceremonial one. When the monarch is not in Canada (which is most of the time), her powers are exercised by the Governor-General. At the provincial level, the lieutenant-governors are the Queen's representatives.

The power that resides formally in the monarchy is in reality held by the Crown's advisers, the Privy Council. The **Privy Council** formally includes all members of the present and past cabinets. However, only present members of cabinet exercise the powers of the Privy Council, and these people are usually elected members of the legislature. At the head of the cabinet is the Prime Minister. The structure of Canada's Parliament is shown in Figure 5.1.

Parliament comprises, then, both the *executive* and *legislative* branches of government. Those who actually exercise the executive power are

Figure 5.1   The Structure of Parliament in Canada

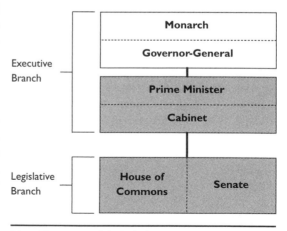

Note: The structure is basically the same at the provincial level, with two differences. The monarch's powers are exercised by a lieutenant-governor and the legislature consists of a single elected chamber.

drawn from the legislature. In deciding who among those elected members of Parliament (MPS) and appointed senators will become members of the government, the rule is quite simple. The leader of the political party with the most seats in the elected House of Commons has the right to try to form a government that has the support of a majority of MPS. If at any time the government loses its majority support in the House, tradition requires that it resign. At this point a fresh election would be called or, if there is a possibility that another party could put together a government that would be supported by a majority of MPS, the Governor-General could call on the leader of that party to try to form a government.

Responsible Government

In order to govern, therefore, the Prime Minister and cabinet require the confidence of the elected House of Commons. This constitutional principle is called **responsible government**. If a government loses the confidence of the House—this would be through either a defeat on an important piece of legislation (i.e., the annual budget or legislation related to government spending) or on a motion of no confidence proposed by an opposition party—it loses the right to govern. This may appear to place enormous power in the hands of MPS, capable of making and breaking governments at will. It does not. The reason why the constitutional theory of responsible government does not translate into governments tremulous before their legislatures is because of **party discipline**. This is another tradition of British parliamentary government, according to which the MPS of a party generally vote as a unified block in the legislature. In Canada, however, party discipline is conformed to more rigidly than in the British Parliament.

Of the 37 governments that were elected between 1867 and 2000 only five fell because of a defeat in the legislature. In all five cases these were *minority governments*: governments that depended on the support of another party's MPS in order to win votes in the legislature. But even in these apparently precarious circumstances, it was usually the government that finally determined when an election would occur. On only one occasion has a government been defeated in the Commons and then had its request denied for a dissolution of Parliament and a fresh election. That was in 1926, and the denial provoked a constitutional crisis over the appropriate role of the Governor-General. There was at least the chance of history repeating itself when the Progressive Conservative government's budget was defeated in 1979. The government had been in office a mere nine months, and the possibility of a minority Liberal government supported by the NDP was not totally outrageous. As it happened, however, Governor-General Ed Schreyer granted Prime Minister Joe Clark's request for a new election, although Schreyer claimed afterwards that he seriously considered asking the leader of the opposition to try to form a government.

Responsible government is not just a constitutional relic. It operates today, but not in the narrow sense of legislatures making and defeating cabinets. Instead, it suffuses the parliamentary process in the form of the *rights of the legislature* and the corresponding *obligations of the government*. The legislature has the right to scrutinize, to debate, and to vote on policies proposed by the government. In order to carry out these activities the legislature has the general right to question the government and to demand explanations for its actions and for those of bureaucratic officials who act in the government's name. The government, for its part, has a constitutional obligation to provide opportunities for legislative scrutiny of its policies and to account for its actions before Parliament. These rights and obligations are to a large extent codified in the *standing orders*—the rules that govern parliamentary procedure.

Responsible government, then, is part of the living constitution. But its formal definition bears little resemblance to the reality of modern parliamentary government. Disciplined political parties and dominant prime ministers ensure that cabinets seldom are defeated at the hands of unco-

Party discipline, an unwritten convention of Canadian parliamentary procedure, undermines the legislature's control over the government. (Roy Peterson, *Vancouver Sun*)

operative legislatures. But if the ultimate sanction that underlies the notion of responsible government has been lost—it really only operated for a brief period in Canadian history, between 1848 and 1864 in the legislature of the United Canadas—the practice of cabinet government that is accountable to the elected legislature remains.

Ministerial Responsibility

The accountability of the government to the legislature is the reason behind another principle of British parliamentary government, that of **ministerial responsibility**. It entails the obligation of a cabinet minister to explain and defend policies and actions carried out in his or her name. This individual accountability of cabinet ministers rests on a combination of constitutional law and parliamentary tradition. Section 54 of the Constitution Act, 1867 gives to cabinet the exclusive right to put before the legislature measures that involve the raising or spending of public revenue. In practice, such measures are introduced by particular members of the government. For example, changes to the tax system are proposed by the

Minister of Finance. The Constitution also requires that any legislation that involves raising or spending public money must originate in the elected House of Commons. This reflects the liberal democratic principle of no taxation without representation. Only the people's elected representatives—legislators who can be removed in a subsequent election—should have the right to propose laws that affect voters' pocketbooks. The accountability of ministers is, therefore, to the people's elected representatives.

Two fundamental principles of British parliamentary government, i.e., strong executive authority and democratic accountability, come together in the concept of ministerial responsibility. Strong executive authority is a tradition that dates from an era when the monarch wielded real power and the principle that these powers depended on the consent of the legislature was not yet established. When the legislature finally gained the upper hand in the seventeenth century, the tradition of strong executive power was not rejected. Instead, it was tamed and adapted to the democratic principle that government is based on the consent of the governed. Since then, individual ministers and cabinet as a whole have exercised the powers that, symbolically, continue to be vested in the Crown. But they do so in ways that enable the people's elected representatives to vote on their proposals and to call them to account for their policies (see Figure 5.2).

In recent times the constitutional principle of ministerial responsibility has come under increasing pressure. The enormous volume of decisions taken in a minister's name and the fact that much of the real power to determine government policy has passed into the hands of unelected officials mean that no minister can be well-informed about all the policies and actions undertaken in his or her name. According to some, the solution is to locate accountability where decision-making power really lies. This is reasonable for most actions and decisions. But elected members of the government must remain directly accountable for the general lines of policy and for major decisions; otherwise, a vital link in the chain of accountability that joins the people to those who govern is lost.

Parliamentary Supremacy versus Constitutional Supremacy

Another central feature of British parliamentary government is that of **parliamentary supremacy**. This means that Parliament's authority is superior to that of all other institutions of government. In concrete terms, this means that the courts will not second guess the right of Parliament to pass any sort of law, on any subject. Parliament embodies the popular will, and unpopular laws can always be defeated by changing the government at the next election. In a federal system like Canada's there is one complication. Law-making powers are divided between the national and provincial and territorial governments. But so long as Ottawa acts within its spheres of constitutional authority, and the provincial governments within theirs, both the federal and provincial parliaments are supreme.

This was the situation in Canada until 1982. When called on to determine whether a law was constitutional or not, the courts almost always

Figure 5.2   The Constitutional Roots of Ministerial Responsibility

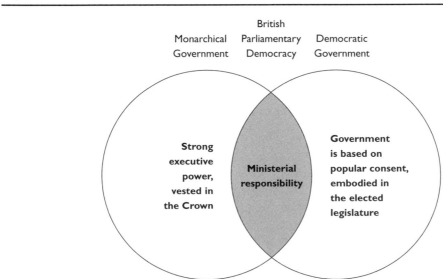

Monarchical Government

British Parliamentary Democracy

Democratic Government

Strong executive power, vested in the Crown

Ministerial responsibility

Government is based on popular consent, embodied in the elected legislature

referred to the federal division of powers set down in the Constitution Act, 1867. If a legislature was not intruding onto the constitutional territory of the other level of government, its actions were by definition constitutional. The only exception to this rule was in the case of laws or actions that ran afoul of procedural rules of the common law, such as the principles of natural justice. The substance of laws, on the other hand, would not be questioned.

Parliamentary supremacy was dealt a major blow by the Charter. Those who opposed the Charter argued that entrenching rights and freedoms in the written Constitution would result in a transfer of power from legislatures to the courts. This is indeed what has happened. Since 1982 the Supreme Court has struck down numerous federal and provincial laws on the grounds that they violate the guarantees set forth in the Charter. The defenders of parliamentary supremacy claim that a system of court-protected rights and freedoms is fundamentally undemocratic. Their reasoning is that it substitutes the decisions of non-elected judges for those of the people's elected representatives.

What is beyond doubt is that parliamentary supremacy has been replaced in Canada by **constitutional supremacy**. The Constitution Act, 1982 makes this very clear. Section 32 declares that the Charter applies to both the federal and provincial governments and to all matters under their authority. Section 52 (1) is even more categorical. It states that 'The Constitution of Canada is the supreme law of Canada, and any law that is inconsistent with the provisions of the Constitution is, to the extent of the inconsistency, of no force or effect.' A vestige of Parliament's former superiority is retained, however, through s. 33 of the Charter. This is the so-called 'notwithstanding clause'. It enables either Parliament or a provincial legislature to declare that a law shall operate even if it violates the fundamental freedoms, legal rights, or equality rights sections of the Charter. Such a declaration must be renewed after five years, otherwise the Constitution reasserts its supremacy.

Judicial Independence and the Separation of Powers

The role of the judicial branch of government is based on constitutional convention rather than law. The Constitution Act, 1867 includes several sections that deal with the system of provincial courts, including how judges shall be selected, how they may be removed, when provincial Superior Court judges must retire (age 75), and who will determine judicial salaries.[24] But there is no mention of the Supreme Court of Canada or of any other federal courts. Instead, section 101 authorizes Parliament to establish a 'General Court of Appeal for Canada', which it did in 1875 (the Supreme Court of Canada) and again in 1970 (the Federal Court of Canada).

Canadian constitutional law is silent on the powers, indeed on the very existence and composition, of this country's highest court of appeal. Nor is the relationship between the judicial and other branches of government described in much detail. This stands in sharp contrast to the American Constitution, in which lengthy descriptions of the powers of Congress (the legislative branch) and the President (the executive branch) are followed by Article III on the judicial branch of government. In Canada, however, the role of the judiciary is based largely on constitutional convention and statute law. The fundamental principles that underlie that role are judicial independence and separation of powers.

Judicial independence means that judges are to be free from any and all interference in their decision-making. Former Chief Justice Brian Dickson declared that the core of this principle involves 'the complete liberty of individual judges to hear and decide the cases that come before them.'[25] It is particularly important that judges be protected from interference by the government. Despite the fact that the principle of judicial independence is deeply embedded in Canada's political culture and enshrined in laws on contempt of court and in guidelines for ministerial conduct, doubts have been raised over whether these protections are adequate. The fact that court budgets are determined by governments represents, in the eyes of some, a potential limitation on judicial autonomy.[26]

The principle of **separation of powers** guarantees the special role of the judiciary. This role is to interpret what the law and the Constitution mean when disputes arise. As in the case of judicial independence, this principle relies more on cultural norms, statute law, and constitutional convention than it does on constitutional law. There is, however, at least one important reference to the role of the judicial branch in the Constitution. This is section 24 of the Constitution Act, 1982, which declares that the enforcement of the Charter shall be through the courts. The perception that the courts represent a check on the powers of Parliament and the provincial legislatures—a perception that has taken hold since the Charter's passage in 1982—reflects an Americanizing trend in Canadian politics. The concept of checks and balances between the three branches of government is basic to the American Constitution. It is not, however, part of British parliamentary democracy.

The separation of the judiciary's role from that of Parliament is not watertight. The ability of the federal and provincial governments to refer a resolution or draft legislation to the courts for a decision on its constitutionality does not, strictly speaking, respect the principle of separation of powers. These constitutional reference cases enable governments to use the provincial and Canadian supreme courts to receive advisory opinions before acting or to thrust a politically volatile issue into the hands of judges. The separation of powers is also breached when judges step outside their role as interpreters of the law's meaning to advocate some position or reform. This occasionally happens (see Box 5.3).

Relations between the House of Commons and the Senate

When the founders designed Canada's Parliament, they took the bicameral structure of Britain's legislature as their model. Accordingly, the legislative branch was comprised of two bodies, an elected House of Commons (the lower house) and an appointed Senate (the upper house). A literal reading of the Constitution suggests that their powers are roughly equal. The major difference is that money bills must be introduced in the House of Commons. In fact, however, the superiority of the elected House of Commons has been clear from day one. The unelected character of the Senate has always sat uneasily in Canada's democratic political culture. This fact, along with the brazen patronage of most government appointments to the Senate, undermined its legitimacy.

The superiority of the House of Commons over the Senate is reinforced by several constitutional conventions. Probably the most important of these involves the selection of the Prime Minister and other members of the government. Constitutional law does not require that they be drawn from the House of Commons, but it is unthinkable today that the Prime Minister not be an elected MP. It occasionally happens that one or two senators are appointed to cabinet, but this usually is because the party in power has few (or no) MPs from a particular region of the country. And occasionally the Prime Minister will appoint to cabinet someone who is neither an MP nor a senator. By tradition, however, this person will very soon afterward seek election to the House of Commons.[27] The whole system of democratic accountability would crumble if the Prime Minister and other members of the government were not elected officials, removable by the electorate.

Another convention that reinforces the House of Commons' superiority is found in the legislative process itself. All bills must pass both the Senate and the House of Commons before they become law. Moreover, the stages through which a bill must pass are identical in both houses of Parliament. But until recently it was generally accepted that the Senate did not have the right to obstruct or reject the will of the elected House of Commons. On occasion the Senate would suggest minor revisions to legislation, sending it back to the House of Commons for reconsideration. After

---

BOX 5.3   Chief Justice McLachlin praises new cash for bilingualism programs

Canada's chief judge says that the country's bilingualism policy is worth every penny because minority-language rights are a 'fundamental plank' of the Canadian identity.

'It goes much beyond cost, it goes much beyond economics, it is really the foundation of what we are as a nation', Chief Justice Beverley McLachlin said in an interview. 'It's moving beyond any short-term calculation.'

McLachlin made her comments on the eve of the federal government's announcement of a strengthened policy that will put hundreds of millions of dollars toward increased bilingualism in schools, health services, and the federal public service.

. . .

McLachlin made her comments in an interview that coincided with a weekend speech in which she emphasized the need for society to be more inclusive in its treatment of minorities and disadvantaged groups, including women, Aboriginals, and French-speaking Canadians.

. . .

'The modern world holds out the promise of inclusion, but delivers the reality of exclusion', she told a symposium at Dalhousie University in Halifax. 'We must tame the dark side of difference.'

McLachlin, who is Canada's first female chief justice and one of the most powerful women in the country, reserved much of her criticism for society's historical mistreatment of her gender.

Windsor Star, 11 Mar. 2003, A16.

---

the 1984 election of the Progressive Conservative government, however, the Senate—dominated by people appointed during over two decades of almost unbroken Liberal government—became more recalcitrant. On legislation dealing with such matters as drug patents, government spending, Unemployment Insurance, the Goods and Services Tax, and the Canada–United States Free Trade Agreement the Senate delayed and in some cases rejected bills coming from the House of Commons. Constitutional law gives senators this right; constitutional convention suggests that they should not try to exercise it.

The Biases of British Parliamentary Government

Along with people, pop music, and the English language, Westminster-style parliamentary gov-

ernment has been one of Britain's chief exports. It is one of the main legacies bequeathed to that country's former colonies, Canada included. We have described the major features of British parliamentary government, as adapted to Canadian circumstances. Let us now consider whether this system tends to favour certain interests and outcomes more than others. In discussing ministerial responsibility we noted that the pre-democratic tradition of strong executive authority was never abandoned under British parliamentary government. Instead, it was adapted to the democratic principle that government is based on the consent of the people, a principle embodied in the powers of an elected legislature and in the doctrine of responsible government. When we recall that the legislature that embodied the popular will originally was elected by and accountable to only a fraction of the people, i.e., property-owning males, this adaptation does not appear very revolutionary or particularly democratic. Of course, universal male suffrage arrived by the latter half of the nineteenth century, and females were enfranchised early in the twentieth century, extending participatory rights to all adult citizens and not simply a privileged group of them. This democratization of citizenship rights did not, however, fundamentally alter the non-participatory biases already embedded in the structure of British parliamentary government.

Following Philip Resnick's arguments in *Parliament vs. People*, we may label these biases *statism*. A statist political tradition is one characterized by a relatively strong political executive and by a population that tends to be deferential towards those in power. The adoption of British parliamentary government, first in the colonial legislatures during the mid-1800s and then through the Constitution Act of 1867, mainly reaffirmed the tradition of centralized executive authority that had existed before the elected legislature's approval was needed to pass laws. This reaffirmation of strong executive power is, Resnick argues, apparent throughout Canada's founding Constitution Act. 'What our Founding Fathers were doing', he maintains,

> was consolidating an orderly . . . move from direct colonial rule to House Rule. . . . They had a particular kind of [political] order in mind, the parliamentary system as it had evolved in Britain, combining the interests of monarchs, lords and commoners. If by the latter part of the 19th Century this system was increasingly responsive to the wishes of an electorate, restricted or enlarged, it was by no means a servant of the electorate.[28]

Some might say, that was then but this is now. Yet the institutions of government adopted through the Confederation agreement, and, equally important, the expectations of the political elites who controlled the levers of state power, reached forward to shape the future course of Canadian politics. Parliament was sovereign, but Parliament was not merely the people. It also included the Crown, the traditional seat of state

authority whose powers came to be exercised by a Prime Minister and cabinet with few serious checks from the legislature. 'Parliamentary sovereignty', Resnick argues, 'fostered attitudes in the population which were nominally participatory but maximally deferential towards those exercising political power. The mystique of British Crown and Constitution helped make illegitimate all forms of political activity not sanctioned or channeled through parliamentary institutions.'[29] This is an important point. Resnick is arguing that the more deferential political culture of Canada, as compared to the United States, did not simply happen. It was generated to some degree by parliamentary institutions that discouraged popular participation in politics, beyond the rituals of voting, and enshrined a sort of top-down philosophy of governance.

The evidence suggests that Resnick is right. There have, of course, been influential currents of participatory politics in Canadian history, particularly coming out of western Canada. But these populist urges have had to struggle against a parliamentary tradition that concentrates political power in the hands of the Prime Minister (or premiers) and cabinet. This style of governance is epitomized in the long tradition of elite deal-making that has characterized federal-provincial relations. But it also surfaces when this country's political leaders reject referendums or constituent assemblies on constitutional change as being 'un-Canadian' or foreign to our political tradition. Indeed, the statist political tradition fostered by British parliamentary government is apparent in a multitude of ways, large and small. 'Our governments', argues Resnick, '. . . become the organizers of our civic consciousness. National celebrations like Expo have to be staged; nationalist propaganda is transmitted across the airwaves, through the newspapers, along with our social security cheques.'[30] Many argue that the Canadian state's orchestration of culture has been a defensive response to the Americanizing pressures from mass media industries centred in the United States. To some degree this is certainly true. But this explanation of state-centred nationalism in Canada does not pay adequate attention to the possibility that the state's efforts may pre-empt those of groups in civil society and encourage a climate of dependence on government to, in Resnick's words, 'organize our civic consciousness'. If governments had done less, and private citizens more, to construct the identities that are part of Canadian culture, perhaps national unity would be less fragile.

To the extent that the Charter of Rights and Freedoms modifies British parliamentary government in Canada, by replacing parliamentary supremacy with constitutional supremacy and helping to generate a greater consciousness of rights among members of the public, it has shifted Canadian politics away from its elitist past towards a more participatory model. Indeed, it is now commonplace to claim that the Charter ushered in a new era in Canadian politics characterized by far less deference to elites. There is some truth in this claim, but the impact of the Charter on Canada's political future is often exaggerated. The British parliamentary system that operates in Canada, albeit modified by the Charter and the principle of constitutional supremacy, continues to concentrate power in the hands of the Prime Minister and cabinet and still provides few opportunities for direct public participation in governance beyond voting in elections. More importantly, the statist culture of governance that Resnick associates with the British parliamentary system is not fundamentally challenged by the fact that, because of the Charter, the courts have become more important venues for resolution of political issues and thus many groups now bypass electoral and legislative politics. Politics waged in the courts is not necessarily more democratic and accessible than these other forms and forums for politics, as many, on both the left and right of the political spectrum, concede.[31]

CHANGING THE CONSTITUTION

Constitutions are meant to last a very long time, but they seldom do. Among the 47 countries whose independence predates 1900, only about a third have constitutions that date from before 1950.[32] Canada's 1867 Constitution Act is one of the oldest and most durable. Only the United States (1787), Sweden (1809), the Netherlands (1814), and the United Kingdom (1832) have older constitutions.

A *coup d'état* is one way of changing a constitution. More peaceful means may also accomplish dramatic change, including the wholesale replacement of one constitution by a fundamentally different one. But radical alteration of the fundamental rules and structures of government is much less common than constitutional reform. Reform aims at changing some aspect(s) of the existing constitution, leaving the basic constitutional structure intact. Limited change of this sort is generally accomplished through a formal procedure set down in the constitution. Reforms that result from such a process are called *constitutional amendments*.

When does constitutional reform become constitutional upheaval? This is difficult to pinpoint, but the line has certainly been crossed when as a result of change a constitution is no longer recognizably what it was before. For example, the 1982 Constitution Act did three main things: (1) it transformed Canada's written Constitution from a set of British laws into Canadian constitutional law; (2) it entrenched the Charter of Rights and Freedoms in the Constitution; and (3) it established formal mechanisms for changing the Constitution. As important as these changes were, they did not amount to a new Constitution. Most features of parliamentary government and of federalism remained the same. On the other hand, the replacement of parliamentary government by American-style congressional government, the elimination of federalism, or—least far-fetched of all—the political independence of Quebec would in each case represent a radical transformation of Canada's Constitution.

Constitutional change may also come about through the gradual evolution of principles and practices. For example, the principle that the Governor-General should accept the advice of the

Prime Minister on when Parliament should be dissolved and a new election called was one that emerged imperceptibly as Canada shook off the vestiges of its colonial relationship to Great Britain. It was only when this principle was breached by Governor-General Lord Byng in 1926 that it became clear that this relationship between the Prime Minister and the Governor-General was part of the Constitution. The clear superiority of the House of Commons over the Senate on matters of legislation is another constitutional convention that became clearer with the passage of time. Those appointed to the Senate in 1867 were largely prominent politicians from the new provinces. It was during this early period that the Senate became known as the chamber of 'sober second thought'. Over time, however, the practice of patronage appointments, the emergence of assertive provincial governments as spokespersons for regional interests, and changing ideas about democracy and representation all contributed to the Senate's decline vis-à-vis the Commons.

Amending the Constitution before 1982

The Constitution Act, 1867 gave Ottawa a very modest power to amend the Constitution of Canada regarding matters that concerned only the federal government.[33] In practical terms, all this power amounted to was the ability to change electoral districts and boundary lines. The Act gave the provincial governments a similar power.[34] Canada's founders, however, omitted to establish an amending procedure that could be used to change the division of powers and all the other important matters that could not be changed using the very limited amendment powers conferred by sections 91(1) and 92(1) of the Constitution Act, 1867. They did not even discuss such a procedure, a curious oversight in view of the fact that the federal Constitution of the United States—the only federal model that existed at the time—was very clear on the procedures for amending the Constitution. In the case of Canada, the only clear requirement was that a request

would have to be made to the British Parliament in order to change the Constitution. The reason for this was, of course, that the Canadian Constitution was in fact a British law, originally passed as the British North America Act, 1867.

What was not clear, however, was who would have to agree here in Canada before a resolution could be sent to London. Would all provincial governments have to agree if a proposed amendment affected their powers? Did Quebec or Ontario or any other province enjoy a special right to veto amendments? Just how much provincial consent was needed to change the Constitution? It was not even clear what would happen if all 10 provincial legislatures and the House of Commons agreed to an amendment, but the Senate rejected it. Formally, at least, the Senate appeared to have the power to block constitutional change.

After decades of uncertainty, the issue was finally decided by the Supreme Court in 1981. The background to this decision was the stalemate in constitutional negotiations between Ottawa and the provinces. The Liberal government of Pierre Elliott Trudeau wanted to patriate the Constitution, entrench in it a Charter of Rights and Freedoms, and establish a formal procedure for future constitutional amendments. Only the governments of Ontario and New Brunswick supported Ottawa's proposal. The conflict ended up in the courts when the governments of Manitoba, Newfoundland, and Quebec each decided to ask their provincial supreme courts whether Ottawa's actions were constitutional. There was some variation in the questions and wording of these provincial references. Nonetheless, they all asked (1) whether Ottawa's proposed amendments affected provincial powers and (2) if provincial consent was constitutionally required to make such changes. Quebec's reference also asked whether that province had a special veto over amendments. These decisions were then appealed to the Supreme Court of Canada.

In its ruling in *Re Constitution of Canada*[35] the Court made the following points:

- Some level of provincial consent was required for changes affecting provincial powers. This requirement was a constitutional convention, not part of constitutional law. It could not, therefore, be enforced by the courts.
- The level of required provincial consent was not at all clear. It was the Court's view that a majority of the provinces certainly had to agree, but unanimous consent was not necessary.
- In constitutional law, no province had a special right of veto over constitutional change. The Court did not give an opinion on whether such a right existed as a matter of constitutional convention.
- Ottawa did not need provincial consent before requesting the British Parliament to change Canada's Constitution in ways affecting provincial powers. If the federal government chose to act without the consent of the provinces, or with the support of only a few of them, this would be legal—but at the same time unconstitutional!

Both Ottawa and the dissenting provinces claimed victory as a result of the Court's decision. Legally, the way was clear for Ottawa to act with or without the consent of the provinces. Politically, unilateral action remained a risky option, particularly in light of the Court's acknowledgement that some level of provincial consent was required by constitutional convention. All 11 governments returned to the bargaining table, each side conscious of the constitutional turf occupied by itself and its opponents. In November 1981, 10 of them were able to reach agreement on a compromise document that became the Constitution Act, 1982. Only the PQ government of Quebec rejected the proposed changes. Despite Quebec's refusal to sign the 1981 agreement, the Constitution Act, 1982 is constitutional law in that province just as it is elsewhere in Canada. A 1982 Supreme Court decision confirmed this.[36]

Amending the Constitution since 1982

The uncertainties surrounding constitutional amendment have been largely dispelled by the Constitution Act, 1982. Part V of the Act lays down the amendment procedures. In fact, it establishes four different procedures, each of which applies to certain types of constitutional change. These procedures, and when they are used, are explained in Table 5.1.

Any of the four amendment procedures may be set in motion by either Ottawa or a provincial government (s. 46[1]). But because intergovernmental agreement is crucial to the success of most amendments, the most likely scenario is that the Prime Minister and the provincial premiers will first reach an agreement, which will then be submitted to their respective legislatures. This was the procedure that led to the Meech Lake Accord, the first proposal for constitutional amendment under the 1982 rules. Negotiations and deal-making between governments—the pre-legislative stage of the amendment process—are as crucial now as when the amendment process was governed by convention. The new procedures have not formally expanded the opportunities for public participation, nor have they enlarged the legislature's role in the process.

Not content with the distinction of having four different procedures for amending the Constitution, the 10 governments who agreed to the 1982 Constitution Act included another extraordinary feature in the amendment rules. This is the 'opting-out' section (s. 40). Under this section, a provincial government that does not agree to an amendment that transfers powers relating to education or other cultural matters from the provinces to Ottawa is not obliged to give up this power. Moreover, Ottawa is required to provide 'reasonable compensation' to any dissenting province. The Meech Lake and Charlottetown Accords would have expanded the opting-out section, guaranteeing a dissenting province the right to reasonable compensation in the case of any transfer of legislative powers from the provinces to Ottawa. In fact, this would only have enshrined in the Constitution a practice that has existed in Canada since 1964.

The first effort at amending the Constitution using the 1982 rules ended in acrimonious failure. The proposed amendment was in fact a group of changes collectively known as the Meech Lake Accord. The Accord was a 1987 agreement between Prime Minister Brian Mulroney and the 10 provincial premiers. It was a response to a series of five demands that the Quebec government of Robert Bourassa wanted met before it was willing to sign the 1981 agreement that produced the Constitution Act, 1982. The main changes proposed by the Meech Lake Accord included: recognition of Quebec as a distinct society; constitutional recognition of a provincial (i.e., Quebec) right to control its own immigration policy (something Quebec had had since a 1978 agreement between Ottawa and Quebec); provincial power to nominate justices for the Supreme Court of Canada; constitutional entrenchment of a provincial right to opt out of federal-provincial shared-cost programs and to be reimbursed for running parallel programs of their own; certain

Table 5.1   Amending the Constitution

Procedure	Requirement	Application
1. General ss. 38, 42	• Resolution passed by the House of Commons and the Senate* • Two-thirds of the legislatures of the provinces that together comprise at least half the population of all the provinces	• Reduction or elimination of powers, rights, or privileges of provincial governments or legislatures • Proportionate representation of the provinces in the House of Commons • Senate • Supreme Court of Canada (except its composition) • Extension of existing provinces into the territories • Creation of new provinces
2. Unanimous Consent s. 41	• Resolution passed by the House of Commons and the Senate* • Resolution passed by every provincial legislature	• Queen • Governor-General • Lieutenant-Governors • Right of each province to at least as many seats in the House of Commons as it has in the Senate • Use of the English or French language (except changes that apply only to single province) • Composition of the Supreme Court • Changing the amending procedures of the Constitution
3. Ottawa and one or more provinces s. 43	• Resolution passed by the House of Commons and the Senate* • Resolution passed by the legislature of each province where the amendment applies	• Alteration of boundaries between provinces • Use of French or English in a particular province or territory
4. Ottawa or a province acting alone ss. 44, 45	• If Ottawa, a resolution passed by the House of Commons and the Senate* • If a province, a resolution passed by its legislature	• Executive government of Canada, the Senate, and the House of Commons, subject to the limits established by ss. 41 and 42 of the Constitution Act, 1982

*If after 180 days the Senate has not passed a resolution already passed by the House of Commons, Senate approval is not necessary.

changes to constitutional amendment procedures and categories (see Table 5.1).

After three years of wrangling marked by both an anti-French backlash in parts of English Canada and a revival of separatist nationalism in Quebec, the Accord expired when the legislatures of Manitoba and Newfoundland failed to ratify it by the 23 June 1990 deadline imposed on the process by the Constitution. Both the birth and the death of the Accord suggested that not much had changed as a result of formalizing the amendment process. The proposed changes that made up the Accord represented a deal struck by 11 heads of government with no public participation or legislative debate. In fact, the Prime Minister and some of the provincial premiers were very insistent that their agreement could not be altered in any respect. It was submitted to their legislatures for ratification, not for possible modification. Public participation was solicited only very late in the process, and then only because the Accord seemed destined for defeat. Indeed, there was little to suggest that any of the governments saw public participation as anything more than a resource to use when convenient. Groups and individuals opposed to the Accord's provisions denounced this process as undemocratic.

The critics may have been right. But it was also clear that any change to the 1987 first ministers' agreement would have required that a new resolution be submitted to Parliament and all the provincial legislatures, and the ratification process would have to start over again. Debate and popular participation *after* an amendment resolution has been agreed to by governments are almost certain to prolong the amendment process, and probably reduce the chances of reaching an agreement.

The death of the Meech Lake Accord likewise suggested that the process of constitutional amendment remained largely as it had been before 1982. The final several months leading up to the ratification deadline were marked by acrimonious debate and some ad hoc efforts to salvage the Accord, and finally ended with Quebec being largely isolated from the other provinces There was a sense of déjà vu about the whole affair. Quebec had been similarly isolated in 1971 when the first Bourassa government suddenly withdrew its acceptance of the Victoria Charter amendments, and then again in 1981 when René Lévesque claimed to have been betrayed by a last-minute deal concocted between the other provinces and Ottawa. In each case agreement ran aground because the Quebec government and some of the governments of English Canada were unable to settle their differences on Quebec's status within Canada. Meech Lake came to grief because of the same obstacle that had blocked previous efforts at constitutional change.

The next two years saw dozens of government-organized public hearings on the Constitution and hundreds of conferences and forums organized by academics, political parties, and interest groups. Ottawa and the provinces were determined to avoid the charges of elitist deal-making that had been levelled at the Meech Lake process. In this they failed. Although there were ample opportunities for citizens and groups to express their views on constitutional reform, the proposals presented to Canadians in the 26 October 1992 referendum were widely viewed as yet another instance of the elites cutting a deal and trying to foist it on the public.

The Charlottetown Accord, as these proposals were referred to, represented the culmination of what the federal government rather misleadingly called the 'Canada round' of constitutional negotiations (the period leading up to Meech Lake having been labelled the 'Quebec round'). In fact, however, the desire to get the Quebec government's political agreement to the constitutional changes of 1982 and worry over the post-Meech Lake resurgence of support for separatism were the chief reasons why the constitutional issue dominated Canadian politics with a vengeance between 1990 and 1992. Moreover, the deal ultimately struck at Charlottetown in August 1992 bore a striking resemblance to the Meech Lake Accord in some important respects.

Besides certain carry-overs from Meech, such as Quebec's 'distinct society' status, Supreme Court nominations, and provinces' ability to opt out of shared-cost programs without penalty, the main features included:

- a Canada clause listing the fundamental characteristics of Canadian society;
- entrenchment of the right to Aboriginal self-government;
- an elected Senate with equal representation from the provinces and, eventually, special seats for Aboriginal representatives;
- francophone veto in the Senate regarding bills affecting the French language or culture;
- a guarantee to Quebec of at least 25 per cent of the seats in the House of Commons;
- confirmation of the provinces' exclusive jurisdiction in several policy areas, and some decentralization of powers to the provinces in the areas of immigration and labour policy.

A sense of the potentially far-reaching changes proposed in the Charlottetown Accord is conveyed by the Canada Clause (see Box 5.4). This provision sought to express the fundamental values of Canadians. Had the Accord been passed the Canada Clause would have been included as section 2 of the Constitution Act, 1867 and would have given the courts guidance in their interpretation of the entire Constitution, including the Charter of Rights and Freedoms. It is impossible to know how judges would interpret many of the provisions of the Canada Clause. What is certain, however, is that it would have given to the courts a whole new field of opportunity, on top of that already provided by the Charter, to involve themselves in the policy-making process. It requires little imagination, for example, to predict that subsection (1)f of the proposed Canada Clause, committing Canadians to 'respect for individual and collective human rights and freedoms of all people', could become the legal basis for challenges to social spending cuts, or that subsection (1)b on the Aboriginal peoples of Canada could become the basis for legal claims on tax resources

and distinctive legal rights for Aboriginal Canadians. The Canada Clause, whatever its impact on Canadian society would have been, was certainly a constitutional lawyer's paradise.

In the national referendum on the Charlottetown Accord, a majority of Canadians (54.5 per cent) rejected the proposed reforms, including provincial majorities in British Columbia, Alberta, Saskatchewan, Manitoba, Quebec, and Nova Scotia, as well as the Yukon. The result in Ontario was virtually a dead heat. During the impassioned referendum campaign it was clear that many English Canadians said 'no' to the Charlottetown Accord because they thought it gave Quebec too much and/or because of its decentralizing tendencies, which effectively gave all provinces what it proffered to Quebec, while many Québécois rejected the deal because they believed it gave them too little! Indeed, the only serious question asked by members of the Quebec media and the province's politicians during the campaign was 'Did Quebec get enough in the Charlottetown Accord?' Although the 1992 agreement provided the Quebec government with more than had been proposed by the Meech Lake Accord, this was not enough in the nationalist political climate that prevailed in the post-Meech years.

While it is always treacherous and somewhat misleading to talk about Quebec or any society as though it has a single set of aspirations, the failure of the Meech Lake and Charlottetown proposals confirmed that a wide gap existed between those of francophone Quebecers and their compatriots in the rest of the country.

CITIZEN PARTICIPATION IN CONSTITUTIONAL REFORM

For most of Canada's history the only direct actors in constitutional reform were governments. This changed during the negotiations and debates that led to the Constitution Act of 1982, when a number of citizens' interest groups played an active role through lobbying government and attempting to influence public opinion. These groups,

BOX 5.4   The Canada Clause

(1) The Constitution of Canada, including the *Canadian Charter of Rights and Freedoms*, shall be interpreted in a manner consistent with the following fundamental characteristics:

   a) Canada is a democracy committed to a parliamentary and federal system of government and to the rule of law;

   b) the Aboriginal peoples of Canada, being the first peoples to govern this land, have the right to promote their languages, cultures and traditions and to ensure the integrity of their societies, and their governments constitute one of three orders of government in Canada;

   c) Quebec constitutes within Canada a distinct society, which includes a French-speaking majority, a unique culture and a civil law tradition;

   d) Canadians and their governments are committed to the vitality and development of official language minority communities throughout Canada;

   e) Canadians are committed to racial and ethnic equality in a society that includes citizens from many lands who have contributed, and continue to contribute, to the building of a strong Canada that reflects its cultural and racial diversity;

   f) Canadians are committed to a respect for individual and collective human rights and freedoms of all people;

   g) Canadians are committed to the equality of female and male persons; and,

   h) Canadians confirm the principle of the equality of the provinces at the same time as recognizing their diverse characteristics.

and many others inspired by the opportunities created by the Charter, were instrumental in bringing about the death of the Meech Lake Accord. During the two years of consultation and negotiation that preceded the signing of the Charlottetown Accord these citizens' interest groups were very much part of the process. Informally at least, Ottawa and the provincial governments appeared to have conceded the legitimacy of a more inclusive style of constitution-making.

What they did not concede, however, was a direct role for public participation and consent. Under the old elitist policy-making style popular consent was mediated by the heads of govern-

ment. Under the more inclusive policy-making style that emerged in the early 1980s popular consent was mediated by these heads of government *plus* certain interest groups claiming to speak on behalf of women, ethnic and racial minorities, Aboriginal Canadians, the disabled, official-language minorities, and so on. But not until the decision was taken in the late summer of 1992 to submit the Charlottetown reforms to the people in a national referendum was popular consent unmediated and the public given a direct role in the constitutional amendment process. This represented a remarkable break from Canada's elitist tradition of constitution-making. With few exceptions, mainly from western Canada, the idea of a referendum to approve constitutional change had been rejected throughout Canada's history. When a formal procedure for constitutional amendment was being debated in the 1930s one of the country's most prominent constitutionalists dismissed the suggestion of a referendum as being inconsistent with cabinet government and a device for 'passing the buck'.[37] Frank Underhill, expressing the views of most intellectuals, argued that average citizens were generally incompetent to decide matters of constitutional change and that their elected representatives usually held more advanced views on public affairs. Legislatures, not citizens, he argued, should be required to ratify constitutional reforms.[38]

The idea of a referendum on the Meech Lake Accord surfaced from time to time in the English-language media but was dismissed by Prime Minister Mulroney and most of the provincial premiers as being alien to Canada's political tradition. This view was as likely to be expressed by those on the social democratic left, such as the national New Democratic Party leader Ed Broadbent and Manitoba's NDP Premier Howard Pawley, as by those more to the right on the political spectrum.

But in the flood of condemnation that followed the death of the Meech Lake Accord the idea that popular ratification should be sought in any future attempt to change the Constitution gathered force. Quebec's provincial government committed itself to holding a provincial referendum on whatever agreement it reached with Ottawa. British Columbia also passed a law requiring provincial ratification of reform proposals. However, most politicians remained steadfast in their opposition. Ottawa's decision, after much hesitation and obvious reluctance, to introduce legislation enabling Parliament to authorize a referendum (really a plebiscite, in that the vote would be formally non-binding) reflected practical necessity more than principled conviction. The powerful Quebec caucus of the governing Conservative Party opposed such legislation. The Minister of Intergovernmental

Affairs, Joe Clark, had often expressed serious reservations about a referendum. But Quebec and British Columbia were both committed to holding referendums, and there was a good chance that the reform proposals would be rejected in both provinces. A national referendum campaign and a favourable vote in most regions was a possible way of legitimizing reform proposals in this climate of division.

The decision to hold a referendum on the Charlottetown Accord and the decision to abide by what was, legally speaking, a non-binding popular vote, appeared to mark the beginning of a new era in Canadian constitution-making. Most commentators believed so, arguing that governments would in the future find it impossible to ignore the 1992 precedent of a popular ratification vote.

Such predictions may be premature. A country's political culture and ways of conducting politics do not change abruptly as a result of a single experience. First ministers will continue to be the key players in any future effort at constitutional reform. Both political tradition and the formal amendment procedure ensure their dominance. But a repeat of the Meech Lake process—an accord negotiated and agreed to without public consultation—has become virtually unthinkable. It is fair to say that a process of consultation and opportunities for public participation in some form have become necessary preconditions for any future agreement.

It remains to be seen, however, whether governments will feel obliged to submit future agreements to the electorate for ratification, or whether the Charlottetown experience was an aberration that has left no mark on Canada's political culture. In British Columbia and Alberta, which have more of a populist tradition, the political pressure for constitutional referendums may be irresistible. In the case of Quebec, the idea that any major change in that province's constitutional status must be approved by the electorate is now firmly established. These provinces are the ones most likely to insist on popular ratification of constitutional reform. If they do, it becomes very awkward for Ottawa not to concede a role for direct public participation through a national referendum, as happened in 1992.

Does Quebec Have the Constitutional Right to Secede? (and Does It Matter?)

On 20 August 1998 the Supreme Court of Canada handed down its much awaited decision on the constitutionality of Quebec separation. In the eyes of some, the most remarkable aspect of the ruling was that it was made at all. The separation of Quebec, if and when it comes about, is a political matter that will be determined by politicians and the people, not by nine appointed judges in Ottawa. This was certainly the view of most Quebec nationalists and of Quebec's Parti Québécois government, whose disdain for the process was such that it refused to send lawyers to argue the case for the constitutionality of Quebec secession. Indeed, the Supreme Court's involvement in this matter was widely viewed by francophone Quebecers as unwarranted meddling in the internal affairs of the province.

Ottawa's decision to refer the issue of the constitutionality of Quebec secession to the Supreme Court was prompted by the actions of Montreal lawyer Guy Bertrand. A one-time separatist, Bertrand had already begun legal proceedings in Quebec challenging the constitutionality of unilateral secession by Quebec. Ottawa's 1996 decision to refer the question to the Supreme Court was, in part, due to the simple fact that Bertrand's private action had already released the genie from the bottle. Nonetheless, there were political risks associated with Ottawa's involvement in a court challenge to Quebec secession. The Liberal government's decision to push forward, despite these risks, was consistent with what had come to be known as the 'Plan B' approach to Quebec separatism. Whereas Plan A had involved efforts to satisfy moderate Quebec nationalists with promises of distinct society status for Quebec and some decentralization of powers to the provinces, Plan B was a hard-line approach that relied on

convincing Quebecers that separation would carry significant economic costs and that some parts of the territory of Quebec might not fall under the authority of an independent Quebec state (this was the partition threat, made by predominantly anglophone communities and Aboriginal groups in Quebec, and occasionally expressed by Stéphane Dion, the Liberal Minister of Intergovernmental Affairs). The court challenge to Quebec secession became a major component of the Plan B strategy.

In the reference submitted by Ottawa to the Supreme Court, three questions were asked. They were:

Question 1: Under the Constitution of Canada, can the National Assembly, legislature or government of Quebec effect the secession of Quebec from Canada unilaterally?

Question 2: Does international law give the National Assembly, legislature or government of Quebec the right to effect the secession of Quebec from Canada unilaterally? In other words, is there a right to self-determination in international law that applies to Quebec?

Question 3: If there is a conflict between international law and the Canadian Constitution on the secession of Quebec, which takes precedence?

The Court decided that there was no conflict, and so only questions #1 and #2 were addressed.

The Court's answer to the first question was a model of ambiguity that provided both federalists and separatists with congenial arguments. In strictly legal terms, said the Court, the secession of Quebec involves a major change to the Constitution of Canada that 'requires an amendment to the Constitution, which perforce requires negotiation.'[39] However, the Constitution of Canada consists of more than the Constitution Acts passed between 1867 and 1982. 'Underlying constitutional principles', said the Court, 'may in certain circumstances give rise to substantive legal obligations . . . which constitute substantive limitation upon government action.'[40] These underlying constitutional principles provided the basis for the Court's argument that if a clear majority of Quebecers voted 'yes' to an unambiguous question on Quebec separation, this would 'confer legitimacy on the efforts of the government of Quebec to initiate the Constitution's amendment process in order to secede by constitutional means'[41] (see Box 5.5). These underlying constitutional principles also impose on Ottawa and the provincial governments outside of Quebec an obligation to negotiate the terms of secession, if and when Quebecers and their provincial government express the democratic will to separate.

So who wins on the first question? The answer is that both federalists and separatists found enough in the Supreme Court's ruling to allow them to claim victory. Federalists emphasized that there is, legally speaking, no constitutional right for Quebec to secede unilaterally, and that even if separatists were to win a referendum the Court specified that a 'clear majority' on an 'unambiguous' question would be required before such a vote could be considered an expression of the democratic will of Quebecers on so weighty a matter. Separatists—or at least those willing to acknowledge the Court's ruling—emphasized that the Court had agreed that the democratically expressed will of Quebecers had to be taken into account in determining whether unilateral secession was constitutional, and that if Quebecers were to express their clear support for separation the rest of Canada would be constitutionally bound to respect this decision and negotiate the terms of secession.

The Court's answer to the second question of whether international law gives Quebec the right to secede was both shorter and less ambiguous. The Court said no. While acknowledging that the right of self-determination of peoples exists in international law, the Supreme Court held that this right did not apply to Quebec.

The Court did not answer the contentious question of whether the Quebec population, or a part of it, constitutes a 'people' as understood in international law. It argued that such a determination was unnecessary because, however the Que-

---

BOX 5.5   Can Quebecers Vote Their Way Out of Canada?

Although the Constitution does not itself address the use of a referendum procedure, and the results of a referendum have no direct role or legal effect in our constitutional scheme, a referendum undoubtedly may provide a democratic method of ascertaining the views of the electorate on important political questions on a particular occasion. The democratic principle identified above would demand that considerable weight be given to a clear expression by the people of Quebec of their will to secede from Canada, even though a referendum, in itself and without more, has no direct legal effect, and could not in itself bring about unilateral secession. Our political institutions are premised on the democratic principle, and so an expression of the democratic will of the people of a province carries weight, in that it would confer legitimacy on the efforts of the government of Quebec to initiate the Constitution's amendment process in order to secede by constitutional means. In this context, we refer to a 'clear' majority as a qualitative evaluation. The referendum result, if it is to be taken as an expression of the democratic will, must be free of ambiguity both in terms of the question asked and in terms of the support it achieves.

Supreme Court of Canada, *Reference re the Secession of Quebec* (1998)

bec people might be defined, it is clear that Quebecers are neither denied the ability to pursue their 'political, economic, social and cultural development within the framework of an existing state',[42] nor do they constitute a colonized or oppressed people (a claim that is a staple of contemporary Quebec historiography). The Court's pronouncements on these matters are found in Box 5.6.

Does the Supreme Court ruling make a difference? Probably not, or at least not much of one, as the Court seemed to acknowledge at various points in its decision. On the issue of what would constitute a 'clear majority' and an 'unambiguous question' in a referendum on Quebec independence, the Court admitted that 'it will be for the political actors to determine what constitutes a

BOX 5.6   International Law and the Self-Determination of Quebec

There is no necessary incompatibility between the maintenance of the territorial integrity of existing states, including Canada, and the right of a 'people' to achieve a full measure of self-determination. A state whose government represents the whole of the people or peoples resident within its territory, on a basis of equality and without discrimination, and respects the principles of self-determination in its own internal arrangements, is entitled to the protection under international law of its territorial integrity.

The Quebec people is not the victim of attacks on its physical existence or integrity, or of a massive violation of its fundamental rights. The Quebec people is manifestly not, in the opinion of the *amicus curiae*, an oppressed people.

For close to 40 of the last 50 years, the Prime Minister of Canada has been a Quebecer. During this period, Quebecers have held from time to time all the most important positions in the federal Cabinet. During the 8 years prior to June 1997, the Prime Minister and the Leader of the Official Opposition in the House of Commons were both Quebecers. At present, the Prime Minister of Canada, the Right Honourable Chief Justice and two other members of the Court, the Chief of Staff of the Canadian Armed Forces and the Canadian ambassador to the United States, not to mention the Deputy Secretary-General of the United Nations, are all Quebecers. The international achievements of Quebecers in most fields of human endeavour are too numerous to list. Since the dynamism of the Quebec people has been directed toward the business sector, it has been clearly successful in Quebec, the rest of Canada and abroad.

The population of Quebec cannot plausibly be said to be denied access to government. Quebecers occupy prominent positions within the government of Canada. Residents of the province freely make political choices and pursue economic, social and cultural development within Quebec, across Canada, and throughout the world. The population of Quebec is equitably represented in legislative, executive and judicial institutions. In short, to reflect the phraseology of the international documents that address the right to self-determination of peoples, Canada is a 'sovereign and independent state conducting itself in compliance with the principle of equal rights and self-determination of peoples and thus possessed of a government representing the whole people belonging to the territory without distinction'.

Reference re the Secession of Quebec (1998)

"clear majority on a clear question".[43] Likewise, the practical meaning of the constitutional obligation of the rest of Canada to negotiate the terms of separation with Quebec, the Court said, would be for political actors to determine. Finally, in response to the argument that a unilateral declaration of independence by Quebec would be effective regardless of whether the Court's test of a clear majority on a clear question was met, the judges could say only that this might well be true, but the action would be unconstitutional nonetheless. One suspects that separatists would not lose much sleep over the constitutionality of such a declaration, particularly, as seems very likely, if France and certain other countries were to immediately recognize the new Quebec state.

NOTES

1. Canada, Constitution Act, 1982, s. 16(1).
2. Pierre Elliott Trudeau, *Federalism and the French Canadians* (Toronto: Macmillan, 1968), 187.
3. Constitution Act, 1867, preamble.
4. Constitution Act, 1867, s. 121.
5. Constitution Act, 1867, s. 145 (repealed in 1893).
6. Constitution Act, 1982, s. 36.
7. Supreme Court of Canada, *Reference re Secession of Quebec*, Aug. 1998, at p.18 of on-line decisions. Available at: <www.droit.umontr.ca>.
8. Supreme Court of Canada, *OPSEU v. A.G. of Ontario*, 1987, 2 S.C.R. 2, S7.
9. *Reference re Secession of Quebec*, 19.
10. Ibid., 20.
11. Ibid., 21.
12. Ibid., 22.
13. Supreme Court of Canada, *R. v. Oakes*, 1986, 1 S.C.R. 103, 136.
14. *Reference re Secession of Quebec*, 22.
15. Ibid., 23.
16. Ibid.
17. Ibid., 25.
18. Constitution Act, 1982, s. 6(3) (6).
19. Ibid., s. 6(4).
20. Supreme Court of Canada, *Morgentaler, Smoling and Scott v. The Queen* (1988), 37 C.C.C. (3rd) 449.
21. Constitution Act, 1982, s. 15(1).
22. Ibid., s. 15(2).
23. Constitution Act, 1867, preamble.
24. Ibid., ss. 96–100.
25. *The Queen v. Beauregard* (1986), 2 S.C.R. 56.
26. This was the basis of a 1986 court action brought against the Quebec government by several Provincial Court judges and the Chief Justice of the Quebec Superior Court.
27. This occurred, for example, with the appointment to cabinet of Stéphane Dion and Pierre Pettigrew shortly after the Chrétien Liberal government took office in 1993. Both subsequently were elected to the House of Commons in special by-elections.
28. Philip Resnick, *Parliament vs. People* (Vancouver: New Star Books, 1984), 19.
29. Ibid., 25.
30. Ibid., 38.
31. For critiques of the courts from two rather different perspectives on democracy, see Rainer Knopff and F.L. Morton, *The Charter Revolution and the Court Party* (Peterborough, Ont.: Broadview Press, 2000), and Michael Mandel, *The Charter of Rights and the Legislation of Politics in Canada* (Toronto: Thompson Educational Publishing, 1994).
32. Charles Lewis Taylor and Michael Hudson, *World Handbook of Political and Social Indicators*, 2nd edn (New Haven: Yale University Press, 1972), 26–7, Table 2.1.
33. Section 91(1). Repealed by the Constitution Act, 1982.
34. Section 92(1). Repealed by the Constitution Act, 1982.

35. Supreme Court of Canada, *Re Constitution of Canada* (1981), 125 D.L.R. (3rd) 1.

36. *Re Attorney General of Quebec and Attorney General of Canada* (1982), 140 D.L.R. (3rd) 385.

37. Cited in Paul Gerin-Lajoie, *Constitutional Amendment in Canada* (Toronto: University of Toronto Press, 1950), 241.

38. Cited ibid., 234.

39. *Reference re Secession of Quebec*, 26.

40. Ibid., 19.

41. Ibid., 27.

42. Ibid., 35.

43. Ibid., 4.

SUGGESTED READINGS

Alan Cairns, *Constitution, Government, and Society in Canada: Selected Essays* (Toronto: McClelland & Stewart, 1988). Several of Cairns's most insightful and widely cited articles are here, including his 1977 presidential address to the Canadian Political Science Association on the impact of political and bureaucratic self-interest and the Constitution on federalism and intergovernmental conflict.

Peter W. Hogg, *Constitutional Law of Canada* (Scarborough, Ont.: Carswell, 2000). This is perhaps the leading text on Canadian constitutional law, widely used in political science and law courses alike.

Bayard Reesor, *The Canadian Constitution in Historical Perspective* (Toronto: Prentice-Hall, 1992). Reesor presents a meticulous historical examination, clause by clause, of the Constitution Acts, including the Charter.

Peter Russell, *Constitutional Odyssey: Can Canadians Become a Sovereign People?*, 2nd edn (Toronto: University of Toronto Press, 1993). This is an excellent survey of constitutional struggles in Canada, culminating in the failed Charlottetown Accord, by one of Canada's leading constitutional scholars.

Review Exercises

1. The cartoon at page 133 caricatures party discipline. What are the pros and cons of this practice? How do you think our constitutional system would change if all votes in the House of Commons were free votes?

2. Draft a 'Canada Clause' to be added at the beginning of the Constitution Act, stating in no more than 100 words the core principles and values that Canada stands for and that should guide interpretation of the Constitution. Compare yours to those drafted by other members of your class.

3. Compare the topics, controversies, and key terms covered in this chapter to those in the constitution chapter of an American politics text (for example, Wilson and DiIulio's *American Government*, published by Houghton & Mifflin, the table of contents for which is available at <http://www.hmco.com/college/polisci/index.html>. Identify some of the similarities and differences in coverage.

Since the Charter of Rights and Freedoms was entrenched in the Constitution, the Supreme Court of Canada has assumed a much more prominent role in our political system. (Greg Vickers)

In modern democracies, political demands are often expressed in the language of rights and freedoms. This chapter examines some of the controversies associated with rights and freedoms, and considers the impact of the Canadian Charter of Rights and Freedoms on Canadian politics. Topics discussed include:

- ❏ What do rights and freedoms mean?
- ❏ The origins and meanings of rights.
- ❏ The pre-Charter era: 1867–1981.
- ❏ The Charter and constitutional supremacy.
- ❏ The 'notwithstanding' clause.
- ❏ Applying the Charter.
- ❏ Individual rights and freedoms.
- ❏ Equality and the Charter.

CHAPTER SIX

RIGHTS AND FREEDOMS

Like the Ten Commandments, rights and freedoms are usually expressed in uncompromising language. Those who argue the case for a woman's right to control her body, a fetus's right to life, a person's freedom of conscience, or an individual's right not to be discriminated against on the basis of race, gender, or some other personal attribute that is beyond one's control typically advance their claims as moral absolutes. Moral absolutes, like biblical injunctions, are non-negotiable. Either a right or freedom exists or it does not. And if it exists, it must be respected in all cases and not simply when governments or the majority find it convenient to do so.

In reality, however, no right or freedom is absolute. There are two reasons for this. One is that rights and freedoms may collide, necessitating some compromise. For example, does freedom of expression protect the right of an individual to shout 'Fire!' in a crowded theatre? This hypothetical case was used by American Supreme Court Justice Oliver Wendell Holmes to explain when and why limits on free speech are justified. Holmes established the 'clear and present danger' test,[1] according to which freedom of expression could legitimately be curtailed when it posed an unmistakable and immediate danger to others. Falsely shouting 'Fire!' in a crowded theatre obviously endangers the safety of others. To guarantee an individual's freedom of expression in such circumstances could jeopardize the right of other individuals to be protected from unreasonable danger.

In fact, the trade-offs between competing values are seldom this simple. Should freedom of expression protect people who publicly communicate statements that 'willfully promote hatred'[2] against some group distinguished by race, ethnicity, language, or religion? When do national secu-

rity considerations or society's interest in preventing trafficking in drugs warrant wiretaps and other violations of the individual's right to privacy? How far should the public's interest in minimizing fraudulent claims on the public purse be allowed to justify intrusions into the homes and lives of welfare recipients? Is affirmative action a legitimate means for promoting social equality, or is it reverse discrimination against those who are not members of the groups targeted for special consideration? When does one right or freedom 'trump' another? Who should determine these issues, the courts or the people's elected representatives?

A second reason why no right or freedom can be treated as an absolute is because this is often impractical. If, for example, a constitution guarantees the right of official-language minorities to public education or services in their mother tongue, does that mean that all government services, everywhere in the country, should be available in each of the official languages? Does it mean that minority-language education should be provided in a community with a bare handful of families demanding their own school? Common sense suggests that there are limits to how far, and in what circumstances, the principles of linguistic equality and minority rights should apply.

What about administrative procedures determined by budget and personnel restrictions that impose hardship on individuals? For example, in 1990 an Ontario Superior Court judge decided that the time spent by many accused persons in jail or on bail while waiting for their trial date violated s. 11(b) of the Charter, i.e., the right 'to be tried within a reasonable time'. Given the existing number of judges and the limits on court resources, enormous backlogs had developed. He proceeded to dismiss hundreds of cases that had been in the dock for months. Can the bureaucratic procedures and budget constraints that lead to these delays and inflict real hardship on individuals be justified as 'practical limitations' on rights? Or are they matters of mere administrative convenience or policy that should not take precedence over individual rights?

Dilemmas like these await us at every turn. Despite this, and despite the passions usually unleashed by such controversies, rights and freedoms have had a low profile in Canadian politics for most of this country's history. The courts were reluctant to question the authority of elected legislatures to pass laws, whatever their content and effects, except to decide whether the matter in question constitutionally belonged to Ottawa or the provinces. As a result, civil liberties issues were transformed—deformed, some would say—into squabbles over the federal-provincial division of powers.

This changed with the passage of the Charter of Rights and Freedoms in 1982. As we noted in Chapter 5, the Charter entrenched various rights and freedoms in the Constitution. Moreover, by establishing the principle of constitutional supremacy (sections 32 and 52[1] of the Constitution Act, 1982), the 1982 constitutional reforms placed these rights more or less beyond the interference of governments because section 1 of the Charter states that these rights and freedoms are 'subject only to such reasonable limits prescribed by law as can be demonstrably justified in a free and democratic society', and section 33(1) enables either Parliament or a provincial legislature to declare that a particular law or provision of a law shall operate even if it violates rights or freedoms guaranteed in sections 2 or 7 to 15 of the Charter. Together, sections 1 and 33 operate to maintain some measure of parliamentary supremacy over the courts and the Charter.

There is little doubt, however, that the Charter has decisively changed the face of Canadian politics. The authority of elected legislatures has receded before the authority of the Constitution and the courts. A transformation has taken place in the venues and language of Canadian politics.

The discourse of 'rights', always a part of the political scene, has assumed much greater prominence since passage of the Charter. Individuals, organized interests, and even governments have turned increasingly to litigation as a means of influencing public policy. It has been estimated that an average of roughly 1,000 Charter cases a year are decided by Canadian courts,[3] reflecting the increased importance of the courts as a forum for political conflict. Since the Charter's passage the Supreme Court of Canada has handed down approximately 200 Charter rulings, including many that have had major effects on public policy. As Michael Mandel puts it, 'the Charter has legalized our politics.'[4]

With what consequences? Which groups (leaving aside lawyers) have won as a result of Charter politics, and which have lost ground? Has Canadian society become more democratic as a result of the unprecedented prominence accorded to rights and freedoms since the Charter's passage? These are crucial questions for which there are no easy answers. Let us begin by examining the concepts of rights and freedoms. We will then examine the history of rights and freedoms in Canada, pre- and post-Charter.

COMING TO TERMS: WHAT DO RIGHTS AND FREEDOMS MEAN?

Although there is a long tradition in Western constitutional law of distinguishing between rights and freedoms, often the distinction is not so straightforward in practice. An individual's freedom to believe something or to behave in a particular way is often expressed in terms of a right. 'I have a right to picket this employer' (freedom of assembly), or 'I have a right to distribute pamphlets explaining that the [you fill in the blank] are responsible for most of the evils that beset the world' (freedom of expression). Likewise, the right to fair and equal treatment by the law is often framed in terms of the conditions necessary to ensure an individual's freedom. For example, an accused person's right to be tried within a reasonable time—a right guaranteed by section 11(b) of the Charter—is probably violated if he or she has to spend a year in prison or 'free' but under onerous bail restrictions before the case comes to trial. Obviously, this individual's personal freedom is seriously compromised in such circumstances. Or consider the case of abortion. Those who argue against legal restrictions on a woman's access to abortion claim that such laws violate a woman's right to control her body, an important dimension of the right to privacy. In this case the right being claimed is nothing less than freedom from interference by the state, or what civil liberties lawyer Alan Borovoy calls the 'right to be left alone'.

Rights and freedoms are not, therefore, watertight compartments in reality. Nevertheless, constitutional experts usually reserve the term 'rights' for those individual and group entitlements that 'are considered so fundamental to human dignity that they receive special protection under the law and usually under the constitution of a country.'[5] Freedoms involve an individual's liberty to do or believe certain things without restraint by government. Whereas the defence of rights often requires some government action, the protection of freedoms requires that government refrain from interfering in certain matters. Rights suggest an active role for government, freedoms a limited one.

Civil liberties or *civil rights* are terms that are sometimes used to refer to all the basic rights and freedoms of citizens. Under the influence of the United Nations' Universal Declaration of Human Rights (1948), the term **human rights** has become the more commonly used designation for this bundle of rights and freedoms. Included among them are the following:

- *Political rights/fundamental freedoms.* These include freedom of association, assembly, expression, the media, conscience and religion, and the right to privacy.
- *Democratic rights.* Among these are the rights of all adult persons to vote and stand for public office. Requirements that elections periodically be held

and that the law apply equally to those who govern and those who are governed are also important democratic rights.

- *Legal rights.* These are essentially procedural rights intended to ensure the fair and equal treatment of individuals under the law. They include, *inter alia*, the right to due process of law, freedom from arbitrary arrest, the right to a fair hearing, the right to legal counsel, and the right not to be subjected to cruel or unusual punishment.
- *Economic rights.* Although they usually are not listed as a separate category of entrenched rights, economic rights occupy an important place in all capitalist democracies. They include the right to own property and not to be deprived of it without fair compensation, the right to withhold one's labour, and freedom of contract.
- *Equality rights.* This is the most recent and probably the most controversial category of rights. The American Constitution, the first modern constitution to include an entrenched guarantee of equality rights, refers only to every person's right to 'equal protection of the laws'.[6] The more recent tendency, however, has been to enumerate the proscribed bases of legal discrimination, such as race, religion, ethnicity, gender, and age. Canada's Charter also includes mental or physical disability and has been interpreted by the courts to prohibit discrimination based on sexual orientation.

These five categories by no means exhaust the rights that may be protected by law. *Language rights* represent an important category of group rights in many societies, Canada included. Other group rights, such as for religious minorities or Native peoples, may also be protected by law. Some argue that *social rights*, or what are sometimes called *entitlements*, including the right to a job, economic security, decent housing, and adequate health care, should also have the status of entrenched constitutional rights. *Environmental rights* have also been advocated by some groups, including the Canadian Bar Association.

In Canada, many of the main categories of human rights are entrenched in the Charter. Table

6.1 identifies the sections of the Charter that correspond to each of them. A word of warning: this classification should be read as a general guide to the location of specific rights in the Charter. Due to the imagination of lawyers, the complex circumstances of particular cases, and the inevitable overlap that exists between different rights claims, the basis for a particular right may be found under what appears to be an unrelated heading.

For example, unions have argued that collective bargaining is a right that belongs to working people. They have claimed (unsuccessfully) that it should be implied by and protected under section 2(d) of the Charter, which guarantees 'freedom of association'. Business interests have argued (successfully) that section 8 of the Charter, which guarantees 'the right to be secure against unreasonable search and seizure', limits the search powers that were being exercised by a government agency with responsibility for investigating collusive business practices.[7] Protection for economic rights was found under a legal rights guarantee. Tobacco companies challenged a federal law banning the advertising of their products by arguing that it violated the Charter's guarantee of 'freedom of expression' (s. 2[6]).[8] An economic right was disguised as a fundamental freedom. But perhaps the most striking case of one sort of right—again, an economic one—being claimed under a different category of rights involved business's successful challenge to the federal Lord's Day Act.[9] Hardly anyone seriously believed that the case had anything much to do with the Charter's guarantee of freedom of religion (s. 2[a]). It had a lot to do, however, with the right to make money on Sundays.

It is no accident that cases involving what obviously are economic claims are packaged in the language of other rights. Except for the Charter's reference to mobility rights, a right intended to guarantee the free movement of Canadian citizens between provinces, it is silent in regard to economic rights. Moreover, the Supreme Court of Canada has declared on a number of occasions that the Charter does not include economic and property rights. '[T]he overwhelming preoccupation of the Charter', declared the majority in a 1987 decision denying the right to strike, 'is with individual, political, and democratic rights with conspicuous inattention to economic and property rights.'[10] This interpretation of the Charter has also worked against business interests on occasion. In particular, business's efforts to find some protection for property rights in the Charter's guarantee of security of the person (s. 7) have been expressly rejected by the Court.[11]

Denied explicit constitutional recognition of their rights, economic interests have urged their claims under what appear to be non-economic provisions of the Charter. This has produced some curious distortions, as the protagonists to a political conflict attempt to fit their claims into the categories available under the Charter and the interpretative tendencies of judges. Legalized politics, Mandel argues, inevitably favours established interests and serves to reinforce the status quo because of the biases built into the law and the legal/judicial profession (see Chapter 8). Yet, 'the legalization of politics' does not express strongly enough the *deformation* of politics that the Charter has encouraged. This deformation is not limited to economic conflicts. Moreover, it is not clear, despite Mandel's claims, that established interests have been the chief beneficiaries of Charter politics. Ted Morton argues that groups located primarily on the left of the political spectrum, groups that he labels 'the Court Party', have been far more successful than so-called establishment interests in using the Charter to win political victories.[12]

ON THE ORIGINS AND MEANINGS OF RIGHTS

There is no inevitability to either the precise rights recognized by the Constitution or the meanings that come to be associated with them. Rights, like a society's notions of justice, are constructed out of concrete historical circumstances. The rights claimed in present-day Canada and the rights discourses that emerge around these claims and

Table 6.1   Human Rights and the Charter

Rights Category	Pre-Charter Protections	Charter Protections
1. Political rights/fundamental freedoms	Common-law protections implied in the preamble of the Constitution Act, 1867	s. 2
2. Democratic rights	Constitution Act, 1867, ss. 41, 50, 84, 85	ss. 3-5
3. Legal rights	Common law, criminal code	ss. 7-14
4. Economic rights	Common-law rights re: contract, property, etc.	s. 6 (and implied under some other sections)
5. Equality rights	Common law; s. 93 of Constitution Act, 1867 guaranteeing educational rights of religious denominations	ss. 15, 28
6. Language rights	Constitution Act, 1867 s. 133	ss. 16-23
7. Aboriginal rights	Treaties	s. 25; also s. 35 of Constitution Act, 1982
8. Social rights	None	None

counterclaims are very different from those of even a generation ago. And much of Canadian rights discourse would be unrecognizable in a society like Iran, where very different religious, cultural, and economic forces have contributed to the recognition of and meaning ascribed to rights. There are, therefore, no absolute rights that may be adduced from human history. What may appear to be the most obvious and uncontroversial rights claims—for example, the right to vote or the right to express one's personal beliefs—are denied in many societies.

Rights come from political struggles. A claim made by an individual or a group will be expressed as a right only when it is denied or placed in jeopardy by the words or actions of some other party. For example, the claim that a woman has a right to abort her pregnancy arises because of legal and practical restrictions on access to abortion. The experience of limitations on freedom of speech, religion/conscience, or association produced calls for their constitutional protection. Likewise, when a linguistic group claims the protection or promotion of its language

as a right, this is an indication that conflict exists between linguistic groups in that society.

Political struggle is a necessary condition for rights claims. It is not, however, a sufficient condition. Only some political conflicts acquire the character of rights issues. To be recognized as legitimate, a rights claim must be successfully linked to one or more of a society's fundamental values. These fundamental values operate as limits on rights discourse.

Consider the familiar issue of abortion. Those who argue for a woman's right to abort her pregnancy when she chooses have often linked this rights claim to individual freedom of choice, a fundamental value in liberal democratic society. Those who oppose abortion, or who favour serious restrictions on access to it, often argue that the human fetus has a right to life, the most fundamental of rights in any civilized society. Those who favour access to abortion would, of course, object to the imputation that they do not value human life, just as those who oppose abortion would deny that they undervalue individual freedom. Behind these rights, as behind all of the rights widely recognized in democratic political systems, are one or more fundamental values, such as the equality of human beings, the autonomy of the individual, and, most importantly, the nature of the good society.

The abortion issues illustrates well how rights claims tend to be squeezed into existing ideological and legal categories and how unconventional political discourses are discouraged by legalized politics. When individual women, women's organizations, and abortionists like Henry Morgentaler have been successful in challenging legal restrictions on access to abortion, this has been because their case has been framed in legal arguments and moral claims that fall within the dominant ideology. Beginning in the 1970s, Morgentaler was involved in a number of court cases where he was charged with violating section 251 of Canada's Criminal Code, which placed limits on a woman's access to abortion. He was acquitted by juries on a number of separate occasions, each time successfully invoking the 'defence of necessity'. This common-law principle, applied to medical procedures, provides immunity from criminal prosecution if the procedure is necessary to save the life of the patient. Pregnancy was treated, in these cases, as an illness and abortion as a medical procedure necessary to deal with it.

The passage of the Charter opened up new legal avenues to abortion advocates. In a 1983 Ontario trial, Morgentaler's lawyer argued that Canada's existing abortion law violated a long list of rights and freedoms that the Charter had entrenched in Canada's Constitution. These included freedom of conscience and expression, the rights to life, liberty, and security of the person, and the right not to be subjected to cruel and unusual treatment. Anti-abortion activist Joe Borowski was busy invoking some of the same rights, i.e., the Charter's section 7 guarantee of life, liberty, and security of the person, arguing that the unborn fetus should be considered a legal person entitled to these rights.[13] Canada's abortion law was eventually ruled unconstitutional by a 1987 Supreme Court decision in which the majority ruled that it violated security of the person. But the same majority agreed that the state has an interest in protecting the fetus, although at what stage of fetal development and in what circumstances the Court did not say. This acknowledgement of fetal rights provided some encouragement to the anti-abortion coalition, whose political strategy focused increasingly on claiming the personhood of the unborn.

When appealing to public opinion and in arguing their case before the courts, both pro- and anti-abortion forces have resorted to symbols and values that are well established in the dominant ideology. The political temptation to do so is overwhelming. But the consequences of fitting a group's objectives into the available framework of rights discourse, including the concepts and interpretations that the legal system provides, tend to be conservative in two main ways.

First, the issue may be misdefined or, what amounts to the same thing, defined in terms that conform to prevailing notions of what rights are legitimate and what strategies are appropriate for pursuing them. This delegitimizes alternative ways of conceptualizing the issue—and even what is really at issue—and the discourses associated with these alternatives. For example, is the abortion issue primarily about 'security of the person' and about procedural fairness in the application of the law? These are the rights that have provided the basis for successful legal challenges to Canada's abortion law. Or is the struggle over abortion really just an element in a larger political struggle involving male domination of women and/or competing notions of the good society? Most feminists would take the latter position, arguing that legal restrictions on access to abortion and the tendency in law to treat abortion as a health problem are manifestations of the social dominance of males, in this instance, of males defining female experiences. Frontal attacks like this tend, however, to be labelled—and largely dismissed—as radical and unrepresentative of majority opinion. Moreover, the sweep and general character of such critiques pose a strategic dilemma. 'Patriarchy' is not a concept recognized by the law. The law does, however, recognize various individual rights. Strategically, then, it makes sense for women's groups to use the legal tools available in order to make a difference in the short term. But in succumbing to what Carol Smart calls the 'siren call of law',[14] the sweep and character of feminist demands may be changed.

The second way in which recourse to rights discourse and the law may result in conservative consequences involves the idea that legal solutions to a problem are possible and desirable. '[I]n engaging with law to produce law reforms', argues Smart, 'the women's movement is tacitly accepting the significance of law in regulating social order. In this process the idea that law is the means to resolve social problems gains strength and the idea that the lawyers . . . are the technocrats of an unfolding Utopia becomes taken for granted. . . . while some law reforms may benefit women, *it is certain that all law reforms empower law*.'[15] (See Box 6.1.) But the law and the legal/judicial profession, as argued in Chapter 8, have some inherent biases towards the status quo.

RIGHTS AND THEIR PROTECTION

During the 1980–1 debate on constitutional reform, critics of an entrenched charter of rights warned that entrenchment would lead to the Americanization of Canadian politics. Since then, they have lamented that their prediction has come true. The 'Americanization' they warned of, and that many still regret, has two main aspects. One involves a more prominent policy role for unelected judges and a related decline in the status of elected legislatures. The other is an increase in recourse to the courts to solve political disputes.

Some of those who opposed entrenched rights argued that rights and freedoms are better protected by elected legislatures, accountable to the electorate for their actions, than by unelected judges. By 'better' they meant that the decisions of elected politicians are more likely to correspond with the sentiments of citizens—or at least that if they do not there exists a democratic mechanism, i.e., elections, to hold politicians accountable for their choices. Rights, the opponents of entrenchment argued, should not be interpreted independently of popular opinion. Nor should important political controversies be determined by unelected officials.

What the critics denounced as the undemocratic flaws of entrenchment, advocates of the Charter acclaimed as its virtues. Rights, they argued, should not be subject to the vicissitudes of public opinion as registered in the legislature. The fact that judges are not elected and are virtu-

---

BOX 6.1   Lawyers and the Charter

The support of legal academics for the Charter is part of the modern trend of the transfer of political influence to professional 'experts'. Keren has observed that all professionals 'derive their status from their possession of esoteric and easily monopolized skills and their political engagement may be seen as a means to increase the scope of issue areas in which those skills can be demonstrated. . . . The more social matters are discussed in professional terms, the more symbolic assets are translated into economic and political gains.' In the context of the Canadian Charter (and 'rights instruments' in other Western democracies), lawyers have a vested interest in redefining policy issues as rights issues, since the latter call into play their 'expertise' and marginalize the non-expert opinions of most legislators and voters.

F.L. Morton and Rainer Knopff, *The Charter Revolution and the Court Party* (Peterborough, Ont.: Broadview Press, 2000), 145.

ally unremovable before the age of 75 serves to protect, not undermine, democracy. What sort of democracy, entrenchment advocates ask, would permit rights and freedoms to depend on shifting popular sentiments and politicians' calculations of political expediency?

The difference between the opponents and advocates of entrenchment is not over the importance of rights. It is not even primarily about the appropriate balance between the rights of individuals and minorities versus those of the majority. As unflinching a civil libertarian as Alan Borovoy, general counsel of the Canadian Civil Liberties Association, argues against the entrenchment of rights.[16] The difference between these two positions is over how best to *protect rights*. Those who advocate the American model of entrenched rights prefer to put their faith in the Constitution and the judges who interpret it. Those who prefer the British model of parliamentary supremacy are more dubious about judge-made law and more inclined to place their trust in the prudence and democratic responsiveness of elected governments.

Does the record of rights enforcement in different countries permit us to draw conclusions about whether the American or British model is 'best'? Has the Charter made a difference in how well rights are protected in Canada? There are no easy answers to these questions. Rights activists are themselves divided in their assessment of the impact of entrenchment. But if definitive answers are elusive, we can at least attempt to understand how rights have been argued and enforced in Canadian politics. The Charter, we will see, represents an important watershed.

The Pre-Charter Era: 1867–1981

There is not a single reference to the subject of rights in R. MacGregor Dawson's *Constitutional Issues in Canada, 1900–1931*, published in 1933.[17] In Dawson's *The Government of Canada* (1947), the first textbook on Canadian government, one finds a mere handful of references to fundamental rights

and liberties.[18] J.A. Corry and J.E. Hodgetts's *Democratic Government and Politics* (1946)[19] pays greater attention to rights, devoting an entire chapter to a comparison of civil liberties in Britain, the United States, and Canada. Generally, however, rights issues occupied a distinctly marginal place in Canadian political science and even in legal circles until the middle of this century.

A couple of factors were responsible for blunting the profile of rights questions. The most important was undoubtedly federalism. The Constitution Act, 1867 contains few references to the rights and freedoms of Canadians. It does, however, include a detailed catalogue of the 'rights' of governments, i.e., the legislative and fiscal powers of Ottawa and the provinces. Faithful to the principle of parliamentary supremacy, the courts were unwilling to overrule the authority of elected legislatures. As a result, throughout most of Canada's history issues that clearly involved the protection of rights and freedoms were dealt with by the courts as federalism questions. To have a chance at success, therefore, rights claims had to be packaged in the constitutional categories of federalism. The resulting jurisprudence was bizarre, to say the least. Consider the following cases:

- *Reference re Alberta Statutes* (Alberta Press case, 1938).[20] The law in question was the Accurate News and Information Act, passed by the Alberta legislature in 1937. It imposed censorship restrictions on the province's newspapers, based on the Social Credit government's belief that the press was unfairly critical of its policies. Ottawa referred this and two other pieces of Social Credit legislation to the Supreme Court for a ruling on their constitutionality. The Court was unanimous in striking down the press censorship law. Two of the judgements in this case referred to the 'right of free public discussion of public affairs' as being a right fundamental to parliamentary democracy and implied under the preamble to the Constitution Act, 1867, which states that Canada is adopting 'a Constitution similar in principle to that of the United Kingdom'. But both of these judgements, although using somewhat different reasoning, suggested that the federal government possessed the authority to impose restrictions on freedom of the press. The Alberta law was struck down essentially on federalism grounds.

- *Saumur v. City of Quebec* (1953).[21] Quebec City had passed a bylaw forbidding the distribution in the streets of any printed material without the prior consent of the chief of police. Without explicitly singling out any group, this bylaw was intended to curb proselytizing activities by the Jehovah's Witness sect, whose activities and teachings strongly offended Catholic Church authorities. In a five-to-four decision, the Court struck down the bylaw. An analysis of the judges' reasoning reveals just how disinclined they were to place the protection of fundamental freedoms over the authority of government. On the majority side, four of the five justices decided that the bylaw was ultra vires (i.e., beyond the legal authority of the government in question). The fifth was willing to concede that the regulation fell within provincial jurisdiction, but felt that the right to disseminate religious material was protected by Quebec's Freedom of Worship Act. On the dissenting side, two of the judges argued that the bylaw fell within the province's jurisdiction over civil rights. No one suggested that freedom of religious expression ought to be protected from interference by any level of government.

- *Switzman v. Elbling* (Padlock Case) (1957).[22] In 1937 the Quebec government had passed a law declaring illegal the use of a house for the propagation of Communism, authorizing the Quebec police to put a padlock on premises where such activities were suspected. The Supreme Court of Canada ruled that the impugned Act had the effect of making the propagation of Communism a crime. Since criminal law is under the exclusive jurisdiction of Ottawa, the 'Padlock Law' was struck down as being ultra vires. The issue of political censorship was raised by a couple of justices, but this was not the basis for the Court's ruling.

- *Attorney General of Canada and Dupond v. Montreal* (1978).[23] This case involved a Montreal bylaw that restricted freedom of assembly in public places. The bylaw was used during the 1960s to prevent public demonstrations during a period of political turmoil and occasional terrorist incidents. By a five-to-three vote the Supreme Court upheld the constitutionality of this restriction. The majority argued that the impugned bylaw regulated matters of a local or private nature and therefore came under the authority of the province. Interestingly, the dissenting judges did not focus on the issue of freedom of assembly. Instead, they argued that the Montreal bylaw was ultra vires because it represented a sort of 'mini-Criminal Code' and thus intruded on Ottawa's exclusive authority to make criminal law. As a final note, the judgement in this case was unequivocal in dismissing the relevance of the 1960 Canadian Bill of Rights. 'None of the freedoms referred to', wrote Justice Beetz, 'is so enshrined in the constitution as to be above the reach of competent legislation.'[24]

Federalism was not the only factor responsible for the relatively low profile of rights issues until well into this century. Public opinion was generally sanguine about the treatment of rights and freedoms in Canada. The feeling of most informed Canadians was probably that rights were best protected by legislatures, the common law, and a vigilant public—the system that Canada had inherited from the United Kingdom. But increasing doubts about the adequacy of these guarantees were being expressed during the 1940s and 1950s. These doubts were sown by such apparent rights violations as Quebec's infamous 'Padlock Law' (1937), the Alberta government's attempt to censor the press (1937), the threatened deportation of Japanese Canadians in 1945–6, and the arbitrary measures taken during the Gouzenko spy affair of 1946. These constituted, according to political scientist Norman Ward, 'disturbing signs of a weakening concern by Dominion and provincial governments for personal rights and liberties'.[25] Corry and Hodgetts agreed, arguing that the protections provided under British parliamentary government were not sufficient in a young country facing the challenge of absorbing large numbers of persons of diverse ethnic origins and cultural backgrounds.[26]

This growing concern over civil liberties was shared by influential groups like the Canadian Bar Association. The solution, they argued, was a bill of rights that would be entrenched in the Constitution. Canada's participation in the United Nations, and the human rights commitments entered into through the UN, reinforced the voices of those calling for constitutionally entrenched rights. When the Conservative Party came to power in 1957 under the leadership of John Diefenbaker, who had long been an outspoken advocate of entrenched rights, the timing for a Bill of Rights seemed propitious.

But there was a major snag. A constitutional Bill of Rights would affect the powers of both Ottawa and the provinces and, it was believed, would therefore require provincial consent. It was clear that some of the provinces would oppose entrenchment, and consequently the Conservative government chose to introduce the Bill of Rights as a statute, requiring only the approval of the House of Commons and the Senate. The Bill of Rights became law on 10 August 1960.

The Bill of Rights proved to be a major disappointment for civil libertarians. The first Supreme Court decisions on its application were very conservative. In a 1963 case involving a challenge to the federal Lord's Day Act, the Court took the position that the Bill of Rights only reaffirmed the rights and freedoms status quo that existed at the time it became law. Speaking for the majority, Justice Ritchie declared that '[The Canadian Bill of Rights] is not concerned with "human rights and fundamental freedoms" in any abstract sense, but rather with such "rights and freedoms" as they existed in Canada immediately before the statute was enacted.'[27]

After nearly a decade of judgements that, to paraphrase Saskatchewan former Chief Justice Emmett Hall, whittled away at the Bill of Rights,[28] the Supreme Court suddenly gave evidence of abandoning its cautious approach. The case involved an Indian, Joseph Drybones, who was convicted under section 94(b) of the Indian Act. This provision of the Act made it an offence for an Indian to be intoxicated off a reserve. In challenging this provision, Drybones's lawyer argued that it conflicted with the Canadian Bill of Rights guarantee of 'equality before the law', subjecting Indians to criminal sanctions that other people were not exposed to. This was obviously true. But if the Court remained faithful to its earlier interpretation, this would not be sufficient to render the discrimination unconstitutional.

By a five-to-three vote the Supreme Court used the Bill of Rights to strike down section 94 of the Indian Act.[29] This proved, however, to be an aberration. Perhaps realizing the Pandora's box they were opening through this more activist interpretation of the Bill of Rights, a majority of the judges retreated from this position after Drybones. This became crystal clear in the 1974 Lavell case,[30] where the majority upheld the constitutionality of another provision of the Indian Act against a challenge that it denied equality before the law.

Another nail was hammered into the Bill of Rights' coffin by the Court's decision in Hogan v. The Queen (1975).[31] In Hogan, a person suspected of driving while intoxicated refused to take a breathalyzer test before seeing his lawyer. He ultimately took the test and this evidence was key to his conviction. The question before the Supreme Court was whether evidence should be excluded if it has been obtained in an improper manner. Under the common law, Canadian judges had followed the rule that such evidence would be admitted so long as it was relevant to the case at hand. But the Canadian Bill of Rights included a number of legal rights, including in section 2(c)(ii) the right of an accused or detained person 'to retain and instruct counsel without delay'.

The Supreme Court was unwilling to apply the Bill of Rights in this case. It appeared, therefore, that the Bill of Rights could not be used to strike down conflicting federal legislation—at least not laws on the books before 1960—and that the Bill of Rights did not take precedence over established rules of the common law. Chief Justice Laskin's dissenting argument that the Bill of Rights should be interpreted as a 'quasi-constitutional instrument' was never supported by a majority of his colleagues. The glimmer of hope that the *Drybones* decision had sparked was extinguished during the 1970s, producing renewed calls for constitutionally entrenched rights.

Before passage of the Charter, the only rights entrenched in Canada's Constitution were associated with religion and language. Section 93 of the Constitution Act, 1867 declares that the educational rights of denominational minorities may not be diminished from what they were when a province entered Confederation. Section 133 establishes the equal standing of French and English in Parliament and in federal courts, and in the Quebec legislature and in the courts of that province. Neither of these sections proved to be very effective in protecting minority rights.

The major test of section 93 involved the Manitoba Public Schools Act. This law eliminated the Catholic and Protestant schools that had existed in the province and replaced them with a single public school system. In *Barrett*,[32] the Judicial Committee of the Privy Council decided that this law did not violate the educational rights of the Roman Catholic minority because Catholics, like the members of any religious denomination, were free to set up their own private schools. Of course they would have to pay for them out of their own pockets, in addition to having to pay the local and provincial taxes that financed the public schools. This, in the JCPC's view, did not diminish the rights they had enjoyed when both Protestant and Catholic schools were financed out of public revenues.

In two other cases involving section 93, the courts refused to accept the argument that this section also protected the educational rights of language minorities. The argument had at least a ring of plausibility because of the fact that, historically, the Roman Catholic schools in Manitoba were predominantly francophone and in Ontario they were often francophone, while Quebec's Protes-

tant schools were anglophone. Thus, when in 1913 the Ontario government issued regulations banning the use of French as a language of instruction in both public and separate (Catholic) schools, this had a negligible impact on public schools but dealt a major blow to the predominantly francophone Catholic schools of eastern Ontario. The issue arose again in the 1970s when the Quebec government passed Bill 22, restricting access to the province's English-language schools, most of which were under the control of Protestant school boards. In both instances the courts rejected outright the claim that section 93 should be read as a protection for linguistic rights in addition to denominational ones.[33]

From the standpoint of promoting bilingualism outside of Quebec, the courts' unwillingness to read language rights into section 93 represented a real setback. On the other hand, the 'victories' for language rights in a pair of Supreme Court decisions handed down in 1978 and 1979 produced little in the way of practical consequences. Both of these decisions involved the limited guarantee of bilingualism established by section 133 of the Constitution Act, 1867. In both cases the Court declared that this guarantee was beyond the interference of governments, thus repudiating the idea that no action lay outside the competence of Parliament or a provincial legislature so long as it did not encroach on the constitutional powers of the other level of government.

In *Attorney General of Quebec v. Blaikie*,[34] the Court upheld a Quebec Superior Court decision that had ruled unconstitutional those sections of Quebec's Bill 101 that attempted to make French the sole official language in that province. While Bill 101 did not ban the use of English from the legislature and the province's courts, and the Quebec government continued to print and publish laws and legislative documents in both languages, the law's clear intent was to make French the only official language for all government activities and the dominant language in the province's courts. This, the courts decided, violated the spirit—if not the strict letter—of section 133.

The issue in *Attorney General of Manitoba v. Forest* (1979)[35] was essentially the same, although the circumstances were quite different. In 1890, the Manitoba legislature had passed a law making English the sole official language of the province's government and courts, and took the further step of actually banning the use of French in the legislature and the courts. This flatly contradicted the Manitoba Act, 1870 (an Act of the British Parliament creating the province of Manitoba), which imposed on Manitoba the same language requirements that section 133 of the Constitution Act, 1867 imposed on Quebec. Ironically, Manitoba's Official Language Act, 1890 had been ruled unconstitutional by a lower court judge in 1892 and then again in 1909. These rulings were apparently ignored by the provincial government. The successful challenge in the *Forest* case was a hollow victory, to say the least. In the words of René Lévesque, Quebec's Premier at the time, the decision came 90 years too late to make a difference for Manitoba francophones.

Life in the Charter Era

It is probably fair to say that the changes generated by the Charter have far exceeded the expectations of all but a few of the politicians and experts who presided at its birth. On a quantitative level, the Charter has been the direct stimulus for explosive growth in the number of rights cases that come before the courts. On average, about 1,000 Charter cases are decided by Canadian courts each year, and about a two dozen of these are rulings by the Supreme Court or one of the provincial superior courts. About 50 federal statutes have been challenged using the Charter in cases that reached the Supreme Court of Canada. In some cases, for example, the Immigration Act and the Income Tax Act, there have been dozens of Charter-based rulings handed down by the Supreme Court. An even greater number of provincial laws have been the subject of Supreme Court Charter rulings. In 2001 about one-fifth of the appeals heard by the Supreme Court were constitutional and about three-quarters of these were based on the Charter.[36]

In terms of 'quality', the change produced by the Charter has been no less pronounced. The previous pattern of deciding rights issues as federalism cases, asking only whether a government was transgressing the jurisdictional turf of the other level of government, has been abandoned. Rights issues are now dealt with head on, argued by litigants and decided by judges on the basis of the Charter. Moreover, the courts have shed some of their traditional reluctance to question the substance of duly enacted laws and regulations. Emboldened by the Charter's unambiguous declarations that the 'Constitution is the supreme law of Canada' and that the courts have exclusive authority to interpret and enforce the Charter's guarantees, judges have struck down provisions in dozens of federal and provincial statutes. As we will see, although judges are quite aware of the expanded role they play in the political process, they continue to exercise a measure of self-restraint when it comes to second-guessing elected governments.

REASONABLE LIMITS AND THE CHARTER

The courts are 'invited' to exercise self-restraint by the opening words of the Charter. Section 1 declares that the guarantees set forth in the Charter shall be 'subject only to such reasonable limits prescribed by law as can be demonstrably justified in a free and democratic society'. What are these 'reasonable limits'? The Supreme Court established a test in the case of *The Queen v. Oakes* (1986).[37] The first part of this test asks whether a government's objective in limiting a right is of sufficient importance to warrant such an encroachment. The second part of the test asks whether the extent of the limitation is proportionate to the importance of the government's objective. In order to satisfy this second criterion, a limitation must meet three conditions: (1) it must be rationally connected to the government's objective;

(2) it should impair the right in question as little as is necessary to meet the government's objective; and (3) the harm done to rights by a limitation must not exceed the good that it accomplishes.

In *Oakes*, the Court was asked to determine whether a 'reverse onus' provision in the Narcotic Control Act violated the presumption of innocence set forth in section 11(d) of the Charter. Under that Act, a person found guilty of possessing drugs was automatically considered guilty of trafficking unless he could prove his innocence on this more serious charge. The Court did not question the importance of the objective associated with this provision of the Act, i.e., to prevent drug trafficking. But in applying the second part of the test, the justices decided that the means was disproportionate to the end.

The separation of legislative ends, part one of the *Oakes* test, from an assessment of the means used to accomplish them may appear to be a way around the thorny problem of judges second-guessing the decisions of duly elected governments. In fact, however, it is not possible to answer such questions as whether a right is impaired as little as possible in the circumstances or whether the means are proportionate to the ends without trespassing into the realm of political value judgements. Since *Oakes*, the courts have been reluctant to question the ends associated with laws and regulations limiting rights. But they have not been shy about using the second part of the *Oakes* test to dismiss governments' section 1 justifications.

This was apparent in the Supreme Court's decision in *Ford v. Attorney General of Quebec* (1988).[38] The case involved a challenge to those sections of Quebec's Bill 101 that prohibited commercial advertising in languages other than French. The Quebec government argued that this limitation was necessary to preserve the economic value of the French language and the predominantly French character of the province. The Court accepted that this was a perfectly legitimate policy goal (it passed part one of the *Oakes* test), but argued that the Quebec government had not

shown that 'the requirement of the use of French only is either necessary for the achievement of the legislative objective or proportionate to it.'[39] Not content to let matters rest here, the Court suggested what the Quebec government perhaps should have done to accomplish its legislative purpose in a way acceptable under section 1 of the Charter. 'French could be required', it suggested, 'in addition to any other language or it could be required to have greater visibility than that accorded to other languages.'[40]

In fairness to judges, why shouldn't they give legislators an idea of how the law needs to be changed to bring it into line with their interpretation of the Constitution? The point is, however, that means and ends are not neatly separable in the real world of politics. Moreover, tests like means being proportional to the ends just beg the question: who should determine how much or little of something is enough? Is proportionality an appropriate matter for unelected judges to decide, or should this be determined by elected legislatures?

These questions resurfaced with a vengeance when the Supreme Court ruled on 21 September 1995 that the federal ban on tobacco advertising violated the Charter's guarantee of freedom of expression. The total ban did not, in the eyes of the majority of the Court, satisfy the second part of the *Oakes* test. 'The government had before it a variety of less intrusive measures when it enacted the total ban on advertising', observed Madam Justice Beverley McLachlin. Commenting on the government's refusal to allow the Court to see documents pertaining to advertising and tobacco consumption, including one on the alternatives to a total ban on advertising, she added, 'In the face of this behaviour, one is hard-pressed not to infer that the results of the studies must undercut the government's claim that a less invasive ban would not have produced an equally salutary result.'[41] Anti-smoking groups responded to the decision by calling on Ottawa to use the notwithstanding clause to override Charter protection for tobacco advertising. Many staunch Charter boosters became skeptics overnight. They were awakened by the tobacco advertising decision to a basic truth of constitutionally entrenched rights: the price of entrenchment is that judges assume a more important role in political life.

THE NOTWITHSTANDING CLAUSE: SECTION 33

'What the Charter gives, the legislature may take away.' This appears to be the meaning of section 33 of the Charter, the 'notwithstanding clause'. It states that either Parliament or a provincial legislature may expressly declare that a law shall operate even if it offends against section 2 or sections 7–15 of the Charter. This provision was not part of Ottawa's original Charter proposal but was inserted at the insistence of several provinces. Indeed, it appears that federal-provincial agreement on the constitutional deal that produced the Charter would have died without this concession.[42]

Although the notwithstanding clause appears to provide governments with a constitutional escape hatch from much of the Charter, it is not clear that it actually has this effect. It has been resorted to on only a handful of occasions. Why have governments generally been reluctant to use section 33 to avoid or reverse court decisions declaring their laws to be in violation of the Charter? In the words of civil libertarian Alan Borovoy, 'The mere introduction of a bill to oust the application of the Charter would likely spark an enormous controversy. . . . Without solid support in the legislature and the community, a government would be very reluctant to take the heat that such action would invariably generate.'[43]

Borovoy's confidence that public support for the Charter and vigilant media provide adequate protection against section 33 is not shared by everyone. Civil liberties groups and the legal profession have generally been outspokenly critical of the notwithstanding clause, to the point that a court challenge was launched against it immediately after the Charter was proclaimed.[44] The basis of this challenge was that if the Constitution is the supreme law of the land, as the Constitu-

tion Act declares, then no part of it should be placed beyond the powers of judicial review. By this reasoning, a legislature's decision to invoke section 33 should itself be reviewable, and therefore able to be overturned, by the courts. In a 1985 ruling, the Quebec Court of Appeal agreed. This decision, however, was overruled by the Supreme Court of Canada in *Ford v. Attorney General of Quebec* (1988). The Court pronounced in favour of a literal interpretation of section 33—which also happens to correspond with the intentions of those provincial governments that insisted on the notwithstanding clause—requiring only that a legislature expressly declare its intention to override the Charter.

It appears, therefore, that there are no serious legal roadblocks in the way of a government using section 33 to circumvent the Charter. Nonetheless, it has been invoked on only a couple of occasions—if one does not take into account the PQ's policy, between 1982 and 1985, of inserting the notwithstanding clause into all laws passed by the Quebec legislature and retroactively into all existing provincial statutes. (These actions were part of a symbolic and legal strategy against the constitutional reforms of 1982, to which the PQ government had not agreed.) It would appear, then, that significant political barriers forestall its use. Quite simply, governments do not want to give the appearance of denying rights to their citizens. There are, however, circumstances where the denial of rights inflicts little political damage on government and may even produce political dividends.

This was certainly true of the Quebec Liberal government's decision to use the notwithstanding clause to re-pass, with some modifications, the provisions of Bill 101 that had been ruled unconstitutional by the Supreme Court (see Chapter 12). Public opinion, the province's francophone media, and the opposition PQ were all strongly supportive of legislative restrictions on the use of languages other than French. While the government's move precipitated the resignation of three anglophone cabinet ministers and drove many English-speaking voters into the arms of the newly formed Equality Party in the next provincial election, there is no doubt that the political costs of not overriding the Charter would have been far greater.

The political costs were also negligible when Saskatchewan's Conservative government inserted section 33 in a 1986 law passed to force striking public servants back to work. The government feared that, without the notwithstanding clause, the courts might rule that back-to-work legislation infringed the freedom of association guaranteed by section 2 of the Charter. Rather than run this risk, it chose to act pre-emptively to override this right. (As it turned out, the Supreme Court later decided that collective bargaining and strike action are not protected by the Charter.) Denying government employees the right to strike is popular with the public. Some analysts suggest that the Saskatchewan Conservatives' use of section 33 against public servants may even have produced a net gain in votes for the party in the election that followed about a year later.[45]

So do public opinion and vigilant media provide adequate protection against legislative abuses of the notwithstanding clause? Ultimately, the answer depends on our expectations for democracy. For some, the mere fact that public opinion may be overwhelmingly supportive of a law that denies rights to some persons is not a legitimate basis for invoking section 33. They would argue that if the Charter does not protect rights when they are vulnerable, guarding them from the 'tyranny of the majority', then it fails what should be the real test of its worth. Rights are either entrenched against popular passions and legislative assault, they would insist, or they are not. But for others, the notwithstanding clause is a mechanism for asserting the popular will in exceptional circumstances. The only other way of overcoming an unpopular court decision on the Charter would be to amend the Constitution, a difficult and time-consuming process. The controversy over section 33 is, in the final analysis, nothing less than the familiar debate over parliamentary versus constitutional supremacy.

APPLYING THE CHARTER

News stories of yet another attempt to use the Charter to challenge some law or administrative procedure have become routine. These attempts range from matters whose social importance is obvious to challenges that appear trivial, even by charitable standards. Only a small fraction of the hundreds of trial court rulings on the Charter ultimately reach the provincial superior courts, and fewer still are appealed to the Supreme Court. Even so, a large share of the workload of these courts is now consumed by cases requiring them to apply the Charter. 'The sheer mass of Charter litigation', observes Michael Mandel, 'and the speed with which its influence is colonizing every corner of Canadian life [make a comprehensive account of the Charter's impact] an impossible quest.'[46] Nevertheless, it is possible to identify the main tendencies in judicial interpretation of the Charter.

To understand these tendencies, three issues are of special significance. First, how have the courts interpreted the Charter's scope and authority? Second, what difference has the Charter had on the relationship between the state and individuals? Third, what have been the Charter's effects on equality in Canada? The last two issues are, of course, fundamental to our assessment of Canadian democracy.

Scope and Authority

In one of its first Charter decisions, *Law Society of Upper Canada v. Skapinker* (1984), the Supreme Court made clear its position on judicial review of the Charter. Consciously modelling its position along the lines of *Marbury v. Madison* (1803), the landmark American Supreme Court ruling that established that Court's supervisory role over the US Constitution, the Supreme Court of Canada declared its intention to assume a similar role in applying the Charter. 'With the Constitution Act 1982', wrote Justice Willard Estey, 'comes a new dimension, a new yardstick of reconciliation between the individual and the community and their respective rights, a dimension which, like the balance of the Constitution, remains to be interpreted and applied by the Court'.[47]

How far would the Court be willing to go in using the Charter to strike down laws passed by elected legislatures? Here, too, the ruling in *Skapinker* borrowed from *Marbury v. Madison*. Although the Constitution must be considered the supreme law of the land, judges should interpret it in ways that 'enable [the legislature] to perform the high duties assigned to it, in the manner most beneficial to the people.'[48] In other words, judges should not be too quick to second-guess elected lawmakers.

Skapinker was more a broad statement of intent than a clear signpost. But a year later the Court was given the opportunity to show how activist it was prepared to be in applying the Charter. The case involved a challenge to procedures under Canada's Immigration Act, whereby applicants for political refugee status were not given an automatic right to a hearing. By a 6–0 vote, the Supreme Court decided that this violated fundamental principles of justice. However, three of the justices based their ruling on a section of the Canadian Bill of Rights that guarantees the 'right to a fair hearing', while the other three went further in arguing that the right to a hearing is implied under section 7 of the Charter, guaranteeing 'the right to life, liberty and security of the person and the right not to be deprived thereof except in accordance with the principles of fundamental justice'. Justice Bertha Wilson took the most aggressive approach to the Charter, arguing that 'the guarantees of the Charter would be illusory if they could be ignored because it was administratively convenient to do so.'[49] At least some of the judges, then, demonstrated their willingness to take a hardline approach to the Charter, whatever the administrative and political effects on government policy might be. As it transpired, the *Singh* decision resulted in thousands of additional cases being added to what was already a huge backlog of refugee claims and precipitated the introduction of a new law intended to limit refugees' access to Canada.[50]

Singh was followed by a string of 1985 rulings that defined in sharper hues the Supreme Court's approach to the Charter. In *The Queen v. Big M Drug Mart* (1985), the Court struck down the federal Lord's Day Act on the grounds that it violated the Charter's guarantee of freedom of religion. From the standpoint of the interpretive rules being developed by judges in applying the Charter (see Box 6.2), the most significant feature of the *Big M* case was the willingness of all of the justices to inquire into the purposes associated with the rights and freedoms set forth in the Charter. The Court signalled its readiness to go beyond the simple words of the Charter and the stated intentions of those who drafted it to interpret the historical meaning and social purposes of a concept such as, in this particular case, freedom of religion. This is the very hallmark of judicial activism.

The issue of what the Charter's drafters actually intended was raised again in *Reference re Section 94(2) of the Motor Vehicle Act (B.C.)* (1985).[51] In this case, British Columbia's Attorney General argued that section 7 protection for the 'principles of fundamental justice' was meant by the governments who agreed to the Charter to be a guarantee of procedural fairness (the issue raised in *Singh*). It was not, he argued, intended to enable the courts to assess the fairness of the 'substance' of laws. In rejecting the government's argument, the Court quite correctly reasoned that it is not always possible to separate substance and procedure. For example, a law whose substance is the denial of a procedural right associated with the principles of fundamental justice is both procedurally and substantively unfair. The majority was quick to add, however, that judicial review under section 7 should be limited to the criminal law and legal rights, and should not extend to general public policy. This declaration was intended to prevent section 7 from being used by any individual or group who believed that a law treated them unfairly.

On the question of what the Charter's drafters had intended for section 7, the Court ruled that arguments about intentions could not be binding for two reasons. First, it is not possible to state categorically what legislative bodies intended for the Charter as a whole or for particular provisions of it. Second, if the original intentions were treated as binding on the courts, then 'the rights, freedoms and values embodied in the Charter in effect becomes [*sic*] frozen in time to the moment of adoption with little or no possibility of growth, development and adjustment to changing societal needs.' This implies, of course, that judges will determine what constitute 'changing societal needs' (see Box 6.2).

As reasonable as these arguments about legislative 'intentions' sound, it should be pointed out that the Court has sometimes taken lawmakers' intentions very seriously. This was true in the *Quebec Protestant School Board* (1984)[52] ruling, where the Court relied on the drafters' intentions for section 23 of the Charter in striking down the education provisions of Quebec's Bill 101. It has also been evident in other decisions, including *Re Public Service Employee Relations Act* (1987).[53] In denying that the right to strike is protected by the Charter, the Court argued that the drafters of the Charter were deliberately silent on economic rights. (The court changed its mind on this in the 2001 *Dunmore* decision, discussed below.) It appears, then, that legislative intentions do matter when judges find them convenient.

The issue of the Charter's scope was the focus of another of the Court's 1985 decisions, *Operation Dismantle v. the Queen*.[54] A coalition of groups opposed to testing of the cruise missile in Canada argued that these tests violated the Charter's guarantee of the right to life and security of the person by making nuclear war more probable. The Court rejected this argument on the grounds that the alleged facts in the plaintiff's claim were in fact unprovable speculations. But the other question before the Court was whether cabinet decisions—the decision to allow cruise missile tests was taken by cabinet—and foreign policy defence issues are reviewable by the Courts. The federal government argued that cabinet decisions are 'Crown prerogatives' and there-

fore off limits to the courts. The Supreme Court disagreed. It argued that section 32 of the Charter should be interpreted to apply to all government actions. On the precise question of whether foreign policy and defence issues are inherently political and beyond the reach of judicial review, the Court did not express an opinion.

There is an additional feature of the Court's approach to the Charter's scope that deserves mention. This involves its insistence that the Charter applies only to relationships between the state and citizens, not to private-sector relationships. Thus, the Charter cannot be used by someone who believes that he has been denied a job or an apartment because of his race, or by a person whose private-sector employer requires that she retire at the age of 65. Forms of discrimination like these are pervasive throughout society, but they are not inequalities that can be overcome using the Charter. The Supreme Court has on several occasions articulated this distinction between public (covered by the Charter) and private, as in *Dolphin Delivery* (1986)[55]: '[The Charter] was set up to regulate the relationship between the individual and the government. It was intended to restrain government action and to protect the individual.'[56] This position is, in fact, faithful to the intentions of those who framed and agreed to the Charter.

The Court's refusal to recognize economic rights is related to this public/private distinction. As noted earlier, the Charter is deliberately silent on economic and property rights, except for the qualified protection it extends to the right to live, work, and be eligible for social benefits in any province. Claims that certain economic rights are implied by provisions of the Charter have generally received a cold reception. For example, the courts have expressly rejected business's arguments that corporations should fall within the ambit of section 7 of the Charter, which guarantees the 'right to life, liberty and security of the person'. The economic rights claims of workers have fared no better at the hands of judges. In a 1987 ruling on whether a right to strike exists, the Supreme Court declared that 'The constitutional guarantee of freedom of association . . . does not include, in the case of a trade union, a guarantee of the right to bargain collectively and the right to strike.'[57] The right to bargain collectively and to strike are not, the Court ruled, fun-

---

BOX 6.2   Some General Principles of Interpretation that Guide the Courts in Charter Cases

The Charter is designed and adopted to guide and serve the Canadian community for a long time. Narrow and technical interpretation, if not modulated by a sense of the unknowns of the future, can stunt growth of the law and hence the community it serves. It is clear that headings were systematically and deliberately included as an integral part of the Charter for whatever purpose. At the very minimum a court must take them into consideration when engaged in the process of discerning the meaning and application of the provisions of the Charter.

The task of expounding a constitution is crucially different from that of construing a statute. A constitution is drafted with an eye to the future. Its function is to provide a continuing framework for the legitimate exercise of governmental power and, when joined by a bill or a charter of rights, for the unremitting protection of individual rights and liberties. It must be capable of growth and development over time to meet new social, political and historical realities often unimagined by its framers. The judiciary is the guardian of the Constitution and must, in interpreting its provisions, not 'read the provisions of the Constitution like a last will and testament lest it become one.'

Neither before nor after the Charter have the courts been enabled to decide upon the appropriateness of policies underlying legislative enactments. In both instances, however, the courts are empowered, indeed required, to measure the content of legislation against the guarantees of the Constitution.

It was never intended that the Charter could be used to invalidate other provisions of the Constitution, particularly a provision such as s. 93 of the Constitution Act, 1867, which represented a fundamental part of the Confederation compromise.

In *The Queen v. Big M Drug Mart*, Dickson J. elaborated on how the interests which are intended to be protected by a particular Charter right are to be discovered: 'in my view this analysis is to be undertaken, and the purpose of the right or freedom in question is to be sought by reference to the character and the larger objects of the Charter itself, to the language chosen to articulate the specific right or freedom, to the historical origins of the concepts enshrined, and where applicable, to the meaning and purpose of the other specific rights and freedoms with which it is associated within the text of the Charter.'

A hierarchical approach to rights, which places some over others, must be avoided, both when interpreting the Charter and when developing the common law. When the protected rights of two individuals come into conflict, as can occur in the case of publication bans, Charter principles require a balance to be achieved that fully respects the importance of both sets of rights.

Canada, Department of Justice, *Canadian Charter of Rights Decision Digest*, Appendix A: http://www.canada.justice.gc.ca/Publications

damental rights or freedoms that deserve the constitutional protection of freedom of association under the Charter. 'They are', the majority declared, 'the creation of legislation, involving a balance of competing interests',[58] and their scope and limitations are appropriately determined by legislatures. To put it very simply, economic rights were viewed as subordinate to political ones.

It is sometimes seen that yesterday's dissent becomes today's law. This appears to be true in the matter of the Supreme Court's interpretation of freedom of expression, guaranteed by section 2(d) of the Charter, and workers' rights. In *Dunmore et al. v. Attorney General for Ontario* (2001),[59] the Court struck down as unconstitutional an Ontario law that excluded agricultural workers from collective bargaining rights available to other groups of workers (see Box 6.3). In reaching this decision the majority borrowed from the reasoning of the dissent in the 1987 *Reference re Public Service Employee Relations Act (Alberta)*, thereby rejecting the view that the fundamental freedoms in the Charter are intended to protect political freedoms but not economic ones. Those who

cling to a view of judges as rightful defenders of the pro-business status quo were dismayed by the Court's shift in this regard.

It may seem, then, that the courts have not strongly favoured either business or labour in their interpretation of the Charter, supporting arguments for economic rights in some limited instances but denying them in others. In fact, this appearance of neutrality is deceiving for two reasons. First, business interests have been able to use some of the 'political' rights in the Charter to protect property rights, in some cases arguably at the expense of workers, consumers, or other community interests. Second, much of the inequality that exists in society is generated by private economic relations—relations between employers and employees, men and women in the workplace, landlords and tenants, buyers and sellers. To declare that the Charter recognizes only 'political' and 'democratic' rights but not 'economic' ones, as the courts have done, could have the effect of freezing the inequalities that currently exist in society and in the economy. Dominant groups tend to win from this public/private

---

BOX 6.3   On Freedom of Association and Collective Activities

The law must recognize that certain union activities—making collective representations to an employer, adopting a majority political platform, federating with other unions—may be central to freedom of association even though they are inconceivable on the individual level. This is not to say that all such activities are protected by s. 2(d), nor that all collectivities are worthy of constitutional protection; indeed, this Court repeatedly excluded the right to strike and collectively bargain from the protected ambit of s. 2(d). It is to say, simply, that certain collective activities must be recognized if the freedom to form and maintain an association is to have any meaning. As one author puts it, the per se exclusion of collective action reduces employee collectives to mere 'aggregates of economically self-interested individuals', rather than 'co-operative undertakings where individual flourishing can be encouraged through membership in and co-operation with the community of fellow workers'. This would surely undermine the purpose of s. 2(d), which is to allow the achievement of individual potential through interpersonal relationships and action.

Dunmore et al, v. Attorney General for Ontario (2001), S.C.C. 94.

distinction, which places important sources of inequality beyond the authority of the Charter, while subordinate groups lose. The *Dunmore* ruling suggests, however, that the Supreme Court has become less conservative on the subject of economic rights than it was in the past.

It is true, of course, that every major Supreme Court ruling on the Charter serves to clarify the scope and authority of judicial review. We have focused on several early Charter decisions to demonstrate that the Court very quickly assumed the mantle of judicial activism. How far judges go in using the Charter to strike down laws and administrative practices is, to a large extent, up to them. Two provisions of the Charter, however, were intended to rein in the courts' authority. One is the 'reasonable limits' clause (s. 1) and the other is the 'notwithstanding clause' (s. 33). In practice, neither of these has been very effective in limiting the scope of judicial activism.

Individual Rights and Freedoms

Some individual rights and freedoms are better protected today as a result of the Charter. Court decisions have expanded the rights of, among others, those accused of crimes, immigrants, women seeking abortions, and business people wanting to advertise in English in Quebec. On the other hand, Supreme Court decisions have declared that the Charter's freedom of association does not provide unionized workers with the right to strike; upheld the constitutionality of terribly vague provincial anti-hate laws against claims that they violate freedom of expression; and ruled that secularly worded Sunday closing laws have the effect of being an 'indirect and unintentional' violation of freedom of religion, but that they qualify as 'reasonable limits' under section 1 of the Charter. The Court came down on the side of freedom of expression over anti-hate restrictions in the *Zundel* decision (1992) and over the federal ban on tobacco advertising (1995). In a major ruling on obscenity, the Supreme Court decided that Criminal Code restrictions on the distribution and sale of obscene materials violated freedom of expression, but that this restriction could be justified under the reasonable limits section of the Charter. (*R. v. Butler*, 1992; see Box 6.4). In a 2001 decision the Court ruled that the Criminal Code's prohibition on possession of child pornography could in some circumstances violate the individual's right to privacy and could not be justified under s. 1 of the Charter. However, while indicating that possession of child pornography is in some instances protected by section 2 of the Charter, the thrust of the Supreme Court ruling in *Sharpe* was to uphold the constitutionality of the general decriminalization of possession as a reasonable limit of free speech. In the end the courts have not unleashed a torrent of individualism on Canadian society, but it is fair to say that individual rights claims tend to do better, and certainly do no worse, under the Charter than previously.

This was certainly true in the *Big M* case, when the Supreme Court was called upon to decide whether the federal Lord's Day Act violated the freedom of religion guarantee set down in section 2 of the Charter. The Court had little trouble in deciding that it did. What could not be achieved using the Canadian Bill of Rights became possible under the Charter.

The courts' rulings on legal rights challenges to Canada's criminal law provide another clear illustration of the more liberal treatment of individual rights in the Charter era. Charter decisions have produced many important changes in law enforcement practices, including the following:

- 'Reverse onus' provisions, requiring a defendant to prove his innocence of a charge, have been ruled unconstitutional.
- Evidence obtained by inappropriate means, such as confession obtained without informing an accused person of his right to legal counsel, cannot be used to help convict that person.
- Writs of assistance, under which the police were able to enter premises at any time without a search warrant, were ruled unconstitutional.

BOX 6.4   When Are Limitations on Freedom of Expression Reasonable? The Case of Obscenity

The *R. v. Butler* case involved a store owner accused of selling and renting hard-core video-tapes and magazines, as well as 'sex toys' and devices, in contravention of s. 163 of the Criminal Code. Section 163 states that 'any publication a dominant characteristic of which is the undue exploitation of sex, or of sex and any one or more of . . . crime, horror, cruelty and violence, shall be deemed to be obscene.' The key words here are 'undue exploitation'.

The majority on the Court agreed that s. 163 of the Criminal Code infringes the Charter's guarantee of freedom of expression, but they stated that this was a reasonable limitation on the grounds that governments have a legitimate responsibility to protect the community and groups in the community from harmful behaviour. Here is part of what they said:

> There is a sufficiently rational link between the criminal sanction, which demonstrates our community's disapproval of the dissemination of materials which potentially victimize women and restricts the negative influence which such materials have on changes in attitudes and behaviour, and the objective. While a direct link between obscenity and harm to society may be difficult to establish, it is reasonable to presume that exposure to images bears a causal relationship to changes in attitudes and beliefs. Section 163 of the Code minimally impairs freedom of expression. It does not proscribe sexually explicit erotica without violence that is not degrading or dehumanizing, but is designed to catch material that creates a risk of harm to society. Materials which have scientific, artistic or literary merit are not caught by the provision. Since the attempt to provide exhaustive instances of obscenity has been shown to be destined to fail, the only practical alternative is to strive towards a more abstract definition of obscenity which is contextually sensitive. The standard of 'undue exploitation' is thus appropriate. Further, it is only the public distribution and exhibition of obscene materials which is in issue here. Given the gravity of the harm, and the threat to the values at stake, there is no alternative equal to the measure chosen by Parliament. Serious social problems such as violence against women require multi-pronged approaches by government; education and legislation are not alternatives but complements in addressing such problems. Finally, the effects of the law do not so severely trench on the protected right that the legislative objective is outweighed by the infringement.

> *R. v. Butler*, [1992] 1 S.C.R.

• Search and seizure powers have been restricted.
• Thousands of persons accused of criminal offences have had the charges against them dismissed because of an Ontario Superior Court ruling that lengthy delays in getting them to trial contravened their s. 11(b) right 'to be tried within a reasonable time'.

In probably the most publicized Charter decision to date, the Supreme Court in 1988 struck down Canada's 20-year-old abortion law. Under section 251 of the Criminal Code a woman wanting an abortion required the approval of a hospital's therapeutic abortion committee. In most communities, however, the local hospital(s) did not have such a committee and did not perform abortions. Even in communities where hospitals performing abortions existed (about 20 per cent of all hospitals at the time), there was considerable difference between them in the likelihood that an abortion would be permitted. The majority in *Morgentaler* (1988)[60] ruled that the obvious practical inequalities in the application of the law violated section 7 of the Charter, guaranteeing the principles of fundamental justice.

Is there an identifiable pattern in the Court's interpretation of the individual rights guaranteed by the Charter? Aside from what most commentators characterize as a moderately activist approach, the Court has shown few sharply pronounced tendencies. In the *Morgentaler* case, for example, the Court's decision was supported by

three distinct sets of reasons. This is not uncommon, nor is it rare for the Court to be sharply divided in its interpretation of important provisions of the Charter. Even where the Court has adopted what appears to be a clear interpretation rule, it is difficult to predict how it will be applied in particular circumstances. Finally, it needs to be kept in mind that the Court is sometimes sharply divided in its approach to individual rights, as was seen in its 1995 ruling on Ottawa's tobacco advertising ban (see Box 6.5).

Equality and the Charter

Some Charter decisions have contributed to greater equality in Canadian society, but others clearly have not. Any attempt to assess the Char-

---

BOX 6.5   A Court Divided

The Decision
The Supreme Court rules in a 5–4 decision that the 1988 Tobacco Products Control Act is unconstitutional because Ottawa's near-total advertising ban violates the industry's right to free speech.

What It Means
Tobacco companies are free to resume all forms of advertising, including the television and radio ads that they voluntarily pulled in 1972.

Bold unattributed health warnings, such as 'Smoking can kill you', are unconstitutional and may disappear.

Companies can put their logos and trademarks back on promotional items such as T-shirts and cigarette lighters. The federal government must pass a new law if it wants to continue to restrict tobacco advertising.

What Was Said
'. . . there was no direct evidence of a scientific nature showing a causal link between advertising bans and decrease in tobacco consumption.' Madam Justice Beverley McLachlin

'The harm engendered by tobacco and the profit motive underlying its promotion, place this form of expression as far from the core of freedom of expression values as prostitution, hate mongering, or pornography and thus entitle it to a very low degree of protection under [section 1 of the Charter].' Mr Justice Gerard La Forest, one of the four dissenters on the Court

ter's overall impact on equality is fraught with difficulties. But given that its supporters have always claimed that the Charter represents a major victory for democracy in Canada, and given the undeniable importance of many Charter rulings for public policy, the issue needs to be addressed.

Section 15 of the Charter deals explicitly with equality rights. Those who drafted this section, the precise wording of which provoked as much controversy as anything in the Charter, expected that it would have significant consequences for the laws and administrative practices of governments. For this reason the equality section did not become operative until three years after the Charter was proclaimed. But in fact, section 15 has had less of an impact on equality in Canada than some other sections of the Charter and less of an impact than the federal and provincial human rights codes.

First and most importantly, it does not extend to discrimination in private-sector relationships. We have already discussed the practical consequences of limiting the Charter to abuses of governmental power. As constitutional expert Peter Hogg puts it:

> The real threat to civil liberties in Canada comes not from legislative and official action, but from discrimination by private persons—employers, trade unions, landlords, realtors, restaurateurs and other suppliers of goods or services. The economic liberties of freedom of property and contract, which imply a power to deal with whomever one pleases, come into direct conflict with egalitarian values.[61]

Although section 15 cannot be used to fight these private forms of discrimination, provincial human rights codes enforced by commissions do cover private-sector relations.

The potential impact of section 15 is also limited by the courts' unwillingness to treat equality rights as superior to other rights in the Charter or to other parts of the Constitution. Not only must the courts balance equality rights against the 'reasonable limits' provision of the Charter—this is a tightrope they must walk with all of the rights set

Many court decisions on the Charter have been highly controversial. (Roy Peterson, *Vancouver Sun*)

forth in the Charter—they must also weigh section 15 rights against other rights and freedoms. How to strike this balance was the issue before the Supreme Court in *Re Education Act* (1987),[62] which dealt with the constitutionality of an Ontario law extending full public funding to that province's Roman Catholic schools.[63] The Supreme Court ruled that the equality of religion guaranteed by section 15 did not override provincial governments' authority to grant special educational rights to Catholics and Protestants under section 93 of the Constitution Act, 1867.

In the final analysis the Charter and the courts send out mixed and sometimes confusing signals about equality. The same can be said, of course, about governments. Despite the courts' willingness to go beyond formal legal equality to see whether the effects of a law meet the requirements of the Charter (as the Supreme Court did in *Morgentaler*), the usefulness of the Charter as an instrument for overcoming the most prevalent and deeply rooted forms of social and economic inequality is limited.

Nevertheless, there have been cases where the equality guarantees of the Charter have provided the basis for fairly dramatic and controversial reversals of long-standing public policy. This was true of the Supreme Court's ruling in *M. v. H.* (1999), a case that involved a challenge to the heterosexual definition of spouses in Ontario's Family Law Act. In earlier decisions the Court had ruled that discrimination on the basis of sexual orientation is analogous to the enumerated grounds for discrimination proscribed by s. 15 of the Charter (*Egan v. Canada*, 1995). It came as no surprise, therefore, when the Supreme Court decided that the heterosexual definition of a cohabiting couple under the Family Law Act was unconstitutional because it denied the same status and rights to homosexual couples. The Court determined that the exclusion of same-sex relationships from the spousal support provisions of the Family Law Act was not rationally connected

to the objectives of the Family Law Act and thus could not be justified under the reasonable limits section of the Charter. Federal Justice Minister Alan Rock had already announced the government's intention to change the law so as to provide same-sex couples with the same status as heterosexual ones. The ruling in *M. v. H* simply made this job easier.

After a decade and a half of considering equality cases without a systematic and consistent framework for assessing s. 15 claims, the Supreme Court developed just such a framework in *Law v. Minister of Human Resources Development*.[64] This case involved a 30-year-old woman who was denied survivor's benefits under the Canada Pension Plan. Had she been 45 or older she would have qualified for the full benefit and between the ages of 35 and 45 she would have received a partial benefit. Ms Law claimed age discrimination under s. 15 of the Charter. The Court disagreed, arguing that not all forms of differential treatment that may appear to violate equality rights are unconstitutional. The key question, said the Court, is whether the differential treatment of the members of a group under the law is demeaning to human dignity. Recall that the Supreme Court has been very explicit since the early years of the Charter in insisting that the rights and freedoms guaranteed by the Charter should not become tools that the advantaged and well-heeled can use to protect their status. In the Charter, and especially in its equality sections, the Court has suggested what might be described as an 'ameliorative' or 'progressive' purpose. The interpretive framework articulated in the *Law* decision is another step in the direction of the courts interpreting the Constitution with an eye to its impact on social relationships.

On balance, there is little doubt that what Morton and Knopff call 'equality seeking groups'—a category that includes women, visible and religious minorities, the mentally and physically disabled, and homosexuals—have won victories using s. 15 of the Charter that probably could not have been won in a non-judicial forum and without the benefit of constitutionally entrenched equality rights.

In their interpretation of s. 15 of the Charter, judges have been sensitive to the social and economic context of the inequalities that appear before them as Charter claims. Indeed, many of the major Charter rulings read like sociological or historical treatises.[65] This is precisely what alarms many of the Charter's critics, who recoil at what they see as judicial usurpation of the legislature's function (see Box 6.6). Moreover, experience under the Charter has shown that society's 'haves', as well as the 'have nots', are able to use the Charter to advance their interests.

BOX 6.6   The Charter Revolution

Just as the 1960s are remembered by Canadian historians as the decade of Quebec's 'Quiet Revolution', so the 1980s and 1990s will be remembered as the period of Canada's 'Charter Revolution'. Since the adoption of the Charter of Rights and Freedoms in 1982, Canadian politics has been transformed. A long tradition of parliamentary supremacy has been replaced by a regime of constitutional supremacy verging on judicial supremacy. On rights issues, judges have abandoned the deference and self-restraint that characterized their pre-Charter jurisprudence and become more active players in the political process. As Chief Justice Lamer observed in 1998, 'There is no doubt that [with the adoption of the Charter] the judiciary was drawn into the political arena to a degree unknown prior to 1982.' Encouraged by the judiciary's more active policymaking role, interest groups, many funded by the very governments whose laws they challenge, have increasingly turned to the courts to advance their policy objectives. As a result, policymakers are ever watchful for what a Justice Department lawyer describes as judicial 'bombshells' which 'shock . . . the system'. In addition to making the courtroom a new arena for the pursuit of interest group politics, in other words, Charter litigation—or its threat—also casts its shadow over the more traditional arenas of electoral, legislative, and administrative politics. Not only are judges now influencing public policy to a previously unheard of degree, but lawyers and legal arguments are increasingly shaping political discourse and policy formation.

F.L. Morton and Rainer Knopff, *The Charter Revolution and the Court Party* (Peterborough, Ont.: Broadview Press, 2000), 12.

NOTES

1. *Schenck v. United States*, 249 U.S. 47 (1919).
2. These are the words used in the 'anti-hate' section of Canada's Criminal Code.
3. University of Calgary, *Charter Database*.
4. Michael Mandel, *The Charter of Rights and the Legalization of Politics in Canada* (Toronto: Wall and Thompson, 1989), 4.
5. Walter S. Tarnopolsky, 'Human Rights', in *Canadian Encyclopedia*, 2nd edn (Edmonton: Hurtig, 1988), vol. 2, 1024.
6. United States Constitution, 14th amendment, 1868.
7. *Hunter et al. v. Southam Inc.* (1984), 11 D.L.R. (4th) 641.
8. *RJR-MacDonald Inc v. Canada* (1995), 3 S.C.R. (4th)
9. *R. v. Big M Drug Mart* (1985), 18 D.L.R. (4th) 321.
10. *Public Service Alliance of Canada et al. v. The Queen in Right of Canada et al.* (1987), 38 D.L.R. (4th) 249 (Supreme Court of Canada).
11. Mandel, *The Charter of Rights*, 218.
12. F.L. Morton, 'The Charter Revolution and the Court Party', *Osgoode Hall Law Journal* 30, 3 (Fall 1992): 634–5.
13. *Borowski v. Attorney General for Canada* (1987), 39 D.L.R. (4th) 731; *R. v. Morgentaler, Smoling and Scott* (1985), 48 C.R. (3rd) 1 (Ontario Court of Appeal).
14. Carol Smart, *Feminism and the Power of Law* (London: Routledge, 1989), 160.
15. Ibid., 161.
16. Alan Borovoy, *When Freedoms Collide: The Case for Our Civil Liberties* (Toronto: Lester & Orpen Dennys, 1988), ch. 10.
17. R. MacGregor Dawson, *Constitutional Issues in Canada, 1900–1931* (London: Oxford University Press, 1933).
18. R. MacGregor Dawson, *The Government of Canada* (Toronto: University of Toronto Press, 1947).
19. J.A. Corry and J.E. Hodgetts, *Democratic Government and Politics* (Toronto: University of Toronto Press, 1946).
20. *Reference re Alberta Statutes* (1938), S.C.R. 100.
21. *Saumur v. Quebec and Attorney General of Quebec* (1953), 2 S.C.R. 299.
22. *Switzman v. Elbling and Attorney General of Quebec* (1957), S.C.R. 285.
23. *Attorney General of Canada and Dupond v. Montreal* (1978) 2 S.C.R. 770.
24. Quoted in Peter H. Russell, *Leading Constitutional Decisions*, 4th edn (Ottawa: Carleton Library Series, 1987), 390.
25. Norman Ward, *The Government of Canada* (Toronto: University of Toronto Press, 1987), 84.
26. Corry and Hodgetts, *Democratic Government and Politics*, 462.
27. *Robertson and Rosetanni v. The Queen* (1963), quoted in Russell, *Leading Constitutional Decisions*, 399.
28. Quoted in Walter S. Tarnopolsky, *The Canadian Bill of Rights*, 2nd edn (Toronto: McClelland & Stewart, 1975), 132.
29. *R. v. Drybones* (1970), S.C.R. 282.
30. *Attorney General of Canada v. Lavell* (1974), S.C.R. 1349.
31. *Hogan v. The Queen* (1975), 2 S.C.R. 574.
32. *City of Winnipeg v. Barrett* (1892), A.C. 445.
33. *Ottawa Roman Catholic Separate School Trustees v. Mackell* (1917), A.C. 62; *Protestant School Board of Greater Montreal v. Minister of Education of Quebec* (1978), 83 D.L.R. (3d) 645.
34. *Attorney General of Quebec v. Blaikie* (1979), 2 S.C.R. 1016.
35. *Attorney General of Manitoba v. Forest* (1979), 101 D.L.R. (3d) 385.
36. www.scc-csc.gc.ca/statistics/ecourt.htm
37. *R. v. Oakes* (1986), 26 D.L.R. (4th) 20.
38. *Ford v. Attorney General of Quebec* (1988).

39. Quoted in F.L. Morton, Rainer Knopff, and Peter Russell, *Federalism and the Charter* (Ottawa: Carleton University Press, 1989), 578.

40. Ibid., 579.

41. Quoted in 'Tobacco ad ban struck down', *Globe and Mail*, 22 Sept. 1995, A1, A11.

42. Roy Romanow et al., *Canada . . . Notwithstanding: The Making of the Constitution 1976–1982* (Toronto: Carswell, 1984), 211.

43. Borovoy, *When Freedoms Collide*, 211–12.

44. *Alliance des Professeurs de Montreal et al. v. Attorney General of Quebec* (1983), 9 C.C.C. (3d) 268.

45. F.L. Morton, 'The Political Impact of the Canadian Charter of Rights and Freedoms', *Canadian Journal of Political Science* 20, 1 (Mar. 1987): 47.

46. Michael Mandel, *The Charter of Rights and the Legalization of Politics in Canada*, 2nd edn (Toronto: Thompson Educational Publishing, 1994), xi.

47. Morton, Knopff, and Russell, *Federalism and the Charter*, 446.

48. Ibid., 389.

49. *Singh v. Minister of Employment and Immigration* (1985), 17 D.L.R. (4th) 469.

50. Morton, Knopff, and Russell, *Federalism and the Charter*, 446.

51. *Reference re Section 94(2) of the Motor Vehicle Act (B.C.)*, [1985] S.C.R. 486.

52. *Attorney General of Quebec v. Quebec Protestant School Boards* (1984), 10 D.L.R. (4th) 321.

53. *Reference re Public Service Employee Relations Act, Labour Relations Act and Police Officers Collective Bargaining Act* (1987), 38 D.L.R. (4th) 161.

54. *Operation Dismantle Inc. et al. v. The Queen* (1985), 18 D.L.R. (4th) 481.

55. *Retail, Wholesale & Department Store Union, Local 580 et al. v. Dolphin Delivery Ltd.* (1986), 33 D.L.R. (4th) 174.

56. Quoted in Mandel, *The Charter of Rights*, 204.

57. *Reference re Public Service Employee Relations Act* (Alberta), quoted in Morton, Knopff, and Russell, *Federalism and the Charter*, 496.

58. Quoted in Mandel, *Charter of Rights*, 193.

59. *Dunmore et al. v. Attorney General for Ontario and Fleming Chicks* (2001), S.C.C. 94.

60. *Morgentaler, Smoling and Scott v. The Queen* (1988), 37 C.C.C. (3d) 449.

61. Peter Hogg, *Constitutional Law of Canada*, 2nd edn (Toronto: Carswell, 1988), 786.

62. *Reference re An Act to Amend the Education Act* (Ontario) (1987), 40 D.L.R. (4th) 18.

63. Before the law was passed, provincial support to Roman Catholic schools ended after grade 10.

64 . *Law v. Minister of Human Resources Development*, [1999] 1 S.C.R. 497.

65. See, for example, the majority and dissenting judgements in the right-to-strike case, *Reference re Public Service Employee Relations Act* (1987), and in the Ontario Roman Catholic high school funding case, *Reference re An Act to Amend the Education Act* (1987).

SUGGESTED READINGS

Donald Abelson, Patrick James, and Michael Lusztig, eds, *The Myth of the Sacred: The Charter, the Courts and the Politics of the Constitution in Canada* (Montreal and Kingston: McGill-Queen's University Press, 2002). This collection of critical perspectives on the Charter challenges the idea of judges as neutral arbiters of the Constitution and argues that the Charter has been used by various groups to institutionalize their particular notions of justice and rights.

Alan Cairns, *Disruptions: Constitutional Struggles, from the Charter to Meech Lake* a(Toronto: McClelland & Stewart, 1991). These essays of one of Canada's pre-eminent political scientists focus on the consequences of the Charter for Canadian politics and were written between the 1976 election of the Parti Québécois and the 1990 demise of the Meech Lake Accord.

Christopher Manfredi, *Judicial Power and the Charter: Canada and the Paradox of Liberal Constitutionalism*, 2nd edn (Toronto: Oxford University Press, 2001). Manfredi examines the tension between the political accountability of elected legislatures and the increasing power of the courts in one of the most up-to-date analyses of Charter decisions.

F.L. Morton and Rainer Knopff, *The Charter Revolution and the Court Party* (Peterborough, Ont.: Broadview Press, 2000). In this highly critical account of how the Charter has affected Canadian politics, Morton and Knopff argue that state-funded interest groups, an activist component of the legal profession, and judges themselves have been successful in using the Charter to advance a minority agenda.

Robert Sharpe, Kent Roach, and Katherine Swinton, eds, *The Charter of Rights and Freedoms*, 2nd edn (Toronto: Irwin Law, 2002). This work presents a balanced and comprehensive treatment of the history of the Charter, the legitimacy of judicial review, and interpretation of virtually all significant sections of the Charter.

Review Exercises

1. Find a story in the media that deals with the Charter. Summarize it, covering as many of the following points as are relevant:
    (a) What are the circumstances?
    (b) Who are the people or organizations involved?
    (c) What law/regulation/action/practice is being challenged?
    (d) At what stage is the challenge?
    (e) Are lawyers or other experts interviewed? Who are they?
    (f) What right or freedom of the Charter is at stake in this story?

2. What is the background of a Supreme Court judge? Visit the Supreme Court of Canada's Web site <www.scc-csc.gc.ca>. Click on 'About the Court', then, under 'Member of the Court', click on the name of a particular judge. In a paragraph or two, provide a profile of one of the current justices. (If you prefer, you may use a recent edition of *Who's Who* to acquire this information.)

3. What are the pros and cons of requiring that at least some judicial nominations—e.g., those for the Supreme Court and for provincial appeals courts—should be subject to open public scrutiny and the approval of a body independent of the Prime Minister? How might such a process be structured?

The view of Ontario and Quebec is not the same as from other parts of Canada, a fact that westerners in particular claim federal politicians too often ignore. (Roy Peterson, *Vancouver Sun*)

Canada's Constitution establishes two levels of government—national and provincial—both of which have important law-making and taxation powers. This system of divided jurisdiction is known as federalism. In this chapter some of the major issues associated with federalism are discussed, including the following:

- ❑ What is federalism?
- ❑ The origins, maintenance, and demise of federal states.
- ❑ The origins of Canadian federalism.
- ❑ The federal division of powers.
- ❑ The courts and federalism.
- ❑ Quebec's impact on federalism.
- ❑ Centre-periphery relations.
- ❑ Intergovernmental relations.
- ❑ Financing federalism.
- ❑ The federal spending power and national standards.

CHAPTER SEVEN

FEDERALISM

When the proposal to create an independent Canada was discussed at Charlottetown (1864) and Quebec (1867), the main subject of debate was the relationship between the new national and regional governments. Two decades of self-government and the constitutional traditions imported from Britain provided the colonies with ready guideposts for most other features of the Constitution. Federalism, by contrast, was uncharted territory. Most of the practical knowledge Canada's founders had of the principles and operation of federalism was based on their observation of the United States. The lessons they took from the American experience were mainly negative. Secession of the Confederacy and the bloody Civil War of 1861–5 did not inspire much confidence in the American model. Despite all this, Canada's founders opted for a federal system of government.

WHAT IS FEDERALISM?

A federal system of government is one in which the constitutional authority to make laws and to tax is divided between a national government and some number of regional governments. Neither the national government acting alone nor the regional governments acting together have the authority to alter the powers of the other level of government. They are co-ordinate and independent in their separate constitutional spheres. Citizens in a federal state are members of two political communities, one national and the other coinciding with the boundaries of the province, state, canton—the name given to the regional units of a federal state vary between countries— in which they reside.

Federalism is a legal term, and its existence is based on the constitution. If a single govern-ment controls all legislative and taxation powers in a country, then no amount of administrative decentralization or variation in the economic, social, or cultural characteristics of its regions will make it a federal state. Federalism is chiefly a property of constitutions, not of societies. Nonetheless, some political scientists refer to 'federal-type' societies, a tendency that has been labelled the *sociological approach* to federalism. Its most prominent advocate, American political scientist William S. Livingston, argues that 'the essence of federalism lies not in the constitutional or institutional structure but in the society itself.'[1] 'Federalism', Livingston declares, 'is a function of societies.'[2]

Which understanding of federalism is correct, the constitutional or sociological one? The answer must be the constitutional approach, for two reasons. First, if federalism is primarily a quality of societies, not of constitutions, then relatively few countries are not federal. After all, most societies have politically significant ethnic or linguistic minorities, often concentrated in particular regions of the country. In fact, most of world's ethnically and linguistically diverse countries have unitary, not federal, constitutions. According to a now somewhat dated ranking of those political systems with federal constitutions, only India placed in the world's top 10 countries ordered according to their level of ethnic and linguistic diversity. Canada was 19th, Belgium 49th, Switzerland and the United States tied at 54th place, and Australia came in at 69th.[3]

The second reason for preferring the constitutional approach to federalism involves the dynamic of state power. A federal constitution institutionalizes regional divisions by associating them with different governments. The regionalism responsible for the adoption of a federal constitution in the first place is reinforced by political and administrative rivalries between the national and regional governments. Regional politics can certainly take place in the absence of a federal constitution. But the political significance of regional differences tends to be elevated by associating them with different political jurisdictions and the governments/bureaucracies that preside over them.

Federalism divides political authority along territorial lines. It is not, however, the only form of government to do so. Important policy-making and administrative powers may be exercised at the regional level even in a unitary state. The extent to which these activities are *decentralized*, i.e., placed in the hands of regional officials, or remain *centralized* at the national level is determined by the particular social, geographic, and political conditions of a country. This is also true of federal states, where the constitution provides only a partial and sometimes very misleading guide to the real division of powers between governments. Political authority is also linked to territory in *confederations* and *economic communities*. These are formal groupings of independent states that have agreed to assign certain legislative and administrative functions to a common institution or set of institutions. All member states have a say—though not necessarily an equal say—in the decision-making of such a body, while they retain their ultimate sovereignty (see Box 7.1).

THE ORIGINS, MAINTENANCE, AND DEMISE OF FEDERAL STATES

Only about 20 of the 191 member countries of the United Nations have a federal system of gov-

---

BOX 7.1   Territory and Political Authority

In the unitary form of government, even when there is a good measure of administrative or legislative devolution or decentralization, sovereignty or competence resides exclusively with the central government, and regional or local governments are legally and politically subordinate to it.

In the federal form of government, sovereignty or competence is distributed between central and provincial (or state) governments so that, within a single political system, neither order of government is legally or politically subordinate to the other, and each order of government is elected by and exercises authority directly upon the electorate.

In the confederal form of government, even where there is a considerable allocation of responsibilities to central institutions or agencies, the ultimate sovereignty is retained by the member-state governments and, therefore, the central government is legally and politically subordinate to them. Furthermore, the members of the major central institutions are delegates of the constituent state governments.

An economic association, when it has common organizing institutions, is a confederal type of government in which the functions assigned by the participating states to the common institutions are limited mainly to economic co-operation and co-ordination.

Canada, Task Force on Canadian Unity
Coming to Terms: The Words of the Debate
(Hull, Que.: Supply and Services Canada, 1979), 21–2.

ernment. We say 'about 20' because the determination of whether a political system is federal is not an exact science. Using the definition of federalism offered in the previous section, one can identify 17 countries with federal constitutions, five confederal political systems, and at least one with a constitution that recognizes the autonomy of a particular region within its national borders (see Table 7.1). Some of these choices may be open to challenge. For example, both the Mexican and Argentine governments have sometimes interfered with the autonomy of state governments. But the precise membership of the club is less important than the fact that it is a small one. Unitary government is far more popular, even in countries where regionally based political conflicts are strong.

What are the circumstances that lead to the adoption of a federal political system? Although there is no simple answer, it is possible to identify a very general condition present at the birth of all federal states and vital to the continued health of a federal union. This involves agreement among the regional components of the federal state that the benefits of being part of the union exceed whatever costs membership may impose. A federal state is based, therefore, on a *consensus of regions*. Students of international law and federalism disagree over whether any part of a federal state has a legal right to break away from the union. But the political facts are that when a region no longer shares the national consensus on which federalism is based, its separation becomes a real possibility.

'Federalism', declared Pierre Trudeau, 'has all along been a product of reason in politics. . . . it is an attempt to find a rational compromise between the divergent interest-groups which history has thrown together; but it is a compromise based on the will of the people.'[4] This is why federal unions are often referred to as 'pacts', 'contracts', or 'bargains.' The key role of consent may be seen in the case of the former Soviet Union. As part of the post-World War II deal between the Soviet Union and the US-led Western democracies, the countries of Estonia, Latvia, and Lithua-

Table 7.1   Federal, Confederal, and Quasi-Federal Political Systems, 2003

1. Federal	2. Confederal	3. Quasi-Federal*
Argentina	European Union	Spain
Australia	Senegambia (Senegal & Gambia)	
Austria	Serbia and Montenegro	
Belgium	Trinidad and Tobago	
Botswana	United Arab Emirates	
Brazil		
Canada		
Germany		
India		
Malaysia		
Mexico		
Nigeria		
Pakistan		
Saint Kits and Nevis		
Switzerland		
United States		
Venezuela		

*Catalon has the status of an autonomous region within Spain's borders.

nia were made members of the Soviet 'federal' state against their will. Their unwilling entry into the Soviet Union, combined with the fact that Moscow dominated the regional republics through the Communist Party's monopoly on power, exposed the hollowness of the Soviet Union's federal pretensions. But with the 1989 abolition of the Communist Party's legal monopoly on power and the greater autonomy enjoyed by the regional republics, the Soviet Union fell apart. Without even a minimal consensus on the desirability of maintaining the central government, and without the Communist Party and Red Army to keep them in check, republic after republic declared national independence.

Trudeau's argument that federalism is the product of reason will not convince Quebec separatists, whose view of 1867 is of a sell-out by an elite of 'cannibal kings'[5] who were willing to collaborate with the Anglo-Saxon oppressor. Nor does reason appear to be the chief factor explaining why disgruntled regions remain part of a federal union when their politicians and their people clearly believe that they are treated unfairly and exploited for the benefit of other regions—a century-old view in western Canada. Some argue that the 'reason' that leads to or sustains federal union may indeed be in the self-interest of some groups, but that federalism may not be reasonable from the standpoint of other groups' self-interest.

Nevertheless, the origins of federal democracies lie in compromise. The fact that some regions are more enthusiastic than others about the federal compromise—indeed, some may enter such a political arrangement only because of despair at the lack of viable alternatives—does not diminish the fact that the voluntary consent of the regions forms the basis of a federal union. Once established, however, a federal state may achieve a new dynamic. The existence of a national government and the idea of national citizenship can be centralizing factors that offset the decentralizing pull of regional interests. Federalism is sustained, then, not by sheer rational calculations on the part of regional populations and politicians. Instead, it is

sustained by a *sense of political nationality*. According to Donald Smiley, perhaps Canada's foremost expert on federalism in the previous generation, political nationality 'means that Canadians as such have reciprocal moral and legal claims upon one another that have no precise counterparts in their relations with others, and that Canadians as such have a continuing determination to carry out a significant number of important common activities together.'[6] It is, in short, a sense of political community that transcends regional, ethnic, and linguistic identifications (though it does not replace or necessarily overshadow the other identities that citizens have of themselves).

Federalism is ultimately sustained by the sense of political nationality—or community—that develops around the national state. By the same token, the breakup of a federal state is sure to be presaged by the deterioration of this sense of community. Sometimes a sense of political nationality is never solidly established in the first place, as it was not in post-independence Nigeria (1961–5). In other cases a fragile political nationality may be destroyed by a particularly divisive regional conflict, as American federalism was split asunder by the slavery issue. The most stable federal systems are those where regional communities share in a sense of political nationality that dampens the decentralizing tendencies produced by regional differences. Switzerland, the contemporary United States, and Austria are good examples of this. The Swiss case in particular demonstrates the fact that regionally based ethnolinguistic divisions do not necessarily prevent the development of a strong political nationality.

To say that a weak sense of political nationality is associated with unstable federalism really just begs the question: What determines the strength of political nationality? Why do regional divisions acquire the status of independence movements in some federal states but not in others? Several factors come into play, but the most basic is regional inequality. If the citizens of a particular region feel strongly that existing federal structures discriminate against their interests economically and politically, this places a strain on the sense of political nationality. Sentiments like these, however, are very common. A 2001 survey by the Centre for Research and Information on Canada found that Ontarians were about twice as likely as Atlantic Canadians to believe that their province was treated with the respect it deserved.[7] Such feelings do not, however, prevent people from feeling positively about Canada. A 1989 Maclean's-Decima poll rediscovered what earlier surveys had found, namely that large majorities in all provinces except Newfoundland and Quebec thought of themselves as Canadians first and provincial citizens second.[8] Predictably, Ontarians were more likely than others to place their Canadian identity before their provincial one. But the ratio of those who said they thought of themselves as Canadians first to those who placed their provincial identity first was at least five to one in every province west of Ontario, including Alberta, the centre of gravity for western feelings of alienation and resentment against Ottawa. As Alberta political scientist Roger Gibbins observes, with the exception of Quebec it is probably a mistake to think of national and provincial loyalties as competitive. 'Even western alienation', he writes, 'is primarily a frustrated sense of Canadian nationalism. Western Canadians want to play more rather than less of a role in Canadian life.'[9]

The likelihood that regional grievances may threaten the stability of federalism is greatest when they are linked to a nationalist movement. Nationalism is usually accompanied by territorial claims. These claims can range from demands for outright independence to more moderate calls for greater autonomy for the region where members of the national community are concentrated. What distinguishes nationalism from regionalism is that nationalism makes its demands on behalf of both a territory and a community that shares some ethnic, linguistic, or other cultural traits. This is far more difficult to accommodate within a federal state than are a region's complaints of unfair treatment. Indeed, nationalism linked to the social and cultural characteristics of a group is fundamental-

ly at odds with the concept of political nationality on which a viable federal state depends.

THE ORIGINS OF CANADIAN FEDERALISM

Canada's federal Constitution was a compromise. Most of the anglophone Fathers of Confederation favoured a unitary system of government under which all power would be in the hands of a new national parliament. They were opposed, however, by two groups. The strongest opposition came from the French-Canadian representatives of Canada East, what today is Quebec. This group, led by Sir George-Étienne Cartier, insisted on constitutional protection for their cultural community. They believed that the most effective way to protect their interests was through a federal union that gave exclusive jurisdiction over linguistic and cultural matters to the provincial governments. Federalism was also the preferred constitutional option of Maritime politicians. Maritimers had developed strong local identities that they were unwilling to see submerged under unitary government. Besides, in an era when politics and patronage were virtually synonymous it was only reasonable that provincial politicians would want to retain control over such important sources of contracts as roads and public works, as well as bureaucratic sinecures.

Although the anglophone politicians of Ontario and Quebec tended to be much less enthusiastic about federalism, some of them saw merit in the idea of dividing legislative powers between two levels of government. For example, Grit politician George Brown expressed the view that conflict between the English Protestant and French Catholic communities—conflict that had produced government instability and political deadlock in the legislature of the United Canadas, and that was one of the reasons behind the Confederation movement—would be reduced by assigning local matters to the provincial legislatures.[10] Ottawa would deal with matters of national interest, like trade and commerce, immigration, defence, and transportation. The presumption that sectional rivalries and local interests would not enter into deliberations on these national issues was naive, to say the least.

The forces pushing the colonies of British North America towards political union required a strong national government. Commercial interests, particularly railroad promoters, wanted unification because their ability to raise investment capital abroad was linked to Canada's creditworthiness. A larger union with a wider revenue base and an integrated national economy were crucial to the railroad promoters' interests and to those of the Canadian financial institutions linked to them. Likewise, a strong central government was needed if British North America was to assume the burden of its own military defence and if expansion into the sparsely populated region between Ontario and British Columbia was to be accomplished. Tugging in the opposite direction were the facts of cultural dualism and the existence of colonial administrations and regional societies unwilling to be completely submerged in a unitary state that would inevitably be dominated by Ontario and Quebec. Federalism was a necessary compromise between these contradictory tendencies.

What sort of federal union did the founders envisage? Obviously, different politicians had different expectations. Some, such as Canada's first Prime Minister, Sir John A. Macdonald, anticipated that the provincial governments would be little more than glorified municipalities, subordinate to Ottawa. Others, like Oliver Mowat, who as Ontario's Premier led the movement for provincial rights during the 1870s and 1880s, clearly did not share this centralist vision.[11] Individual expectations aside, the agreement the founders reached gave what then were the most important legislative powers and sources of public revenue to the federal government. Ottawa was given authority over trade and commerce, shipping, fisheries, interprovincial transportation, currency and banking, the postal service, and several other subjects related to managing the economy. Responsibility for immigration and agriculture were divided between

the federal and provincial governments, but in the event of a conflict Ottawa's legislation would prevail. The federal government was also assigned the duty to build an intercolonial railway connecting Montreal to Halifax. Together, these powers appeared to establish Ottawa's clear superiority over the provinces in economic matters. When we consider that promoting economic growth and military defence (also a federal responsibility) were two of the chief functions of the nineteenth-century state—maintaining public order was the third, and this responsibility was divided between Ottawa and the provinces—there is little doubt that Ottawa was assigned the major legislative powers of that era.

Ottawa's superiority was also clear on the taxation front. Donald Smiley notes that customs and excise taxes—indirect forms of taxation—accounted for about three-quarters of colonial revenues prior to Confederation. The Confederation agreement made these the exclusive preserve of the federal government, which could '[raise] Money by any Mode or System of Taxation' (s. 91[3]). The provinces were restricted to the less developed field of 'Direct Taxation' (s. 92[2]), as well as royalties on provincially owned natural resources (s. 109). Not only were provincial revenue sources meagre compared to those of the federal government, the Confederation agreement also established the practice of federal money transfers to the provinces (s. 118, repealed in 1950). The dependence of the economically weaker provinces on subsidies from Ottawa began in 1867 and continues to this day (see the discussion later in this chapter).

In addition to all this, the Confederation agreement included several provisions that have been described as *quasi-federal*. They appear to establish a nearly colonial relationship between Ottawa and the provinces by permitting the federal government to disallow laws passed by provincial legislatures. Sections 55, 56, and 90 of the Constitution Act, 1867 give provincial lieutenant-governors, appointees of Ottawa, the authority to reserve approval from any act passed by a provincial legislature for a period of up to one year, or to disallow the act at any time within a year of its passage. These were widely used powers during the first few decades after Confederation and were used periodically during the first half of the twentieth century. In most instances Ottawa was reacting to provincial economic policies that challenged its own priorities and jurisdiction. Moreover, Section 92(10c) gives the federal government the authority to intervene in a provincial economy by declaring that the construction of a 'public work' (this could be anything from a road to an oil field) is in the national interest. This power has been used 470 times, but has not been used since 1961. Finally, Section 93(3)(4) actually gives Ottawa the power to pass laws respecting education, an area of provincial jurisdiction. It may do so where education rights that denominational minorities held when a province entered Confederation are abrogated by provincial law. This power has never been used.

Assuming that it is even possible to sort out the founder's intentions, do they really matter? Legally, no. In interpreting the federal division of powers the courts have generally been unreceptive to arguments about what the Fathers of Confederation really had in mind.[12] Indeed, the Supreme Court of Canada's ruling in the 1981 Patriation Reference, *Re Constitution of Canada*, declared flatly that 'arguments from history do not lead to any consistent view or any single view of the nature of the British North America Act. So, too, with pronouncements by political figures or persons in other branches of public life. There is little profit in parading them.'[13]

Politically, however, arguments about intentions can matter. The argument most frequently made about Canadian federalism is that it represents a compact between French and English Canada or, alternatively, a contract between the provinces that agreed to give up certain powers to a new national government of their creation. Both the compact and contract theories of federalism maintain that the federal 'bargain' cannot be changed without the mutual consent of those who agreed to it. In the case of the compact theory, this means that Quebec—the province in which most francophones reside and the only province in which they are in the majority—should have a veto over any constitutional change that affects either the federal distribution of powers or the relative weight of Quebec in Parliament and on the Supreme Court (where three of the nine justices must be members of the Quebec bar). This argument was rejected by the Supreme Court of Canada in the 1981 Patriation Reference.

Those who argue that federalism is a contract between the provinces claim that each of them has the right to veto constitutional change that affects provincial powers or national representation. In fact, there are three variants of contract theory. One would restrict the right of veto to the original signatories (Nova Scotia, New Brunswick, Quebec, and Ontario). A second extends it to all provinces, regardless of when they joined Canada. The third takes the position that the unanimous consent of the provinces is not required to change the federal distribution of powers, but that 'substantial provincial agreement' is necessary. Like compact theory, none of these variants of contract theory has any legal foundation.

The political importance of these compact/contract theories may be seen in the fact that Canadian governments for nearly 50 years were unable to agree on a formula for amending the Constitution. Between the first serious attempt in 1935 and the 1982 promulgation of the Constitution Act, it proved impossible to get all the provincial governments to agree to an amendment formula. Unanimous provincial consent appeared to be a political requirement for enacting such a formula (although if one or two of the smaller provinces had been the only dissenters this 'requirement' might have been overcome). Moreover, many constitutionalists and political scientists came to assume—wrongly, it turned out—that unanimity or something close to it was also a legal requirement.

The compact interpretation of Canadian federalism continues to carry political weight. The Quebec government's refusal to agree to the Constitution Act, 1982 was widely viewed as a serious blow to the Constitution's legitimacy. Former Prime Minister Brian Mulroney regularly, if misleadingly, spoke of bringing Quebec into the Constitution. Legally, of course, the 1982 reforms applied right across Canada. But politically the Prime Minister had a point. The government of Quebec, whose claim to speak on behalf of one of the country's two founding nations rests on the fact that the province is home to about 90 per cent of Canadian francophones, did not consent to far-reaching constitutional changes. Both of Quebec's major provincial political parties, the Parti Québécois and the Quebec Liberal Party, insist that Canadian federalism must be understood as a compact between founding nations, a view that enjoys diminishing support in the rest of Canada. Indeed, diminished support for the idea of Canada as a binational compact is precisely the problem, claimed Claude Ryan, former leader of the Quebec Liberal Party. 'If the movement in favor of sovereignty was able to put down its roots and develop itself in Quebec,' Ryan argued, 'it is precisely because more and more Quebecers came to the conclusion that this equality, which had been the dream of many generations, will never be realized within the Canadian federation.'[14]

The contract theory of Canada lives on politically in the idea of the formal equality of the provinces. Section 2 of the Calgary Declaration, an agreement on the parameters for future constitutional negotiations that all of the provinces, except Quebec, agreed to in 1997, states that 'All provinces, while diverse in their characteristics, have equality of status.' The Declaration also stated that any constitutional amendment that confers powers on one province must make these powers available to all provinces. This involves a fundamentally different view of Canadian federalism than that which flows from the compact theory. The idea that provinces are and ought to remain formally equal—a contract theory view of federalism—is not easily squared with the notion of Quebec as a distinct society—a compact theory perspective on federalism.

THE FEDERAL DIVISION OF POWERS

Whatever the intentions of the founders may have been when they drafted the British North America Act, it is clear today that both levels of government exercise wide-ranging legislative and taxation powers. Their ability to do so ultimately rests on the responsibilities assigned to them by the Constitution. Canada's founders took exceptional pains to specify the responsibilities of each level of government. But a literal reading of the division of powers they decided on, and of the formal changes that have been made to it since then, provides at best a partial and at worst a misleading guide to Canadian federalism. In some cases policy areas were unthought of when the federal division of powers was framed—electronic communications, air transportation, and environmental protection would be examples—and so are not explicitly assigned to either Ottawa or the provinces. In other cases, what were minor responsibilities in the nineteenth and early twentieth centuries have assumed greater importance as a result of economic and societal changes, and of changes in the state itself.

The heart of the federal division of powers is found in sections 91 and 92 of the Constitution Act, 1867. Each of these sections contains a detailed list of enumerated powers that belong exclusively to Parliament (s. 91) or the provincial legislatures (s. 92). Combined with several other sections that also deal with the division of powers, this is the constitutional foundation of Canadian federalism. An examination of who holds what powers reveals that both Ottawa and the provinces have the capacity to act in most of the major policy fields (see Table 7.2).

Some of the constitutional powers listed in Table 7.2 could reasonably have been placed under more than one policy heading. The authority to tax, for example, has been used to promote economic growth, to redistribute income between groups, and to subsidize all sorts of special interests. Employment Insurance is both an econom-

Table 7.2   The Federal Division of Powers under the Constitution Acts

Public finance	Ottawa	Provinces
	Ottawa	**Provinces**
	(1867)	(1867)
	• 91(3): authority to raise money by any 'Mode or System of Taxation'	• 92(2): authorizes direct taxation within the province
	• 91(4): authority to borrow money	• 92(3): authority to borrow money
	(1982)	• 92A(4): permits provinces to use 'any mode or system of taxation' in the case of non-renewable natural resources, forestry resources, and electrical energy
	• 36(2): commits Ottawa to the principle of equalizing public revenue levels in the provinces	
Managing the economy	(1867)	(1867)
	• 91(2): regulation of trade and commerce	• 92(9): authority to issue commercial licences
	• 91(2A): unemployment insurance	• 92(10): public works within the province
	• 91(5): post office	• 92(11): incorporation of companies with provincial objects
	• 91(10, 12): navigation, international waters, and offshore resources	• 92(13): property and civil rights
	• 91(14, 15, 16, 18, 19, 20): national monetary system	• 92A: reaffirms provincial authority over natural resources within their borders
	• 91(17, 22, 23): commercial standards	• 95: agriculture, but federal law takes precedence
	• 92(10.c): authority to intervene in a provincial economy by declaring a public work to be in the national interest	• 109: establishes provincial ownership of natural resources within their borders
	• 95: agriculture	
	• 121: prohibits provincial taxes on imports from other provinces, thus reinforcing the concept of a national economic union	
	(1982)	(1982)
	• 6(2): guarantees the economic mobility of citizens anywhere within Canada, reinforcing the concept of a national economic union	• 6(4): permits provinces to favour provincial residents in hiring if the rate of unemployment in that province is above the national average
Social policy and the quality of life	(1867)	(1867)
	• 91(24): Aboriginal Canadians	• 92(7): hospitals
	• 91(26): marriage and divorce	• 92(12): solemnization of marriage
	• 93(3, 4): authority to protect the educational rights of denominational minorities	• 93: education
	• 94A: old age pensions, but provincial law prevails	• 94A: public pensions
	• 95: immigration	• 95: immigration, but federal law prevails
Cultural policy	(1867)	(1867)
	• 133: official bilingualism of Parliament	• 92(16): all matters of a merely local or private nature
	(1982)	• 93: education
	• 16(l), 19, 20: establishes official bilingualism in all institutions of the federal government	• 133: official bilingualism of Quebec legislature
		(1982)
		• 16(2), 17(2), 18(2), 19(2), 20(2): establishes official bilingualism in all institutions of the New Brunswick government

Table 7.2 continued

Administration and enforcement of law	Ottawa (1867)	Provinces (1867)
	• 91(27): criminal law • 91(28): penitentiaries • 96: appointment of judges of provincial courts • 100: authority to set judicial salaries • 101: authority to establish a general court of appeal for Canada, and other federal courts	• 92(14): administration of justice and the organization of courts within the province • 92(15): authority to establish penalties for violations of provincial laws
International relations and defence	(1867) • 91(7): military and defence • 132: authority to enter foreign treaties and perform obligations under them	(1867) • Since the Supreme Court's decision in the *Labour Conventions* case of 1937, it appears that provincial consent is required to implement foreign treaty obligations involving matters of provincial jurisdiction. There is, however, no consensus on this.
Other legislative authority	(1867) • 91 (preamble): authorizes Parliament to make laws for the 'peace, order, and good government' of Canada • 91(29): matters not falling under the enumerated powers of the provinces come under Ottawa's jurisdiction	(1867) • 92(8): municipal institutions • 92(16): all matters of a local or private nature in the province

ic policy, tied to manpower retraining and a claimant's job search activities, and a social policy that has the effect of redistributing income to less affluent regions of the country. Immigration policy has always been harnessed to the needs of the Canadian economy and has also been tied to cultural policy through citizenship services and language training for immigrants.

At the same time, governments have sometimes found the authority to legislate in powers that are implied, rather than stated, in the Constitution. The most important example of this involves the federal government's spending power. Ottawa spends billions of dollars annually on programs that fall under the jurisdiction of provincial and municipal governments. The feds also provide money to universities (for research and student scholarships) and to school boards (for language instruction), even though these organizations fall under the constitutional author-

ity of the provinces, and to individuals for purposes that might appear to fall under provincial jurisdiction (e.g., tax benefits for child care). Ottawa's constitutional 'right' to spend money for any purpose has never been definitely established in the courts.[15] Nevertheless, the spending power today provides the constitutional basis for such major federal grants to the provinces as the Canada Health and Social Transfer (CHST) and equalization payments.

THE COURTS AND FEDERALISM

Only the layperson expects constitutional terms like 'trade and commerce', 'property and civil rights', and 'direct taxation' to have straightforward meanings. This view has not been shared by constitutional lawyers, governments, and the private interests that have challenged federal and provincial laws. For these groups the federal division of powers is a dense thicket of contradictory and contested meanings and opportunities, and the interpretation attached to a particular enumerated power is often a matter to haggle over in the courts. The judicial decisions that have resulted from these disputes have played an important role in shaping the evolution of Canadian federalism. Among the many contentious sections of the Constitution, the courts' interpretation of Ottawa's authority to 'make laws for the peace, order, and good government of Canada' (POGG) and the federal government's 'trade and commerce' power have had the greatest impact on the division of powers. We will look briefly at each of these.

Peace, Order, and Good Government

The courts have tended to place a narrow interpretation on the federal Parliament's general authority to make laws for the 'peace, order, and good government of Canada'. This has been reduced over time to an emergency power that can provide the constitutional basis for federal actions in special circumstances. It cannot, however, be used to justify federal laws during 'normal' times. This narrow interpretation of POGG began with the *Local Prohibition Case* (1896). The Judicial Committee of the Privy Council ruled that POGG could not be used by Ottawa to override the enumerated powers of the provinces. The decision also marked the introduction into Canadian constitutional law of the 'national dimensions' test. Lord Watson wrote:

> Their Lordships do not doubt that some matters, in their origin local or provincial, might attain such dimensions as to affect the body politic of the Dominion, and to justify the Canadian Parliament in passing laws for their regulation or abolition in the interest of the Dominion.[16]

When does a matter acquire 'national dimensions'? This question was dealt with in a series of three decisions handed down in 1922, 1923, and 1925. In *Re Board of Commerce Act and Combines*

and Fair Prices Act 1919 (1922), the JCPC struck down two federal laws introduced after World War I to prevent business monopoly and hoarding of essential commodities. For the first time the JCPC articulated the 'emergency doctrine', according to which Parliament could pass laws under the authority of POGG only in the case of a national emergency. Writing for the majority, Viscount Haldane declared that:

> [C]ircumstances are conceivable, such as those of war or famine, when the peace, order and good Government of the Dominion might be imperilled under conditions so exceptional that they require legislation of a character in reality beyond anything provided for by the enumerated heads in either s. 92 or s. 91.[17]

Essentially, the JCPC ruled that some national crisis must exist before federal laws can be based on POGG. The fact that a matter has acquired 'national dimensions' would not, by itself, be sufficient to justify such exceptional legislation.

Despite the JCPC's admission that peacetime circumstances could conceivably warrant Ottawa acting under the authority of POGG, subsequent rulings suggested that POGG was really a wartime power. In the first of these decisions, *Fort Frances Pulp and Power Co. v. Manitoba Free Press* (1923), the JCPC declared that war-related circumstances were sufficient to warrant legislating under POGG. Moreover, Viscount Haldane's opinion in *Fort Frances* indicated that the courts should be reluctant to question Parliament's judgement that a war-related emergency exists. Rulings in 1947 by the JCPC and in 1950 by the Supreme Court of Canada repeated this view.[18]

In those cases where the courts have rejected POGG as a valid basis for federal legislation, the impugned laws were intended to deal with peacetime circumstances. The first of these was the decision in *Toronto Electric Commissioners v. Snider* (1925). Relying on the 'emergency doctrine' that it had developed in the *Board of Commerce* case, the JCPC struck down Canada's major industrial relations law, the Industrial Disputes

Investigation Act, 1907. The JCPC again rejected peacetime recourse to POGG in the 1937 reference decision on Ottawa's Employment and Social Insurance Act, 1935.[19] The federal government's attempt to justify this law under POGG, on the grounds that unemployment was a matter of national concern and, moreover, that it threatened the well-being of the country was considered inadequate by the JCPC.

Confronted with broadly similar reasoning in the 1970s, the Supreme Court of Canada found that POGG could be used to justify federal laws during peacetime. The Court was asked to rule on the constitutionality of Ottawa's Anti-Inflation Act, 1975. A majority of the Court accepted the federal government's argument that mounting inflationary pressures constituted an emergency justifying legislation that encroached on provincial jurisdiction. Not only was the 'emergency doctrine' liberated from war-related circumstances, the Court also indicated its reluctance to challenge Parliament's judgement on when emergency circumstances exist. The result, according to constitutionalists such as Peter Russell, is that Ottawa now appears to have fairly easy access to emergency powers under this doctrine.[20] Constitutionally this may be so. Politically, however, any federal government would think twice before legislating under this contentious power. In the 28 years since Ottawa won this constitutional victory there has not been a single instance where the federal government has relied on POGG as the basis for an alleged intrusion into provincial jurisdiction.

Trade and Commerce

On the face of it, Ottawa's authority over the regulation of trade and commerce (s. 91[2]) appears rather sweeping. Any economic activity or transaction would seem to fall within its scope. In fact, however, court decisions have construed the trade and commerce power to be much narrower, limited largely to interprovincial and international trade. At the same time, provincial jurisdiction over property and civil rights in the province (s.

92[13]) has been interpreted as the provinces' own 'trade and commerce' power. This line of judicial interpretation began with the decision in *Citizens' Insurance Co. v. Parsons* (1881). Based on its view that a broad, literal interpretation of s. 91(2) of the Constitution Act, 1867 would bring any and all aspects of economic life under the authority of Ottawa, leaving the provinces powerless to affect business, the JCPC interpreted 'regulation of trade and commerce' to include 'political arrangements in regard to trade requiring the sanction of parliament, regulation of trade in matters of interprovincial concern, and it may be that they would include general regulation of trade affecting the whole Dominion'.[21] To construe Ottawa's trade and commerce power otherwise, the JCPC argued, would be to deny the 'fair and ordinary meaning' of s. 92(13) of the Constitution Act, 1867, which assigns property and civil rights in the province to the provincial governments.

The legacy of *Parsons* has been that Ottawa's authority to regulate trade and commerce has been limited to interprovincial trade, international trade, and general trade affecting the whole of Canada. But even this definition of federal jurisdiction has presented problems of interpretation. For example, what about a federal law whose principal goal is to regulate trade that crosses provincial borders but has as an incidental effect the regulation of some transactions that occur wholly within a province? Is such a law constitutional under s. 91(2)? Until the 1950s the courts' answer was 'no'.[22] But a series of Supreme Court decisions, culminating in *Caloil v. Attorney General of Canada* (1971), signified a broader interpretation of Ottawa's power to regulate interprovincial trade.[23] In *Caloil*, the Court acknowledged that a federal law prohibiting the transportation or sale of imported oil west of the Ottawa Valley interfered with local trade in a province. Nevertheless, the Court upheld the federal law on the grounds that its 'true character' was 'the control of imports in the furtherance of an extraprovincial trade policy'.[24] Ottawa's authority was given an additional boost by a 1971 reference decision of the Supreme

Court. In the *'Chicken and Egg' Reference*—no kidding, 'Chicken and Egg'—the Court ruled unconstitutional a provincial egg-marketing scheme that restricted imports from other provinces on the grounds that it encroached on Ottawa's trade and commerce power. Justice Bora Laskin, who would later become Chief Justice of the Supreme Court, referred specifically to the trend towards a more balanced interpretation of federal and provincial jurisdiction over trade.[25] Laskin went on to argue that 'to permit each province to seek its own advantage . . . through a figurative sealing of its borders to entry of goods from others would be to deny one of the objects of Confederation . . . namely, to form an economic unit of the whole of Canada.'[26] The current situation may be described as *Parsons + Caloil* = 'trade and commerce'.

What of the *Parsons* allusion to general trade affecting the whole of Canada? Constitutional expert Peter Hogg suggests that its meaning remains obscure, but that it could conceivably provide the basis for federal laws regulating business. In both *MacDonald* v. *Vapor Canada Ltd.* (1977) and *Attorney General of Canada* v. *Canadian National Transportation* (1983), the Court raised the question of when trade affects the whole country, thereby justifying, per *Parsons*, federal regulation under the trade and commerce power. It has not yet given a definitive answer.[27]

The Impact of Judicial Decisions

Court rulings seldom put an end to conflicts between Ottawa and the provinces. Instead, they typically become part of the bargaining process between governments. Consider the following examples:

- *Employment and Social Insurance Act Reference* (1937). The JCPC struck down a federal statute establishing a program to deal with national unemployment. This was followed by negotiations between the federal and provincial governments, leading to a 1940 constitutional amendment that gave Ottawa authority over unemployment insurance.

- *Public Service Board v. Dionne* (1978). The Supreme Court confirmed Ottawa's exclusive jurisdiction to regulate television broadcasting. Immediately after the decision was handed down, the federal Minister of Communications announced Ottawa's willingness to negotiate some division of authority with the provinces.

- *CIGOL v. Government of Saskatchewan* (1978). In *CIGOL*, a provincial tax on natural gas was found to be a direct tax and therefore outside the jurisdiction of the province. When Ottawa and the provinces were negotiating constitutional reform in 1980–1, the issue of provincial control over natural resources was on the table. The result was s. 92A of the Constitution Act. It appears to permit the form of resource taxation that was ruled ultra vires in the *CIGOL* decision.

- *Re Constitution of Canada* (1981). The Supreme Court ruled that Ottawa's proposal to patriate the British North America Act and to change it in ways affecting provincial powers was legal, but that it was unconstitutional in the conventional sense (see Chapter 5). The decision gave the federal government a legal victory, at the same time as the provinces were given the moral high ground. Within weeks all governments were back at the table trying to find a negotiated solution.

- *Reference re Secession of Quebec* (1998). On the face of it, this appeared to be a victory for Ottawa and federalist forces generally. The Supreme Court ruled that neither the Canadian Constitution nor international law confers on the government and National Assembly of Quebec the right to secede from Canada unilaterally. The Court added, however, that a 'clear majority vote in Quebec on a clear question in favour of secession would confer democratic legitimacy on the secession initiative which all of the other participants in Confederation would have to recognize.' So who really won, the separatists or the federalists? As was also true of the Court's ambiguous 1981 pronouncement in the Patriation Reference, both sides were able to claim a victory of sorts. The 1998 ruling did not resolve the issue of Quebec separation—indeed, no one expected that this would be its result. Instead, by clarifying some of the constitutional questions associated with Quebec secession the Court provided all sides in this ongoing political struggle with ammunition for future sniping.

EVOLVING FEDERALISM

It is generally believed that judicial decisions have pushed Canadian federalism in a more decentralist direction than the Fathers of Confederation planned, but that this tendency has been attenuated since 1949 when the Supreme Court became Canada's highest court of appeal. Some bemoan the judiciary's decentralizing influence, particularly that of the JCPC during Canada's first half-century. Others maintain that the limits placed on Ottawa's general legislative authority (POGG) and trade and commerce power, and the broad interpretation of such provincial powers as property and civil rights, have reflected the political reality of Canada. As Pierre Trudeau observed, 'it has long been the custom in English Canada to denounce the [Judicial Committee of the] Privy Council for its provincial bias; but it should perhaps be considered that if the law lords had not leaned in that direction, Quebec separatism might not be a threat today: it might be an accomplished fact.'[28]

Judicial review is only one of the factors that have shaped the evolution of federalism. In fact, legal disputes over the division of powers are only symptomatic of underlying tensions at the root of intergovernmental conflict. These tensions have three main sources: (1) the status of Quebec and the powers of the Quebec state; (2) relations between the more heavily industrialized and populous centre of the country and the outlying western and eastern regions; and (3) the political and administrative needs of governments.

Quebec

'What does Quebec want?' The question has been asked countless times over the years by English Canadians, some of whom genuinely wanted to know and others who asked it out of exasperation, believing all along that the answer would be unacceptable. The complementary question— 'What does English Canada want?'—has seldom been posed. Yet neither question makes sense in isolation from the other. To understand what Quebec wants from Canada it is also necessary to consider what the rest of Canada expects from, and is willing to concede to, Quebec. Quebec's unique role in Canadian federalism derives from two factors. One is its predominantly French-speaking character. About 85 per cent of the provincial population claims French as their mother tongue, and about 90 per cent of all Canadian francophones reside in Quebec. The second factor is Quebec's size. At Confederation it was the second most populous province and Montreal was the hub of Canada's commercial and financial industries. Although its weight relative to the rest of Canada is much less today, Quebec is still Canada's second most populous province, accounting for slightly less than one-quarter of Canada's population. Economically, Quebec's gross provincial product and its importance as a centre for finance and manufacturing are surpassed only by Ontario.

Quebec's distinctive social and cultural fabric explain why it has made special demands on Canadian federalism. Because it is a large province with the second largest bloc of seats in the federal Parliament and because francophones have always been able to control Quebec's provincial legislature, the demands of Quebec have had a significant impact on the evolution of Canadian federalism. This impact has been experienced on two main fronts: the Constitution and the financial and administrative practices of federalism. We will examine Quebec's impact on the financial and administrative dimensions of federalism later in this chapter.

Quebec's influence on the Constitution predates the Confederation agreement. Between 1848 and 1867 Ontario and Quebec formed the United Canadas, governed by a single legislature in which the two colonies held equal representation. It was during this period that the *double-majority* practice developed. To become law, a bill had to be approved by a majority of members on both the Ontario and Quebec sides of the legislature. This was Canada's first experience with the federal principle of regional representation. Predominantly francophone Quebec and predominantly anglophone Ontario were joined in a legislative partnership that required the agreement of both regional communities in order to work. It turned out, however, to be a failure. Quebec's influence on the Constitution was strongly evident in the Confederation agreement. Its representatives were the most insistent on a federal constitution for Canada, under which the provincial government would have authority over those matters considered vital to the preservation of the language, religion, and social institutions of Quebec. Indeed, for decades the clerical and political leaders of French Canada were unanimous in viewing Canadian federalism as a pact between two peoples. 'Canadian Confederation', declared Henri Bourassa, 'is the result of a contract between the two races in Canada, French and English, based on equality and recognizing equal rights and reciprocal duties. Canadian Confederation will last only as long as this equality of rights is recognized as the basis of the public right in Canada, from Halifax to Vancouver.'[29]

The equality Bourassa had in mind did not last very long. It was violated in Manitoba, where the status of French in the provincial legislature and the educational rights of francophone Catholics were swept away a couple of decades after that province entered Confederation. It was also violated in Ontario, where Regulation 17 (1913) banned French instruction from the province's public schools. These developments contributed to the identification of French Canada with Quebec, the only province in which francophones were in the majority and where they could effectively defend their rights and preserve their culture.

The constitutional consequences of limiting French Canada to the boundaries of Quebec became apparent by the middle of the twentieth century. As Ottawa became increasingly involved in areas of provincial jurisdiction, particularly through its spending power but also by monopolizing the field of direct taxation between 1947 and 1954, the Quebec government became more and more protective of what it argued were exclusive provincial powers under the Constitution. But not until the Quiet Revolution of the 1960s, marking the eclipse of the conservative anti-statist nationalism that had dominated Quebec politics for more than a century, was Quebec's resentment towards Ottawa's encroachment onto provincial territory matched by aggressive constitutional demands. The first major indication of this occurred during the federal-provincial negotiations on a public old-age pension scheme (1963–5). Quebec Premier Jean Lesage stated that his government would only agree to a constitutional amendment giving Ottawa the authority to pass pension legislation if Quebec were able to opt out of the federal plan. Ottawa agreed, and so was born the Canadian practice of provinces being able to opt out of federal shared-cost programs without suffering any financial loss.

Quebec's constitutional demands appeared to become even more ambitious a few years later. The 1966 provincial election saw the Union Nationale (UN) run on the slogan 'Quebec d'abord!' (Quebec first!) The party's leader, Daniel Johnson, had authored a book entitled *Egalité ou indépendance*, and in the election campaign the UN called for major constitutional reform that included the transfer of virtually all social and cultural matters to the province, constitutional recognition of Canada's binational character, and exclusive provincial control over the major tax fields then shared with Ottawa. In fact, however, these demands were not pursued with much vigour during the party's time in power (1966–70). The one constitutional issue on which the UN government did confront Ottawa was that of international representation for Quebec. But as Kenneth McRoberts observes:

In purely symbolic terms Quebec's demands seemed very significant; Quebec was seeking to assume what many regarded as the trappings of sovereignty. Yet . . . these demands did not directly attack the real distribution of power and responsibilities to the extent that various Lesage demands, such as a separate Quebec Pension Plan, had.[30]

Despite the lack of substantive change in Quebec's constitutional status and powers during this period, the province's nationalist undercurrent was gaining momentum. The creation of the Parti Québécois (PQ) in 1968, under the leadership of René Lévesque, brought under one roof most of the major groups committed to the eventual political independence of Quebec. The Liberal Party of Quebec remained federalist, but advocated what amounted to special status for Quebec within Canadian federalism. 'Un fédéralisme rentable' (profitable federalism) was the passionless way in which Liberal leader Robert Bourassa explained Quebec's commitment to Canada.

Constitutional negotiations between Ottawa and the provinces had been ongoing since 1968. The 1970 election of a Liberal government in Quebec appeared to provide an opportunity to bring these talks to a successful conclusion. But when the 11 governments got together at Victoria in 1971, it became apparent that Quebec's price for agreeing to a constitutional amendment formula and a charter of rights was higher than Ottawa was willing to pay.[31] The impasse was over social policy. Quebec demanded constitutional supremacy in an area in which Ottawa operated several major programs, such as Family Allowances, Unemployment Insurance, manpower training, and old-age pensions. Moreover, the Quebec government wanted the fiscal means to pay for provincial policies in these fields. Ottawa went some way towards meeting these demands. The Trudeau government refused, however, to concede the principle of provincial supremacy over social policy and would not provide a constitutional guarantee that provinces would receive financial compensation for operating their own programs in these areas. The federal-provincial compromise reached in Victoria fell apart days later in Quebec, where the deal was widely seen as constitutional entrenchment of an unacceptable status quo.

After Quebec's rejection of the Victoria Charter, the Bourassa government adopted a piecemeal strategy for changing federalism, negotiating with Ottawa on single issues like Family Allowances, social security, and telecommunications. It was unsuccessful, however, in extracting any major concessions from a federal government that believed provincial powers were already too great and that was staunchly opposed to special status for Quebec.

A rather different strategy was followed by the PQ government of René Lévesque after it came to power in 1976. The PQ was committed to holding a provincial referendum on its option of political sovereignty for Quebec, combined with some form of economic association with the rest of Canada. But instead of simple confrontation with Ottawa, the Lévesque government pursued an *étapiste* (gradualist) strategy of providing 'good government'—which required some degree of co-operation with Ottawa because of the intricate network of intergovernmental programs and agreements—while attempting to convince the Quebec population that its best interests lay in sovereignty-association. The two governments co-operated on dozens of new capital spending projects, on management of the economy, and on immigration policy. The PQ government even participated in federal-provincial talks on constitutional reform in 1978–9.[32] All of this occurred against the background of the looming referendum on the PQ's separatist option.

Sovereignty-association was rejected by Quebec voters in May 1980. But they re-elected the PQ in 1981. It was thus a PQ government that participated in the constitutional negotiations towards 'renewed federalism' that the federal Liberal government had initiated after the Quebec referendum. But it was also a PQ government that refused to sign the final product of these talks, the November 1981 accord that became the Constitution Act, 1982. The PQ's refusal was hardly surprising in light of the fact that none of the demands that Quebec governments had made since the 1960s were included in the 1981 constitutional accord. Indeed, the province's Liberal opposition also found the accord to be unacceptable. The Constitution had undergone its most dramatic reform since its passage in 1867, but the provincial government of the country's second largest province and home to 90 per cent of Canada's francophones had not agreed to these changes. Although the legality of the Constitution Act, 1982 was not in doubt, its political legitimacy was.

This was the situation when Robert Bourassa and the provincial Liberals were returned to power in 1985. Their election appeared to reflect the muted tenor of Quebec nationalism in the post-referendum era. Change had also taken place in Ottawa. Prime Minister Brian Mulroney, elected in 1984, did not share Pierre Trudeau's view that the provinces were already too powerful for the good of the national economy and political unity. Nor was he viscerally opposed to some form of special status for Quebec, as Trudeau was. Conditions seemed propitious, therefore, for 'bringing Quebec into the constitutional family'—a phrase favoured by Prime Minister Mulroney.

It was not to be. The Quebec government put forward a package of five demands that had to be met before it would agree to the constitutional reforms passed in 1982. These proposals were agreed to by Ottawa and all of the provincial premiers on 30 April 1987, forming the basis for what became known as the Meech Lake Accord. As we have seen in Chapter 5, these constitutional proposals died on the drawing board, and two years later, in 1992, the Charlottetown proposals for constitutional reform, which offered Quebec even more and also brought Aboriginal Canadians to the table, were defeated in a national referendum.

In the wake of the Charlottetown Accord's rejection, politicians of all stripes fled from the constitutional issue. Indeed, the whole question of constitutional reform was conspicuously absent from the Liberal Party's 1993 'Red Book', its official statement of policy positions and promises. Nor was it an issue in the 1993 federal election campaign, at least not outside Quebec. In Quebec, however, these matters were kept before the voters by the Bloc Québécois, under the leadership of Lucien Bouchard. The Bloc's raison d'être was, of course, to achieve political independence for Quebec. Their success in capturing 54 of Quebec's 75 seats in the House of Commons may not have been a surrogate vote for separation, but it certainly demonstrated the depth of Quebec voters' dissatisfaction with the federal government and existing constitutional arrangements.

Despite their obvious wish to avoid the constitutional quagmire, the Liberals were forced to confront the issue as a result of the 1994 election of the PQ in Quebec. The PQ was committed to holding a referendum on Quebec independence within a year of their election. When the referendum campaign began in September 1995, the *indépendantiste* side got off to a sputtering start. There appeared to be a little enthusiasm among Québécois for the PQ's separatist vision, and the early polls showed the 'no' side to be leading by a margin of as much as 20 percentage points. The federalist campaign relied on messages intended to convince Quebecers that they would suffer economically if the province voted 'yes'. Federal Minister of Finance Paul Martin and prominent business spokespersons warned Quebec voters that the days after separation would be dark ones.

About halfway through the campaign, however, leadership of the 'yes' side passed from Quebec Premier Jacques Parizeau to Bloc Québécois leader Lucien Bouchard. Support for independence took off, no doubt due in large measure to Bouchard's charismatic style and unsurpassed ability to connect emotionally with francophone Quebecers, but also due to what in retrospect can be seen to have been a terribly uninspired campaign by the federalists. Prime Minister Jean Chrétien chose to stay on the sidelines until the last couple of weeks of the campaign, when polls showed the 'yes' side to be leading. His previous refusal to make any concrete constitutional offer to Quebec wavered during the period before the vote, when he suggested that he supported constitutional recognition of Quebec as a distinct society and a Quebec veto over constitutional reform. On 30 October 1995, the 'yes' side emerged with the narrowest of victories: 49.6 per cent against independence, 48.5 per cent for, with spoiled ballots accounting for the rest.

The federal government's reluctance to deal with the issue of constitutional reform and Quebec's demands, before the 1995 referendum forced its hand, was due in great measure to its realization that Canadians' reactions to the constitutional issue tended to range from indifference to deep hostility. But as their uncertain performance in the referendum campaign showed, the Liberals' silence may also have been due to their inability to formulate a positive response to the sovereignty option proposed by Quebec nationalists.

This inability can be traced to the Liberal model of federalism that took shape during the Trudeau era. Although not centralist in any absolute sense—Canada is surely among the least centralized federal systems in the world—this model assumes that a strong central government is essential to the maintenance of Canadian unity. Moreover, it is in general opposed to what is called 'asymmetrical federalism', i.e., the constitutional recognition of differences in the status and powers of provincial governments; in particular, it is against constitutional entrenchment of special status for Quebec. The Constitution Act of 1982, particularly the Charter and the denial of a right of constitutional veto to any single province, embodies this vision of federalism.

This model is, of course, hotly contested. The main challenge comes from Quebec nationalists, not only from separatists but also from Quebec's nationalist-federalists. This latter group, which includes the Liberal Party of Quebec, maintains that constitutional reforms, including, at a minimum, recognition of Quebec's special responsibility for the protection and promotion of the French language in Canada and a Quebec veto over constitutional change, are necessary to keep Quebecers interested in Canadian federalism. The federal Liberals, since Trudeau stepped down as party leader in 1984, have shown a willingness to concede much of what the nationalist-federalists demand, as seen in the party's support for the Meech Lake and Charlottetown Accords. However, their enthusiasm for these constitutional reforms has been tempered both by a realization that they receive mixed reviews among voters in Ontario and generate downright hostility in western Canada, and by a vestigial loyalty among many Liberals to Trudeau's brand of no-special-status-for-Quebec federalism.

In the wake of the close call experienced by federalists in the 1995 Quebec referendum, where a clear majority of francophones voted for the sovereignty option, the federal Liberal Party showed that it was ready to cut the cord connecting it to the Trudeau era. Only weeks after the referendum the Liberal government introduced a motion recognizing Quebec as a distinct society, assigning the province a veto over constitutional change (Ontario and British Columbia were also assigned veto power, as were the prairie and Atlantic regions if at least two provinces representing more than 50 per cent of the regional population opposed a proposed amendment), and transferring to Quebec some authority for job training. The first two of this trio of reforms have clear constitutional implications. The federal motion does not, of course, change the written Constitution. However, to the extent that Ottawa allows its behaviour to be governed by what the Liberal government characterized as a constitutional offer to Quebecers, it does change the Constitution in an informal way.

This, in fact, marks a return to a tradition of Canadian federalism that predates Pierre Trudeau's entry into federal politics. It is a tradition familiar to students of the British Constitution and of Canadian federalism alike, whereby constitutional change is not the result of formal amendments to the written Constitution but of developments in policy and practice whose status is greater than that of ordinary laws but not quite that of tablets brought down from Mount Sinai.

Centre-Periphery Relations

Canada spans five and a half time zones and occupies the second largest land mass of any country, and yet the narrow belt that runs between Windsor and Montreal—the 'industrial heartland' of Canada—is home to over 55 per cent of Canada's population and generates over 60 per cent of national income and production. Ontario and Quebec together account for just under 60 per cent of the 301 seats in the House of Commons. No national political party can hope to form a government without considerable support from the voters of at least one, and usually both, of these provinces. They comprise Canada's centre, in terms of both their political and economic power.

Predictably, the provincial governments of Ontario and Quebec carry greater weight in Canadian federalism than do those of the other provinces. The other eight provincial governments preside over regions whose interests have usually been subordinated by Ottawa to those of central Canada. In this sense these other provinces constitute Canada's *peripheries*, situated on the edge—sometimes precariously so—of national politics. Resentment against central Canada and the federal government has deep roots in the politics of these provinces, particularly in the West. Their litany of historical grievances includes, to mention only a few: tariff policy that for a century protected manufacturing jobs and corporate profits in Ontario and Quebec; the perceived insensitivity of the country's Toronto- and Montreal-based financial institutions when it comes to western interests; Ottawa's treatment of the petroleum resources that are concentrated in the West; investment and spending decisions by the federal government; official bilingualism and what westerners in particular perceive to be Ottawa's favouritism towards Quebec's interests.

No one can seriously doubt that the peripheral provinces have a case. As Donald Smiley has written, 'there are dangers that Canadian problems will be resolved almost entirely within the framework of the heartland of the country with the progressive alienation from national affairs of those who live on the peripheries.'[33]

The federal principle of regional representation is embodied in the Canadian Senate and is practised assiduously by prime ministers in selecting cabinet ministers and in making certain other federal appointments, yet this federal deference to regionalism has not provided these regions with what they believe to be an adequate voice in national politics. **Intrastate federalism**—the representation and accommodation of regional interests within national political institutions—has been an abysmal failure in Canada. Deprived of significant influence in Ottawa, the peripheral regions of the country have tended to rely on their provincial governments for the protection and promotion of their interests.

The fact that more MPs are elected from Ontario and Quebec than from all the other provinces combined has always been the root cause of Ottawa's tendency to favour central Canadian interests. This political factor has been reinforced by the ideological bias of Canadian politics, a bias that has tended to interpret Canadian history and identity in terms of experiences that are more germaine to central Canada than to the peripheral regions. The very concept of 'Canada' has usually been associated with a counter-revolutionary or Loyalist tradition based on a rejection of the values and political institutions of the United States and with the cultural dualism so important to the political history of central Canada. Neither of these experiences is central to the identity and political consciousness of western Canadians.[34] In the East, too, the national myths, symbols, and identities associated with 'Canada' often have had little relationship to the experience of Maritimers.[35]

The dominance of Ontario and Quebec in national politics and the subordinate status of the interests and cultural values of the peripheral regions of the country have always been reflected in relations between Ottawa and the provincial governments of the peripheries. For example, although Ottawa has exercised its constitutional power to disallow provincial laws 112 times, only a few of these were laws passed by Ontario or Quebec.[36] When Manitoba joined Confederation in 1870 it did so without control over public lands situated in the province.[37] Ottawa retained control in order to promote its own nation-building strategy relating to railway construction and western settlement. Similarly, when Saskatchewan and Alberta became provinces in 1905 they did not immediately acquire control over public lands and natural resources within their borders.[38] Ottawa kept these powers to itself, using the argument that this was necessary to accomplish its immigration and settlement objectives for western Canada. All of these provinces received subsidies from Ottawa as compensation for the revenue they were deprived of by not controlling public lands and, in Alberta and Saskatchewan, natural resources. Their governments did not consider this to be adequate recompense for the quasi-colonial status imposed on them by Ottawa.

There is nothing subtle about the disallowance power, or about denying some provinces constitutional powers possessed by other provincial governments. Today's list of grievances against Ottawa is comprised of less blatant forms of policy discrimination against the interests of the peripheries. Among the items perennially on this list are claims that Ottawa does too little to support prairie grain farmers or the east coast fishing industry, and that the federal government's spending decisions unfairly favour Ontario and Quebec. Even in provinces like Alberta and British Columbia, which are wealthy by Canadian standards, a sense of powerlessness in the face of central Canadian dominance is a major component of their provincial politics. 'The West', observes Alberta historian Doug Owram, 'has never felt in control of its own destiny. None of the wealth of recent years has eased this feeling.

In fact, the tremendous wealth of the region merely sharpens the contrast with the political powerlessness that exists on the national level.'[39]

This contrast between the economic strength and political weakness of the West, or at least of British Columbia and Alberta, is more likely to sharpen than diminish in the future. Between 1994 and 2002 British Columbia's population grew by about 500,000 persons, Alberta's by roughly 400,000, but Quebec's by only about 250,000. British Columbia has become Canada's fastest-growing province, and the combined population of British Columbia and Alberta is poised to surpass that of Quebec within the next several years. Moreover, the economic muscle of these westernmost provinces has also increased in recent years. About one-third of the 100 largest industrial firms in Canada have their head offices in either British Columbia or Alberta, compared to about 60 per cent in Ontario and Quebec. The West's share has increased significantly over the last decade. At the level of major cities, the economic prosperity and buoyant growth that have characterized Vancouver and Calgary for most of the last two decades contrasts sharply with the obvious economic decline of Montreal, the hub of Quebec's economy.

It would appear unlikely that the West, aware of its economic strength and its growing population, will become less resentful of what it perceives to be the domination of national politics by Ontario and Quebec.

State Interests and Intergovernmental Conflict

The fact that Quebec is overwhelmingly francophone, while the other provinces are not, gives it a special set of interests that any Quebec government feels bound to defend. Likewise, grain farming in Saskatchewan, petroleum in Alberta, the automotive industry in Ontario, and forestry in British Columbia shape the positions taken by the governments of these provinces on taxation, trade, and other policies affecting these interests.

Each province comprises a particular constellation of economic, social, and cultural interests that together influence the demands its provincial government makes on federalism. Intergovernmental conflict, then, is to some extent the clash of conflicting regional interests.

This is, however, only part of the explanation. Governments do not simply reflect societal interests. They actively shape these interests through their policies, sometimes deliberately and other times inadvertently. Moreover, governments have their own political and administrative interests, the pursuit of which may have nothing to do with the interests of those they represent. 'Canadian federalism', Alan Cairns has argued, 'is about governments, governments that are possessed of massive human and financial resources, that are driven by purposes fashioned by elites, and that accord high priority to their own long-term institutional self-interest.'[40] This state-centred interpretation of federalism maintains that conflicts between governments are likely to be generated, or at least influenced, by the 'institutional self-interest' of politicians and bureaucrats.

The evidence in support of this view is overwhelming. Intergovernmental turf wars, over their respective shares of particular tax fields and over which level will have jurisdiction over what matters, often seem remote from the concerns of Canadian citizens. For example, in 1998 the federal government proudly announced the creation of the Millennium Scholarship to provide financial assistance to university students. Provincial governments immediately cried foul, pointing out that education falls under provincial jurisdiction and that Ottawa had not even consulted them on this new initiative. One suspects that for the students eligible to receive the money, its source was a matter of total irrelevance. But from the point of view of governments, how revenue sources and legislative competence are divided between them affects the ability of politicians to pursue their interest in re-election, career advancement and personal prestige, and their own conception of the public interest. So, too, with bureaucratic offi-

cials, we may assume that they are not indifferent to matters that influence the future of the organizations and programs to which their personal career fortunes and ambitions, and their own conception of the public interest, are tied.

When the political and administrative needs of governments are reinforced by the demands of provincially oriented economic interests this may give rise to what has been called **province-building**. As the term suggests, this is the provincial counterpart to the nation-building orientation of Sir John A. Macdonald's post-Confederation government. Province-building has been defined as the 'recent evolution of more powerful and competent provincial administrations which aim to manage socioeconomic change in their territories and which are in essential conflict with the central government.'[41] The concept generally has been associated with the provincial governments of Alberta and Quebec.[42] The Ontario government is as 'powerful and competent' as these other provincial states, and no one would accuse Ontario governments of being indifferent to the direction of 'socio-economic change' within their borders. Ontario's pivotal status in Canadian politics, however, based on its large population and economic importance, has meant that it generally has been able to count on a sympathetic hearing in Ottawa. With the exception of the NDP government of Bob Rae (1990–5), aggressive and persistent 'fed-bashing' has not been a popular blood sport among that province's politicians, simply because it has not been necessary for the achievement of their goals. In other respects, however, Ontario governments have not lagged behind their more aggressive counterparts, and in fact have often been at the forefront in expanding the political and administrative reach of the provincial state.

Intergovernmental Relations

The Constitution, we have seen, does not establish a neat division of legislative and taxation powers between Ottawa and the provinces. All of the chief sources of public revenue—personal and

The Kyoto Accord is *dat* way.

The *gold* is that way!

CANADIAN PAIRS

Intergovernmental relations are complicated by the often conflicting agendas and interests of Ottawa and some of the provinces, as the feud between Ottawa and Alberta over the Kyoto Accord demonstrated. (Roy Peterson, *Vancouver Sun*)

corporate income taxes, payroll taxes, sales taxes, and public-sector borrowing—are shared between the two levels of government. Likewise, both the federal and provincial governments are involved in all the major policy fields. Defence and monetary policy come closest to being exclusive federal terrain, although provincial governments do not hesitate to express their views on such issues as the location of Canadian Forces bases, major defence purchases, and interest rates. On the provincial side, snow removal, refuse collection, and sidewalk maintenance are the sorts of local activities that are free from federal involvement. But not entirely: the money that Ottawa transfers annually to the provinces affects the amounts that provincial governments pay to their municipalities, thereby having an impact on municipalities' ability to carry out these local functions.

Divided jurisdiction has given rise to a sprawling and complicated network of relations linking the federal and provincial governments. This network has often been compared to an iceberg, only a small part of which is visible to the eye. The 'visible' tip of intergovernmental relations involves meetings of the Prime Minister and provincial premiers (first ministers' conferences) and meetings of provincial premiers. These meetings, which have become less frequent in recent years, always generate considerable media attention and some part of their proceedings usually takes place before the television cameras. Less publicized, but far more frequent, are the hundreds of annual meetings between federal and provincial cabinet ministers and bureaucrats. Many of these meetings take place in the context of ongoing federal-provincial structures like the Continuing Committee on Economic and Fiscal Matters, established in 1955, and the Economic and Regional Development Agreements negotiated between Ottawa and the less affluent provinces. Others are generated by the wide range of shared-cost activities that link the two levels of government, from major spending programs such as the Canada Health and Social Transfer to smaller federal subsidies such as for official minority-language education.

Executive federalism is a term sometimes used to describe the relations between cabinet ministers and officials of the two levels of government. The negotiations between them and the agreements they reach are usually undertaken with minimal, if any, input from either legislatures or the public. The secrecy that generally cloaks this decision-making process, combined with the fact that the distinction between federal and provincial responsibilities is often blurred by the deals it produces, has generated charges that executive federalism is undemocratic. It is undemocratic because it undermines the role of elected legislatures whose role, if they have one at all, is usually limited to ratifying *faits accomplis*. Second, an agreement to finance jointly the cost of a program or to share a particular tax field or legislative power makes it difficult for citizens to determine which level of government should be held responsible for what policies. Third, executive federalism provides no meaningful opportunities for public debate of intergovernmental issues that affect the standard of health-care services, welfare, post-secondary education, local taxation, and other matters of real concern to citizens. Political parties, interest groups, and individual Canadians are generally excluded from a decision-making process dominated by cabinet ministers and intergovernmental affairs specialists of the two levels of government.

In addition to these indictments of executive federalism, Donald Smiley lists three others.[43]

- *It distorts the political agenda.* Executive federalism has a territorial bias. It reinforces the significance of territorially concentrated interests and of the provincial governments that represent them, and at the same time it undervalues the importance of other interests.
- *It fuels government expansion.* Competitive relations between Ottawa and the provinces have produced inefficient duplication, as each level of government has its own bureaucracy to pursue similar goals.
- *It perpetuates intergovernmental conflict.* The increasing sophistication of executive federalism, conducted through specialized bureaus staffed by intergovernmental affairs specialists, reduces the likelihood of resolving federal-provincial disputes. This is because specialized intergovernmental affairs bureaus, which exist in all provinces and at the federal level, and the experts who staff them tend to perceive issues in terms of the powers and jurisdiction of their particular government. Intergovernmental conflict is in a sense institutionalized by the fact that what is perceived to be at stake is the power/resources/prestige of one's government.

In the face of this lengthy catalogue of allegations, executive federalism and its practitioners are left to rely on the defence of necessity. Overlapping powers are an unavoidable fact of life under Canada's federal Constitution. In light of this, is it realistic to imagine that complex administrative and financial agreements can be negotiated in public forums? And besides, much of policy-making is carried on in a closed fashion, dominated by cabinet ministers and bureaucratic elites. Why condemn executive federalism for traits that are deeply embedded in Canadian policy-making generally? The fact of the matter is, however, that the characteristics of executive federalism are out of sync with the less deferential political culture that has evolved in Canada over the last generation. Governments will continue to conduct much of their negotiations behind closed doors and the constitutional division of powers will continue to be characterized by overlap, competition, and ambiguity. But public acceptance of this and other elitist forms of policy-making is today much weaker than in the past.

Financing Federalism

From the very beginning, money has been at the centre of intergovernmental relations. The Confederation agreement included an annual per capita subsidy that Ottawa would pay to all provincial governments.[44] Moreover, the new federal government agreed to assume liability for the debts of the provinces as they stood in 1867.[45] Taxation powers were divided between the two levels of government, with Ottawa receiving what were at the time the major sources of public revenue.

These financial arrangements have never been adequate. At the root of the problem is the fact that the provinces' legislative responsibilities proved to be much more extensive and expensive than the founders had anticipated. This has been referred to as the *fiscal gap*. Provincial governments attempted to fill this gap between their revenues and their expenditure requirements through an increasing array of provincial taxes. Licence fees, succession duties, and personal and corporate income taxes were all used to increase provincial revenues. In addition, the provinces pressed Ottawa for more money. Indeed, only two years after Confederation the federal subsidy paid to Nova Scotia was increased. An important precedent was thereby established: federal-provincial financial relations are determined by governments, not by the Constitution.

Today, combined provincial and local revenues exceed those of the federal government (see Figure 7.1). The revenue position of the provinces improved steadily between the 1950s and the

Figure 7.1   Public Finance in Canada: Revenue and Expenditure as Percentages of GDP for Each Level of Government, 1950 and 2001

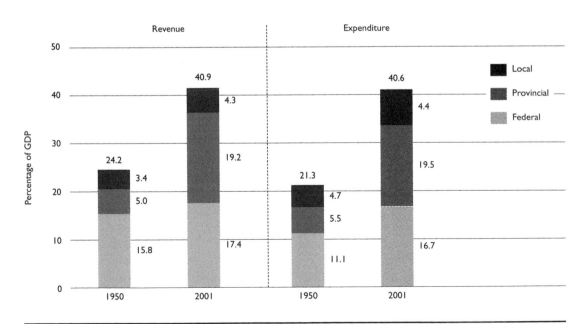

Sources: Figures provided in Department of Finance, *Quarterly Economic Review*, Annual Reference Tables; and Statistics Canada, *Canadian Economic Observer*, Historical Statistical Supplement 1994–5, cat. 11–210.

1970s, as Ottawa conceded *tax room*—i.e., an increasing share of particular revenue sources like the personal income tax—to aggressive provincial governments. But at the same time, provincial dependence on subsidies from Ottawa remains high in several provinces. In the case of the poorest provinces, money from Ottawa currently accounts for about half of their total revenue. Part of this dependence has been encouraged by Ottawa through **shared-cost programs**, provincially administered programs where Ottawa's financial contribution is geared to how much a province spends. In the past Ottawa agreed to match provincial spending dollar for dollar. Until 1995 the major shared-cost program in Canada was the Canada Assistance Plan, which financed welfare and other provincial social services. The federal budget of that year replaced CAP with the Canada Health and Social Transfer to the provinces, the amount of which is not geared to provincial spending. Federal grants for health care and post-secondary education also were launched on a shared-cost basis, but were converted by Ottawa into **block funding** programs through the Federal-Provincial Fiscal Arrangements Act of 1977. The federal government argued, reasonably enough, that the shared-cost formula did not encourage the provinces to control program costs. Under block funding, Ottawa's financial contribution is geared to the previous year's subsidy plus an amount calculated on the basis of growth in the recipient province's gross provincial product. Ottawa is not obliged to match provincial spending, and indeed the effect of the switch to block funding has been to transfer an increasing share of the burden of health care and post-secondary education costs onto the shoulders of the provinces.

What could possibly be wrong with the provinces carrying more of the costs for programs that fall under their constitutional jurisdiction? First, provincial governments argue that Ottawa encouraged them to spend more on social services by offering to share program costs on a matching basis. It is unfair, they claim, for the federal government to try to back out of financing policy areas whose growth it encouraged. Second, the provinces' ability to increase their own-source revenues to compensate for reduced federal transfer payments is limited by the fact that they share all of the major taxes fields with Ottawa. Unless the federal government is willing to give up some tax room (i.e., some of its share of total tax revenue from a particular source) to the provinces, provincial governments face the hard choice of increasing the total tax burden on their citizens, charging or increasing user fees (e.g., tuition fees), or cutting back on program expenditures. Third, any reduction in Ottawa's commitment to financing provincial social services hurts the poorer provinces more than it does the wealthier ones. The Maritime provinces in particular are dependent on federal transfers in order to offer a level of social services comparable to that in other provinces. Figure 7.2 shows federal transfers to the provinces in 2001 as a percentage of provincial gross revenues.

Some of the money that Ottawa transfers to the provinces carries conditions as to how it must be spent. These are called conditional grants. Transfers that have no strings attached are called unconditional grants. Important examples of both include the following:

- Provincial social assistance programs must be based exclusively on need and must not make previous residency in the province a condition for receiving benefits.
- The block transfer that Ottawa makes to the provinces under the Canada Health and Social Transfer must be spent on health care, post-secondary education, and social services previously covered under CAP.
- The Canada Health Act, 1984 includes a provision that reduces Ottawa's payment to provincial governments that permit physicians to extra-bill their patients. The terms of the CHST also specify that provinces must respect the principles of the Canada Health Act, 1965 (portability of coverage between provinces, comprehensiveness of provincial plans, universality, public funding, and public

Figure 7.2   Federal Transfers* as Percentage of Provincial Gross Revenues, 2001

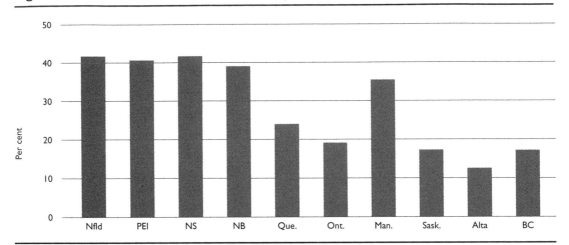

*Includes cash transfers and tax points.

Source: OECD, *OECD Territorial Reviews: Canada* (Paris, 2002).

administration). Ottawa's contribution to provincial health-care spending is, therefore, subject to some conditions.

- Equalization grants are paid to provincial governments whose per capita tax revenues (according to a complex formula negotiated between Ottawa and the provinces) fall below the average of the two most affluent provinces. Equalization accounts for about one-quarter of all federal transfers to the provinces and about a quarter of the total revenue of the poorest provincial governments. It carries no conditions as to how it must be spent. Figure 7.3 provides a breakdown of federal transfers to the provinces.

The adequacy of federal transfers is not the only issue that has set Ottawa against the provincial governments. Another long-standing complaint of the provinces is that shared-cost programs distort provincial spending priorities because of the enticement of matching federal grants. Ottawa's spending power, they argue, permits undue federal interference in matters of provincial jurisdiction. The government of Quebec has been most insistent about this. Indeed,

during the 1950s the provincial government of Maurice Duplessis refused to accept federal money for the construction of Quebec's portion of the Trans-Canada Highway and for universities, and was not even compensated for the fact that Canadian taxpayers residing in Quebec were paying for these programs in the other provinces. In 1965 the Quebec government of Jean Lesage opted out of the new Canada Assistance Plan (although Quebec has never been freed from the fairly minimal program standards that Ottawa sets) and some other conditional grant programs, receiving compensation in the form of tax room surrendered by Ottawa to the province. Both the Meech Lake and Charlottetown Accords included a provision that would have obligated Ottawa to provide 'reasonable compensation' to any provincial government choosing not to participate in a new national shared-cost program, so long as the province's own program was 'compatible with the national objectives'. Critics argued that this opened the door for an erosion of national standards in social policy. Defenders claimed that this particular section merely constitutionalized a long-standing practice in Canadian federalism.

THE FEDERAL SPENDING POWER, NATIONAL STANDARDS, AND THE SOCIAL UNION

In the 1990s it became popular to vilify certain provincial governments, particularly the Klein government in Alberta and the Harris government in Ontario, for having undermined national standards in social programs. In fact, however, one of the major threats to national standards came from Ottawa's shrinking financial commitment to provincially administered social programs. Federal transfers as a share of provincial program spending fell from 21 per cent in 1986–7 to 16 per cent in 1996–7.[46] The wealthier provinces, including Ontario, Alberta, and British Columbia, faced the largest burden of these federal cuts, starting with Ottawa's 1990 decision to limit the annual increase in CAP payments to these provinces to 5 per cent.

Ottawa's retreat from financing provincial social programs became unmistakable with the 1995 federal budget. Described as a 'new vision of confederation' by Liberal Finance Minister Paul Martin, the 1995 budget replaced the shared-cost programs that pay for welfare and social services under the CAP and the Extended Programs Financing (EPF) for health and post-secondary education with a single block transfer called the Canada Health and Social Transfer. The CHST institutionalized the ad hoc freezes and caps on transfers that both Liberal and Tory governments imposed from the early 1980s. It did so, in Ottawa's words, by ensuring that 'the amounts transferred will not be determined by provincial spending decisions (as under cost-sharing).'[47] Caps and freezes also had this effect, the difference being that Ottawa could always excuse what were effectively transfer cuts by citing their 'temporary' nature. The CHST appeared to put the decisive nail in the coffin of shared-cost programs and thus to mark a retreat from Ottawa's commitment to maintain national standards in social policy, a commitment that has always depended on the federal spending power.

Figure 7.3   Federal Transfers* to Provinces and Territories, 2002–3

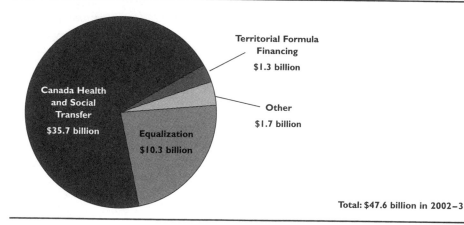

Total: $47.6 billion in 2002–3

*Equalization associated with the tax transfers under CHST is included in both CHST and Equalization. Total has been reduced by $1.4 billion to avoid double-counting.

**The federal government provides assistance to provinces and territories under other programs, such as official languages and grants in lieu of municipal taxes.

Source: Department of Finance, 'Federal Transfers to Provinces and Territories', www.fin.gc.ca/fedprove/ftpe.html

The appearance may, however, be deceptive. The Liberals' determination to rein in federal transfers to the provinces has not been matched by a corresponding rhetoric of decentralization. On the contrary, in recent years the Liberal government has refused to concede ground on the issue of national standards, particularly in regard to the health-care system (see Box 7.2). Their

BOX 7.2   Health Care and Federalism: Canada's Second Longest-Running Soap Opera

After the issue of Quebec's constitutional status, health care has a pretty reasonable claim to being Canadian federalism's second longest-running soap opera. Elements of intrigue, betrayal, good, and evil intermingle in a story that reveals much about the nature of intergovernmental relations.

A 'soap opera digest' summary of how the story has unfolded might go something like this. Ottawa and the provincial governments co-operated during the 1960s to create a national health-care system that would be administered by the provinces, but where they would share the costs with the federal government. Ottawa, flush with revenue in the 1960s and disposed to encourage provinces to spend money on social programs that fell under provincial jurisdiction, agreed to match provincial spending on health care, a formula that provided little incentive for the provinces to control costs. The feds began to back away from this open-ended commitment to health care in the late 1970s. Over the next 20 years the federal contribution to health care, as a share of total public spending on health, would drop dramatically, from about 50 per cent to 20 per cent.

Provincial cries of betrayal were met with federal accusations of provincial treachery, as Ottawa accused some of the provinces of allowing creeping privatization and the beginning of 'American-style' health care. No one could agree on the numbers. Ottawa protested that its contribution was much greater than the provinces claimed, if the mysterious phenomenon of 'tax points' was included. Ottawa threatened to withhold dollars from the province of Alberta in a struggle that it characterized as nothing short of good compassionate Canadianism versus evil individualistic conservatism.

By the end of the 1990s Ottawa and several of the provinces launched major studies of the health-care system, producing duelling reports on what was wrong and what to do about it. Alberta's Mazankowski Report recommended greater room for private elements to operate alongside the public health-care system. Ottawa's Romanow Report recommended more spending—much more spending—as a major part of the solution to the system's woes. In early 2003, Ottawa and the provinces reached a deal whereby $12 billion in new health-care funding is to be transferred to the provinces during the period 2003–8.

Well into roughly its fourth decade, there is little likelihood that the Canadian health-care soap opera will disappear from the prime-time schedule anytime soon. The stakes are too high for both levels of government, both financially and politically. If there is a lesson in federalism to be learned from the last 30 years of intergovernmental conflict over health care it is this: sharing the costs of an expensive policy area is a prescription for political and bureaucratic rivalry, muddied accountability, and mutual recriminations.

message to the provinces has been this: 'We will give you fewer and fewer dollars with which to pay for your health-care services, but we will continue to set conditions on how those services must operate.'

The Liberals' resolve was put to the test by the Conservative government of Alberta, which allowed the establishment of private clinics for certain health services like cataract operations, where patients, for a price, can jump the queue that they would otherwise face in the publicly funded system. At the end of the day, however, all Ottawa could do was withhold some of the health-care dollars Alberta received from the feds. This may be a penalty without much sting. As economist Paul Boothe observed, 'The amount of money coming from Ottawa compared to the total health budget is trivial.'[48] In the case of Alberta, federal cash transfers amount to only about 10 per cent of provincial revenue.

In explaining the advantages of the CHST, the 1995 budget documents stated that it would 'end the intrusiveness of previous cost-sharing arrangements.'[49] More specifically, the transition to block funding under the CHST was argued to have the following beneficial effects:

- Provinces will no longer be subject to rules stipulating which expenditures are eligible for cost-sharing or not.
- Provinces will be free to pursue their own innovative approaches to social security reform.
- The expense of administering cost-sharing will be eliminated.
- Federal expenditures will no longer be driven by provincial decisions on how, and to whom, to provide social assistance and social services.[50]

Provinces would not, however, be free to do whatever they pleased under the new fiscal arrangements. The Liberal budget mentioned health care and social assistance as two areas where national standards would be maintained. In the case of social assistance this amounted only to an interdiction on minimum residency requirements. In regard to health care, the Liberals insist-

ed that provinces would have to respect the principles of the Canada Health Act. But even if Ottawa was able to enforce national standards on the provinces, critics noted that the lumping together of Ottawa's transfer for health care, social assistance, and post-secondary education under the CHST would permit provinces greater room to redistribute their spending between politically unpopular welfare programs and more popular health-care and education spending.

Ottawa's retreat from its financial commitment to provincially administered social programs—a retreat, it should be said, that was motivated more by the Liberal government's desire to reduce its budget deficit rather than by what Finance Minister Martin grandly called a 'new vision of federalism'—was not well received by provincial governments. Ottawa's success in transforming budget deficits into surpluses was largely due to cuts in transfers to the provinces, the use of Employment Insurance fund surpluses as general revenue, and increased federal tax revenues during the mid- to late 1990s. Very little of the turnaround in federal finances was due to cuts in Ottawa's program spending, although the Liberal government certainly conveyed this impression. From the provinces' point of view, Ottawa's deficit-cutting strategy was at their expense, leaving provincial governments with the politically difficult choice between raising taxes or cutting services (or doing a bit of both!). Moreover, the Liberal government's insistence that national standards for health care and welfare would have to be respected was particularly galling, ignoring as it did the old adage that he who pays the piper calls the tune.

This was the background to the idea of a Canadian *social union*, a concept that emerged in the wake of the transfer cuts announced in Ottawa's 1995 budget. Although the meaning attributed to the term depends on who is defining it, it is fair to say that the social union involves some new set of arrangements for funding and determining program standards in the areas of health, welfare, and post-secondary education. Alberta and Ontario, whose per capita payments under the CHST are the lowest in Canada, tend to see the social union as a commitment to national standards in social policy that are not federally imposed standards but, rather, are negotiated between the provinces and Ottawa in a spirit that reflects the provinces' constitutional authority in matters of social policy. This is a decentralized version of the social union, under which the balance of control over and money to fund social programs would shift to the provinces. Ottawa and some of the more transfer-dependent provinces view the social union differently, insisting on a central role for the federal government in maintaining the interprovincial uniformity of social program standards, limiting provincial barriers against citizens from other provinces when it comes to social services (for example, provincial residency requirements such as those BC maintains as a condition for welfare eligibility or the higher tuition fees that Quebec universities charge out-of-province Canadian students), and maintaining a strong federal role in financing social programs. The Quebec government kept its distance from the formal social union negotiations, insisting on a principle that has long been defended by provincial governments of various party stripes in Quebec, namely, that neither Ottawa nor the other provinces have any constitutional authority to interfere with Quebec's autonomy in setting its standards for social policy.

Ideology was never very far from the surface of debates on the social union. To the degree that the social union was associated with a redistribution of power and money away from Ottawa and towards the provinces, it was often characterized as being part of a market-oriented agenda that was hostile to entitlements and the welfare state. This characterization, however, was always overly simplistic and misleading. While it certainly is true that the ideologically conservative governments of Ontario and Alberta preferred a version of the social union that would increase their autonomy in determining standards in provincial social policy and, relatedly, weaken Ottawa's ability to set and enforce national standards, the NDP govern-

ment in British Columbia and the PQ government in Quebec—neither of which were ideological soulmates of their Ontario and Alberta counterparts—also supported more provincial autonomy.

On 4 February 1999, Prime Minister Chrétien and nine of the 10 provincial premiers agreed to the Social Union Framework Agreement (SUFA). Quebec's separatist Premier, Lucien Bouchard, was present but refused to sign the agreement, maintaining that Ottawa's retention of the right to set national standards in social policy and to penalize provinces that refused to conform to those standards represented an unconstitutional intrusion into matters of provincial jurisdiction. In taking this stand Premier Bouchard remained faithful to a position that all Quebec governments, separatist and non-separatist, have insisted on since the 1960s.

The willingness of Alberta, Ontario, and British Columbia to agree to a social union pact that saw Ottawa formally retain its right to withhold money from any province that, in its view, violates the principles of the social union and to initiate new federal programs in the area of social policy, was probably due to money. Ottawa promised the provinces about $2.5 billion per year in new health-care funding—really a reinstatement of federal transfers that had been cut over the previous few years, said the deal's critics. Only Quebec, for political reasons, was able to reject this enticement. The Quebec government was alone in insisting that the SUFA include the right of a province to get out of new national social programs with financial compensation to operate its own programs free of federal dollars and standards. Ottawa has insisted that the SUFA is binding on Quebec, despite that province's unwillingness to sign it. In this case 'binding' has meant that the Quebec government received some new health-care funding, just like the other provinces, but otherwise it is difficult to see how Ottawa could compel an unco-operative Quebec government into complying with the other provisions of the deal.

With the defeat of the separatist Parti Québécois government by the Quebec Liberal

Party under Jean Charest in Quebec's April 2003 election, expectations arose that a new flexibility and pragmatism would come to characterize financial relations between Ottawa and Quebec. This was certainly true in Ontario after Mike Harris was replaced by Ernie Eves as the Conservative Premier of that province. Under Harris, Ontario took a hard line in resisting Ottawa's efforts to set program standards as conditions for receiving federal dollars. Eves proved to be much more ready to deal and more concerned with receiving money than with defending ideological principles and constitutional turf. In the spring of 2003 the provincial government did an about-face on child-care funding, agreeing to accept Ottawa's condition that the money it offered be used only for publicly regulated child-care places. 'Show me the money' appeared to have become the new principle in federal-provincial financial relations.

NOTES

1. William S. Livingston, *Federalism and Constitutional Change* (Oxford: Clarendon Press, 1956), 2.
2. Ibid., 4.
3. Based on the ranking system used in Charles Lewis Taylor and Michael C. Hudson, *World Handbook of Social and Political Indicators*, 3rd edn (New Haven: Yale University Press, 1972), 271–3, table 4.15.
4. Pierre Elliott Trudeau, 'Federalism, Nationalism and Reason', in Trudeau, *Federalism and the French Canadians* (Toronto: Macmillan, 1968), 195.
5. The term is a translation of 'rois-nègres', coined by André Laurendeau in 'A Search for Balance', *Canadian Forum* (Apr. 1963), 3–4.
6. Donald Smiley, *The Canadian Political Identity* (Toronto: Methuen, 1967), 30–1.
7. Centre for Research and Information on Canada.
8. Canadian Institute for Public Opinion, *Gallup Poll*, 13 Aug. 1991.
9. Roger Gibbins, 'Letting Quebec Go: Would It Matter to Alberta?' Available at: www.uni.ca/ gibbins.html, at p. 4.
10. Peter Waite, *The Life and Times of Confederation 1864–1867* (Toronto: University of Toronto Press, 1962), 96.
11. The diversity of expectations was reflected in newspaper accounts of the Confederation agreement. See ibid., 111.
12. There are some exceptions. In *Citizens Insurance Co. v. Parsons; Queen Insurance Co. v. Parsons* (1881), the Judicial Committee of the Privy Council ruled that Ottawa's trade and commerce power did not take pre-eminence over enumerated provincial powers. In the words of Sir Montague Smith, '[The founders] could not have intended that the powers exclusively assigned to the provincial legislature should be absorbed in those given to the dominion parliament.' Reproduced in Peter H. Russell, ed., *Leading Constitutional Decisions*, 4th edn (Ottawa: Carleton University Press, 1987), 35.
13. Ibid., 527.
14. *Amicus curiae* concerning Certain Questions Relating to the Secession of Quebec, 31 Jan. 1998.
15. See the discussion in Keith G. Banting, *The Welfare State and Canadian Federalism*, 2nd edn (Montreal and Kingston: McGill-Queen's University Press, 1987), 52–4.
16. *Attorney General of Ontario v. Attorney General of Canada* (Local Prohibition Case), 1896, in Russell, *Leading Constitutional Decisions*, 59.
17. *Re Board of Commerce Act and Combines and Fair Prices Act*, 1919, 1922, ibid., 75.
18. *Co-operative Committee on Japanese Canadians v. A.G. Canada*, 1947, A.C. 87; *Reference re Validity of Wartime Leasehold Regulations*, 1950, S.C.R. 124.

19. *Attorney General of Canada v. Attorney General of Ontario* (Employment and Social Insurance Act Reference), 1937.
20. See Peter Russell, 'The Anti-Inflation Case: The Anatomy of a Constitutional Decision', *Canadian Public Administration* 10, 4 (Winter 1977).
21. Constitution Act, 1867, s. 91(2).
22. Ibid., s. 92(13).
23. Russell, *Leading Constitutional Decisions*, 39.
24. *The King v. Eastern Terminal Elevator Co.* (1925) S.C.R. 434; *A.G. of British Columbia v. A.G. of Canada* (Natural Products Marketing Reference) (1937) A.C. 377; *Canadian Federation of Agriculture v. A.G. of Quebec* (Margarine Reference) (1951) A.C. 179.
25. *Ontario Farm Products Marketing Reference* (1957) S.C.R. 198; *R. v. Klassen* (1959) 20 D.L.R. (2nd) 406 (Manitoba Court of Appeal); *Caloil v. A. G. of Canada* (1971) S.C.R. 543.
26. *Caloil*, 551.
27. Peter Hogg, *Constitutional Law of Canada* (Toronto: Carswell, 1998), 479–82.
28. Trudeau, 'Federalism, Nationalism, and Reason', 198.
29. Henri Bourassa, 'The French Language and the Future of Our Race', in Ramsay Cook, ed., *French Canadian Nationalism* (Toronto: Macmillan, 1969), 141.
30. Kenneth McRoberts, *Quebec: Social Change and Political Crisis*, 3rd edn (Toronto: McClelland & Stewart, 1988), 214.
31. See Richard Simeon, *Federal-Provincial Diplomacy* (Toronto: University of Toronto Press, 1972), 115–22.
32. McRoberts, *Quebec*, 293–7.
33. Quoted in George Woodcock, *Confederation Betrayed!* (Vancouver: Harbour Publishing, 1981), 8.
34. This argument is developed by Barry Cooper in 'Western Political Consciousness', in Stephen Brooks, ed., *Political Thought in Canada* (Toronto: Irwin, 1984), 213–38.
35. James Bickerton, *Nova Scotia, Ottawa, and the Politics of Regional Development* (Toronto: University of Toronto Press, 1990).
36. G.V. LaForest, *Disallowance and Reservation of Provincial Legislation* (Ottawa, 1955).
37. Ottawa ceded control to Manitoba in 1930.
38. Alberta and Saskatchewan acquired these powers in 1930.
39. Doug Owram, 'Reluctant Hinterland', in Larry Pratt and Garth Stevenson, eds, *Western Separatism* (Edmonton: Hurtig, 1981), 61.
40. Alan Cairns, 'The Governments and Societies of Canadian Federalism', in Cairns, *Constitution, Government, and Society in Canada* (Toronto: McClelland & Stewart, 1988), 153–4.
41. R.A. Young, Philippe Faucher, and André Blais, 'The Concept of Province-Building: A Critique', *Canadian Journal of Political Science* 17, 4 (Dec. 1984): 785.
42. Two of the major works using this concept are John Richards and Larry Pratt, *Prairie Capitalism* (Toronto: McClelland & Stewart, 1979), and McRoberts, *Quebec*.
43. Donald Smiley, 'An Outsider's Observations of Federal-Provincial Relations', in R.D. Olling and W.M. Westmacott, eds, *Perspectives on Canadian Federalism* (Scarborough, Ont.: Prentice-Hall Canada, 1988).
44. Constitution Act, 1867, s. 118.
45. Ibid., s. 111.
46. Paul Boothe and Derek Hermourtz, 'Paying for ACCESS: Province by Province', paper delivered before the Political Economy Research Group, University of Western Ontario, 24 Oct. 1997, Figure 3b.
47. Department of Finance, *Budget 1995: Key Actions and Impacts*, unpaginated.
48. *Western Report*, 3 Apr. 1995, 19.
49. *Budget 1995*.
50. Ibid.

SUGGESTED READINGS

Herman Bakvis and Grace Skogstad, eds, *Canadian Federalism: Performance, Effectiveness, and Legitimacy* (Toronto: Oxford University Press, 2002). This is the best recent reader on Canadian federalism and inter-governmental relations.

Alan Cairns, *Charter versus Federalism: The Dilemmas of Constitutional Reform* (Montreal and Kingston: McGill-Queen's University Press, 1992). The essays in this collection examine the demise of the older elite accommodation-style politics and the dominance of federalism issues and the ascendance of what Cairns calls 'Charter Canadians', whose identities and demands on government are powerfully influenced by the Charter.

Stéphane Dion, *Straight Talk: On Canadian Unity* (Montreal and Kingston: McGill-Queen's University Press, 1999). In these speeches and writings Canada's Minister of Intergovernmental Relations discusses the spirit and practice of federalism, identity, and secession.

Richard Simeon, *Political Science and Federalism: Seven Decades of Scholarly Engagement* (Kingston: Institute of Intergovernmental Relations, Queen's University, 2002). This is an engaging survey of the study of federalism in Canada since the Great Depression.

Donald Smiley, *The Federal Condition in Canada* (Toronto: McGraw-Hill Ryerson, 1987). Although somewhat dated, this survey of the development, nature, and challenges associated with Canadian federalism, written by arguably the most astute observer of the subject, remains worthwhile reading.

Pierre Elliott Trudeau, *Federalism and the French Canadians* (Toronto: Macmillan, 1968). In these classic essays, written before he became Prime Minister, Trudeau considered the meaning and significance of Canadian federalism, the protection of French language rights, the role of Quebec in Canadian federalism, and the development of nationalism in French Canada.

Review Exercises

1. Visit the Web site maintained by the Institute on Governance and the Public Service Commission <http://learnet.gc.ca>. Go to 'The Learning Centre'. Click on 'How Government Works', found under the heading 'Self-Directed Learning Online'. What sections of this document deal with federalism? In a couple of paragraphs, summarize the main points concerning the impacts of federalism on governance.

2. Visit the primary Web site for the government of Canada <www.gc.ca>. Click on 'About Government' and then 'Provincial and Territorial Governments'. Click on to a province or territory that is not your own. Make a list of the main public issues discussed at the site. What information is provided about the relationship of the province's/territory's finances and programs to Ottawa?

3. Draw up a list of issues that would have to be resolved if Quebec were to separate from the rest of Canada. Attach a level of difficulty to each, ranging from 1 (very easily resolvable) to 10 (almost impossible to resolve).

4. Does it matter which level of government pays for what share of health-care costs and which level or levels set the rules for health policy? In answering this question be sure to address the issues of constitutionality, political accountability, Canadian values, and taxpayer interests.

Parliament Hill is the symbolic centre of Canada's system of government, but many of the important decisions that affect the lives of Canadians are taken next door at the Supreme Court and in parts of the bureaucracy scattered throughout the National Capital Region. (Greg Vickers)

Modern government is a complicated affair. This chapter examines the key components of the machinery of government, including the following topics:

- ❏ The monarch and Governor-General.
- ❏ The Prime Minister and cabinet.
- ❏ Central agencies.
- ❏ The bureaucracy.
- ❏ Departments.
- ❏ Public enterprise.
- ❏ Regulatory agencies.
- ❏ The legislature.
- ❏ The influence and activities of MPs.
- ❏ The courts.
- ❏ How a law is passed.

CHAPTER EIGHT

THE MACHINERY OF GOVERNMENT

Like a Rube Goldberg invention, modern government appears to be an unwieldy and complicated apparatus. Many of its parts seem to perform no useful function, and the overall impression is one of unco-ordinated and often pointless activity. It appears to have been assembled piece by piece, without much planning and without discarding old parts to make room for new ones. The purpose of the machinery is easily lost sight of in its Byzantine complexity, and it seems certain that there must be a more efficient way of doing whatever the apparatus is intended to accomplish.

But for all its inelegance and appearance of muddling, the machinery does produce results. Laws are passed, regulations are applied, applications are dealt with, cheques are issued, and the innumerable other specific tasks performed by government are carried out. How well these tasks are done, whether some of them should be done at all, and what other things should be done by public authorities are important questions. But before we can answer them, we need an understanding of the machinery itself—of its individual parts, the functions they perform, and the relations between them.

In this chapter we will focus on state institutions at the national level. But Canadians also encounter the machinery of government at the provincial and local levels, where the state's activities affect their lives in ways that often seem more direct and significant than those of Ottawa. Hospitals, doctors' services, schools, rubbish collection and disposal, water treatment, police, roads, and urban mass transit: these are all primarily the responsibilities of provincial and local governments. Together, provincial and local governments out-spend and out-tax the federal government.

The formal organization of the government of Canada is shown in Figure 8.1. Portrayed this way, the structure appears to be quite simple—deceptively simple, as it turns out! The three branches of government coincide with three major functions of democratic governance. The legislature is responsible for making the laws. The executive branch is responsible for implementing the laws. And the role of the judicial branch is to interpret the laws.

In reality, however, these compartments are not watertight. The legislature does indeed debate and pass laws, but these laws typically originate in the executive branch as bills that are seldom expected to change much, if at all, as they make their way through the legislative mill. The legislature is, in fact, dominated by a small group of its members—the Prime Minister and cabinet—who oversee the executive branch. The judicial branch of government does not, strictly speaking, involve itself in the making of laws. In recent times, however, Canadian courts have played a major role in the determination of policy on such matters as Sunday shopping, abortion, Aboriginal landownership, the collective bargaining rights of workers, and same-sex benefits such as pension rights for gays and lesbians. The courts may truly be said to have made policy on many important public issues. Is the distinction between making policy and making law really a distinction without a difference and, if so, can we say that through their responsibility for interpreting the law the courts become involved in what amounts to lawmaking? The bureaucrats whose job it is to implement the laws passed by their political masters in the executive branch often have enormous discretion in determining the actual meaning of laws that provide them with only vague guidelines about what they are expected to do. When elected officials delegate discretion to non-elected

Figure 8.1   The Formal Organization of Canadian Government

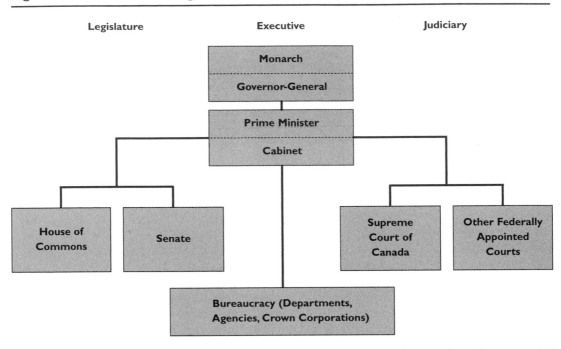

bureaucrats are they not also delegating part of their law-making function?

The actual operations of the machinery of Canadian government are, therefore, more complex than its formal organization suggests. Nevertheless, the respective roles of the legislative, executive, and judicial branches are significantly different and their differences are rooted in our expectations for democratic government. These expectations can be briefly summarized as follows:

The legislative branch shall . . .

- represent the people and be accountable to them through periodic elections;
- debate public issues and provide a forum for competition between political parties;
- make laws.

The executive branch shall . . .

- implement the laws;

- ensure that the public's business is carried out efficiently, accountably, and in accordance with the law;
- be non-partisan at the bureaucratic level, such that non-elected officials faithfully carry out the policies of whatever party forms the government of the day.

The judicial branch shall . . .

- be non-partisan and free from interference by the government;
- interpret the law's meaning;
- not substitute its preferences for those of elected public officials in matters of public policy, as distinct from legal and constitutional interpretation.

Democratic expectations are not, however, immutable. Today, many people expect that the bureaucracy should be representative of the population it serves, an expectation that may affect bureaucratic recruitment and promotion policies. Some argue that it is neither realistic nor desirable to expect non-elected officials to be politically neutral, and that accountability for policy (as distinct from its implementation) should be shared between politicians and bureaucrats. The elevated status of Canadian courts in the political process since the Charter of Rights and Freedoms was passed in 1982 has been welcomed by those who see judges as more likely than politicians to protect rights and promote democracy. Others, clinging to more traditional expectations, lament that the courts have come to trespass on turf that properly belongs to the people's elected and accountable representatives. The courts are also expected by many to be representative, instead of being dominated by white males. The under-representation of women and minorities on the bench, these critics say, undermines the courts' ability to reflect the diverse interests and values of Canadians.

Expectations for our institutions of government are not chiselled in stone. In this chapter we will discuss the main characteristics and roles of the institutions that comprise the machinery of Canadian government, including the changes that have taken place in their roles and the controversies associated with these changes.

THE EXECUTIVE BRANCH

The Monarch and Governor-General

Canada is a constitutional monarchy. The monarch, currently Queen Elizabeth II, embodies the authority of the Canadian state. Any action of the government of Canada is taken in the Queen's name.[1] The monarch is responsible for appointing the Prime Minister and for deciding when Parliament will be dissolved and a new election held. When she is not in Canada, which is of course most of the time, her duties are carried out by the Governor-General, currently Adrienne Clarkson. Although the strict letter of the Constitution suggests that the role of the monarch in Canada's system of government is a formidable one, most Canadians realize that the Queen and Governor-General perform mainly symbolic functions. The real decision-making powers of the executive are exercised by the Prime Minister, who is the head of government, and cabinet.

In matters such as the selection of the Prime Minister and the dissolution of Parliament, constitutional convention is far more important than the discretion of the monarch. For example, when one party wins a majority of the seats in an election, the choice of Prime Minister is automatic. Even when no party has a majority, it is understood that the leader of the party with the most seats will be given the first opportunity to try to form a government that has the support of a majority in the legislature. If, however, it is clear that the members of the other parties will not support a government led by this person, the monarch's representative may turn directly to the leader of another party. This happened in Ontario after the 1985 provincial election. Whatever the legislative scenarios appear to be, it is understood that a newly elected legislature must at least be given the opportunity to meet. The monarch's representative cannot simply decide that there is no point in convening the legislature and that a new election should be held immediately.

Likewise in the case of dissolving Parliament, the monarch's discretion is limited by constitutional conventions that have developed over time. Normally, the Prime Minister's request that Parliament be dissolved and a new election held will be granted automatically. It is remotely conceivable, although highly improbable, that in circumstances of minority government the monarch's representative could refuse such a request and instead ask the leader of another party to try to form a government. The last time this happened was in 1926, when Governor-General Lord Byng refused Prime Minister Mackenzie King's request for a new election. This refusal provoked a minor constitutional crisis. Since then, the view of most constitutional experts has been that the monarch's representative is required to accept the 'advice' given by the Prime Minister.

The monarch and Governor-General play no significant role either in setting the government's policy agenda or in the subsequent decision-making process. Royal assent to legislation is virtually automatic. It has never been withheld from a law passed by Parliament. On the occasions when the monarch's provincial representatives, the lieutenant-governors, used the disallowance and reservation powers, this was almost always at the behest of the elected government in Ottawa.[2]

What role, then, does the monarchy play in Canada's system of government? We have said that the monarch's role today is primarily a symbolic one. This does not mean that the functions performed by the Queen and Governor-General—and lieutenant-governors at the provincial level—are unimportant. The ceremonial duties that are part of government must be performed by someone, and it may be that assigning them to a head of state who is above the partisan fray reduces the possibility of too close an association between the political system itself—the state—and the leadership of particular political factions within it. As James Mallory argues, '[the monarchy] denies to political leaders the full splendor of their power and the excessive aggrandizement of their persons which come from the undisturbed occupancy of the centre of the stage.'[3] Perhaps, but it must be admitted that these state functions are performed by an elected president in countries like the United States and France without there being much evidence that this has imperilled those democracies. On the other hand, both the American and French political systems have legislative checks on executive power that do not exist in a British parliamentary system. Mallory may, therefore, be correct in his belief that a non-elected head of state serves as a buffer against the self-aggrandizing tendencies of elected politicians. Paradoxically, then, a non-democratic institution, i.e., an unelected head of state, may contribute to the protection of a democratic social order.

But the monarchy has not always been an uncontroversial pillar of stability in Canadian politics. Despite the constitutional fact that the monarch's status in Canada's system of government is that of the King or Queen of Canada, not of the United Kingdom, the institution of monarchy has been perceived by some as an irritating reminder of Canada's colonial ties to Britain and of the dominance of Anglo-Canadians in this country's politics. This was particularly true during the 1960s, when royal visits to Quebec acted as lightning rods for the anti-federalist grievances of Quebec nationalists. Ancient memories of British domination and French subordination have faded, but have not disappeared. The failure of the Meech Lake Accord in 1990 led many francophone politicians to call for the cancellation of the Queen's scheduled visit to Montreal. When French-English tensions run high, the issue of which groups in Canada are symbolically represented by the monarch resurfaces. But despite occasional imbroglios over royal visits, we should not exaggerate the institution's contribution to national disunity.

A new sort of controversy has been associated with the position of Governor-General since the 1999 appointment of Adrienne Clarkson. Clarkson's spouse is John Ralston Saul, a well-known philosopher-historian and author. Saul's writing and public pronouncements on contemporary issues, as when he was critical of the American reaction to the terrorist attacks of 11 September 2001 and expressed skepticism about George W. Bush's competence as a leader, have focused attention on the question of whether his relationship to the Governor-General ought to limit his forays into political matters. While his defenders noted that he was a private citizen, entitled to the same freedom of speech to which any other citizen is entitled, this was somewhat disingenuous. Like Governor-General Clarkson, Saul is referred to as 'His Excellency' and makes use of the publicly financed staff and other facilities that are part of the office of Governor-General. Whether this reality ought to limit his participation in the more controversial side of public life is a matter on which there is disagreement.

Perhaps more importantly, Adrienne Clarkson has shown occasional signs of wanting to reshape the boundaries of the Governor-General's role in public life. For example, in 2001 Clarkson sent a message of congratulations to a gay couple in Ontario who were wed in Toronto's Metropolitan Community Church, at a time when there was much public controversy over the legal definition of marriage. Critics charged that as a non-elected and non-partisan head of state, Clarkson should not have expressed views that could have been construed as critical of existing law and therefore politically divisive.

THE PRIME MINISTER AND CABINET

In contrast to the passive and principally symbolic roles of the monarch and Governor-General, the Prime Minister (PM) and cabinet are at the centre of the policy-making process. The PM is the head of government in Canada. By convention, this person is the leader of the dominant party in the House of Commons. One of the PM's first duties is to select the people who will be cabinet ministers. In the vast majority of cases these will be other elected members of the House of Commons, although it occasionally happens that a senator or two are appointed to cabinet to give the government representation from a region where the governing party has elected few or no members, or because of the special abilities of a senator. In the British parliamentary tradition, cabinet members are always drawn from the same political party as the PM. In recent years, the size of the federal cabinet has ranged from a low of 20 to a high of almost 40 members. Provincial cabinets are somewhat smaller.

The power of the PM and cabinet rests on a combination of factors. One of these is the written Constitution. Section 11 of the Constitution Act, 1867 states that 'There shall be a Council to aid and advise in the Government of Canada, to be styled the Queen's Privy Council for Canada.' Section 13 of that Act goes even further to specify that the actions of the monarch's representative in Canada, the Governor-General, shall be undertaken 'by and with the Advice of the Queen's Privy Council for Canada'. The Privy Council is, of course, the cabinet, under the leadership of the PM. Although, formally, anyone who has ever been a member of cabinet retains the title of privy councillor after leaving government, only those who are active members of the government exercise the powers referred to in the Constitution.

These powers include control over the budget. Section 54 of the Constitution Act, 1867 requires that any legislation or other measure that involves the raising or spending of public revenue must be introduced by cabinet. In fact, cabinet dominates the entire legislative agenda of Parliament, not just money matters. MPs who are not members of the cabinet have the right to introduce private members' bills, but the meagre time allocated to considering these bills and the operation of party discipline combine to kill the prospects of most of these initiatives.

More important than these written provisions of the Constitution, however, are constitutional conventions relating to the PM and cabinet. Although the position of Prime Minister is not even mentioned in the written Constitution, it is understood that the person who leads the dominant party in the House of Commons has the power to decide the following matters:

- who will be appointed to, or removed from, cabinet;
- when a new election will be held;
- the administrative structure and decision-making process of government;
- the selection of persons to a wide array of appointive positions, including deputy ministers, judges of all federal and provincial courts, senators, members of federal regulatory agencies and of the boards of directors of federal Crown corporations, ambassadors, etc.

These are formidable powers. They help to explain why the PM is always the pre-eminent figure in Canadian government, even when his or her decision-making style is a collegial one that encourages the participation of other members of cabinet. The PM's pre-eminence is reinforced by constitutional conventions on accountability. Although individual cabinet ministers are separately accountable to Parliament for the actions of their departments and the entire cabinet is collectively accountable for government policy, the PM cannot avoid personal accountability for the overall performance of government and for all major policies. The opposition parties and the media ensure that the PM takes the heat for these matters.

Responsible government is another constitutional convention that strengthens the power of the PM and cabinet. As we noted in Chapter 5, responsible government encourages party discipline. This means that the elected members of a party will tend to act as a unified bloc on most matters, particularly when voting on budget measures and important government legislation. If the members of the governing party break ranks, the government will fall. Party discipline, therefore, ensures that members of the governing party will normally be docile in their support of the government's policies. And when the government has a majority in both the House of Commons and the Senate, the automatic backing of the government party's backbenchers (i.e., MPs who are not cabinet ministers) enables the PM and cabinet to move their legislative agenda through Parliament without serious impediment. Cabinet dominance may be attenuated, however, during periods of minority government and when different parties control the House of Commons and the Senate.

The weakness of Canada's political party organizations is another factor that reinforces the dominance of the PM and cabinet. Parties, particularly the Liberal and Progressive Conservative parties, are geared primarily towards running election campaigns. They usually have little influence on the policies adopted by the party leadership when it forms the government. There are two main reasons for this. One is the parties' efforts to attract a broad base of support. This requires that a party's leadership be allowed a large margin of manoeu-

vre in communicating the party's policies to different groups. A second reason involves the absence, except in the case of the NDP, of formal affiliations between the parties and organized interests. Since 1961 the NDP has been formally affiliated to the Canadian Labour Congress. Formal affiliations usually have the effect of narrowing a party's electoral appeal and increasing the weight in a party's internal affairs—including leadership selection and policy-making—of the affiliated group(s). But when they have been in power provincially, NDP governments have not been willing to tie themselves rigidly to the party's platform.

Statute law is not an important source of prime ministerial power. It provides, however, a significant legal basis for the authority and responsibilities of individual cabinet ministers. The statute under which a government department, agency, or Crown corporation operates will always specify which minister is responsible for the organization's actions. Legislation may also assign to a particular minister special powers over a part of the bureaucracy, such as a right of approval or veto of all or some category of the organization's decisions, or the right to order an agency or Crown corporation to base its decisions on particular guidelines or to act in a specific way. In fact, this sort of intervention is more likely to come from the PM and cabinet acting collectively, rather than being the initiative of an individual minister.

The constitutional and statutory foundations of prime ministerial and cabinet powers are reinforced by the relationship between the political executive and the media. This relationship is close and mutually dependent. The PM and members of cabinet regularly speak 'directly' to the people or to targeted publics via the media. Even when presenting or defending the government's policies in the House of Commons, they are aware of the wider audience to whom their words and behaviour are communicated by television cameras and the parliamentary press corps. For their part, journalists typically turn first to the PM and the responsible ministers when reporting on politics. In doing so, the media contribute to the personalization of politics and, more particularly, to the popular identification of government with the PM and cabinet. These tendencies have become even more pronounced as a result of the visual character of television—the medium that most Canadians depend on for national news—and modern electioneering techniques that focus on the party leaders.

The reality of direct communications between the PM and cabinet and the public has undermined the role of the legislature and political parties. When public sentiment can be gauged through public opinion polls and when the PM and cabinet ministers can speak to either the general public or targeted groups via the media and personal appearances, there is no perceived need to communicate through government MPs and the party organization. The result is that Parliament often seems to be little more than a procedural sideshow. This infuriates some constitutional purists, for whom Parliament is the proper conduit between the state and society. They argue that the practice of responsible government, the bedrock of the British parliamentary system, is subverted by direct communications between the government and the people. But the fact is that responsible government is already attenuated by party discipline. And, in any case, there is no reason to believe that a diminished communications role for Parliament and MPs has reduced the democratic accountability of government from what it was before images of the PM and other government members flickered nightly across television screens.

The communications role of the PM and cabinet is related to their representative functions. From the beginnings of self-government in Canada, cabinet formation has been guided by the principle that politically important interests, whenever possible, should be 'represented' by particular cabinet ministers. Adequate representation of different regions and even particular provinces has always been considered important, as has representation of francophones (see Figure 8.2).

The numerical dominance of anglophones has always ensured that they would be well represented in any government. Representation from the business community—the Minister of Finance has often been a person with professional connections to either the Toronto or Montreal corporate elite—and the inclusion of ministers perceived to be spokespersons for particular economic interests, particularly agriculture and occasionally labour, have also been significant factors in making appointments to particular cabinet positions. Some representational concerns, such as the inclusion of various religious denominations, have diminished in importance while others, like the representation of women and non-French, non-British Canadians, have become increasingly significant.

Representational concerns also surface in the case of the PM. These concerns are particularly important when a party is choosing its leader. Candidates are looked at, by party members and the media, in terms of their likely ability to draw support from politically important regions and groups. At a minimum, an aspiring leader of a national political party cannot be associated too closely with the interests of a single region of the country. Moreover, he or she must be at least minimally competent in French. In practical terms, this means being able to read parts of speeches in French and to answer questions in French. Given the numerical superiority of anglophone voters, it goes without saying that any serious leadership candidate must be able to communicate well in English.

Being the leader of a national political party or even PM does not automatically elevate a politician above the factional strife of politics. Conservative Prime Minister John Diefenbaker (1957–63) was never perceived as being particularly sensitive to Quebec's interests, despite the fact that his party held a majority of that province's seats in the House of Commons between 1958 and 1962. Liberal Prime Minister Pierre Elliott Trudeau (1968–79, 1980–4) was never able to convince western Canada—not that he always tried very hard—that he shared their perspectives on Canadian politics. For westerners, Trudeau and the

Liberals represented the dominance of 'the East' and favouritism towards Quebec. Conservative Prime Minister Brian Mulroney was more successful than Trudeau in drawing support from all regions of the country. But he, too, came under attack, particularly from the West, for allegedly neglecting western interests in favour of those of central Canada, especially Quebec. In the end, the political weight of Ontario and Quebec is such that any PM, regardless of his or her background, is bound to be accused of favouring central Canada. The alternative is to risk losing the support of the region that accounts for 60 per cent of the seats in the House of Commons.

Figure 8.2   Regional Representation in the 1985 Mulroney and 2002 Chrétien Governments

A. 2002 CHRÉTIEN CABINET

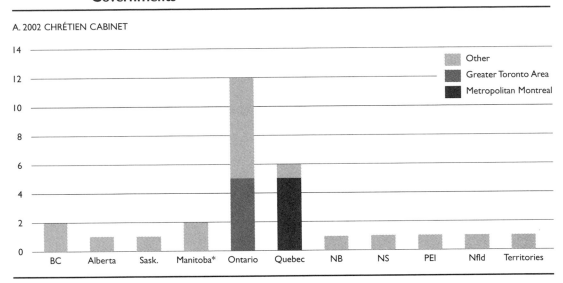

*One of Manitoba's two members of cabinet was Senator Sharon Carstairs.

B. 1985 MULRONEY CABINET

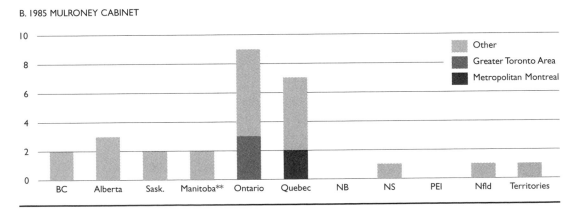

**One of Manitoba's two members of cabinet was Senator Duff Roblin.

Liberal Prime Minister Jean Chrétien was widely perceived as being more successful than his predecessors in attracting the support of both French and English Canadians. In fact, however, under Chrétien's leadership the Liberal Party did less well in Quebec than during the Trudeau years—the Liberals were outpolled by the Bloc Québécois in both 1993 and 1997—and ran a distant second to the Canadian Alliance west of Manitoba. Chrétien's popularity and the success of his party in recent years rested largely on the federal Liberals' strength in Ontario and on the fact that the right-of-centre vote has been divided between the Alliance and Conservative parties. Like Pierre Trudeau and Brian Mulroney before him, both of whom were also Quebecers, Chrétien walked a delicate tightrope between satisfying francophone Québécois that he understood their cultural aspirations and distinct status within Canada and, on the other hand, showing English Canada that he represented all of Canada without what would be viewed as undue favouritism towards any province. It is a tough performance, as every Prime Minister since Sir John A. Macdonald has learned.

Representation is about power. The PM and cabinet wield considerable power through the machinery of government, which is why representation in the inner circle of government is valued by regional and other interests. This power is based on the agenda-setting role of the PM and cabinet and on their authority within the decision-making process of the state.

Each new session of Parliament begins with the Speech from the Throne, in which the Governor-General reads a statement explaining the government's legislative priorities. This formal procedure is required by the Constitution.[4] Although a typical Throne Speech will be packed with generalities, it will also contain some specific indications of the agenda that Parliament will deal with over the ensuing months. For example, the 2002 Throne Speech included the following goals and promises:

- doubling the amount of developmental assistance by 2010, with at least half of the increase earmarked for African countries;
- reforming health care, including an increased federal spending commitment to health care, improved health services for Aboriginals, and financial support for those who take time away from their jobs to care for an ill or dying family member;
- increasing the National Child Benefit for poor families;
- establishing Headstart and improving educational programs for Aboriginal children on reserves;
- ratifying of the Kyoto Protocol on limiting greenhouse gas emissions;
- increasing investment in the infrastructure of cities;
- creating new ethics guidelines for public officials;
- changing the election financing laws.

Budgets represent a second way in which the PM and cabinet define the policy agenda. Every winter, usually around late February, the Minister of Finance tables the **estimates** in the House of Commons. This is what students of public finance call the *expenditure budget*. It represents the government's spending plans for the forthcoming fiscal year (1 April–31 March). Given that most public policies involve spending, changes in the allocation of public money provide an indication of the government's shifting priorities. The government can also use the expenditure budget to signal its overall fiscal stance. Increased spending may be part of an expansionary fiscal policy. Spending restraint and cutbacks, more typical in recent years, may signal the government's concern that the total level of public spending and the size of the public-sector deficit are damaging the economy.

From time to time, usually every two years, the Minister of Finance will present in Parliament either a **revenue budget** or a major *economic statement*. The former outlines the government's plans to change the tax system. An economic statement provides the government's analysis of the state of the economy and where the government plans to steer it. Both revenue budgets and economic statements are major opportunities for the government to shape the economic policy agenda.

Even when the bills and budget proposals of government have not originated in cabinet—they often have been generated within some part of the bureaucracy—or when they appear to be simple reactions to politically or economically pressing circumstances, these initiatives must still be accepted and sponsored by the government. In deciding which initiatives will be placed before Parliament, the priorities among them, and the strategies for manoeuvring policies through the legislature and communicating them to the public, the government influences the policy agenda. As Figure 8.3 shows, cabinet and cabinet committees, particularly the Treasury Board, are central players in the budget-making process.

Agenda-setting is part of the decision-making process in government. It is a crucial part, being that early stage during which public issues are defined and policy responses are proposed. The

Figure 8.3   The Expenditure Management System, 1999

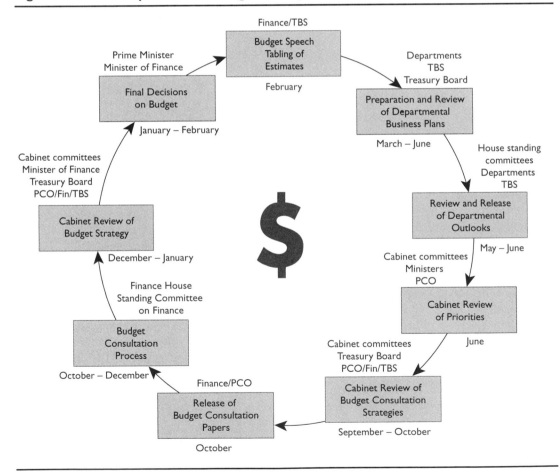

Source: Canada, Treasury Board, 'The Expenditure Management System of the Government of Canada' (1999).

role of the PM and cabinet at this and other stages of the policy process is institutionalized through the formal structure of cabinet decision-making. Between 1968 and 1993 the key committee of cabinet in terms of establishing the government's policy and budget priorities was the Priorities and Planning (P&P) Committee. It was chaired by the Prime Minister and included only the most influential members of cabinet. This formal distinction between a sort of inner and outer cabinet was abolished under Prime Minister Kim Campbell (1993) and has not been re-instituted. Gone, too, is the elaborate system of formal committees created during the Trudeau years. The structure of cabinet decision-making was streamlined under the Chrétien Liberals to include only five permanent subcommittees of cabinet: Economic Union, Social Union, Treasury Board, Government Communications, and the Special Committee of Council. Ad hoc committees were created and disbanded as circumstances required.

The formal structure of cabinet decision-making, including its committee structure, has never been more than a very imperfect guide to who has influence over what within the government of the day. The one reliable rule of thumb is this: ministers are influential to the degree that the Prime Minister allows them to be influential and supports their favoured projects and initiatives. A minister who has a reputation for having the PM's ear and being part of his favoured circle, as was true of John Manley during the third Chrétien government, acquires enhanced status among his or her colleagues in Parliament and in the eyes of the media. Other factors are important, too, such as a base of support within the party or being in charge of a powerful part of the bureaucracy, but the personal relationship between the PM and a minister is always a significant determinant of a minister's influence. The decision-making process in cabinet does not occur only through formal committee meetings. One-on-one conversations in the corridors of the Langevin Building (the location of the Privy Council Office), in the PM's office in the West Block (Prime Minister Chrétien's preferred office),

over the phone, or however and wherever they may take place have always been crucial in the decision-making process. No organizational chart can capture this informal but crucial aspect of ministerial influence. Nor can it convey the extent to which the Prime Minister is the dominant player in this decision-making process. Political observers have long characterized the PM's status in cabinet as *primus inter pares*—first among equals. But as Donald Savoie notes, there is no longer any *inter* or *pares*. There is only *primus*, the PM, when it comes to setting the government's agenda and taking major decisions.[5]

Ministerial control over the bureaucracy is another dimension of cabinet's decision-making authority. The word 'control' should be used carefully, however. Ministers are virtually never involved in the day-to-day running of the departments that fall under their nominal control. Moreover, policy initiatives are more likely to be generated within the bureaucracy than to spring from the fertile imagination of the responsible minister. Inevitably, most ministers, most of the time, act as cabinet advocates for the interests of their departments, their budgets and programs, and for the groups that depend on them. We should not succumb, however, to the caricature of wily, powerful bureaucrats manipulating their hapless political 'masters'—a caricature popularized by the British television program *Yes, Prime Minister*. Departments and other parts of the bureaucracy are created and restructured as a result of cabinet initiatives, and changes to their budgets and programs are often undertaken in spite of bureaucratic opposition. Anyone who doubts this need only look at the restructuring of the federal bureaucracy carried out under Kim Campbell in 1993 and the major program cuts instituted by Prime Minister Chrétien and Finance Minister Paul Martin in the mid-1990s.

Central Agencies

Cabinet has always been a decision-making body. But when John A. Macdonald and the first cabinet met in 1867, they dealt with a workload that was only a fraction of that which faces government today. There were only a handful of departments, no Crown corporations, no regulatory agencies, and federal-provincial relations were still relatively uncomplicated. The scope and complexity of contemporary government are vastly wider. In order to deal with the sheer volume of information that comes before cabinet and the hundreds of separate decisions that it takes annually, cabinet needs help. This help is provided by central agencies.

Central agencies are parts of the bureaucracy whose main or only purpose is to support the decision-making activities of cabinet. More concretely, this means that they perform such functions as providing cabinet with needed information, applying cabinet decisions in dealing with other parts of the bureaucracy, and communicating cabinet decisions and their implications to the public, to provincial governments, or to other organizations within the federal state. The general character of their policy role, their direct involvement in cabinet decision-making, and their ability to intervene in the affairs of departments have led political scientists Colin Campbell and George Szablowski to refer to the senior officials of central agencies as 'super-bureaucrats'.[6] The main organizations usually considered to have central agency status are the Department of Finance, the Privy Council Office, the Treasury Board Secretariat, the Prime Minister's Office, and, within the PCO, Intergovernmental Affairs.

Department of Finance

The Department of Finance plays the leading role in the formulation of economic policy. Its formal authority is found in the Department of Finance Act, 1869 and in the Financial Administration Act. The authority that the law confers on Finance is reinforced by the department's informal reputation within the state. Although comparatively small— it employs about 700 persons—Finance has always been a magnet for 'the best and the brightest' within the public service because of its unrivalled status in all aspects of economic policy-making.

The Finance Department has what amounts to almost exclusive authority over the preparation of the revenue budget, budget speeches, and economic statements delivered in Parliament by the Finance Minister. Whatever input other parts of the bureaucracy and interests outside of government have is at the discretion of the Minister of Finance and the department.[7] New initiatives in taxation and trade policy and in managing the level of government spending and debt will often be generated within Finance. Even when a new policy idea originates elsewhere, it is unlikely to reach the legislation stage if Finance is steadfastly opposed.

Finance officials are able to influence the entire spectrum of government policy through their role in the annual formulation of the expenditure budget. They are involved at the very beginning of the expenditure budget process, providing projections on the future state of the economy and the fiscal framework within which spending choices will have to be made. A Finance forecast of weak economic activity and lean taxation revenues will impose across-the-board restraint on departments jostling for scarce funds. But in addition to this macro-level influence on policy, Finance officials may also be involved in micro-level decisions about programs and in setting the policy agenda. In the words of one senior federal bureaucrat:

> Budget cutting tends not to be 'take 10 per cent off your budget and do what you will.' The Department of Finance tends to say 'you will take so much off such-and-such a program in such-and-such a way, in such-and-such a time frame', and once they've said all of those things, you really have a fairly small box to start playing in. . . . The Speech from the Throne might be a Speech from the Throne, but I can tell you that there is an awful lot of Finance finger in the pie. . . . There's nothing in there that they haven't figure out how to finance.[8]

The dominant status of Finance was reinforced during the 1990s, once deficit reduction and debt management became Ottawa's overriding priorities. When Ottawa turned the corner on the deficit issue and began to accumulate considerable budget surpluses during the late 1990s, many believed that Finance's stranglehold on the government's agenda would loosen under pressure from those who believed that Ottawa could afford to restore spending on some of the programs that had been cut during the mid-1990s. In fact, however, Finance appears to have lost none of its authority at the centre of the policy-making universe. As Donald Savoie observes:

> the budget has come to dominate policy and decision-making in Ottawa as never before. This holds significant advantages for the centre of government. It enables the prime minister and the minister of Finance to introduce new measures and policies under the cover of budget secrecy and avoid debate in Cabinet—and perhaps, more importantly, long interdepartmental consultations and attempts to define a consensus.[9]

In other words, the unrivalled status of Finance within the federal bureaucracy is one factor that effectively reinforces the power of the PM, who, along with his or her Minister of Finance, is the only member of the government to be intimately involved in the process that leads up to the making of a budget or economic statement in the House of Commons.

Finance has only a handful of programs for which the department is directly responsible, but they are important, big-ticket ones. One of these is *fiscal equalization*, under which unconditional payments are made to provincial goverments whose revenues fall below a level agreed to by Ottawa and the provinces. These payments amount to over $10 billion per year. Finance oversees the entirety of federal transfers to the provinces, of which equalization is a part, including the Canada Health and Social Transfer. The CHST was worth about $36 billion in 2002. Changes in the conditions under which these and other transfers are made and in the size of the transfer do not happen without the close involvement of Finance.

The Privy Council Office

The Privy Council Office (PCO) is the cabinet's secretariat and a principal source of policy advice to the Prime Minister. Donald Savoie characterizes it as 'the nerve centre of the federal public service'.[10] The PCO was formally created by Order-in-Council in 1940. The position of Chief Clerk of the Privy Council was put on a statutory basis in 1974, without any specification of the duties associated with this position. The authority of this person, who is the head of the public service, and the influence of the PCO derive mainly from their intimate and continuous involvement in cabinet decision-making (see Box 8.1).

In their study of central agencies, Campbell and Szablowski argue that the PCO is the lead agency for 'strategic planning and formulation of substantive policy'.[11] The PCO's role is 'strategic' because it is situated at the confluence of all the various policy issues and decisions that come before cabinet.

In terms of its organization, the PCO is divided into a number of secretariats that provide support services for the various committees of cabinet. These services range from such mundane functions as scheduling and keeping the minutes of committee meetings to activities that carry the potential for real influence, such as providing policy advice and dealing directly with government departments. Perhaps more than any other single component of the bureaucracy, the PCO is capable of seeing 'the big picture' of government policy. This picture embraces policy *and* political concerns. A former head of the PCO, Gordon Robertson, has summarized the different roles of the PCO and the Prime Minister's Office in the following way: 'The Prime Minister's Office is partisan, politically oriented, yet operationally sensitive. The Privy Council Office is non-partisan, operationally oriented yet politically sensitive.'[12]

Although Robertson's characterization of the different roles of PCO and PMO was made three decades ago, it continues to be apt. As Donald Savoie observes, 'the office briefs the prime minister on any issue it wishes, controls the flow of papers to Cabinet, reports back to departments on the decisions taken, or not taken, by Cabinet, advises the prime minister on the selection of deputy ministers . . . on federal-provincial relations and on all issues of governmental organization and ministerial mandates.'[13] If the government of Canada is a railway, the PCO is Grand Central Station. Savoie argues that the title 'Clerk of the Privy Council' is in some ways a misnomer as this most senior member of the federal bureaucracy in fact serves and reports to the PM, not to cabinet as a whole. Along with the PM's chief of staff in the PMO, the Clerk of the PCO is the only official who meets almost daily with the PM when he is in Ottawa. 'The clerk', Savoie observes, 'has direct access to the prime minister as needed.'[14] The Clerk of the Privy Council is, effectively, a sort of deputy minister to the Prime Minister and, as such, is always one of the most influential persons in the federal government.

The Treasury Board Secretariat

The Treasury Board Secretariat (TBS) is an administrative adjunct to the Treasury Board, which in turn is the only cabinet committee that has a statutory basis, going back to 1869. The Treasury Board is, in a sense, guardian of the purse strings, but it performs this function in more of a micro fashion compared to Finance's macro authority in relation to spending matters. The Treasury Board is also the government's voice on employment and personnel matters and on administrative policy within the federal government. Its authority is, in a word, extensive. But although the responsibilities of the TBS are wide-ranging and important, it occupies the shadows of the policy-making and agenda-setting process when compared to Finance and the PCO. Donald Savoie quotes a senior federal official who compares the roles of Finance, the PCO, and the TBS this way: 'PCO looks after the broad picture and resolves conflicts between ministers and departments. Finance looks after the big economic and budgeting decisions. The Treasury Board looks after the little decisions.'[15]

'Little' should not be considered unimportant, however. Particularly from the standpoint of program managers within the federal bureaucracy, the activities and decisions of the Treasury Board and TBS are quite significant. The TBS includes the Office of the Comptroller General of Canada (OCG), whose functions include departmental audits, establishing and enforcing accounting standards in government, and the evaluation of particular programs. As government employer, the Treasury Board negotiates with federal public-

---

BOX 8.1   A Former Chief Clerk of the PCO Describes His Job

The Privy Council Office provides non-partisan, public service support to the Prime Minister and the Cabinet. Under the direction of the Clerk of the Privy Council and Secretary to the Cabinet, the Office assists the head of government in meeting his other responsibilities for keeping the Ministry united and on course. In this context, the Prime Minister looks to the PCO for advice and support in choosing the principal ministerial and official office-holders, in balancing ministerial mandates, in providing the machinery that the Cabinet requires to serve the process of collective decision-making, in providing management for the public service, and in giving general direction to government policy. In addition, when Governments change, the Privy Council Office ensures a smooth transition from one administration to the next.

Paul Tellier, Clerk of the Privy Council (personal communication, 1991)

sector unions, establishes the rules for recruitment and promotion, is involved in implementing the terms of the Official Languages Act relating to the representation of francophones and the use of French in the public service and the availability of services to the public in both official languages, and is responsible for setting rules for increasing the representations of women, visible minorities, disabled persons, and Aboriginals in the Canadian public service. These clearly are important functions.

TBS officials formulate the expenditure outlook that, along with the economic outlook and fiscal framework developed by Finance, is the starting point in the annual expenditure budget exercise. The expenditure forecasts provided by TBS are used by cabinet in making decisions on the allocation of financial resources between competing programs. The involvement of TBS officials does not stop here. Along with the spending committees of cabinet, they assess the spending proposals and plans that departments are required to submit each year. Preparation of the main estimates—the detailed spending plans that the government tables in the House of Commons each winter—is the responsibility of the Treasury Board. Because the TBS has the deepest ongoing knowledge of government spending programs of all central agencies, it is often turned to by the PCO and Finance—its more muscular and glamorous cousins—for information and advice.[16]

The Prime Minister's Office

Unlike the other central agencies, the Prime Minister's Office (PMO) is staffed chiefly by partisan appointees rather than by career public servants. These officials are the Prime Minister's personal staff, performing functions that range from handling the PM's correspondence and schedule to speech writing, media relations, liaison with ministers, caucus, and the party, and advice on appointments and policy. Gordon Robertson's observation that the PMO is 'partisan, politically oriented, yet operationally sensitive'[17] captures well the role of this central agency. It serves as the

PM's political eyes and ears, and has the added distinction of being able to speak on behalf of the PM. The PMO is headed by the PM's chief of staff. No other non-elected official is in such regular contact with the PM.

Since the expansion in the PMO that took place under Pierre Trudeau three decades ago, the size of the Prime Minister's staff has varied from about 80 to 120 persons. Some people may wonder what could possibly justify such a large staff, but the demands on the Prime Minister's time are enormous and the process of co-ordinating the PM's activities, providing him or her with briefing and advice, and dealing with the volume of communication that flows into and from the Prime Minister's Office are daunting, to say the least. The bottom line for all staffers in the PMO, from the chief of staff to those who answer the phones, is summed up by a former PMO staff member in these words: 'Our job is quite simple really, we make the PM look good.'[18] This can, of course, be a challenge.

To give but one example of how PMO officials perform this job, let us consider the preparation that takes place before Question Period in the House of Commons. In Canada it is expected that the Prime Minister will attend Question Period, held shortly after 2:00 p.m. on Monday through Thursday and shortly before noon on Fridays, when the House is sitting and when he is in Ottawa. Moreover, the Prime Minister is expected to remain in the House for all of Question Period. He or she is the star of the show and Question Period occupies the central place in media coverage of Parliament and in Canadians' idea about the process of government because of this understanding that the Prime Minister should be present to answer questions about the activities and policies of the government.

Question Period is, potentially, a political minefield, a fact attested to by the presence of journalists in the gallery, few of whom ever bother to be physically present for any of the debates or committee proceedings that take up most of Parliament's working day. Given the stakes,

Reduced to its essentials, the function of the PMO is to protect the PM and project the best image of their boss. This is sometimes a challenge, as was true after some of the PM's comments that seemed to blame US policies for 9/11. (Roy Peterson, *Vancouver Sun*)

preparation of the PM and his or her ministers is crucial. Within the PMO a handful of staffers arrive each day before sunrise to begin the process of sifting through the day's newspapers and the broadcast media's coverage from the previous day and that morning, identifying those issues that the opposition parties are most likely to pounce upon during Question Period. But their job does not stop there. They also craft responses to the anticipated questions, a process that involves considerable partisan and tactical thinking. The most successful response to an opposition member's question is, of course, one that turns the tables and puts the opposition on the defensive or in some way embarrasses the questioner and his or her party. Staffers in the PMO have done their job well when they provide the boss with the ammunition for just such a response.

Although the PMO is clearly the most partisan of the central agencies, it would be quite wrong to think of the PMO as being unconcerned with policy matters. Protecting the Prime Minister and making him or her look good necessarily involves PMO officials in issues of policy, large and small. 'Senior PMO staff', says Savoie, 'will get involved in whatever issue they and the prime minister think they should.'[19] It simply is not possible to draw a line between drafting a speech for the Prime Minister, a function that typically will take place in the PMO, and providing policy advice. But how involved PMO officials are in shaping policy and what their influence is vis-à-vis other control agency officials and departmental managers will, as always, depend on the Prime Minister. Ultimately, the Prime Minister decides from whom he or she will seek advice and who will be a player on any particular issue.

Intergovernmental Affairs (formerly the Federal-Provincial Relations Office)

Perhaps the most surprising thing about this central agency is that it did not exist before 1975. Federal-provincial relations did not suddenly become complex and the political stakes high in the 1970s. Before the Federal-Provincial Relations Office (FPRO) was created, its functions had been carried out within the PCO. What, then, prompted Prime Minister Pierre Trudeau to create a new agency to deal with intergovernmental affairs? According to Colin Campbell, the reason had to do with a 'staffing' problem. Trudeau wanted to appoint Michael Pitfield as Chief Clerk of the Privy Council, but was faced with the dilemma of what to do with Gordon Robertson, Pitfield's predecessor and perhaps the most widely respected official in the public service. The solution was to create the Federal-Provincial Relations Office (FPRO) and to appoint Robertson as the first Secretary to the Cabinet for Federal-Provincial Relations.[20] The episode provides a nice illustration of the role played by serendipity in government decision-making.

After its launch, and despite the prestige of its first head, the FPRO never achieved the influence of other central agencies like Finance, the TBS, and the PCO. Indeed, only two years after the FPRO was established, the cabinet position of Minister for Federal-Provincial Relations and the cabinet committee on federal-provincial relations were abolished. The FPRO was to have been the support staff for this minister and the secretariat to this committee, but their elimination did not result in the dismantling of the FPRO. It continued to provide information and advice to cabinet committees on issues that had an intergovernmental dimension. The precise functions performed by the FPRO depended on the PM. For example, the FPRO played a major role in the development of the Meech Lake Accord proposals. Its lesser stature in the universe of central agencies was largely due to the fact that the FPRO did not hold a monopoly over advice on federal-provincial matters.

Under Prime Minister Chrétien, the FPRO was restructured when the Liberals returned to power in 1993. The functions of the FPRO were reintegrated into the PCO through its Intergovernmental Affairs Office. Intergovernmental Affairs provides policy advice to the Prime Minister and the Minister of Intergovernmental Affairs on issues ranging from health and social programs to national unity and Aboriginal matters. The mandate of the office includes the following objectives:

- To provide advice and strategic planning related to national unity, federal-provincial relations, and constitutional and legal issues.
- To provide communications support on issues with federal-provincial dimensions.
- To work with the provinces and provide advice on the basis of provincial priorities, by monitoring files with intergovernmental dimensions and seeking to forge broader partnerships and new agreements with the provinces and territories to renew the federation.
- To develop policies with respect to Aboriginals and ensure that Aboriginal concerns are taken into consideration in Canadian constitutional development. [21]

The influence of the Intergovernmental Affairs Office waxes and wanes, depending in large measure on the stature of the minister with responsibility for intergovernmental relations and on the nature of the issues it is permitted to deal with. 'Permitted' is the key word because whether Intergovernmental Affairs and its minister take the lead or a leading role on an issue will depend on the Prime Minister. With Stéphane Dion as minister, the Intergovernmental Affairs Office played an important role in the communications—negotiations they were not!—with Quebec over the future terms of a referendum on Quebec independence, which eventually produced the Clarity Bill. Likewise, Dion and the Intergovernmental Affairs Office played an important role in the federal-provincial negotiations that produced the 1999 Social Union

Framework Agreement. Under a minister with less clout on Ottawa-Quebec relations—Dion was recruited into the Liberal Party with the promise of a cabinet post precisely because of his views on Quebec's place in Canadian federalism—it is entirely imaginable that Intergovernmental Affairs would find it difficult to make its voice heard and its presence felt in the central agency universe.

Prime Ministerial Government

For decades various commentators on the Canadian political scene have asked whether Canadian prime ministers were becoming more 'presidential' in their stature and power. The question, however, was always based on the false premise that an American President is more powerful in relation to the country's legislation and his own party than is a Canadian Prime Minister. In fact, there have always been fewer checks on the behaviour of a Canadian Prime Minister than on an American President, and any occupant of the White House would envy the sort of constitutional latitude enjoyed by the leader of the Canadian government. Canadian commentators who purported to see a creeping presidentialization occurring in Canada's system of government were, in fact, mistakenly attributing to the American head of state powers beyond those actually held by the US President.

In recent years this rather wrong-headed debate has come to a close. Indeed, it is now widely recognized that the Canadian Prime Minister has far more clout within the Canadian system of government than the President has in the American system and, moreover, that power has become increasingly centralized in the hands of the PM and those around him. These days, if one looks for counterweights to the PM's power they are more plausibly found in the courts, the media, and in some of the provincial capitals than in Parliament. This centralization of power has advanced to such a degree that some of Canada's most astute political commentators now characterize Canada's system of government as *prime ministerial* rather than

parliamentary government.[22] Donald Savoie and Jeffrey Simpson are among those who argue that not only has the influence of Parliament been effectively eclipsed by the growth of prime ministerial government, but cabinet, too, has been left on the margins of the policy-making process, 'a kind of focus group for the prime minister', in the words of a recent Liberal cabinet minister,[23] or what Jeffrey Simpson calls a 'mini-sounding-board'[24] where decisions already approved by the PM and his advisers in key central agencies are rubber-stamped (see Box 8.2).

THE BUREAUCRACY

For policies to have an impact, they must be implemented. The Employment Insurance (EI) program, for example, depends on the administrative efforts of thousands of public servants employed in Canada Employment centres across the country, the adjudicative work of hundreds of EI appeals commissioners, and the Employment Insurance Commission, which is responsible for making and applying regulations under the Employment Insurance Act. Educational policy is implemented through bureaucratic structures at the federal (student loans, support for research), provincial (ministries of education), and local (school boards) levels. Policies aimed at supporting Canadian industry are administered through a staggering array of separate programs—with their own budgets and bureaucracies—at all levels of government.

Policy implementation is the role of the bureaucracy. Implementation is not, however, an automatic process of converting legislative decisions into action. Unelected officials often wield enormous discretion in applying laws and administering programs. Moreover, their influence is not restricted to the implementation stage of policy-making. It begins at the agenda-setting stage, when problems and possible responses are being defined. Bureaucratic influence is felt at numerous points in the decision-making process prior to the actual introduction of a bill in Par-

BOX 8.2   The Reality of Prime Ministerial Government

Cabinet has now joined Parliament as an institution being bypassed. Real political debate and decision-making are increasingly elsewhere—in federal-provincial meetings of first ministers, on Team Canada flights, where first ministers can hold informal meetings, in the Prime Minister's Office, in the Privy Council Office, in the Department of Finance, and in international organizations and international summits. There is no indication that the one person who holds all the cards, the prime minister, and the central agencies which enable him to bring effective political authority to the centre, are about to change things. The Canadian prime minister has little in the way of institutional check, at least inside government, to inhibit his ability to have his way.

Donald Savoie, *Governing from the Centre*, 362.

liament. Often, the decision-making process has no parliamentary stage, or at least Parliament has minimal involvement in the process. Here, the power of unelected officials is seen in its most naked form.

The original meaning of the word 'bureaucracy'—*bureaucracie*, coined by the French writer Vincent de Gournay in the mid-eighteenth century—involved rule by unelected officials. The first formal definition of the word appeared in 1798 in the Dictionary of the French Academy. It read: 'Power, influence of the heads and staff of governmental bureaux'. Ever since, the political power of unelected officials has been a chief concern of those who study bureaucracy.

The Structure of the Canadian Bureaucracy

The federal public sector employs close to 400,000 people working in close to 400 different organizations (all figures as of 1999). About 221,000 of these people work directly for government departments and agencies. They are public servants, in the narrow legal sense of this term. Their employer is the Treasury Board and the organizations they work for fall directly under the authority of a cabinet minister. Another approximately 70,000 people are employed

by federally owned Crown corporations and about 89,000 work in some capacity in the Canadian Forces. The organizations they work for receive all or part of their funding from the federal government and are subject to rules that it sets, but these organizations operate with some degree of autonomy.

Public-sector employment is even greater at the provincial and local levels. In 1999, provincial governments employed about 207,000 public servants and local governments roughly 249,000. There are hundreds of provincially owned Crown corporations, some of which, like Hydro One Networks in Ontario and Hydro-Québec, are among the biggest employers and capital investors in the Canadian economy. If we define the public sector broadly to include all those organizations that receive all or a major part of their operating revenues from one or more levels of government, an estimated one in four Canadian workers is employed in the public sector. It includes nurses, teachers, firefighters and police officers, workers for Children's Aid Societies and at some women's shelters, and so on.

Even in these days of downsized government, the public sector is quite extensive. That part of it that is often labelled the 'bureaucracy' may be divided into three main components: the public service (chiefly departments); independent and semi-independent agencies and tribunals; and Crown corporations.

Public service. About half of those employed in the federal public sector work in the public service. It includes all statutory departments and other organizations whose members are appointed by the Public Service Commission (PSC) and who, formally, are employees of the Treasury Board. This is the part of the bureaucracy that is most directly under the authority of cabinet.

Agencies and tribunals. These organizations perform a wide variety of regulatory, research, and advisory functions. Among the most widely known federal regulatory agencies are the Canadian Radio-television and Telecommunications Commission (CRTC), which regulates communications and broadcasting, the National Transportation Agency (air, water, and rail transportation), and the National Energy Board (energy when it crosses provincial and international boundaries). It is important to note that many important areas of regulation, including trucking, public utilities within provincial boundaries, and most labour relations, are controlled by provincial governments.

These organizations have a greater degree of independence from government than those that fall under the public service. With few exceptions their members are not appointed by the PSC, nor are they employees of the Treasury Board. The precise degree of autonomy enjoyed by an agency or tribunal varies, but in some cases it is almost total.

Crown corporations. These organizations, in most cases, perform commercial functions and typically operate at 'arm's length' from the government of the day. They hire their own employees, determine their own internal administrative structures, and in many instances behave much like privately owned businesses. Over the last couple of decades some of the largest of these corporations, notably Air Canada, Canadian National, and Petro-Canada, have been privatized.

These three categories do not cover the entire federal bureaucracy. Some relatively small but important parts of that bureaucracy, including the Auditor General's Office and the Commissioner of Official Languages, are independent of cabinet, reporting to Parliament. The Royal Canadian Mounted Police also has a distinct legal status, as does the Canadian Forces.

Together, this vast administrative apparatus has responsibility for implementing public policy. At the most prosaic level—the level where virtually all of us have made personal contact with the state—officials deal with passport applications, meat inspections, public queries regarding Employment Insurance benefits, job seekers at Canada Employment centres, and a vast number of similarly routine administrative tasks. But at the top of the bureaucratic pyramid are men and women whose relationship to public policy is much more active. Senior officials within the departmental bureaucracy, particularly deputy ministers and assistant deputy ministers, interact frequently with cabinet ministers and senior officials in central agencies. They are called on to testify before committees of the legislature. These officials often deal directly with the representatives of organized interests. They are universally acknowledged to have influence in shaping public policy, although the extent of their influence is a matter of debate

The bureaucracy is not a uniform structure. One can identify several different functions performed by organizations within the administrative system. These include:

- the provision and administration of services to the public, often to narrow economic, social, or cultural clientele groups;
- the provision of services to other parts of the bureaucracy;
- the integration of policy in a particular field, or the generation of policy advice;
- the adjudication of applications and/or interpretation of regulations (such as product safety standards, or the determination of what constitutes morally offensive scenes of sex or violence on films);

- the disbursement of funds to groups or individuals, as with the grants to artists and cultural organizations administered by the Canada Council;
- the production of a good or the operation of a service that is sold to buyers.

These functions are not mutually exclusive. A large and organizationally complex department like the federal Department of Transport is involved in service delivery, the regulation of transport standards, and the development of policy. Almost all government depart ments, regardless of their primary orientation, have a policy development capacity. During the 1970s this was formalized—although not necessarily enhanced—with the creation of policy analysis units, usually at the assistant deputy minister level. An informal policy advisory capacity, however, has always existed at the level of senior officials. This role is based on their expert familiarity with the programs administered by the department and on the fact that, typically, they remain within a particular policy field longer than their nominal superiors in cabinet. The turnover rate for deputy ministers and other senior bureaucrats has increased since the era of the Ottawa 'mandarins' from the 1940s to the 1960s, when a coterie of top officials whose careers were associated with particular parts of the bureaucracy exercised an extraordinary influence on the direction of federal policy. The more recent emphasis has been on senior officials as managers, whose management skills are transferable across policy fields. Combined with the more rapid turnover of deputy ministers since the early 1980s, it is often argued that the policy influence of senior bureaucrats has diminished.

In fact, it would be more accurate to say that this power has become more diffuse. The days when a mere handful of key deputy ministers could dominate the policy-making process are gone. Today, bureaucratic influence is distributed more widely, in large part because of the increased importance of central agencies such as the Privy Council Office and the Treasury Board Secretariat, but also because it is rare for a deputy minis-

ter to remain in charge of a particular department for more than a few years. Nevertheless, there is little doubt that senior bureaucrats continue to be principal players in policy-making.

Neither the passing of the mandarinate nor the development of central agencies as an alternative source of expert policy advice to cabinet has undermined the fundamental basis of bureaucratic influence on policy. This influence rests on the following factors:

- Departments are repositories for a vast amount of information about current and past programs and about the day-to-day details of their administration. While the aphorism 'Knowledge is power' is too simplistic and implies a sort of rationality that usually is not characteristic of policy choices, ministers invariably depend on the permanent bureaucracy for advice on policy. Senior bureaucrats occupy strategic positions in the policy process because of their ability to shape the information and recommendations reaching the minister.
- The relationship of a department to the social or economic interests that benefit from the programs it administers is a source of departmental influence on policy. Departmental officials clearly are not indifferent in their sympathies towards conflicting societal interests. Moreover, the bureaucracy is an important target for professional lobbyists and interest group representatives who wish to influence policy.
- 'Ministers', observes Savoie, 'do not manage.'[25] Their deputy ministers perform this job. Given the competing pressures on a minister's time, the deputy minister inevitably assumes the job of senior manager of the department over which a cabinet minister presides. In many instances the chief responsibility for policy direction also will be assumed by the deputy minister.
- Most laws contain provisions delegating to bureaucrats the authority to interpret their general terms in application to actual cases (see Box 8.3). This is also true of other statutory instruments that have the force of law (for example, the thousands of Orders-in-Council that issue from

BOX 8.3   The Delegation of Discretion

The Broadcasting Act is the key law regulating television, radio, and telecommunications in Canada. Like many laws it delegates to non-elected officials the power to make rules that flesh out the very general terms of the statute they implement. For example, officials with the Canada Broadcasting Corporation, a Crown corporation, and with the Canadian Radio-television and Telecommunications Commission, the regulatory agency that licenses broadcasters, must determine the meaning of the following vague objectives set down in the Broadcasting Act:

3. (1) It is hereby declared as the broadcasting policy for Canada that . . .

   (d) the Canadian broadcasting system should

      (i)   serve to safeguard, enrich and strengthen the cultural, political, social and economic fabric of Canada,

      (ii) encourage the development of Canadian expression by providing a wide range of programming that reflects Canadian attitudes, opinions, ideas, values and artistic creativity, by displaying Canadian talent in entertainment programming and by offering information and analysis concerning Canada and other countries from a Canadian point of view,

      (iii) through its programming and the employment opportunities arising out of its operations, serve the needs and interests, and reflect the circumstances and aspirations, of Canadian men, women and children, including equal rights, the linguistic duality and multicultural and multiracial nature of Canadian society and the special place of aboriginal peoples within that society, and

      (iv) be readily adaptable to scientific and technological change;

In addition,

   (l) the Canadian Broadcasting Corporation, as the national public broadcaster, should provide radio and television services incorporating a wide range of programming that informs, enlightens and entertains;

  (m) the programming provided by the Corporation should

      (i)   be predominantly and distinctly Canadian,

      (ii) reflect Canada and its regions to national and regional audiences, while serving the special needs of those regions,

      (iii) actively contribute to the flow and exchange of cultural expression,

      (iv) be in English and in French, reflecting the different needs and circumstances of each official language community, including the particular needs and circumstances of English and French linguistic minorities,

      (v) strive to be of equivalent quality in English and in French,

      (vi) contribute to shared national consciousness and identity,

      (vii) be made available throughout Canada by the most appropriate and efficient means and as resources become available for the purpose, and

    (viii) reflect the multicultural and multiracial nature of Canada. . . .

Broadcasting Act, Chapter B-9.01 (1991, c.1 1)

cabinet each year). The task of implementation— applying the law to actual cases—is not a neutral one. In some cases this discretion is exercised at a low level in the bureaucratic hierarchy (for example, decisions by local custom officials on whether a particular video cassette constitutes obscene material and therefore should be prohibited entry into Canada).

To summarize, the bureaucracy enters the policy process both early and late. Bureaucrats are the people who actually administer the programs established by law. In doing so they regularly exercise considerable discretion, a fact that often leads special interests to focus at least part of their attention on the bureaucracy. Departmental officials are also involved in the early stages of the policy process because of the intimate knowledge they have of existing programs and the daily contact between bureaucrats and the groups directly affected by the programs they administer. Moreover, the annual expenditure budget, which provides a fairly reasonable indication of a government's policy priorities, is based largely on the information provided by departments. New legislation is invariably influenced by the input of senior permanent officials. These officials are both managers and policy advisers, and they are very clearly part of the inner circle of policy-making that extends outward from cabinet.

On top of all the other expectations held for the bureaucracy in democratic societies, it is also expected to 'represent' the population. This means that the composition of the bureaucracy should reflect in fair proportion certain demographic characteristics of society. Affirmative action programs and quota hiring are the tools used in pursuit of this goal. The basic reasoning behind arguments for 'representative' bureaucracy is that it will have greater popular legitimacy than one that is not, and that its representative character will help ensure that the advice bureaucrats give to politicians and the services they provide to their clienteles are sensitive to the values and aspirations of the governed.

As reasonable as this may sound, the idea and implementation of representative bureaucracy have always been problematic. Which groups should be singled out for representation? What constitutes 'fair proportion'? To what extent are other values like efficient performance and equal rights for all compromised by such a policy? Can the idea of a representative bureaucracy be squared with that of a politically neutral one?

Problems aside, it is clear that a grossly unrepresentative bureaucracy can pose problems. The fact that comparatively few French Canadians were found at the senior levels of the federal bureaucracy was already a controversial matter in the 1940s, 1950s, and 1960s, and led to major public service reforms and Canada's first policy of representative bureaucracy under Lester B. Pearson and Pierre Elliott Trudeau. On the other hand, most students of British bureaucracy agree that the strongly upper-class character of that country's public service did not prevent it from co-operating with the post-World War II Labour government in implementing reforms opposed by the upper class. Nor has the unrepresentative and elitist character of the French bureaucracy been considered a major problem in that country.

One thing is certain: governments that have instituted policies of affirmative action and quota hiring have done so chiefly for political reasons, not because the intellectual arguments offered in support of such policies are demonstrably true. Among the most important political reasons is national unity. In Canada it has long been recognized that the merit principle, which ignores the ascriptive characteristics of individuals and looks only at their job-related achievements and skills, should not interfere with what one writer called 'a tactful balance of national elements'.[26] Until fairly recently, this balancing act chiefly involved ensuring adequate francophone representation in the management ranks of the bureaucracy. Indeed, it is fair to say that until the 1970s this was the only serious representational factor taken into account in public service recruitment and promotion. John Porter's analysis of the senior federal bureaucracy during the 1950s showed that only the British, French, and Jewish ethnic groups were significantly represented, and those of British origin were clearly dominant.[27] Women and what are today labelled visible minorities were almost completely absent from the senior levels of the public service.

As the ethnic composition of Canadian society has changed—people of non-British, non-French ancestry now comprise over one-quarter of the population—and especially as the discourse of collective rights and group identities has achieved greater prominence, the old concern with 'fair' linguistic representation has been joined by efforts to recruit and promote women, visible minorities, Aboriginal Canadians, and the disabled. Affirmative action programs are established by the Treasury Board and monitored by the Public Service Commission. During the 1980s their programs relied mainly on a system of employment targets rather than on mandatory quotas for group representation. Ottawa and the provincial governments continue to use targets and incentives to encourage senior managers to hire and promote members of designated groups, but they also use quota systems—euphemistically labelled 'employment equity' policies. In 2002 the federal government, through the Treasury Board, issued an employment directive to departmental managers that required them to increase the proportion of visible minorities—defined by the Treasury Board as someone other than an Aboriginal who is non-white—on their staffs to 20 per cent and calling for one out of every five appointments to the executive category of the public service to be from visible minorities by 2005. Some interpret 'fair representation' as a proportion of the bureaucracy equal to a group's share of the population. This is, for example, the position taken by the New Democratic Party (NDP) and by feminist organizations in Canada. To this day, however, Canadian governments have not attempted to implement this vision of fairness.

THE LEGISLATURE

The legislature is a study in contrasts. Its physical setting is soberly impressive, yet the behaviour of its members is frequently the object of derision. Its constitutional powers appear to be formidable, yet its actual influence on policy usually is much less than that of the cabinet and the bureaucracy. All major policies, including all laws, must be approved by the legislature, but the legislature's approval often seems a foregone conclusion and a mere formality. One of the two chambers of the legislature, the House of Commons, is democratically elected. The other, the Senate, has long had an unenviable reputation as a sinecure for party hacks and other appointed unworthies.

The contradictions of the legislature have their source in the tension between traditional ideas about political democracy and the character of the modern state. Representation, accountability to the people, and choice are the cornerstones of liberal democratic theory. An elected legislature that represents the population either on the basis of population or by region—or both—and party competition are the means by which these democratic goals are to be accomplished. But the modern state, we have seen, is characterized by a vast bureaucratic apparatus that is not easily controlled by elected politicians. Moreover, while the Prime Minister's power has always been vastly greater than that of other members of Parliament, the concentration of power in and around the office of the Prime Minister appears to have reached unprecedented levels. As the scale and influence of the non-elected parts of the state have grown and prime ministerial government has been consolidated, the inadequacies of traditional democratic theory—centred on the role of the legislature—have become increasingly apparent.

Is there an alternative? A more representative and democratically responsive bureaucracy is sometimes viewed as the solution to the problem of power without accountability. Reforms in this direction are certainly useful. They cannot, however, substitute for elections that enable voters to choose those who will represent them. If one begins from the premise that the free election must be the cornerstone of political democracy, the role of the legislature is crucial.

One way of ensuring that the legislature better performs its democratic functions is to improve its representative character. Possible ways through which this could be done include reform of the political parties' candidate selection process, instituting a system of proportional representation (see Chapter 9), or by the creation of a reformed Senate. Another option is to tighten the legislature's control over the political executive and the non-elected parts of the state. This may be done by increasing the legislature's access to information about the intentions and performance of the government and bureaucracy, providing opportunities for legislative scrutiny and debate of executive action, and enabling legislators to influence the priorities and agenda of government.

Canada's legislature has two parts, the House of Commons and the Senate. Representation in the elected House of Commons is roughly according to population—roughly, because some MPs represent as few as 30,000 constituents, while others represent close to 200,000. Each of the 301 members of the House of Commons—scheduled

to become 308 in 2004—is the sole representative for a constituency (also known as a 'riding').

Senators are appointed by the government of the day when a vacancy occurs. They hold their seats until age 75. Representation in the Senate is on the basis of regions. Each of the four main regions (Ontario, Quebec, the four western provinces, and the Maritimes) has 24 seats. Newfoundland has six, and there is one from each of Yukon, the Northwest Territories, and Nunavut, for a total of 105 seats. Eight temporary seats were added by the Mulroney government in 1988 to overcome Liberal opposition in the Senate to the Goods and Services Tax, thus raising the total number of senators for a while from 104 to 112.[28] In recent years there have been suggestions that senators be elected and that a certain number of Senate seats be reserved for women and Aboriginal Canadians.

In law, the powers of the House of Commons and Senate are roughly equal. There are, however, a couple of important exceptions. Legislation involving the spending or raising of public money must, under the Constitution, be introduced in the House of Commons. And when it comes to amending the Constitution, the Senate can only delay passage of a resolution already approved by the Commons. But all bills must pass through

---

BOX 8.4   The Ambivalence of Parliament

[The] House of Commons is the true heart of Canada. It reflects every passing mood, sensation, pleasure, and pain in the vast, sprawling body of the nation, and articulates it within a few hours. Yet Parliament, on its green hill, lives strangely aloof, floating in a warm, comfortable vacuum. National politics is a craft apart, and its life is separated from the ordinary life of the nation and even Ottawa, just outside its stone gates, by a gulf as wide as the sea. It is a separate and wondrous craft unknown to the layman, hidden from the ordinary citizen, who sees only the outward ripples, never the inward movements; a complicated and mysterious process utterly foreign to the life of the people, which it yet manages to reflect, in legislation and government, like a true and clear mirror.

Bruce Hutchison, *The Unknown Country*, 1942, 80.

identical stages in both bodies before becoming law (see the Appendix at the end of this chapter).

Despite the similarity of their formal powers, the superiority of the elected branch is well established. For most of its history, the Senate has deferred to the will of the Commons. This changed after the 1984 election of a Conservative majority in Parliament. On several occasions the Liberal-dominated Senate obstructed bills that had already been passed by the Commons. When the Senate balked at passage of the politically unpopular GST the government decided it had had enough. Using an obscure constitutional power it appointed eight new Conservative senators, thereby giving the Conservative Party a slender majority. Under the Chrétien government the partisan balance in the Senate has shifted back to a Liberal majority. The squabbles that often occurred after 1984, when the House of Commons was controlled by one party and the Senate by another, have become rare.

The legislature performs a number of functions that are basic to political democracy. The most fundamental of these is the passage of laws by the people's elected representatives. Budget proposals and new policy initiatives must be placed before Parliament for its approval. The operation of party discipline ensures that bills tabled in the legislature are seldom modified in major ways during the law-passing process. This does not mean, however, that Parliament's approval of the government's legislative agenda is an empty formality. The rules under which the legislature operates ensure that the opposition parties have opportunities to debate and criticize the government's proposals.

Robert Jackson and Michael Atkinson have argued that those involved in the pre-parliamentary stages of policy-making anticipate the probable reactions of the legislature and of the government party caucus before a bill or budget is tabled in Parliament.[29] While this may have been true in the past, it no longer appears that those who actually take policy decisions and draft legislation lose much sleep over what they think

will be the reaction of backbench MPs. On the influence of caucus, Savoie states that government party MPs 'report that they are rarely, if ever, in a position to launch a new initiative, and worse, that they are rarely effective in getting the government to change course. They also do not consider themselves to be an effective check on prime ministerial power.'[30] In the words of one government party MP, 'We simply respond to what Cabinet does, and there are limits to what you can do when you are always reacting.'[31] In short, there is little evidence from recent years to suggest that the Prime Minister and those around him who are involved in making policy pay much attention to the preferences of those in the legislature, on either the government or opposition side of the aisle. They are, however, very likely to pay attention to the results of surveys and focus groups that have been commissioned to gauge public reaction to a policy.

Although the legislature may often, indeed usually, play second fiddle to more direct means used by government to take the public pulse on issues, it is far from being irrelevant in the policy-making process. Functions performed by the legislature include scrutiny of government performance, constituency representation, debate of issues, and legitimation of the political system.

Scrutinizing Government Performance

Various regular opportunities exist for the legislature to prod, question, and criticize the government. These include the daily Question Period, the set-piece debates that follow the Speech from the Throne and the introduction of a new budget, and Opposition Days, when the opposition parties determine the topic of debate. Committee hearings and special parliamentary task forces also provide opportunities for legislative scrutiny of government actions and performance, although the subjects that these bodies deal with are mainly determined by the government. Party discipline is a key factor that limits the critical tendencies of parliamentary committees, particularly during periods of majority government.

Earlier we said that Question Period has become, for better or for worse, both the centrepiece of Parliament's day and the chief activity shaping the ideas that most Canadians have of what goes on in Parliament. The introduction of television cameras into the legislature in the late 1970s has reinforced the stature of Question Period as the primary forum through which the opposition can scrutinize and criticize the government on matters big and small. This is the opposition parties' main chance to influence the issues that will be discussed in the media and how the government will be portrayed by the press. In fact, however, the dynamic of Question Period involves reciprocal influences between the media and opposition parties. It has often been said that this morning's *Globe and Mail* headline becomes this afternoon's leading volley in Question Period, but things are not this simple. Journalists also react—although not always in the way that opposition parties may like—to the questions and lines of attack that opposition parties launch against the government. For example, during the spring of 2002 the opposition parties, particularly the Canadian Alliance and the Conservative Party, carried out a sustained assault on the government and, in particular, a handful of its members, charging that there was widespread evidence of corruption and influence-peddling in the awarding of government advertising contracts. This was clearly part of an opposition campaign to generate as much negative publicity for the Chrétien government as possible and to create (or reinforce) a public perception of the government as corrupt. To what degree this issue was media-driven as opposed to being driven by the opposition parties is impossible to say. What is clear is that this sort of critical scrutiny of the government serves the interests of both the opposition parties, who wish to see the government embarrassed and its popular support drop, and the media, who know that controversy and the scent of wrongdoing attract more readers and viewers than do reports that all is well with the world.

Committees of the House of Commons, whose membership is generally limited to about 20 MPs, may appear to be forums where the lack of party discipline can be loosened and backbench MPs may acquire some expertise in particular policy areas that will enable them to assess the merits of legislation in a more informed and less partisan manner. Students of American politics know that congressional committees are where the real action is in Congress and where what enters one end of the committee sausage-grinder may not bear much resemblance to what emerges from the other end, if it emerges at all. In Canada's Parliament, however, committees seldom modify in more than marginal ways what is placed before them and virtually never derail any bill that the government has introduced in the House. Far from being a source of opportunity and satisfaction for MPs who wish to see themselves as being truly engaged in the law-making process, there is much evidence to suggest that committees are a source of frustration for many MPs and that they do not provide a serious vehicle through which the legislature can scrutinize the activities of government and call it to account for its actions. In his study of MPs' behaviour and perceptions of their jobs, David Docherty states that 'several rookie Liberals indicated that the failure of their own executive to treat committee work and reports seriously was the single most frustrating (and unexpected) aspect of their job as an MP.'[32] Docherty found that frustration with House committees was not limited to government party members. Opposition MPs also expressed disappointment with the inability of committees to make more than a marginal and occasional difference.

Party discipline is at the root of this dissatisfaction. Despite some tinkering over the last couple of decades, the ostensible goal of which was to increase the independence of committees and thereby augment the influence of the legislature, the fact that party discipline operates in committee just as it does on the floor of the House of Commons undoes all of these reforms. Moreover, all but a small fraction of what committees do is reactive, responding to a bill tabled in Parliament by the government, spending proposals submitted by the government, or some investigative task assigned to a committee by the government. Within this straitjacket there can be little wiggle room for non-partisan consideration of the government's record and proposals.

Senators argue that life is different in the red chamber. They point to the Senate's long string of committee and task force studies on topics ranging from corporate concentration in Canada's media industries to the proposed decriminalization of marijuana possession. Being appointed to serve until the age of 75, most of them argue, loosens the constraint of party discipline. Not having to worry about whether their party leader will sign their nomination papers at some future election and being unconcerned with how their actions will affect their prospect of being appointed to cabinet, senators can behave with far greater independence than their House of Commons colleagues.

This argument, while not totally false, is both naive and self-serving. It is naive in that it ignores the palpable reality that most senators have demonstrated pretty firm and unswerving loyalty to the party, and especially to the Prime Minister who appointed them. This is not surprising when one looks at who becomes a senator and why. Most are people who have served their party long and well, and it would be more than a bit unusual if they were suddenly, after appointment to the Senate, to change the patterns of loyalty that got them there in the first place. To be sure, there are mavericks and 'characters' in Canada's Senate whose idiosyncrasies and speechifying in that chamber would not be tolerated by their party in the House. But how many Canadians know or care about this? The truth is that the media seldom report this side of the Senate and, to senators' disappointment, few are paying attention but themselves.

The self-serving aspect of the argument about senators' greater independence enabling them to scrutinize and criticize the government to a degree not permitted in the House of Commons is pointed out by Jeffrey Simpson.[33] Simpson notes that senators routinely point to their many committee reports on important policy matters, undertaken at arm's length from the government, as proof of the significant role the unelected Senate performs in Canada's system of government. This is, Simpson rightly observes, a sort of *faute de mieux* argument. Lacking other plausible justifications for the existence of an appointed Senate stuffed with those whose appointments represent a form of patronage bestowed by the Prime Minister, senators point to their committees and their products. While their committee reports have often influenced the contours of public debate on an issue and the independence often associated with these reports could not have occurred in the House, there is no reason to believe that only the Senate as currently constituted could make this contribution to the process of scrutinizing government policy, investigating important issues, and proposing legislative change. Indeed, the committee work that senators point to as their proudest accomplishment and chief raison d'être usually just covers the same ground that think-tanks, academic studies, and government-commissioned studies have mapped.

Representation

The House of Commons is both symbolically and practically important as a contact point between citizens and government. Symbolically, the elected House embodies the principle of government by popular consent. The partisan divisions within it, between government and opposition parties, have the additional effect of affirming for most citizens their belief in the competitive character of politics. At a practical level, citizens often turn to their elected representatives when they experience problems with bureaucracy or when they want to express their views on government policy.

Unlike the elected Commons, the Senate does not perform a significant representational role in Canadian politics despite the fact that senators are appointed to represent the various provinces. The unelected character of Canada's upper house and the crassly partisan criteria that prime ministers have usually relied on in filling

Senate vacancies have undermined whatever legitimacy senators might otherwise have achieved as spokespersons for the regions. Provincial governments, regional spokespersons in the federal cabinet, and regional blocs of MPs within the party caucuses are, in about that order of importance, vastly more significant in representing regional interests.

Debate

The image that most Canadians have of Parliament is of the heated exchanges that take place across the aisle that separates the government and opposition parties. Parliamentary procedure and even the physical layout of the legislature are based on the adversarial principle of 'them versus us'. This principle is most clearly seen in the daily Question Period and the set-piece debates that follow the Speech from the Throne and the introduction of a new budget. At its best, the thrust and riposte of partisan debate can provide a very public forum for the discussion of national issues, as well as highlight the policy differences between the parties. Unfortunately for the quality of political discourse in Canada, parliamentary debate is more often dragged down by the wooden reading of prepared remarks, heckling and personal invective, and occasional blatant abuses of either the government's majority or the opposition's opportunities to hold up the business of Parliament.

It is a mistake to imagine that the purpose of parliamentary debate is to allow for a searching discussion of issues in a spirit of open-mindedness. Generally, MPs' minds are made up when a measure is first tabled in Parliament. So what is the point of the long hours spent criticizing and defending legislative proposals and the government's record, all at taxpayers' expense?

There are two reasons why legislative debate is important. First, outcomes are not always predictable. Even when the government party holds a commanding majority in Parliament or when the policy differences between government and opposition are not significant, the dynamic of debate on an issue is not entirely controllable by the government or by Parliament. Media coverage of the issue, reporting of public opinion polls, and the interventions of organized interests, other governments, and even individuals who have credibility in the eyes of the media and public all can have a bearing on the trajectory of parliamentary debate.

Parliamentary debate is also important because it reinforces the popular belief in the open and competitive qualities of Canadian democracy. The stylized conflict between government and opposition parties, which is the essence of the British parliamentary system, emphasizes disagreements and differences. Adversarial politics obscures the fact that these partisan disagreements usually are contained within a fairly narrow band of consensus on basic values and that the words and deeds of the opposition, when it holds power, usually bear a strong resemblance to those of its predecessor. Parliamentary debate, therefore, produces an exaggerated impression of the open and competitive qualities of Canadian politics. This provides valuable support for the existing political system, while papering over the obstacles that non-mainstream interests face in getting their concerns and views onto the public agenda.

Political scientist Gerald Baier has noted, however, that even this legitimation function of parliamentary debate has been severely weakened in recent years by the 'precipitous decline' in the number of days that Parliament and provincial legislatures are in session. This decline, it would seem, poses a potentially serious threat to the concept of responsible government, or what Baier terms 'parliamentary democracy'. In 2002, for example, the Ontario legislature had only 28 sitting days when parliamentary debate of any kind was possible.[34] When a government faces the opposition in debate for so few days over the course of a year, the democratic principles inherent to parliamentary government can fall victim to unchecked rule by the executive.

Legitimation

Parliament is both a legislative and a legitimizing institution. Laws must pass through the parliamentary mill before being approved, and thus Parliament deserves to be called the legislative branch of government. But it is also the legitimizing branch of government because most of the mechanisms of democratic accountability are embodied in the structure and procedures of Parliament: it represents the people; it scrutinizes the actions of government; and it debates public issues. Along with elections and judicial review of the Constitution, Parliament appears to be one of the chief bulwarks against the danger that government will abuse its powers.

How well Parliament performs its democratic functions is another matter. But the structures and procedures of the legislature are built around the ideas of open government and popular consent and the idea that the actions of government must be approved by Parliament. These factors help to legitimize the political system and the policies it produces. If, however, most people hold the view that the legislature is a farce, then its contribution to the perceived legitimacy of Canadian government would be undermined. Canadians do not hold this view. Their cynicism about the integrity of politicians does not appear to undermine their faith in parliamentary institutions.

Although the concentration of power in and around the Prime Minister has reached unprecedented levels, the legislature is not the helpless pawn of the executive. Using the rules of parliamentary procedure, opposition parties are able to prod, question, and castigate the government; all in front of the parliamentary press gallery and the television cameras in the House of Commons. The opposition's behaviour is usually reactive, responding to the government's proposals and policies. Nevertheless, the legislature's function as a talking shop—the *parler* in 'parliament'—enables it to draw attention to controversial aspects of the government's performance. MPs are not quite the 'nobodies' that Pierre Trudeau once labelled them. But they are far from having the policy influence of their American counterparts, who, because of loose party discipline and very different rules governing the law-making process, are often assiduously courted by interest groups and the President himself.

Earlier, we said that **caucus**, the body of elected MPs belonging to a particular party, generally does not have much influence on the party leadership, at least not in the government party. When Parliament is in session, it is usual for a party's caucus to meet at least weekly. Caucus is not, however, considered unimportant by party leaders. The Prime Minister regularly attends caucus meetings, as do members of his or her cabinet when they are in Ottawa. These meetings often amount to little more than what one MP describes as 'bitching sessions' and, moreover, it is almost never the case that MPs challenge the Prime Minister behind the closed doors of the party's weekly meeting.[35]

Some insiders argue, however, that the government caucus provides a real opportunity for backbench members to influence government policy through frank debate. This may occasionally be true. But the limits on caucus's influence are readily apparent from two facts. First, policies that are extremely unpopular with the public, as was the GST, but that are priorities of the government, are not affected by caucus opposition. The same is true of policies that create sharp divisions in a party's caucus, such as the Liberal government's 1995 gun control law. If the policy is a high priority, the prospect that a caucus revolt will defeat or substantially change it is extremely remote. Members who fail to toe the line are likely to experience the fate of those Liberal MPs who voted against the government's gun law in 1995: the loss of committee assignments. Expulsion from caucus is another sanction that may be used to punish recalcitrant backbenchers. Second, caucus—like the legislature as a whole—usually enters the policy-making process late, after much study, consultation, and negotiation have already taken place. Embedded in the legislation that the members of the government party caucus are asked to vote for is a complex fabric of compromises and accommodations between government and interest groups, different agencies of government, or even Ottawa and the provinces. It is unlikely that the government will be willing to see this fabric unravelled because of caucus opposition.

What Does an MP Do?

It is almost certainly true that most Canadians believe that their MPs are overpaid and underworked. Stories of 'gold-clad' MPs' pensions and of senators who slurp at the public trough while living in Mexico help to fuel this widespread but generally unfair charge. Most backbench MPs work very long hours, whether in Ottawa or at home in their constituencies (Box 8.5). The demands on their time ratchet upward in the case of members of the government and party leaders, all of whom are required to travel extensively in carrying out

their jobs. But what does a typical MP do? For most MPs, the single largest bloc of their working day is devoted to taking care of constituency business. David Docherty reports that the MPs he surveyed from the 34th (1988–93) and 35th (1993–7) parliaments claimed to devote just over 40 per cent of their working time to constituency affairs. The second largest block of time was spent on legislative work, such as committee assignments and attending Question Period and debates. This activity runs a fairly distant second, however, to constituency work, as shown in Figure 8.4.

In performing their functions, all MPs are provided with a budget that enables them to hire staff in Ottawa and in their riding office. How they allocate these resources is up to them, but most MPs opt to have two staffers in Ottawa and two in the constituency office. MPs also receive public funds to maintain their constituency offices and are allowed an unlimited regular mail budget and four mass mailings to constituents—known as 'householders'—per year. Although these resources are

Figure 8.4   How an MP Spends the Day (per cent of working time devoted to different tasks)

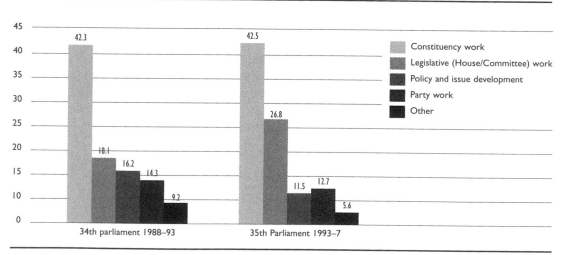

Source: David Docherty, *Mr. Smith Goes to Ottawa: Life in the House of Commons* (Vancouver: University of British Columbia Press, 1997), 129.

paltry compared to those at the disposal of United States representatives and senators, they are superior to those of legislators in the United Kingdom, Belgium, France, and many other democracies. And while they are adequate to enable an MP to carry out his or her constituency duties, they are not sufficient to pay for high-powered policy analysts and other research staff.

Docherty found that MPs who were new to Parliament tended to spend more time on constituency work than those who had been in the legislature for a longer period of time. '[T]he longer members serve in office', he observes, 'the less time they will devote to constituency work.'[36] This shift from constituency to policy-oriented work does not, however, mean that a veteran MP's constituents are less well served than those of an MP who is new to Parliament. Docherty found that the Ottawa staff of veteran MPs tended to make up the difference, spending more of their time on constituency business as the focus of the MPs shifted to policy concerns. 'No matter what stage of their career,' Docherty states, 'members of parliament see helping individuals as their most crucial duty.'[37] In this, MPs show themselves to be realistic about the limits on their ability to be lawmakers.

THE COURTS

Responsibility for Canada's judicial system is divided between Ottawa and the provinces. While the Constitution gives the federal government the exclusive right to make criminal law, it assigns responsibility for the administration of justice and for law enforcement to the provinces. Consequently, all provinces have established their own courts that interpret and apply both federal and provincial laws.

The Constitution also gives Ottawa the authority to create courts. This authority was used in 1875 to create the Supreme Court of Canada. Since 1949 the Supreme Court has been Canada's highest court of appeal. Ottawa again used this constitutional power in 1971 to create the Feder-

al Court of Canada. It has jurisdiction over civil claims involving the federal governments, cases arising from the decisions of federally appointed administrative bodies like the Immigration Appeal Board, and matters relating to federal income tax, copyrights, and maritime law—all of which fall under the legislative authority of Ottawa. The structure of Canada's court system is shown in Figure 8.5.

Courts apply and interpret the law. They perform this role in matters ranging from contested driving offences to disputes over the most fundamental principles of the Constitution. The decisions of judges often have profound implications for the rights and status of individuals and groups, for the balance of social and economic power, and for the federal division of powers. It is crucial, therefore, that we understand the political significance of the judicial process and the methods of interpretation typically used by the courts.

The independence of judges is the cornerstone of the Canadian judicial system. Judges are appointed by governments. But once appointed they hold their office 'during good behaviour'.[38] What constitutes a lapse from 'good behaviour'? A criminal or a serious moral offence could provide grounds for removal, as could decisions of such incompetence that they undermine public respect for the law and the judiciary. In such circumstances the appointing government may launch removal proceedings against a judge. In fact, however, this has seldom happened. Formal proceedings have seldom been initiated and have never been prosecuted to their ultimate conclusion, i.e., the actual removal of a judge by resolution of Parliament or a provincial legislature. Judicial independence is also protected by the fact that judges' salaries and conditions of service are established by law. Consequently, governments cannot single out any individual judge for special reward or punishment.

But as Ralph Miliband puts it, to say that judges are 'independent' begs the question, 'Independent of what?' As members of the societies in which they live—usually successful members of

BOX 8.5   A Day in the Life of a Backbench MP

There really is no such thing as a typical day in the life of an MP. In fact, most MPs will say that they have three sorts of days: days spent in their constituency; days spent in the House of Commons, when it is in session; and days spent on the road, at conferences, seminars, conventions, or other travel related to their job as an MP.

Most Canadians probably believe that when the House is not sitting, MPs have little to do. But as the following log of a constituency day in the life of Alliance MP Scott Reid shows, this is far from the truth.

- Today was typical of a constituency day. After getting out of bed I spent about half an hour, in my pyjamas, reviewing and correcting constituent correspondence on my laptop from home. I have arranged for my correspondence assistant to draft responses to all letters that come into the office and to send me copies by e-mail for my approval. If I want to make any changes, I do so in the text of the e-mail and send it back to her. In this way, every letter that is sent out from our office is reviewed by me. By putting the approval system on e-mail, we have made it possible for me to proofread and edit correspondence with my constituents from anywhere in the world.

- I next had to e-mail my report for the office's daily meeting. Each morning, every staff member, myself included, files a report listing any changes to my schedule for the next month. At this meeting I also assign new tasks to each staff member and we review the previously assigned tasks to see which ones are done and which ones are running late. The report was e-mailed from home, and each staff member had read it and e-mailed his or her own list to every other staff member in time for our 9:30 a.m. conference call. I conducted the call from my Parliament Hill office and my Hill staffers and I were joined over the phone by the staff from my constituency office manager from his desk in Carleton Place. The meeting took about half an hour. My goal is to have all such meetings done in ten minutes or less—I'm a great believer in frequent, but highly structured (and therefore very short) meetings.

- Most of the morning was spent in routine tasks. It's remarkable how much of an MP's time is consumed by the most routine items: signing letters, reviewing office budgets, and so on. I did spend about half an hour writing a letter to the editor of a major newspaper, criticizing a government minister for making what I regard as misleading statements in my portfolio area.

- At 11:20 I drove from Parliament Hill to a restaurant in a rural part of my riding in order to have lunch with a reporter for a local weekly newspaper. One of the joys of having an Ottawa-area riding is that I can work on Parliament Hill and not lose touch with the riding. And not having to travel back and forth across the country each week is the equivalent of having an entire extra day in my work week. Nonetheless, I am busy enough that I don't get much time for recreational reading, so today I supplemented it, as I usually do on long car trips, by listening to an audiobook on my car stereo.

- I was supposed to end the luncheon appointment at 1:20 p.m. in order to be back on Parliament Hill in time for a 2:00 p.m. conference call. However, I am not the best at cutting conversations short and the reporter needed to spend a few extra minutes taking a photo of me (reporters for local newspapers normally do all of their own photography). As a result, I arrived back at my Hill office about fifteen minutes late. As it turned out, however, the 2:00 p.m. meeting had been cancelled, since one of the participants was suddenly unavailable. This is a frequent occurrence in politics; I'd say that around one-third of the meetings we schedule get cancelled at the last minute, which makes it very difficult to plan one's day.

- The remainder of the afternoon was spent in a series of office tasks: Designing a mailing to constituents, reviewing the text of a draft manual of office procedures to assist new staffers to learn the ropes at our office, and arranging to get my letter to the editor published. I was also able to buttonhole one of my party's MPs in the hallway outside my office, and to lobby to get some time set aside in the House next week so that I can make a statement on an issue of local importance.
- At 5:00 p.m. the staff left the office. I spent an additional 90 minutes at my desk, reviewing letters and invitations which my office manager has set aside for me. Then I went out to buy groceries—my fridge is still empty as a result of last month's travelling—and returned to my house by 8:00 p.m. I took a break to watch TV for a while, but at 9:00 p.m. I was back on my computer at my home office, editing more correspondence until 10:00 p.m.

the middle and upper-middle classes—they cannot be neutral in the values they bring to their task. Judges, observes Miliband, 'are by no means, and cannot be, independent of the multitude of influences, notably of class origin, education, class situation and professional tendency, which contribute as much to the formation of their view of the world as they do in the case of other men.'[39] Thus, when one says that the judiciary is 'independent' this should be understood as a description of its formal separation from the executive and legislative branches of the state. But in regard to the dominant value system of their society, judges are no more independent than are the members of any other part of the state elite. Leaving aside the socio-economically unrepresentative character of the legal profession and the effects of formal training in the law, in British parliamentary systems all judges are appointed by governments.[40] One would hardly expect these governments to appoint radical critics of society, even supposing that a significant number of such individuals existed within the legal profession. Moreover, governments control promotion within the court system—who will be promoted from a district court to a superior court, and so on. This fact may also exert a chilling effect on unconventional judicial behaviour.

The socio-economic background of judges and the process by which they are selected have been argued by some to introduce conservative

tendencies into the judiciary. But they are not the only factors, nor are they necessarily the most important ones, that may incline the courts towards protection of the status quo. The law itself is often a powerful conservative force. We are used to thinking of the law as simply 'the rules made by governments' that 'apply to everybody in society'.[41] But the law is more than this. It represents values that have accumulated over a long period of time. The concepts, meanings, precedents, and interpretive rules that shape judicial decision-making tend to inhibit sharp breaks with the past.

Judges work within the embedded premises of the law. Among the most important of these premises, in terms of their impact on the distribution of power in society, are the rights of the individual, the rights associated with private property, and the concept of the business corporation. Individualism is woven throughout the legal fabric of Canadian society. As a practical matter, respect for individual rights tends to be more important for the privileged than for the disadvantaged. While this is obviously true in the case of property rights—protection for these rights matters more to those who have something to lose than to those who do not—it has also tended to be true in matters like individual freedom of expression. For example, a series of court decisions handed down between 1983 and 2001 have ruled unconstitutional sections of the federal Elections Act that prohibited advertising by organizations other than registered political parties during federal election campaigns. In the abstract this represented a victory for freedom of expression. Critics charge, however, that these victories matter most to well-heeled organizations—championed by the ideologically conservative National Citizens' Coalition, which has led the challenges to these restrictions—with the means to pay for such advertising.

The powerful tug of liberal individualism on judicial reasoning was clearly demonstrated in a 1987 Supreme Court of Canada decision on the right to strike. A majority of the justices decided that 'The constitutional guarantee of freedom of association . . . does not include, in the case of a trade union, a guarantee of the right to bargain

collectively and the right to strike.'[42] The right to bargain collectively and to strike were not, the Court ruled, fundamental rights or freedoms that deserved the constitutional protection of section 2(d) of the Charter. 'They are', the Court said, 'the creation of legislation, involving a balance of competing interests',[43] and their scope and limitations are appropriately determined by legislatures. To put it very simply, economic rights were viewed as subordinate to political ones. The Court said as much: 'the overwhelming preoccupation of the Charter is with individual, political, and democratic rights with conspicuous inattention to economic and property rights.'[44] But what 'conspicuous inattention' meant in practical terms was that the existing balance of power and rights

Figure 8.5   The Structure of Canada's Court System

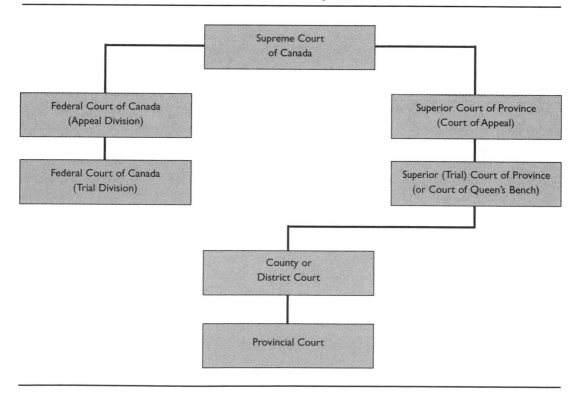

Source: Canada, Department of Justice, *Canada's System of Justice* (Ottawa: Supply and Services, 1988), 20.

between employers and workers was considered to be correct, and that workers and unions could not count on the courts to defend their rights against governments intent on diminishing them.

On the other hand, judges are not always insensitive to the structural inequalities that exist in society and in the economy. Particularly at the highest levels of the judicial system, judges are generally quite aware of the socio-economic and political consequences of their decisions. In his dissent from the majority decision in the 1987 right-to-strike case, Chief Justice Dickson observed that 'Throughout history, workers have associated to overcome their vulnerability as individuals to the strength of their employers. The capacity to bargain collectively has long been recognized as one of the integral and primary functions of associations of working people.'[45] Collective bargaining, according to Dickson, requires that workers have the right to strike. Moreover, in a 1989 decision the Supreme Court rejected the traditional liberal notion of equality as identical treatment before the law in favour of what is sometimes called **substantive equality**. This requires that individuals be looked at in terms of their group characteristics and the possible advantages or disadvantages they may have experienced as a result of these attributes. Liberal individualism does not have the field all to itself in Canadian society. Moreover, it is far from being uncontested in legal and judicial circles.

The biases of liberal individualism are also embedded in the judicial process. While all judicial systems are adversarial, in the sense that one party (the plaintiff in civil cases; the prosecution in criminal ones) brings an action against another (the defendant), common-law systems like Canada's represent the most extreme form of this adversarial process. In civil cases the onus is placed on the individual parties—plaintiff and defendant—to make their respective cases before the court. In criminal proceedings the state is responsible for prosecuting the case against an individual or organization, but that individual or organization is responsible for his own defence.

In both civil and criminal proceedings, the role of the court is to hear and weigh the evidence, not to participate actively in the development of either side to the action.

It is up to a plaintiff or defendant to make his or her most persuasive case. Their ability to do so will depend, in part, on their access to competent legal counsel. In criminal proceedings, the state will pay for legal counsel for defendants who cannot afford to hire a lawyer. Legal aid is available in all provinces for those who cannot afford the legal costs of a civil action. But these forms of subsidized legal assistance by no means equalize access to effective legal counsel. The difference between an Edward Greenspan and a court-appointed lawyer is not simply, or even mainly, their skills in the courtroom. The high-priced Edward Greenspans of the legal profession are backed up by the resources of a large law firm, which include other high-priced lawyers with particular areas of expertise, extensive research capabilities, and both broad and deep networks of potentially influential relationships. A large corporation or a wealthy individual can afford to pay for these resources, but they are beyond the means of most people.

Although the judicial system is hardly a level playing field, it would be wrong to suggest that it serves only the interests of the wealthy and powerful. Indeed, particularly since the addition of the Charter of Rights and Freedoms to Canada's Constitution, groups representing women, Aboriginal Canadians, the disabled, gays and lesbians, and other interests that could hardly be described as being near the epicentre of power in Canadian society have frequently achieved successes in the courts that were not possible in legislative and electoral forums. For example, the Supreme Court's unanimous 1997 ruling on Native landownership produced a victory for the Gitksan and Wet'suwet'en peoples, and by extension for other Aboriginal communities claiming a historic right of occupancy and use to land not covered by a treaty, that years of political negotiation had not been able to achieve.

Some argue that recourse to the courts to achieve ends that cannot be accomplished through the political process is fundamentally undemocratic. It is simply wrong, however, to conceive of the courts as being outside the political process. Even before the Charter, the courts were very much a part of politics and policy-making in Canada. Their rulings on the federal-provincial division of powers and on all manner of policy questions have always been part of Canadian politics. Quebec nationalists have long complained that the Supreme Court of Canada has a pro-federal bias, a claim that—true or not—reflects the inescapable involvement of the Court in the politics of federalism. The fact that by law three of the Supreme Court's nine judges must be members of the Quebec bar, and that by tradition three should be from Ontario, two from the West, and one from Atlantic Canada, shows that the essentially political issue of regional representation has been considered important for the judicial branch, just as it is important in the executive and legislative branches of government.

In recent years the issue of representation on the bench, particularly on the Supreme Court, has become even more politically charged. The 1998 retirement of Justice John Sopinka unleashed a flurry of behind-the-scenes lobbying and public advocacy on behalf of particular candidates for the vacancy on Canada's highest court. The formal retirement of Justice Peter Cory in 1999 likewise was preceded by active lobbying in legal circles, particularly on behalf of female candidates for the job. Gender and judicial ideology appear to have become more prominent criteria in the Supreme Court selection process, at least in the eyes of many advocacy and rights-oriented groups.[46]

If we accept, then, that the courts are unavoidably part of the political process, is there any basis for the claim that recourse to the courts may be undemocratic? The short answer is 'yes'. Several decades before the Charter, James Mallory argued that business interests cynically exploited the federal division of powers in the British North America Act, 1867 to oppose increased state interference in their affairs, regardless of which level of government was doing the interfering.[47] Respect for democratic principles and the Constitution was the cloak behind which business attempted to conceal its self-interest.

In the Charter era similar criticisms have been expressed. Charter critics like Ted Morton and Rainer Knopff argue that recourse to the courts by abortion rights advocates, gay and lesbian rights groups, and Aboriginals, among others, has produced rulings that often elevate the preferences of special interests over more broadly held values. More importantly, from the standpoint of our examination of the machinery of government, they agree with Michael Mandel's argument that the Charter era has witnessed the 'legalization' of Canadian politics.[48] Emboldened by the entrenchment of rights in the Constitution and the declaration of constitutional supremacy in section 52 of the Constitution Act, 1982, judges have been less deferential to governments and legislatures than in the past. Moreover, a network of rights-oriented advocacy groups, law professors, lawyers, journalists, and bureaucrats working within the rights apparatus of the state (from human rights commissions to the ubiquitous equity officers found throughout the public sector) has emerged that, in the words of Morton and Knopff, 'prefers the policy-making power of the less obviously democratic governmental institutions.'[49] The institutions they are referring to are the courts and quasi-judicial rights commissions and tribunals.

The era of judges deferring to the will of elected officials is over. The Charter was the catalyst for what both critics and supporters see as an enormous increase in the policy role of the courts. The issue of when and how far judges should involve themselves in the determination of public policy has become increasingly prominent. Critics from both the right and the left of the spectrum have attacked what they believe to be an overwillingness on the part of many judges to use the Charter to strike down government policies. By 1998 the chorus of criticism had become so loud and frequent that former Justice

Antonio Lamer of the Supreme Court of Canada stated publicly that 'court-bashing' was damaging the reputation of the judicial system. Like their counterparts on the United States Supreme Court during the 1960s and 1970s—an era that saw America's highest court expand the rights of the criminally accused, declare that women had a constitutional right to abortion, ban prayer from public schools, and require the busing of children to achieve racial integration in schools—the justices of Canada's Supreme Court have discovered that judicial activism is not always well received by all segments of the public.

In an apparent response to a downdraft of negative media commentary about judges alleged to be arrogant and indifferent to public sentiment, eight of the nine members of the Supreme Court took the unprecedented step of travelling together to Winnipeg in April 1999. Their trip was widely perceived as a public relations exercise, intended to show that the Court was willing to break out of the cocoon of the nation's capital and get closer to the people. The fact that the judges spent their time in meetings with other members of the legal profession generated some cynicism about their idea of what it means to reach out to the public.

But in fairness to the judges of the Supreme Court and of all the other courts in Canada, interpreting the Constitution is not supposed to be a popularity contest. If minority rights were to be protected by the courts only when it is popular to do so, these rights would be extremely precarious. Similarly, it is notoriously the case that the works and deeds of 'degenerate' artists, political 'radicals', religious 'oddballs', and all manner of non-conformists enjoy little sympathy in the court of public opinion. Entrenching rights and freedoms in the Constitution and then assigning judges the role of deciding when the actions of elected governments infringe these constitutional guarantees is fundamentally at odds with majoritarian democracy. It enables the views of a minority to triumph over public opinion—and sometimes the public reaction is one of outrage.

At the same time, however, it must be acknowledged that public support for the Charter has remained high across Canada. When judges use the Charter to make unpopular decisions, as in the case of a 2001 Supreme Court ruling on the possession of child pornography, public ire is directed chiefly at judges rather than at the Charter. What critics too seldom realize is that the phenomenon of 'judicial imperialism', a phenomenon that is far from being uniquely Canadian, is to some degree an unavoidable result of entrenching rights in the Constitution. In France and Germany, both of which have constitutionally entrenched bills of rights, criticism that judges have encroached on the policy-making prerogatives of elected governments is not uncommon. This is, of course, a long-standing complaint in the United States, particularly from conservatives.

But why, one might ask, don't judges show greater deference to elected governments, as section 1 of the Canadian Charter of Rights and Freedoms would clearly allow them to do? The answer to this question is complex and would require an analysis of the sociology and psychology of the legal profession, from law school to the bench. Suffice it to say that under the influence of the Charter a new generation of lawyers and judges has acquired a more activist conception of the appropriate role of judges than existed in the past. Whether this is a good or bad thing is for each of us to decide (see Box 8.6).

APPENDIX: HOW A LAW IS PASSED

The law takes various forms. A statute passed by the House of Commons and the Senate, and given royal assent by the Governor-General, is clearly a law. But decisions taken by cabinet that have not been approved in the legislature also have the force of law. These are called Orders-in-Council. Thousands of them are issued each year, and they are published in the *Canada Gazette*. The decisions of agencies, boards, and commissions that receive their regulatory powers from a statute also

BOX 8.6   Chief Justice McLachlin Defends the Court's Involvement in Making Social Policy

The fact that judges rule on social questions that affect large numbers of people does not, however, mean that judges are political. There is much confusion on this point in the popular press. Judges are said to be acting politically, to have descended (or perhaps ascended) into the political arena. Judges, on this view, are simply politicians who do not need to stand for election and can never be removed.

This misapprehension confuses outcome with process. Many judicial decisions on important social issues—say affirmative action, or abortion, or gay rights—will be political in the sense that they will satisfy some political factions at the expense of others. But the term 'political' is used in the context to describe an outcome, not a process. While the outcomes of cases are inevitably political in some broad sense of the term, it is important—critical, even—that the process be impartial. It is inescapable that judges' decisions will have political ramifications but it is essential that they not be partisan. In their final form, judgments on social policy questions are often not that different from legislation. It is the process by which the judgments are arrived at that distinguishes them. Legislation is often the product of compromise of conflict between various political factions, each faction pushing its own agenda. The judicial arena does not, and should not, provide simply another forum for the same kind of contests. *Judges must maintain the appearance and reality of impartiality.* It is impartiality that distinguishes us from the other branches of government, and impartiality that gives us our legitimacy.

. . . changing society affects the work of judges. The nature of the questions they decide, and the public expectation that they will decide them fairly and well, place new demands on judges. It no longer suffices to be a competent legal scholar sensitive to a broad range of social concerns. They must possess a keen appreciation of the importance of individual and group interests and rights. And they must be in touch with the society in which they work, understanding its values and its tensions. The ivory tower no longer suffices as the residence of choice for judges.

Remarks of the Right Honourable Beverley McLachlin on 'The Role of Judges in Modern Society', 5 May 2001. Available at: <http://www.scc-csc.gc.ca/aboutcourt/judges/speeches/role-of-judges_e.html>.

have the force of law. Finally, there are the regulations and guidelines issued and enforced by the departmental bureaucracy in accordance with the discretionary powers delegated to them under a statute. These also have the force of law.

In a strictly numerical sense the statutes passed annually by Parliament represent only the tip of the iceberg of laws promulgated each year.

Nevertheless, virtually all major policy decisions—including budget measures and the laws that assign discretionary power to the bureaucracy—come before the legislature. The only exception has been when the normal process of government was suspended by passage of the War Measures Act. This happened during World War I, again during World War II, and briefly in 1970 when Ottawa proclaimed the War Measures Act after two political kidnappings in Quebec by the Front de libération du Québec. The War Measures Act was replaced by the Emergencies Act in 1988.

During normal times the law-making process involves several stages and opportunities for debate and amendment. The steps from the introduction of a bill in Parliament to the final proclamation of a statute are set out in Figure 8.6.

There are two types of bills, private members' bills and government bills. Private members' bills originate from any individual MP, but unless they

Figure 8.6   From Bill to Statute

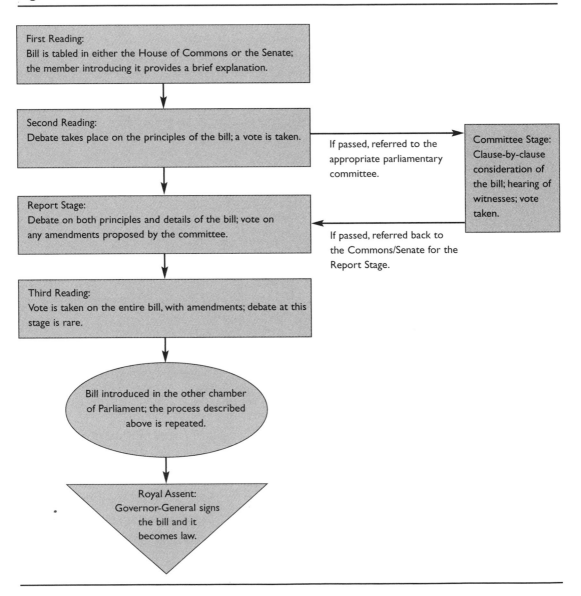

First Reading:
Bill is tabled in either the House of Commons or the Senate; the member introducing it provides a brief explanation.

Second Reading:
Debate takes place on the principles of the bill; a vote is taken.

If passed, referred to the appropriate parliamentary committee.

Committee Stage:
Clause-by-clause consideration of the bill; hearing of witnesses; vote taken.

Report Stage:
Debate on both principles and details of the bill; vote on any amendments proposed by the committee.

If passed, referred back to the Commons/Senate for the Report Stage.

Third Reading:
Vote is taken on the entire bill, with amendments; debate at this stage is rare.

Bill introduced in the other chamber of Parliament; the process described above is repeated.

Royal Assent:
Governor-General signs the bill and it becomes law.

get the backing of government they have little chance of passing. Government bills dominate Parliament's legislative agenda. When major legislation is being proposed, a bill is sometimes preceded by a White Paper. This is a report for discussion, based on research by the bureaucracy (and sometimes the legislature as well), and serves as a statement of the government's legislative intentions.

Once a bill has been drafted by government, it is introduced into the Senate, or more usually, into the House of Commons. Here, it is given *first reading*, which is just a formality and involves no debate. Then the bill goes to *second reading*, when the main principles of the bill are debated and a vote is taken. If the bill passes second reading it is sent to a smaller legislative committee, where the details of the bill are considered clause by clause. At this *committee stage*, amendments can be made but the principle of the bill cannot be altered. The bill is then reported back to the House, where all aspects, including any amendments, are debated. At this *report stage* new amendments can also be introduced. If a bill passes this hurdle it then goes to *third reading* where a final vote is taken, sometimes after further debate. Once a bill has been passed in the House, it is then sent to the Senate where a virtually identical process takes place. If a bill was first introduced in the Senate, then it would now be sent to the House. Finally, a bill that has been passed in both the House and the Senate can be given royal assent and become law.

NOTES

1. 'The Executive Government and Authority of and over Canada is hereby declared to continue and be vested in the Queen.' Constitution Act, 1867, s. 9.
2. In the provinces, the Crown's authority is exercised through the lieutenant-governors, who are appointed by the Governor-General to serve five-year terms.
3. James Mallory, *The Structure of Canadian Government*, rev. edn (Toronto: Gage, 1984), 42–3.
4. Constitution Act, 1867, s. 54.
5. Donald Savoie, *Governing from the Centre: The Concentration of Power in Canadian Politics* (Toronto: University of Toronto Press, 1999), ch. 4.
6. Colin Campbell and George Szablowski, *The Super-Bureaucrats: Structure and Behaviour in Central Agencies* (Toronto: Macmillan, 1979).
7. See David A. Good, *The Politics of Anticipation: Making Canadian Federal Tax Policy* (Ottawa: School of Public Administration, 1980).
8. Leslie Pal, *Beyond Policy Analysis* (Toronto: Nelson Canada, 1998), 92.
9. Savoie, *Governing from the Centre*, 189.
10. Ibid., 109.
11. Campbell and Szablowski, *The Super-Bureaucrats*, 29.
12. Gordon Robertson, 'The Changing Role of the Privy Council Office', *Canadian Public Administration* 14 (Winter 1971): 506.
13. Savoie, *Governing from the Centre*, 109.
14. Ibid., 121.
15. Ibid., 195.
16. Ibid.
17. Robertson, 'The Changing Role of the Privy Council Office', 506.
18. Savoie, *Governing from the Centre*, 101.
19. Ibid., 103.
20. Colin Campbell, *Governments under Stress* (Toronto: University of Toronto Press, 1983), 90.
21. At <www.pco.gc.ca>.
22. Both Donald Savoie in *Governing from the Centre* and Jeffrey Simpson in *The Friendly Dictatorship* (Toronto: McClelland & Stewart, 2001) make the case for this characterization.
23. Savoie, *Governing from the Centre*, 260.
24. Simpson, *The Friendly Dictatorship*.
25. Savoie, *Governing from the Centre*, 248.

26. Alexander Brady, *Democracy in the Dominions* (Toronto: University of Toronto Press, 1947), 82.

27. John Porter, *The Vertical Mosaic* (Toronto: University of Toronto Press, 1965).

28. The total number of Senate seats rose from 104 to 105 with the creation of the new territory of Nunavut on 1 April 1999.

29. Robert J. Jackson and Michael A. Atkinson, *The Canadian Legislative System*, 2nd edn (Toronto: Gage, 1980), 22.

30. Savoie, *Governing from the Centre*, 91.

31. Ibid., 92.

32. David C. Docherty, *Mr. Smith Goes to Ottawa: Life in the House of Commons* (Vancouver: University of British Columbia Press, 1998), 234.

33. Simpson, *The Friendly Dictatorship*, 23.

34. Gerald Baier, St Thomas University, interview on CBC Radio, *Sounds Like Canada*, 27 Mar. 2003.

35. Savoie, *Governing from the Centre*, 91–2.

36. Docherty, *Mr. Smith Goes to Ottawa*, 204.

37. Ibid., 206.

38. See the Constitution Act, 1867, s. 99(1). This phrase, or reference to 'misbehaviour', is found in the federal and provincial statutes that govern the removal of judges.

39. Ralph Miliband, *The State in Capitalist Society* (London: Quartet Books, 1973), 124.

40. Judges of county courts and all higher courts are appointed by Ottawa. Provincial court judges are appointed by the provinces. See Figure 8.5 in the text.

41. Canada, Department of Justice, *Canada's System of Justice* (Ottawa: Supply and Services, 1988), 7.

42. *Reference re Public Service Employee Relations Act* (Alberta) (1987), 38 D.L.R. (4th) 161.

43. Ibid., 200.

44. Ibid., 232.

45. Ibid., 200.

46. See Tonda MacCharles, 'Top court speculation begins anew', *Toronto Star*, 19 Jan. 1999.

47. James Mallory, *Social Credit and the Federal Power* (Toronto: University of Toronto Press, 1954).

48. Michael Mandel, *The Charter and the Legalization of Canadian Politics*, 2nd edn (Toronto: Nelson, 1994).

49. Rainer Knopff and Ted Morton, *Charter Politics* (Toronto: Nelson Canada, 1992), 79.

SUGGESTED READINGS

Stephen Brooks and Lydia Miljan, *Public Policy in Canada*, 4th edn (Toronto: Oxford University Press, 2003).This text examines the forces that shape Canadian public policy and surveys several policy fields, including health, Aboriginal, social, economic, family, and water policy.

David Docherty, *Mr. Smith Goes to Ottawa: Life in the House of Commons* (Vancouver: University of British Columbia Press, 1997). Based largely on surveys of MPs, this is the best analysis of legislative behaviour and influence in the House of Commons to be written in last 20 years.

G. Bruce Doern, ed., *How Ottawa Spends 2003–2004* (Toronto: Oxford University Press, 2003). This annual publication of the School of Public Administration at Carleton University includes contributions on various structures, processes, and current issues relating to the federal government.

Christopher Dunn, ed., *The Handbook of Canadian Public Administration* (Toronto: Oxford University Press, 2002). Virtually all key aspects of the structures and processes of Canadian public administration are covered in this fine collection, with contributions from some of the foremost students of Canadian bureaucracy and policy-making.

Donald Savoie, *The Politics of Public Spending in Canada* (Toronto: University of Toronto Press, 1990). Savoie unpacks and lays bare the structural factors within the bureaucracy, cabinet, and federal-provincial relations that pull in the direction of increased public spending.

Donald Savoie, *Governing from the Centre: The Concentration of Power in Canadian Politics* (Toronto: University of Toronto Press, 1999). Here Savoie makes the case that the concentration of power in and around the Prime Minister's Office has reached unprecedented and undemocratic levels. This is a 'must read' for those interested in the inner workings of the machinery of government.

Review Exercises

1. Visit the government of Canada Web site <www.gc.ca>. Click on 'About Government'. Now click on 'Government of Canada Institutions' (listed alphabetically). Choose a government institution and click on its Web site. Find the following information for the institution you have chosen.

    (a) number of employees
    (b) budget
    (c) cabinet minister responsible for the department/agency/Crown corporation
    (d) major programs or functions.

2. Choose one of the following:

    (a) If Parliament is in session while you are taking this course and you have either cable or satellite television , turn to CPAC (the parliamentary channel) and watch an hour of debate or Question Period. In a paragraph or two, summarize the proceedings and your impression of them.

    (b) If Parliament is not in session or if you do not have cable television or a satellite dish, visit the Parliament of Canada Web site <www.parl.gc.ca>. Click on 'Reference Material', then, under the heading 'Parliament', click on 'Speech from the Throne'. In two or three paragraphs, summarize the major goals indicated in the speech. What is your overall impression of the Throne Speech, given at the opening of each session of Parliament?

3. Put together a list of the various governmental organizations (federal, provincial, municipal) you have been in contact with during your life and the reasons for the contact(s). Think hard—the list is probably longer than you imagine at first.

4. Draw up a list of reasons for and against the abolition of the Canadian Senate. See the background material on Senate reform at <www.cric.ca/en_html/guide/senate/senate.html>. How would Senate abolition or reform affect how power is distributed in Canada's system of government?

PART FOUR

PARTICIPATION IN POLITICS

The national party system that Canadians had known for generations was shaken up by the 1993 election. (Party logos courtesy of the five political parties)

Political parties and elections are essential features of modern democracy. This chapter examines the characteristics and influence of these institutions in Canadian political life. The following topics are covered:

- ❑ The origins and evolution of the Canada's party system.
- ❑ Brokerage politics.
- ❑ The role of minor parties.
- ❑ The 1993, 1997, and 2000 federal elections.
- ❑ Is the party system undergoing fundamental realignment?
- ❑ The electoral system and its consequences.
- ❑ Party finances and special interests.

CHAPTER NINE

PARTIES AND ELECTIONS

Elections and the political parties that contest them represent the main contact points between most citizens and their political system. Most adult citizens vote at least some of the time, although perhaps not in every election and probably more often federally than in provincial and local elections. This may be, in fact, the extent of their participation in politics, short bursts of attention to candidates and their messages and occasional visits to the polls, interspersed around lengthier periods of inattention and political inactivity. Only about one-third of eligible voters actually cast their ballots in the last two federal elections, but even among those who did not vote we can probably assume that most were at least aware that an election was taking place.

Elections remind us that we live in a democracy in which those who wish to govern must win the support of the governed—or at least of some considerable number of the governed. Elections are the cornerstone of democratic governance, yet it is widely believed they have become meaningless and even farcical affairs in which political parties and their candidates serve up sound bites instead of sound policy in campaigns orchestrated by the same people who put together marketing campaigns for cars and deodorants. Political parties have for years ranked among the lowest of social institutions in public esteem. It would seem, therefore, that democracy's cornerstone suffers from some worrisome cracks.

Doubts about the democratic qualities of democracy's showpiece are not new. One of the oldest fears is that those with money are more likely than those without it to be able to influence voter behaviour. In the nineteenth century the influence of money often took such petty forms as candidates buying beer or whisky for voters, a practice facilitated by the fact that voters cast their ballots in public. But the role of money also assumed more dramatic forms, as when Hugh Allan essentially bankrolled the Conservative Party in the 1873 federal election in exchange for a promise from John A. Macdonald that Allen would be made president of the railroad company chartered to build a transcontinental railroad linking Ontario to the Pacific coast. Over a century ago Liberal cabinet minister Israël Tarte remarked that 'Elections are not won with prayers', a fact of political life that has become even truer in the age of television campaigning. But fact of life or not, if parties and votes can be purchased by those with deep pockets this surely undermines the democratic credibility of the electoral process.

Money is not the only factor that stands accused of defiling democracy's temple. Political parties and candidates have often been criticized for avoiding important issues and framing electoral discourse in ways that deflect attention from major divisions in society, oversimplifying the issues, and trivializing politics by substituting style and image for substance. The 'dumbing down' of public life has been facilitated—some would argue necessitated—by the fact that modern elections are fought largely through the medium of television, a medium that by its very nature elevates images over ideas. But the claims that parties and candidates avoid certain divisive issues and attempt to frame electoral discourse in ways that privilege certain interests while marginalizing others are long-standing ones in Canada.

The criticisms occasionally levelled at parties and elections in Canada may appear petty when viewed alongside the problems of one-party states and the practices of ballot fraud, voter intimidation, and bribery that are routine in many countries where elections are held. But Canadians are not used to comparing their democratic institutions and processes to those of Nigeria, Mexico, or Haiti. We place the bar higher than this and measure the performance of our political parties and our electoral system against ideas of equality and participation that have evolved out of our liberal democratic tradition. Judged against these values, the Canadian experience is not perfect, although critics differ over the nature and extent of its shortcomings.

PARTIES: DEFINITION AND FUNCTIONS

Political parties may be defined as organizations that offer slates of candidates to voters at election time. To this end they recruit and select party candidates, raise money to pay for their campaigns, develop policies that express the ideas and goals that their candidates stand for, and attempt to persuade citizens to vote for their candidates. In a democracy parties are not created by, nor are they agents of, the state. They are, in Eugene Forsey's words, 'voluntary associations of people who hold broadly similar opinions on public questions'.[1]

It is usual to give as one of the distinguishing characteristics of political parties their attempt to 'elect governmental office-holders'.[2] This is, however, somewhat misleading. While most parties do hope to elect candidates to office, and some even have a realistic prospect of electing enough candidates to form a government, other parties may contest elections chiefly to get their ideas onto the public stage, without any expectation of garnering more than a small fraction of the vote. This would seem to be true of the Natural Law Party, which supports 'yogic flying' as a method for resolving various sorts of public policy problems, and the Marxist-Leninist Party, whose quixotic advocacy of global revolution by the proletariat remains largely unchanged from Karl Marx and Friedrich Engels's *Communist Manifesto* of 1848. The now defunct Rhinoceros Party ran candidates in many Canadian ridings during the 1970s and 1980s, injecting welcome humour

into elections—the party stood for the repeal of the law of gravity, among other things—without any serious expectation of electing candidates to office. (As an aside, the Rhinoceros Party's candidates outpolled Progressive Conservative Party candidates in several Quebec ridings during the 1980 election.)

John Meisel, one of Canada's foremost experts on parties and elections, identifies seven functions that political parties play in a democracy.[3]

1. *Integrating citizens into the political system.* Historically, parties have served as important linkages between citizens and the governmental system. Through voting for parties and thinking about public affairs in terms of policies and ideologies represented by parties, citizens develop attachments to the political system more generally. This connection, Meisel argues, has weakened as political parties have fallen in public esteem and have come to be perceived by many as simply another distant and unaccountable institution in a political system characterized by alienating institutions.

2. *Developing policy.* In many democracies different parties represent clear ideological and policy options. Moreover, party members and their deliberations are key sources of the policies that a party will seek to implement when in power. Canada's historically dominant parties, the Liberal and Conservative parties, have seldom been sharply different from one another in either ideological terms or in their behaviour when in power. They have occasionally stood for significantly different policies during election campaigns, as was true in 1988 when the Liberals opposed the Canada–United States Free Trade Agreement that had been negotiated by the Conservative government. Once in office, however, neither party has felt tied to the policy platforms developed by the extra-parliamentary wing of the party—witness the Liberal government's refusal to either scrap or reform the GST after winning the 1993 election, despite what was generally perceived to be a firm commitment to do so in the party's 'Red Book' of election promises.

The New Democratic Party and the Canadian Alliance provide voters with clearer policy choices than do the historically dominant parties. The NDP has also been, of all Canada's national parties, the one characterized by the greatest involvement of the party's extra-parliamentary membership in policy development.

3. *Elite recruitment*. With rare exceptions, those elected to federal and provincial office in Canada are associated with a political party and run as the official candidates of their parties. Parties choose their candidates and their leaders, and in doing so they determine the pool of persons from which elected public officials, including members of the government, will be drawn.

4. *Organization of government*. Governing parties propose; opposition parties oppose. This somewhat oversimplified formula expresses an important fact about the role that parties play within the system of government. They provide a partisan structure to the process of law-making and the debate of public affairs. Under the British parliamentary system that exists in Canada, this partisan structure is by design an adversarial one, from the physical layout of the legislature, in which the government benches face those of the opposition parties, to the traditions and procedures observed in conducting the business of Parliament.

5. *Structuring the vote*. Just as parties lend structure to the activities of the legislature and allow for the identification of the government with a particular party (or coalition of parties in some democratic systems), they also serve to structure the vote in elections. The fact that only a handful of political parties are serious contenders for citizens' votes simplifies enormously the information-gathering task facing voters. Instead of having to determine what every individual candidate stands for they can—and most people do—rely on party labels as a sort of shorthand for the ideas and policies that a candidate represents. Each party represents, in a sense, a particular selection on a limited menu. The parties will differ from one another in their voter appeal with different segments of the population, and most voters can be said to have

most-favoured and least-favoured political parties. These partisan inclinations at the weak end, or loyalties and identifications at the strong end, provide a degree of continuity in voting behaviour. This continuity can, however, be quickly shattered, as the 1993 collapse of the federal Conservative vote and the dramatic growth of the Reform Party—now called the Canadian Alliance—and Bloc Québécois vote showed.

Until the 1993 election it had been common to characterize Canada as having a two and one-half party system. The Liberal and Conservative parties both had a realistic chance of forming a government, and between them usually accounted for about 85 per cent of the popular vote. The NDP accounted for the balance. This fairly stable structure to the vote and to the parliamentary status of the parties dissolved in 1993, for reasons discussed later in this chapter.

6. *Organizing public opinion*. Parties are often characterized as right wing, left wing, or centrist; as liberal, conservative, or socialist; or by some other labels signifying that they occupy particular places on the ideological map. Parties reflect, but may also help to create or at least reinforce, divisions within society. They do so through the issues they identify as important, the way they frame these issues, and the policies they propose.

Canada's two historically dominant political parties have avoided ideological appeals in favour of a flexible centrist style of politics often labelled **brokerage politics**. They have avoided talking the language of class politics—rich versus poor, bosses versus workers, corporations versus unions—and have attempted to accommodate the preferences of major interests, regions, and communities through their flexible policy style. Of course, politics has to be about something, and even the most centrist and waffling of parties cannot avoid taking positions on some divisive issues. Historically, language, religion, and region have been among the key issues distinguishing the Liberal from the Conservative Party, the Liberals doing better among francophones, Catholics, and in the provinces east of Manitoba, and the Conservatives doing better among Protestants and western Canadians. Parties have helped to organize Canadian public opinion on religious (in the past), linguistic, and territorial lines. The NDP and its predecessor, the Co-operative Commonwealth Federation, have been the only significant parties presenting voters with a class-based definition of Canadian politics. In recent years the ability of the historically dominant parties to organize public opinion in ways that preserve their dominance by bridging major divisions in Canadian politics has been challenged by the Canadian Alliance, which emerged out of westerners' dissatisfaction with the older parties, and by the Bloc Québécois, whose success in Quebec is testimony to the failure of brokerage politics to accommodate Quebec nationalism.

7. *Interest aggregation.* Organizations representing secondary school teachers, gays, or advocates for wetlands preservation may be influential in politics. However, the narrowness of their respective agendas and the fact that each represents only a small segment of the population mean that they could not hope to elect a Teachers' Party, Gay Rights Party, or Save-the-Ducks Party to power. Parties, especially parties that hope to form a government, must aggregate different interests. This requires that they be willing to reach compromises on issues, bringing together under the party roof a coalition of different interests sufficiently broad to win election.

In order to be electorally successful it is not necessary that a party bring all major groups or regions under its roof. The Liberal Party, the most successful of Canada's national parties during the twentieth century, has often formed a government with little representation from western Canada. In fact, history shows that it is seldom possible to avoid playing off one region against another in Canadian politics. Interest aggregation that produces a winning result in a federal election does not always promote unity. Paradoxically, the practice of interest aggregation may reinforce regional division.

THE ORIGINS AND EVOLUTION OF CANADA'S PARTY SYSTEM

The Nature of Brokerage Politics

The origins of Canada's two oldest political parties—the Conservatives and the Liberals—can be traced back to the shifting coalitions and alignments in the United Province of Canada in the 1840s and 1850s.[4] Although these groups were much more amorphous and unstable than modern political parties and would not really coalesce into cohesive organizations until the 1880s, they did represent distinct political tendencies. On the one hand was the governing coalition of Liberal-Conservatives (which would eventually drop the 'Liberal' from its official name) under the leadership of Sir John A. Macdonald in Canada West and his French-Canadian counterpart, Sir George-Étienne Cartier, in Canada East. This disparate organization encompassed a number of distinct groups: moderate Reformers from what was to become Ontario, moderate Conservatives (the *bleus*) from Canada East (Quebec), the commercial and industrial interests of English-speaking Quebec, and the remnants of the old ruling oligarchies in Upper and Lower Canada, the Family Compact and the Château Clique. Many of these groups had potentially conflicting interests (Catholics and Protestants, French and English, urban and rural elements), but the organization was held together largely by the political dexterity of Macdonald and by the gradual development of a unifying vision, one based on the nation-building program eventually enshrined in the National Policy of 1878–9. The key elements of this program were the implementation of a protective tariff designed to promote the growth of indigenous manufacturing in Ontario and Quebec, the encouragement of western settlement to open up a market for the products of central Canadian industry and to protect this territory from American encroachment, and the creation of a transcontinental railroad to ship the manufactured goods of the centre to the newly opened western territories.[5]

On the other hand was an even looser opposition coalition, comprising the Clear Grits of Canada West and the *rouges* of Canada East. Both of these groups shared a common admiration for the republican and individualist ideas of the United States and both advocated free trade with the Americans. They also shared an unrelenting hostility to the commercial and banking interests linked to Macdonald's governing party. But the two groups made for rather uneasy partners, since the Grits were vocally critical of the Roman Catholic Church. So were the *rouges*, for that matter (and their anti-clericalism placed serious obstacles in the path of electoral success in their home province of Quebec), but there was nonetheless considerable ethnic and religious tension between the two groups. It was only when Wilfrid Laurier assumed the leadership of the Liberal Party in 1887 that these diverse elements were moulded into a relatively cohesive political organization.

It would be a mistake to make too much of the doctrinal differences between Liberals and Conservatives during the formative years of the Canadian party system (roughly 1880 to 1920). Admittedly, the Liberals were identified with free trade and provincial rights, and after 1885 (when Louis Riel was hanged for treason following the failed Northwest Rebellion) they appeared to be 'more sensitive to the interests of French Canada' than the Tories.[6] They were also more sympathetic to the plight of the farmer than were the Conservatives. The latter, meanwhile, were generally thought of as the party of the British connection, the party of privilege—in the sense that its leading spokesmen claimed that all healthy and stable societies are ruled by a *natural* governing elite—and the party of centralization and economic protection. But these ideological differences, far from constituting fundamental clashes of world outlooks on which the two sides sought to mobilize their supporters, were almost always subordinated to the central preoccupation of Canadian politics: **patronage**.

The scramble to control the distribution of government largesse was undoubtedly the dominant feature of Canadian politics during the 1860s and 1870s, when a number of provisions in our electoral law helped to force political life into that mould. In particular, the use of the open ballot, whereby voters simply declared their choice at the polls in the presence of a government official (and anybody else who happened to be in the room at the time!), provided numerous opportunities for bribery, coercion, and intimidation, and made it difficult for anybody whose livelihood was dependent on government contracts to vote against candidates supported by the ruling cabinet (see Box 9.1). Non-simultaneous or staggered elections, which permitted the government to call elections in safe ridings before having to work its way into more doubtful territory, forced candidates in many ridings to be *ministerialists*, so called because their 'politics were not to support a party but a ministry and any ministry would do.'[7] This non-partisan stance was the surest way to provide for a steady flow of government patronage into the successful candidate's constituency.

The elimination of the open ballot and deferred elections by the late 1870s, along with the gradual standardization of electoral regulations across the different provinces, did not reduce the importance of patronage in federal politics—far from it. Despite the removal of some of the crasser forms of electoral corruption by the 1880s, the two federal parties still operated in a political environment characterized by the absence of civil service reform (the merit principle), a highly restricted franchise, and a weak working class (from an organizational and numerical standpoint). All of these factors, it has been suggested, predispose political parties to appeal to potential supporters through networks of patron-client relations (where votes are exchanged for certain 'favours') rather than on the basis of collectivist or solidaristic appeals (class-based ideologies).[8]

This is precisely the situation described by the French political sociologist, André Siegfried, when he visited Canada in the early part of the

BOX 9.1   The Open Ballot

The Liberals, for reasons that are not hard to discern, favoured the secret ballot, and every year after 1869 saw a Liberal motion for the adoption of the ballot fall by the wayside. The opportunities for bribery of voters, the coercion of employees by their superiors and of civil servants by the Conservatives, and the open interference of the clergy in Quebec, were all cited as arguments by the Liberals. The Conservatives tacitly admitted the justice of the opposition's case, but yielded nothing. One staunch party man went so far on one occasion as to observe with commendable frankness that, after all, elections could not be carried on without money, and 'under an open system of voting, you can readily ascertain whether the voter has deceived you.' The Prime Minister thought the [secret] ballot 'un-British.' Another was critical of it on the ground that it would let a dishonest elector sell his vote to two or three different parties, instead of just one. With these and other cogent reasons for preserving electoral purity, the open system of voting was allowed to last until 1874.

Norman Ward, *The Canadian House of Commons*
(Toronto: University of Toronto Press, 1950), 158.

twentieth century. Siegfried complained that the preoccupation with questions of 'material interest' and 'public works' tended to 'lower the general level of political life' in Canada. He also noted that Canadian politics was hardly lacking in substantive issues—rivalries between Catholics and Protestants, French and English, for example—that could have been addressed by the two major parties, but that the party leaders 'prefer that they should not be talked about. The subjects which remain available for discussion are not numerous. In addition, the parties borrow one another's policies periodically, displaying a coolness in this process that would disconcert us Europeans.'[9]

Siegfried's comments on the nature of party competition in Canada, written almost a century ago, are still remarkably relevant (see Box 9.2). Although the NDP might be considered a 'labour' party and the Bloc Québécois represents 'French' (i.e., nationalistic Quebec) interests in the federal Parliament, if Siegfried were somehow transported back to present-day Canada, he would probably conclude that there have been few substantive changes in our party system since he published his work in 1906. The emphasis on

accommodating the diverse interests—regional, linguistic, ethnic, class, religious—of the electorate through the prudent employment of 'public works' and individual material incentives is still a characteristic feature of federal and provincial politics. Elections are usually preceded by a barrage of new government programs and spending initiatives in various parts of the country—ill-disguised attempts by the party in power to purchase electoral support in key ridings. As well, the nonchalant borrowing of elements of one party's program by another party, which Siegfried found so disconcerting, is still going on today. Among the more flagrant recent examples of this habit we might mention the 1974, 1984, and 1993 federal elections. In the first case, Pierre Trudeau's Liberal government implemented wage and price controls in an attempt to cure inflation, only a few months after an election in which the Liberals had castigated the Conservatives and their leader, Robert Stanfield, for proposing just such a policy. In 1984, the new leader of the Conservatives, Brian Mulroney, is widely thought to have scored a decisive win in the television debate with his Liberal counterpart, John Turner, on the issue of patronage appointments. Voters were seemingly impressed by the Tory leader's display of moral outrage at Turner's feeble attempt to justify appointing a raft of Liberals to plum positions at the tail end of the Trudeau dynasty. But not long after the election, the Tories themselves were practising pork-barrel politics on a scale that made their predecessors look like rank amateurs.

During the 1993 election campaign the Liberal Party under Jean Chrétien promised to eliminate the despised GST and reopen negotiations with the Americans on the Free Trade Agreement (FTA), both of which were part of the Conservatives' legacy. To no one's surprise the Americans indicated that they were not interested in renegotiating the FTA, and the Liberals retreated from their campaign bravado. In the case of the GST,

---

BOX 9.2   An Early Illustration of the Brokerage Theory of Canadian Politics

...The fact that in the Dominion parties exist apart from their programmes, or even without a programme at all, frequently deprives the electoral consultations of the people of their true meaning. In the absence of ideas or doctrines to divide the voters, there remain only questions of material interest, collective or individual. Against their pressure the candidate cannot maintain his integrity, for he knows that his opponent will not show the same self-restraint. The result is that the same promises are made on both sides, following an absolutely identical conception of the meaning of power. Posed in this way, the issue of an election manifestly changes. Whoever may be the winner, everyone knows that the country will be administered in the same way, or almost the same. The only difference will be in the personnel of the government. This is the prevailing conception of politics—except when some great wave of opinion sweeps over the whole country, covering under its waters all the political pygmies....

The reason for this ...is easy to understand. Canada, we know, is a country of violent oppositions. English and French, Protestant and Catholic, are jealous of each other and fear each other. The lack of ideas, programmes, convictions, is only apparent. Let a question of race or religion be raised, and you will immediately see most of the sordid preoccupations of patronage or connection disappear below the surface. The elections will become struggles of political principle, sincere and passionate. Now this is exactly what is feared by the prudent and far-sighted men who have been given the responsibility of maintaining the national equilibrium. Aware of the sharpness of certain rivalries, they know that if these are let loose without any counter-balance, the unity of the Dominion may be endangered. That is why they persistently apply themselves to prevent the formation of homogeneous parties, divided according to race, religion, or class—a French party, for instance, or a Catholic party, or a Labour party. The clarity of political life suffers from this, but perhaps the existence of the federation can be preserved only at this price.

André Siegfried, *The Race Question in Canada*,
ed. Frank Underhill (Toronto: McClelland & Stewart,
Carleton Library edition, 1966
[originally published in French, 1906]), 113–14.

after two years in power it became apparent that what the Liberals really meant by elimination of the GST was the harmonization of this tax with its provincial counterparts into a single sales tax. This was not exactly what voters had been led to believe. These kinds of flip-flops by the older parties on key issues—and many more examples could be cited—only serve to fuel the electorate's cynicism about politics in general and their distrust of politicians in particular.

The electoral opportunism exhibited by both the Liberals and the Tories in recent years should not to be taken to mean that the two older parties have no principles or ideological commitments whatsoever. Just as was the case when Siegfried was studying the Canadian party system, in recent times Canada's oldest parties have represented somewhat distinct traditions, particularly on matters concerning federalism and Canada–US relations. With the accession of Pierre Trudeau to the party leadership in 1968, the Liberals became identified in the minds of most Canadian voters with a strong central state (hence the ongoing battles between Ottawa and the provinces over control of natural resource revenues), with economic nationalism (Petro-Canada, the National Energy Program, the Foreign Investment Review Agency [FIRA]), and with 'French power'. The Tories, meanwhile, came increasingly to be associated with political decentralization. Joe Clark, when he was leader of the party and briefly Prime Minister in 1979, described Canadian federalism as a 'community of communities', which Trudeau sarcastically rejected as 'shopping-mall' federalism. The Conservatives also came to embrace the notion of free trade with the United States; this represented a dramatic reversal of the party positions on the subject in the late nineteenth and early twentieth centuries, when the Liberals strongly advocated continentalist economic policies. Finally, the neo-conservatism of the 1980s, spearheaded by British Prime Minister Margaret Thatcher and US President Ronald Reagan, found its most receptive audience among the Conservatives during the Mulroney years.

Despite these apparent differences in the policy orientations of the two older parties in recent times, Siegfried's central contention about the Canadian party system remains indisputable. The historically dominant parties have continued to be much more flexible, opportunistic, dominated by their leaders (see Box 9.3), and wary of ideological appeals to the electorate than those in most European nations. The nature of our electoral system and the norms that govern party competition in this country are such that the Liberals and Conservatives can usually fight elections without having to worry too much about keeping their principles intact or consistent. Many observers of the Canadian party system have attached a specific label to this type of flexible, non-ideological party system: it is a *brokerage* party system. That is, the two older parties at the federal level act as 'brokers of ideas . . . middlemen who select from all the ideas pressing for recognition as public policy those they think can be shaped to have the widest appeal'.[10] Each of the parties attempts to cobble together a winning coalition of voters at election time; the voting support for the two major parties, therefore, does not come from stable, well-defined social groups, as is the case in many Western European countries. Most importantly, politics in Canada lacks an obvious *class* dimension. Conflicts between the working class and capitalists over the political and economic rights of workers, and over the distribution of national wealth, take a back seat to other issues—those arising out of religious, ethnic, and regional rivalries, for instance.

This peculiarity of Canadian politics has led some observers to describe the Canadian party system as less developed or less modern than those of most other industrial nations. Robert Alford, for example, declared in his classic study of voting behaviour in the Anglo-American democracies (the United States, Canada, Great Britain, and Australia) that Canada had the lowest level of class voting.[11] Alford's explanation of this situation echoes the one advanced by

BOX 9.3   The Historical Importance of the Leader in Canadian Party Politics

...it is of the first importance to the success of a party that it should be led by someone who inspires confidence, and whose mere name is a programme in itself. As long as the Conservatives had Macdonald for their leader, they voted for him rather than for the party. So it is with Laurier and the Liberals of today. If Laurier disappeared, the Liberals would perhaps find that they had lost the real secret of their victories.... Canadians attach themselves rather to the concrete reality than to the abstract principle. They vote as much for the man who symbolizes the policy as for the policy itself.

Siegfried, *The Race Question in Canada*, 136.

Siegfried almost 60 years earlier: 'Class voting is low in Canada because the political parties are identified as representatives of regional, religious, and ethnic groupings rather than as representatives of national class interests, and this, in turn, is due to a relative lack of national integration.'[12] Class divisions and antagonisms are certainly not absent in Canada, Alford observed, and he predicted that once the issue of national unity had been resolved, class voting would increase and Canada would come to resemble other modern democracies—Great Britain, for instance.

In the roughly 40 years since Alford's book was written, it should be noted, his prediction has simply not come true: the issue of class is still subordinated to questions of national unity and regional or ethnic grievances. The two older parties do not normally appeal to specific class constituencies and still evade class issues when possible. Moreover, the self-described left-wing party in Canada, the New Democratic Party, receives nowhere near a majority of the votes of blue-collar workers.

Brokerage theory, then, makes two fundamental claims about Canada's two historically dominant political parties: first, they do not appeal to specific socio-economic groupings, and they lack cohesive ideological visions (especially those based on class interests and identity); sec-

ond, the parties are flexible and opportunistic because this sort of behaviour is necessary to preserve the fragile unity of the nation. This brings to mind Siegfried's observation that there are all kinds of pressing issues in Canadian politics, but that the prudent and cautious leaders of the two main parties do not want them to be discussed, for fear of inflaming group jealousies and thereby jeopardizing the stability of the country.

An alternative explanation for the absence of class politics in Canada is advanced by Janine Brodie and Jane Jenson in their book, *Crisis, Challenge, and Change*.[13] They argue that brokerage theory tends to view political parties as more or less passive transmission belts for societal demands. In the vocabulary of empirical social science, brokerage theorists consider parties to be *dependent variables*: their behaviour is shaped by the divisions that exist in society—in Canada's case, the most important divisions being those of language, ethnicity, region, and religion. Brodie and Jenson call for a more nuanced view of parties that treats them simultaneously as *dependent* (influenced by society) and *independent* (actively shaping societal demands) variables. The most important aspect of the independent, creative function of political parties in liberal democracies like Canada is their role in creating a *definition of politics*:

through which people make sense of their daily lives. Because issues are raised and choices provided in particular ways, this cultural construction defines the content and sets the limits of partisan politics. Social problems never included within the bounds of partisan political debate remain invisible and confined to the private sector or private life for resolution. From a myriad of social tensions the definition of politics identifies and selects those susceptible to 'political' solutions. Political parties, in other words, by defining the political, contribute to the organization and disorganization of groups in the electorate.[14]

Brodie and Jenson argue that in the period immediately following Confederation, class, religion, language, and other social differences competed with each other—more or less equally—as potential support bases for the two federal parties. Since both of these parties drew the bulk of their support from the same social group—the bourgeoisie—they tended to avoid the issue of class in their competition for votes. As a strategy for differentiating their 'product' from that of the governing Conservatives, the Liberals gradually seized on the issue of ethnic, religious, and linguistic differences, and 'became the party of French Quebec (and later of other ethnic minorities) while the Conservatives solidified their base among Anglophone Canadians.'[15] In later years, the authors claim, the two traditional parties would frequently try to avoid discussing class issues such as the rights and place of workers in Canadian society by redefining them as regional or cultural concerns. The NDP, they contend, has not been able or willing to challenge the prevailing definition of politics in Canada, and therefore is forced to compete with the Liberals and Conservatives under conditions that permanently handicap it and leave a significant portion of the Canadian electorate effectively disenfranchised.

Brodie and Jenson's explanation of the non-class nature of the Canadian party system is an important contribution to our understanding of politics in this country. Nevertheless, it does seem

somewhat overdrawn, since it appears to downplay or minimize the pre-eminence of religious and ethnic divisions in Canadian society in the late nineteenth century and to exaggerate the extent to which the parties have been able to play up the issues of language and culture for their own electoral advantage. One important reason that class identity came so slowly and unevenly to Canadian workers was precisely the role played by religious institutions—the Catholic Church and the Orange Order, most notably—in organizing the working class. The Orange Order appealed to workers as Scottish or Irish Protestants, while the Catholic Church stressed the spiritual mission of French-Canadian workers and was reluctant to define society in terms of antagonistic classes (as socialists did). All of this helped to ensure that for large numbers of Canadian workers their class identity was intermingled with their ethnic and religious allegiance. A large part of the explanation of the relative unimportance of class issues in Canadian politics, therefore, must be found in the social organization of the working class itself, and not simply attributed to the major parties' manipulation of the definition of politics.

The Role of Minor Parties in the Brokerage System

By the summer of 1991, almost three years into its second mandate, the Progressive Conservative government of Prime Minister Brian Mulroney had sunk to historic lows in public opinion polls, with barely 15 per cent of the electorate indicating that they would vote for the Tories if an election were held at that time. In fact, the Conservatives were being rivalled in voter popularity by a fledgling organization that was beginning to capture a great deal of voter and media attention: the Reform Party of Canada. Under the leadership of Preston Manning, the son of the former Social Credit Premier of Alberta, Ernest Manning, the Reform Party was founded in late 1987, primarily as a vehicle for western discontent (its original slogan was 'The West Wants In').

The Reform Party, now called the Canadian Alliance, is thus the latest in a string of western protest movements—its most successful predecessors having been the Progressives in the 1920s, Social Credit and the CCF in the 1930s and 1940s, and the Western Canada Concept in the early 1980s—that have tapped into the powerful feelings of economic and political alienation in the western provinces. These feelings originate in the firm conviction that the West is getting the short end of the stick, economically speaking: many westerners believe that existing federal arrangements allow Ontario and Quebec to siphon off the resource wealth of the West in order to fuel growth and prosperity in the centre. The two major parties are seen as co-conspirators in this vicious circle of exploitation, since they are beholden to the powerful economic interests in the metropolitan areas and are compelled to enact policies that favour those regions where the bulk of the seats are to be won in a federal election.

This deep-seated suspicion among westerners of central Canada and national political institutions was briefly dispelled by the 1984 federal election. Although the new Prime Minister, Brian Mulroney, was himself a bilingual Quebecer, for the first time since the Diefenbaker interlude of the 1950s a large number of prominent westerners were placed in key cabinet positions. 'At last', western voters seemed to be saying to themselves, 'we're getting a government that will understand and respond to our concerns, and not treat us like second-class citizens.' Gradually, however, this guarded optimism gave way to a shattering disillusionment, as the Conservative government made a number of policy decisions that were viewed as detrimental to western interests. Without a doubt the most publicized instance of 'biased' government decision-making was Ottawa's awarding of a multi-million-dollar maintenance contract for the CF-18 fighter aircraft to a Quebec-based firm, despite the fact that Bristol Aerospace of Winnipeg had presented what federal officials acknowledged was a technically superior bid. This enraged not only Manitobans,

but most westerners, and the CF-18 decision quickly joined the National Energy Program as a symbol of regional resentment and injustice.[16] Many westerners drew the conclusion from this affair that no matter how many representatives they sent to the House of Commons, the system itself—especially the 'national' parties—was biased against the West. A new voice, therefore, that of a regionally based protest party like the Reform Party, was necessary to extract favourable policies from central Canada.

Although the Reform Party began its life as a strictly regional organization—its constitution originally even included a prohibition on fielding candidates east of Manitoba—it quickly capitalized on the public's growing disenchantment with so-called 'traditional' political parties to make inroads into Ontario, the bastion of central Canadian power. The percentage of Canadians expressing 'a great deal' or 'quite a lot' of confidence in political parties had dropped from 30 per cent in 1979 to only 7 per cent in 1991.[17] Reform attacked existing political institutions as being unresponsive, unaccountable, and elitist, and attempted to portray itself as a populist movement rather than a political party. Rigid party discipline—which various governments have promised to relax without much noticeable effect—was singled out by both voters and the Reform Party as one of the biggest culprits in driving a wedge between the individual citizen and the political system. Under the Mulroney Conservatives, two Tory backbenchers who were publicly critical of the GST found themselves expelled from the party's caucus. Likewise, and despite Jean Chrétien's promise to relax party discipline, those Liberal MPs who opposed the government's 1995 gun control law were stripped of their parliamentary committee assignments. Such incidents remind voters that under the traditional parties those they elect to Parliament are expected to vote as the party brass decides, even if this collides with the strongly held desires of their constituents.

There is also a generalized suspicion, fuelled by occasional sordid conflict-of-interest scandals that have befallen governments in Ottawa and in many of the provincial capitals as well, that politicians have become overly concerned with furthering their own careers or lining their pockets, at the expense of their primary duty of representing the wishes and interests of their constituents. The issue of MPS' pensions is a lightning rod for this popular sentiment. The Reform Party made much of its commitment to opt out of what it considered to be the unfairly generous terms of MPS' pensions, and in 1995 all but one of the party's MPS chose not to participate in the pension plan. Finally, there is declining tolerance among voters for the kind of closed-door, elitist decision-making that traditionally has characterized Canadian politics under Liberal and Conservative governments.

Responding to the widely held demands among the electorate for greater accountability and a more democratic political structure, the Canadian Alliance has followed in the path of its populist predecessors, the Progressives and Social Credit, and has called for the implementation of a number of institutional reforms that would increase the individual citizen's control over his or her representatives. The Alliance advocates greater use of referendums and citizen initiatives; the right of constituents to recall their MPS should they be deviating too obviously from their wishes; and relaxation of party discipline so that most votes in Parliament would be 'free' votes. The Alliance's ideology is conservative, and it regularly finds itself alone as the sole political party advocating radical change to the policy status quo. For example, during the 1993 election campaign it was the only party to advocate a major reduction in Canada's annual intake of immigrants during times when the economy was weak. It was also the only party to insist that deficit reduction, to be achieved mainly through spending cuts, should be Ottawa's top priority (a policy that the Liberal government subsequently embraced). Reformers were the main critics in Parliament of the 1995 gun control law requiring the registration of all firearms. The party also has stood alone in its opposition to official multiculturalism and bilingualism.

Although the Conservatives, Liberals, and NDP all initially tried to ignore or downplay the significance of the Reform Party, by the summer of 1991—when the report of the Spicer Commission was released, documenting the deep dissatisfaction of many Canadians with the functioning of their traditional democratic institutions, especially the political parties—this protest movement was simply too powerful to be casually dismissed as a sort of political chinook. If the Conservatives and the New Democrats hoped to hold onto at least some of their traditional electoral strongholds in the Prairies, then they had to respond to the policy concerns raised by Preston Manning's organization, no matter how distasteful or 'populist' they considered them to be. This is exactly what happened during previous cycles of regional protest: the major parties were eventually compelled to head off the electoral challenge of a nascent protest movement (whether it was the Progressives, the CCF, or Social Credit) by endorsing policies that appealed to the new party's supporters. In the case of the Progressives, for instance, the party was opposed to the National Policy tariff (which kept the price of central Canada's manufactured goods relatively high and drove up the costs of farming) and to the discriminatory freight rates charged by the CPR (which made it cheaper to ship manufactured goods from central Canada to the West than to send grain eastward). After the Progressives' meteoric rise to prominence in the 1921 federal election, however, the protest they represented was gradually dissipated by the skilful manoeuvring of the Liberal Prime Minister, Mackenzie King, who made relatively minor changes in the tariff and in freight rate policy and managed to buy off some of the Progressives' leaders with offers of cabinet posts in his government. This was largely the fate of the Co-operative Commonwealth Federation (CCF) as well: Mackenzie King sought to take the wind out of the socialist party's sails by implementing a number of social welfare policies that its supporters were advocating, including old age pensions and unemployment insurance.

'Minor' parties perform an important function in our brokerage party system: they provide a much-needed source of policy innovation, goading the major parties into acting on the concerns of regions, classes, or significant social groups that they have traditionally ignored or underestimated. Walter Young, in his history of the national CCF, described the contribution of third parties to the Canadian political system in the following way:

> By providing . . . the kind of ideological confrontation which is typically absent in contests between the two major parties, [minor parties] have served to stimulate the older parties and reactivate their previously dormant philosophies. . . . Two parties alone cannot successfully represent all the interests or act as a broker—honest or otherwise. Attempts to represent a national consensus have been usually based on the assessment of a few with limited access to the attitudes of the whole. The result has been that the national consensus has in fact been the view of the most dominant voices in the old parties. And these are the voices at the centre; historically, the voices of the elite or the establishment.[18]

The Party System Since 1993: The End of Brokerage Politics?

Since 1993, it no longer seems appropriate to refer to the Liberal and Progressive Conservative parties as Canada's two 'major' parties. Before the 1993 election it was common to speak of Canada's 'two and one-half' party system. The Liberals and Conservatives were the parties that had a realistic chance of forming a government, while the NDP was a stable minority party on the federal scene, regularly winning 15–20 per cent of the popular vote and occasionally holding the balance of power during a period of minority government. The distinction between major and minor parties was rooted in the realities of electoral competition.

The old certainties were shattered by the 1993 election results. The Liberals won a solid majority, taking 177 of the 295 seats in the House of Commons and 41.3 per cent of the popular vote. Neither the Conservatives nor the NDP elected enough MPs to qualify for official party status in the House of Commons. On the other hand, the Reform Party jumped from one seat that had been won in a by-election to 52 seats. The Bloc Québécois, created in 1990 by the defections of several Tory and Liberal MPs, went from seven seats to 54. Not since 1921, when the Progressives came second to the Liberals, had the national party system received such a jolt by voters.

With the Conservatives and NDP reduced to near irrelevance in the Commons, and two strong opposition parties, neither of which gave signs of being interested in brokerage-style politics, it was natural that political analysts should talk of the realignment taking place in Canada's national party system. Realignment suggests a durable change, not one caused by transient and unusual factors. Those who interpreted the 1993 election results as evidence of a realignment based this reading on what they saw as voters' dissatisfaction with brokerage-style politics, the weakness of party loyalties among voters, and erosion of the NDP's support across the country. This interpretation was greeted skeptically or even rejected by others. Critics of the realignment argument pointed to such factors as the monumental unpopularity of former Conservative Prime Minister Brian Mulroney, the erosion of NDP support in Ontario, where an unpopular NDP government was in power, a wave of western disaffection with the major parties, and the unusual and presumably passing phenomenon of the Bloc Québécois, spawned in the bitter wake of the 1990 defeat of the Meech Lake Accord.

Textbook writers engage in prognostication at their peril, and only time will determine who is right. Nevertheless, one might argue that the elements for a durable party realignment exist. One of these involves the low esteem in which parties and politicians are held by voters. In the words of the Royal Commission on Electoral Reform and Party Financing:

Canadians appear to distrust their political leaders, the political process and political institutions. Parties themselves may be contributing to the malaise of voters. . . . whatever the cause, there is little doubt that Canadian political parties are held in low public esteem, and that their standing has declined steadily over the past decade. They are under attack from citizens for failing to achieve a variety of goals deemed important by significant groups within society.[19]

The wave of cynicism that has been building in the Canadian electorate has weakened attachments to the traditional parties, as may be seen in Table 9.1, which summarizes results for the 19 federal elections since 1940.

A second element that may presage a realignment of the party system involves what might be described as the shrinking centre in Canadian politics. The traditional dominance of the Liberals and Progressive Conservatives, centrist parties that differed very little from one another in terms of their principles and policies, depended on the existence of a broad popular consensus on the role of government and on their ability to keep political debate within the familiar confines of language, regionalism, and leadership. This popular consensus has become frayed, and so the parties' ability to keep political conflict within 'safe' boundaries has been diminished.

The consensus that developed during the post-World War II era was based on the welfare state, an active economic management role for government, and official bilingualism. The Liberals and Conservatives, but particularly the Liberal Party in its role as the government for most of this era, were the architects of the policies that were the practical expressions of this consensus. Commenting on Canada's national party system in the early 1980s, Seymour Martin Lipset argued that there was no right-wing party but that all the parties were part of the left-of-centre consensus. The British weekly *The Economist* made the same point in commenting on the 1988 election. It observed that the leaders of the Conservatives, Liberals, and NDP were 'all to the left of the

Table 9.1   Summary of Election Results, 1940–2000

A. Percentage of Vote* and Candidates Elected by Political Party at Canadian General Elections, 1940–2000

Party	1940	1945	1949	1953	1957	1958	1962
Liberal	54.9%	41.4%	50.1%	50.0%	42.3%	33.8%	37.4%
	181	127	193	172	106	48	99
PC	30.6%	27.7%	29.7%	31.0%	39.0%	53.7%	37.3%
	40	68	41	51	112	208	116
CCF/NDP	8.5%	15.7%	13.4%	11.3%	10.8%	9.5%	13.4%
	8	28	13	23	25	8	19
Social Credit	2.7%	4.1%	3.9%	5.4%	6.6%	2.6%	11.7%
	10	13	10	15	19	—	30
Bloc Populaire	—	3.3%	—	—	—	—	—
	—	2	—	—	—	—	—
Others	3.3%	7.8%	2.9%	2.3%	1.3%	0.4%	0.2%
	6	7	5	4	3	1	1
Total valid votes	4,620,260	5,246,130	5,848,971	5,641,272	6,605,980	7,287,297	7,690,134
Total seats	245	245	262	265	265	265	265

Table 9.1 continued

A. Percentage of Vote* and Candidates Elected by Political Party at Canadian General Elections, 1940–2000 (cont'd)

Party	1963	1965	1968	1972	1974	1979	1980	1984	1988	1993	1997	2000
Liberal	41.7%	40.2%	45.5%	38.5%	43.2%	40.1%	44.3%	28.0%	31.9%	41.3%	38.5%	40.8%
	128	131	155	109	141	114	147	40	83	177	155	172
PC	32.8%	32.4%	31.4%	34.9%	35.4%	35.9%	32.5%	50.0%	43.0%	16.0%	18.8%	12.2%
	95	97	72	107	95	136	103	211	169	2	20	12
NDP	13.1%	17.9%	17.0%	17.7%	15.4%	17.9%	19.8%	18.8%	20.4%	6.9%	11.0%	8.5%
	17	21	22	31	16	26	32	30	43	9	21	13
Créditistes	—	4.6%	4.4%	—	—	—	—	—	—	—	—	—
	—	9	14	—	—	—	—	—	—	—	—	—
Social Credit	11.9%	3.7%	0.8%	7.6%	5.0%	4.6%	1.7%	0.1%	**	—	—	—
	24	5	0	15	11	6	0	0	0	—	—	—
Bloc Québécois	—	—	—	—	—	—	—	—	—	13.5%	10.7%	10.7%
	—	—	—	—	—	—	—	—	—	54	44	38
Reform/Alliance	—	—	—	—	—	—	—	—	2.1%	18.7%	19.4%	25.5%
	—	—	—	—	—	—	—	—	0	52	60	66
Others	0.4%	1.2%	0.9%	1.2%	0.9%	1.5%	1.7%	3.0%	2.6%	3.6%	1.6%	2.2%
	1	2	1	2	2	0	0	0	0	1	1	0
Total valid votes	7,894,076	7,713,316	8,125,996	9,667,489	9,505,908	11,455,702	10,947,914	12,548,721	13,175,599	13,667,671	12,985,964	
Total seats	265	265	264	264	264	282	282	282	295	295	301	

Note: The election of 1945 was the first in which the name Progressive Conservative was used. The New Democratic Party first participated in the election of 1962.

* Columns may not add up to 100 per cent due to rounding.

** Less than 0.1 per cent.

Table 9.1 continued

B. Percentage of Vote and Candidates Elected by Party and Province, 2000

Province	Liberal	Progressive Conservative	NDP	Alliance	Bloc Québécois	Others	Totals, Province
Nfld	44.9%	34.5%	13.1%	3.9%	—	3.6%	229,498
	5	2	—	—	—	—	7
NS	36.5%	29.1%	24.0%	9.6%	—	0.8%	435,269
	4	4	3	—	—	—	11
NB	41.7%	30.5%	11.7%	15.7%	—	0.3%	383,012
	6	3	1	—	—	—	10
PEI	47%	38.4%	9.0%	5.0%	—	0.5%	74,464
	4	—	—	—	—	—	4
Que.	44.2%	5.6%	1.8%	6.2%	39.8%	2.4%	3,456,898
	36	1	—	—	38	—	75
Ont.	51.5%	14.4%	8.3%	23.6%	—	2.3%	4,452,605
	100	—	1	2	—	—	103
Man.	32.5%	14.5%	20.9%	30.4%	—	1.8%	487,832
	5	1	4	4	—	—	14
Sask.	20.7%	4.8%	26.2%	47.7%	—	0.6%	433,697
	2	—	2	10	—	—	14
Alta	20.9%	13.5%	5.4%	58.9%	—	1.2%	1,255,999
	2	1	—	23	—	—	26
BC	27.7%	7.3%	11.3%	49.4%	—	4.3%	1,614,721
	5	—	2	27	—	—	34
Yukon, NWT, and Nunavut	39.8%	8.6%	28.4%	22.7%	—	0.2%	33,778
	2	—	1	—	—	—	3
Totals	5,252,031	1,566,998	1,093,868	3,276,929	1,377,727	290,220	12,857,774
Party	172	12	13	66	38	—	301

*Rows may not add up to 100 per cent due to rounding.

American Democratic team, Mr. Michael Dukakis and Mr. Lloyd Bentsen. . . . Most Canadian voters, too, are committed to a quasi-welfare state.'[20] On constitutional issues, too, the traditional parties were capable of broad agreement. This was evident in the support that all three parties gave to both the Meech Lake Accord and the Charlottetown Accord, a unanimity that certainly was not found in the Canadian population.

Popular consensus on the Keynesian welfare state and activist government has unravelled since the 1980s. Issues like deficit reduction, welfare reform, and lower taxes are the rallying points for dissent from the post-war consensus. Opposition to what is perceived to be state-sponsored pluralism through official multiculturalism and bilingualism provides another pole for this dissent. In broadening its organization from the West to include Ontario and eastern Canada, the Reform Party was clearly attempting to provide a voice for this dissent, a voice that many voters believed was not being provided by the Conservative Party. Reform's second-place finish in Ontario in the 1993 election, capturing 20 per cent of the popular vote, cannot be explained in terms of 'western alienation'. These appeared to be voters who had defected from the Conservative Party in search of a party that defined the issues in a way they believed responded to the country's true problems. At the provincial level this dissent contributed to the election of the Conservatives under Ralph Klein in Alberta and under Mike Harris in Ontario, provincial Conservative governments that were much closer to the outlook of the Reform Party than they were to the national Conservative Party under Jean Charest (1993–8) and Joe Clark (1998–2003).

Only the Liberal Party succeeded in practising the old brokerage-style politics. It emerged from the 1993 election as the only truly national party, electing members from every province and territory and receiving no less than one-quarter of the votes cast in any province. The Liberals did only slightly less well in 1997, failing to elect a member only in Nova Scotia and Yukon. In the 2000 election Liberal support ranged from a low of 20.7 per cent of the popular vote in Saskatchewan to a high of 51.5 per cent in Ontario. The party won seats in every province and territory, no other party coming close to this accomplishment. The lesson may be that there is no longer enough space in the centre of the Canadian electorate to support two centrist brokerage parties. Given the national Conservative Party's long history and continuing organizational resources, as well as its strength at the provincial level, it would be rash to write its obituary. But it seems likely that the PCs will have to reposition themselves ideologically by competing for the votes that Reform/Canadian Alliance siphoned off in the 1993, 1997, and 2000 elections. It cannot afford to remain a near-clone of the Liberal Party, especially since the Liberals in power have created some distance between them-

selves and the Keynesian welfare state they were instrumental in building. The electoral success of right-leaning Conservatives in Alberta and Ontario suggests that the future of the national party may lie in this direction.

Some critics of the realignment interpretation of the post-1993 party system argue that the success of the Bloc Québécois was the chief factor that knocked the party system off its usual orbit. Assuming that the Bloc is a temporary phenomenon, they argue, the national party system will return to two-party dominance once the Bloc has passed from the scene. After all, most of those who voted for the Bloc in 1993, 1997, and 2000 had voted for the Conservatives in 1984 and 1988, when the latter party captured fully half of the popular vote in Quebec. Eliminate the Bloc from the picture, they argue, and many of these voters will have nowhere to go except to the Conservatives, thereby re-establishing the Conservative Party's national status.

Perhaps. But there are a couple of serious problems with this scenario. One is that in order to recapture voters who have supported the BQ in recent years, the Conservatives would have to offer Quebecers something different from the federalist philosophy of the Liberals. It is unlikely that they could do this in a way that would appeal to nationalist sentiment in Quebec without in the process angering voters in the rest of Canada. The other problem is that re-establishing Conservative support in Quebec still would not solve the party's difficulties in the rest of Canada. Since 1993 the Reform Party/Canadian Alliance has outpolled the Conservatives in Ontario in every federal election and, moreover, in the four western provinces Reform/Alliance candidates have received about four votes for every one cast for the Tories. If the popular consensus on which two-party dominance in English Canada rested really has come apart, and therefore the electoral space for brokerage politics has shrunk, then the Conservatives will require more than cosmetic surgery to regain their voter appeal west of Quebec. The challenge is made all the more difficult by the fact

Y'alright?

Y'alright?

Since the 1993 election, the fact that the Conservative and Alliance parties have split the centre-right vote has helped the Liberals win majorities with barely more than 40 per cent of the popular vote. (Roy Peterson, *Vancouver Sun*)

UNITING THE RIGHT
(The Plot So Far)

that the Liberals, masters of the art of borrowing ideas and policies when this is expedient, have shown a willingness to move to the right on such matters as government spending and welfare reform. As this is being written, Paul Martin appears poised to become the next leader of the Liberal Party. Martin was the chief architect of the Liberal government's policy of spending cuts and deficit reduction during his nine years as Finance Minister (1993–2002). Between a Liberal Party led by Paul Martin and the fiscal conservatism of Alliance leader Stephen Harper there is not much room for a national Conservative Party leader to stake out some distinctively right-of-centre turf. Nor has there been much indication that the recent leadership of the party has wanted to move the party in that direction.

The 1997 general election was a replay of 1993 in several important respects. The Liberals won another majority, albeit a reduced one, sweeping all but one of Ontario's 103 seats. The Reform Party dominated in the West, taking 57 of the 74 seats in Saskatchewan, Alberta, and British Columbia. The Reform share of the vote in Ontario remained stable at slightly less than 20 per cent, but the Conservative share of the Ontario vote recovered to almost equal that of Reform. The Bloc Québécois continued to be the most popular party in Quebec, but it lost some ground in both share of the vote and seats to the Liberals.

More significant than these nuanced changes were the election results in the Atlantic provinces. Twenty-one of the 32 seats in the four Atlantic provinces were won by the NDP and the Conservatives. Indeed, the Conservative Party emerged from the 1997 election appearing to be almost as much an Atlantic Canada party as Reform appeared to be a western Canadian party. Thirteen of the PCs' 20 seats were won in Newfoundland, Nova Scotia, and New Brunswick. The NDP, which historically had achieved only minor inroads in Atlantic Canada, won eight seats in the region, representing about 40 per cent of the party's caucus in Parliament. The loss of several Liberal seats and the ascendance of the Conservatives and the NDP in the region were almost certainly due to voters' unhappiness with federal spending cuts, particularly in transfers to provincial governments, that were felt more deeply in their region than in more affluent parts of Canada. The message of fiscal conservatism that the Liberals preached, particularly after the 1995 federal budget, was an unnerving one in provinces whose job markets and public services have long been sustained by a life-support system of federal assistance.

Just as the Progressives' mercurial rise to official opposition party in 1921 proved to be short-lived, and the sweep of Quebec by the Conservative Party of John Diefenbaker in 1958 amounted to a fleeting blip on the radar screen, and then the Mulroney Conservatives' dominance of Quebec between 1984 and 1992 was vaporized by that party's disastrous 1993 showing, it may be premature to speak of a permanent realignment in Canadian party politics. If nothing else, however, the rise of Reform/Canadian Alliance in the West and of the Bloc Québécois in Quebec tells us that the party loyalties of many Canadian voters are not very durable.

The Reform Party, joined by some elements from the national and provincial Conservative parties, sought to capitalize on the apparent softness of party loyalties through a movement to create the United Alternative. Formally launched in 1998, the roots of the United Alternative go back to the 1993 election. The Liberals won a strong majority on the strength of only 41.3 per cent of the popular vote. Combined popular support for the PCs and Reform came to 34.7 per cent. While not all Reform voters were disaffected Conservatives, it is safe to conclude that most were. Those on the right of Canada's political spectrum were quick to lament the division of the conservative vote, a sit-

uation that enabled the Liberal Party to win seats that it probably would not have won, particularly in many Ontario ridings. The combined popular vote of the Conservative and Reform parties in 1997 came to 38.2 per cent, just a hair less than the Liberals' 38.5 per cent of the vote. At this point the talk of the need for a 'unite the right' movement to defeat the Liberals became more persistent.

Spearheaded intellectually by conservative political writer David Frum and organized by the Reform Party, the United Alternative was created in 1998 and held a national convention in February 1999. The convention certainly gave the appearance of inter-party co-operation to unite conservative political forces against the governing Liberal Party. An Ontario cabinet minister, Tony Clement, was the convention co-chair. Conservative Premier Ralph Klein gave the keynote address. Prominent Quebecer and former Liberal Jean Allaire spoke to the convention. The fly in the ointment, from the standpoint of the UA and its goal of realigning Canada's national party system, was that with the exception of only a couple of Conservative MPs, the national Conservative Party kept its distance from the UA. Conservative leader Joe Clark repeatedly refused to respond to Preston Manning's public invitations to join forces in a new party. This was not surprising in light of Clark's long history as a product and practitioner of brokerage politics, who very clearly nurtured the vision of re-establishing the Conservative Party's status as Canada's other brokerage party. Consequently, about all the United Alternative initiative managed to achieve, apart from some fleeting publicity for the right-wing cause, was to rename the Reform Party as the Canadian Reform Conservative Alliance Party, euphemistically called CRAP by the pundits since the federal Conservatives had hardly participated and now generally known as the Canadian Alliance.

The 2000 Election: Alliance Stalled?

It is generally conceded by all but the most loyal supporters of Jean Chrétien that the 2000 election was called for no better reason than what appeared to be its winnability. The main opposition party, the Canadian Alliance, had just gone through a fairly divisive leadership race that resulted in the defeat of the party's founder, Preston Manning, and his replacement by another Alberta politician, Stockwell Day. The Alliance's new leader was a born-again Christian with a reputation for social conservatism. The Liberals could have continued in power for almost two more years before calling an election. But Day appeared vulnerable and so an election was called.

The rest, as they say, is history. The Liberals were re-elected with a larger majority than they held before the election. The Alliance failed to make its much-desired breakthrough in Ontario and so continued to be seen as a party of western protest. Stockwell Day's performance in the campaign was generally seen as ineffective, leaving him open to criticism within his own party. This criticism continued to build during the year after the election until the pressure on Day to resign became irresistible. Day stepped down as leader and ran as a candidate in a new leadership race held less than two years after he had defeated Preston Manning. This time Day lost to yet another Albertan—although born and raised in Ontario—Stephen Harper.

What makes this story strange are the following facts, virtually ignored by most members of the media and academic commentators on the 2000 election:

- Alliance's share of the popular vote increased from 19.4 per cent in 1997 to 25.5 per cent in 2000.
- The party's share of the popular vote in Ontario increased from 19.1 per cent in 1997 to 23.6 per cent in 2000.
- Alliance increased its seats in the House of Commons from 60 to 66.
- Alliance's share of the popular vote in Ontario exceeded that of the NDP and Progressive Conservative Party combined.

Given these facts, the obvious question is why the 2000 election was widely interpreted as a setback for Alliance and a personal defeat for its leader, Stockwell Day.

The answer to this question reveals much about Canadian politics. What an outsider, viewing the Canadian electoral scene for the first time, might interpret as clear progress by the Canadian Alliance was viewed as a setback by most of the country's opinion-makers because of the party's failure to pick up seats in Ontario. Winning only two out of Ontario's 103 seats, and nothing in the eastern reaches of Canada, seemed to reconfirm the party's image as just the latest in a line of western protest parties. Of course, the distortions created by Canada's electoral system—about which more will be said in the next section—are largely responsible for this image of Reform/Alliance. Nevertheless, the simple fact of the matter is that the bar had been set at an Ontario breakthrough. When this did not happen due to the Alliance and the Conservative parties splitting the right-of-centre vote, it appeared that the Alliance was stalled. Three successive elections had left it pretty much where it began in 1993.

Why the blame for this should come to rest largely on the shoulders of Stockwell Day provides another insight into Canadian politics. During the election campaign *Maclean's* magazine ran an issue with Day's picture and the question, 'The Scare Factor: Is Stockwell Day too extreme for mainstream Canadian voters?' The cover story focused on the Alliance leader's religious beliefs and his social conservatism, and included claims that Day believed in the literal truth of the book of Genesis and thus rejected evolutionary theory and evidence that the Earth is older than 5,000 years.[21] The fundamental questions posed by the piece were, one, whether Day's ideas were significantly out of sync with those of most Canadians and, two, whether, if he became Prime Minister, Day could be trusted not to try to foist an agenda of social conservatism onto Canadian society.

Most Canadians do not read *Maclean's* and it is probably a fair bet that among those who do, support for the Alliance is not very high to begin with. But the *Maclean's* story was only part of a broader pattern of media questioning of Day's religious beliefs and what the political implications of these might be. Questions like these are, of course, reasonable enough but they were not asked in connection with any of the other party leaders. Day may have been singled out for scrutiny because his born-again Christianity placed him further from the safe centre of Canadian spiritual life than the other leaders. But this merely illustrates the point: the constituency for social conservatism is far from being large enough in Canada to elect a like-minded leader. Moreover, whether a majority of Canadians consider such a leader to be 'scary' is an open question, but there is not much doubt that most of their opinion leaders do and that they believe Canadians should as well. Once the social conservative label was stuck to him, Day was no longer considered viable in Ontario. For Alliance eventually to make its breakthrough beyond the comfortable confines of the West it needed a leader who could not be portrayed, subtly or otherwise, as a religious nut.

In terms of the more general implications of the 2000 election, it remained unclear whether the party *dealignment* that began in 1993 had been succeeded by a reasonably durable *realignment* of the national party system and voter support. The odds appeared to be against it. The Bloc Québécois continued to capture a significant share of the Quebec electorate—about 40 per cent of the vote—and support for both the NDP and the Progressive Conservatives remained weak. Indeed, the Conservative Party appeared to have become a party of Atlantic Canada, winning about one of every three votes in the four Atlantic provinces and nine of their 12 seats from this region. This was achieved by positioning the party *to the left* of the Liberals in Atlantic Canada, criticizing the Chrétien government's spending cuts and their negative impact on the region. This red Tory message is one that probably can only be sold in Atlantic Canada. The idea that the Conservative Party can re-establish itself nationally by outflanking the Liberals on the left is pretty far-fetched. Emerging from the 2000 election with the smallest share of the popular vote in its history on the national political stage, the Conservative Party and its leadership seemed to be clinging pathetically to the hope that the Alliance would somehow implode and wayward Alliance MPs and voters would return to their proper home in the Conservative Party.

As for the NDP, the 2000 election marked the third consecutive one in which the party's national support was in the single digits. The long-simmering debate over whether the way out of marginal status in national politics could be found in moving the party further to the left or in recapturing the centrist orientation it had under leaders like Ed Broadbent and, before him, David Lewis, eventually led to the resignation of NDP leader Alexa McDonough. The ensuing leadership race pitted a strongly left-wing Toronto politician, Jack Layton, against a less strident long-time Saskatchewan MP, Bill Blaikie. Layton's victory suggested that the party was pinning its hopes on a shift to the left.

All that is clear is that the old pre-1993 party system is history. Given the decline in the strength of party loyalties over the last generation, it would probably be foolish to expect some durable party realignment to emerge and persist for several decades. Meanwhile, the fragmentation of voter support and the nature of Canada's electoral system enable the Liberal Party to capture solid majorities in the House of Commons with only 40 per cent of the popular vote. This situation generated renewed calls for reform of the electoral system, with spokespersons for both the right and the left advocating change. To understand why, we need to look more closely at how the electoral system works.

THE ELECTORAL SYSTEM AND ITS CONSEQUENCES

Many Canadians were shocked and even scandalized when George W. Bush was elected President of the United States in 2000, even though he received about one-half million fewer votes than

Al Gore. What they did not realize is that such an outcome can and has happened in Canada. In 1979 the Liberal Party received about 4 per cent more of the popular vote than the Conservatives, but the Conservatives won 22 more seats and formed the government. In the 1998 provincial election in Quebec the Quebec Liberal Party won 43.7 per cent of the popular vote compared to 42.7 per cent for the Parti Québécois. Despite this the PQ won a strong majority of seats in Quebec's National Assembly. It occasionally happens that the party that wins a provincial or federal election in Canada is not the party that wins in the popular vote. Even more common, however, is the situation where the governing party is elected on the strength of only 38–40 per cent of the popular vote. Canadians who were scandalized by George W. Bush's victory in 2000 would do well to consider that Bush won a larger share of the eligible electorate than did Jean Chrétien's Liberal Party in the Canadian election of 2000. But few voices contested the legitimacy of Chrétien's victory. (Of course, in Canada today there are several national or viable regional parties besides the Liberals—PCs, NDP, Alliance, BQ—that draw measurably significant percentages of the vote, whereas the US historically has had a two-party system.)

Canada's electoral system does not reward parties in proportion to their share of the popular vote. The Liberal Party, whose candidates received just under 41 per cent of the popular vote in the 2000 election, won about 57 per cent of all seats in the House of Commons. The Progressive Conservatives received 12.2 per cent and the NDP 8.5 per cent of the popular vote, which translated into 4.3 and 4.0 per cent, respectively, of seats in the Commons. The Alliance received a share of seats (22 per cent) roughly equal to its 25.5 per cent of the popular vote, but this concealed the fact that the party's candidates won almost a quarter of the votes cast in Ontario but under 2 per cent of that province's seats. The Bloc Québécois, which only ran candidates in Quebec, received just under 11 per cent of the national vote and 12.6 per cent of all seats in the legislature.

To understand what happened in these elections, we must first describe the Canadian electoral system, the principal features of which are the same at both the federal and provincial levels. It is based on the **single-member, simple-plurality electoral system**: one person is elected to represent the citizens of a particular geographic area, called a constituency or riding. The candidate who receives the most votes in a constituency election becomes the member of Parliament (or provincial legislator) for that constituency. A majority of votes is not necessary and, given the fragmentation of votes between the various parties, is, in fact, the exception rather than the rule.

A political party's representation in the House of Commons will depend, therefore, on how well its candidates fare in the 301 constituency races that make up a general election. It regularly happens that, nationally, the leading party's candidates may account for only about 40 per cent of the popular vote and yet capture a majority of the seats in the Commons. Indeed, the advocates of the single-member, simple-plurality electoral system point to this as the system's chief virtue. It manages, they claim, to transform something less than a majority of votes for a party into a majority of seats, thereby delivering stable majority government. (In fact, however, the system's performance on this count has been rather mediocre. Six of the 15 general elections from 1957 to 2000 produced minority governments.)

The chief alternative to the single-member, plurality electoral system is some form of **proportional representation** (PR). Under a PR system, the number of members elected by each party about coincides with its share of the popular vote. This sounds eminently fair, but PR has its critics. Detractors criticize it on three main counts. First, they claim that it promotes a splintering of the party system, encouraging the creation of minor parties that represent very narrow interests and undermining the development of broad-based national parties capable of bridging sectional rivalries and the differences between special interests. Second, proportional representation is said to produce unstable government. The unlikelihood that any party will have a majority of seats creates the need to cobble together and maintain a coalition government, resulting in more frequent elections. And even between elections, the inter-party deals necessary to maintain a coalition government may paralyze cabinet decision-making. Countries such as Italy and Belgium, where governments often last only a year or two, are said to illustrate the horrors of PR (curiously, proportional systems with a relatively low level of executive turnover, including the Netherlands and Germany, are seldom mentioned by the critics).

A third standard criticism of PR systems is that they encourage ideological polarity and enable extremist parties to achieve representation in the legislature. There is no doubt that countries having proportional electoral systems do tend to have more political parties than those with plurality systems, and the ideological distance between the extreme ends of the party spectrum will inevitably be greater than that separating Canada's major parties, or Democrats and Republicans in the United States (another plurality electoral system). In fact, however, the ideological distance between those parties in proportional systems that are likely to be the senior partners of any government coalition tends to be no greater than between, say, the Liberal Party and the NDP in Canada. Moreover, not everyone would agree that more, rather than less, ideological dispersion between parties is a bad thing. One might argue that it improves voters' ability to distinguish between parties on the basis of the values and policies they represent. The prospect that extremist parties will infiltrate the legislature through a proportional system is also less worrisome than is claimed by detractors. Both theory and experience suggest that the closer a party gets to membership in a governing coalition, the more moderate its behaviour will be.[22]

The 'winner-take-all' electoral system that exists in Canada is not without its own detractors. In a classic analysis, Alan Cairns identifies several consequences for Canada's party system and national unity that flow from the single-member, simple-plurality system.[23] They include the following:

- It tends to produce more seats than votes for the strongest major party and for minor parties whose support is regionally concentrated.
- It gives the impression that some parties have no or little support in certain regions, when in fact their candidates may regularly account for 15–30 per cent of the popular vote.
- The parliamentary composition of a party will be less representative of the different regions of the country than is that party's electoral support.
- Minor parties whose appeal is to interests that are distributed widely across the country will receive a smaller percentage of seats than votes.

Cairns concludes that the overall impact of Canada's electoral system has been negative. The system has, he argues, exacerbated regional and ethnolinguistic divisions in Canadian political life by shutting out the Conservative Party in Quebec for most of this century and giving the impression that the Liberal Party was the only national party with support in French Canada. Cairns's article on the electoral system's effects was written in the late 1960s. If it was written today it would also mention, among other consequences, the gross underrepresentation of the Liberals in western Canada over the last couple of decades, despite their receiving between one-quarter and one-third of western votes in most elections, and the failure of the Reform Party to elect a single member from Ontario in 1997 and Alliance's election of a mere two MPs in 2000, despite receiving more votes in that province than in the three westernmost provinces combined. As William Irvine observes, 'the electoral system confers a spurious image of unanimity on provinces. By magnifying the success of the provincial vote leader, the electoral system ensures that party caucuses will overrepresent any party's "best" province.'[24] And this is not the only quirk of our electoral system.

Along with the distortions that Canada's electoral system produces, another argument for the system's reform is that it leaves many voters feeling disempowered and contributes to low levels of voter turnout. This is a view that has become increasingly popular in recent years. Voter turnout in federal elections has declined over the last several elections, reaching bottom at about 60 per cent of the eligible electorate in 2000. This decline in voter participation, however, could be caused by factors—such as a general dissatisfaction with parties and politics—other than any sense that one's vote may be futile because of the electoral system. There is absolutely no definitive proof that voters' perceptions of the impact of the electoral system on the probable consequences of each person's vote influence the likelihood that they will go to the polls on election day.

Historically, the party that has stood to gain most from the replacement of Canada's electoral system by some form of proportional representation has been the CCF-NDP. It received a smaller percentage of total seats in the Commons than its share of the national vote in every one of the 17 elections between 1935 and 1988. This was again true in 1993, but the collapse of the NDP vote from its usual 15 to 20 per cent to just under 7 per cent was clearly more significant than the fact that the electoral system once again 'under-rewarded' the party (it won nine seats, or 3 per cent of the total). The Conservative Party, which historically was one of the chief beneficiaries of the biases of the electoral system, has been the biggest loser since 1993. In the 2000 election it received a share of seats in the Commons (4 per cent) that was only a third of its share of the popular vote (12.2 per cent). Irvine's point about the tendency of the electoral system to magnify the success of the most popular party in a province and punish those parties whose share of the vote does not achieve some critical mass has certainly been borne out by recent election results. Reform received 20 per cent of the Ontario vote in 1993, coming in second behind the Liberals' 53 per cent, but was rewarded with only one seat to the Liberals' 98. Reform's share of the Ontario vote dropped by only one percentage point in 1997,

but it failed to elect a single member from the province. In the 2000 election Alliance candidates captured almost one-quarter of the votes cast in Ontario, good enough for only two Ontario seats (just under 2 per cent of the province's total). This helped fuel the misperception of Alliance as being merely a western party, when in fact over one million votes, representing about one-third of all votes cast for the Canadian Alliance, were received in Ontario. Given the realities of political life, however, there is no reason to imagine that the Liberal Party or—should it happen—a revitalized Conservative Party would show much enthusiasm for electoral reform, let alone adopting proportional representation. Their dominance would almost certainly be eroded by such a system.

Canadians probably will just have to live with the regionally divisive effects of the existing electoral system. The best hope for overcoming the negative consequences that Cairns, Irvine, and many others have pointed to may be reform of the Canadian Senate. An elected Senate whose members would be chosen according to some system of proportional representation within each province—so that a party's share of Senate seats would be determined by its share of the provincial popular vote—could go some way towards overcoming the regionally unrepresentative character of parties' caucuses in the House of Commons. This would depend, however, on the Senate becoming a more respected and effective branch of the legislature than it is at present.

Giving it an elected basis would certainly increase its legitimacy in the eyes of Canadians and would probably improve the calibre of representatives found in the Senate. If this happened, it is easily conceivable that senators would routinely be appointed to cabinet, rather than exceptionally as is currently the practice. In such circumstances no major party should have difficulty in putting together a government with a fair share of representation from all regions of the country. At the same time, an unreformed House of Commons would have the virtue of retaining the Canadian tradition of individual representatives for citizens—MPs who are accountable to electors in local constituencies. Unfortunately, little in our recent political history suggests that major reforms to the Senate, and therefore to our entire parliamentary system, can squeeze by the formidable constitutional and partisan obstacles in their path.

PARTY FINANCES AND SPECIAL INTERESTS

Throughout their history, the Liberal and Progressive Conservative parties have relied heavily on corporate contributors to finance their activities. The NDP, by contrast, has depended mainly on contributions from individuals and on the financial support of affiliated trade unions. Corporate donations to the national NDP have always been minuscule.

It is difficult to attach precise numbers to party finances before 1974, for the simple reason that parties were not legally required to disclose their sources of revenue. A study done by Khayyam Paltiel for the federally appointed Royal Commission on Election Expenses (1966) estimated that, before the 1974 reforms, the older parties depended on business contributions for between 75 and 90 per cent of their incomes,[25] a figure that did not even include the value of services in kind that they received from businesses, particularly from advertising and polling firms during election campaigns.[26] Not only did the Liberals and Conservatives depend on business for all but a small share of their revenue, but most of this corporate money was collected from big businesses in Toronto and Montreal.[27] Other students of party finances have confirmed this historical pattern of dependence on big financial and industrial capital.[28]

Passage of the Election Expenses Act in 1974 signalled a watershed in Canadian party finance. The Act included spending limits for individual candidates and political parties during election campaigns, changes to the Broadcasting Act requiring radio and television stations to make available to the parties represented in the House of Commons both paid and free broadcast time during election campaigns,[29] and a system of reimbursement for part of their expenses for candidates who receive at least 15 per cent of the popular vote. This last reform has the effect of subsidizing the three main parties at taxpayer expense, a consequence that can only be defended on the grounds that this public subsidy helps to weaken parties' financial dependence on special interests.

But from the standpoint of the parties' sources of income, the most important reforms brought in by the Election Expenses Act involved tax credits for political contributions and public disclosure requirements for candidates and political parties. On the first count, changes to the Income Tax Act allow individuals or organizations to deduct from their taxable income a percentage of their donation to a registered political party or candidate, up to a maximum tax credit of $500. There is no limit on the size of political donations, but the maximum tax credit is reached with a donation of $1,150.[30] On the second count, parties and candidates are required to provide the chief electoral officer with a list of all donors who have contributed $100 or more in money or services in kind, as well as an itemized account of their expenditures. Openness has its limits, however. Parties are not required to disclose how much they spend on important activities such as fundraising and polling between elections, although available evidence suggests that these are very expensive functions.[31]

Perhaps the most striking consequence of the 1974 reforms has been the dramatic increase in the importance of donations by individuals. These contributions were always the mainstay of NDP finances. Now, because of the tax credit for political donations and the older parties' adoption of sophisticated direct-mail techniques of fundraising first developed in the United States,[32] contributions by individuals are a major source of income for all three main political parties. Contributions from individuals have exceeded business contributions to both the PC and Liberal parties in several of the years since the tax credit came into effect. The same is true of candidates' revenue. NDP candidates receive very little from corporate donors, but depend heavily on trade union contributions. The Canadian Alliance relies overwhelmingly on contributions from individuals, as does the Bloc Québécois. Figure 9.1 shows the chief sources of revenue for the five parties represented in the House of Commons in 2000. Figure 9.2 provides information on party spending during the election.

On the face of it, then, the Liberal and Conservative parties' traditional financial dependence on business appears to have been diluted. This should not blind us, however, to the continuing importance of corporate donations for the older parties. They still account for close to half of total contributions during election years and roughly 40–50 per cent between elections. Moreover, very large corporate contributions still account for a sizable share of the older parties' total revenues. If we define a large corporate donation as being at least $10,000, we find

Figure 9.1   Sources of Contributions to the Bloc Québécois, Liberal, Alliance, New Democratic, and Progressive Conservative Parties, 2000

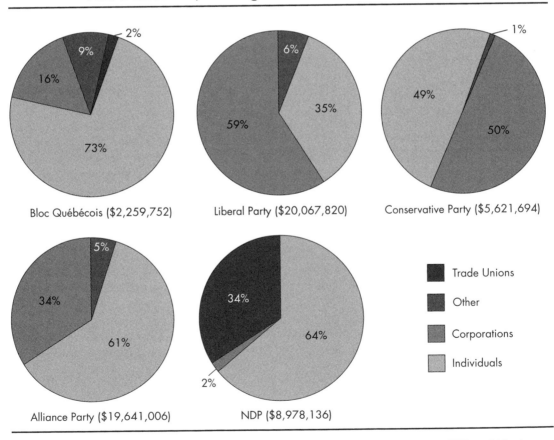

Bloc Québécois ($2,259,752)

Liberal Party ($20,067,820)

Conservative Party ($5,621,694)

Alliance Party ($19,641,006)

NDP ($8,978,136)

■ Trade Unions
■ Other
■ Corporations
□ Individuals

Source: Canada, Elections Canada, Contributions to registered political parties by donor category, 2000, available at www.elections.ca

Figure 9.2   Election Spending by Political Parties, Including the Percentage Spent on Print and Broadcast Adverstising* (in millions)

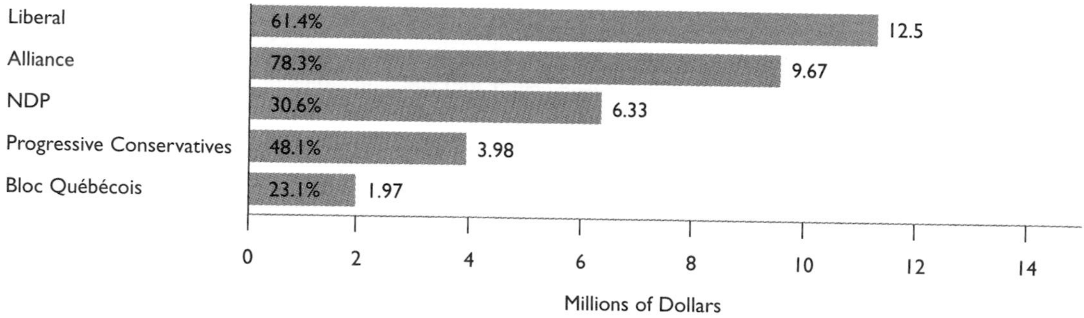

Note: These amounts do not include spending by individual candidates.

*The percentage spent on broadcasting and other forms of advertising is shown within each bar.

Source: Elections Canada, Breakdown of Election Expenses of Registered Political Parties, 2000 election, www.elections.ca

that these contributions have accounted for about 15–30 per cent of total contributions for both the Liberals and Conservatives in recent years. This is a dramatic change from the days when party 'bagmen' collected all but a small fraction of party funds from the Toronto and Montreal corporate elites.

The most important consequence of special interest contributions to parties and individual politicians may be the access to policy-makers it buys for contributors. Although cases of influence-peddling come to light from time to time, it is usually a mistake to think of political contributions as payments offered in the expectation of receiving some particular favour. There are, no doubt, instances where firms that rely on government contracts for some part of their revenue, or hope to receive government business in the future, find it prudent to donate money to parties or candidates. But for most corporate contributors, and certainly for large donors like the banks and those leading industrial firms that are perennial contributors to the two older parties, there is no expectation of a specific quid pro quo.

So why do they bother? One explanation is that corporate political donations represent a sort of insurance premium. As the late Conservative strategist and political adviser Dalton Camp put it:

> For the wise donor, the financing of the political system may very well be a duty and an obligation to the system, but it is, as well, insurance against the unlikely—such as the ascendancy of socialism—or against occasional political aberration, a Walter Gordon budget, say, or a Carter report on tax reform [both perceived to be anti-business policies]. When such contingencies arise, the price for access is modest indeed.[33]

What Camp calls 'a duty and an obligation to the system' might also be described as an investment in two-party dominance. Business interests are often at loggerheads with both Liberal and Conservative governments over specific policies. But generally speaking, both of the two older parties are congenial towards corporate enterprise. Business can live with either a Liberal or Conservative government, and has a material interest in supporting the centrist politics that characterize the Canadian political system and in avoiding the polarization of party politics between the right and the left (as happened in the United Kingdom several decades ago).

In addition to helping finance a party system generally congenial to business interests, it has long been understood that donations help buy access. In the words of Dalton Camp: 'Toronto money merely [*sic!*] maintains access to the parties, keeping open essential lines of communication, corporate hotlines, so to speak, to the right ears at appropriate times.'[34] In many cases the sheer size and importance of a corporation will be sufficient to ensure a hearing when the corporation feels its interests are at stake. In any given year about half of the largest 100 industrial firms in Canada do not even contribute to either of the two older parties. It would be ridiculous to conclude that their lack of generosity cuts them off from direct access to political decision-makers. But all things being equal, contributions probably open the door a bit wider (see Box 9.4).

Is the distinction between bribery—contributions given in the expectation of a specific favour—and paying for access really a piece of hair-splitting sophistry? After all, if we acknowledge that contributions confer on the donor an advantage that is not available to those who cannot afford to donate thousands of dollars to political parties, are we not thereby acknowledging that party donations reinforce inequalities based on money? It is widely accepted that access is an important component of influence on policy. The fact that corporate donations are neither given nor received in the expectation that a particular contract or a specific legislative or regulatory output will ensue does not mean that there is no exchange. Money helps buy access. Obviously, it does not always ensure a sympathetic hearing. But in a political system in which groups are clamouring to be heard so that they may make their case to those who will ultimately make policy decisions, access to political decision-makers is a valuable commodity. As Camp observes, party donations are a modest price to pay for this advantage.

The link between party contributions and access has become more controversial with the increasing prominence of 'paid access opportunities'. These are fundraising events such as dinners and cocktail parties where, for an admission price that can range up to several thousand dollars, donors receive the opportunity to rub shoulders and exchange views with party leaders and other members of the government. Money obviously acts as a filter in determining who is likely to participate in such events, as does the party's invitation list. These fundraising events have been supplemented by an American invention, special clubs for large contributors. Both the Republican and Democratic parties have operated such clubs for years, where, for an individual contribution of thousands of dollars (higher for a corporate membership), the donor receives the chance to meet with important politicians, such as congressional committee chairpersons.[35] In Canada, the Progressive Conservatives were the first to establish such a club, their '500 Club'. The national Liberal Party operates a similar paid-admission elite network, as do many provincial parties.

In the eyes of some, paid access opportunities such as these raise an ethical question: at what point does the ability to pay for special access to political decision-makers subvert the democratic process by favouring those with the money to make their views known directly? Parties need funds to carry out their activities. Even with a tax credit for political contributions, only a small portion of all Canadian taxpayers contribute money directly to parties or candidates. The money has to come from somewhere, and such developments as paid access opportunities represent the parties' innovative search for stable sources of funds. One alternative would be to impose severe restrictions on how much money parties can spend, so that the relatively small contributions from individuals (publicly subsidized by the tax credit) and the public subsidy that candidates receive from the reimbursement provision of the Election Expenses Act would be sufficient to finance their activities. This would require that current levels of spending by the major parties and their candidates be cut back. Of course, the public subsidy to the parties

BOX 9.4   Do Corporate Donations Buy Access?

Nick Taylor, a former long-time Alberta Liberal Senator and party bagman, says big corporate money plays a critical role in getting access to the country's top policy-makers, adding that sometimes this access is translated into real influence.

Despite the fact that Prime Minister Jean Chrétien says he wants to end [the assumption] 'that money buys influence in politics', Mr Taylor said it's not just a perception, it's real.

'Money does have influence through access, money has too much influence, way too much. After all, we have a capitalist society. Access means you get in to tell your story. No cabinet minister could meet everybody in Canada. He or she [has] only so many hours in a day and maybe he could meet six to eight people each day, and if not him, the deputy minister, and if not him, the assistant deputy minister, and if not him, the director. In other words, there's this hierarchy that they have a say in a decision on [for example] what helicopters to buy for military or for taxes for construction and energy [sectors]. So, you want to put your case forward', Mr Taylor told *The Hill Times* last week.

'The banking industry has managed to run nearly a monopoly in Canada. They want to make more of a monopoly now. They want to merge. I don't think there's any bank president who doesn't have an access to any cabinet minister. The Canadian Bankers' Association throws one of the best parties on the Hill. I was chairman of a committee and everybody wants to appear before the committee but you can't hear everybody so you have to restrict it and those people [bankers] are seldom restricted. So, they get their chance to make their case.'

Asked why, if banks have so much influence, they can't simply succeed in their merger proposals, Senator Taylor said: 'I am not saying that a person with money succeeds every time they go. In other words, sometimes, it's a Chinese torture effect. They don't just suddenly jump on their private jet and fly to Ottawa and get what they want to get and go out again. It's a continuous process. That's why they have big departments, some people call them political action departments or public affairs. Every large corporation has a department whose sole job is to lobby.'

Moreover, Mr Taylor said cabinet ministers' aides go out of their way to help big corporations to get access and to arrange meetings with cabinet ministers because he said many hope that they might be hired by these corporations.

Mr Taylor said he thinks that there should be some law to stop cabinet ministers' assistants from going on to work for big private corporations for a certain number of years after they leave their jobs as aides to cabinet ministers.

'One of the problems in Ottawa and Edmonton are the assistants who are barely above the subsistence wage. They bend over backwards that access goes to large corporations. There should be a waiting period between working for a cabinet minister and then working for a large corporation.'

Adapted from *The Hill Times*:
<http://www.thehilltimes.ca/2003/february/17/rana/>.

could be increased. But this would serve to institutionalize the existing party system further, a criticism that has already been made of the public subsidies provided for in the 1974 reforms.

Despite sharp criticism from within his own party, Liberal Prime Minister Jean Chrétien introduced legislation that proposed to limit corporate and union contributions to parties, their candidates, and contenders for the leadership of registered political parties to $1,000 per year. The bill, scheduled to take effect on 1 January 2004, would also limit individual contributors to parties and candidates to $10,000 per year and move the public disclosure threshold for contributions to $200 from the current level of $100. To ease the pain of life with less private donation revenue, the Chrétien government also proposed to double the amount of the public subsidy to registered parties and candidates. Each party would receive an annual public subsidy of $1.50 for every vote obtained in the previous election.

Critics were quick to charge that these reforms, while perhaps having the salutary effect of reducing the parties' dependence on money from special interests, will also privilege the existing parties because the financing formula is based on results of the last election. Moreover, the Liberal Party is by far the biggest winner under this reformed system of party financing, a fact that led some to challenge Chrétien's claim that the reforms were only about cleaning up the tarnished image of parties beholden to special interests.

After all is said and done, however, we should not exaggerate the importance of corporate political contributions as a lever of influence on the behaviour of parties when in power. As Jeffrey Simpson observes:

> Even large corporations, in the era after reforms to the Elections Act, often spent more money on trade associations, the Business Council on National Issues, or lobbying firms than they did contributing to the non-socialist political parties. For them political contributions are a kind of civic duty whereas the money spent on lobbyists and the like can directly reward self-interest.[36]

These other paths of influence are discussed in the next chapter.

NOTES

1. Eugene A. Forsey, *How Canadians Govern Themselves* (Ottawa: Supply and Services Canada, 1982), 32.

2. Leon Epstein, *Political Parties in Western Democracies* (New Brunswick, NJ: Transaction Books, 1980 [1967]), 9.

3. John Meisel, 'Decline of Party in Canada', in Hugh G. Thorburn, ed., *Party Politics in Canada*, 4th edn (Scarborough, Ont.: Prentice-Hall, 1979).

4. This section was co-written with Professor A. Brian Tanguay, Wilfrid Laurier University.

5. George M. Hougham, 'The Background and Development of National Parties', in Hugh G. Thorburn, ed., *Party Politics in Canada* (Toronto: Prentice-Hall, 1963), 3.

6. Ibid., 13.

7. Escott Reid, 'The Rise of National Parties in Canada', in Hugh G. Thorburn, ed., *Party Politics in Canada*, 5th edn (Scarborough, Ont.: Prentice-Hall, 1985), 12. See also Norman Ward, *The Canadian House of Commons* (Toronto: University of Toronto Press, 1950), 157–62.

8. See, in particular, Martin Shefter, 'Party and Patronage: Germany, England, and Italy', *Politics and Society* 7, 4 (1977): 403–51; Epstein, *Political Parties in Western Democracies*, ch. 5.

9. André Siegfried, *The Race Question in Canada* (Toronto: McClelland & Stewart, Carleton Library Edition, 1966 [English translation first published 1907]), 114.

10. J.A. Corry, *Democratic Government and Politics*, 2nd edn (Toronto: University of Toronto Press, 1951), 22. Variations on this theme can be found in R.M. Dawson and Norman Ward, *The Government of Canada*, 5th edn (Toronto: University of Toronto Press, 1987), 430–3, and Hugh G. Thorburn, 'Interpretations of the Canadian Party System', in Thorburn, ed., *Party Politics in Canada*, 5th edn, 20–40. For a critique of the adequacy of brokerage theory, see Janine Brodie and Jane Jenson, *Crisis, Challenge and Change: Party and Class Revisited* (Ottawa: Carleton University Press, 1988), ch. 1.

11. Robert Alford, *Party and Society* (Westport, Conn.: Greenwood Press, 1963), 250–1. Alford computed his index of class voting by subtracting the percentage of non-manual workers voting for left parties (in Canada, the Liberals and the NDP, according to Alford) from the percentage of manual workers voting for the left parties, on the assumption that a party of the left should receive the bulk of its support from the traditional 'blue-collar' (manual) occupations. See the discussion ibid., chs 4 and 5. Obviously, Alford's index leaves a great deal to be desired and has been subjected to substantial criticism over the years. Many critics of his work are particularly exercised by his classification of the Liberal Party of Canada as a party of the left.

12. Ibid., 251.

13. Brodie and Jenson, *Crisis, Challenge and Change*.

14. Janine Brodie and Jane Jenson, 'Piercing the Smokescreen: Brokerage Parties and Class Politics', in Alain G. Gagnon and A. Brian Tanguay, eds, *Canadian Parties in Transition: Discourse, Organization, and Representation* (Scarborough, Ont.: Nelson, 1989), 28.

15. Ibid., 34.

16. Robert M. Campbell and Leslie A. Pal, *The Real Worlds of Canadian Politics* (Peterborough, Ont.: Broadview Press, 1989), 5.

17. Canadian Institute of Public Opinion, *The Gallup Report*, 'Confidence in Political Parties Declines', 1 Feb. 1989; 'Government Increas-ingly Becoming Object of Scorn Among Canadians', 20 Feb. 1991.

18. Walter Young, *The Anatomy of a Party: The National CCF, 1932–61* (Toronto: University of Toronto Press, 1969), 298, 300.

19. Canada, Royal Commission on Electoral Reform and Party Financing, *Reforming Electoral Democracy*, vol. 7 (Ottawa: Supply and Services Canada, 1991), 221.

20. 'Bleeding-Heart Conservatives', *The Economist*, 8 Oct. 1988, 4.

21. John Geddes, 'The Scare Factor: Is Stockwell Day too extreme for mainstream Canadian voters?', *Maclean's*, 10 July 2000.

22. William P. Irvine, *Does Canada Need a New Electoral System?* (Kingston: Institute of Intergovernmental Relations, Queen's University, 1979), 46–7.

23. Alan Cairns, 'The Electoral System and the Party System in Canada, 1921–1865', *Canadian Journal of Political Science* 1, 1 (Mar. 1968): 55–80.

24. Irvine, *Does Canada Need a New Electoral System?*, 14.

25. See Khayyam Paltiel, *Political Party Financing in Canada* (Toronto: McGraw-Hill Ryerson, 1970), 19–75.

26. These services are discussed by Reg Whitaker, *The Government Party: Organizing and Financing the Liberal Party of Canada, 1930–1958* (Toronto: University of Toronto Press, 1977), 204–6, 216–63.

27. According to Khayyam Paltiel, 'For the 1972 [national] election half the funds raised in Ontario by the Liberal Party were collected personally by the chairman of the party's Treasury Committee from 90 large corporations.' 'Campaign Financing in Canada and its Reform', in Howard Penniman, ed., *Canada at the Polls: The General Election of 1974* (Washington: American Enterprise Institute, 1975), 182.

28. See A.B. Stevenson, *Canadian Election Reform: Dialogue on Issues and Effects* (Toronto: Ontario Commission on Election Contributions and Expenses, 1982); Whitaker, *The Government Party*.

29. The number of hours per network and the division of time between the parties is determined by the CRTC. In deciding how much time each party receives the CRTC is guided by a formula weighted according to each party's share of the seats and popular vote in the previous election.

30. The Income Tax Act includes a graduated schedule of tax credits: 75 per cent for donations up to $100; 50 per cent for contributions between $100 and $550; and 33.3 per cent for amounts over $550, to a maximum tax credit of $500.

31. Khayyam Paltiel, 'Political Marketing, Party Finance, and the Decline of Political Parties', in Gagnon and Tanguay, eds, *Canadian Parties in Transition*, 342.

32. See Larry Sabato, *The Rise of Political Consultants* (New York: Basic Books, 1981), esp. ch. 4.

33. Dalton Camp, *Points of Departure* (Toronto: Deneau and Greenberg, 1979), 91.

34. Ibid.

35. Sabato, *The Rise of Political Consultants*, 279.

36. Jeffrey Simpson, *Spoils of Power* (Toronto: Collins, 1988), 372.

SUGGESTED READINGS

John Courtney, *Do Conventions Matter? Choosing National Party Leaders in Canada* (Montreal and Kingston: McGill-Queen's University Press, 1995). This is the single best source on party leadership selection by Canada's foremost expert on the subject.

William Cross, ed., *Political Parties, Representation, and Electoral Democracy in Canada* (Toronto: Oxford University Press, 2002). These essays, by many of Canada's leading students of political parties and elections, cover topics including leadership selection, western populism, television campaign coverage, and the relationship between parties and interest groups.

Hugh G. Thorburn and Alan Whitehorn, eds, *Party Politics in Canada*, 8th edn (Toronto: Prentice-Hall, 2001). Probably the most comprehensive reader on Canadian parties, this collection includes a mix of classic and more recent analyses.

Lisa Young, *Feminists and Party Politics* (Vancouver: University of British Columbia Press, 2000). Young provides a good analysis of the impact of feminism on party politics, including female representation, in Canada and the United States.

Review Exercises

1. Based on data available at the Web site of the Chief Electoral Officer of Canada <www.elections.ca> determine the following:

   (a) the number of seats each party would have received in the last general election under a straight proportional representation system; and

   (b) the number of votes and percentage of the vote received by each candidate in your constituency during the last federal election.

2. Visit the Web sites of two of the political parties represented in the House of Commons. To locate the parties' Web sites, go to <www.ccsd.ca/links.html>. Look under the heading 'Government', subheading 'Federal Parties'. Compare the depth and breadth of information provided about each party's history, current leader, and present policies.

3. How do Canadian political parties select their candidates? For information on this, visit the Web sites of a couple of the national political parties. Click on the party's constitution, looking for the rules on candidate selection.

Parliament Hill is a favourite site for interest group demonstrations, as in the case of this coalition of anti-abortion groups that gathered in Ottawa in May 2003.

Politics does not stop between election campaigns. Much of the effort to influence the actions of government is channelled through interest groups. This chapter examines their characteristics and the role they play in Canadian politics. Topics include the following:

- ❏ How many groups, representing what interests?
- ❏ The bias of the interest group system.
- ❏ Perspectives on interest groups.
- ❏ Ingredients of interest group success.
- ❏ The impact of federalism on interest groups.
- ❏ Strategies for influence.
- ❏ Advocacy advertising.
- ❏ Lobbying and lobbyists.

CHAPTER TEN

INTEREST GROUPS

Elections are democracy's showpiece. But as important as they are, the influence of elections on what governments do is usually rather blunt and indirect. Policies are far more likely to be determined by forces generated within the state and by the actions of organized groups outside of it than by the latest election results. Indeed, it may often seem that special interests dominate the policy-making process in democracies. Their attempts to influence government are unremitting. The resources they marshal are often impressive. And their access to policy-makers is, in the case of some organized interests, privileged. Compared to this, the role of elections and the influence of voters often appear feeble.

Interest groups or *pressure groups*—the terms may be used interchangeably—have been defined as 'private associations . . . [that] promote their interests by attempting to influence government rather than by nominating candidates and seeking responsibility for the management of government'.[1] They arise from a very basic fact of social life, the reality of diversity in the interests and values of human beings. This diversity, in turn, gives rise to what James Madison called **political factions**: groups of citizens whose goals and behaviour are contrary to those of other groups or to the interests of the community as a whole.[2] If these factions, or special interests as we are apt to call them today, appear to overshadow the public interest in democracies, there is a simple explanation for this. The tug of one's personal interests—as an automotive worker, teacher, farmer, or postal worker—tend to be felt more keenly than the rather nebulous concept of the public interest. Arguments that appeal to such general interests as consumer benefits or economic efficiency are unlikely to convince the farmer whose income is protected by the production quotas and price floors set by a marketing board. But economic interests are not the only basis for factionalism in politics. Such group characteristics as ethnicity, language, religion, race, gender, and shared values may also provide the basis for the political organization of interests.

Economically based or not, interest groups are distinguished by the fact that they seek to promote goals that are not shared by all members of society. Paradoxically, however, their success in achieving these goals often depends on their ability to associate their efforts with the broader public interest. 'What is good for General Motors is good for America'[3] may or may not be true. Nevertheless, the slogan makes good sense as a strategy for promoting the interests of GM, North American automobile producers, and business interests generally.

CHARTING THE TERRITORY

The world of interest groups is both vast and characterized by enormous variety. Although no unified reliable list of interest groups exists for Canada or any other democracy, some idea of the sheer number of groups may be had from *Associations Canada*.[4] Its 2002 edition lists almost 20,000 organizations, not all of which would meet the criterion of attempting to influence government action. Many groups focus exclusively on non-political activities like providing services and information to their members. But several thousand perform political functions for their members on a regular or occasional basis.

Almost every imaginable interest is represented by an organization. There are several hundred women's associations across Canada, close to

1,000 environmental groups, over 2,000 business associations, perhaps 500 organizations representing agricultural interests, about 200 that focus on Aboriginal issues[5]—the range of organized interests and the sheer number of groups within each general category of interests are enormous. Impressive as these figures may seem, they do not provide a complete map of Canada's associational system. They do not, for example, include those transitory groups that emerge briefly around a single issue and then disappear from the scene. Nor do they include international organizations that may attempt to influence the actions of Canadian governments. But however we draw its boundaries, the universe of organized interests is vast.

While it is impossible to say exactly how many of these associations qualify as interest groups, there can be no doubt that a large number of them are politically active. One way to get a sense of this is to look at the list of groups that make representations to a legislative body or government-sponsored commission considering some issue. For example, well over 1,000 groups made representations and submitted briefs to the Royal Commission on Aboriginal Peoples during its six months of public hearings in 1993. The Commission on the Future of Health Care in Canada received submissions from 429 groups and associations during the public consultation phase of its work in 2001. Alternatively, one may look at the composition of some politically active organizations. Approximately 700 women's organizations are represented by the National Action Committee on the Status of Women, which lobbies governments on their behalf. The Canadian Chamber of Commerce, one of whose main functions is to influence government policies, represents over 500 community and provincial chambers of commerce and boards of trade, as well as close to 100 trade and professional associations and many international organizations (such as the Canada-Taiwan Business Association). In short, the size of the interest group system is considerable.

THE BIAS OF THE INTEREST GROUP SYSTEM

The notion that the pressure system is automatically representative of the whole community is a myth. . . . The system is skewed, loaded and unbalanced in favor of a fraction of a minority.[6]

It goes without saying that some interest groups are more influential than others. But which ones are the most powerful? Why? Is the interest group system biased 'in favor of a fraction of a minority', as E.E. Schattschneider claims?

Schattschneider argues that the interest group system—he calls it the pressure system—has a business and upper-class bias. Writing about American politics in the early 1960s, he observed that business associations comprised the single largest group of organized interests in American society, they were far more likely than other interests to lobby government, and they tended to spend much more money on attempting to influence policy-makers than other interest groups. Moreover, Schattschneider cites impressive evidence demonstrating that 'even non-business organizations reflect an upper-class tendency.'[7] Those with higher than average incomes and/or years of formal education are more likely to belong to organized groups than those lower down the socio-economic ladder. He explains the business and upper-class bias of interest group politics as being a product of both superior resources and the relatively limited size and exclusive character of these special interests. 'Special-interest organizations', he argues, 'are most easily formed when they deal with small numbers of individuals [or corporations] who are acutely aware of their exclusive interests.'[8] This awareness of special interests that are vital to one's material well-being or the well-being of one's organization is characteristic of trade associations like the Canadian Association of Petroleum Producers, the Canadian Bankers' Association, and a broader-based business organization like the Alliance of Canadian Manufacturers and Exporters Canada (formerly the Canadian Manufacturers' Association and the Canadian Exporters

Association), and also characterizes producer and occupational groups like the Quebec Dairy Association and the Ontario Medical Association. It is less likely to characterize organizations that represent more general interests.

Most social scientists and political journalists agree with Schattschneider. Charles Lindblom argues that business occupies a 'privileged position' in the politics of capitalist societies. In his book *Politics and Markets*,[9] Lindblom attributes this pre-eminence to business's superior financial resources and lobbying organization, greater access than other groups to government officials, and, most importantly, propagandistic activities that—directly through political advertising and indirectly through commercial advertising—reinforce the ideological dominance of business values in society.

One of the key factors most often cited by those who argue that business interests are politically superior is the **mobility of capital**. Investors enjoy a wide although not absolute freedom to shift their capital between sectors of the economy and from one national economy to another. The epitome of this mobility is found in the transnational corporation—an enterprise whose activities span a number of national economies and whose international character often is used as a lever in dealing with the government of a particular country. In addition to being territorially mobile, investment capital also has the capacity to expand and contract in response to investors' perceptions of the political-economic climate for business. Short of imposing punitive tax rates on savings, governments cannot force business and private investors to invest. Governments in all capitalist societies are concerned with levels of business confidence and are reluctant to take actions that carry a high risk of causing a cutback in investment. The consequences of such a cutback are felt politically by governments. Weak economic activity tends to translate into popular dissatisfaction and a loss of political support.[10]

The mobility of capital gives rise, in turn, to concern with *business confidence*. Politicians need

to care about business confidence because of the very real possibility that they will not be re-elected if business's unwillingness to invest causes unemployment and falling incomes. But another factor that gives pause even to governments that can count on strong popular backing is the state's financial dependence on business. A decline in the levels of investment or profit will soon be felt as a drop in government revenues from the taxation of corporate and employment income, payroll taxes, and the taxation of consumption. The problem of falling revenues is almost certain to be compounded by an increase in state expenditures on social programs, the costs of which are sensitive to changes in the level of economic activity. Borrowing on the public credit is only a temporary solution to this dilemma, and experience has shown this to be both costly and subject to the limits of international investor confidence.

Neither Lindblom nor anyone else would argue that business interests 'win' all of the time, or even that powerful business groups cannot experience major defeats. Instead, they maintain that there is a tendency to favour business interests over others because of systemic characteristics of capitalist societies. This is one of the few propositions about politics that manages to cut across the ideological spectrum, attracting support from the left and right alike (if rather more heavily from the left).[11] There are, however, dissenters.

Those who teach or write for a business school audience, for example, are likely to view business interests as being simply one set of interests in a sea of competing interest group claims on government.[12] Business historian Michael Bliss argues that whatever privileged access business people may have enjoyed in the corridors of political power and whatever superiority business interests may have had in relation to rival claims on government had largely disappeared by the 1980s. 'Groups with powerful vested interests,' he writes, 'including trade unions, civil servants, tenured academics, and courtesanal cultural producers, perpetuated a hostility toward business enterprise rooted in their own fear of competition on open markets.'[13]

In what is perhaps the most compelling rebuttal to the 'privileged position' thesis, David Vogel argues that, on balance, 'business is more affected by broad political and economic trends than it is able to affect them.'[14] Although Vogel focuses on the United States, he develops a more general argument about the political power of business interests in capitalist democracies. Popular opinion and the sophistication of interest group organization, he maintains, are key to understanding the political successes and failures of business and other interest groups. Vogel argues that business's ability to influence public policy is greatest when the public is worried about the long-term strength of the economy and weakest when the economy's ability to produce jobs and to increase incomes is taken for granted.

The political organization of business interests is the second key to understanding the ebb and flow of business influence. Vogel maintains that the victories of environmental, consumer, and other public interest groups in the 1960s and 1970s were largely due to their ability to read the Washington map and work the levers of congressional and media politics. Business interests, by comparison, were poorly organized and amateurish. Since then, however, the political mobilization of business has been without equal. But despite its organizational prowess, divisions within the business community have generally served to check its influence on public policy.

Another factor that prevents business interests from dominating politics is what James Q. Wilson has called 'entrepreneurial politics'.[15] This involves the ability of politicians and interest groups to identify issues around which popular support can be mobilized in opposition to business interests. The opportunities for entrepreneurial politics are fewer in Canada than in the United States because of the tighter party discipline in Canada's legislature. Entrepreneurial politics, however, is practised by interest groups on issues ranging from the protection of seals off the coast of Newfoundland to the promotion of social justice issues. Astute use of the media and adept packaging of a group's message to generate public awareness and support for its goals are central to entrepreneurial politics.

So who is right? Are business interests perched securely atop the heap of the interest group system in capitalist societies, or do business groups have to slug it out in the political trenches just like other groups and with no more likelihood of victory? Perhaps neither position is right. This is the conclusion suggested by much of the recent work on Canadian interest groups, what Paul Pross calls *post-pluralism* and others have called *neo-institutionalism*.

This approach is based on a simple observable fact: policy-making generally involves the participation of a relatively limited set of state and societal actors, a **policy community** centred around a sub-government; i.e., that set of state institutions and interest groups usually involved in making and implementing policy in some field. We will have more to say about the approach later in the chapter. For now, the point is simply that groups representing business interests may or may not be members of a sub-government or policy community. Whether they are and how influential they are depends on the policy field in question and on the particular configuration of interests that are active in the policy community. Moreover, neo-institutionalists tend to emphasize the capacity of state actors to act independently of the pressures and demands placed on them by societal interests. This capacity will vary across policy sectors. But the bottom line of the neo-institutionalist approach is that state actors in some policy communities may be quite capable of resisting pressures coming from highly organized, well-heeled business interests—or from any societal interests, for that matter.

PERSPECTIVES ON INTEREST GROUPS

Pluralism

Pluralism or group theory may be defined as an explanation of politics that sees organized interests as the central fact of political life and that explains politics chiefly in terms of the activities of groups. It is a societal explanation of politics in that it locates the main causes of government action in the efforts and activities of voluntary associations—trade associations, labour unions, churches, PTAS, etc.—outside the state. When it turns its attention to considering the role and character of the state in democratic societies, pluralist theory draws two main conclusions. First, the state itself is viewed as a sort of group interest or, more precisely, as an assortment of different interests associated with various components of the state. Second, despite the possibility that the state may have interests of its own, its chief political function is to ratify the balance of group interests in society and to enforce the policies that embody this balance of power. As Earl Latham graphically put it: 'The legislature referees the group struggle, ratifies the victories of the successful coalition, and records the terms of the surrenders, compromises, and conquests in the form of statutes.'[16]

The purest embodiment of group theory is found in the work of Arthur Bentley. Society, Bentley argues, can only be understood in terms of the groups that comprise it. He views government as simply a process of 'groups pressing one another, forming one another, and pushing out new groups and group representatives (the organs or agencies of government) to mediate the adjustments.'[17] This is an extremely reductionist approach. Pluralists after Bentley, figures like David Truman, Robert Dahl, and John Kenneth Galbraith,[18] have certainly been aware of the danger of trying to squeeze too much explanation out of a single cause. But they have remained faithful to a couple basic elements of pluralist theory, one empirical and the other normative. The empirical element is the claim that politics is a competitive process where power is widely distributed, there is no single ruling elite or dominant class, and the interaction of organized interests outside the state is the chief force behind the actions of government. The normative element suggests that the

outcome of this competitive struggle among groups represents the public interest and, indeed, that this is the only reasonable way of understanding the public interest in democracy.

Pluralism begat *neo-pluralism*. The neo-pluralist assault took issue with both the empirical and normative claims of group theory. Writers like E.E. Schattschneider, Theodore Lowi, and Charles Lindblom had little difficulty in showing that the interest group system was much less open and competitive than the earlier pluralists had argued. Regarding pluralism's normative features, Lowi took aim at its equation of the public interest with the outcome of struggles between special interests. He argued that the special interest state—what Lowi called interest group liberalism—actually trivializes the public interest and ends up undermining it by pretending that it is no more than the latest set of deals struck between the powerful through the intermediary offices of government. 'Interest group liberalism', he argued, 'seeks pluralistic government, in which there is no formal specification of means or of ends. In pluralistic government there is therefore no substance. Neither is there procedure. There is only process.'[19]

As if these indictments were not enough, pluralism also stands accused of misunderstanding the true character of political power. By focusing on group competition, their critics argue, pluralists are inclined to see political life as relatively open and competitive because they emphasize the observable struggles between groups and the decisions of governments. But as Bachrach and Baratz suggest, 'power may be, and often is, exercised by confining the scope of decision-making to relatively "safe" issues.'[20] Non-decision-making, the ability to keep issues unformulated and off the public agenda, is a form of power. Considered from this angle, the interest group system appears much less competitive.

Class Analysis

Viewed through the prism of class analysis, interest groups do not disappear, but their edges become blurred and they take a back seat to the class interests these groups are argued to represent. Some of the major works of contemporary Marxist scholarship do not even mention such terms as 'interest group', 'pressure group', or 'social group'.[21] There is no heading for interest groups in either the table of contents or the index to *The New Practical Guide to Canadian Political Economy*, a bibliographic reference book for class analysis writings in Canada.[22] Nor are interest groups given more than an occasional mention in a standard collection on Canadian class analysis.[23]

This is not to say that the reality of organized interests in politics is either denied or ignored by class analysis. Ralph Miliband has written that:

> Democratic and pluralist theory could not have achieved the degree of ascendancy which it enjoys in advanced capitalist society had it not at least been based on one plainly accurate observation about [pressure groups], namely that they permit and even encourage a multitude of groups and associations to organize openly and freely and to compete with each other for the advancement of such purposes as their members may wish.[24]

Miliband's *The State in Capitalist Society* devotes an entire chapter to the role of organized interests in an attempt to refute the pluralist model. Some Canadian examples of how class analysis can include a careful analysis of interest groups include Wallace Clement's *The Challenge of Class Analysis*[25] and Rianne Mahon's study of Canada's textile industry. Clement examines the complex network of unions, co-operatives, and associations in Canada's coastal fisheries in order to, in his words, 'lend understanding to the material basis of class struggle'.[26] In *The Politics of Industrial Restructuring*, Mahon develops a sophisticated analysis of trade associations and labour unions in the textile sector in terms of the fundamental class interests they represent, the organizational capacity of these interests, and their ideological characteristics.[27]

But interest groups, from the perspective of class analysis, are not the basic units of society

and political life; classes are. And so organized groups are seen as the bearers of more fundamental interests and ideologies, namely those of classes and their factions. This enables one to acknowledge the uniqueness of individual groups and associations while focusing on larger collective interests represented by individual groups. An association like the Canadian Council of Chief Executives, which represents 150 of the largest private-sector corporations in Canada, would be seen as a representative of 'monopoly capital'. The Alliance of Canadian Manufacturers and Exporters, although it represents over 3,000 corporations spanning virtually all manufacturing industries and ranging in size from thousands of employees to a mere handful, is viewed as an organizational voice for the manufacturing faction of the capitalist class. In fact, some class analyses characterize this organization of manufacturers and exporters as an instrument of the oligopolistic, American-oriented faction of the capitalist class. Labour unions are, of course, viewed from this perspective as representative of subordinate class interests and ideologies, as are groups representing women, Natives, and ethnic and racial minorities.

Corporatism

Corporatism is a political structure characterized by the direct participation of organizations representing business and labour in public policymaking. 'In its core,' states Jurg Steiner, 'corporatism in a modern democracy deals with the interactions among organized business, organized labor, and the state bureaucracy. These three actors cooperate at the national level in the pursuit of the public good.'[28] Such structures are associated to varying degrees with several of the capitalist democracies of Western Europe, including Sweden, Austria, the Netherlands, Germany, and Switzerland.

The distinctiveness of corporatism as an interest group system is based on three characteristics. One is the existence of *peak associations* for business and labour. These are organizations that can credibly claim to represent all significant interests within the business and labour communities, respectively, and that have the ability to negotiate on behalf of the interests they represent. A second characteristic of a corporatist interest group system is the formal integration of business and labour into structures of state authority. Under corporatism, these interests do not simply have privileged access to state policy-makers, they have *institutionalized access*. A third characteristic of corporatism is its ideology of social partnership. As William Coleman says of corporatist ideology in Austria, 'There is a commitment to allow class conflict to grow only so far before it is internalized and addressed in ways judged a "fair" compromise.'[29] Compared to pluralism, which is characterized by an intensely competitive interest group system that stands outside the state, a corporatist system is more consensus-oriented and obliterates the barriers between the state and the societal interests represented through corporatist decision-making structures.

What possible relevance can the corporatist model have to an understanding of interest groups in Canada? The peak associations of business and labour necessary to make corporatism work do not exist in Canada. The most inclusive of Canadian business associations, the Canadian Chamber of Commerce, is on closer inspection just a loose federation of provincial and local chambers, individual corporations, and trade associations. The national organization exercises no control over its members, and the sheer range of interests represented within the CCC obliges it to focus mainly on very general issues—lower corporate taxation, cutting the level of government spending, reducing the amount of government regulation of business—where there is broad consensus among business people.[30] On labour's side, the ability of an association to claim to represent Canadian workers is weakened by the fact that fewer than four out of 10 members of the labour force belong to a union. The Canadian Labour Congress is the largest of Canada's labour associations, with close to 100 affiliated unions that represent about 2 million workers. This is only about 15 per cent of the total labour force. Unions representing mainly francophone workers have preferred to affiliate with the Confédération des syndicats nationaux.

The two other requirements for corporatism—tripartite decision-making structures bringing together the state, business, and labour, and an ideology of social partnership between business and labour—are also absent from the Canadian scene. Indeed, Gerhard Lehmbruch, one of the leading students of corporatism, places Canada in the group of countries having the fewest characteristics of corporatism.[31] Canadian political scientist William Coleman agrees with this assessment, although he notes that corporatist policy-making networks are found in the agricultural sector of the Canadian economy.[32]

Some observers have claimed to detect elements of corporatism in various tripartite consensus-building efforts launched by governments in Canada and in the practice of labour and business organizations being invited to appoint representatives to various public boards and tribunals. Past examples have included the Economic Council of Canada and the Canadian Labour Market and Productivity Centre—both of which are now defunct—and task forces on industrial restructuring orchestrated by Ottawa between 1975 and 1978. Some of the provinces, particularly Quebec, have experimented with tripartite consensus-building, and the periodic 'economic summits' organized by Ottawa and several of the provinces from time to time have been interpreted by some as signs of incipient corporatism.[33] None of these has produced any fundamental change in the process of economic policy-making. The obstacles to corporatism in Canada are enormous, including such factors as British parliamentary structures that centralize power in the hands of the Prime Minister and cabinet, a political culture that does not encourage the interventionist planning associated with corporatism, the decentralization of authority in both the business and labour communities, and the division of economic powers between Ottawa and the provinces. Whether or not corporatist-style interest mediation is desirable or not is a different question.[34]

Neo-Institutionalism

Neo-institutionalism is a perspective on policy-making that emphasizes the impact that structures and rules, formal and informal, have on political outcomes. '[T]he preferences and rules of policy actors', argue Coleman and Skogstad, 'are shaped fundamentally by their structural position. Institutions are conceived as structuring political reality and as defining the terms and nature of political discourse.'[35] What does this mean and how does it help us understand the behaviour and influence of interest groups?

First, what has been called neo-institutionalism or the new institutionalism is not so much a model of politics and policy-making as a theoretical premise shared by an otherwise diverse group of perspectives. The premise is, quite simply, that institutions—their structural characteristics, formal rules, and informal norms—play a central role in shaping both the actions of individuals and of the organizations to which they belong. This 'insight' is neither very new nor very surprising. The founders of modern sociology knew the importance of institutions in determining behaviour, a relationship that is most pithily expressed in Robert Michels's aphorism, 'He who says organization, says oligarchy.'[36] Moreover, few of us would blink at the rather bland assertion that 'where you stand depends on where you sit.' So where is the 'neo' in neo-institutionalism, and what special contribution can it make to understanding interest groups? Let us begin by examining the diverse roots of the neo-institutionalist approach. They include the following.

Economics
Rational choice theory forms the bedrock of modern economics. Beginning in the 1950s and 1960s, economists began to apply systematically the concepts of individual (limited) rationality and market behaviour to the study of elections, political parties, interest groups, bureaucracy, and other political phenomena.[37] The economic theory of politics that has developed from this work emphasizes the role played by rules, formal and informal, in shaping individual choices and policy outcomes. Viewed from this perspective, 'institutions are bundles of rules that make collective action possible.'[38]

Organization Theory
Appropriately enough, organization theory has been an important source of inspiration and ideas for the neo-institutionalist approach. One of the first political scientists to apply the behavioural insights of organization theory to Canadian politics was Alan Cairns. His 1977 presidential address to the Canadian Political Science Association relied heavily on organization theory in arguing that Canadian federalism is influenced mainly by state actors, the 'needs' of the organizations they belong to, and the constitutional rules within which they operate.[39] James March, Herbert Simon, and Johan Olsen are among the organization theorists frequently cited by neo-institutionalists.[40] The spirit of the organizational perspective is captured in Charles Perrow's declaration that 'The formal structure of the organization is the single most important key to its functioning.'[41]

Society-Centred Analysis
The rising popularity of neo-institutional analysis can be attributed in part to a reaction against explanations of politics and policy-making that emphasize the role of such societal factors as interest groups, voters, and social classes. This reaction has produced an enormous outpouring of work on the autonomy of the state (i.e., the ability of state actors to act on their own preferences and to shape societal demands and interest configurations rather than simply responding to and mediating societal interests). Neo-institutionalism, which focuses on the structural characteristics of and relationships between

political actors, has been inspired by this same reaction. This is not to say that neo-institutionalism is a state-centred explanation of politics. But in ascribing a key role to institutions, structures, and rules, it inevitably takes seriously the structural characteristics of the state.

Neo-institutionalism deals intensively with what might be called the interior lives of interest groups: the factors responsible for their creation, maintenance, and capacity for concerted political action. James Q. Wilson identifies four categories of incentives that underlie the interior dynamics of interest groups.[42] They include:

- *material incentives*—tangible rewards that include money and other material benefits that clearly have a monetary value;
- *specific solidarity incentives*—intangible rewards such as honours, official deference, and recognition that are scarce, i.e., they have value precisely because some people are excluded from their enjoyment;
- *collective solidarity incentives*—intangible rewards created by the act of associating together in an organized group and enjoyed by all members of the group, such as a collective sense of group esteem or affirmation;
- *purposive incentives*—Wilson describes these as being 'intangible rewards that derive from the sense of satisfaction of having contributed to the attainment of a worthwhile cause'.

Economists have also attempted to explain what Mancur Olson first called the logic of collective action, including how the interior character of a group affects its capacity for political influence.

Neo-institutionalism tends to agnosticism when it comes to the old debate on whether societal or state forces are more important determinants of political outcomes. Such concepts as *policy communities*—the constellation of actors in a particular policy field—or *policy networks*[43]—the nature of the relationships between the key actors in a policy community—are the building blocks of the neo-institutional approach. Embedded in them is the irrefutable claim that 'the state'

is in fact a fragmented structure when it comes to actual policy-making. So, too, is society. Those who are active and influential on the issue of abortion, for example, are very different from those who are part of the official-language policy community. What Coleman and Skogstad describe as the 'diversity in arrangements between civil society and the state'[44] inspires agnosticism on the state versus society debate. The reality is that the relative strength of state and societal actors and the characteristics of policy networks vary between policy communities in the same society and, moreover, the line between state and society often is not very distinct. Paul Pross's visual depiction of what a policy community looks like conveys a good sense of the complexity and potential for fluidity in the relations between interest groups and the state (see Figure 10.1).

A group's capacity for influence within a policy community will depend on both its internal characteristics and its external relationships to the larger political system and the state. Philippe Schmitter and Wolfgang Streeck call these the logics of membership and influence, respectively.[45] We have already mentioned some of the factors that may be relevant to understanding a group's interior life. On the logic of influence, Coleman and Skogstad argue that the key determinant of a group's influence is 'the structure of the state itself at the sectoral level',[46] i.e., within a particular policy community. Perhaps. But *macro*-political factors like political culture, the dominant ideology, and the state system's more general characteristics are also important to understanding the political influence of organized interests. Policy communities are perhaps best viewed as solar systems that are themselves influenced by the gravitational tug of cultural and institutional forces emanating from the centre of the larger galaxy in which they move. In this way the diversity of state-society relations between policy communities can be reconciled with larger generalizations about the interest group system, such as Lindblom's claim that business interests occupy a privileged position within this system.

THE INGREDIENTS OF INTEREST GROUP SUCCESS

There is no magic recipe for group influence. Successful strategies and appropriate targets will depend on the issue, the resources and actions of other groups, the state of public opinion, and characteristics of the political system. But although there is no single formula for influence, it is nevertheless possible to generalize about the factors

Figure 10.1   Policy Community 'Bubble Diagram'

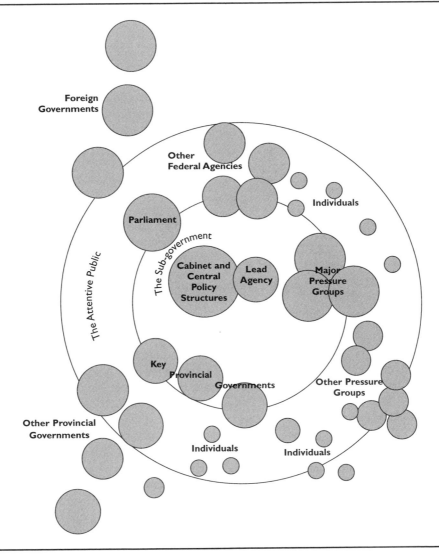

Source: Paul Pross, 'Pressure Groups: Talking Chameleons', in M.S. Whittington and G. Williams, eds, *Canadian Politics in the 1990s* (Toronto: Nelson, 1995), 267.

associated with powerful interest groups. As we will see, these factors are more likely to characterize business groups and their dealings with government than any other set of societal interests.

Organization

It may seem a trite observation, but organized interests are usually more influential than unorganized ones and are always better equipped to apply sustained pressure on policy-makers. A lone person who writes a letter to the Prime Minister demanding that the government act in a particular way is unlikely to make much of an impact, even if that person is someone of national stature. Tens of thousands of people writing to the Prime Minister and taking to the streets are more likely to get the Prime Minister's attention. Their impact will be even greater if it is channelled through an organization or organizations that can credibly claim to speak on behalf of these thousands of like-minded people, and that are skilled at media and government relations. The unco-ordinated efforts of individuals and the fury of a spontaneous mob can have an impact on policy-makers. But this impact is unlikely to be sustained without organization.

Paul Pross, Canada's foremost student of interest groups, points to the character of modern government and the policy-making process in explaining why organization is crucial. Modern government, he observes, is a sprawling, highly bureaucratized affair in which the power to influence policy is widely diffused. When government was smaller, the number of policies and programs affecting societal interests were fewer, power was concentrated in the hands of a small group of senior bureaucratic officials and cabinet, and groups did not require sophisticated organizational structures to manage their dealings with government. This was the era of the 'mandarins', the tightly knit group of deputy ministers who dominated the policy process.[47] Pathways to influence were relatively uncomplicated. A conversation with the minister or deputy minister in

the restaurant of the Chateau Laurier or at the Five Lakes Fishing Club was the preferred method of communicating a group's views. Access at this rarefied level was, however, restricted largely to members of the corporate elite and those representing their interests.

This era began to pass into history during the 1960s. The more complex interventionist state that emerged was not as amenable to the informal, discreet style of influence that powerful economic interests had grown used to during the 1940s and 1950s. As the scope of state intervention widened and its regulation of economic and social matters deepened, it became increasingly imperative that groups have the ongoing capacity to monitor government and deal with it at those levels where power resided. Inevitably, a large intrusive state means that power is more widely diffused throughout the administrative apparatus of government, in the hands of officials who draw up regulatory guidelines, interpret and administer technical matters delegated to them under the authority of vaguely worded statutes, and provide advice on programs and policies that influence the options considered by those nominally in charge, i.e., the members of cabinet.

To deal with the reality of the modern administrative state, groups require organization. And organize they have. William Coleman shows that close to half of the associations representing business interests have been created since 1960.[48] A veritable explosion of associations representing environmental concerns, consumer interests, women, ethnic groups, official-language minorities, and other interests has occurred over the last few decades. Interest groups acquired prominence later in Canada than in the United States, and when they did it was largely due to a defensive reaction against a state that, like Kafka's castle, was fast becoming more impenetrable and mysterious—not to mention hostile from the standpoint of those in the business community.

The increasing size and complexity of the public sector spawned organized interests in another way as well. The active role of government in promoting the creation of associations that would in turn represent and articulate the interests of their group interests is well documented. It is a phenomenon that appears to have begun in World War I, when the federal Department of Trade and Commerce encouraged the creation of trade associations to represent corporations in the same industry.[49] During the 1960s and 1970s, the Department of Secretary of State was instrumental in the creation and proliferation of a large number of organizations representing women, ethnic groups, and official-language minorities, particularly through the provision of core funding to finance the activities of these groups.[50] In many cases it appears that the motivation of the state agencies that encouraged the creation of interest groups was at least partly self-serving. They were helping to organize the interests that depended on their programs and budgets and thereby created constituencies whose support could be useful to the bureaucracy in protecting its policy and budgetary turf.[51]

This practice of state funding for organized groups continues today. For example, Canadian Parents for French, a group that is active in promoting French-language schools in English-speaking Canada, receives a large part of its budget from the Official Languages Support Programs Branch of the Department of Canadian Heritage. The Multiculturalism Program of Canadian Heritage funds a wide array of ethnic, racial, religious, and cultural organizations in Canada, many of which lobby government officials or attempt to influence public opinion on matters of concern to them. Many Aboriginal and human rights groups receive a large part of their funding from the Canadian government. The Court Challenges Program has provided funding for over 20 years to organizations representing 'members of historically disadvantaged groups' or official-language minorities. The Women's Legal Education and Action Fund (LEAF), a regular and prominent intervener in Charter cases involving alleged sexual discrimination, has often received funding under this program, usually between $35,000 and $50,000 per case.

Despite some setbacks in the courts, Ottawa has persisted in its effort to restrict the ability of groups and individuals other than political parties and their candidates to advertise during election campaigns. Under revisions to the Canada Elections Act passed in 2000—opposed only by Canadian Alliance MPs—so-called 'third parties' may not spend more than about $150,000 nationally on campaign advertising that 'promotes or opposes a registered party or the election of a candidate, including by taking a position on an issue with which the registered party or candidate is associated.' The limit that may by spent on advertising in a particular election district is about $3,000. By way of comparison, the Elections Act limits any registered party and its candidates to $12 million nationally during the official 36-day federal election campaign and another $18 million locally, in addition to free air time that broadcasters are required to provide. The 2000 reforms also impose on groups and individuals who spend on campaign advertising a system of registration regulation and reporting requirements broadly similar to that which exists for registered parties and candidates. The National Citizens' Council immediately launched a court challenge to these restrictions, which they and other critics call a 'gag law', and in June 2001 an Alberta court struck down the spending limits as unconstitutional but upheld the registration and regulation requirements imposed on third-party campaign advertisers. The Alberta court decision was appealed in May 2002 and may well reach the Supreme Court.

Sophisticated organization has become a *sine qua non* for sustained group influence. Paul Pross uses the term **institutional groups** to describe those interests that possess the highest level of organization. These groups have the following characteristics:

- They possess organizational continuity and cohesion.
- They have extensive knowledge of those sectors of government that affect their clients, and enjoy easy communications with those sectors.

- They have stable memberships.
- They have concrete and immediate objectives.
- The overall goals of the organization are more important than any particular objective.[52]

While many different types of groups can lay claim to having these characteristics, there is no doubt that business associations are more likely to conform to Pross's criteria for institutionalized groups than are those representing other interests. Indeed, associations like the Canadian Council of Chief Executives, the Alliance of Manufacturers and Exporters, the Canadian Chamber of Commerce, the Conseil du Patronat du Québec, the Canadian Federation of Independent Business, and many of the major trade associations in Canada are among the most organizationally sophisticated interest groups in this country.

Resources

Lots of money is no guarantee of interest group success—but it usually doesn't hurt. It is no accident that the most organizationally sophisticated groups, which enjoy easy access to policy-makers and have the best track records of success in protecting and promoting the interests they represent, tend also to be well-heeled. Money is necessary to pay for the services that are vital to interest group success. A permanent staff costs money—a good deal of money if it includes lawyers, economists, accountants, researchers, public relations specialists, and others whose services are needed to monitor the government scene and communicate with both the group's membership and policy-makers. The services of public relations firms, polling companies, and

When NHL team owners in Canada, and their players, asked for government assistance in 1999, many Canadians saw them as just another special interest hoping to feed from the public trough. (Roy Peterson, *Vancouver Sun*)

professional lobbyists are costly and certainly out of the reach of many interest groups.

It hardly requires demonstration that interest groups representing business tend to have more affluent and stable financial footings than other groups. Their closest rivals are major labour associations, some occupational groups such as physicians, dentists, lawyers, university professors, and teachers, and some agricultural producer groups (see Figure 10.2). The budgets of some non-economic groups may also appear to be considerable. For example, in 2001 Pollution Probe had a budget of nearly $2.5 million. The National Action Committee on the Status of Women had a budget of roughly $500,000 for the same year. But there are three important differences between the monetary resources of the major business interest groups and those of other organized interests.

First, the members of business interest groups typically do not rely on their collective associations for political influence to the extent that the members of other interest groups do. Large corporations usually have their own public affairs departments that, among other functions, manage the organization's relations with government.

Moreover, corporations will often act on their own in employing the services of a professional lobbying firm or other service that is expected to help them influence policy-makers. Indeed, the clientele lists of such firms as Hill and Knowlton (formerly Public Affairs International), Government Consultants International, and Executive Consultants Ltd read like a 'Who's Who' of the Canadian corporate elite (with many non-Canadian corporate clients in the bargain). Corporations are also major contributors to the Liberal and Progressive Conservative parties—business associations seldom donate at all—and annual contributions in the $50,000–$100,000 range are not unusual. This is another channel of influence—purchasing access is a better way of describing it—that can be afforded by the individual members of business associations but seldom by the members of other types of interest groups.

The second important difference in the monetary resources of business and non-business associations relates to stability. Simply put, business groups rest on more secure financial footings. They are less subject to the vicissitudes of economic recession and because they do not

Figure 10.2   Annual Expenditures of Selected Associations, 2001

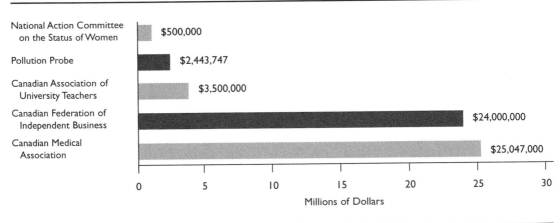

Note: Exact expenditure figures were provided by the CMA and Pollution Probe. Amounts for the other three associations are close estimates.

depend on government funding they are not exposed to the vagaries of cutbacks and budgetary shuffles. Many other groups cannot make this claim. 'We live and die on people in the street supporting wildlife conservation', said the president of the World Wildlife Fund in 1992. 'If Canadians don't have discretionary income', he added, 'it shows [in our revenues].'[53] Women's groups face a somewhat different problem. Their dependence on government funding became a liability during years of fiscal restraint and under a Conservative government that probably was tired of being attacked by women's groups. Core funding for these groups was slashed in the late 1980s and continued to fall in the mid-1990s under the Liberals. The National Action Committee on the Status of Women, which once depended on federal subsidies from Ottawa for most of its budget, today no longer receives any federal funding.

A third difference involves the ability of business and non-business groups to raise money to deal with a 'crisis' issue. Free trade and the federal election campaign of 1988 represent a case in point. Although no hard numbers exist, no one seriously denies that business associations in favour of the Canada–US Free Trade Agreement outspent their opponents by a wide margin in an attempt to influence public opinion on the deal and thereby ensure the election of the Conservatives, the only party that supported the FTA. Much of the pro-FTA money was spent through the Canadian Alliance for Trade and Job Opportunities, an ad hoc association financed by 112 Canadian-based corporations. Most of the major contributors to the Alliance were members of the elite Business Council on National Issues (see Box 10.1). The Alliance spent a good deal of money, probably at least $2 million, purchasing television and newspaper ads in the year before the election.[54] When a Conservative victory seemed in doubt, the Alliance financed a media blitz during the last three weeks of the 1988 campaign.

BOX 10.1 King of the Interest Group Hill: The CCCE

The Canadian Council of Chief Executives began life in 1976 as the Business Council on National Issues. It was modelled after the Business Roundtable, created in the United States two years earlier. Like the Business Roundtable, the CCCE was created in response to the perception in the corporate elite that big business was under attack from consumers' groups, environmentalists, and governments wedded to taxation and regulation policies. An organization representing the heavy hitters of the corporate world was needed to articulate big business's points of view and to defend its interests in the corridors of power.

The CCCE is composed of the 150 CEOs of major companies operating in the Canadian economy. Most of them do some part of their business outside of Canada and many are truly international in their production and sales activities. The CCCE has never included a government-controlled firm. As of 2002 member companies of the CCCE controlled about $2.1 trillion in assets, had yearly revenues of more than $500 billion, and employed close to 1.5 million Canadians.

As the senior voice of Canadian big business, the CCCE takes positions on a range of public policy issues, not simply economic ones. It was, for example, supportive of the Charlottetown Accord in 1992. The CCCE is believed by many to have been instrumental in persuading the Conservative government to propose free trade talks to the United States in 1985.

Deep pockets, however, will not always get the job done. During the late 1990s the Canadian corporate elite and its lead association, the Canadian Council of Chief Executives (CCCE), lobbied hard for the Multilateral Agreement on Investment. The MAI was a proposed treaty among the wealthy industrialized countries that would have imposed serious restrictions on governments' ability to discriminate against foreign investors through, for example, requirements that they source materials locally or meet other conditions for investing in a nation's economy. In the end, opposition to the MAI from labour unions and anti-globalization groups in Canada and abroad led the governments who were championing the MAI to abandon their efforts. The superior resources of the corporate backers of the MAI were not enough to win this particular battle.

Money is not the only resource that is useful in promoting an interest group's objectives. John Kingdon identifies several other resources that enable a group to influence what gets on (or stays off) the policy agenda and the alternatives considered by policy-makers.[55] These include electoral influence, the capacity to affect the economy negatively, and group cohesion.

Electoral Influence

The perceived ability to swing a significant bloc of votes is an important group resource. While all interest group leaders claim to speak on behalf of the group's membership, politicians know that the claim is more credible in some cases than in others. The sheer size of a group's membership can be an important resource, as can the status or wealth of its members and their geographic distribution. The distributional factor can cut in two ways. In political systems like Canada's, characterized by the election of a single member from each constituency, the concentration of a group's members in a particular region will, other things being equal, increase the political influence of that group. Candidates and parties are likely to see the advantage of proposing policies that are attractive to such a regionally concentrated group, whose votes are crucial to winning the seats in that region. On the other hand, geographic dispersion of a group's membership may also be advantageous, even under an electoral system like Canada's. A group's claim to speak on behalf of members who are found across the country, and who can be mobilized to vote in a particular way, can be an impressive electoral resource. It is, for example, an argument regularly used by the Canadian Federation of Independent Business, which has close to 100,000 members across Canada.

Capacity To Inflict Damage on the Economy

The ability to 'down tools', close businesses, scale down investment plans, refuse to purchase government bonds, or in some other way inflict harm on the economy or public finances (or both!) can be a powerful group resource. It is a resource possessed mainly by business groups. Unions and other occupational groups, such as physicians or agricultural producers, have a more difficult time using 'economic blackmail' to influence policy-makers. There are two reasons for this. First, when nurses, teachers, dockworkers, postal workers, truckers, or doctors attempt to tie up the economy or some important public service by withholding their labour, the linkage between the behaviour of such a group and the social or economic consequences of their actions is extremely visible. Regardless of the factors that led to their action, the general public is likely to perceive the situation as one where the *special* interest of such a group stands in sharp contrast to the *public* interest. A union or other occupational group that attempts to use the threat of economic or social chaos to back up its demands should not count on favourable public opinion. On the contrary, public support for or indifference towards a group's demands is likely to change to hostility in such circumstances. In the case of unions, they suffer from the additional disadvantage of being held in very low esteem by Canadians. Surveys regularly show that public confidence in labour unions is lower than for most other major social institutions.

A second reason why business interests are better able than other economic interest groups to use successfully the threat of economic damage in pursuing their objectives has to do with culture. In a capitalist society like ours, the fundamental values that underpin the strength of business interests—the belief in private property, the importance of profits, and faith in markets as the best mechanism for generating and distributing wealth—lend legitimacy to the general interests of business. Particular industries or corporations may be perceived as being greedy or socially irresponsible, but the general values associated with a capitalist economy enjoy widespread support. When workers strike to apply pressure in support of their demands, there is a good chance that their action will be interpreted as being irresponsible. But if business refuses to invest in new plant and machinery, lays off workers, or relocates, the reactions of policy-makers and the public are likely to be quite different. After all, most of us accept that business is about making a profit. The damage that a failure of business confidence may do to an economy may be regrettable, but business people are less likely to be accused of being irresponsible because they are just acting in accordance with the rules of a system that most of us accept.

Group Cohesion

'United we stand, divided we fall' has always been a pretty sound rule of interest group influence. Other things being equal, an association's hand will be strengthened if it is able to convince policy-makers that it speaks with a single voice and genuinely represents the views of its membership. This is not always easy. We have already noted that both labour and business interests are highly fragmented in Canada and represented by a large number of associations, not one of which can credibly claim to speak on behalf of all labour or business interests. The same is true for many other collective interests in Canadian society. Hundreds of organizations represent different groups of agricultural producers. Native Canadi-

ans are represented by many associations, the largest of which is the Assembly of First Nations. Its ability to speak on behalf of all Aboriginal groups is limited, however, by the fact that it does not speak for Métis and non-status Indians (who are represented by the Native Council of Canada) or for the Inuit (represented by Inuit Tapiriit Katatami and, most significantly, by the Nunavut government). Cohesion may appear to be greatest in the women's movement. The National Action Committee on the Status of Women is the umbrella association that represents about 700 smaller women's organizations. This appearance, however, is somewhat deceiving. The NAC has been beset by internal divisions for more than a decade and the confrontational style that it has favoured much of the time has not been supported by some groups within the women's movement.

Group cohesion typically becomes less problematic as the number of members represented by an organization grows fewer and the similarity between members increases. But what is gained in cohesion may, of course, be lost as a result of the perception that an association represents a very narrow special interest. As well, it is easier to present a united front when an association is speaking on behalf of just one group. Alliances with associations representing other groups may be politically useful, but the downside is, again, the problem of submerging group differences in such a common front.

A rather different problem of cohesion involves the relationship between a group's leaders and its membership. Evidence of a gap between the goals of leaders and those they purport to represent will undermine an association's credibility in the eyes of policy-makers. A variation of this problem exists when an interest group claims to speak on behalf of a collectivity that is largely unorganized, or where there are good reasons for doubting that the group actually expresses the views of those they claim to represent. For example, women's groups like the NAC have sometimes been accused of not expressing the views of a large part of Canada's female population. Labour unions' claims to speak on behalf of Canadian workers are weakened, in the eyes of some, by the fact that they represent fewer than four out of every 10 workers.

The dynamics of group cohesion tend to favour certain types of interests more than others. As is also true of the other group resources we have examined, the primary winners are business interest groups. To understand why this is the case, consider two widely accepted propositions about interest group cohesion.[56] First, as the number of members in an organization increases, the likelihood that some individuals will believe they can reap the benefits of the organization's actions without having to contribute to it also increases. This is called the **free-rider problem**. Other things being equal, smaller groups are more cohesive than larger ones. Second, groups able to offer exclusive benefits to their members, i.e., benefits only available to members of the organization, will be more cohesive and more capable of concerted political pressure than those that rely on collective benefits, i.e., benefits that will accrue to society as a whole. A corollary of this second proposition is that organizations relying on material incentives to attract and retain members, which therefore can motivate members with the prospect of shared material benefits, will be more cohesive than groups that rely on non-material incentives.[57]

If we turn now to the actual interest group system, we find that business groups tend to be smaller than other interest associations. Indeed, some are quite small, particularly those representing companies in oligopolistic industries. For example, the Canadian Boiler Society represents only 11 boiler manufacturers, the Canadian Pulp and Paper Association has only 39 members, and the Canadian Bankers' Association has 66 member organizations. Some business associations, such as the Chamber of Commerce, the Canadian Federation of Independent Business, and the Alliance of Canadian Manufacturers and Exporters Canada, have large memberships. But it is also true that these organizations represent more general interests of the business commun-

ty, while the more specific interests of corporations are represented through trade associations with smaller memberships.

In regard to the incentives that groups use to attract, maintain, and motivate members, business groups are not the only ones to rely on exclusive benefits and material incentives. Labour unions, agricultural producer groups, and professional associations do as well. But one needs to remember that cohesion is only one group resource. Farmers' groups or labour unions may be as cohesive as business associations but still inferior to business in terms of the other resources at their disposal.

Safety in the Shadows

Placard-waving animal rights activists, a blue-suited spokesperson for some organization presenting a brief to a parliamentary committee, or a full-page newspaper ad promoting a particular policy are all highly visible manifestations of interest groups in action. They are not, however, necessarily the most effective pathways of group influence. Often it is what does not happen—the absence of visible signs of groups exerting themselves in order to influence policy—that tells us most about the strength of organized interests. In the jungle that is the interest group system, there is often safety in the shadows.

The fact that the status, privileges, and interests of some group are not matters of public debate tells us something about the power of this group. As E.E. Schattschneider writes, 'The very expression "pressure politics" invites us to misconceive the role of special-interest groups in politics.'[58] 'Private conflicts', he argues, 'are taken into the public arena precisely because someone wants to make certain that the power ratio among the private interests most immediately involved shall not prevail.'[59] The point is, on reflection, obvious and yet profoundly important. Society's most powerful interests would prefer to avoid the public arena where they have to justify themselves and respond to those who advocate changes that would affect their interests. They are safe in the shadows. But when the light of public debate is shone on them they become prey to attacks from other groups and they lose their security. Conflict, Schattschneider notes, always includes an element of unpredictability. Consequently, even private interests with impressive group resources may suffer losses in their status and privileges, depending on what alliances form against them, the shape of public opinion, and the behaviour of political parties. Indeed, when previously unquestioned interests have reached the public agenda and are recognized as group interests, this registers a loss of influence on the part of such a group.

When the security of the shadows is lost, the relative safety of a fairly closed policy community is a decent substitute. In the United States, the concept of an **iron triangle** has been used to describe the closed system of relations between an interest group and the administrative agencies and congressional committees with which it routinely deals. Most commentators agree that the 'iron triangles' that may have characterized policy-making in the United States have become less rigid over the last few decades. Moreover, because these triangular relationships were based on the power of legislative American politics, the 'iron triangle' concept never travelled very well beyond the United States. The terms 'sub-governments', 'policy communities', and 'policy networks' are now more commonly used in both the United States and elsewhere to describe the reality of relatively exclusive constellations of state and societal actors who dominate routine policy-making in a particular field. Indeed, the ability to maintain the routine nature of policy-making is vital to preserving the privileged status of the dominant actors in a policy community.[60]

THE IMPACT OF FEDERALISM ON INTEREST GROUPS

Hardly a corner of Canadian political life is not somehow affected by federalism, the interest group system included. Because the Constitution

divides political authority between two levels of government, one of the first challenges facing an interest group is to determine where jurisdiction lies or, as is often the case, how it is divided between the national and provincial governments. An extensive literature has developed on federalism and interest groups in Canada.[61] We will examine three of the more general propositions that emerge from this work.

The first has been labelled the *multiple crack hypothesis*.[62] According to this interpretation, the existence of two levels of government, each of which is equipped with a range of taxing, spending, and regulatory powers, provides interest groups with an opportunity to seek from one government what they cannot get from the other. Business groups have been the ones most likely to exploit the constitutional division of powers, and there are many well-documented cases where they have done so successfully.[63]

A second interpretation of federalism's impact on interest groups argues that a federal constitution tends to weaken group influence by reducing the internal cohesion of organized interests. According to this argument, divided authority to make policy on matters that affect a group's interests will encourage it to adopt a federal form of organization.[64] Although this may seem a politically prudent response to the realities of divided legislative authority, it may reduce the ability of groups to speak with a single voice and to persuade governments that they have the capacity for collective action to back up their demands. A group's influence may be weakened even further when the two levels of government are in serious conflict, a situation that may spill over to create division within the group itself (for example, on regional lines) and between its representative associations.[65]

A third proposition about federalism and interest groups involves what might be called the statist interpretation of federalism's impact. According to this view, governments and their sprawling bureaucracies increasingly dominate the policy-making scene, particularly when jurisdictional issues are involved. Societal groups, even those with considerable resources, may be largely frozen out of the process of intergovernmental relations. Alan Cairns implies as much in arguing that modern Canadian federalism is mainly about conflicts between governments and their competing political and organizational goals.[66] Leslie Pal draws similar conclusions—although he is careful not to overgeneralize his findings—from his study of the historical development of Canada's unemployment insurance program. Pal finds that the impact of societal groups on the original form of UI and on subsequent changes to the program was minor compared to the role played by bureaucratic and intergovernmental factors.[67] Unlike the 'federalism as opportunity' view, this interpretation sees federalism—at least the modern federalism of large, bureaucratic state structures at both the national and regional levels—as a constraint on the influence of business and other societal interests.

The 'federalism as opportunity' and 'federalism as constraint' views are best thought of as representing the two ends of a continuum along which actual cases fall. Examples can be found to support either of these interpretations. Between them are other instances (probably the majority) where the federal division of powers and the intergovernmental rivalry that it sets up provide opportunities for interest groups (the 'multiple cracks' referred to earlier) but also place limits on their influence. Opportunity or constraint, federalism does have some influence on how interests organize for political action, the strategies they adopt when trying to influence policy, and the likelihood of their success.

STRATEGIES FOR INFLUENCE

There are three basic strategies open to interest groups. One is to target policy-makers directly, through *lobbying* in personal meetings with officials, briefs, and exchanges of information. Another strategy is to target *public opinion* in the expectation that policy-makers will respond to indications that there is considerable popular support for a group's position. The media play a crucial role here because they are the channel by which a group's message will be communicated to the wider public. A variation of the public opinion option involves alliance-building. By building visible bridges with other groups on some issue, a group may hope to persuade policy-makers that its position has broad support. A third strategy involves *judicial action*. By its very nature this is a confrontational strategy because it involves a very public challenge and an outcome that is likely to leave one side a winner and the other a loser. For some groups it tends to be an option of last resort, used after other strategies have failed. But for other groups, such as LEAF, the Sierra Legal Defence Fund, and the Canadian Civil Liberties Association, litigation is a basic weapon in their arsenal of pressure tactics (see Box 10.2).

These strategies are not mutually exclusive. A group may use more than one of them at once or switch from one strategy to another. Nor can one draw firm conclusions about the relative effectiveness of different influence strategies. Much depends on the nature of the issue and the character of the policy community within which a group's actions reverberate. Despite the contingent quality of group influence, a few generalizations are possible.

- Everyone recognizes that one of the keys to influence is being involved early in the policy-making process, when ideas are just being considered and legislation has not yet been drafted. Lobbying is the generally preferred strategy at this stage of the policy process. Confrontation and visibility are relatively low, and the importance of thorough preparation and credible technical information is high.
- Groups that are well-established members of a policy community, routinely consulted by government officials, will tend to prefer a lobbying strategy. More public and confrontational strategies involve the risk of bringing unpredictable elements into the policy-making process and will be used only as measures of last resort.

BOX 10.2 Influence through Litigation

It is now more than 12 years since Sierra Legal first opened its doors. From an original staff of two in Vancouver, Sierra Legal has grown into a national organization of more than 40 lawyers, scientists and support staff at our offices in Vancouver and Toronto. Sierra Legal is a non-profit, charitable organization funded by public donations and foundation grants and currently has over 20,000 individual supporters across Canada.

As Canada's pre-eminent advocate for the environment, Sierra Legal is now a cornerstone in the strategic plans of campaign groups throughout the country. Our lawyers and scientists represent not only environmentalists, but also labour groups, First Nations and citizens' organizations.

We continue to tackle some of the most significant environmental cases in the country and choose our cases strategically to set important precedents in Canada's burgeoning body of environmental law—and we are getting results. From the lower courts to the Supreme Court of Canada, environmental cases are being heard and won.

Litigation in critical environmental cases is an absolute necessity that: levels the playing field, forcing offenders to obey environmental laws; establishes crucial precedents that serve to protect the environment in the years ahead; and provides a last line of defence for the environment.

Today, Canadians are more aware of the environmental threats that confront them and they are seeking ways to protect themselves. Sierra Legal is working with communities across the country and has been instrumental in providing strategic counsel in several successful grassroots campaigns.

Sierra Legal Defence Fund Web site:
http://www.sierralegal.org/aboutsierralegal.html

* Groups that are not well established within a policy community are more likely to rely on confrontation, media campaigns, and other public strategies to get policy-makers to pay attention and respond to the interests they represent.
* Where a group's interests are significantly affected by regulation, lobbying strategies that rely on research and technical information supplied to the bureaucratic officials doing the regulating will be most successful.
* The era of vested interests relying on lobbying strategies has passed. Lobbying remains a very important influence strategy, but even groups enjoying regular high-level access to policy-makers now often find that lobbying is not enough.

* A successful influence strategy is usually quite expensive. This is true whether one is talking about lobbying (which often involves hiring a professional government relations firm), aiming at public opinion (which may involve the use of paid advertisements and the services of public relations and polling experts), or going to court. Business groups tend to be better able to pay for these expensive strategies than other groups.

Just what is the price of influence? The business-financed National Citizens' Coalition paid the bills for a community college teacher's legal challenge to the practice of requiring all workers at unionized establishments to pay union dues even if they choose not to belong to the union. By the time the Supreme Court of Canada handed down its decision, the NCC had paid in the ballpark of $1 million in legal bills. This price tag is not unusual for a case that reaches Canada's highest court. Expenses like these are, however, beyond the means of many groups.

A campaign directed at influencing public opinion can also be costly. We have already mentioned the multi-million dollar campaign waged by the pro-FTA Canadian Alliance for Trade and Job Opportunities—probably over $2 million spent even before the final blitz during the 1988 federal election campaign. But business groups are not the only ones to spend lavishly in an effort to shape public opinion. Quebec's Cree Indians spent an estimated $500,000 on paid advertisements and the services of a New York public relations firm in an effort to stop the construction of the Great Whale hydroelectric project in Quebec. The public opinion they were targeting was in New York, the people who would be the consumers of power generated by Great Whale and exported to the United States. In the months preceding the announcement of the 1999 Ontario election, the Canadian Automobile Workers and the province's teacher unions spent heavily on billboard and broadcast advertising in an effort to mobilize public opposition to the ideologically conservative government of Mike Harris. The Alberta government spent $1.5 million in 2002 on an advertising campaign against Canadian ratification of the Kyoto Protocol. Ottawa launched its own national ad campaign on television and in newspapers, spending at least as much attempting to persuade the public that Kyoto was a good thing as Alberta spent on raising concerns about the accord.

The purchase of newspaper/magazine space or broadcast time to convey a political message is called **advocacy advertising**. As the Great Whale and Ontario election cases show, business interest groups are not the only ones to buy advertising in an effort to influence public opinion on some issue. But among societal groups, business uses advocacy advertising most extensively. The crucial question raised by any form of advertising that carries a political message is whether the ability to pay for media time/space should determine what views get expressed. The critics of advocacy advertising were quick to denounce the blitz of pro-free trade advertising by business during the 1988 election campaign. They argued that the deep pockets of the corporate interests ranged behind free trade made a sham of the democratic political process and totally undermined the intention of the statutory limits on election spending by political parties. The Royal Commission on Elections agreed. Its 1992 report recommended that spending by organizations other than registered political parties be limited during elections (something that Parliament tried to accomplish through a law passed a decade earlier, which the courts struck down as unconstitutional).

The defenders of advocacy advertising claim that it is a way for business to overcome the anti-business bias of the media and to bridge the 'credibility gap' that has developed between business and the public. Mobil Oil, one of the pioneers of this advertising technique, has called it a 'new form of public disclosure',[68] thereby associating it with freedom of information. Business and economic issues are complex, and advocacy advertising—most of which is done through the print media—provides an opportunity for business to explain its actions and to counter public misconceptions. And in any case, argue corporate spokespersons, the biggest spender on advocacy advertising is government, whose justification for this spending is essentially the same as that of business![69]

There is no doubt that strategies aimed at influencing public opinion have become increasingly important to interest groups. In fact, in discussing advocacy advertising we have only scratched the surface of these strategies.[70] Important as they are, however, strategies that target public opinion usually take a back seat to the lobbying strategies that target policy-makers directly.

Lobbying may be defined as any form of direct or indirect communication with government that is designed to influence public policy.[71] Although the term conjures up images of smoke-filled rooms, 'old boy networks', and sleazy deal-making, this is a somewhat unfair caricature of lobbying on two counts. First, lobbying is a basic democratic right. When a group of citizens organizes to demand a traffic light at a dangerous neighbourhood corner and meets with their local city councillor to express their concerns, this is lobbying. When the president of a powerful business association arranges a lunch rendezvous with an official in the Prime Minister's Office with whom he went to law school, this, too, is lobbying. The fact that lobbying is often associated in the minds

of the public and journalists with unfair privilege and even corruption should not obscure the fact that it is not limited to organizations representing the powerful and, second, that in principle there is nothing undemocratic about lobbying.

A second way in which the 'sleaze' caricature of lobbying conveys a wrong impression is by associating it with practices that, in fact, constitute only a small part of what lobbyists actually do. Direct meetings with influential public officials are certainly an aspect of lobbying. Likewise, there is no shortage of evidence that ethically dubious and sometimes downright illegal relations occasionally exist between lobbyists and policy-makers. But lobbying involves a much wider set of activities than simply buttonholing

---

BOX 10.3 What Does a Government Relations Firm Sell?

In today's increasingly vigilant and information-driven marketplace, communications become a cornerstone of success. Our strategic counsel—delivered by a team of dedicated, experienced and seasoned professionals—is helping many of the world's leading corporations and organizations, large and small, react quickly and creatively to challenge, giving them the insight to turn unexpected risk into competitive advantage.

Using traditional methodologies as well as cutting-edge technologies, we develop integrated communications strategies consistent with clients' overall business and marketing strategies, and deliver relevant messages to target audiences.

Our dedication and commitment to client service combined with our depth of expertise and breadth of experience ensures that all our work meets the highest standards of excellence, creativity and quality delivering measurable results.

For great strategic thinking, you need a great strategic team. Hill & Knowlton Canada has sought out of the top strategic minds in Canada, for the sole purpose of adding value and depth to your decision-making power. Our team includes talented and knowledgeable players with first-hand experience in your industry. And our first order of business is to understand the strategic pressures and subtleties of your corporation in its present situation.

By hiring the best and brightest in the industry, and by fostering through our ongoing training and mentoring programs constant innovation, creativity and strategic thinking Hill & Knowlton Canada continues to be widely recognized for the knowledge, ideas and expertise we deliver to clients.

Hill & Knowlton Web site: http://www.hillandknowlton.ca/publicaffairs.htm

BOX 10.4   What Do the Clients of a Government Relations Firm Buy?

Michael Coates, President and CEO of Hill & Knowlton Canada

Mr. Coates' career in consulting began in 1983 as Public Affairs International (PAI) consultant for transportation and privatization. He rose to become its Vice President of Marketing before PAI merged with Hill and Knowlton in 1989.

Since that time, he has managed a number of major clients, mainly in the areas of export financing, privatization and government procurement.

Prior to consulting, Mr. Coates was the PC Party's Director of Voter Research, where he developed and administered its Public Opinion Research Program. His political career started as Executive Assistant to the Hon. Perrin Beatty. Mr. Coates continues to play an active role in politics and has served on three national campaign committees and the PC Canada Fund, and is past National Secretary and National Treasurer of the PC Party. He has also served as a member of former Prime Minister Campbell's Transition to Government Committee, and is currently a director of the PC Canada Fund.

Brian Mersereau, Executive Vice-President and General Manager

Brian's primary consulting focus is in the fields of government procurement and industrial development.

Since joining the firm in 1983 he has been engaged by industry as an advisor for many of the government's largest federal procurements including the competition for the Corporate Credit Card, Travel Services, Flying Training (NFTC), Search and Rescue Helicopter and light trucks.

He brings to Hill & Knowlton more that 15 years of direct experience negotiating major Crown contracts, including the $9B Canadian Patrol Frigate Contract, with the now Department of Public Works and Government Services Canada.

Jo-Anne Polak, Senior Vice-President

Polak is a senior VP and National Service Director for H&K Canada's National Crisis Communications division. She oversees a national team of crisis experts who deliver crisis preparedness and response for H&K's clients worldwide. Ms. Polak is also a core member of H&K's global crisis communications team. She began her career as political assistant at Queen's Park during the Bill Davis era. She then worked for two communications agencies and then became General Manager of the Ottawa Rough Riders of the Canadian Football League. Polak left this job to go into broadcasting, joining H&K in 1994. Her professional accomplishments have often been recognized including the International Association of Business Communications President's Awards.

Hill & Knowlton Web site: http://www.hillandknowlton.ca

cabinet ministers or their senior officials. Most professional lobbyists, whether they work for a company or interest group, or for a government relations firm that sells its lobbying expertise to clients, spend the better part of their time collecting and communicating information on behalf of the interests they represent. They monitor the political scene as it affects their client's interests. An effective lobbyist does not simply react, but instead is like an early warning system, providing information about policy when it is still in its formative stages and tracking public opinion on the issues that are vital to a client's interests. Lobbyists provide information about how and where to access the policy-making system and strategies for influencing policies or winning contracts. They may also provide advice and professional assistance in putting together briefs, press releases, speeches, and other communications, as well as public relations services such as identifying and targeting those segments of public opinion that influence policy-makers on some issue. Helping to build strategic coalitions with other groups is another function that lobbyists may perform.

Most interest groups lobby government on their own. But for those who can afford it, the services of a professional lobbying firm may also be purchased. The 2003 Ottawa telephone directory lists 35 firms under the 'Government relations consultants' heading of the Yellow Pages. They range from large firms like Hill & Knowlton Canada, which employ dozens of professional staff and have annual billings in the tens of millions of dollars, to small operations that employ a handful of persons. In addition, many law firms and accounting companies, including such prominent ones as Osler Hoskins & Harcourt, McCarthy Tetrault, MacMillan Binch, and Pricewaterhousecoopers, do lobbying work. The line between legal representation and lobbying is often non-existent, a fact attested to by the presence of many law firms on the public registry of lobbyists.

Since 1989, those who are paid to lobby federal public office-holders have been required to register with a federal agency. The Lobbyists Registration Act, amended in 1996, provides for three categories of lobbyists:

- *Consultant lobbyists* are those who, for a fee, work for various clients. As of 31 March 2002 there were 858 such individuals registered as active consultant lobbyists.
- *Corporate in-house lobbyists* are those who work for a single corporation and who lobby federal officials as a significant part of their duties. As of 31 March 2002 there were 233 individuals registered as in-house corporate lobbyists.
- *Organization in-house lobbyists* are the senior paid officers and other employees of organizations— business, labour, environmental, charitable, etc.—whose activities would include lobbying federal officials. As of 31 March 2002 there were 351 in-house organization lobbyists registered with the Lobbyists Registration Branch of Industry Canada.

The majority of active consultant and in-house organization lobbyists represent corporations and business associations (it goes without saying that the in-house corporate lobbyists represent business). The clientele lists of Canada's leading government relations firms read like a 'Who's Who' of the Canadian and international corporate world. Hill & Knowlton Canada, for example, boasts that it represents such clients as Microsoft, SHL Systemhouse, De Beers, Rio Algom, Kraft, Glaxo Wellcome, Deutsche Bank Canada, and Standard Life.[72] Box 10.5 lists some of Canada's most prominent consultant lobbyists and some of the clients they work for.

BOX 10.5   Who Do Government Relations Firms Represent?

Lobbyist	Company	Clients
Ronald Atkey	Osler, Hoskins & Harcourt	Time Canada Time Warner Viacom Warner Brothers Canada
Brian Mersereau	Hill & Knowlton Canada	Amex Canada Bombardier General Dynamics Rockwell International
Herb Metcalfe	The Capital Hill Group	AT & T Canada Canadian National Canadian Association of Broadcasters Lockheed Martin Trimark Investment
David Angus	The Capital Hill Group	British Airways Hewlett Packard Canada Japanese Automobile Manufacturers Association of Canada
Harry Near	Earnscliffe Strategy Group	Molson Canada RBC Dominion Securities Canadian Pacific Labatt Breweries Petro-Canada Microsoft Canada
William Neville	Strategies Group	Canadian Tobacco Manufacturers Council Federal Express Canada General Synod of the Anglican Church in Canada

Industry Canada, Lobbyists Registration Branch, on-line public registry.

NOTES

1. V.O. Key, *Politics, Parties, and Pressure Groups*, 4th edn (New York, 1958), 23.
2. James Madison, *The Federalist Papers, no. 10* (New York: New American Library, 1961).
3. This slogan is attributed to Thomas Sloan, a former chairman of GM during the 1920s.
4. *Associations Canada: An Encyclopedic Directory* (Mississauga: Canadian Almanac & Directory Publishing Co., 1999).
5. Estimates based on ibid.
6. E.E. Schattschneider, *The Semi-Sovereign People* (New York: Holt, Rinehart and Winston, 1960), 35.
7. Ibid.
8. Ibid.
9. Charles E. Lindblom, *Politics and Markets* (New York: Basic Books, 1977), esp. chs 13–16.
10. Bruno S. Frey, *Modern Political Economy* (New York: John Wiley & Sons, 1978), ch. 11.
11. For example, Diane Francis, editor of the *National Post*, argues that the concentration of corporate power 'has become so significant that the country is hurtling towards a new form of economic and political feudalism.' This is a position that Canadian socialists, not generally counted among the admirers of the *National Post*, would approve wholeheartedly. See Francis, *Controlling Interest: Who Owns Canada?* (Toronto: Macmillan, 1986), 3.
12. Business's ideological and academic spokespersons adopt an essentially pluralistic position on the matter of interest group influence. William Stanbury's remarks are typical: 'The relationship between business firms and governments in either positive or normative terms cannot be characterized in a single phrase. It is inevitably plural and diverse. Depending upon the industry, the time, the other issues on the public policy agenda, the individuals involved, and what each "side" is seeking to do vis-à-vis the other, the relationship might be characterized as adversarial, cooperative, symbiotic, supportive, or protective.' Stanbury, *Business-Government Relations in Canada* (Toronto: Methuen, 1986), 9.
13. Michael Bliss, *Northern Enterprise: Five Centuries of Canadian Business* (Toronto: McClelland & Stewart, 1987), 578.
14. David Vogel, *Fluctuating Fortunes: The Political Power of Business in America* (New York: Basic Books, 1989), 193.
15. James Q. Wilson, 'The Politics of Regulation', in Wilson, ed., *The Politics of Regulation* (New York: Basic Books, 1980), 370.
16. Earl Latham, *The Group Basis of Politics* (New York: Octagon Books, 1965), 35.
17. Arthur F. Bentley, *The Process of Government* (Evanston, Ill., 1935), 208.
18. David B. Truman, *The Governmental Process* (New York: Alfred A. Knopf, 1951); Robert Dahl, *Who Governs?* (New Haven: Yale University Press, 1961); John Kenneth Galbraith, *Countervailing Power* (Boston: Houghton Mifflin, 1956).
19. Theodore Lowi, *The End of Liberalism* (New York: W.W. Norton, 1969), 97.
20. P. Bachrach and M. Baratz, 'Two Faces of Power', *American Political Science Review* 56, 4 (1962): 948.
21. This is true of Nicos Poulantzas, *Political Power and Social Classes* (London: New Left Books, 1973); Fred Block, *Revising State Theory* (Philadelphia: Temple University Press, 1987); Bob Jessop, *The Capitalist State* (New York: New York University Press, 1982). Interest groups are given some passing mention in James O'Connor, *The Fiscal Crisis of the State* (New York: St Martin's Press, 1973); Claus Offe, *Contradictions of the Welfare State* (Cambridge, Mass.: MIT Press, 1984). Among the leading Marxist intellectuals, it is perhaps fair to say that only Ralph Miliband has very much to say on interest groups. See Miliband, *The State in Capitalist Society* (London: Quartet Books, 1973).

22. Daniel Drache and Wallace Clement, eds, *The New Practical Guide to Canadian Political Economy* (Toronto: Lorimer, 1985).

23. Wallace Clement and Glen Williams, eds, *The New Canadian Political Economy* (Montreal and Kingston: McGill-Queen's University Press, 1989).

24. Miliband, *The State in Capitalist Society*, 131.

25. Wallace Clement, *The Challenge of Class Analysis* (Ottawa: Carleton University Press, 1988), chs 7 and 8.

26. Ibid., 132.

27. Rianne Mahon, *The Politics of Industrial Restructuring: Canadian Textiles* (Toronto: University of Toronto Press, 1984).

28. Jurg Steiner, *European Democracies* (New York: Longman, 1986), 221.

29. William D. Coleman, *Business and Politics: A Study of Collective Action* (Montreal and Kingston: McGill-Queen's University Press, 1988), 224.

30. It occasionally happens, however, that the CCC is capable of taking a firm position on issues that are more divisive in the business community. Its support for the Canada–US Free Trade Agreement was an example of this.

31. Gerhard Lehmbruch, 'Concertation and the Structure of Corporatist Networks', in John Goldthorpe, ed., *Order and Conflict in Contemporary Capitalism* (Oxford: Clarendon Press, 1984), 65–6.

32. Coleman, *Business and Politics*, ch. 6.

33. These tripartite initiatives are discussed in detail in Pierre Fournier, 'Consensus Building in Canada: Case Studies and Prospects', in Keith Banting, research coordinator, *The State and Economic Interests*, vol. 32 of the research studies for the Royal Commission on the Economic Union and Development Prospects for Canada (Ottawa: Supply and Services, 1986), 291–335.

34. William Coleman is among those who argue that such structures would benefit Canada economically. See Coleman, *Business and Politics*, ch. 13.

35. William D. Coleman and Grace Skogstad, 'Introduction', in Coleman and Skogstad, eds, *Policy Communities and Public Policy in Canada* (Toronto: Copp Clark Pitman, 1990), 2.

36. Michels's argument was that the specialization of function that accompanies organization inevitably results in domination of the organization by a minority and, therefore, creates the likelihood that the goals pursued by the organization will more closely reflect those of its leadership than its membership. Robert Michels, *Political Parties* (London: Jarrold, 1915).

37. Some of the classics of this literature include Anthony Downs, *An Economic Theory of Democracy* (New York: Harper and Row, 1957); Mancur Olson, *The Logic of Collective Action* (Boston: Harvard University Press, 1965); James M. Buchanan and Gordon Tullock, *The Calculus of Consent* (Ann Arbor: University of Michigan Press, 1965); Anthony Downs, *Inside Bureaucracy* (Boston: Little, Brown and Company, 1967).

38. Michael Atkinson, 'How Do Institutions Constrain Policy?', paper delivered at the conference 'Governing Canada: Political Institutions and Public Policy', McMaster University, 25 Oct. 1991, 8.

39. Alan Cairns, 'The Governments and Societies of Canadian Federalism', *Canadian Journal of Political Science* 10, 4 (Dec. 1977): 695–725.

40. These works include James G. March and Herbert Simon, *Organizations* (New York: John Wiley, 1958); James G. March, *Decisions and Organizations* (Oxford: Basil Blackwell, 1988); James G. March and Johan P. Olsen, 'The New Institutionalism: Organizational Factors in Political Life', *American Political Science Review* 78 (1984): 734–49; James G. March and Johan P. Olsen, *Rediscovering Institutions: The Organizational Basis of Politics* (New York: Free Press, 1989).

41. Charles Perrow, *Complex Organizations: A Critical Essay*, 3rd edn (New York: Random House, 1986), 260.

42. James Q. Wilson, *Political Organizations* (New York: Basic Books, 1973), 3–4.

43. These definitions are the ones used in Coleman and Skogstad, 'Introduction'. They are not,

however, agreed upon by everyone who mines this vein.

44. Ibid., 25.
45. Ibid., 23.
46. Ibid., 24.
47. J.L. Granatstein, *The Ottawa Men* (Toronto: Oxford University Press, 1982).
48. William D. Coleman, 'Canadian Business and the State', in Banting, *The State and Economic Interests*, 260, fig. 5–2.
49. O. Mary Hill, *Canada's Salesman to the World: The Department of Trade and Commerce, 1892–1939* (Montreal and Kingston: McGill-Queen's University Press, 1977), 172.
50. Leslie A. Pal, *Interests of State* (Montreal and Kingston: McGill-Queen's University Press, 1992), ch. 6.
51. A. Paul Pross, *Group Politics and Public Policy* (Toronto: University of Toronto Press, 1986), 68–9.
52. Ibid., 114–16.
53. Quoted in Erik Heinrich, 'Recession chills out of green groups', *Financial Post*, 10 Feb. 1992, 8.
54. G. Bruce Doern and Brian W. Tomlin, *Fear and Faith: The Free Trade Story* (Toronto: Stoddart, 1991), 219.
55. John W. Kingdon, *Agendas, Alternatives, and Public Policies* (Boston: Little, Brown and Company, 1984), 54–7.
56. Mancur Olson, *The Logic of Collective Action* (Cambridge, Mass.: Harvard University Press, 1965).
57. James L. Wilson, *Political Organizations* (New York: Basic Books, 1973), 36–8.
58. E.E. Schattschneider, *The Semi-Sovereign People* (New York: Holt, Rinehart and Winston, 1960), 37.
59. Ibid., 38.
60. Good analyses of several Canadian policy communities are found in Coleman and Skogstad, eds, *Policy Communities and Public Policy in Canada*.
61. This literature is brought together in Hugh G. Thorburn, *Interest Groups in the Canadian Fed-*

eral System, vol. 69 of the research studies for the Royal Commission on the Economic Union and Development Prospects for Canada (Ottawa: Supply and Services, 1985).
62. Richard J. Schultz, *Federalism, Bureaucracy and Public Policy: The Politics of Highway Transport Regulation* (Montreal and Kingston: McGill-Queen's University Press, 1980), 148.
63. See, for example, M.W. Bucovetsky, 'The Mining Industry and the Great Tax Reform Debate', in A. Paul Pross, ed., *Pressure Group Behaviour in Canadian Politics* (Toronto: McGraw-Hill Ryerson, 1975), 89–114.
64. The long-accepted claim that Canadian federalism has led most associations to adopt a federal form of organization is not supported by the facts—at least not in the case of business associations. A survey by William Coleman found that about three-quarters of business associations have unitary structures. Coleman's conclusion is that Canada's industrial structure has a far greater impact on how business associations organize themselves than does the Constitution. See Coleman, *Business and Politics*, 260.
65. See Schultz, *Federalism, Bureaucracy and Public Policy*, esp. ch. 8.
66. Alan Cairns, 'The Governments and Societies of Canadian Federalism', in Cairns, *Constitution, Government, and Society in Canada* (Toronto: McClelland & Stewart, 1988), 167.
67. Leslie A. Pal, *State, Class, and Bureaucracy* (Montreal and Kingston: McGill-Queen's University Press, 1988).
68. Quoted in Duncan McDowall, ed., *Advocacy Advertising: Propaganda or Democratic Right?* (Ottawa: Conference Board of Canada, 1982), v.
69. For example, a former federal Minister of Justice defended his government's advertising on proposed constitutional reforms by saying, 'Government is too complex nowadays to rely on policy by press release. Programs must be explained—not by reporters but by people who created them.' Ibid., 7.
70. Privately funded think-tanks like the C.D. Howe Institute, the Fraser Institute, and the Confer-

ence Board of Canada are another way of promoting group interests, in this case the general interests of business, by producing studies and funding experts whose perspectives and options for public policy are favourable to those interests. Direct-mail campaigns targeted at selected groups whose opinions and actions may, in turn,

affect policy-makers are another technique employed mainly by business groups.

71. A fascinating account of lobbying in Canada is John Sawatsky, *The Insiders: Government, Business, and the Lobbyists* (Toronto: McClelland & Stewart, 1987).

72. http://www.hillandknowlton.ca/letter.htm

SUGGESTED READINGS

Robert Campbell and Leslie Pal, *The Real Worlds of Canadian Politics*, 3rd edn (Peterborough, Ont.: Broadview Press, 1994). Although the case studies are a bit dated, this book provides rich accounts of the policy-making process in Canada, including the behaviour and influence of interest groups.

William Coleman, *Business and Politics: A Study of Collective Action* (Montreal and Kingston: McGill-Queen's University Press, 1988). This remains one of the leading empirical contributions to the study of interest groups in Canada.

Leslie A. Pal, *Interests of State: The Politics of Language, Multiculturalism and Feminism in Canada* (Montreal and Kingston: McGill-Queen's University Press, 1993). Testing various models of interest group influence, Pal explains the complex interaction between group interests and identity formation and the interests and goals of public officials.

Donley T. Studlar, *Tobacco Control: Comparative Politics in the United States and Canada* (Peterborough, Ont.: Broadview Press, 2002). This work presents an excellent comparative analysis of the actions and influence of the tobacco lobby in Canada and the United States.

Review Exercises

1. Find a newspaper story that discusses an interest group. Based on this article, answer as fully as you can the following questions:
    (a) What is the name of the group?
    (b) Who does the group represent?
    (c) Why is the group in the news?
    (d) Can anything about the group's demands or values be determined from the article?

2. How many organized groups do you or have you belonged to or contributed to in some way? Make a list. Which of these do you think attempt to influence public opinion or policy? If you are having trouble coming up with a list, just think about jobs that you may have had (were they unionized?), churches, clubs, or associations that you may have belonged to, causes to which you might have donated money, petitions you may have signed, etc.

3. Make a list of the various political activities engaged in by different interest groups. Which activities do you consider to be strongly democratic, somewhat democratic, and undemocratic, explaining your reasons.

The media do not merely report political news, they are influential players in shaping the public agenda. (Greg Vickers)

Media impact on modern political life is profound. In this chapter the following aspects of media influence on politics are examined:

- ❏ Shaping the political agenda.
- ❏ What do the media produce?
- ❏ What determines the mass media product?
- ❏ The economic filter.
- ❏ The technological filter.
- ❏ The legal-regulatory filter.
- ❏ The organizational filter.
- ❏ The ideological filter.
- ❏ The media and democracy.

CHAPTER ELEVEN

THE MEDIA

Few readers of this book will have met the Prime Minister of Canada. Even fewer have met the President of the United States. However, virtually all readers will have ideas about these two leaders and many will have strongly held views on their character, abilities, and performance despite never having exchanged a word with them. What most of us know and believe about presidents and prime ministers, the facts upon which we form our ideas and judgements concerning them, is based on third-hand information at best. The same may be said, of course, about how we acquire our knowledge and beliefs about most of the world outside of our own neighbourhoods. We rely on the images and information offered to us on television, in newspapers, over the radio, and via many other media in our information-saturated society.

The fact that our ideas are based largely on third-hand information means that we should pay careful attention to the character of the 'hands' that communicate this information. Think for a moment about the typical political story on the late-evening television news. It may amount to 60–90 seconds of images and words of the Prime Minister, other cabinet ministers, and opposition critics, probably in the House of Commons during Question Period or in the foyer near the entrance to the Commons, where journalists and cameras await the Prime Minister and other politicians as they exit the House after Question Period. The story may include brief segments involving politicians, experts, and interest group spokespersons responding to the Prime Minister's remarks. Some portion of the story will consist of the reporter's own narration of what is happening and what it means. The entire news clip has involved a large number of choices by those who assign the stories to be covered and those who edit and package them in the television network's

newsroom. This is why the information is described as third-hand. The viewer is not personally a witness to the action or occurrence covered in the story. The reporter's account of what happened is shaped by the decision of others who play a part in packaging the story for the television news. Consequently, what the viewer ultimately sees has been influenced by a number of people whose choices contribute to what might be described as the news.

There is nothing particularly new in all this. Most citizens have always depended on the media for much of their ideas and information about life. What is more recent is our awareness of the possibilities for selection, distortion, and manipulation in the process of reporting the news. Long-standing fears that media might have a partisan bias or that propaganda might subvert democratic politics by depriving citizens of independent sources of information and varied perspectives on their societies have been joined in recent years by worries that the biases of the media are more deeply rooted and insidious than ever before. The 'seductions of language', says media expert Neil Postman, are trivial compared to the seductions and manipulative powers of the image-based media.[1]

The media are crucial to the health of democracy. The founders of the American republic knew this, which is why freedom of the press, along with freedom of speech, religion, and assembly, was specifically mentioned in the First Amendment to the United States Constitution. Freedom of the press was, in fact, already enshrined in several of the state constitutions. For example, Virginia's 1776 Bill of Rights stated 'That the freedom of the press is one of the great bulwarks of liberty, and can never be restrained but by despotick government.'[2] Canada's founders devoted little

'Scrum' is a rugby term that is also used to describe the rather chaotic mingling of politicians, journalists, and cameramen that takes place after question period in the House of Commons each day. It provides the media with one of the day's main opportunities to ask questions and gives politicians the chance to get some television time.

attention to freedom of the press, or other freedoms for that matter, assuming instead that these would be adequately respected under the system of parliamentary government they adopted from Britain and that a democratic society had no need to inscribe in tablets of stone the principles that it lived by. (Some of the American founders were of the same view. In the *Federalist Papers*, no. 84, Alexander Hamilton argued that freedom of the press ultimately depended on public opinion and 'the general spirit of the people and of the government', and that no explicit constitutional guarantee would be able to protect this or any other freedom in a hostile political culture.)

The ability of those in the media to report on public affairs as they see fit—within the limits of defamation law and recognizing that the public disclosure of some government information could be prejudicial to legitimate national security or policy-making interests that state officials are expected to protect—is crucial to democracy. If a broadcaster, Internet site, newspaper, or other media organ can be shut down, censored, or pun-

ished because public officials do not like the information it conveys, the free discussion of public issues is diminished and democracy suffers. Likewise, when governments get into the business of broadcasting, publishing, and advertising, fears are often expressed that public dollars may be spent on partisan and propagandistic purposes.

At the same time, there is no country in the world in which the media system is not regulated in some way by the state. This is particularly true of broadcasting, where the airwaves have been defined as public property throughout the world and where there have been technological reasons for restricting the number of broadcasters in order to protect the quality of the television or radio signals reaching consumers. But even this traditional argument for regulation has been challenged by newer technologies that rely on cables and satellites, which have produced an explosion in the quantity of messages that can be sent and received at any time. The Internet is the most recent culmination of these technological developments, resulting in a situation where, in the words of

David Jones, president of Electronic Frontier Canada, 'On the Internet, everyone's a publisher.'[3]

But state regulation of the media is not, in the eyes of some critics, the only or even the main threat to freedom of the press and the health of democracy. A more serious threat than state control and censorship, critics argue, is the economic censorship that may result when too few owners control too many media organs that account for too great a share of the market, as is certainly the case in Canada today. Moreover, they point to the dependence of most mass media organs on advertising as a key factor that operates to filter out certain forms of controversial, critical, and non-mainstream coverage of political, economic, and social affairs. Whether censorship results from governmental *diktat* or from the working of capitalist markets, they insist, it is censorship just the same.

The relationship of the media to politics generates enormous controversy. Before we attempt to make sense of this relationship, let us begin by examining the mass media's role in social learning and the chief characteristics of Canada's media system.

'THE PICTURES IN OUR HEADS'

The media are creators and purveyors of images and information. As such, they play a role in social learning, i.e., the process of acquiring knowledge, values, and beliefs about the world and ourselves. This is a role the media share with other agents of social learning: the family, schools, peer groups, and organizations that one belongs to. Studies of social learning, including those that focus on the acquisition of politically relevant attitudes and personality characteristics, have long concluded that the family is the most important agent of social learning. It has a crucial influence on the development of an individual's sense of self-esteem, trust, and disposition towards authority, all of which have been linked to political attitudes and behaviour. As well, the family typically has a major impact on one's acquisition of communication skills, class identification, and social attitudes (e.g., gender roles). Although none of this learning is about politics per se, it has important consequences for politics.

While the family and other agents of social learning all contribute to what Walter Lippmann called 'the pictures in our heads', none of them rivals the media in its impact on the political agenda. Lippmann wrote, 'The only feeling that anyone can have about an event that he does not experience is the feeling aroused by his mental image of that event.'[4] The contours of modern political discourse are largely determined by the mass media as they process and report on 'reality'. Moreover, when it comes to matters that are remote from one's personal experience and daily life—political turmoil in the countries of the former Soviet Union, global pollution, conflict in the Middle East, or the latest Canadian federal budget—the media provide the only source of images and information about the events, issues, and personalities involved. Politicians and generals realize the media's importance, which is why one of the first steps taken in any serious *coup d'état* is to seize control of broadcasting and either shut down or muzzle any newspapers not sympathetic to the new regime.

It has often been remarked that the media do not determine *what we think* so much as *what we think about*. This is, of course, a formidable power. It is the power to shape the public consciousness by conveying certain images and interpretations and excluding others. The responsibility that accompanies such power is enormous. A 'free press' has been viewed as a necessary ingredient of democratic politics since the American Revolution. The reasoning behind this view is that all other groups and individuals—political parties, candidates for public office, corporations, labour unions, government officials, and so on—are self-interested. They cannot be counted on to give an objective assessment of their goals and actions. Too often their interests will be best served through concealment, deception, and manipulation—by **propaganda** that espouses a particular ideology or policy through the public dissemination of selected information and/or misinformation. Only the media, so the argument goes, have an interest in presenting the facts. They may perform this function imperfectly, and particular media organs may have political biases that reflect the views of their owners, the values of their editors, producers, and journalists, or the prejudices of their readership/viewership (would one expect the Christian Broadcasting Network to give positive coverage to pro-choice abortion groups or equal time to atheists?). But competition ensures that all significant points of view reach the public.

Is this an accurate picture of the media's role in political democracies? How well do the media cover all significant points of view? Who determines the facts, or are they self-evident? Regardless of what the intentions of those in the media might be, what are the actual consequences of their behaviour for politics? Let us start by considering the 'products' of the mass media.

WHAT DO THE MEDIA PRODUCE?

Only a small portion of television and radio time is devoted to public affairs. Most programming, including during the prime-time periods when people are most likely to be watching or listening, aims to entertain rather than inform. Despite the existence of a hard-core minority who tune in mainly or exclusively for news and public affairs, television and radio are essentially entertainment media. Most television viewing and radio listening time is spent watching drama, comedy, game and talk shows, and sports, and listening to music. According to data collected by the Bureau of Broadcast Measurement, about 70 per cent of anglophone Canadian television viewing time is spent watching American programs (compared to about two-thirds of francophone viewing time devoted to Canadian programs).[5]

The pattern is similar for radio. Private broadcasters account for about 90 per cent of the market, and most of what they offer is music. Although the Canadian Radio-television and Telecommunications Commission (CRTC), the industry's regulatory watchdog, requires all radio stations to carry news, only the largest privately owned stations generate any significant amount of news themselves. Most rely on information supplied by wire services and newspapers, as well as local sports and weather, to meet their news quota. Only stations affiliated with the state-owned Canadian Broadcasting Corporation and Radio-Canada, its French-language counterpart, broadcast a significant amount of national and international public affairs programming that has been generated by their own staff.

Like most radio stations, newspapers are geared primarily to the local market. Although all dailies carry national and international news, much of their space is devoted to community affairs. Studies suggest that newspapers are considered by the public to be better than either television or radio as a source of community information, while television is believed to be the best source of information for international, national, and even provincial news. Television is also judged to be the most up-to-date, fair and unbiased, believable, influential, and essential to the country.[6]

Newspapers are relied on by most readers chiefly as a source of local information. Only the Toronto-based *Globe and Mail* and *National Post* do not conform to this community mould. Of all Canadian dailies, these two conservative papers are the only ones that have significant national circulations. The emphasis on national and international news is greater in the *Globe and Mail* and *National Post* than in other dailies. The *Globe's* daily 'Report on Business' section and the 'Financial Report' section of the *Post* also distinguish them from community-oriented papers. The *Globe's* self-proclaimed reputation as English Canada's 'national' newspaper—a reputation the *Post* has attempted to challenge since it began publication in 1998—has been acquired in part because of high-calibre journalism. The political columnists and editorial writers of both the *Globe* and the *National Post* are influential players in defining the country's political agenda. Montreal-based *Le Devoir* plays a similar role in Quebec.

Critics of Canadian newspapers have focused on a number of specific concerns relating to industry structure. First, concentrated ownership is said to limit the range of ideas and the information that reach the public. We would argue, however, that weak competition has less impact on the range of media information than the need to make profits and the organizational structure of news-gathering and reporting. The organizational filter through which the media product must pass is discussed in a subsequent section. As well, newspapers that are part of larger corporate networks that include non-media interests may be reluctant to cover stories and interpret events in ways that put their owner's other interests in a bad light. Again, the empirical proof for this claim is weak. Incidents of owner interference or, more often, self-censorship that appears clearly to be based on media people's sensitivity to their owner's interests do occasionally happen.[7] But as Edward Herman and Noam Chomsky argue, it is too simplistic to look for direct correlations between ownership and how *particular* issues or stories are handled by the media. Instead, they maintain, owners exercise their influence more diffusely through 'establishing the general aims of the company and choosing its top management'.[8] Finally, ownership will produce a certain uniformity in the partisan orientations of newspapers within the chain. This claim, while superficially plausible, is not supported by the evidence. Studies carried out by researchers at the University of Windsor have found no proof that chain ownership is associated with either the patterns of news reporting or editorial policy.[9] The differences one finds between newspapers are determined far more by their readership characteristics than by who owns them. Moreover, their market shares do not appear to coincide with political divisions, unlike the situation in countries like France, Belgium, and Italy, where particular papers have distinct partisan or ideological readerships.

In the case of magazines, foreign ownership, rather than concentrated ownership, is the major political issue. The best-selling ones include scandal sheets like the *National Enquirer*, current affairs weeklies like *Newsweek*, *Time*, *Maclean's*, and *Sports Illustrated*, monthlies like *National Geographic* and *Reader's Digest*, and magazines directed mainly at a female readership such as *Ladies' Home Journal*, *Cosmopolitan*, *Elle*, and *Chatelaine*. All of these sell hundreds of thousands of copies monthly or weekly. In fact, despite the enormous number of magazines sold in Canada, a mere handful representing a limited number of genres accounts for the majority of total magazine sales.[10] Most of them are not oriented towards coverage of politics and public affairs, and several of the most popular ones are American-based, including *Time*, *Newsweek*, *Sports Illustrated*, *Cosmopolitan*, *Elle*, and *Maxim*. Those that focus on 'hard news' and that have large circulations, such as *Time*, *Newsweek*, and *Maclean's*, occupy the conventional middle ground of Canadian and American politics.

Compared to the media we have discussed so far, film may appear relatively insignificant. The average Canadian goes to the cinema only about four or five times per year (more often among those who live in major cities). But some of the time he or she spends in front of the television is spent watching films. Cable television, direct broadcast satellites, pay-TV, and the VCR/DVD player have all increased the market penetration of films, expanding the movie industry beyond the theatre and bringing its product directly into the home of the consumer. In a sense, this new technology has produced a new 'golden age' for the film industry, enabling it to recapture some of the prominence it held between the 1930s and the 1950s, before the television set became a standard feature of most households.

Film is at the centre of the modern imagination. If a person has not read the book, he or she probably has seen its film adaptation. Indeed, recent years have seen the emergence of the ultimate tribute to the power of the visual medium, the book based on the motion picture. Blockbusters like the *Star Wars* films, the adventures of *Indiana Jones, ET, The Lion King, Spider Man,* and *Titanic* are familiar to most of us. The stories they tell, the characters they contain, and the stereotypes they convey both shape and reflect our popular culture. At the extreme, life imitates art as when gangs of British youths copied the random violence seen in Stanley Kubrick's adaptation of *A Clockwork Orange,* and in the Littleton, Colorado, massacre where teenage members of the 'Trenchcoat Mafia' styled themselves after Leonardo DiCaprio in *The Basketball Diaries.* In the 1980s US President Ronald Reagan borrowed from *Star Wars* to label the Soviet Union the 'evil empire' and to call for a 'star wars' defence system (formally referred to as the Strategic Defence Initiative). The archetypes and icons of popular culture are more likely to be associated with movies than with any other mass medium.

What does the film industry offer the viewing public? With hundreds of new releases every year from the studios of Hollywood and thousands more from independents in the US, Canada, and elsewhere, one might assume that the industry produces a richly varied product. It does. But only a narrow band of the entire range of film production is made easily available to movie viewers. This band represents the commercial feature film. The genre may vary, but what distinguishes such a film is the fact that it must appeal to a large mass audience in order to recoup the millions of dollars— often running to the tens and even hundreds of millions of dollars (*Titanic* reputedly cost about US $300 million to make)—spent on its production and marketing. Documentary and artistic films generally cost much less to make, but they also generate smaller revenues. They usually are made by small independent film companies or by state-owned filmmakers such as Canada's National Film Board. Little is spent on marketing them and public access to non-commercial films is limited by the fact that the distributors do not want to show them and relatively few movie rental stores stock them.

The images and stories purveyed by the commercial film industry are often disturbing and occasionally critical of 'the system'. Indeed, one of the most popular motifs of popular film has long been the lone good man versus the bad system. Bruce Willis, Denzel Washington, Clint Eastwood, Sylvester Stallone, and Harrison Ford are among the more successful. *It's a Wonderful Life* is a classic example of this simple theme, as are the archetypal westerns *Shane* and *High Noon*. Other examples of older and more recent vintage include *To Kill a Mockingbird, Places in the Heart, Silkwood, Grand Canyon,* and *Erin Brokovitch*. But on balance, commercial film does much more to reinforce dominant values and institutions than it does to challenge them. The economics of the industry make this inevitable, as we will explain later in this chapter.

Advertisements are another important part of the media product. Most people are exposed to hundreds of ads each day. Television and radio are heavily laced with them. Newspapers and magazines are fairly bursting with them. Even films have become vehicles for advertising, with companies willing to pay thousands of dollars for fleeting glimpses of their products in a favourable context. Billboards, storefront signs, pamphlets, flyers, Internet banners . . . there is no escape. The estimated amount spent on mass media advertising worldwide exceeds the value of Canada's GNP. The advertising assault is so massive and unremitting that the vast majority of it fails to pierce our consciousness. Advertisers have long been aware of this and search continually for ways to capture the attention of the viewers, listeners, or readers to whom they want to sell something. Whether we pay attention or tune out, advertising constitutes a continuous 'buzz' in the background of our daily lives. What is it telling us?

In the case of most advertising, the intended message is 'buy this'. We say 'most' because some advertising aims to persuade people to vote or think in particular ways, or simply provides them with useful information (much public service advertising by governments would fall into this last category). The vast majority of advertising, however, aims to affect our behaviour as consumers.

But there is much more to commercial advertising than the intended message, 'buy product X'. We are urged to buy, period. The high-consumption economy is sustained by the frenetic materialism that pervades our culture. This materialism, in turn, is reinforced by the mass media through advertising and entertainment programming. When the message 'buy this' is hurled at us hundreds of times a day from the time we are quite young, the cumulative impact is to instill and sustain a high-consumption mindset.

This is only one of the incidental messages communicated through commercial advertising. Gender stereotyping and the use of sexual imagery and innuendo are rampant. The youthful, the slender, the muscular, the large-breasted, the extroverted, the materially successful, and the 'cool' are far more likely to appear in television, magazine, and billboard ads than are those who appear to be deficient in these qualities. Who and what are excluded from visual advertising—and the same holds true for all visual media—are as important as who and what are included. The silences and blind spots of advertising and of all

mass media include the poor, visible minorities, men and women who do not conform to fairly standard stereotypes, the physically unattractive, and the socially non-conforming. There are, of course, exceptions. But in general, advertisers find it more profitable to appeal to conventional beliefs and prejudices and to very basic emotional needs and insecurities (see Box 11.1).

WHAT DETERMINES THE MASS MEDIA PRODUCT?

'The facts of modern life do not spontaneously take a shape in which they can be known. They must be given a shape by somebody.'[11]

No one except the naive and those with a professional interest in self-deception believes that the mass media simply mirror reality. Confronted with more information than can possibly be conveyed to their readerships/audiences, those who produce the media product must choose what stories, images, and 'facts' to communicate. What ultimately is offered to the media consumer is a selec-

---

BOX 11.1 The Art of Selling

The principles underlying this [commercial advertising] are extremely simple. Find some common desire, some widespread unconscious fear or anxiety; think out some way to relate this wish or fear to the product you have to sell; then build a bridge of verbal or pictorial symbols over which your customer can pass from fact to compensatory dream, and from the dream to the illusion that your product, when purchased, will make the dream come true. 'We no longer buy oranges, we buy vitality. We do not buy just an auto, we buy prestige.' And so with all the rest. In toothpaste, for example, we buy, not a mere cleanser and antiseptic, but release from the fear of being sexually repulsive. . . . In every case the motivation analyst has found some deepseated wish or fear, whose energy can be used to move the consumer to part with cash and so, indirectly, to turn the wheels of industry. Stored in the minds and bodies of countless individuals, this potential energy is released by, and transmitted along, a line of symbols carefully laid out so as to bypass rationality and obscure the real issue.

Aldous Huxley, *Brave New World Revisited*
(New York: Harper Brothers, 1958), 63–4.

tive pastiche, an abridged and inevitably somewhat distorted version of a 'reality' that is constructed in the process of being communicated.

The choices made by reporters, editors, producers, and others who contribute to the media product are not random. Several factors influence how reality is processed and how news is reported by the media. These factors may be understood as a series of filters that are more likely to let through certain information and images than others. To oversimplify a great deal, information and images that threaten the privileges of dominant social and economic groups are less likely to make it through these media filters than those that are fairly orthodox and non-menacing. This will strike many readers as being an absurd claim, conditioned as most of us are to believe that the media are independent and frequently critical of the powerful. On balance, however, the media do much more to support the status quo, including the distribution of power in society and the economy, than they do to erode it. In other words, their role in politics is essentially conservative.

The Economic Filter

Most media organs are privately owned, and as such they are subject to the iron law of the marketplace. That law is very simple: they must be able to sell a product that will attract enough subscribers, advertisers, buyers, or patrons—the exact source of revenue depends on the media product—to cover production costs and, usually, earn a competitive return on invested capital. Given the high costs involved in producing a daily newspaper, a slick magazine, a television series, or a feature film, profitability requires a mass market. No media organ needs to appeal to everyone in order to survive, and none tries. But particularly when a marketplace is competitive, there will be a tendency to avoid programming or content that seems likely to have limited appeal in favour of that which will hold onto, or even increase, sales.

State ownership alters, but does not eliminate, the economic pressures to which the mass media are exposed. Publicly owned broadcasters must be sensitive to charges of elitism. This is particularly true of television broadcasting, where the costs of producing high-quality entertainment programming are great. Few politicians will be willing to risk the loss of votes in order to subsidize broadcasting that attracts a tiny audience. Market influences become even greater when a publicly owned broadcaster is required to raise some part of its revenues from advertising or viewer/corporate support.

Economic pressures have an important impact on what the mass media produce. They cannot, however, explain all of media behaviour. What is finally offered to viewers, readers, and listeners is also affected by regulatory requirements, the legal system, and the cultural norms of society.

The economic filter operates mainly through the influence that advertising and industry structure have on the media product. Without advertising dollars, privately owned and even (to a lesser degree) publicly owned media companies are not economically viable. These media companies are in competition for the advertising patronage of business. It follows, then, that they will be sensitive to their patrons' needs and will tend to avoid reporting or programming that reduces their attractiveness in the eyes of advertisers. In the words of an American network executive, television 'is an advertising-supported medium, and to the extent that support falls out, programming will change.'[12] The advertising base of a newspaper or radio broadcaster is typically more local than that of a television network, but the maxim still holds: advertisers' preferences cannot be ignored by an ad-dependent media system.

How is this relevant to politics? First of all, dependence on advertising may reduce the likelihood that powerful economic interests will be portrayed in a negative light. This is not to imply that advertisers hold a power of economic blackmail over the heads of media organs. There have, however, been occasions when particular programs were boycotted by corporate sponsors or where their broadcast was followed by advertiser reprisals. In some instances, the anticipated reaction of corporate advertisers is enough to either kill a story or moderate its tone. But the influence of advertising is much more subtle and pervasive than these occasional incidents might suggest. When a typical 30-second commercial spot during prime time on a major American network can cost roughly US $200,000 (much more in the case of a special broadcast that pulls in extraordinary audience numbers, like the final episode of *Seinfeld* in 1998 or the Super Bowl), the economic costs of broadcasting material that offends powerful corporate advertisers obviously are great. Those who make programming decisions certainly are aware of this.

There is little evidence, however, to support the occasionally expressed view that news report-ing is 'censored' or slanted as a result of advertiser interference. In *News from Nowhere*, Edward Jay Epstein declares that none of the hundreds of correspondents and production personnel he interviewed for his study could recall an incident of sponsor interference in a network news broadcast. On the contrary, Epstein observes that stories that directly conflicted with the interests of major sponsors were not uncommon.[13] The fear that advertisers may withhold their business, he argues, has little impact on the content of national news programming, although it may occasionally affect news documentaries and other public affairs programs.

The influence of advertising operates in a second, more powerful way. Most television broadcasting and most viewing time are, we have seen,

From its earliest days as the Reform Party, Alliance Party politicians and those who support them have claimed that the media based in central Canada, are biased against them. (Roy Peterson, *Vancouver Sun*)

devoted to entertainment programming. Natural-ly, the most lucrative advertising slots are associ-ated with this sort of programming. There is, therefore, an economic pressure on ad-dependent broadcasters to maximize the amount of high audience-appeal programming during prime-time hours. Most public affairs programming does not have the draw of a popular sitcom or drama, and consequently is subject to pressures that it be marginalized (relegated to off-peak viewing times, or left up to state-owned or viewer-supported broadcasters) or that it adopt an entertainment format. The emergence of what has been called 'infotainment' or 'soft news'—news that is pack-aged using an entertainment, celebrity journalist format—has become prevalent in the United States. Infotainment is clearly linked to the high price fetched by advertising spots during popular viewing hours. The Canadian industry has not gone as far in breaking down the traditional bar-riers between entertainment and public affairs programming. But the economics of broadcasting in Canada also work against the viability of pro-gramming that does not attract a mass audience.

State-owned media organs like the CBC, TV Ontario, and Radio-Québec in Canada and the viewer-supported Public Broadcasting System (PBS) in the United States are not immune from the influence of advertising. Both the CBC and Radio-Québec rely on advertising for part of their revenue. In the case of the CBC, advertising income accounts for about one-quarter of its annual budget. Viewer-supported broadcasters like the American PBS system rely on state subsi-dies (directly and through the tax system) and corporate sponsorship of programs for part of their revenue needs. Some critics have argued that corporate sponsorship, like advertising, tends to filter out socially divisive and controversial pro-gramming, including criticism of powerful eco-nomic interests and the capitalist system.

Dependence on state subsidies does not nec-essarily remove all constraints on media content. Public broadcasters must constantly be sensitive to charges of bias and ideological favouritism.

Over the years CBC television programs like *This Hour Has Seven Days*, *the fifth estate*, *Marketplace*, and the various programs hosted by environ-mentalist David Suzuki, notably *The Nature of Things*, have been accused of having a leftist polit-ical bias and of being anti-business. The in-house monitoring of CBC broadcasting for 'fairness' has reached unprecedented levels of sophistication. Much of this, as during election campaigns, is intended to ensure that the CBC is even-handed in its treatment of the major political parties and their leaders. But monitoring also focuses on the portrayal and coverage of social and economic groups, including business. In the world of pub-lic broadcasting, culturecrats' and politicians' aversion to controversy may substitute for the check that dependence on advertising imposes on private broadcasters.

Industry structure is the second component of the economic filter. As the costs associated with producing a newspaper have increased, competi-tion has suffered. The daily newspaper industry in Canada (as in the United States) is characterized by local monopoly. In only nine Canadian cities (Halifax, Quebec, Montreal, Ottawa, Toronto, Winnipeg, Calgary, Edmonton, and Vancouver) is there competition between same-language, mass-circulation dailies that have different owners. Chain ownership is a feature of both the English- and French-language markets. Most daily news-paper circulation in English Canada is controlled by the Southam, Thomson, and Sun Media chains. In French-speaking Quebec all but a tiny share of the daily newspaper market is controlled by Québecor (Pierre Peladeau), Power Corpora-tion (Paul Desmarais), and Unimédia.

Television and radio markets, to say nothing of the Internet, are much more fragmented than the newspaper market. The days when a handful of American broadcasters, plus the CBC, dominat-ed television broadcasting are long past. Cable and satellite technology, and more recently the development of the Internet, have created unprecedented opportunities for niche program-ming targeted at more limited audiences than the traditional broadcasters require to ensure profitability. The economics of electronic media are significantly different from those of print media, such that concentrated ownership is not as prominent an issue in broadcasting as in newspaper markets.

Instead, the ownership issue in broadcasting and news media, like the Internet, is framed chiefly as an issue of American penetration into Canadian markets. There may indeed be hundreds of television stations that Canadian viewers have access to through direct broadcast satellite (DBS) or modern cable technology, but the fact remains that the most popular ones either originate in the United States or rely heavily on programming, often heavily promoted through advertising, produced in the United States. Issues of ownership in the United States and internationally are thereby imported into Canada.

One of these issues involves the new corporate convergence in mass media, particularly in electronic media industries. As the nationalist Friends of Canadian Broadcasting puts it, 'large media multinationals are getting larger, concentrating their market power, crossing over into new lines of [media] business and crossing national borders with unprecedented ease.'[14] The most prominent example of such a multi-media giant is Time Warner, whose corporate empire spans the older media of books, magazines, television broadcasting, and films, the newer media of cable, pay-per-view, and shop-at-home TV, and the ownership of intellectual property rights. Critics argue that multi-media convergence and the growth of giants like Time Warner will accelerate the erosion of national cultures like that of Canada.

A world in which such multinationals as Time Warner, Sony, IBM, Philips NV, and Disney dominate the electronic media food chain, from the production of the entertainment and information products through the means for distributing and receiving them, is not likely to provide much opportunity for the expression of distinctively Canadian values, perspectives, and stories. Or is it? There is, after all, little doubt that more Canadian programming is produced and available today than ever before. This has been largely due to government regulation and subsidies, to which we now turn.

The Legal/Regulatory Filter

Print media in Canada and in most other democracies are basically free from direct regulation by government. Unlike radio and television broadcasters and cable system companies, they do not require a special licence to do business. Newspapers and magazines essentially regulate themselves through press councils created and operated by the industry. These councils receive and investigate complaints; they do not systematically monitor performance. Calls for greater state regulation of their behaviour invariably provoke cries of censorship from those in the newspaper and magazine business.

A number of indirect forms of regulation, however, may affect content in the print media. Most of these involve measures whose ostensible aim is to promote Canadian values through newspapers and magazines. For example, the federal Income Tax Act permits advertisers to deduct from their taxable income only the cost of ads placed in newspapers or magazines that are at least 75 per cent Canadian-owned. This explains why foreign ownership of Canadian newspapers has never been an issue, despite the fact that the industry has been extremely profitable over the years and might therefore have been expected to attract foreign capital.

It is doubtful, however, whether the provisions of the Income Tax Act favouring Canadian-owned publications have much of an impact on newspaper content. With the chief exceptions of the *Globe and Mail*, the *National Post*, and *Le Devoir*, newspapers are geared to local markets. Community news and classified ads account for a large share of these papers. Their profitability depends on a large local readership that they can 'sell' to local advertisers. This, and not the nationality of their owners, will influence newspaper content.

One might argue, however, that the owner's nationality could influence the way a newspaper covers national and international news, as well as sports and comics—two of a paper's most read sections—but even Canadian-owned papers depend heavily on news that they purchase from foreign news agencies like the Associated Press wire service, particularly for international news and sports. Most comic strips—and we should not dismiss comics and cartoons as purveyors of values—are produced by American cartoonists. The economics of news-gathering, not the nationality of the owners, is responsible for this dependence on foreign sources of news. In the end, the Income Tax Act almost certainly does more to promote Canadian ownership than Canadian culture. The situation in the magazine industry is quite different. Despite the fact that the Canadian ownership provisions of the Income Tax Act also apply to magazines, the English-Canadian market is dominated by magazines and split-run publications. *Sports Illustrated* is an example of a split-run publication, where the magazine is based outside of Canada, most of its editorial and other production costs are incurred outside of Canada, and most of its circulation is non-Canadian. A split-run edition of such a magazine can be produced at a very low cost by importing the American version via satellite, adding a few pages of Canadian content, and qualifying for the lower Canadian advertising rates that Canadian magazines are able to offer advertisers.

In 1997 the World Trade Organization, responding to an American complaint, ruled that laws subsidizing Canadian magazines and treating foreign periodicals differently in terms of taxation and postal rates violated Canada's international trade obligations. In response, the federal government introduced Bill C-55, which proposed heavy fines for any magazine publisher selling ads in Canadian editions of foreign magazines, a measure that was clearly targeted at the highly profitable split-run issues of US magazines. This was met by loud protests from American magazines publishers, Canadian advertisers, and

the American government. By the summer of 1999 a compromise of sorts was negotiated, requiring that split-run editions include a majority of Canadian content in order to sell advertising space at the lower Canadian rate.

The split-run issue encapsulates the essential regulatory dilemma for Canadian policy-makers grappling to preserve Canadian culture and promote domestic cultural industries. It boils down to this: the much larger American market enables US magazine publishers to produce a glossier product and pay better rates for articles at a lower cost than their small-market Canadian counterparts. Moreover, Canadians have shown over the years that they like what American magazines offer. An estimated 80 per cent of the magazine titles available on Canadian newsstands are American, and US-based publications account for about 70 per cent of total magazine sales in Canada. Availability of Canadian magazines is not the problem. According to the Canadian magazine industry's own figures there are roughly 1,500 magazines published in Canada.[15] But with low cultural barriers between English Canada and the United States, no language barrier, and a high level of consumer and media integration between the two societies, American magazines do not seem to be foreign in the way that British or other English-language ones do.

State regulation is much more intrusive in the case of the electronic media. The original reason for treating broadcasting differently from print media was the need to prevent chaos on overcrowded airwaves. Controlling entry in a market through the licensing of broadcasters seemed the only practical solution to this potential problem. At the same time, however, broadcasting policy has always been based on the assumption that only extensive state intervention can prevent complete American domination of the Canadian market.[16]

The American 'threat' is a matter of simple economics, and content regulations for both radio and television constitute one of the pillars of Canadian broadcasting policy. The CRTC establishes and enforces a complicated set of content guidelines that all licensed broadcasters must observe. The idea behind them is to ensure that more Canadian content reaches the airwaves than would be available without regulation (see Box 11.2).

Whether or not the system works depends on what one means by 'Canadian content'. If this signifies that some of the major people involved in the production of a television program or piece of music are Canadian, then the policy has been a success. But if Canadian content is taken to mean the subjects, values, and ideas conveyed through these media, then the verdict is rather different. In fact, the *Report* of the Task Force on Broadcasting (1986) characterized the content system applied to television broadcasters as 'regulatory tokenism'. Many of the programs that qualify as Canadian content, it observed, 'could be mistaken for American productions and seem to have been made on the assumption that references to their Canadian origin would hurt their appeal to audiences outside Canada, particularly

---

BOX 11.2   What Is Canadian Content?

Radio:

According to the Canadian Radio-television and Telecommunications Commission (CRTC), a musical selection qualifies as Canadian content if it meets any two of the following critieria:

- The music is composed entirely by a Canadian.
- The lyrics are written entirely by a Canadian.
- The music is or lyrics are performed principally by a Canadian.
- The live performance is performed wholly in Canada and broadcast live in Canada or recorded wholly in Canada.
- The musical selection was performed live or recorded after 7 September 1991 and a Canadian who has collaborated with a non-Canadian receives at least 50 per cent of the credit as composer and lyricist.

For AM radio, at least 35 per cent of all music aired must meet this definition of Canadian content. In recognition of FM radio's diversity of formats (and the corresponding supply of appropriate Canadian-content recordings), the CRTC allows different levels of required Canadian music content. The quota is as low as 7 per cent in the case of ethnic radio stations.

In the case of French-language radio stations, at least 65 per cent of the music played must have French vocals, a quota that drops to 55 per cent between 6:00 a.m. and 6:00 p.m.

Television:

To be considered Canadian, a television program must have a Canadian producer and must earn a minimum 6 of a possible 10 points based on key creative positions. The CRTC awards points when the duties of these positions are performed by Canadians. There are additional criteria regarding financial and creative control for programs involving foreign production partners. The CRTC requires that Canadian progams be used to fill at least 60 per cent of the overall schedules of both public and private television broadcasters. Moreover, Canadian content must fill at least 50 per cent of evening programming hours for private broadcasters and 60 per cent for public broadcasters.

in the United States.'[17] The same may be said of content regulations for radio. The economics of the recording industry encourage products that are marketable outside of Canada. Radio stations typically deal with Canadian content requirements by relying heavily on recordings by performers like the Bare Naked Ladies, Céline Dion, Shania Twain, Alanis Morissette, and Avril Lavigne, whose music seems as at home in Boston as Toronto, and by marginalizing much of their Canadian content to off-peak hours.

Governments also affect the content of the electronic mass media through subsidies paid to Canadian film and television producers and through their direct participation in the industry as broadcasters and filmmakers. The Canadian content quotas established by the CRTC are, in the case of television, met largely through sports, news, and public affairs programming. But most viewing time is spent watching entertainment programs. Very few of these programs are Canadian, again, simply because it makes economic sense to purchase an American-made product for a fraction of its production costs—a product that, moreover, benefits from the inevitable spillover into Canada of advertising that American networks use to promote audience interest. In English-speaking Canada only the CBC broadcasts a significant amount of Canadian-made entertainment programming. Indeed, beginning in 1996 the CBC stopped broadcasting any American programs during prime time.

To compensate for the unfavourable economics of domestic production, Ottawa offers subsidies. This is done chiefly through Telefilm Canada, which helps finance the production of Canadian-made feature films (over 200 of them since 1986), television programs (more than 1,500 television programs and series since 1968), documentary films, and animation. Telefilm Canada also invests in international co-productions. If you look closely at the credits that scroll across the screen at the end of a Canadian-made television documentary, dramatic series, or children's program, chances are good that you will see

that it was subsidized by Telefilm Canada. While the publicly owned CBC, Radio Canada, TV Ontario, and Radio-Québec have been among the major recipients of money provided through Telefilm Canada over the years, private television and film producers have also drawn on this source of public money. Fears have long been expressed that they typically use these subsidies to produce what has been called 'American clone programming', films and television programs that are as unrecognizably Canadian as possible so as not to alienate potential American audiences. Again, the economies of profitability in broadcasting and film work against the goal of producing and promoting distinctively Canadian cultural products. Even with the maximum level of public support that Telefilm Canada is allowed to provide, the typically low licence fees paid by Canadian broadcasters still leave a production company with a significant share of production costs uncovered. There are, therefore, economic pressures to turn out an exportable product in order to recoup costs through foreign (this will usually mean American) sales. In the case of feature films the problem is largely that the two major distribution chains, Famous Players and Cineplex Odeon, do little to promote Canadian-made films, nor do the companies producing them have the resources to advertise widely to generate audience interest.

Despite the unfavourable economics of producing recognizably Canadian programs, a situation that subsidies appear not to correct, such programs do get produced. In the end it falls to public broadcasters and the National Film Board to carry most of the burden of showing Canadians what is distinctive about their society and culture. Indeed, this is what these organizations were intended to do. Under the Broadcasting Act the CBC is required to be 'a balanced service of information, enlightenment and entertainment for people of different ages, interests and tastes covering the whole range of programming in fair proportion'. The CBC, through its English- and French-language divisions, has done far more to Canadianize the airwaves than any other broadcaster, particularly when it comes to dramatic programming and during prime viewing hours. Its ability to do so, however, is threatened by budget cuts that began in the late 1970s. The CBC has responded by increasing its dependence on advertising. This places Canada's main public broadcaster between a rock and a hard place. On the one hand, the CBC is required to rely on Canadian programming. On the other hand, it is increasingly dependent on the revenues from the sale of advertising time, which requires that the CBC's programming achieve audience ratings that will attract and retain advertisers.

The National Film Board's mandate is to 'interpret Canada to Canadians and the rest of the world' (Film Act). For almost 65 years the NFB has done this to critical and international acclaim, turning out documentaries and serious drama that the private sector has been unwilling to produce. There is, of course, a very simple reason why private companies have not invested in these sorts of productions: the major theatre chains do not want to show them and ad-dependent television stations do not want to broadcast them. As in the case of the CBC, the burden of showing Canadians images of themselves falls to a publicly owned corporation.

Media content is also affected through federal and provincial laws dealing with obscenity, pornography, and what is called hate literature. None of these terms is defined very precisely in Canadian law, but the federal Criminal Code and the Customs Act, as well as provincial statutes dealing with hate literature, restrict the sorts of printed matter and films that may enter Canada or be distributed here, as well as the media products that individuals may possess. This last restriction became extremely controversial in January 1999 when a British Columbia Supreme Court judge ruled that a 1993 federal law prohibiting the possession of child pornography violated the right to individual privacy guaranteed under the Charter. A firestorm of protest greeted the ruling, part of which ultimately was upheld by the Supreme Court of Canada. Civil liberties groups were critical of the law for being too general.

The issue of when and how to restrict media content raises issues of censorship, individual privacy, freedom of expression, public morality, and the safety of certain groups, such as the children who become fodder for pornographic films, magazines, and Internet sites. These issues have become increasingly complex and traditional methods used to regulate media content have been challenged by the new media of satellite communications and the Internet. It has been estimated by the European Union and other organizations that, as of 2002, between 2,000 and 3,000 Web sites were dedicated to promoting hate. Thousands more are devoted to child pornography. Proposals to regulate media content on the Internet have ranged from making service providers responsible for the content of their Web sites and e-mail carried over their networks to a law that would require the labelling of all on-line information to identify the degree of adult content. To this point, however, regulation of the Internet remains relatively slight in Canada and other democracies. This is not, however, true throughout the world. Not until 2002 did the government of Iraq allow citizens, other than authorized officials, Internet access. Not surprisingly, countries in which traditional media are state-controlled have been unwilling to let their populations have full and open access to Web-based sources of information.

The Technological Filter

Few things date more quickly than news. The technology of broadcasting is instantaneous and that of newspapers involves a matter of hours. The mass media are thus capable of providing their audiences with the latest developments, and indeed our general expectations are that they will communicate what is happening now. What is happening now, of course, can be reported in the context of the larger background against which events unfold. The practical problem is that stories must be edited down to a length suitable for inclusion in a 30-minute news program or the pages of a newspaper.

Television, we have already noted, is the medium relied upon by most people for their knowledge of national and international events. The visual character of this medium lends itself to the personalization of reality—an emphasis on individuals and personalities at the expense of broad social forces that are not captured by the eye of a camera. Consequently, the media, in particular television, are disposed towards the personal, the immediate, and the concrete. Reality becomes a constantly shifting pastiche of images, as though those who produce the news assume that the average viewer has an attention span that lasts a minute or two at best. Entertainment programming tends to assume the same faster-than-life character. According to Morris Wolfe, this is because of what he calls the First Law of Commercial Television: 'Thou shalt give them enough jolts per minute (jpm's) or thou shalt lose them.'[18] Too few jpm's and viewers will lose interest and change channels—and ratings will suffer. And if ratings suffer, advertising revenue will fall and profits will drop. But are the networks simply giving the viewers what they want? And what difference does it make for politics if, in Wolfe's words, 'all television increasingly aspires to the condition of the TV commercial'?[19]

Industry people are doubtless correct when they claim that many viewers are easily bored and that a rapid pace and frequent jolts are necessary to capture and hold their attention. But it may also be true that viewers have come to expect the sort of high jpm product at which commercial television and film excel. Morris Wolfe again: '[A] steady diet of nothing but high jpm television tends to condition viewers' nervous systems to respond only to certain kinds of stimulation. Their boredom thresholds are frequently so low that TV viewers find it difficult to enjoy anything that isn't fast-paced.'[20] (As an aside, some psychologists argue that the explosive growth in what is labelled attention deficit disorder is, in fact, a result of the impact of television and video games on the central nervous systems of children.[21]) Whatever the cause, it can hardly be denied that most television

shows (including news programs) and commercial films have the staccato rhythm and jumped-up energy level that Wolfe and countless other media watchers have commented on.

Wolfe's First Law of Commercial Television captures only part of the explanation for what he calls the 'TV wasteland'. The technology of television and film is also responsible. It is often said that one picture is worth a thousand words. This is doubtless true—sometimes. But it is often the case that the moving images on the screen capture only the surface of events, and this substitutes for an explanation that is more complicated and *non-visual* than the medium can deal with. Of course, people can turn to newspapers, magazines, and books to fill in those parts of the picture that are not covered well by television. But there are good reasons for believing that most do not. We mentioned earlier that a clear majority of Canadians rely on television for their knowledge of national and international affairs and, furthermore, believe this medium to be the most unbiased and believable. In other words, they count on what they see before their eyes.

Politicians and others who regularly come under the eye of the camera have long understood the biases of the visual medium. Photo opportunities and highly structured, controllable events are among their ways of using television's need for the immediate, the personal, and the visual to their own advantage. Television has had an enormous impact on how elections are fought, how special interests attempt to influence public policy, and how public officials communicate with the people. One of the masters of the medium, the American social activist Jesse Jackson, remarked over three decades ago on the importance of speaking in short memorable sentences—'sound bites' as they are called today. They conform to the needs of television technology; long, rambling, or complex statements do not (see Box 11.3).

Those who produce television programs, including the news, operate on the assumption that action and motion are far more likely to hold viewer attention than are 'talking heads'. There is,

BOX 11.3   The Philosophy Behind the 30-Second TV News Story

Because the television commercial is the single most voluminous form of public communication in our society, it was inevitable that Americans would accommodate themselves to the philosophy of television commercials. By 'accommodate,' I mean that we accept them as a normal and plausible form of discourse. By 'philosophy,' I mean that the television commercial has embedded in it certain assumptions about the nature of communication that run counter to those of other media, especially the printed word. For one thing, the commercial insists on an unprecedented brevity of expression. One may even say, instancy. A sixty-second commercial is prolix; thirty seconds is longer than most; fifteen to twenty seconds is about average. This is a brash and startling structure for communication since, as I remarked earlier, the commercial always addresses itself to the psychological needs of the viewer. Thus it is not merely therapy. It is instant therapy. Indeed, it puts forward a psychological theory of unique axioms: the commercial asks us to believe that all problems are solvable, that they are solvable fast, and that they are solvable fast through the interventions of technology, techniques and chemistry. This is, of course, a preposterous theory about the roots of discontent, and would appear so to anyone hearing or reading it. But the commercial disdains exposition, for that takes time and invites argument.

Neil Postman, *Amusing Ourselves to Death: Public Discourse in the Age of Show Business* (New York: Penguin, 1985), 130–1.

therefore, an exaggerated emphasis on action, and particularly on two-sided conflict. As Edward Jay Epstein explains:

> . . . the high value placed on action footage by executives leads to a three-step distillation of news happenings by correspondents, cameramen and editors, all of whom seek the moment of highest action. Through this process, the action in a news event, which in fact may account for only a fraction of the time, is concentrated together and becomes the central feature of the happening. This helps explain why news on television tends willy-nilly to focus on activity.[22]

The visual character of television introduces other biases as well, including dependence on stereotypes and emphasis on confrontation.

Dependence on a repertory of stereotypes. Writing early in the twentieth century, Walter Lippmann argued that newspaper reporting consisted largely of fitting current news to a 'repertory of stereotypes'. There are cultural reasons for this that we will discuss later. But in the case of a visual medium, there are also technological reasons for this dependence. 'Viewers' interest', observes Epstein, 'is most likely to be maintained through easily recognizable and palpable images, and conversely, most likely to be distracted by unfamiliar or confusing images.'[23]

Emphasis on confrontation. From the standpoint of a visual medium, confrontation has two virtues. First, it involves action, which is one of the requirements of most television news and public affairs coverage. Second, conflict helps to present a story in a way that viewers can easily grasp. Epstein notes that 'Situations are thus sought out in network news in which there is a high potential for violence, but a low potential for audience confusion.'[24] When the events themselves do not include the necessary visual drama, this can always be provided through the use of file film—action in the can and ready to go!

The Organizational Filter

News-gathering and reporting are carried out by organizations. The needs and routine procedures of these organizations influence the content of the news: both what is reported and how it is covered. The organization's dilemma is that news developments are not entirely predictable, yet it does not have the resources to be everywhere news might break or to cover all stories equally well. News organizations rely on various strategies to deal with this dilemma.

In the case of television, several criteria help to impose predictability on the news. Those who have a reputation for being influential or who occupy an official position of some power are more likely to make the news than those whose public profile is lower or whose position does not, in the eyes of news-gatherers, automatically confer on them a mantle of credibility. Prime ministers, premiers, and the leaders of opposition parties are automatically assumed to be newsworthy, as are mayors and leading councillors when the news item is local. Spokespersons for what are considered to be important organizations—the Canadian Council of Chief Executives (formerly the Business Council on National Issues), the Canadian Labour Congress, the Women's Legal Education and Action Fund, the Catholic Church, and so on—are also considered to be newsworthy and can count on being sought out when an issue falls into their sphere of concern.

Government officials and powerful private interests understand that news organizations operate within a system of routines and requirements including, for example, the need to have the evening news film footage in the can by a certain hour to allow time for editing. Accommodating the media's needs through well-timed press conferences, photo opportunities, news releases, and staged events—what Daniel Boorstin has called 'pseudo-events'—is simple prudence from the standpoint of groups that want to affect public opinion. This practice has been called **news management**. Obviously, governments and the public affairs/media relations bureaucracies of the powerful are not able to control the news agenda. But they are able to influence news reporting.

Publicly acknowledged experts will also be sought out by the media. What makes one a 'publicly acknowledged expert'? Affiliation with a respectable institution is one of the key determinants of this status. Specialists associated with an established think-tank such as the C.D. Howe Institute, the Canadian Centre for Policy Alternatives, the Fraser Institute, or a university—particularly a university located in a city where a network has production facilities—are most likely to be considered newsworthy. The point here is not that only 'establishment' voices will be heard on an issue, but that spokespersons for mainstream views are almost certain to receive a hearing because their institutional affiliation confers on them the status of 'acknowledged expert', while spokespersons for marginal groups and unconventional views are much less certain to be deemed newsworthy.

The mass media's demand for the ideas and information generated by experts is based on a combination of factors. One of these is the media's self-image as dispenser of the news, reporter of the facts. Fulfillment of this role requires access to sources of information whose credibility is sound and whose claim to objectivity is generally accepted. Related to this is a second factor: the media's need for low-cost information and instant analysis. To conduct their own analysis would be expensive and time-consuming, and most journalists are in any case not trained as professional economists, sociologists, political scientists, or whatever other field of expertise a story may call for. It therefore makes economic sense to tap the knowledge of those whose training, reputation, and/or institutional affiliation confer on them the social standing of 'expert'. Third, to protect themselves against charges of bias and lawsuits, media organizations and reporters need information 'that can be portrayed as presumptively accurate'.[25] Expert knowledge meets this requirement, and that provided by those with socially respected professional or institutional credentials is particularly useful. In fact, the media's need for expert opinion and information helps to confer this social respectability on individuals and institutions, and in many instances probably serves to reinforce the political status quo.

Predictability is important in determining what become 'news'. Any news organization operates within the framework of a budget and the limited resources—camera crews, journalists, researchers, and so on—that this implies. Other things being equal, it makes sense to concentrate organizational resources where news is most likely to happen: Parliament Hill, the provincial capitals, Toronto and Montreal, and internationally as resources permit. Of course, this becomes a bit of a self-fulfilling prophecy. The unplanned, especially unexpected happenings that occur too quickly or too far away to send a journalist and film crew are less likely to be covered than scheduled events that take place near where a news crew is stationed. As Epstein puts it, 'The more predictable the event, the more likely it will be covered.'[26]

Visual appeal is also important. Television obviously needs pictures. But some subjects are more telegenic than others. Epstein writes:

> . . . priority is naturally given to the story in a given category that promises to yield the most dramatic or visual film footage, other things being equal. This means, in effect, that political institutions with rules that restrict television cameras from filming the more dramatic parts of their proceedings are not routinely assigned coverage.[27]

Canadians see much more of what is happening in the House of Commons, particularly Question Period, than they do of the Supreme Court. And yet the Court's decisions have an enormous impact on public policy, in many instances more of an impact than the fairly predictable antics of parliamentarians. Likewise, closed meetings of first ministers, the proceedings of regulatory commissions, and the institutions of the bureaucracy generally are either inaccessible to cameras or lack the sort of visual spice that is usually considered a crucial ingredient of televised news. The result, therefore, is to overemphasize the importance of those actors and individuals who can be filmed in action—action that is often stage-managed by the actors themselves—and to underemphasize the significance of those who are more reclusive or who do not lend themselves to confrontational or sensational visual bites.

A news organization's need for stories that are newsworthy, predictable, and visually appealing produces a situation where 'the news selected is the news expected.'[28] Along with the other filters we have discussed, the organizational one creates biases that affect media content. Simple dramatized confrontation, familiar players and issues, and a relatively narrow range of locales where most news happens are among these biases.

The Ideological Filter

Those who report the news are often accused by conservatives and business people of having liberal-left and anti-business biases. They are more likely, it is argued, to favour stories and groups that challenge established authority. The CBC in general and some of its programs in particular have occasionally been accused of ideological bias against the Canadian Alliance, conservatism, and big business (especially American business). Similar charges have been heard in the United States, where Republicans, conservatives, fundamentalist Christians, and business interests have often accused the major networks, and journalists generally, of harbouring liberal biases.

Studies seem to confirm these claims. An American study that looked at the social backgrounds, personality traits, ideologies, and world views of business and media elites found that media respondents typically gave more liberal responses to such statements as 'Government should substantially reduce the income gap between rich and poor.'[29] The researchers concluded that 'leading journalists seem to inhabit a symbolic universe which is quite different from that of businessmen, with implications for the manner in which they report the news to the general public.'[30] Several American studies have confirmed that those in the media, particularly the electronic media, tend to be more liberal than members of the general population. A study of CBC radio, directed by Barry Cooper, concluded that 'on the whole, [the CBC] adopted a left-wing, rather than right-wing critical stance.'[31] His study of CBC television news coverage arrives at a similar conclusion, although Cooper expresses it rather differently. 'The CBC,' he argues, 'like all modern media, has directed its energies towards the production of a specific configuration of opinion—namely progressive opinion—and not towards the provision of reliable information about the world.'[32]

This conclusion is reinforced by what is probably the most systematic study to date of Canadian journalists' values and beliefs.[33] Based on a survey of 270 electronic and print journalists and a sample of the general public (804 respondents), Cooper and Lydia Miljan draw two main conclusions. First, English-Canadian journalists tend to be more left-of-centre than the general public, a finding that corroborates Cooper's earlier studies. Second, the left-leaning proclivities of journalists affect the way news stories are reported, a finding that may appear unsurprising but that does not exactly square with the media's credo of objectivity. Among the ways in which English-Canadian journalists differ from their audiences and readerships are the following:

- Journalists are less religious than the public, 57 per cent saying that they did not belong to a religion and 32 per cent saying that they definitely believed in God compared to 39 per cent (no religious affiliation) and 56 per cent (definitely believe in God) for the university-educated public.
- Although the ideas of private-sector journalists on the desirability of capitalism, free markets, and

private property are broadly the same as those of the general public, the views of the public-sector CBC journalists are significantly to the left.
- The public is more conservative on social issues than those in the media. For example, journalists are more likely than the general public to believe that abortion should be considered a moral and legal right and a much greater share of the public than journalists believes that gay and lesbian issues receive too much media attention.
- Journalists are considerably more likely than the general public to vote for the NDP, the highest level of NDP support by far being among CBC radio journalists.

Miljan and Cooper also note that French-Canadian journalists are closer to their audience/readership in their political and social views than are English-Canadian journalists to theirs, a circumstance that may reflect a more secularized, libertarian, and left-leaning society in Quebec than is found in English Canada.

Although it is pretty clear that left-of-centre political and social views are more often found among those in the media than in Canadian society as a whole, this ideological gap needs to be understood in the context of what 'left' and 'right' mean in Canadian society. 'Left' does not mean fundamental opposition to the basic institutions of the capitalist economy. To be on the left in the predominantly liberal societies of Canada and the United States has always meant to be ambivalent about business—to distrust excessive concentrations of economic power, to believe that business must be regulated—and to favour an active welfare state that can support the disadvantaged in society, while accepting the superiority (in most circumstances) of private property and the market system of allocation. But this is the ambivalence of family members who do not see eye to eye on all matters at all times.

News and public affairs reporting focuses on conflict and controversy, often involving government officials and powerful private interests, so this naturally gives the impression that those in the media are anti-establishment critics. The impression is somewhat misleading. Ralph Miliband is almost certainly correct when he observes that only a minority of those in the mass media have strong left-wing or right-wing commitments. This is certainly true in Canada. Those on the right, such as David Frum and Mark Steyn, and those on the left, such as Linda McQuaig and Judy Rebick, are relatively rare in Canadian journalism. The majority occupy various locations towards the middle of the ideological spectrum and generally experience little difficulty in accommodating themselves to the needs of the organization within which they work. 'They mostly "say what they like",' says Miliband, 'but this is mainly because their employers mostly like what they say, or at least find little in what they say which is objectionable.'[34]

It bears repeating that most of what the mass media produce does not fall into the categories of news and public affairs. It should not be assumed, however, that the entertainment and information products of the media industry carry no political messages or ideological biases. They do, both through the images, themes, and interpretations they communicate and through their silences. If the mass media are 'more important in confirming or reinforcing existing opinions than they are in changing opinions',[35] as studies generally suggest, this is partly due to the ideological orthodoxy of most writers, producers, editors, and others who have an influence on the media product.

This is not to suggest that there is no place in the mass media for people whose political views lie outside the safer familiar mainstream. The point is, rather, that those in media industries cluster mainly in the uncontroversial centre of the political spectrum. For these cultural workers the other four filters affecting media content are largely beside the point. The conformity of their value systems with that of society's dominant ideology ensures that they seldom, if ever, test the limits of what the system will allow.

THE MEDIA AND DEMOCRACY

> In regard to propaganda the early advocates of universal literacy and a free press envisaged only two possibilities: the propaganda might be true, or it might be false. They did not foresee what in fact has happened, above all in our Western capitalist democracies—the development of a vast mass communications industry, concerned in the main neither with the true nor the false, but with the unreal, the more or less totally irrelevant. In a word, they failed to take into account man's almost infinite appetite for distractions.[36]

The media, it often appears, have few friends except themselves. Politicians, business people, and those on the right of the political spectrum regularly accuse the media of having liberal-left biases, of irresponsible scandal-mongering, and of being inherently and unfairly opposed to established authority. Those on the political left, however, are no less critical of the media. They are apt to view the media as the servile handmaidens of powerful interests, particularly economic ones. Both ideological camps, right and left, accuse the media of having strongly anti-democratic tendencies. Conservatives argue that those in the media tend to be more liberal-left than society as a whole but foist their interests and perspectives on the public behind a smokescreen of journalistic detachment and objectivity. Left-wing critics of the media claim that the media help to 'manufacture consent'[37] for a social system—including political and economic structures—that operates mainly in the interests of a privileged minority. What the mass media foist on the public, leftist critics charge, are less their own ideological biases than the false consciousness of the dominant ideology. In this chapter we have argued that the behaviour of the mass media is shaped by a number of filters. These filters cumulatively determine the sort of 'product' likely to reach the consuming public. Our conclusion is that the products of the mass media are generally supportive of established values and institutions. Thus, the media tend to reinforce the power of those groups whose interests are best served by the status quo. In order to play this role it is not necessary that the media avoid all criticism of powerful interests. This would be a ludicrous claim. All that is necessary is that an overwhelming preponderance of what appears on the page, screen, and over the airwaves conforms to mainstream values. This test is amply met.

On the other hand, it must be admitted that the gains made in recent years by socially marginal, politically weak interests such as Aboriginal Canadians, women, and environmental activists have been in large measure due to media coverage of their demands and spokespersons. This, in turn, has raised public consciousness of the issues and discourse—'equal pay for work of equal value', 'Aboriginal self-government', 'sustainable development'—associated with their demands. Moreover, it can hardly be denied that the media usually do a better job of scrutinizing and criticizing government actions, to say nothing of those of powerful societal groups, than do the opposition parties. Indeed, it is precisely the critical and even irreverent tenor of much public affairs journalism that contributes to the widespread belief in the mass media's independent and anti-establishment character.

Most of what the mass media offer does not have this character. Frank Lloyd Wright's description of television as 'chewing gum for the eyes' is in fact a fairly apt characterization of much of the mass media, electronic and print. Wright's judgement was basically an aesthetic one. But Huxley's argument—that the 'mass communications industry is concerned in the main neither with the true nor the false, but with the unreal, the more or less totally irrelevant'—expresses a political judgement about the mass media. Huxley is suggesting that the media—particularly their entertainment and advertising components—help to foster a false consciousness among the public, the sort of pacified somnolence that characterizes the masses in his *Brave New World*. This may seem rather harsh, but Huxley is certainly right in suggesting that one should not assume that only news and public affairs reporting has political consequences.

On balance, democracy is not very well served by Canada's mass media. The biases of the mass media are towards familiar images and stories—what Lippmann called a 'repertory of stereotypes'—oversimplified conflict, the personalization of events, drama and action, and reliance on established opinion-leaders. These biases are much more supportive than threatening of the status quo. Moreover, as we saw in Chapter 9, the media can be an important channel for the manipulation of public opinion by political parties and well-heeled societal interests, particularly business. Given their enormous importance as mediators of reality for Canadians, one might wish for something better than this.

NOTES

1. Neil Postman, *Amusing Ourselves To Death: Public Discourse in the Age of Show Business* (New York: Penguin, 1985).
2. Henry Commager, ed., *Documents of American History*, 8th edn (New York: Appleton, Century, Crofts, 1968), 104.
3. www.efc.ca/pages/media/globe:08may97.html
4. Walter Lippmann, *Public Opinion* (New York: Harcourt, Brace and Company, 1922), 13.
5. http://friendscb.org/Split_Screen/splt.html
6. Canada, Royal Commission on Newspapers, *Newspapers and Their Readers* (Ottawa: Supply and Services, 1981), 26, table 19.

7. The Royal Commission on Newspapers expressed this view, although only the case of the Irving family in New Brunswick was cited explicitly. See also the comments of the former Premier of Saskatchewan, Allan Blakeney, in Diane Francis, *Controlling Interest: Who Owns Canada?* (Toronto: Macmillan, 1986), 316.

8. Edward Herman and Noam Chomsky, *Manufacturing Consent* (New York: Pantheon, 1988), 8.

9. Walter I. Romanow et al., 'Correlates of Newspaper Coverage of the 1979 Canadian Election: Chain Ownership, Competitiveness of Market, and Circulation', study done for the Royal Commission on Newspapers (Ottawa: Supply and Services, 1981).

10. Audit Bureau of Circulation, *Fas-Fax: United States and Canadian Periodicals and Canadian Circulation of U.S. Magazines* (Toronto, 1999).

11. Lippmann, *Public Opinion*, 345.

12. Quoted in Todd Gitlin, *Inside Prime Time* (New York: Pantheon, 1983), 253.

13. Edward Jay Epstein, *News from Nowhere: Television and the News* (New York: Random House, 1973), 112.

14. Friends of Canadian Broadcasting, 'Split Screen', at http://friendscb.org/Split_Screen/splt7.html

15. www.billc55.com/billc55/about/facts

16. See the discussions in Frank Peers, *The Politics of Broadcasting 1920–1951* (Toronto: University of Toronto Press, 1969); Marc Raboy, *Missed Opportunities: The Story of Canada's Broadcasting Policy* (Montreal and Kingston: McGill-Queen's University Press, 1990).

17. Task Force on Broadcasting, *Report* (Ottawa, 1986), 433.

18. Morris Wolfe, *Jolts: The TV Wasteland and the Canadian Oasis* (Toronto: James Lorimer, 1985), 14.

19. Ibid., 16.

20. Ibid., 18.

21. Richard DeGrandpre, *Ritalin Nation: Rapid-fire Culture and the Transformation of Human Consciousness* (New York: W.W. Norton, 1999).

22. Epstein, *News from Nowhere*, 263.

23. Ibid., 262.

24. Ibid.

25. Herman and Chomsky, *Manufacturing Consent*, 19.

26. Epstein, *News from Nowhere*, 146.

27. Ibid., 147.

28. Ibid., 199.

29. Stanley Rothman and S. Robert Lichter, 'Personality, Ideology and World View: A Comparison of Media and Business Elites', *British Journal of Political Science* 15, 1 (1984): 36.

30. Ibid., 46.

31. Barry Cooper, *Sins of Omission: Shaping the News at CBC TV* (Toronto: University of Toronto Press, 1994), xi.

32. Ibid., 227.

33. Lydia Miljan and Barry Cooper, *Hidden Agendas: How the Beliefs of Canadian Journalists Influence the News* (Vancouver: University of British Columbia Press, 2003).

34. Ralph Miliband, *The State in Capitalist Society* (London: Quartet Books, 1969), 211.

35. Leon Epstein, *Political Parties in Western Democracies* (New York: Praeger, 1967), 237.

36. Aldous Huxley, *Brave New World Revisited* (New York: Harper & Brothers, 1958), 44.

37. The term is used by Herman and Chomsky in their analysis of the political role of the American media. They, in turn, borrow it from Walter Lippmann, who had in mind, however, government's use of propagandistic techniques to cultivate popular acceptance of their rule.

Suggested Readings

Barry Cooper and Lydia Miljan, *Hidden Agendas: How Journalists Influence the News* (Vancouver: University of British Columbia Press, 2003). This is one of the few empirical studies of the nature and causes of media bias, and probably the best.

Paul Nesbitt-Larking, *Politics, Society, and the Media: Canadian Perspectives* (Peterborough, Ont.: Broadview Press, 2001). Nesbitt-Larking offers a compre-hensive examination of the characteristics and political and social impacts of Canada's media system.

David Taras, *Power and Betrayal in the Canadian Media* (Peterborough, Ont.: Broadview Press, 2001). This is a highly critical account of the performance of the Canadian media system by one of its most astute observers.

Review Exercises

1. Keep a two-day record of your media consumption, being sure to write down all the television programs and films you watch, the amount and sorts of radio programming you listen to, the newspapers, magazines, and books you read, and your Internet activity. Try not to change what would be your normal pattern of viewing/listening/reading/surfing. Based on this record, answer the following questions:

    (a) What proportion of your daily media consumption is normally devoted to entertainment? News and public affairs? Other purposes?

    (b) Which medium (or media) do you rely upon most for news about your local community, your country, the international scene?

    (c) If and when you pick up a newspaper, which section do you read first? What else do you look at in the newspaper?

2. Critics sometimes charge that the media mainly cover the same stories, often based on the same news sources. Compare the front pages and editorial pages of the *Globe and Mail* and your local paper or the *Toronto Star* for two successive Saturdays. Make two lists of stories, one of articles that cover a story reported in both papers and the other of stories covered in only one (at least on these pages). Exclude letters to the editor, but include editorials. What conclusions do you draw?

3. Watch the late-evening television news broadcast of one of the main Canadian broadcasters (CBC, CTV, or Global). Make a list of those stories where experts are interviewed, quoted, or referred to (for example, 'A study by the C.D. Howe Institute . . .'). Record the positions and, if possible, affiliations of the experts (e.g., professors, government officials, think-tank researchers, activists, etc.). Can you suggest other sorts of experts or organizations that could have been contacted for any of these stories?

PART FIVE

CONTEMPORARY ISSUES IN CANADIAN POLITICAL LIFE

Groups opposed to Quebec independence have often used the fear of economic loss, as in this image from the 1995 Quebec referendum campaign, to dissuade Quebecers from leaving Canada. (Comité québécois pour le Canada)

Conflict over language has always been a central feature of Canadian politics. This chapter explains why language and the status of Quebec are such prominent issues in Canada. It also examines chief aspects of federal and Quebec language policies. Topics include the following:

- ❏ The demographics of language politics.
- ❏ The shift from French-Canadian nationalism to Quebec nationalism.
- ❏ The Quiet Revolution and its legacy.
- ❏ Language policy in Quebec.
- ❏ Federal language policy.
- ❏ Is Quebec a distinct society?

CHAPTER TWELVE

LANGUAGE POLITICS

Like the theme of unrequited love in an Italian opera, the status of Quebec is an issue that surfaces repeatedly when Canadians and their governments turn their thoughts to constitutional reform. And like Italian opera, elements of tragedy and comedy mingle freely when the related issues of Quebec's constitutional status and language rights are on the table. But unlike an Italian opera, the 'Quebec question'—which might just as fairly be called the 'Canada question' (or at least one of the fundamental Canada questions, the other one being Canada's relationship to the United States)—has no neat finale. Even the scenario of a separate Quebec would not bring down the curtain on the 'Canada/Quebec' question. No one doubts that an enormous number of practical matters would still have to be dealt with, including such thorny issues as the nature of economic relations between the remnants of *l'ancien Canada* and the status of the French language in a Canada without Quebec.

Why are Quebec and language so central to Canadian politics? Why is the issue of language rights so closely tied to that of Quebec's constitutional status? Why do Lord Durham's words about 'two nations warring in the bosom of a single state', words written over 150 years ago, sound so apt today? What does Quebec want from the rest of Canada, and the rest of Canada from Quebec? Why has nationalism always been the key to unlocking the mysteries of Quebec politics?

Questions do not always have answers. These are big questions, and despite all the attention paid them throughout this country's history they are far from being settled. Let us at least try to understand why these particular questions have so often been asked and why answers have been so elusive.

THE DEMOGRAPHICS OF LANGUAGE POLITICS

When New France was formally placed under British control in 1763, francophones outnumbered anglophones by about eight to one in the territory that would become Canada. Forty years later, the two groups were of roughly equal size. During the mid-nineteenth century the English language gained ground on the French because of the wave of immigrants from the British Isles, so that by the 1871 census—Canada's first—Canadians of French origin comprised about one-third of the population.[1] The extraordinarily high birth rate among French-Canadian women enabled francophones to hold their own until the end of the 1950s against an English-speaking population that was buoyed by immigration—immigrants of whatever language group overwhelmingly adopted English as their new language. Since then birth rates have dropped precipitously in Quebec, where the vast majority of francophones reside, and the francophone share of Canada's population has nudged down to its present all-time low of about 23 per cent (see Figure 12.1).

The end of *la revanche des berceaux*—the high birth rate that for close to a century enabled French Canada to maintain its numerical strength against English Canada—coupled with the fact that the vast majority of immigrants have chosen English as their adopted language, finally led to a decline in the francophone share of the Canadian population by the early 1960s. More worrisome from the standpoint of Quebec governments was the fact that demographers began to predict a fall in the francophone share of that province's population, particularly in Montreal where most new immigrants chose to establish themselves. Mon-

Figure 12.1   Mother Tongues of the Canadian Population, 1931–2001

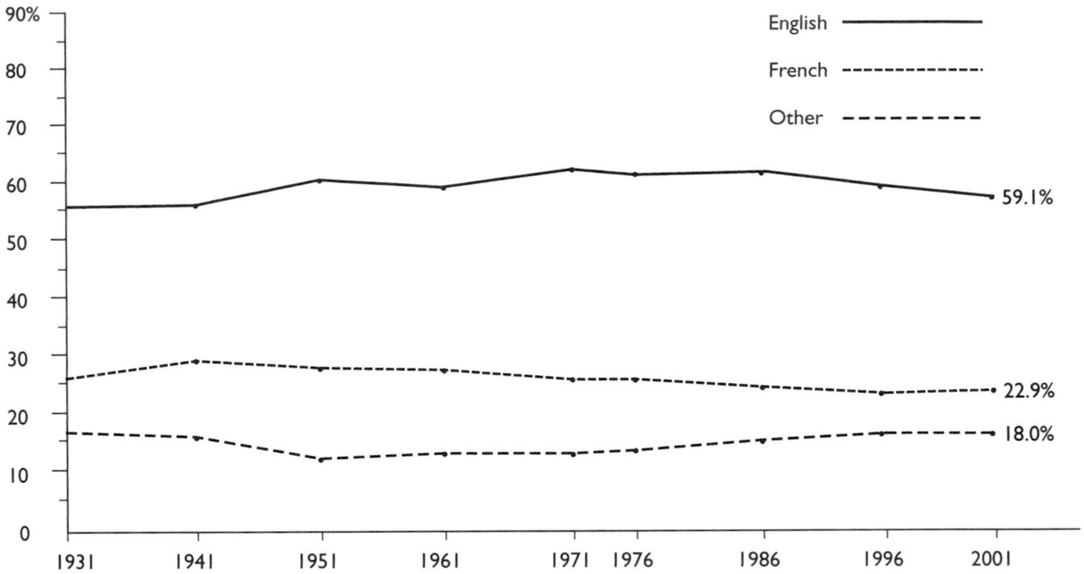

Sources: Leacy, ed., *Historical Statistics of Canada,* Series A185–237; *Canada Year Book 1990,* 2–25; www.statcan.ca/, Catalogue no. 96F0030XIE2001005.

treal, which proudly called itself the second largest French-speaking city in the world (after Paris), according to demographer Jacques Henripin, would be about equally divided between anglophones and francophones by the early twenty-first century.[2] The possibility that francophones would become a minority in Quebec was often raised by Quebec nationalists, although serious demographers like Henripin argued that this possibility was quite remote.[3] Nevertheless, this decline provided the impetus for provincial language laws intended to stem this tide.

The key factor in shifting the linguistic balance of Quebec, it should be emphasized, was immigration. Given that the province's anglophones were no more fecund than francophones, the language choices of allophones—Canadian demographers' unlovely term for those whose native language is neither English nor French— would be crucial in shaping Quebec's future linguistic contours. Immigration became the sole reason for provincial population growth by the 1960s, given that the provincial fertility rate had fallen below the replacement level (i.e., the average number of births per female needed to offset the mortality rate).

With the exception of the relatively few immigrants whose native tongue was French, all other groups overwhelmingly adopted English for themselves and their children. As of the 1961 census, 46 per cent of foreign-born residents of Quebec spoke only English, another 25 per cent spoke English and French, and only 17 per cent spoke only French.[4] Despite provincial language laws that require immigrants to send their children to French schools, make French the sole official language for provincial public services, and promote the use of French in the Quebec economy, evidence points to the fact that many allophones still opt for English. Figure 12.2 shows that the percentage of Quebecers claiming French as their mother tongue is identical to the percentage who speak mainly French in the home. But the percentage speaking English in the home is greater than that which claims English as its mother tongue. The gains made by the English-speaking community can only be explained by the linguistic choices of those whose mother tongue is neither French nor English. New Quebecers have continued to find English an attractive choice, although less often than before the existing provincial language laws were put into place.

Inside Quebec, the current demographic picture includes the following characteristics.

- French is spoken at home by about 82 per cent of the population (2001 census).

- Contrary to projections made in the 1960s and early 1970s, Quebec has not become less francophone. The 81.4 per cent of the population speaking French at home compares to 80 per cent in 1901 and 81 per cent in 1961.

- Most of the province's population increase is due to immigration. The 2001 census study shows that slightly more immigrants in Quebec adopt English as their home language as choose French (22.1 per cent versus 20.4 per cent), despite the provincial *francisation* measures targeted at them.[5]

- Quebec's share of Canada's total population has fallen over the last two decades, from 28 per cent in 1971 to about 23 per cent in 2002.

Outside Quebec the language picture looks very different. With the exceptions of New

You ethnics are free to complain about Quebec's unjust language laws...

... just be sure that you complain twice as loudly in French as you do in English!

The portrayal of Quebec's language laws in English Canada is usually extremely critical. In this cartoon the character in the dark trench coat is evocative of a Nazi, an unflattering image if ever there was one! (Roy Peterson, *Vancouver Sun*)

Brunswick and Ontario, the francophone populations of the other provinces are tiny. In fact, in certain provinces and in all but a handful of Canada's major metropolitan areas outside Quebec, some of the non-official-language communities are considerably larger than the French-speaking minority. For example, in Vancouver native speakers of Chinese outnumber those whose mother tongue is French by a ratio of more than ten to one and in Toronto by a ratio of five to one.

Figure 12.2   Mother Tongue and Language Spoken at Home, 2001

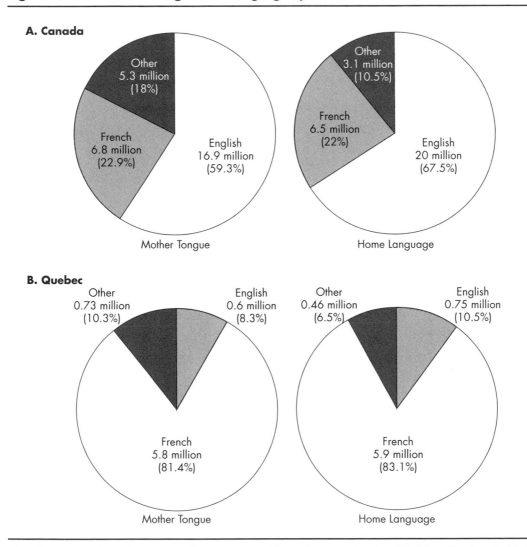

A. Canada

B. Quebec

Note: The category 'Other' includes non-official languages and those who report French and English, or French or English plus a non-official language, as their mother tongue or home language.

Source: *Census of Canada,* 2001.

Native speakers of Italian are as numerous as those of French in Windsor and outnumber francophones by a two-to-one ratio in Hamilton.

In all provinces except Quebec, the French-language community loses some of its members to the English majority. This may be seen from the difference between those for whom French is their mother tongue and those for whom it is their home language. This difference represents the rate of language transfer to the dominant language group (see Table 12.1). Only in Quebec and, to a lesser degree, New Brunswick is the rate of French language retention high. By contrast, the rate of language retention among native English-speakers is high everywhere in Canada.

This is not a recent development. In *Languages in Conflict*, Richard Joy carefully documented the trend towards the assimilation of francophones outside Quebec. Joy was the first to make what today seems an obvious point, namely, that the rate of language transfer is greatest among the younger generations. For example, using data from the 1961 census he found that the transfer rate from French to English in the four western provinces was 25 per cent among those aged 45–54 but 60 per cent for those aged 5–14 and 67 per cent among infants of ages 0–4.[6] Only in what Joy called 'the bilingual belt', the narrow region running from Moncton, New Brunswick, in the east to Sault Ste Marie, Ontario, in the west, was the rate of assimilation among all generations significantly lower. The reason, of course, was the ability to shop, work, go to church, and do the other things that keep a language alive. Outside the bilingual belt, this supportive milieu was seldom encountered. Indeed, the 2001 census shows that the francophone population in every province except Quebec and New Brunswick is older than in Canada as a whole, confirming Joy's prediction that the failure to retain young francophones would contribute to the steady erosion of the community's base.

Table 12.1   Percentage of Francophones* Who Speak English at Home, by Province and Canada less Quebec, 1991 and 2001

	1991	2001	Percentage change 1991–2001 (loss or gain)
Newfoundland and Labrador	54.9	63.6	−15.8
Prince Edward Island	46.7	53.1	−13.7
Nova Scotia	41.7	45.6	−9.3
New Brunswick	9.7	10.5	−8.2
Quebec	1.1	1.0	0
Ontario	36.9	40.3	−9.2
Manitoba	50.1	54.7	−9.2
Saskatchewan	67.6	74.6	−10.4
Alberta	64.6	67.7	−4.8
British Columbia	72.8	72.7	0
Canada less Quebec	35.1	38.1	−8.5

*Francophone: the population with French as mother tongue.
Note: The total of the percentages of francophones speaking English or French most often at home may be smaller than 100 per cent because some of them speak a non-official language most often at home.
Source: Statistics Canada, *Profiles of languages in Canada: English, French and many others*, Catalogue no. 96F0030XIE2001005, 30.

At this point some readers may protest that the gloomy picture Joy drew three decades ago is no longer accurate. They will point to statistics suggesting that bilingualism outside of Quebec has been increasing in recent years. Indeed, bilingualism is today highest among the young, the very group that Joy argued was most likely to transfer to the dominant language group. The rapid expansion of French immersion schools since the 1980s, particularly in Ontario, which accounts for over half of all immersion students in Canada, is responsible for most of this increase. The future of French outside Quebec, they argue, is assured.

What is one to conclude from the fact that while the francophone share of Canada's population outside of Quebec has been declining, the proportion of the population claiming to be bilin-

gual has been increasing? Does this represent a reprieve for French-language minorities? Or are they, as René Lévesque once said, 'dead ducks', or as Quebec writer Yves Beauchemin has characterized them, '*des morts vivantes*' ('warm corpses' would be a reasonable translation)?

The pressures of assimilation continue unabated throughout most of the predominantly English-speaking provinces. A study by Roger Bernard of the University of Ottawa concludes that a combination of aging populations, low birth rates, marriage to non-francophones, and the general lack of supportive social and economic milieux for French speakers will lead to the collapse of many francophone communities outside Quebec within a generation or two.[7] The 2001 census found that about 50 per cent of married francophones living outside Quebec and

Figure 12.3   Bilingualism in Canada, 1931–2001

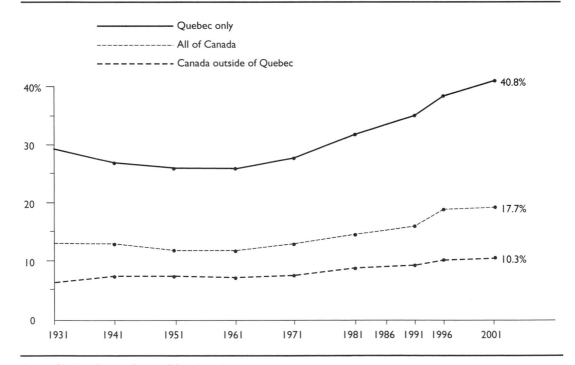

Source: Statistics Canada, *Census of Canada,* various years.

New Brunswick had anglophone spouses. Generally, English becomes the lingua franca and the language of the children in such families. It appears, however, that the fate of larger francophone communities in northern and eastern Ontario and in New Brunswick may be less bleak. Jacques Henripin cautiously suggests that official bilingualism in New Brunswick and the extension of French-language services and education in Ontario may have slowed the assimilationist tide in those provinces.[8]

As for the increasing level of bilingualism in Canada, we would not draw from this the conclusion that the prospects for living in French outside of Quebec have improved. The census question that measures bilingualism ('Can you carry on a conversation in the other official language?') does not provide a measure of languages in use. The fact that increasing numbers of those whose mother tongue is English are 'functionally fluent' in French does not mean that French will be used more often in the home, the workplace, at the pub, and wherever else communication takes place. Indeed, there is a good deal of evidence suggesting that a quarter-century of French immersion education[9] has produced a wave of **receptive bilinguals**—people who are capable of responding to French communications but who do not themselves initiate conversations in French, consume French-language media, or seek out opportunities to live in their acquired second language. There is certainly nothing wrong with this and, indeed, much that is good about the expansion of bilingualism, receptive or otherwise! But the claims made for and conclusions drawn from the immersion experience should be viewed with a certain amount of skepticism (see the discussion later in this chapter).

Moreover, despite the 30 years of immersion education in Canada, the rate of functional bilingualism is still relatively low outside of Quebec, at about 10 per cent for the population as a whole and closer to 15 per cent for young people between the ages of 15 and 24. Over half of all bilingual Canadians reside in Quebec, where the

rate of bilingualism is about four times greater than in Ontario. The increase in the level of bilingualism in Quebec since the 1960s has been sharper than in the rest of Canada. This is simply to say that Canadian bilingualism is to a considerable degree a predominantly Quebec phenomenon. In fact, the most recent census found that the level of bilingualism among anglophones outside Quebec declined in recent years.

Finally, the fact that functional bilingualism appears to be on the rise does not mean that the social and economic milieux outside Quebec have become more supportive for francophones. It is true that provincial government services for the francophone communities of Ontario have improved since the mid-1980s, and those in New Brunswick are quite good. But it is also true that few French-speaking people outside the 'bilingual belt' can manage to shop, work, and do the other daily social activities that help keep a language alive. Even francophone schools in predominantly English-speaking communities experience the pressures of language erosion. René Lévesque's characterization of francophones outside Quebec as 'dead ducks' is somewhat overstated. Lame ducks might be closer to the truth.

THE TRAJECTORY OF NATIONALISM

French-Canadian nationalism, Pierre Trudeau wrote, was originally a system of self-defence. This was certainly true. Conquered by arms, the French-speaking population of New France found themselves subordinated to an anglophone minority about one-eighth its size. English was the language of the new political and commercial elites. The Conquest left French a second-class language within Quebec and francophones largely excluded from the colony's structures of power.

Why did francophones not succumb to assimilationist pressures, as they did in Louisiana after it, too, passed from French control? The answer is complex, but three chief factors can be identified. One involved the policies of the British colonial authorities in New France. By the terms of the Quebec Act, 1774, they granted formal protection to the status of the Roman Catholic religion and the *code civil*, the basis of civil law in New France.[10] Faced with rebellion in the Thirteen Colonies, which two years later successfully declared their independence from Britain, this recognition of the rights of the French-Canadian population may have been motivated chiefly by the desire to ensure the allegiance of the clerical and civil leaders of that population. Regardless, it involved official recognition of the rights of the francophone Catholic majority and reinforced the leadership role of that community's clerical elite.

A second factor that explains the different fates of the French language and culture in Louisiana compared to Quebec is demography. French-speakers in the South of the United States were very quickly swamped by a rapidly growing anglophone population. In Canada, although immigration of Loyalists from the United States and of English-speakers from the British Isles tipped the linguistic balance towards English by the early nineteenth century, the high fertility rate among French Canadians enabled them to hold their ground at about one-third of Canada's population between Confederation and the 1950s.

The defensive posture that Trudeau argued was characteristic of French-Canadian nationalism is the third factor that explains the ability of French Canada to resist the pressures of assimilation. Under the guidance of a clerical elite whose leading social role was strengthened when anglophones occupied the political and commercial elites of the colony, French Canada met the challenge of English domination by remaining loyal to traditional values and institutions. The nationalist ideology that developed in French Canada after the Conquest is summed up in a famous passage from *Maria Chapdelaine*, the classic novel of traditional French Canada:

> Round about us strangers have come, whom we are wont to call barbarians; they have seized almost all the power; they have acquired almost

all the money, but in the country of Quebec nothing has changed. . . . [W]e have held our own, so that, it may be, after several centuries more, the world will turn to us and say: these people are of a race that knows not how to perish. . . . .

In the country of Quebec, nothing shall die, and nothing shall be changed. . . .[11]

Traditional French-Canadian nationalism was guided by the idea of **la survivance**—survival, against the pressures of a dominant culture that was anglicizing, Protestant, materialistic, liberal democratic, and business-oriented. In other words, this dominant English culture was all the things that French Canada, according to the spokespersons for this ideology, was not and should not become. The main ideas expressed in the writings and public pronouncements of the exponents of the traditional nationalism can be summarized fairly briefly:

- French Canada comprised a distinct nation, whose chief characteristics were the Catholic religion and the French language. Preservation of the French language and the Catholic religion were inseparable, as the title of Henri Bourassa's book *La langue, guardienne de la foi*[12] explicitly declared. 'The preservation of language', Bourassa wrote, 'is absolutely necessary for the preservation of a race, its spirit, character and temperment.'[13]
- French Canada had a mission, a special vocation as a people. The mission was to remain faithful to its roots and to resist the lure of materialistic, English, Protestant pressures. The democratic belief in the separation of church and state was ludicrous. It was a lamentable heresy that was spawned by the French Revolution and the American Constitution.
- The character of the French-Canadian people was most secure in the province of Quebec, but French Canada was not restricted to the boundaries of that province. In other words, French Canada was defined by socio-cultural characteristics, not by the territory of Quebec.

While these were the chief characteristics of the nationalist ideology that became dominant in

French Canada during the nineteenth century, a dominance that continued until the middle of the twentieth century, there were voices of dissent. In fact, sociologist Marcel Rioux has argued that the idea of the French-Canadian nation was first developed by the secular elites of Quebec who espoused liberal and often aggressively anti-clerical views.[14] Political scientist Denis Moniére concurs, noting that the authority of the Church was much weaker before and in the decades immediately following the Conquest than is usually believed (especially by English-Canadian historians).[15] He maintains that the 'victory' of the conservative traditional nationalism only became assured after the defeat of Louis Papineau's liberal forces in the Lower Canada Rebellion of 1837. But even after the ideological dominance of the Church and the voices of traditional rationalism was firmly established, liberal voices of dissent were occasionally heard.[16]

The traditional nationalism came under mounting pressure during the middle of the twentieth century. Its chief tenets were increasingly at odds with the economic and social reality of Quebec. The emigration of hundreds of thousands of French-speaking Quebecers to the northeastern United States during the latter half of the nineteenth century demonstrated more clearly than anything the empty idealism of the traditional nationalism's hymn to the pastoral vocation of French Canadians. There simply was not enough arable land to support the rural parish lifestyle that the ideologues of the traditional nationalism clung to so tenaciously. The urban population of Quebec surpassed the rural population in the 1921 census (56 per cent to 44 per cent). Between 1926 and 1950 the number of people employed in Quebec's manufacturing sector increased by about 220 per cent, slightly higher than the rate of increase for Canada as a whole (210 per cent), but significantly higher than the rate for the rest of the country if Ontario—where most new investment in manufacturing was located—is omitted from the picture.[17] By the middle of the twentieth century manufacturing workers

outnumbered farm workers in Quebec by a large margin.[18] In short, even by the early twentieth century the 'typical' Québécois lived in a city or town, worked in a factory, store, or office and had family members who had left the province in search of employment opportunities.

Quebec was following the path of modernization. But the urbanization and industrialization that this involved also produced a political side effect of enormous importance. This was the increasing realization that francophones, despite accounting for about four-fifths of the Quebec population, were largely shut out of the centres of economic decision-making and controlled relatively little of the province's wealth. 'Is there any inherent or unavoidable reason why,' asked Abbé Lionel Groulx in 1934, 'with 2,500,000 French Canadians in Quebec, all big business, all high finance, all the public utilities, all our water rights, forests and mines, should belong to a minority of 300,000?'[19] Although the question was not new—Edouard Montpetit, Errol Bouchette, Étienne Parent, and others had raised basically the same issue in arguing that educated francophones needed to rid themselves of their apparent distaste for careers in industry and finance—it was being asked with increasing frequency between the 1930s and the 1950s.[20]

These decades saw the emergence of the first serious challenge to the conservative ideology since the crushed rebellion of 1837. It brought together a diverse group of university professors and students, journalists, union activists, liberal politicians, and even some elements within the Catholic Church (particularly Action catholique). They were united by their opposition to the so-called 'unholy alliance' of the Catholic Church, anglophone capital, and the Union Nationale party of Maurice Duplessis and, of course, to the conservative nationalism that sought to justify French-Canadians' marginal economic status. Marcel Rioux calls this anti-establishment challenge the ideology of contestation and recoupment.[21] It contested the traditional elites' monopoly over power in the province and what was argued to be their backward characterization of French-Canadian society and culture. Its goal was to recoup lost ground; to bring Quebec's society, economy, and government up to date, a goal that became known in Quebec as *rattrapage* (catching up).

The nerve centre of this challenge to the conservative establishment and ideology included the Faculty of Social Sciences at Laval University; the intellectual revue *Cité libre*, founded by such figures as Pierre Trudeau and Gérard Pelletier; and the provincial Liberal Party. As the political party attempting to depose Duplessis, it was natural that the Quebec Liberal Party would attract the energies of those who saw the Union Nationale under *le chef* as one of the chief obstacles to reform.

Like the dinosaurs, the traditional ideology and the interests it defended were doomed by their failure to adapt to a changing environment. As Marcel Rioux observes, 'the ideology and old power structure in Quebec were becoming anachronistic in the face of the demographic, economic, and social changes that Quebec was experiencing.'[22] They managed to hold on until the 1960s largely because of the tight web of patronage politics that Maurice Duplessis used to keep the ideologically conservative Union Nationale in power between 1945 and his death in 1959. The death of Duplessis was followed by disorder within the governing Union Nationale. Paul Sauvé, who succeeded Duplessis as Premier, died suddenly within a year. The Union Nationale went into the 1960 provincial election under a leader, Antonio Barrette, who was opposed by many powerful members of the party. The Liberal Party's election victory probably owed as much or more to disorder within the Union Nationale as to popular support for change. Regardless, the opportunity for reform had come.

THE QUIET REVOLUTION AND ITS LEGACY

The first several years of the 1960s are justly considered a turning point in the history of Que-

bec.[23] Duplessis's death in 1959 and the election of the provincial Liberals under Jean Lesage in 1960 opened the way for the political reforms and social changes that generally are referred to as the Quiet Revolution. At the heart of these reforms lay an increased role for the Quebec state. It replaced the authority of the Catholic Church in the areas of social services and education, and also acquired a vastly broader range of economic functions. The provincial state was seen as the *moteur principal* of Quebec's attempt to modernize social and political institutions that were ill-suited to the urbanized, industrialized society that Quebec had become. The state, traditionally viewed as a second-class institution in a province where most social services were controlled by the Church and where government was associated with crass patronage, became the focus of nationalist energies.

The nationalism that emerged in the crucible of the Quiet Revolution marked a sharp break with the past. The traditional nationalism had emphasized preservation of the *patrimoine*—the language, the faith, the mores of a community whose roots went back to New France. Although some of its chief spokespersons, such as Abbé Lionel Groulx, associated this community with the region of the St Lawrence River and even with the vision of a Laurentian state whose territory would include what is today the southern region of the province, the essential elements of the traditional nationalism were not defined by either the territory or the powers of the Quebec state.

Rioux has characterized the traditional nationalism as an ideology of conservation. Its goals were the preservation of the traditional values and social structures of French Canada, including the leading role played by the Church in articulating these values and controlling these structures (i.e., the schools, hospitals, labour unions, etc.). The modern welfare state necessarily threatens the dominant social role of the Church and was generally rejected by spokespersons for the traditional nationalism. Although they insisted on constitutional protections for the province's exclusive right to make education policy and put limits on Ottawa's ability to interfere with social affairs in the province, they did not expect that the Quebec state would actively occupy these fields. The traditional nationalism attached no particular value to the Quebec state, except insofar as its powers could be used to ward off federal intrusions that challenged the status of conservative values and the power of the traditional elites—the clergy, anglophone business leaders, and provincial politicians.

Nationalism is always based on some concept of the nation: who belongs to it and who does not. The traditional nationalism did not identify *la nation canadienne-française* with *la société française du Québec*. The boundaries of *la nation* extended beyond Quebec to embrace French Canadians throughout Canada. There were two reasons for this. First, Catholicism and the role of the Church were important elements of the traditional nationalism. Obviously, neither of these stopped at the Quebec border. Second, the anti-statist quality of the traditional nationalism prevented it from associating the French-Canadian nation with the Quebec state.

History had shown that assimilationist pressures and unsympathetic governments faced francophones outside of Quebec. Nevertheless, to identify *the nation* with the Quebec state would have challenged the dominant social role of the Church. The survival of the nation did not depend, according to the traditional nationalism, on the activities of the Quebec state. Instead, it depended primarily on those institutions that were crucial to the continuation from generation to generation of the French language and the Catholic religion—family, school, and parish. Family and parish obviously fell outside the state's authority. And although the schools were under the constitutional jurisdiction of the provincial state, their control was mainly left in the hands of the Church. This did not change until the early 1960s.

The central elements of the traditional nationalism were located outside of the state. This would not be true of the new nationalism that both spurred and was influenced by the Quiet Revolution. Instead of defining *la nation* in terms of language and religion, the ascendant nationalism of the 1960s developed an understanding of Quebec's history, its economy, and its social structure that was based on language and dependency. The dependency perspective portrayed Quebec as a society whose evolution had been shaped and distorted by the economic and political domination of English Canadians.

This secularized version of French-Canadian history, and more particularly of francophone Quebec, cast an entirely different light on the future of the Quebec nation and its relationship to English Canada. If the problem was that Québécois were dominated economically and politically, then the solution required that they take control of their economic and political destiny. To do so, they would have to use the Quebec state. All of the major reforms of the Quiet Revolution—the establishment of a provincial Ministry of Education, the nationalization of privately owned hydroelectric companies, the creation of Crown corporations such as la Caisse de dépôt et placement and la Société générale de financement, and passage of the Quebec Pension Plan—involved using the Quebec state in a newly assertive way.

The replacement of the traditional nationalism by the state-centred nationalism of the Quiet Revolution was not as abrupt as history might suggest, nor was this new nationalism unchallenged. The traditional social order and its values had been crumbling at the edges for at least a couple of decades before the deaths of Duplessis and then of Sauvé finally provided the opportunity for opposition groups to gain power. Once the doors were opened to reform, it quickly became apparent that the anti-Duplessis forces shared little more than a common antipathy towards the old order. They were divided on at least three main levels.

First, there was a split between the federalists and those who advocated either special status or independence for Quebec. The federalists included such prominent figures as Pierre Elliott Trudeau, Jean Marchand, and Gérard Pelletier, all of whom entered federal politics through the Liberal Party in 1965. Leadership of the Quebec autonomy side would fall on René Lévesque, who became the first leader of the Parti Québécois in 1968 and who had been a key minister in the Lesage government of the early 1960s and before that a popular broadcaster. The second division concerned the size and functions of the Quebec state. Even within the reformist Liberal government of Jean Lesage, there were sharp differences over such major policies as the nationalization of the hydroelectricity industry and the role of the province's investment agency, la Caisse de dépôt et placement. Agreement that the provincial state should play a larger role in Quebec society was not matched by consensus on what that role should be. Finally, Quebec separatists were divided on ideological lines. Those who came to form the leadership of the *indépendantiste* Parti Québécois, individuals like René Lévesque, Jacques Parizeau, and Claude Morin, were ideologically liberal. But there were others, within the PQ and in other pro-independence organizations, for whom Quebec independence was inseparably linked to the overthrow of what they argued to be a bourgeois state. PQ members Pierre Bourgault and Robert Burns, for example, wanted the end of *la domination anglaise* of the Quebec economy. Although the electoral strength of these left-wing groups never amounted to much, they managed to have a significant impact on political discourse in Quebec, particularly through the province's universities, labour unions, and in the extra-parliamentary wing of the PQ.

In view of these divisions, two developments justify the claim that a state-centred nationalism emerged out of the Quiet Revolution. First, the identification of French Canada with the territory of Quebec was a view shared by most nationalists. Indeed, the entry of Trudeau and his fellow federalists into national politics was chiefly a reaction to this Quebec-oriented nationalism. The provincial Liberals' 1962 campaign slogan, **Maîtres chez nous**,

captured a nationalist consensus that ever since has been an accepted tenet of Quebec politics. Second, key institutional reforms of the Quiet Revolution, including the Caisse de dépôt et placement, Hydro-Québec, and the jurisdictional terrain that the Quebec government wrested from Ottawa in the areas of social policy, immigration, and taxation, have left an important mark on Quebec nationalism. They constitute the hard core of the provincial state upon which the aspirations summed up in the phrase *Maîtres chez nous* depend.

The Unilingual Approach of Quebec

We are Québécois. . . . At the core of this personality is the fact that we speak French. Everything else depends on this essential element and follows from it or leads us infallibly back to it.[24]

The origins of present-day language policy in Canada lie in developments in Quebec during the 1960s. With the election of the Quebec Liberal Party in 1960, the political obstacles to change were largely removed and the outdated character of the traditional ideology was exposed. It was replaced by an emphasis on catching up with the level of social and economic development elsewhere. As many commentators have observed, the construction of the Manicouagan dam in northern Quebec—engineered and built by Québécois—became a popular symbol for the new confidence in the ability of French-speaking Quebecers to cope with a modern world and to compete economically. The state, traditionally viewed as a second-class institution in a province in which most social services were controlled by the Church and government was associated with crass patronage, became the focus of nationalist energies. The fact that the new nationalism of the Quiet Revolution turned to the provincial state, in which French-speaking Quebecers were unquestionably in the majority, reinforced the identification of French Canada with the territory of Quebec.

The ideology of *rattrapage* and the identification of French Canada with Quebec had important consequences for language policy in that province. As the instrument for economic and social development, the Quebec state assumed functions previously administered by the Church authorities and also expanded the scope of its economic activities. In doing so it provided career opportunities for the growing number of educated francophones graduating from the province's universities. Access to high-paying managerial and technical jobs in the private sector, however, remained blocked by anglophone domination of the Quebec economy. The relative exclusion of francophones from positions of authority above that of foreman and the concentration of francophone businesses in the *petites et moyennes entreprises* sector of the economy had long been known.[25] This situation ran directly counter to the expectations of the Quiet Revolution and became an important political issue when the capacity of the public sector to absorb the increasing ranks of highly educated francophones became strained.

Demographic trends comprised an additional factor that shaped provincial language policy in Quebec. Immigrants to the province overwhelmingly adopted the English language. This fact, combined with the dramatic reduction in the birth rate among francophones, lent credibility to a scenario where francophones might eventually become a minority even within Quebec. Along with evidence of the exclusion of francophones from much of the province's economic structure, these trends formed the basis for the policy recommendations of the Quebec Royal Commission of Inquiry on the Position of the French Language and on Language Rights in Quebec (the Gendron Commission, 1972). That Commission's recommendation that the provincial government take legislative action to promote the use of French in business and in the schools was translated into law under the Quebec Liberal government that introduced the Official Language Act[26] and in the Charte de la langue française[27]—or Bill 101, as it was more commonly known outside Quebec— passed under the subsequent Parti Québécois government. Without going into the detailed provisions of this legislation, three principal features of Quebec language policy since the passage of Bill 101 can be identified.

(1) French is established as the sole official language in Quebec, and therefore the exclusive official language for proceedings of the provincial legislature and the courts and the main language for public administration in the province. In a 1979 decision the Supreme Court of Canada ruled that this section of Bill 101 violated section 133 of the BNA Act, which guarantees the coequal status of the French and English languages at the federal level and in the province of Quebec.[28] Nevertheless, the principal language of provincial government services in Quebec is French, and many provincial and local services are not available in English in much of the province.

(2) Through the requirement that businesses with 50 or more employees receive a *francisation* certificate as a condition of doing business in the province, the Quebec government seeks to increase the use of French as a working language of business in the province. The language charter does not establish linguistic quotas for corporations. Instead, it leaves the conditions of certification a matter for individual negotiations between a firm and the Office de la language française. Despite some initial resistance from the anglophone business community, symbolized by the immediate move of Sun Life's head office from Montreal to Toronto in 1977, this section of Bill 101 has generally been accepted by employers. More controversial have been the provisions requiring that public signs and advertisements be in French only. This blanket prohibition was relaxed in 1983 to make exception for bilingual advertising by 'ethnic' businesses, and in a 1988 decision the Supreme Court ruled that it violated the freedom of expression guaranteed in the Charter of Rights and Freedoms.[29] The signage provisions of Quebec's language law were modified in 1989 through Bill 178, which required that exterior commercial signs be in French only, but allowed bilingual interior signs so long as the French language was more prominently displayed. These provisions were

amended again in 1993 through Bill 86, which states that the rules governing when signs must be unilingual French and when other languages are allowed shall be established by government regulations—a more flexible approach than enshrining the rules in the statute.

(3) The provisions of Bill 101 that initially excited the most controversy were those restricting access to English-language schools in Quebec. Under this law, children could enrol in an English school if one of the following conditions was met: their parents had been educated in English in Quebec; they had a sibling already going to an English school; their parents were educated in English outside of Quebec but were living in the province when the law was passed (1977); they were already enrolled in an English school when the law came into effect. The intent was obviously to reverse the overwhelming preference of immigrants for the English language, a preference that demographers predicted would eventually change the linguistic balance in the province, and even more dramatically in Montreal, which attracted the vast majority of immigrants. In one of the first Supreme Court decisions on the Charter of Rights and Freedoms, the Court held that the requirement that at least one of a child's parents must have been educated *in* English in Quebec violated section 23 of the Charter, a section that clearly had been drafted with Bill 101 in mind. The practical importance of this ruling is small, given the low level of migration to Quebec from other Canadian provinces. More significant is the fact that the Supreme Court was unwilling to accept the Quebec government's argument that the demographic threat to the position of the French language justified this restriction on language rights under the 'reasonable limits' section of the Charter. In 1993 the education provisions of Bill 101 were brought into conformity with s. 23 of the Charter.

Despite some setbacks in the courts, the principles on which Quebec's language policy rests have remained substantially unchanged since the passage of Bill 101. The most publicized reform of the province's language law occurred after the Supreme Court's 1988 ruling that the prohibition on languages other than French for commercial signs in Quebec violated the Charter's guarantee of freedom of expression. Within weeks the Quebec legislature passed Bill 178, which invoked the 'notwithstanding clause' of the Charter in order to reaffirm the ban on languages other than French for commercial signs outside a business. Legal restrictions on commercial signs were removed in 1993, as noted above, although they continue to be maintained through regulations (see Box 12.1). Judged according to its two main objectives—increasing the use of the French language in the Quebec economy and stemming the decline in the francophone share of the provincial population—Bill 101 must be judged a success.[30]

Language policy in Quebec has been shaped by the idea that French Canada is co-extensive with the boundaries of that province. The Office de la langue française and the law it administers build on an approach to language promotion that can be traced back to the early 1960s. The Liberal government of Jean Lesage set out to increase francophone participation in the economy through such provincial institutions as la Société générale du financement, la Caisse de dépôt et placement, Sidérurgie québécoise, and an expanded Hydro-Québec.[31] The common denominator since then has been the use of the provincial state as an instrument for the socio-economic advancement of francophones.

The Bilingual Approach of Ottawa

A very different approach to language policy—one based on a conception of French and English Canada that cuts across provincial borders—has been pursued by successive federal governments since the 1960s. Responding to the new assertive nationalism of the Quiet Revolution, the signs of which ranged from Quebec's demands for greater taxation powers and less interference by Ottawa in areas of provincial constitutional responsibility to bombs placed in mailboxes and at public

BOX 12.1   Signs, Flags, and Political Undercurrents

The picturesque and historic village of Knowlton, Quebec, is located a little more than an hour's drive southeast of Montreal in what are called les cantons de l'est (the Eastern Townships) of Quebec. For almost 200 years the population of Knowlton and the surrounding region was predominantly English. This has changed over the last several decades. Knowlton remains a largely English-speaking community, but the English-speaking population of the region has declined and the French-speaking population has increased. In 2000 Knowlton was at the centre of a language controversy that received national attention. 'The Lyon and Wallrus' antique shop was charged with being in violation of the Charter of the French Language because its outside sign gave equal prominence to French and English. The shop's owners appealed the $500 fine that was imposed on them, but the Quebec Court of Appeal upheld their conviction. After the Supreme Court of Canada refused to hear an appeal of this ruling the Lyon and Wallrus's owners decided in December 2002 to take their case to the United Nations Committee on Human Rights, which has ruled against provisions of Quebec's language legislation in the past. Visitors to Knowlton will notice an unusual number of Canadian flags. One might imagine that this is for the benefit of American tourists who flock to its quaint boutiques, but Quebec nationalists know that the message being conveyed is also, even primarily, a political one directed at them. The Canadian flag is a symbol of division in this town, where an overt expression of Canadian patriotism is seen by many French-speaking Quebecers as gesture of defiance.

BOX 12.2   Do Beer Coasters Threaten French in Quebec?

An Indian restaurateur in Montreal has been told he is violating Quebec's language charter with a cardboard beer coaster. Satyajyoti Bhattacharjee has been ordered by the Commission de Protection de la Langue Française to get rid of Double Diamond beer coasters or face fines of up to $7,000. 'This business is no longer funny', Bhattacharjee, the owner of the Indira Restaurant, said Thursday. Language inspectors have been complaining about his Double Diamond coasters since February 1999, and he's not sure why. True, the oval coasters sing the praises of British ale in English only, but the square English-only coasters touting a German beer seem to be acceptable to the inspectors, Bhattacharjee said. The firm that supplies Indira with imported beers and ales and free promotional coasters was also at a loss Thursday to explain why Bhattacharjee has been singled out. Christian Geadah, sales manager of Premium Beer Co., said about 70 restaurants and bars in the Montreal and Quebec City areas use the free Double Diamond coasters. Jean Saindon, the language inspector who has written three letters to Bhattacharjee about the coasters, said Thursday that he couldn't explain or comment on the case.

Windsor Star, 31 Mar. 2000.

monuments, the Liberal government of Lester Pearson established the Royal Commission on Bilingualism and Biculturalism. As Eric Waddell writes, 'The federal government was facing a legitimacy crisis in the 1960s and 1970s and had the immediate task of proposing a Canadian alternative to Quebec nationalism.'[32] The B&B Commission was a first step towards the adoption by Ottawa of a policy of official bilingualism. This policy was to some degree intended to defuse the *indépendantiste* sentiment building in Quebec, especially among young francophones, by opening Ottawa as a field of career opportunities to rival the Quebec public service.

The alternative Ottawa offered, which was expressed in the federalist philosophy of Pierre Trudeau, was of a Canada in which language rights would be guaranteed to the individual and protected by national institutions. In practical terms this meant changing the overwhelmingly anglophone character of the federal state so that francophones would not have grounds to view it as an 'alien' level of government from which they were largely excluded. These changes have been carried out on two main fronts. First, what Raymond Breton refers to as the 'Canadian symbolic order' has been transformed since the 1960s.[33] Through a new flag, the proclamation of 'O Canada' as the official national anthem, new designs for stamps and currency, and the language neutering of some federal institutions, documents, and celebrations (for example, Trans-Canada Airlines became Air Canada, the BNA Act is now officially titled the Constitution Act, 1867, and Dominion Day is now called Canada Day), a deliberate attempt has been made to create symbols that do not evoke Canada's colonial past and British domination. Second, the passage of the Official Languages Act (1969) gave statutory expression to the policy of bilingualism that had been set in motion under Lester Pearson. This Act established the Office of the Commissioner of Official Languages as a 'watchdog' agency to monitor the three main components of language equality set forth in the Act: (1) the public's right to be served by the federal government in the official language of their choice;

(2) the equitable representation of francophones and anglophones in the federal public service; and (3) the ability of public servants of both language groups to work in the language of their choice. The situation that the Official Languages Act was intended to redress was one where francophone representation in the federal state was less than their share of the national population. Francophone under-representation was greatest in managerial, scientific, and technical job categories (see Figure 12.4). Moreover, the language of the public service—the language that officials worked in and, in most parts of the country, the language that citizens could realistically be expected to be served in—was English. In view of these circumstances, Ottawa's claim to 'represent' the interests of francophones lacked credibility.

Among the main actions taken to increase the bilingual character of the federal bureaucracy have been language training for public servants, the designation of an increasing share of positions as bilingual, and the creation of the National Capital Region as the office blocks of the federal state spread into Hull, Quebec, during the 1970s. Language training for public servants was perhaps the most controversial of these measures. In his annual report for 1984 the Commissioner of Official Languages, D'Iberville Fortier, noted that a relatively small proportion of public servants in positions designated bilingual appeared to have acquired their second-language skills as a result of taxpayer-funded language training. This led Fortier to question the extent to which language training was capable of making public servants, particularly anglophones who were the main consumers of federal language courses, effectively bilingual.[34] Although fewer resources have been devoted to language training programs since then, 31 March 2003 was declared '*Parlez* Both Official Ways Day', when 'nearly all executives in the public service [were] expected to reach an advanced level of bilingualism in French and English.'[35]

In view of the fact that two of the objectives of the Official Languages Act have been to increase the number of francophones recruited into the public service and to improve francophones' opportunities for upward mobility within it, the designation of positions according to their linguistic requirements has been probably the most significant feature of Ottawa's language policy. At the present time about 42 per cent of positions in the public service are designated either bilingual or French (37 per cent bilingual; 5 per cent French).

Evidence on recruitment to the federal public service and upward mobility within it demonstrate that the linguistic designation of positions

has worked to the advantage of francophones. In recent years close to one-third of new appointments to the federal public service have gone to those who claim French as their mother tongue, a level significantly higher than the approximately 23 per cent of the Canadian population comprised of native French speakers. A clear majority of appointments to bilingual positions are filled by francophones. This is true for both new appointments to the public service and for reappoint-

Figure 12.4   Anglophone and Francophone Representation in the Federal Public Service as a Whole, in the Management Category of the Public Service, and in the Canadian Population, Selected Years

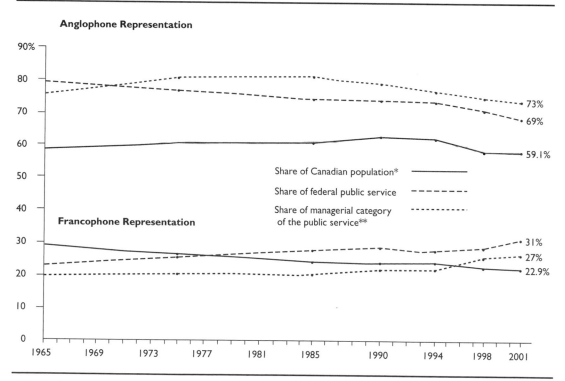

*Data for the representation of French and English language groups in the Canadian population are taken from the censuses for various years. The question refers to mother tongue, and therefore the figures do not add up to 100 per cent.

**The 1965 survey used to determine the language of those in the management category asked respondents to indicate their mother tongue; 5.2 per cent indicated a language other than English or French.

Sources: Figures provided in various annual reports of the Commissioner of Official Languages, the *Canada Year Book*, the *Report of the Royal Commission on Bilingualism and Biculturalism*, volume 3A (Ottawa: Queen's Printer, 1969), 215, table 50, and Treasury Board of Canada Secretariat, *Annual Report on Official Languages 2000–2001*.

ments within the federal bureaucracy, about 70 per cent of each going to francophones. But as the Commissioner of Official Languages regularly observes, increased representation of francophones should not be taken as an indication that French and English are approaching greater equality as *languages of work* in the federal state. Outside of federal departments and agencies located in Quebec, the language of work remains predominantly English. And inside Quebec, the ability of anglophone public servants to work in English is often limited. As the 1998 annual report of the Commissioner of Languages put it:

> Our experience in conducting audits and investigating complaints in this area over the past decade reveals that there has been little or no improvement on the language of work front; many public servants are still unable to exercise their right to work in French in the NCR [National Capital Region] and New Brunswick and, albeit to a lesser extent, in English in Quebec. This is not surprising when one considers that over one-third of federal government executives, to whom employees look for an example . . . do not meet the language requirements of their bilingual positions.[36]

The domination of English as the lingua franca of the bureaucracy persists even in the National Capital Region. This led a previous Commissioner of Official Languages to conclude that French has become a valuable attribute from the standpoint of career advancement without becoming a working language on a par with English.[37]

A recent annual report of the Commissioner's office points to a rather different development, the linguistic polarization of the federal public service on regional lines. It notes that there is 'virtually all-Anglophone recruitment in seven provinces and virtually all-Francophone recruitment in Quebec'.[38] New Brunswick and Ontario—and within Ontario, particularly the Ottawa region—are the only parts of the country where recruitment to the federal public service draws significantly on both official-language communities. This ought not to be surprising, given the very small size of francophone minorities in all provinces except Ontario and New Brunswick.

Ottawa's language policy acquired two additional thrusts in the 1970s. The first of these has involved financial assistance to organizations and individuals seeking to defend or expand the rights of official-language minorities and to local francophone cultural organizations outside of Quebec. Most significant in terms of results has been financial support for court challenges to provincial laws respecting language rights. These challenges have included Supreme Court decisions in 1979 and 1985 that established the official status of French in the province of Manitoba[39] and successful challenges to the restrictions on education and public signs and advertising contained in Quebec's Bill 101.[40] Until 1985, language rights cases were the only ones supported by Ottawa under its Court Challenges Program.

A second thrust of federal policy to promote bilingualism in Canadian society has been through financial assistance for second-language instruction and minority-language schools controlled by the provinces, including French immersion schools and support for summer immersion programs. The immersion phenomenon has seen the proliferation of French immersion schools in cities throughout English Canada. As of 2000–1 about 365,000 students were enrolled in French immersion elementary and secondary schools, compared to roughly 75,000 in 1980. More than half of all French immersion schools and about half of all immersion students in Canada are in Ontario.[41]

The popularity of French immersion education has grown steadily over the last two decades, fuelled by non-francophone parents' perception that bilingualism will give their children an edge in the future competition for good jobs. This perception of greater opportunities for bilinguals, at least in the private sector, remains to be substantiated. Indeed, a 1985 study of bilingual job opportunities by the Commissioner of Languages answered the question, 'Do immersion graduates make good use of their French after high school?'

with 'Yes, they do—in Ottawa.'[42] The 2001 census, the first to ask Canadians about the languages used in the workplace, found that 4 per cent of anglophone Canadians claimed to use French most often or regularly at work. But half of these workers are anglophones in Quebec, the percentage being 2.1 for anglophones outside Quebec. Only among francophones did workers report that they used English often in the workplace, close to one-third of francophones in Quebec saying that they used English most often or regularly and two-thirds of francophones outside Quebec reporting that they used English most often at work. This hardly supports the picture of a Canadian work world in which the opportunities to use French are great, at least outside Quebec.[43]

Moreover, as we noted earlier, studies of immersion graduates demonstrate that the experience tends to produce 'receptive' bilinguals—people who neither initiate conversations in French nor consume French-language newspapers, radio, or television after leaving school. Bilingualism becomes in some sense a badge of social distinction rather than a part of their lifestyle. This has led some to comment on the incidental effects of immersion on social class distinctions. Eric Waddell writes:

> There is much to suggest that the current fascination for French language education is more an expression of class (and indirectly of ethnic class) interests than of a concern to forge a new national identity. French immersion schools give the impression of constituting an elite system of education functioning within the public system. The state, through federal intervention, is in the process of elaborating a dual system, one for tomorrow's leaders and one for the followers. For this 'new' class, the bilingualism that mastery of the French language confers constitutes something profoundly Canadian in the sense of being sophisticated and more 'European'. Hence it serves increasingly to demarcate this class from other social classes and, strikingly, from our southern neighbours.[44]

A DISTINCT SOCIETY?

Does Quebec comprise a distinct society? Is Quebec more distinct from the other nine provinces than any one of those other provinces is from the rest? What is the basis for Quebec's claim to be distinct? Even if Quebecers' claim to distinctiveness is valid, should distinct society status be entrenched in the Constitution? Is this necessary? Is it desirable?

It is a fair bet that few Canadians had heard of 'distinct society' before the late 1980s, when the Meech Lake Accord came to grief over the proposal to recognize Quebec as a distinct society within Canada (see Chapter 5). It is also reasonable to assume that most Canadians are today no wiser about what 'distinct society' means. This, it should be added, is after tens of millions of dollars were spent by a phalanx of federal and provincial task forces, commissions, and committees on the Constitution that sprung into existence in the two years after the failure of the Meech Lake Accord, and after countless hours and column-inches of discussion and debate in the media since the late 1980s. Average Canadians perhaps may be forgiven whatever confusion they have over the distinct society issue. Constitutional experts, political scientists, journalists, and politicians cannot agree on what it means!

After all, it is clear that the demand for constitutional recognition of Quebec as a distinct society has been a non-negotiable item on the agenda of Quebec's political elite since the late 1980s. It is also clear that the issue excites a popular emotional response both inside Quebec and in the rest of Canada that other constitutional proposals—reforming the Senate, tinkering with the Supreme Court, changing the amendment process, and so on—do not. Let us try to understand the controversy over a distinct society clause by addressing the questions posed at the beginning of this section.

Whether or not Quebec is a distinct society depends on what criteria we use in comparing Quebec to the other provinces. How people in

Quebec make their living, the films they watch, the popular novels they read, how and where they spend their vacations, and most other aspects of their lifestyle are not remarkably different from how Canadians work and live in other regions of the country. In fact, if material and lifestyle criteria are used, then there is a good case for arguing that Quebec and Ontario are more similar than, say, Ontario and Newfoundland.

Not everyone agrees. And it is true that one can point to several important social characteristics of the Quebec population that distinguish it from those of the other provinces. Québécois marry less often and later than other Canadians; the percentage of couples living in common-law relationships is about twice the national average and higher than in any other province; a greater percentage of children (about half of first births) are born outside of marriage than in other provinces; a higher percentage of Quebecers than other Canadians report single ethnic origins (about 90 per cent, compared to 70 per cent for all of Canada); they are heavier smokers and drink more wine than their compatriots. Whereas English-Canadian television viewers prefer American-produced programs during prime time, French-speaking Quebecers are likely to be watching Quebec-made dramas and sitcoms. But to base an argument for constitutional recognition of Quebec as a distinct society on such social characteristics trivializes the meaning of distinct society. Many of these phenomena have no political relevance. Moreover, in some cases the differences between Quebec and the rest of Canada are too slight to warrant reading much significance into them.

Another possibility is that the beliefs and values of the Québécois set them apart from other Canadians. As we saw in Chapter 4, the evidence for this claim is mixed. Several early studies on regional variations in political culture concluded that Canada is, in fact, comprised of several distinctive regional political cultures. Richard Simeon and David Elkins found that levels of political trust, efficacy, interest in politics, and participation varied significantly between provinces and that this variation persisted even after eliminating the impact of socio-economic factors (i.e., levels of education and income) known to influence these attitudes/behaviours. The implication is, of course, that while Quebec may be a 'special case'

Some political analysts have argued that many Francophone Quebecers vote for nationalist parties in order to extract greater concessions from Ottawa and the other provinces. (Roy Peterson, *Vancouver Sun*)

I'm against separation, so I'll vote for the separatist candidate!

Why Quebec is a province unlike the others.

in terms of its politically relevant values, it is not the only regional special case.

Conversely, other studies of regionalism conclude that there are no significant attitudinal differences between citizens in different parts of the country. Based on their analysis of data from the 1977 national Quality of Life survey, Bernard Blishen and Tom Atkinson concluded that personal values did not differ significantly between provincial populations.[45] But either way, whether Quebec's political culture is argued to be broadly similar to that in the rest of Canada or if one takes the position that there are several distinct regional cultures in Canada, this weakens the argument for constitutional entrenchment of distinct society status for Quebec.

Nonetheless, one's conclusions may depend on what questions are asked and what values they tap. Surveys that ask Canadians whether they think of themselves as Canadians first or as citizens of their province reveal that those in Quebec are most likely to see their primary attachment as provincial. But Newfoundlanders are just about as provincialist and Prince Edward Islanders are not terribly far behind. Besides, this evidence of strong provincial loyalty may not matter very much given that numerous surveys have shown that Quebecers and other provincial populations are capable of maintaining provincial and Canadian loyalties at the same time. Studies of Canadians' attitudes towards rights and freedoms and the Charter suggest much more similarity than difference between French-speaking Québécois and other Canadians.[46] On the other hand, one of the most rigorous empirical investigations of regional variations in political ideology concludes that 'the extent of ideological differentiation in English Canada is very small' and that 'the ideological difference between Quebec and English Canada is greater than the internal variation within English Canada'.[47] In this study, Michael Ornstein shows that ideological values in Quebec are considerably to the left of those in the other provinces.[48]

In view of these apparently contradictory findings, can we conclude that Quebec comprises a distinct society in terms of the values and beliefs of its citizens? Possibly not. Differences between Quebec and the rest of Canada are sharpest on attitudes relating to language. A 1991 Gallup poll found that 78 per cent of Montrealers, compared to 28 per cent of Torontonians, thought that English-language rights were well protected in Quebec. Asked about the protection of French-language rights outside Quebec, 87 per cent of Torontonians thought they were well protected, compared to only 25 per cent of Montrealers. The two solitudes were perfect in their mutual mistrust! But on other political issues, differences are often slight or non-existent. Even if we concur with those, like Ornstein, who argue that Quebec is more different attitudinally from the rest of Canada than the predominantly English-speaking provinces are from one another, it does not follow that this difference warrants constitutional recognition of special status. Values and beliefs are not set in stone, as any student of changes in Quebec society and French-Canadian nationalism over the last half-century knows.

A third possible argument for Quebec's distinctiveness relies on history. The basic outline of such an argument goes as follows. French-Canadian society goes back to the seventeenth century when the first immigrants came over from France. Most French Canadians are, in fact, descended from those who were already settled in New France at the time of the Conquest. Current generations of French Canadians are heirs to three centuries of tradition and resistance against assimilating pressures. This continuity can be seen in the distinctive French spoken in Quebec (and, for that matter, in the dialects spoken in the French-speaking communities outside of Quebec); in Quebec folk songs, popular music, films, and literature; in such institutions as Quebec's distinctive system of civil law (based on the French civil code rather than English common law); and in the history that children in Quebec learn in school—a history that has always told a rather different story from that learned by students in English schools across

Canada. For example, according to provincial curriculum guidelines in Quebec as of 1999, for grade 9 history, the only two Canadian prime ministers studied are Sir John A. Macdonald (1867–73, 1878–91) and Wilfrid Laurier (1896–1911). After that the focus is exclusively on Quebec.[49] In Ontario, by contrast, the history curriculum for this age group is far less provincially focused—essentially substituting Canadian developments and consequences for the Quebec ones emphasized by Quebec's history curriculum—and includes a unit on the development of western Canada.[50] It is this unique history as one of Canada's two 'founding peoples' that justifies distinct society status for Quebec. Moreover, history has demonstrated that only in Quebec, where francophones have always formed the majority and have been able to control the levers of provincial government, are the distinctive language and traditions of French Canadians secure against anglicizing pressures and discrimination.

Variations on this basic argument are standard features of Quebec government documents on the Constitution and in the literature of both the Quebec Liberal Party and the Parti Québécois. It is a view that is widely shared by francophones in Quebec. Not only does this form the basis of demands for constitutional recognition of Quebec as a distinct society, but historical arguments also are used to make the case for a Quebec veto over constitutional amendments, as indicated by the 1991 *Report* of the Commission on the Political and Constitutional Future of Quebec:

> At its origin, Canada's federal system was founded, from Quebec's point of view, on Canadian duality and the autonomy of the provinces. Canadian duality, which rests on the relationship between the French-Canadian and English-Canadian peoples, is seen as the founding principle of the federal system. The federal union is thus conceived of as a pact between these two peoples, that may only be changed with the consent of each of these parties.[51]

The problem with the historical case for constitutional recognition of Quebec as a distinct society is not that it is based on incorrect or flimsy evidence. Indeed, the historical record speaks for itself. The problem is, rather, that some of the other provinces appear to be convinced that their regional histories are equally distinct. Western Canadians and their governments tend to be unimpressed by arguments that Quebec's history is somehow more distinctive than their own. Newfoundlanders are also unlikely to be convinced. The unsympathetic reception that spokespersons for the predominantly English-speaking provinces give to the historical argument for Quebec as a distinct society has recently been joined by that of Native Canadians. They argue that if any community has a historical right to distinct society status it is theirs. After all, their languages and traditions had been established for centuries before the arrival of Canada's European 'founders'. No discussion of 'founding peoples' or 'distinct societies' is complete, they argue, without recognition of the historical status and rights of Aboriginal Canadians.

The final and most persuasive grounds for arguing Quebec's right to distinct society status is the province's linguistic character. As noted earlier, over 80 per cent of the Quebec population claims French as its mother tongue and an equal percentage report speaking French at home. No other province comes close to this level of French-language dominance; indeed, in no other province do francophones comprise a majority of the population. Close to 90 per cent of all Canadian francophones reside in Quebec. It was no accident that the Commission on the Political and Constitutional Future of Quebec, established by the Bourassa government after the failure of the Meech Lake Accord, emphasized the distinctive linguistic character of Quebec as the first point in the section of its *Report* on Quebec's '*identité propre*' (special or unique identity).[52] Moreover, the distinct society proposals in the Meech Lake Accord and the Charlottetown Accord, and more recently in the motion passed by Parliament in 1995 and in the Calgary Declaration of 1997, were explicit in declaring that what is distinct about Quebec society is primarily its linguistic character (see Appendix 1 to this chapter).

This argument cannot be refuted. Of course, each province has its own distinctive linguistic character. But it requires either a very dull wit or very impressive powers of denial not to appreciate the remarkably unique linguistic character of Quebec within Canada and, for that matter, in all of North America. In no other jurisdiction, provincial or state, is English not the language regularly spoken by a clear majority of the population.

But if the distinct society clauses of Meech Lake and Charlottetown are merely statements of demographic reality, why the fuss? There are a couple of reasons. One is that some people will readily acknowledge Quebec's distinctive linguistic character, but deny that this warrants constitutional recognition of Quebec as a distinct society any more than, say, Saskatchewan deserves to be recognized as a distinct society because of its special economy, history, and demographic character.[53] Why, they ask, should language be elevated above other social characteristics in determining which provincial societies are distinct and which are not?

A second and probably more important reason why some provincial governments, the Alliance Party, and most English-speaking Canadians resist what might appear to be a compelling linguistic argument for a distinct society clause involves the consequences that would follow from entrenching this in the Constitution. Many English Canadians believe that this would give to Quebec legislative powers not possessed by other provinces. Some worry that minority rights—those of non-francophones in Quebec and those of francophones outside the province—would suffer from constitutional recognition of Quebec as a predominantly French-speaking society and of the rest of Canada as predominantly English-speaking. Fears have been expressed that a distinct society clause could undermine Charter guarantees of rights and freedoms in Quebec.

But above all, what probably bothers English-speaking Canadians outside of Quebec more than anything else is their gut sense that distinct society status for Quebec undermines their idea of Canada. 'Two nations' theories of Canada, while enjoying some popularity in certain political parties and

among anglophone political scientists, have never been very popular with the English-Canadian public. In an unarticulated way they sense that distinct society recognition for Quebec is a sort of Trojan horse for a two-nations conception of Canada. This offends against a particular understanding of equality that—again, while usually inarticulate—objects to the idea that there are categories of Canadians instead of Canadians, period. Former Conservative Prime Minister John Diefenbaker probably expressed this best when he inveighed against what he called 'the Anglo-phonies, the Franco-phonies, and all the other phonies' whose insistence on defining Canada in linguistic and ethnic terms, he believed, undermined national unity.

Although many of Canada's national political elite have for years denied that the 'one Canada' aspirations of most English Canadians conflict with the recognition of Quebec as a distinct society, Québécois political leaders suffer from no illusions on this count. The *Report* of the Commission on the Political and Constitutional Future of Quebec made this very clear. The *Report* argued that the 'one Canada' and 'dual societies' conceptions have become increasingly irreconcilable since the passage of the Charter and the other constitutional reforms of 1982. This is because, the *Report* argues, the Constitution Act of 1982 is based on three principles that, while popular outside of Quebec, are fundamentally opposed to the recognition of Quebec as a distinct society (see Appendix 2 to this chapter). These principles are:

- The equality of all Canadian citizens, from one ocean to the other, and the unity of the society in which they live.
- The equality of all cultures and cultural origins in Canada.
- The equality of the 10 provinces of Canada.

Whatever a distinct society clause in the Constitution might mean in practice—and, notwithstanding the confident blusterings of many politicians and constitutional experts, we should have learned from the experience with the Charter that it is often impossible to predict how Canadian judges will interpret important sections of the Constitution—there can be no doubt that the Quebec elites who insist on it expect it to make a difference. They reject the 'one Canada' vision that they argue is represented in the Charter and in the current procedure for amending the Constitution (whereby Quebec does not have a constitutionally entrenched veto). Distinct society is, in their eyes, a corrective against the centralizing implications of the Charter and, moreover, represents a return to the founding spirit of Canada.

Distinct society status and a veto over constitutional change may no longer be enough. Several weeks after the narrow defeat of the separatist option in the 1995 Quebec referendum, the Liberal government passed a motion recognizing Quebec as a distinct society and giving the province (as well as British Columbia, the Prairie provinces, Ontario, and the Atlantic provinces) a veto over constitutional reform. Neither the PQ government in Quebec, the Bloc Québécois in Ottawa, nor Quebec's French-language media were particularly impressed by Ottawa's action. Even the Quebec Liberal Party argued that Ottawa's proposals—the constitutional status of which was uncertain, to say the least—did not go far enough. Ottawa's hope, of course, was to satisfy the demands of enough 'soft nationalists' to undercut the separatists in the next referendum. For their part, the PQ and the BQ have been determined to shift the debate away from distinct society and constitutional vetoes, terms that imply a federalism framework, and onto a different plane. That plane involves political independence and economic association.

Quebec citizens, however, seem to have grown weary of what are by now decades-old debates over political independence, distinct society status, and constitutional reform. Public opinion polls taken throughout 2001–2 showed that about six in 10 Quebecers were opposed to the idea of another referendum on Quebec sovereignty. The defeat of the PQ government by the Liberals in the April 2003 Quebec election, after almost 14 years of PQ rule, was interpreted by many as a sign of Quebecers' dissatisfaction with the PQ's separatist vision. Independence and constitutional reform, according to the conventional wisdom that has emerged over the last few years, is yesterday's political agenda. Many go so far as to pronounce Quebec separatism dead.

This obituary is premature, to say the least. It was common to pronounce Quebec separatism dead or at least harmless in the mid-1980s, until the failure of the Meech Lake Accord and the sudden upsurge in support for independence demonstrated the difference that exists between dead and dormant. It is not difficult to imagine circumstances, such as a major conflict between Ottawa and Quebec, that could trigger an increase in support for separatism among French-speaking Quebecers. Complacency in regard to Quebec's relationship to the rest of Canada is far from being warranted by the facts of the situation. Foremost among these facts is the gulf that continues to separate the one-Canada, equality-of-the-provinces, and multicultural visions of the country that dominate outside Quebec from the insistence by the Quebec 'federalists' and separatists alike that Quebec must be considered a province unlike the others. The art of national unity involves finding ways to bridge this gulf, but no one seriously believes that the gulf is likely to be eliminated. While the bridges may appear fairly sturdy now, the 1995 referendum should serve as a reminder of how precarious they can be.

APPENDIX 1: PROPOSALS FOR A DISTINCT SOCIETY CLAUSE

Version I: Meech Lake Accord (1987)

1. The Constitution Act, 1867 is amended by adding thereto, immediately after Section 1 thereof, the following section:

2. (1) The Constitution of Canada shall be interpreted in a manner consistent with:
   (a) The recognition that the existence of French-speaking Canadians, centred in Quebec but also present elsewhere in

Canada, and English-speaking Canadians, concentrated outside Quebec but also present in Quebec, constitutes a fundamental characteristic of Canada; and, (b) The recognition that Quebec constitutes within Canada a distinct society;

(2) The role of the Parliament of Canada and the provincial legislatures to preserve the fundamental characteristic of Canada referred to in paragraph (1) (a) is affirmed;

(3) The role of the Legislature and Government of Quebec to preserve and promote the distinct identity of Quebec referred to in paragraph (1) (b) is affirmed;

(4) Nothing in this section derogates from the powers, rights or privileges of Parliament or the Government of Canada, or of the legislatures or governments of the provinces, including any powers, rights or privileges relating to language.

Version II: Charlottetown Accord (1992)

The Constitution Act, 1867 is amended by adding thereto, immediately after Section 1 thereof, the following section:

2. (1) The Constitution of Canada, including the Canadian Charter of Rights and Freedoms, shall be interpreted in a manner consistent with the following fundamental characteristics:
. . .
(c) Quebec constitutes within Canada a distinct society, which includes a French-speaking majority, a unique culture and a civil law tradition;
. . .

(2) The role of the legislature and Government of Quebec to preserve and promote the distinct society of Quebec is affirmed.

Version III: Motion Passed by Parliament (1995)

THAT

Whereas the people of Quebec have expressed the desire for recognition of Quebec's distinct society;

(1) the House recognize that Quebec is a distinct society within Canada;

(2) the House recognize that Quebec's distinct society includes its French-speaking majority, unique culture and civil law tradition;

(3) the House undertake to be guided by this reality;

(4) the House encourage all components of the legislative and executive branches of government to take note of this recognition and be guided in their conduct accordingly.

Version IV: The Calgary Declaration (1997)

In Canada's federal system, where respect for diversity and equality underlines unity, the unique character of Quebec society, including its French-speaking majority, its culture and its tradition of civil law, is fundamental to the well-being of Canada. Consequently, the legislature and the Government of Quebec have a role to protect and develop the unique character of Quebec society within Canada.

APPENDIX 2

(from *Rapport de la commission sur l'avenir politique et constitutionnel du Québec*, mars 1991, 38–40; author's translation)

The Constitution Act, 1982 and the principles that it enshrines have in fact given to Canada a centralizing direction unknown previously. This Act has contributed to the reinforcement of certain political ideas about the Canadian federation and to the perception of a Canadian national identity that is difficult to reconcile with the effective recognition and political expression of

Quebec's distinct identity. These political ideas and this perception manifest themselves in the following dimensions [of the Act]:

The equality of all Canadian citizens, from one ocean to the other, and the unity of the society in which they live.

By virtue of this political vision, which is based on the Charter of Rights and Freedoms contained in the Act of 1982, equality is a strictly individual notion and applies uniformly across Canada: it does not allow for the special constitutional recognition of the Quebec collectivity. The concept of Quebec as a distinct society is thus perceived as a source of inequality and as being incompatible with the principle of the equality of all Canadians.

The equality of all cultures and cultural origins in Canada.

This vision proceeds from the principle of multiculturalism enshrined in the Canadian Charter, which promises to maintain and promote the multicultural heritage of Canadians. In the eyes of many, the French language and francophone cultural origins are among the many mother tongues and cultures that form the multicultural heritage of Canada and are equal to them: the French language and francophone cultural origins should not require special recognition or guarantees in the Canadian Constitution. The notions of 'linguistic duality' and of 'two founding peoples' do not reflect the Canadian reality

shared by a large number of Canadians and in which they see themselves reflected.

The equality of the 10 provinces.

This notion has become one of Canada's dominant political principles. It was consecrated in the constitutional amendment procedure adopted in 1982, more precisely in the unanimity rule for certain amendments and in the 'seven provinces representing 50 per cent of the Canadian population' rule that is the general amending formula. . . .

By virtue of this principle of the equality of all provinces, any constitutional change, prerogative, or competence obtained by Quebec must be obtained equally by the nine other provinces. The strict application of this principle thus has the effect of preventing Quebec from achieving a special status.

The equality of the provinces requires, consequently, a uniform decentralization towards all the provinces of any competence or prerogative assigned to Quebec. This decentralizing effect is not acceptable to those who see in it a weakening of the central government.

Under the combined effect of the principle of provincial equality and of positions favouring the centralization of powers in the hands of a single 'national' government that dominates the country, it becomes difficult to respond to the needs of Quebec and accommodate, within the Canadian Constitution, the political recognition of its distinctiveness within the federation.

NOTES

1. Information on mother tongue was first collected with the census of 1931. Before then, the census only asked about ethnic origin. Demographer Jacques Henripin suggests that French ethnic origin was probably a good surrogate measure for language group at the time of Confederation.

2. In fact, Henripin predicted that over 40 per cent of Montrealers would be anglophone by 2001.

   This prediction was based on census data from 1971. See Jacques Henripin, *L'Immigration et le déséquilibre linguistique* (Ottawa: Main d'oeuvre et immigration, 1974), 31, tableau 4.7.

3. Henripin estimated that at the rate of decline experienced in the early 1970s, Quebec would still be 77 per cent French-speaking by 2001.

4. Richard Joy, *Languages in Conflict* (Toronto: McClelland & Stewart, 1972), 58, table 25.

5. Statistics Canada, *2001 Census: Analysis Series*, 'Profiles of languages in Canada: English, French and many others' (Ottawa: Minister of Industry, 2002). Available at: <www.statcan.ca>.

6. Joy, *Languages in Conflict*, 39, table 14.

7. Roger Bernard, *Le choc des nombres* (Ottawa: Université d'Ottawa, 1990).

8. Jacques Henripin, 'The 1986 Census: Some Enduring Trends Abate', *Language and Society* 24 (Fall 1988): 8–9.

9. The first experience with immersion education was in 1975 in St Lambert, Quebec.

10. See Peter C. Waite, *Pre-Confederation* (Toronto: Prentice-Hall, 1965), 54–5.

11. Louis Hemon, *Maria Chapdelaine*, trans. Sir Andrew Macphail (Toronto: Oxford University Press, 1921), 212–13.

12. Henri Bourassa, *La langue, guardienne de la foi* (Bibliothèque de l'action française, 1918).

13. Henri Bourassa, 'The French Language and the Future of Our Race', in Ramsay Cook, ed., *French Canadian Nationalism* (Toronto: Macmillan, 1969), 133.

14. Marcel Rioux, 'Sur l'evolution des ideologies au Quebec', English translation in Richard Schultz et al., eds, *The Canadian Political Process*, 3rd edn (Toronto: Holt, Rinehart and Winston, 1979), 99–102.

15. Denis Monière, *Ideologies in Quebec* (Toronto: University of Toronto Press, 1981), esp. ch. 2.

16. These voices included such figures as Gonzalve Doutre, Errol Bouchette, and Olivar Asselin, and the activities of the Institut Canadien.

17. F.H. Leacy, ed., *Historical Statistics of Canada* (Ottawa: Supply and Services, 1983), R1–22, R81–97.

18. The numbers were about 390,000 in manufacturing compared to 249,000 in agriculture. The figure for the agricultural labour force counts only males.

19. Quoted by Trudeau in 'Quebec on the Eve of the Asbestos Strike', in Cook, ed., *French Canadian Nationalism*, 35–6.

20. Victor Barbeau, *Mesure de notre taille* (1936); Barbeau, *Avenir de notre bourgeoisie* (Montréal: Editions de l'action canadienne française,

1939); Jacques Melançon, 'Retard de croissance de l'entreprise canadienne-francasie', *L'actualite économique* (janvier-mars 1956): 503–22.

21. Rioux, 'Sur l'évolution', 105–8.

22. Ibid., 105.

23. This section draws heavily on Stephen Brooks and Alain-G. Gagnon, 'Managing the French-English Conflict in Canada', *Fédéralisme* 4 (1990): 1–25.

24. René Lévesque, *An Option for Quebec* (Toronto: McClelland & Stewart, 1968), 14.

25. See Melançon, 'Retard de croissance'.

26. Lois du Quebec, 1974, c. 6.

27. Lois du Quebec, 1977, c. 5.

28. See *Attorney General of Quebec v. Blaikie et al.* (1979), 101 D.L.R. (3d) 394 (Supreme Court of Canada).

29. *Ford v. Attorney General of Quebec* (1988), Supreme Court of Canada.

30. Calvin Veltman, 'Assessing the Effects of Quebec's Language Legislation', *Canadian Public Policy* 12, 2 (June 1986): 314–19. Veltman observes that the effectiveness of Bill 101 in promoting the use of French among the children of immigrants varies considerably among ethnic groups.

31. See the discussion of these economic initiatives in Kenneth McRoberts, *Quebec: Social Change and Political Crisis*, 3rd edn (Toronto: McClelland & Stewart, 1988), 132–5.

32. Eric Waddell, 'State, Language and Society: The Vicissitudes of French in Quebec and Canada', in Alan Cairns and Cynthia Williams, eds, *The Politics of Gender, Ethnicity and Language in Canada*, vol. 34 of the research studies for the Royal Commission on the Economic Union and Development Prospects for Canada (Toronto: University of Toronto Press, 1985), 97.

33. Raymond Breton, 'The Production and Allocation of Symbolic Resources: An Analysis of the Linguistic and Ethnocultural Fields in Canada', *Canadian Review of Sociology and Anthropology* 21, 2 (1984): 129.

34. Commissioner of Official Languages, *Annual Report 1985* (Ottawa: Supply and Services, 1986), 50.

35. 'Civil service execs set to hit bilingualism wall', CBC on-line, available at: http://www.cbc.ca/stories/2003/03/31/bilingual_030331

36. http://ocol-clo.gc.ca/e298_3.htm#anchor304

37. 'Francophones in the National Capital Region represent over 35 per cent of the Public Service population but, on average, they work more than 60 per cent of their time in English. In bilingual areas of Ontario the corresponding figures are 23 per cent and 66 per cent; roughly one-quarter of all employees are thus working two-thirds of their time in their second language.' Commissioner of Official Languages, *Annual Report 1985*, 54.

38. http://ocol-clo.gc.ca/e298_3.htm#anchor305

39. *Attorney General of Manitoba v. Forest* (1979), 101 D.L.R. (3d) 385 (Supreme Court of Canada); *Reference re Language Rights under the Manitoba Act, 1870* (No. 1) (1985), 19 D.L.R. (4th) 1.

40. *Attorney General of Quebec v. Quebec Protestant School Boards* (1984), 10 D.L.R. (4th) 321 (Supreme Court of Canada); *Ford v. Attorney General of Quebec* (1988), Supreme Court of Canada.

41. These figures are from the annual reports of the Commissioner of Official Languages.

42. Commissioner of Official Languages, *Annual Report 1985*, 172.

43. Statistics Canada, 'Use of English and French at Work', Catalogue no. 96F00030XIE2001011, Feb. 2003.

44. Eric Waddell, 'State, Language and Society: The Vicissitudes of French in Quebec and Canada', in Cairns and Williams, eds, *Politics of Gender, Ethnicity and Language*, 101.

45. Bernard Blishen and Tom Atkinson, 'Regional and Status Differences in Canadian Values' (Toronto: Institute of Behavioural Research, York University, 1981).

46. Peter Russell et al., 'Liberty, Authority, and Community: Civil Liberties and the Canadian Political Culture', paper presented at the annual meeting of the Canadian Political Science Association, Windsor, Ont., 9 June 1988.

47. Michael Ornstein, 'Regionalism and Canadian Political Ideology', in Robert Brym, ed., *Regionalism in Canada* (Toronto: Irwin, 1986), 78.

48. Ibid., 66, table 2.

49. www.umi.cd/curriculum.html

50. Ontario, Ministry of Education and Training, *The Ontario Curriculum: Social Studies Grades 1 to 6, History and Geography Grades 7 and 8* (Toronto: Queen's Printer for Ontario, 1998), 49–54.

51. Québec, Commission sur l'avenir politique et constitutionnel du Québec, *Rapport* (Québec, 1991), 17.

52. Ibid.

53. Robert Sheppard, 'For a really distinct society, try Saskatchewan, not Quebec', *Globe and Mail*, 20 Nov. 1989.

SUGGESTED READINGS

Ramsay Cook, ed., *French Canadian Nationalism: An Anthology* (Toronto: Macmillan, 1969). This work contains a wide selection of writings from French-Canadian nationalists and about French-Canadian and Quebec nationalists, from the mid-nineteenth century to the Quiet Revolution.

Alain-G. Gagnon, ed., *Quebec: State and Society*, 3rd edn (Peterborough, Ont.: Broadview Press, 2003). A comprehensive reader, this collection includes contributions from many of Canada's leading students of Quebec politics.

Kenneth McRoberts, *Quebec: Social Change and Political Crisis*, 3rd edn (Toronto: Oxford University Press, 1999). McRoberts provides an excellent account of Quebec's historical and political evolution.

Garth Stevenson, *Community Besieged: The Anglophone Minority and the Politics of Quebec* (Montreal and Kingston: McGill-Queen's University Press, 1999). This is a somewhat nostalgic examination of the history and current state of the anglophone minority in Quebec.

Charles Taylor, *Reconciling the Solitudes: Essays on Canadian Federalism and Nationalism* (Montreal and Kingston: McGill-Queen's University Press, 1993). Written by Canada's most internationally renowned philosopher, several of the pieces in this collection deal with Quebec and Quebec nationalism.

Review Exercises

1. In a paragraph or two, explain the message conveyed in the political cartoon at page (357).

2. How bilingual is your community? Make an inventory of the indications that French (or English, if you are in Quebec) language rights are protected and the French language promoted. It might look something like this:

   A. Schools
- French schools

      Names
- Monseigneur Jean Noël
- Ste-Thérèse
- Lajeunesse
- Bellewood

- Immersion schools

   B. Media
- Newspapers
- Radio
- Television

- Le Rempart
- Radio-Canada (540 AM)
- Radio-Canada (54)
- TFO (19, cable)
- TVA (69, cable)
- TVO (70, cable)

      Signs
- stores
- traffic signs
- billboards
- product labels
- government office

   C. Churches
- Catholic

- St Jérome
- Ste-Anne
- St Joseph

   D. Clubs, Bars, Community Centres
- Club Alouette
- Place Concorde

3. What would be the consequences of Quebec independence for official bilingualism in the rest of Canada? Move past the immediate emotion and backlash to consider what possible consequences separation might have for schools, political parties, government services, and the Constitution.

In the wake of the terrorist attacks of II September 2001, Canada's Muslim community felt that the Canadian multicultural mosaic became less welcoming. Events like the open house advertised at this mosque were launched to counter what some saw as an increase in anti-Muslim and anti-Arab sentiment.

Diversity is both a part of the social reality of Canada and one of the leading values associated with Canadian politics. In this chapter we examine the politics of diversity in Canada, with special attention to issues of gender diversity and equality. Topics include the following:

- ❏ The changing ethnic character of Canadian society.
- ❏ Increased awareness of diversity.
- ❏ The institutionalization of diversity.
- ❏ The political representation of ethnic groups.
- ❏ The extent and causes of female under-representation in politics.
- ❏ Early feminism.
- ❏ Contemporary feminism.
- ❏ Organization within the women's movement.
- ❏ Strategies of the women's movement.
- ❏ Feminist achievements.
- ❏ Attitudes regarding gender.

CHAPTER THIRTEEN

DIVERSITY AND POLITICS

Over the last generation respect for diversity has joined equality and freedom as one of the core values of Canadian politics. Indeed, many would go so far as to say that it has become *the* pre-eminent Canadian cultural trait, the quality that more than any other defines what Canada is about and how our society and political life are different from those of other countries, but particularly from the United States. Canada is, as former Prime Minister Joe Clark once put it, 'a community of communities'. Canadians, we are often told, are united by their differences. At first blush this claim appears to be at least paradoxical and possibly even contradictory. What it means, however, is that tolerance, respect, the recognition of group rights, and a belief in the equal dignity of different cultures are central to the Canadian ethos. Indeed, the very idea that there is such a thing as a Canadian ethos is comparatively recent, emerging at the same time as this image of Canada as the pluralistic society par excellence and a model of cultural coexistence.

This image of Canada is not without its ironies and skeptics. Foremost among the ironies is the fact that separatist sentiment in Quebec—diminished in recent years but far from extinguished—challenges this rosy picture of Canada as a model of cultural coexistence. In addition, many critics maintain that the diversity-centred image of Canada, and policies and institutions based on it, do more to undermine Canadian unity than strengthen it. Still others question whether multicultural democracy can work at all, in Canada or elsewhere, except in special circumstances. They note the resurgence of ethnicity-based nationalism in the modern world and the breakup or instability of many countries that combine different cultures within their borders.

Ironies and skepticism aside, there is no denying that the politics of diversity has moved to the centre of Canada's political stage in recent decades. The evidence ranges from official recognition of multiculturalism in the law and under the Constitution to public controversy over the impact of recent immigration on Canadian society. While diversity is nothing new in Canada—Canadian society has always been pluralistic and the official recognition of group rights goes back at least as far as the 1774 Quebec Act, under which the British authorities recognized the religious rights of French Canadians—what is relatively new is the level of awareness of diversity and the idea that it should be recognized, protected, and even promoted through the actions and institutions of the state.

In this chapter we will examine the politics of diversity in Canada, including the important impact that the women's movement has had on Canadian society and public policy. The issues that will be examined include the following:

- how Canada's population characteristics have changed over time;
- the ways in which diversity politics has been institutionalized in state institutions and policies;
- the impact of the women's movement on Canadian society and politics.

FROM FOUNDING NATIONS TO MULTICULTURALISM: THE CHANGING ETHNIC DEMOGRAPHY OF CANADA

The Canada that we know today was built upon two pillars: the displacement and marginalization of Aboriginal Canadians and the settlement and development of what would become Canada by European immigrants. Not only were the vast majority of the immigrants who settled in Canada during the country's formative years European, they were overwhelmingly of French and British Isles origins (although many of the latter came to Canada via the United States in the wave of Loyalists who left America after the War of Independence). The languages that they established in Canada were mainly French and English. With very few exceptions their religions were Christian, either Roman Catholic or Protestant. For much of Canada's history they would unhesitatingly be referred to as the 'founding nations' or 'charter groups', one French and Catholic and the other English and mainly Protestant. At the time of Confederation their virtual monopoly on Canadian public life was symbolized in the partnership of John A. Macdonald, the leading English-Canadian advocate of an independent Canada, and George-Étienne Cartier, the major spokesperson for French Canada. The first Canadian government under Macdonald did not include anyone who was not a member of these so-called charter groups (not to be confused with today's Charter groups).

This image of Canada as a partnership—albeit an unequal one—of two European charter groups survived well into the twentieth century. It was not until the 1960s and, more specifically, the work of the Royal Commission on Bilingualism and Biculturalism (B&B Commission) that the two-nations image of Canada experienced any serious competition. Spokespersons for non-French and non-British groups in Canada argued that this image of Canada and the policies that were based on it excluded them from the Canadian picture. These groups, in the main, were also comprised of Canadians of European origin. Ukrainian spokespersons, for example, were prominent among those who were critical of the two-nations, bicultural image of Canada. Moreover, it is important to emphasize that the demands of these dissenting groups stopped well short of equality of status with English and French for their groups and languages. What they demanded and won was official recognition of Canada as a *multicultural society*, not a bicultural one. This was achieved through the 1971 passage of the Multiculturalism Act and the creation of a

new federal Ministry of State for Multiculturalism, a position that has morphed over the years and that currently falls under the rubric of the Department of Canadian Heritage.

The image of Canada as a sort of New World extension of two European peoples and their value systems was also being challenged by some Canadian intellectuals. John Porter's influential book, *The Vertical Mosaic*,[1] drew attention to the stratified nature of Canada's pluralistic society, in which English Canadians dominated virtually all of the important elites and controlled the channels of recruitment into them. The picture he painted was of a Canada in which influence, status, and wealth were held disproportionately in the hands of one of Canada's two charter groups, and where the members of other groups were largely blocked from access to the opportunities monopolized by Anglo-Canadians. This situation, Porter argued, was inconsistent with the democratic values of openness, socio-economic mobility, and equality preached by Canadian politicians and believed in by the general population. His analysis of the systemic inequality and discrimination that characterized Canadian society would provide much of the inspiration for a generation of social critics who, unlike their predecessors, did not take for granted the domination of the British charter group and the exclusion of increasing numbers of Canadians from the two-nations image of Canada.

The challenges launched by intellectual critics like Porter and the groups that wanted the biculturalism in the B&B Commission to be replaced with multiculturalism would not have had much of an audience or impact had it not been for the changes to Canada's population characteristics that were well underway by the 1960s. These changes have accelerated since then and, moreover, have altered in ways that present even greater challenges to older notions of Canadian pluralism than those first launched in the 1960s. To put it simply, the share of Canada's population with neither French nor British Isles ethnic origins has increased quite dramatically. Immigrants from Eastern and Southern

Europe were becoming increasingly important within Canada's overall immigration picture between the 1950s and 1970s. They have been joined in recent decades by increasing numbers of non-European immigrants, many of whom come from non-Christian cultures. As Figure 13.1 shows, the ethnic composition of Canadian society has changed significantly over the last half-century. This change has been experienced most strikingly in Canada's largest metropolitan areas, magnets for new immigrants, where the new Canadians of neither British nor French ethnic origins have clustered and where the visible minority population has increased significantly in recent years (see Figure 13.2).

Change in the ethnic distribution of Canada's population has been brought about by shifting patterns of immigration. For most of Canada's history the major sources of immigration were

Europe and the United States. In recent years the leading sources of immigration have been Asia, the Middle East, and the Caribbean. Whereas just under 95 per cent of all immigrants to Canada before 1961 were born in Europe or the United States, that figure was only 22.3 per cent for the period 1991–2001. Immigrants from Asia, the Middle East, Africa, and the Caribbean, who together accounted for only 5.5 per cent of all immigrants prior to 1961, grew to about 77.5 per cent of all immigration during the 1991–2001 period. The top 10 countries of birth for immigrants to Canada before 1961 and during the period 1991–2001 are shown in Table 13.1.

Canada remains, even after recent waves of immigration from non-European countries, a predominantly Christian society. As Figure 13.3 shows, three-quarters of Canadians claim an affiliation with either the Catholic Church or a Protes-

Figure 13.1   Ethnic Origins of the Canadian Population, Selected Years

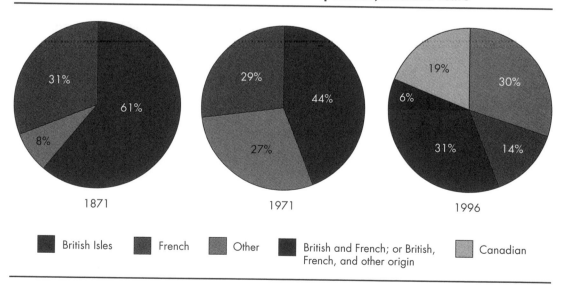

Note: The comparability of the ethnic origins data from the 1996 census with answers prior to 1991 is affected by the fact that since 1991 respondents have been able to provide multiple ethnic origins. The data used in constructing the pie chart for 1996 do not double-count any respondents.

Source: F.H. Leary, ed., *Historical Statistics of Canada*, 2nd edn (Ottawa: Minister of Supply and Services Canada, 1983); Statistics Canada at: <http://www.statcan.ca/english/census96/feb17/eo2can.htm>.

Figure 13.2   Visible Minorities in Canada and in Main Metropolitan Areas, 1991 and 2001

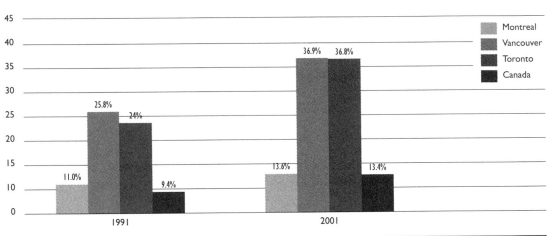

Source: Statistics Canada, *Canada's Ethnocultural Portrait: The Changing Mosaic*, Catalogue no. 96F0030XIE2001008.

Table 13.1   Main Countries of Birth for Immigrants to Canada, before 1961 and 1991–2001

	Immigrated before 1961			Immigrated 1991–2001*	
	Number	%		**Number**	%
Total immigrants	894,465	100.0	Total immigrants	1,830,680	100.0
United Kingdom	217,175	24.3	China, Peoples Republic of	197,360	10.8
Italy	147,320	16.5	India	156,120	8.5
Germany	96,770	10.8	Philippines	122,010	6.7
Netherlands	79,170	8.9	Hong Kong, Special	118,385	6.5
Poland	44,340	5.0	Administrative Region		
United States	34,810	3.9	Sri Lanka	62,590	3.4
Hungary	27,425	3.1	Pakistan	57,990	3.2
Ukraine	21,240	2.4	Taiwan	53,755	2.9
Greece	20,755	2.3	United States	51,440	2.8
China, People's Republic of	15,850	1.8	Iran	47,080	2.6
			Poland	43,370	2.4

*Includes data up to 15 May 2001.
Source: Statistics Canada, *Canada's ethnocultural portrait: The changing mosaic*, Catalogue no. 96F0030XIE2001008, 39.

tant denomination. This is down from all but a sliver of the population at the time of Confederation and even represents some small slippage since 1971, about the time the profile of Canadian immigration began to shift away from traditional European sources. This slippage has been due chiefly to a sharp increase over the last generation in the number of people without a religious affiliation. People belonging to non-Christian religions continue to constitute a rather small minority, at about 6 per cent of the population. Their presence in particular cities, however, such as Sikhs and Hindus in Vancouver and Muslims in Toronto, is much greater than it is nationwide.

Along with greater diversity in the ethnic, religious, and racial composition of Canada, the demographic picture has become more varied in other ways as well. Examples include family composition, sexual orientation, and disability.

Families. Families tend to be smaller today than they were a generation ago and considerably smaller than they were two generations ago.

There are many more single-parent families than in the past (today, roughly one out of every six families) and many more couples who choose not to marry (over 10 per cent of all couples nationally, ranging from a low of about 7 per cent in some provinces to 20 per cent in Quebec). Same-sex couples are more frequent than in the past, although precisely how much more frequent is impossible to say given that virtually no data were collected on such matters until recently.

Sexuality. There probably is no reason to assume that the ratio of those who are heterosexual compared to those who are gay/lesbian has changed significantly over time. What has changed, however, is the willingness of non-heterosexuals to proclaim openly their sexuality and the readiness of a growing number of Canadians to accept this in many, if not all, circumstances. Consequently, sexual diversity is much more apparent today than was the case when social pressures and the law discouraged all but a small number of non-heterosexuals from 'coming out'.

Figure 13.3   Religious Affiliations of the Canadian Population, Selected Years

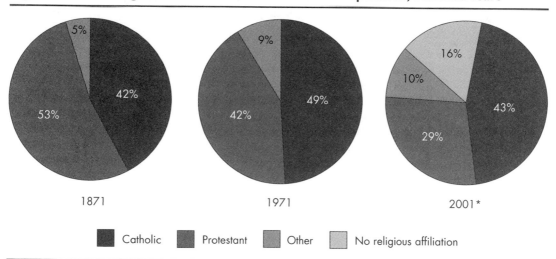

*The 'Other' category for 2001 includes other Christians (2.6%), Christian Orthodox (1.6%), Muslim (2%), Jewish (1.1%), Buddhist (1%), Hindu (1%), and Sikh (0.9%).
Source: F.H. Leary, ed., *Historical Statistics of Canada*, 2nd edn (Ottawa: Minister of Supply and Services Canada, 1983); Statistics Canada, at <http://www.statcan.ca/english/Pgdb/demo32.htm>.

Times have changed, as the tens of thousands who annually line the streets and march in Toronto's Gay Pride parade attest. Canada has openly gay politicians, some of its churches ordain and marry homosexuals, and human rights codes prohibit discrimination based on sexual preference. This is not to imply that this aspect of Canadian diversity is not controversial. As shown in Box 13.1, these matters continue to divide Canadians. The struggle over the legal definition of marriage as excluding same-sex unions is seen by many as the last major legal barrier to the equality of gays and lesbians with heterosexuals. This struggle is being waged in the courts and in the court of public opinion. In the latter case, polls show that Canadians remain divided on this issue. A *Toronto Sun* poll, conducted in the autumn of 2002, found 34 per cent of Canadians in favour, 43 per cent opposed, and 23 per cent indifferent towards same-sex marriages.

Disability. According to statistics, a greater proportion of the population is disabled today than at any point in Canada's history. Health Canada reports that about one in eight Canadians claims to experience either a mental or physical disability. But as in the case of sexuality, it is doubt-

---

BOX 13.1   The Controversy over 'Asha's Mums'

By a 7–2 majority, Canada's highest court unequivocally rejected the Surrey School Board's attempt to ban from the classroom three books depicting same-sex families: *Belinda's Bouquet*, *Asha's Mums*, and *One Dad, Two Dads, Brown Dads, Blue Dads*. The Court referred the question of whether the books should be approved for use in the classroom back to the Board to be made according to 'the broad principles of tolerance and non-sectarianism underlying the School Act'.

'The court today has affirmed the right of children in same-sex parented families to see themselves and their families reflected in the school curriculum', said John Fisher, Egale Canada's Executive Director. 'This is an unequivocal victory not only for lesbian, gay, bisexual and transgender Canadians and their families, but for all Canadians, in that it affirms the right of children to a bias-free curriculum that teaches the values of equality, tolerance and respect for diversity that we as a society hold so dear. The Supreme Court sent the clear message today to educators across the nation that families come in many diverse forms, and that all are equally entitled to be treated with respect. Ultimately, the Court has recognized that children benefit from learning respect for those who are different. In the words of the Chief Justice, "tolerance is always age-appropriate."'

Supreme Court Chief Justice McLachlin, writing for the majority, addressed the core argument of the Surrey School Board. 'It is suggested that, while the message of the books may be unobjectionable, the books will lead children to ask questions of their parents that may be inappropriate for the K–1 level and difficult for parents to answer. Yet on the record before us, it is hard to see how the materials will raise questions which would not in any event be raised by the acknowledged existence of same-sex parented families in the K–1 parent population, or in the broader world in which these children live. The only additional message of the materials appears to be the message of tolerance. Tolerance is always age-appropriate.'

Egale Canada Web site: www.egale.ca

ful whether the actual incidence of Canadians suffering from various forms of disability is greater today than in the past. What has changed, however, is both our society's ideas about what constitute disabilities and the legal definition of what counts as a disabilty for purposes of pensions, workers' compensation, social assistance, employment, housing, and other matters. The recognition of disabledness has increased and, moreover, it has become one of the diversity criteria used by governments in making public policy.

OFFICIAL RECOGNITION AND THE INSTITUTIONALIZATION OF DIVERSITY

Multiculturalism was given its own minister—albeit a minister of state, which is a rung down from a departmental minister—in 1972. But the official recognition of groups of Canadian citizens according to their group characteristics and the institutionalization of diversity go back much further. We have already mentioned that the Quebec Act of 1774 represented the first official confirmation of the status and rights of a particular segment of the population, in this case French-speaking Catholics. But in fact the distinction of 'first' ought probably to be conferred upon the Royal Proclamation of 1763. This document recognized the presence and rights of 'the several Nations or Tribes of Indians with whom we are connected, and who live under our protection'. Aboriginal Canadians were recognized by the Proclamation as distinct rights-bearing peoples under the protection of the British Crown. This relationship continues to the present day—although the Canadian government long ago assumed the obligations that originally belonged to Britain—perpetuated and institutionalized through the Indian Act and s. 35 of the Constitution Act, 1982, which embeds the treaty rights of Aboriginal peoples in Canada.

There is, therefore, a long history of recognizing diversity in Canada. But until the 1960s that recognition extended principally to the French- and English-language communities (s.

133 of the Constitution Act, 1867), the Catholic and Protestant religions for schooling purposes (s. 93 of the Constitution Act, 1867), and Aboriginal Canadians. This changed as a result of the emergence of feminism as a political force in the 1960s and 1970s and the increasing popularity—first among some elites, spreading later to the general population—of multiculturalism and group-oriented thinking about rights.

Leslie Pal argues that the institutionalization of diversity in Canadian public life was leveraged during the late 1960s and throughout the 1970s and 1980s by the activities of a small organization, the Citizenship Branch, within the Department of Secretary of State (SOS).[2] The grants disbursed by the Citizenship Branch through its Official Language Minority Group, Women's Program, and Multiculturalism section helped finance thousands of organizations that, in time, made group-related policy demands on government, raised the profile of diversity issues, and reinforced the idea that government should be protecting and promoting group interests. SOS played a pivotal role in financing diversity advocacy. 'Measured in dollars,' Pal concludes, 'the programs were insignificant. Measured in increased tolerance for minorities and women, they were at best marginally successful.'[3] But their enduring significance, Pal argues, was to help reshape the structures of government and the relationship of the state to groups of citizens in ways that institutionalized diversity.

This process of recognizing and promoting diversity did not stop at SOS. Human rights commissions at both the federal and provincial levels have played a very important role in expanding the concept of minorities. The earlier emphasis on language, religion, and ethnic origins has had to compete in recent years with such non-racialized and non-cultural forms of minority status as gender, sexual orientation, dependence on alcohol and drugs, and social conditions. Human rights commission officials, as Howe and Johnson argue, have been at the forefront of the movement to extend the recognition of diversity through expanding the number of rights-bearing groups:

Human rights commission officials continuously urged expansive legislation and brought test cases forward to stretch the law. But in addition, the educational programs of commissions and the very existence of the legislation and the complaint procedures served to encourage a further growth of equality rights consciousness and societal pressures for stronger leglislation. By providing education about rights, and by publicizing the existence of a system of rights protection, human rights programs and institutions politicized Canadian society in the direction of making demands for wider rights. Rights consciousness and awareness of human rights commissions encouraged more and more groups to pressure for more and more rights. The result was a steady expansion of human rights protections, the entrenchment of human rights legislation, and the institutionalization of human rights commissions, embedded in an increasingly politicized society in which rights-conscious human rights interest groups demanded ever wider rights.[4]

At the federal level the activities of the Canadian Broadcasting Corporation, including its Native language broadcasting operations, the National Film Board, and Telefilm Canada, have all contributed to the public projection of images of Canadian society that reflect the diversity of the country's population and history. The Department of Canadian Heritage has inherited the functions pioneered by the Citizenship Branch of SOS, providing grants to an enormous array of groups and operating as the leader within government for the promotion of Canadian pluralistic identity. In the 2001–2 fiscal year Canadian Heritage disbursed about $850 million to hundreds of groups and projects, ranging from small one-time grants, such as support for a study on 'The economic and ideological bases of racism towards recent Chinese immigrants to Vancouver', to expensive ongoing programs, including the Promotion of Official Languages and Official Languages in Education programs. If Canada's Booker Prize-winning novelist Yann Martel is correct in his description of Canada as the 'world's greatest hotel', then Heritage Canada may be thought of as the marketing arm of this hotel.

DIVERSITY AND POLITICAL REPRESENTATION

The 1878 cabinet of Sir John A. Macdonald had 14 members. All but one were born in Canada. About 80 per cent (11 of 14) had British Isles ethnic origins and the rest were French. All were either Catholic (4 of 14) or Protestant.

In May 2002 the cabinet of Jean Chrétien was not as different from Sir John A.'s government as one might have expected, given the enormous demographic shifts that have occurred in Canadian society. Of its 29 members—this excludes secretaries of state—only a couple were born outside of Canada. The vast majority, about 80 per cent, had French or British ethnic origins. The religious affiliation of MPs is today more difficult to ascertain from public records than it was in the past, but only one or two of the 29 members of cabinet may have had a non-Judeo-Christian religious affiliation. It is probable that a handful had no religious affiliation. On the whole, however, the demographic composition of Chrétien's 2002 cabinet was more similar to than different from the Macdonald cabinet of 1878, except in one striking respect. Chrétien's government included seven women whereas Macdonald's included none.

Forty years ago John Porter remarked that Canada's political elite had been slow to change, failing to reflect the increasing ethnic diversity of the country. It was, he said, still an elite dominated by males from the two charter groups. Members of these groups continue to be disproportionately represented, at least if we define the political elite rather narrowly to include only the federal cabinet. John Diefenbaker appointed to cabinet Canada's first female minister, Ellen Fairclough, and first non-charter group Canadian, Michael Starr, of Ukrainian origin, in the late 1950s. Canada's first Jewish member of cabinet was Herb Gray, appointed Minister without Port-

BOX 13.2   Religious Diversity and the Souls of Soldiers

Religious services in the Canadian forces are controlled exclusively by a few major Christian churches, discriminating against other faiths and minority Christian sects, a Pentecostal minister has charged in a human rights complaint.

The forces have 29 Anglican chaplains—eight times the percentage of Anglicans in the general population—but no Jews, Hindus or Muslims, Reverend Sheldon Johnston notes in his complaint.

The 35-year-old from Castlegar, BC, is getting support from a major Jewish group, which says the Department of National Defence must better represent Canada's Spiritual mosaic.

'What we have right now is a handful of religious groups that are judging other groups and saying that they are not worthy to be represented, which I think is wrong', Rev. Johnston said.

'I think it has a huge impact on minority groups. This is a primary reason why there isn't that much diversity.'

Religions are supposed to be represented in the military chaplaincy based on the number of troops who declare themselves to be members of those churches.

'We know right now that we are not reflective of Canadian society, so we've got a lot of work to do and it's going to take some time', said Lieutenant-Colonel Dave Kettle, a chaplaincy spokesman.

Rev. Johnston, of the Church of God Canada, said the forces must go further and end for good their practice of having quotas for the number of chaplains from different Christian churches.

Tom Blackwell, 'Minister Battles Military Over Faith',
National Post, 21 Feb. 2003, A2.

folio in 1969. But despite the election of increasing numbers of candidates from non-Judeo-Christian backgrounds over the last couple of decades, few have been promoted to cabinet. People from non-European ethnic backgrounds, who today comprise about 12 per cent of the Canadian population, and even those of non-charter group European origins continue to be underrepresented at this highest level.

The situation is not different in the case of the judicial elite and the highest ranks of the federal bureaucracy. If we look at the 74 individuals who have been members of the Supreme Court since its creation, all but three have had British or French ethnic origins and all have had Judeo-Christian backgrounds. The same, broadly speaking, is true of the ranks of deputy ministers in Canada, although members of non-charter groups have made somewhat greater inroads into this elite. The main change to have occurred in both of these elites is the increased presence of women.

By drawing attention to the continuing dominance of these elites by members of the French and British charter groups, we are not suggesting that this is evidence of discrimination against those who come from other backgrounds. A couple of qualifying factors need to be taken into account. First, it takes time for demographic change to work its way through to the top of a political system. Most of the decline in the share of Canada's population claiming either French or British Isles ethnic origin has occurred since the

1970s. It is rare for one to become a member of one of the elites examined above before the age of 40, and most are in their fifties and sixties. As the size of the pool of non-charter group Canadians with the qualifications and other attributes necessary to become a member of one of these elites increases, we might expect to see more of these people selected.

Second, the concept of 'charter group Canadians' has become increasingly problematic. Growing numbers of Canadians have mixed ethnic origins and a considerable share of the population now rejects the traditional ethnic identities, preferring to describe themselves as being of Canadian origin. Consequently, it may be more accurate to say that the political, judicial, and bureaucratic elites in Canada are dominated by persons of French, British, *and* Canadian origins, without there being reason to think that 'Canadian' here is just a substitute label for membership in one of the tradtional charter groups.

THE UNDER-REPRESENTATION OF WOMEN

Women constitute about 52 per cent of the Canadian population and a slightly larger percentage of the electorate. Despite their numerical superiority, only one female, Kim Campbell, has held the office of Prime Minister, and two, Rita Johnson of BC and Catherine Callbeck of PEI, have been provincial premiers. Of these three, only Callbeck led her party to election victory. The number of women who have been elected to the leadership of political parties in Canada can be counted on the fingers of a couple hands. There are, however, some signs of change. The percentage of female candidates nominated by the major political parties has never been as high as it is today, although from 1997 to 2000 there was some slippage. Women comprised close to one-quarter of all candidates for the five main parties in the 1993, 1997, and 2000 federal elections (see Figure 13.4). Yet, while the number of women

(62) elected to the House of Commons in 2000 was the same as in 1997, there were 44 fewer women candidates in 2000 than in the previous federal election. Females comprised about 30 per cent of all NDP candidates in 2000 and about 22 per cent of Liberal candidates. In 1989 the NDP became the first major political party to elect a woman as its leader, again choosing a female leader in 1994.

A similar pattern of under-representation is found in the case of non-elected positions within the state. Before the 1982 appointment of Justice Bertha Wilson, no woman had ever been a member of the Supreme Court of Canada. Since then Justice Claire L'Heureux-Dubé (1987), Justice Beverley McLachlin (1989), Justice Louise Arbour (1999), and Justice Marie Deschamps (2002) have been appointed to the Supreme Court. Overall, however, only a small percentage of judges in Canada are women. Somewhat deeper inroads have been cut into the senior ranks of the bureaucracy. Women account for about 30 per cent of senior management personnel in the federal public service, and their presence is no longer rare on the top rungs of the bureaucratic ladder (deputy ministers and equivalent positions). While it is not uncommon for women to be appointed to the boards of directors of Crown corporations, no woman has ever been the CEO of a major commercially oriented Crown at either the federal or provincial level. In this respect, Crown corporations such as Canadian National, the Canadian Wheat Board, Hydro One Networks in Ontario, Hydro-Québec, and the Caisse de dépôt et placement du Québec simply mirror the pattern of female exclusion that characterizes Canada's corporate elite.

Why are females under-represented in political life? Does it matter that the levers of the state are overwhelmingly in the hands of men? These questions are not new. The reasons behind female under-representation are, however, more easily explained than are its consequences. Let us begin with the relatively uncontroversial part.

Why Aren't More Women Involved in Political Life?

At a superficial level, the riddle of women's under-representation in public life may appear to be simple: they have been less interested than men. Female participation levels have long been about the same as men's for political activities like voting and campaigning, but have been much lower for more demanding activities, such as holding office in a political party and running for public office. 'The higher, the fewer' is how Sylvia Bashevkin has described the political participation gap between males and females.[5] This gap has narrowed over time, but it continues to exist.

If interest is one of the key determinants of participation, what explains different levels of interest? The answer lies in social learning. Traditionally, females learned from the world around them that politics was a predominantly male occupation. The signals were unmistakable. The Prime Minister/President was a man. So, too, were all but a handful of cabinet ministers and elected representatives. More subtle than the evident maleness of the political profession, but probably more important in discouraging most females from seeing themselves in political roles beyond those of voter and perhaps member of the women's auxiliary of Party X, was the sheer weight of social customs and expectations, communicat-

Figure 13.4   Gender of Candidates for the Five Main Parties in the 2000 Election

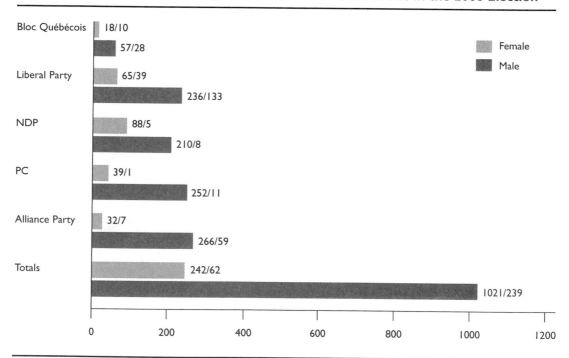

Note: The number of male and female candidates for each party is indicated to the right of each bar, followed by the number of male or female candidates actually elected. The total elected that is indicated here—300—does not include the one independent, John Nunziata, who was also elected.

Source: Based on data provided in the Report of the Chief Electoral Officer of Canada, 37th General Election (2000).

ed in the family, in school, in churches, and through the media. Leadership and an active involvement in the world beyond the family and neighbourhood were associated with masculinity. If females were not actively discouraged from developing an interest in politics, they generally were not encouraged to apply their energies and time to such matters.

The influence of social learning was reinforced by the sexual division of labour in society, particularly in the family but also, and relatedly, in the workplace. The traditional male breadwinner/female homemaker family and the more contemporary two breadwinner/female homemaker household are universally acknowledged by feminists as important sources of female subordination to males, including their comparatively marginal status in politics. This subordination/marginalization operates on two main levels.

1. *Psychological*. Child-rearing and housework are useful and necessary activities. Society's attitude towards them, however, is ambivalent. Because they are forms of unpaid labour, at least when carried out by a household member, there exists no objective yardstick for determining their value. And so they tend to be undervalued, particularly in comparison to paid work outside of the home. A good deal of evidence suggests that society's general failure to recognize the value of domestic work, or to praise it while labelling it 'woman's work', generates frustration and low self-esteem among many women.[6] Moreover, the traditional roles of mother and homemaker have often operated to limit women *spatially* (tied to the physical demands of the domestic routine), *cognitively* (the relevant world and its activities are more likely to centre on the family and household than in the case of men), and *emotionally* (expressive, nurturing, caring functions are associated with the homemaker, while instrumental, active, and rational qualities are associated with the breadwinner). In brief, the consciousness that is likely to be produced by the traditional roles of mother and homemaker is not likely to generate the motivations, interests, and personal resources for political activism.

2. *Status and professional achievements*. Traditionally, women have been under-represented in precisely those occupations from which political office-holders tend to be drawn: law, business,

And...why exactly do you want a sex-change operation?

I'm seeking a Liberal nomination in the next election.

Although all political parties today nominate many more female candidates than a generation ago, roughly four-fifths of all candidates for the five main parties in the 2000 election were men. (Roy Peterson, *Vancouver Sun*)

and the liberal professions. Their formal educational attainments have tended to be less than those of men and they have not been found in significant numbers in fields such as finance, economics, and engineering, which are important professional backgrounds for many senior positions in the public service. But even when women have made what were and (in some cases, such as engineering) still are viewed as non-traditional career choices, the likelihood has been great that they have had to take time out from their career and/or not pursue opportunities that would make greater demands on their time or require them to uproot their families because of the expectation that the nurturing of children and household duties will fall primarily to women.

The sexual division of labour within the household, therefore, has worked to reduce women's opportunities to achieve the sorts of experience and professional status that often provide the basis for recruitment into parties and other political organizations. If, however, a woman has the motivation and the status achievements to break into public life, there is still a good chance that the competing pressures of household responsibilities will limit the scope of her aspirations. It is certainly true that males are less likely to feel the constraining tug of these responsibilities than females.

The traditional male breadwinner/female homemaker family is, of course, much less common than it used to be. About 61 per cent of Canadian women over the age of 15 are in the workforce (2002). The labour force participation rate for married women with children under six years old is about two-thirds, compared to barely more than one-quarter in 1971. Whereas 65 per cent of Canadian families were of the one earner/male breadwinner model in 1961, barely more than 10 per cent conform to this model today. Although the average income for full-time female workers is still less than three-quarters of the average male income (71.7 per cent in 2000, up from 58.4 per cent in 1967), the proportion of women in relatively high-status professions

such as law, accounting, and university teaching and in middle management positions in both the private and public sectors has increased significantly during the last generation. Nonetheless, the traditional sexual division of household labour still places limits on women's opportunities for political participation that men are less likely to experience.

WOMEN IN POLITICS

Women were active in politics before being entitled to vote and run for office. Much of this activity was aimed at achieving full citizenship rights for women. But this was far from being the sole concern of women's groups during the pre-suffrage era. They were also active in demanding a long list of social reforms ranging from pensions for widowed mothers to non-militaristic policies in international relations. By contemporary standards, however, the early women's movement was small and politically weak. Moreover, its demands and values—although radical in the context of the times—today appear to have been quite moderate and in some cases even reactionary.

Although the women's movement of today looks and sounds very different from early versions, elements of continuity span the movement's history. In tracing the history of women's political involvement in Canada, we will focus on the social and ideological forces that have influenced the women's movement, as well as the issues, organizations, strategies, and accomplishments that have characterized the movement at different points in time.

Phase One: The Contradictions of Democracy and Industrialization

Feminist writings and occasional incidents of women mobilizing around particular events or issues before the nineteenth century were quite rare. The democratic impulses released by the overthrow of absolute monarchy in Britain (1688) and by the American (1776) and French revolutions (1789) generated some agitation for equality of political rights, but their consequences were negligible. Although married women did have the right to vote in some societies, it appears that they were expected to follow the lead of their husbands—particularly during an era before the secret ballot. In matters of law and property, a woman was subsumed under the person of her father and, after marriage, her husband.

The origins of the women's movement usually are located in the mid-nineteenth century. As Sheila Rowbotham writes, 'Feminism came, like socialism, out of the tangled, confused response of men and women to capitalism.'[7] The progress of capitalism produced both affluence and misery. As more and more people crowded into the cities whose growth was spawned by factory production, a new set of social problems arose. Working-class women, girls, and children were employed in many industries. In fact, their cheap labour provided the basis for the profitability of such industries as textiles, clothing, footwear, and cigar-making. As historian Terry Copp observes:

> Large numbers of working class women were 'emancipated' from the bondage of unpaid labour at home long before their middle class counterparts won entry into male-dominated high income occupations. There was no need to struggle against an exclusionist policy, since employers were only too happy to provide opportunities for women in the factories, shops, and garment lofts of the city.[8]

Hard numbers on female participation in the workforce do not exist before twentieth-century census-takers began to keep track of such things. It has been estimated, however, that women comprised about 20 per cent of the labour force in Montreal during the 1890s. There is no reason to think that the percentage was lower in other cities. The low wages they invariably received put downward pressure on the wages of all unskilled working people.

Working conditions in most manufacturing establishments were hard, to say the least. There were no laws regulating the hours of work, minimum wages, or safety and sanitation in the workplace. A disabling injury on the job usually meant personal financial disaster. While both men and women suffered under these conditions, the exposure of women—usually single—to the harsh environment of the factory and sweatshop was considered more serious because of the era's views on femininity. A woman's natural place was considered to be the home, and her participation in the wage economy was believed, by political reactionaries and social reformers alike, to be 'one of the sad novelties of the modern world . . . a true social heresy'.[9]

Early industrialization took its toll on women in other ways as well. The brutal grind and crushing squalor that characterized the lives of many working people could be numbed through drink. And in an era before heavy 'sin taxes', beer and spirits were very cheap. Alcohol abuse, although by no means restricted to the working class, was one of the side effects of the long hours of work, inadequate wages, and sordid workplace conditions characteristic of workers' lives. It not only contributed to the ruin of individuals, but to the suffering of their families. Poor sanitation, overcrowding in improperly ventilated housing, and improper diet combined to produce low life expectancy—tuberculosis was a major killer among the urban working class—and high infant mortality.

The harshness of early industrialization was experienced by both men and women. Its manifestations—child labour, poverty, alcohol abuse—became central issues in the early women's movement because of their perceived impact on the family and on prevailing standards of decency. The Woman's Christian Temperance Union, the Young Women's Christian Association, and the Women's Institutes that sprang up in cities across Canada starting in the late nineteenth century were keenly aware of the clash between the material conditions of working-class women and prevailing notions of femininity and family. The social reforms that they urged on government were intended to protect women and the family from what they saw as the corrosive influences of industrial life.

Early feminism was not, however, merely a response to the contradictions that industrialization created for women. The achievement of democracy was also full of contradictions. If democracy was a system of government based on the will of the people that recognized the equal humanity and dignity of human beings, half of the population could not be denied the rights and status enjoyed by the other half.

As John Stuart Mill observed in his essay 'The Subjection of Women',[10] arguments against the political and legal equality of the sexes took several forms. The main ones, and Mill's refutations (*in italic*), included the following:

- Unlike the slavery of one race by another, or the subordination of a defeated nation by its military conqueror, the subjection of women to men is natural. *When hasn't the subordination of one category of the human race by another been labelled 'natural' by members of the dominant group? What is said to be natural turns out to be, on closer examination, merely customary.*

- Unlike other forms of domination, the rule of men over women is accepted voluntarily by the female population. *This is not true. Some women do not accept the subordinate lot of their sex. And if a majority appear to acquiesce in their second-class status, this should surprise no one. From their earliest years women are trained in the habits of submission and learn what male-dominated society expects of them.*

- Granting equal rights to women will not promote the interests of society. *What this means, in fact, is that equality will not promote the interests of male society. It is a mere argument of convenience and self-interest.*

- What good could possibly come from extending full political and legal rights to women? *Leaving aside the good that this would produce for women— for their character, dignity and material conditions— all society would benefit from a situation where the competition for any particular vocation is determined by interest and capabilities. Society loses when any*

group is barred from contributing its talents to humanity. Finally, equality for women would improve the character of men, who would no longer enjoy the sense of being superior to one-half of the human race because of an accident of birth, rather than to any merit or earned distinction on their part.

Despite the compelling quality of Mill's arguments for equality, men who would have been shocked at the imputation that they were anything but democratic continued to ignore and resist demands that women be treated as full citizens. The arguments used to deny political rights for women were intellectually flabby and often amounted to nothing more than 'nice women do not want the vote' or 'my wife doesn't want the vote'.[11] But the logic of democratic rights is universal, and the exclusion of the female half of the population from the enjoyment of these rights was one of the major contradictions of most democracies until well into the twentieth century (see Table 13.2).

The early women's movement focused mainly on three sets of issues: political rights, legal rights, and social reform. Anti-militarism was a fourth, but less prominent, issue on the political agenda of feminists. The social feminism mainstream of the movement was concerned chiefly with what it perceived as threats to the security of women and the family and to the traditional values associated with them. The demands made by organizations like the WCTU and YWCA and by prominent feminists like Nellie McClung were based solidly on the middle-class morality of the times.

The dominant middle-class morality could, and eventually did, accommodate itself to political rights for women. 'Respectable' feminists were those who consented to play by the rules of the game as they found it. Political rights for women were expected to make the political parties and government more sensitive to issues of concern to women, such as working conditions for females, child labour, alcohol abuse, and pensions for widowed mothers. Legal rights enabling a married woman to own property in her own

Table 13.2   Women's Suffrage

Year	Number of countries where men and women could vote in national elections on equal terms
1900	1
1910	3
1920	15
1930	21
1940	30
1950	69
1960	92
1970	127
1975	129

Source: Kathleen Newland, *Women in Politics: A Global Review* (Washington: Worldwatch Institute, 1975), 8.

name or protecting her from disinheritance in the event of her husband's death were demanded in order to provide more economic security for women and their dependent children. Such social reforms as the prohibition of alcohol sales, family allowances, more humane conditions in women's prisons, and labour legislation dealing with women and children were expected to produce a more civilized, compassionate society. Finally, peace issues within the women's movement were tied directly to the image of woman as the giver and nurturer of life, to what were believed to be the maternal instincts of women.

The mainstream of the women's movement was represented by the Woman's Christian Temperance Union, the Young Women's Christian Association, the National Council of Women of Canada, and the Federated Women's Institutes. They were politically moderate organizations in terms of both their goals and their strategies for attaining them. Indeed, it would be fair to say that the goals of social feminism were fundamentally conservative, aimed at protecting women and the family from the corrosive influences of the industrial age. The political discourse of the movement drew upon the middle-class morality of the times. Even Nellie McClung, who was considered a firebrand of the movement, did not in the least sug-

gest that the social roles of man the provider and woman the nurturer be changed. Instead, McClung and most other leaders of the early women's movement wanted to put woman's role on a more secure material footing.

The political tactics employed by mainstream women's groups hardly ever strayed beyond the familiar bounds of accepted practice. Unlike their sisters in Great Britain and the United States, Canadian suffragists did not resort to such confrontational methods as chaining themselves to the fences surrounding Parliament, physically resisting the police, or hunger strikes. Instead, they relied on petitions to government and efforts to persuade public opinion.

After about 40 years of campaigning, the first success came in Manitoba in 1916. The other three western provinces and Ontario followed suit within about a year. In the Maritimes, where the suffrage movement was comparatively weak, the achievement of political rights for women was preceded by much less agitation than in the West. Nova Scotia (1918), New Brunswick (1919), PEI (1922), and Newfoundland (1925) extended political rights to women, although in the case of New Brunswick, women were granted only voting rights. They could not hold provincial public office until 1934. Quebec was the straggler among Canada's provinces. Opposition from the Catholic Church blocked political rights for women until 1940.

Nationally, women became citizens between 1917 and 1919. The Wartime Elections Act of 1917 extended voting rights to the relatively small number of women serving in the military and to the much larger pool of females whose male relatives were in military service. This was broadened in 1918 to include all women aged 21 years and over. The right to hold office in the House of Commons followed a year later, although women appeared to be barred from entry into the non-elected Senate and from holding other appointive public offices, such as judgeships, by virtue of not qualifying as 'persons', as this term was understood in law.

Absurd though it may seem, the personhood of women was considered to be dubious in the years following their enfranchisement.[12] Two prime ministers rejected calls for the appointment of a woman to the Senate on the grounds that women, not being persons as understood in law, were not eligible. The right of females to sit as judges was challenged in the handful of cases where they were appointed to the bench. After a couple of provincial rulings in their favour, the question was placed before the Supreme Court of Canada in 1927. Feminists were shocked when the Court ruled that the legal meaning of 'persons' excluded females.

This decision was reversed on appeal by the Judicial Committee of the Privy Council. Its ruling was blunt: 'The exclusion of women from all public offices is a relic of days more barbarous than ours . . . and to ask why the word [person] should include females, the obvious answer is, why should it not?'[13] While logic and justice won the day in this particular legal battle, they have lost a number of others in the courts. Indeed, some contemporary feminists express strong doubts about the courts and law as vehicles for achieving the movement's goals. Voting rights for women and formal access to the male world of politics and the professions did not change the

fact that society still viewed a woman's place as being in the home. Social feminists never really challenged this belief.

Political rights for women might have provided the basis for the reforms envisaged by feminists if two conditions had existed: (1) a sufficient number of voters were prepared to cast their ballots for candidates and parties who supported the reforms advocated by the women's movement; and (2) a political vehicle existed to articulate the movement's agenda and provide a feminist alternative in electoral politics. Indeed, it appears to have been the belief of many in the women's suffrage movement that the major political parties either would crumble when a flood of independent candidates was elected or would tremble submissively before the demands of reform-minded female voters. But in fact the parties continued to set the agenda of electoral politics along the familiar lines that had long served them so well. That the parties felt no need to respond to the agenda of the women's movement or to recruit more women into their inner circles showed how slight was the impact of feminism on public consciousness.

The major parties' indifference to the demands of the women's movement was matched by the movement's distrust of the party system. Early feminists were reluctant to rely on the established political parties as vehicles for reform. There were two main reasons for this. One involved the attitude of the parties. It was not simply that the Liberal and Conservative parties showed little enthusiasm for the goals of the women's movement, including political rights for women; they were often dismissive and even hostile towards women's concerns and those expressing them. So after achieving the same formal political rights as men, women found that little of substance had changed. They were marginalized within parties dominated by men who, in the words of Canada's first female MP, Agnes Macphail, 'Want to Hog Everything'.[14] This was not surprising. The parties reflected the dominant beliefs of the time, beliefs that made women in public life—or in any of what were traditionally male preserves—appear an oddity. Even the more egalitarian of Canada's male politicians were not immune from sexism when it came to women in politics. J.S. Woodsworth, at the time a Labour MP from Winnipeg, probably summed up male politicians' grudging acceptance of women in *their* game when he said, 'I still don't think a woman has any place in politics.'[15]

A second reason why early feminists were reluctant to work within the framework of the party system was that their movement, like the farmers' movement of the same era, was issue-based. The organizations that formed the core of the movement took hard, uncompromising positions on prohibition, political rights for women, and social reform. Political parties, the two major ones at least, were based on principles that rejected the issue-based approach. One of these principles was partisan loyalty, the chief manifestation of which was the sheep-like obedience of elected members to the policy positions established by their party's leaders. Feminists wanted to be able to take positions based on their perception of what was in the interests of women without having to compromise the movement's goals. This concept of direct representation was shared by the farmers' movement of the time but was discouraged by the partisan rules of British parliamentary government.

The anti-party inclinations of feminists were reinforced by the parties' tendency to avoid if possible, and fudge, if avoidance was not possible, issue stances that might alienate important groups of voters. This has been called 'brokerage politics' (see Chapter 9). It is an approach that had no appeal to single-issue groups like prohibitionists and suffragists, or to the reform-minded women's movement more generally.

But working outside the established party system and the legislature, in an era when the media were less effective channels for political influence than they are today, carried heavy costs. A legislator who sits as an independent is marginalized in British parliamentary government, not sharing in the opportunities for participation that are available to the members of political parties. Moreover, the organizational and financial resources of the parties are important advantages that their candidates have over independents. It very quickly became apparent that non-partyism could not be made to work in practice.

Phase Two: After the Vote, What?

'Is Women's Suffrage a Fizzle?' asked a 1928 article in *Maclean's*. The question reflected the disillusionment experienced by many in the women's movement only years after having won the vote. Little, it seemed, had changed. Men still dominated the political process. The issues that interested women's groups, with the exception of prohibition, were no more prominent than before women's suffrage. And despite having the same formal political rights as men, women were still viewed as a not-quite-appropriate oddity in public life, rather like a dog walking on its hind legs. The dog can do it, but it's unnatural and, anyway, what is the point?

Part of the disappointment felt by feminists was due to their unrealistic expectations. Those who spearheaded the fight for women's suffrage believed—wrongly as it turned out—that the vote would be the tool women would use to change the world. As Nellie McClung put it, 'Women have cleaned up things since time began; and if women ever get into politics there will be a cleaning out of pigeon-holes and forgotten corners, on which the dust of years has fallen, and the sound of the political carpet-beater will be heard in the land.'[16] When the millennial expectations of social feminists were not met, worse than this, when hardly anything appeared to have changed after the victory that was supposed to change so much, frustration and gloom were natural reactions.

It is usual to treat the period from suffrage to the new feminism that gained momentum in the 1960s as one long hiatus in the women's movement.[17] A small number of women did run for public office, and an even smaller number won election. Of those elected or appointed to public office, some achieved national prominence.

Among them were Ottawa mayor Charlotte Whitton, five-time MP and twice Ontario MPP Agnes Macphail, British Columbia judges Emily Murphy and Helen Gregory MacGill, and Conservative cabinet minister Ellen Louise Fairclough. But the distinction of being the first woman to enter what had been an exclusive preserve of men, or to achieve recognition for one's talents and capabilities, had little impact on the political and social status of women in general. The breakthroughs and accomplishments of a few stood in sharp contrast to the unchanged status of the many. A number of plausible reasons help to explain this lack of change, chief among them the nature of early feminism, the party system, and societal attitudes.

The nature of early feminism. The mainstream of the women's movement was essentially conservative. Far from wanting to break down traditional gender roles, social feminists wanted to protect the social values and the family structure on which they rested. Early feminists tended to believe that the political subordination of women was based on their inferior political and legal rights. What they failed to see was that traditional gender roles in the family, the workplace, and other social settings prevented women from participating more fully and effectively in public life.

The party system. We have already explained how the anti-party stance of feminist reformers proved difficult to maintain once they became part of a parliamentary process that was based on partisanship. This was not, however, the only impact that the party system had on women's political involvement. Within the two traditional parties, as well as the CCF-NDP, women's involvement was organized around support services. The women's auxiliary or club was the symbol of the complementary role that women were encouraged to play in parties dominated by men. These separate organizations for women actually predated women's suffrage by a few years.[18] By the 1960s, this segregation of active male roles from supportive female roles—essentially an extension of the gender relations that existed within the family and society—was increasingly seen as an impediment to the equal and effective participation of women in politics.

Societal attitudes. Feminism failed to make a greater mark on social attitudes in part because the social feminist mainstream of the women's movement did not challenge conventional ways of thinking about appropriate gender roles. Outside of the mainstream was a more radical feminist fringe, what William O'Neill calls 'hard-core feminists',[19] who were not satisfied with the political rights and the social reforms that constituted the agenda of social feminism. Hard-core feminists like Flora MacDonald Denison demanded the legal emancipation of women and sexual equality in education, employment, the family: in short, wherever women were systematically subordinated to men.[20] Their ideas were not, however, considered to be 'respectable'.

If mainstream feminism was a weak force in Canadian politics, which it was, hard-core feminism barely scratched the surface of public life and political discourse. Its more radical critique of female subordination was marginalized in left-wing political organizations, which themselves were on the near-irrelevant periphery of Canadian politics. Even within the CCF, the only left-wing political organization that managed to occupy an important place in Canadian politics, hard-core feminism ran up against some intransigent barriers. As historian Joan Sangster writes:

> [E]vidence indicates that women were channelled into [the CCF's] social committees; that women's feminine character was often described as emotional and sensitive, implying a female inability to cope with the 'rational' world of politics; and that women were seen as more apathetic and politically backward than men. Perhaps most important of all, because women's primary responsibility for the family was never questioned, an essential barrier to women's whole-hearted participation in politics remained unchallenged and unchanged.[21]

But this raises the question of why social attitudes about gender roles were slow in changing.

It is a complex issue that cannot be reduced to a single explanation. We would argue, however, that the ability of women to exert some greater degree of control over their reproductive role was a chief factor contributing to this change. Fairly reliable contraceptive devices became widely available and used during the 1950s (mainly condoms and diaphragms) and the 1960s (the birth control pill). It was no coincidence that women began to have fewer children. Smaller families and the ability to be sexually active without fear of becoming pregnant provided the opportunity for women to say in school longer or participate in the workforce for more years of their reproductive lives. Choice in the realm of reproduction was a crucial material condition for women's liberation in other aspects of life.

The pill made it possible, but not inevitable. We still need to understand why the second wave of feminism that became a political force in the 1960s—it already was something of an intellectual force, influenced by writers like Margaret Mead and Simone de Beauvoir—was more critical and, as it turned out, more effective than the early women's movement. The explanation has three parts: sexuality, secularism, and economics.

Sexuality had been the deafening silence of the first wave of feminism. The entire topic of sexuality was shrouded in mystery and taboo before the 1960s. While there still is a good deal of half-baked thinking surrounding the subject, the period since the sixties has been marked by a much greater willingness to talk about sexuality and acknowledge its importance in social relationships. This was a necessary step that opened the way for public debate on such matters as reproductive rights and women's control of their bodies, the possible impact of pornography on violence against women, and sexual stereotyping in education and the media.

Sexuality was not entirely in the closet before the 1960s. The subject had, in fact, received considerable attention from intellectuals since Sigmund Freud based the totality of human experience on males' and females' different struggles to resolve the conflict between their libidinal drives (sexual energy) and the demands of the superego (society's demands and taboos on behaviour). It is no accident that virtually every major intellectual leader of feminism's second wave took direct aim at Freud and what they argued was the patriarchal bias of twentieth-century psychology.[22] Essentially, they argued that Freudian psychology was phallocentric, and that concepts like the 'castration complex', 'penis envy', and 'masculinity complex' were pseudo-scientific justifications for male dominance, not biologically rooted facts of the human condition.

Once conventional beliefs about sexuality were challenged, this opened the door to a re-examination of traditional gender roles and stereotypes throughout society. The position taken by modern feminists was that these roles and their accompanying stereotypes were mainly social constructions rather than facts of nature. This was the reasoning that underlay the movement's slogan, 'The personal is political'. Conventional beliefs about female passivity, maternal instincts, and home-centredness were argued to be the ideological foundations, and the traditional division of labour in the home, workplace, church, and in other supposedly non-political settings the structural foundations, of women's political subordination. Differences that had been largely accepted and even promoted by maternal feminists earlier in the century were flatly rejected by the new feminism of the sixties.

Secularism was a second factor that contributed to the changed character of second-wave feminism. Many of the leading individuals in the first wave of feminism had been women of strong religious conviction and even fervour. As well, some of the key organizations in the suffrage and social feminism movements, such as the WCTU, the Imperial Order of the Daughters of the Empire, and the National Council of Women of Canada, had either direct links or an affinity of views with some of the Protestant churches. Early feminism had strong ties to the social gospel movement of the period between the 1890s and the 1930s, a movement that 'attempt[ed] to apply Christianity to the collective ills of an industrializing society'.[23] Those in the social gospel movement, like the early feminist leaders, believed that a New Jerusalem could be created on earth through social reforms. Their Christianity was secular insofar as it focused on changing conditions in the here and now. But their vision of reform was inspired by traditional Christian ideals.[24]

The second wave of the women's movement was secular in both its goals and inspiration. Its worldly character was broadly in tune with the changed social climate of the post-fifties world, where the traditional moral authority of religion was weaker than previously. In fact, traditional religious values regarding the family, procreation, and appropriate behaviour for males and females, as well as the patriarchal authority structures of most churches, were targets of feminist criticism. While some of the earlier leaders of the women's movement, for example, Nellie McClung,[25] had been outspokenly critical of certain church teachings and practices, they had generally embraced traditional moral values, not seeing them as impediments to equality for women.

Economic change was a third factor that influenced the second wave of the women's movement. Women had long constituted an important part of the labour force. Single women in particular provided a pool of very cheap labour in some manufacturing and service industries. The unpaid domestic work of women helped to subsidize the private economy by reducing the price that employers would otherwise have had to pay to male employees. Moreover, women constituted what has been called a 'reserve army' of labour that could be mobilized in unusual circumstances, as during the two world wars. Their participation in the wage economy was limited, however, by two conventional beliefs: women should not take jobs that could be held by men, and outside employment was fine for single women but should stop after marriage.

These constraints began to weaken during the 1950s and 1960s. As Figure 13.5 shows, the

Figure 13.5   Labour Force Participation Rates, 1901–2001

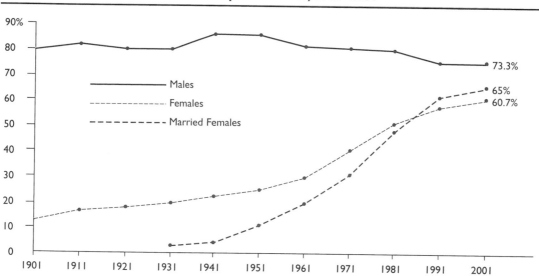

Sources: F.H. Leacy, ed., *Historical Statistics of Canada*, 2nd edn (Ottawa: Supply and Services Canada, 1983), D107–122 and D431–148; Statistics Canada, *Labour Force Annual Averages*, Catalogue no. 71–220 annual; Statistics Canada on-line data at: <www.statscan.ca>.

labour force participation rate of women (i.e., the percentage of working-age women who hold jobs or are looking for jobs outside the home) increased dramatically between 1951 and 1971. Most of this increase was the result of an explosion in the number of married women working outside the home. Their participation rate increased 300 per cent over these 20 years. Women's share of the total labour force also increased sharply.

A number of explanations have been offered to explain this increased participation rate. Economists have favoured three main arguments:

- Falling real family incomes have compelled women to enter the workforce to maintain the household's purchasing power. (This explanation is more plausible for the period since the 1980s. Real incomes for individual workers increased between the 1950s and the 1970s, the period during which the greatest increase in female labour force participation occurred.)
- Labour-saving household appliances and higher female educational attainment have produced feelings of boredom and dissatisfaction in the home, leading more and more women to seek outside employment.
- As the real wages associated with some 'female' jobs increased, outside employment appeared increasingly attractive to women.

There is doubtless some truth in each of these explanations. But as is so often true of conventional economics, it misses the mark by ignoring the obvious. Women had become increasingly restive with their traditional role. Betty Friedan called this 'the problem that has no name'.[26] Although difficult to label and express in a culture that told women they should feel fulfilled in the home, the problem amounted to this: 'I want something more than my husband and my children and my home.'[27] A paying job was often seen to be that 'something more'.

Yet another factor, however, should not be ignored. Most of the new jobs created in advanced industrial economies since World War II have been in service industries. Many of these jobs have been relatively low-paying ones that have been traditionally viewed as female occupations. Expansion of the service economy thus produced an increase in the supply of the clerical, secretarial, retail sales, cashier/teller, and waitressing jobs that were predominantly held by females. Many economists have a difficult time dealing with this factor because their model of the economic world says that if the demand for something increases, in this case secretaries and so on, the price should also increase. This did not happen—underpaid 'female' occupations remained underpaid— because of conventional beliefs that undervalued the work performed by women, seeing it as temporary or merely a supplement to the main (male) breadwinner's income. The world of work is a central part of modern feminism's reform agenda. Of course, the exploitation of female workers had been an important concern of social feminists, but they never questioned the belief that a married woman's proper place was in the home and that marriage was the most desirable estate for a woman. By the 1960s, the material basis of these conventional views had become shaky. The economic forces that caused a growing number of married women to seek wage employment, combined with the psychological impetus for women to seek fulfillment beyond their homemaker role, changed the nature of women's involvement in the economy. The reality of their segregation into low-pay, low-prestige occupations[28] became less and less palatable to women as their participation in the wage economy increased.

Phase Three: The Personal Is Political

The decade of the fifties was like the quiet before the storm. Post-war economic growth and the 'baby boom' combined to reinforce traditional gender roles and stereotypes. Television sitcoms, films, and popular magazines almost unfailingly portrayed the male breadwinner/female homemaker family as the pinnacle of human happiness. Having achieved political rights, it seemed that equality was no longer an issue.

The syrupy bliss of the era, it turned out, was an illusion. By the early sixties voices of discontent were being increasingly heard. Women were challenging the deep-seated beliefs and social structures that limited their participation in the male-dominated world. The 'problem that has no name' was being named, and the name was **sexism**. This is a word that is not found in dictionaries before the 1970s, a fact that reflected the unconscious acceptance by most people of gender role differences as natural and even desirable. 'Sexism' was coined in the 1960s as a label for behaviour that treated males and females unequally for no better reason than their gender. Sexism in its numerous forms and wherever it took place was the target of the women's movement that emerged during these years.

The revival of the women's movement was the result of several factors. Intellectually, writers like Simone de Beauvoir in France, Germaine Greer in Britain, and Betty Friedan and Gloria Steinem in the United States were developing a powerful analysis of women's subordination to men. Their critique went far beyond matters of political and legal rights and social reform, the chief concerns of earlier feminists. Instead, they exposed the social, cultural, and economic roots of inequality. Friedan's approach was typical in its range. In *The Feminine Mystique* she traced the causes of female subordination to the family, the social sciences (particularly psychology, sociology, and anthropology), education, advertising and the media, mass consumption capitalism, and sexual mores.

Anti-establishment ideas always face an uphill struggle. They never triumph by their intellectual weight alone. What saved the feminist critiques of Beauvoir, Friedan, and company from the fate of many interesting but ultimately ineffectual intellectual movements were the supportive material conditions and social climate of the 1960s. With about one out of every three women of working age employed outside the home, including about one out of five married women (1961), and increasing numbers of women enrolled in post-secondary education,[29] sexual

double standards were increasingly apparent to more women than ever before. Articles on the dilemmas facing the 'new woman', telling her how to juggle family, romance, and job, became standard fare in women's magazines like *Chatelaine* and *Redbook*. Terms such as 'women's lib' and 'women's libbers' were more frequently said with a sneer than not, and most women (and men) probably would not have recognized the names of people like Betty Friedan and Germaine Greer. Nevertheless, modern feminism's argument that the personal is political, that the fight for gender equality had to be waged in the workplace, the media, the schools, and over women's bodies, struck a responsive chord with many.

What the lived experience of women confirmed, the social climate of the 1960s encouraged. This was the era of the civil rights movement in the United States, mounting opposition to American military involvement in Vietnam, and anti-establishment political causes generally. Attacks on the 'establishment' and its values were common. Student radicalism, protest marches, sit-ins, and occasional violence were the visible signs of a reaction against the status quo. While the feminist movement did not spearhead the protest movement of the 1960s, it profited from the movement's tendency to see all established power relations as unjust.

The protest politics of the 1960s affected the women's movement in a second, more enduring way as well. Civil rights advocates in the United States argued that **affirmative action** programs were necessary to provide real equality of opportunity for blacks. Quotas and preferential hiring policies for targeted minorities were justified, they reasoned, because these groups were the victims of a systemic discrimination that ensured that few of them would acquire the formal qualifications—degrees, professional school admission scores, job-relevant experience—needed to compete with the members of more advantaged groups. The opponents of affirmative action—'reverse discrimination', as they were more likely to call it—charged that such a policy just shifted the burden of injustice onto the shoulders of the qualified members of advantaged groups who were not personally responsible for the plight of the minority groups targeted for special treatment. But despite considerable opposition, affirmative action policies were widely adopted by governments and educational institutions in the United States.

The arguments and demands of the North American women's movement bear a strong resemblance to those that emerged during the struggle to advance the rights of American blacks. Affirmative action does not have nearly the same prominence in several of the Western European democracies. Part of the explanation for this may have to do with lower barriers to the participation of women in politics and the professions in some European societies than in North America. Also, many European countries have more supportive structures, such as publicly financed schools that accept children from the age of two or younger, enabling women to continue their careers with minimal interruption. But an important part of the answer, we would argue, is the influence that the American civil rights movement has had on the demands of the women's movement and the response of policymakers. Affirmative action for women borrows arguments and policy measures that were pioneered in the struggle to increase the economic and social status of blacks in the United States.

Although Canada had no first-hand experience with racially based affirmative action policies before the 1960s, the concept and practice were not totally imported. Language policies adopted in Quebec during the 1970s aimed to increase the representation of francophones in the managerial ranks of that province's economy through agreements negotiated between the government and private companies. At the federal level, the period from the early 1970s saw an increasing number of administrative positions designated officially bilingual. This policy had the practical effect of favouring francophones who, more often than anglophones, had bilingual skills. During the 1980s, Ottawa began the practice of setting 'targets'—the word 'quotas' was and continues to be rejected—for the representation of particular groups in specified categories of the public service, and eventually of linking the performance evaluation of senior bureaucrats to their success in hitting these targets.

The logic of affirmative action was not, therefore, foreign to Canada. Language policies, in Quebec and nationally, incorporated elements of such an approach by the mid-1970s. Not only was the discourse of group rights already familiar in Canada, largely because of the struggles over language policies and Quebec's constitutional status, but the logic and machinery of targeting groups for preferred treatment was already embedded in the Canadian state.

Contemporary feminism is different from the first wave of the women's movement in more than its analysis and aims. The organizational network of women's groups is much more developed than when female suffrage and social reform were the key issues. Moreover, the movement's strategies distinguish it from its predecessor. We turn now to an examination of the organizations, strategies, and achievements of modern feminism.

ORGANIZING FOR INFLUENCE

Women have long been active in Canadian politics. As may be seen in Appendix 1 to this chapter, several important women's organizations date from the pre-suffrage era. Moreover, the political parties provided a channel—though not a very effective one—for women's participation in political life. Over the last three decades these organizations have been joined by hundreds more, as the organizational network of the women's movement has proliferated. This proliferation has generated, in response, new state structures to deal with 'women's issues' and the groups expressing them.

The organizations listed in Appendix 1 represent only some of the most visible structures through which women's political involvement takes place. Approximately 700 national and local women's groups are represented by the National

Action Committee on the Status of Women (NAC), an umbrella lobbying organization for the women's movement. The National Council of Women of Canada (NCWC), founded in 1893, is a federation of dozens of local, provincial, and national organizations that, in turn, represent hundreds of women's organizations. Both the NAC and the NCWC have consultative status with the Economic and Social Council of the United Nations, an affiliation that has been used to criticize the performance of Canadian governments on gender issues. In addition, there are women's church groups, professional associations, labour associations, and service organizations that are not members of either the NAC or the NCWC, as well as ad hoc groups that spring up around short-term issues.

While the network of women's groups has become denser over the last few decades, some argue that a focus on formal organizations and the structures of women's political involvement is misleading. Historian Anne Firor Scott argues that there has been a long but 'invisible' history of women's struggles against practices and conditions they wanted changed.[30] Many Canadian feminists agree.[31] They maintain that a female political culture operates through contacts and consciousness at the community level—based around issues that affect women in their daily lives—and that it does not rely on the formal political institutions and decision-making processes dominated by men. These grassroots activities tend to be overlooked and undervalued because the dominant political culture 'puts a premium on formal, institutionalized political processes, predictable and regulated levels and types of participation and both bureaucratic and hierarchical structures.'[32] Some argue that women's influence diminishes and their perspective on issues becomes blunted when they play by the rules of a political game established by men.

Although it is common to refer to the women's or feminist movement, such a label conceals the often profound divisions that exist between women's groups on matters ranging from ideology to political tactics. Just as there is an enormous range of perspectives within feminism, the real world of women's organizations reflects diversity rather than a monolithic bloc. Perhaps the most prominent and arguably the most crippling division within the Canadian women's movement in recent years has been between the predominantly white middle-class feminists, who have led the movement since the second wave of feminism took off in the 1960s, and non-white feminists whose ties are to less privileged ethnic groups and classes. This second group emphasizes race and class as central themes of their feminist vision. In the words of one-time NAC president Judy Rebick, 'an organization like NAC, which has been dominated by white middle class women, must transform almost everything we do to respond to the needs of doubly oppressed women.'[33] At the extreme, some have argued that white middle-class feminists are incapable of truly understanding and representing the circumstances and aspirations of women who are black, Aboriginal, poor, or from some other historically oppressed group.

This claim has generated considerable controversy within the feminist movement and in particular organizations such as the NAC and LEAF. Since Judy Rebick's departure over a decade ago, the NAC's presidents have been from visible minorities and the orientation of the organization very definitely has shifted towards an emphasis on the special problems of poor women from visible minorities. Whether this is a laudable change of direction is not the point. What is clear, however, is that the NAC's redefinition of the feminist project and division among feminists themselves have made it easier for governments to question, as they now regularly do, whether the NAC truly represents the concerns and values of a majority of Canadian women.

STRATEGIES

'There are fifty-six whooping cranes in Canada and one female federal politician.'[34] So began a 1971 article by Barbara Frum in *Chatelaine*. Half a century after winning the same political rights as men, the inroads made by women in Canada's political parties were pitifully small. Their participation was still channelled mainly into the activities of women's auxiliaries/associations, whose role was to provide support services for the party mainstreams. Although vital to the parties, these activities—social, administrative, fundraising, and campaigning—had low prestige and were remote from the policy- and strategy-oriented structures of the parties. Separate women's associations were singled out by the Royal Commission on the Status of Women as a serious barrier to the full participation of women in party politics. The Commission recommended that they be abolished.

Support-oriented women's associations within the parties were redolent of the sexual division of labour that modern feminism condemned. They have been eliminated at the national and provincial levels in all of the major parties. The trend since the late 1960s has been to replace the traditional women's associations with new women's groups dedicated to increasing women's representation and policy influence. As Sylvia Bashevkin notes, this transition has not been frictionless.[35] Nevertheless, if men still dominate within Canada's political parties—which they do—and if the feminist political agenda is still resisted—which it is to varying degrees in all of the main national parties except the NDP—the internal structures of the parties are no longer to blame.

Attempting to increase the representation and influence of women in parties that aspire to govern is a rather blunt strategy for achieving feminist goals. Parties in power, or even within sight of being elected to govern, are disinclined to alienate those voters and organized interests who object to such elements of the feminist agenda as the elimination of legal restrictions on abortion, affirmative action in hiring, and a national program of publicly subsidized daycare. Consequently, the women's movement has sought influence and change by other means.

One of these means has been the courts. Litigation in support of sexual equality claims has a long history in Canada, going back to the turn of the century when women challenged barriers to their entry into certain professions. But with the notable exception of the 1929 *Persons* case, in which the JCPC overruled Canadian courts in determining that women were persons in law, most of the pre-Charter litigation on sexual equality resulted in defeats for women's claims.[36] Given this dismal track record in the courts, plus the high cost of litigation—several pre-Charter cases reached the Supreme Court only because certain lawyers were willing to freely donate their time[37]—it comes as no surprise that this strategy was seldom chosen by women.

The Charter was expected to change all this. Indeed, women's groups fought hard and successfully for the inclusion of section 28 of the Charter, which states that 'the rights and freedoms referred to in [the Charter] are guaranteed equally to male and female persons.' Their efforts had already ensured that the equality section of the Charter (s. 15) proscribed discrimination based on sex. With sections 15 and 28 in hand, it appeared that women's groups would turn to the courts as never before.

They have, but with mixed results. In the first years after the equality section came into effect (1985–9), 44 cases of sexual discrimination under section 15 were decided by the courts. Most of these cases were instigated by or on behalf of men. In only nine cases were equality claims made by women. Despite victories in some of these cases feminist legal scholars quickly became dubious about the usefulness of section 15. Michael Mandel uses the term 'equality with a vengeance' to describe the tendency of courts, and of governments responding to court decisions, to interpret the Charter's equality provisions in ways that can backfire against women.[38]

Feminists have argued that the sexual equality guarantees of the Charter are undermined by two aspects of judicial interpretation. One is the courts' unwillingness to elevate equality rights over other rights and freedoms guaranteed in the Charter. For example, in *Casagrande v. Hinton*

Roman Catholic Separate School District (1987),[39] a Catholic school board's decision to fire an unmarried pregnant teacher was upheld on the grounds that section 15 equality rights took a back seat to the rights of 'denominational, separate or dissentient schools' that are also guaranteed by the Constitution. Second, and more serious according to feminists, is the tendency of judges to interpret equality in **formal** rather than **substantive** terms. What they mean by this is that judges will be satisfied that no discrimination has occurred if laws treat similarly persons who are similarly situated. This is an 'equality before the law' approach that, according to feminists, fails to understand the real mechanisms through which discrimination occurs. **Systemic discrimination**—the inequality created and maintained through social practices and beliefs—cannot be overcome by ensuring that the law is blind to the sex or other group characteristic of a section 15 claimant. Substantive equality, they argue, requires that judges determine whether a claimant belongs to a disadvantaged group and, second, 'whether the impugned law, policy or practice is operating to the detriment of [that disadvantaged group]'.[40]

In fact, however, this claim is not entirely fair. As early as 1984 the Supreme Court of Canada had declared its intention to look beyond the formal words of Charter sections to consider the interests they were meant to protect.[41] In *Edwards Books* (1986),[42] the majority expressed the view that 'the courts must be cautious to ensure that [the Charter] does not simply become an instrument of better situated individuals to roll back legislation which has as its object the improvement of the condition of less advantaged persons.'[43] A year later, Justices Dickson and Wilson argued that one of the important purposes of the Charter was to assist social and economic 'underdogs'.[44] These intimations of judicial activism were acted on in the *Morgentaler* abortion decision (1988), where the majority was willing to look at the actual effects of Canada's abortion law to determine whether it violated the 'liberty' and 'security of the person' guarantees in section 7 of the Charter.

Then, in *Law Society of British Columbia v. Andrews and Kinersley* (1989),[45] Canada's highest court showed that it was prepared to go beyond the wooden requirements of formal equality in interpreting section 15 of the Charter. The Supreme Court argued that the Charter's equality section prohibits laws that have had a discriminatory impact on the members of some group or groups. The decisions written by Justices Wilson and McIntyre both cited approvingly an American Supreme Court precedent that identified 'discrete and insular minorities' as groups requiring the protection of constitutional equality guarantees. In fact, the formal equality test so maligned by feminist legal scholars was explicitly rejected by all of the Supreme Court justices.[46] The substantive equality test is now routinely used by the courts in applying s. 15 of the Charter (see Box 13.3).

Activist Penney Kome identifies several political strategies, including legal action, that are open to women's groups. They range across grassroots organizing to deal with emergencies (e.g., a rash of sexual assaults in a neighbourhood) or chronic local problems (e.g., inadequate public transportation or pollution), representations through official channels, lobbying campaigns directed at decision-makers and potential supporters, and use of the media.[47] Lacking the financial resources and the personal access that characterize many business and professional interest groups, the women's movement has made extensive use of all of these political action strategies.

Like many groups that lack the financial resources and personal access to the corridors of power to carry on effective behind-the-scenes lobbying, women's organizations have often resorted to very public and sometimes confrontational strategies intended to generate media coverage of their issues and demands. Such strategies come with no guarantee of success. The representations that the NAC and other women's groups have made to the United Nations Committee on Economic, Social and Cultural Rights and to international meetings on women's issues have

---

BOX 13.3   When Is a Sexual Double Standard Protected by the Charter?

[Note: This case involved a male prisoner who objected to cross-sex frisk searches and the presence of female guards when being strip-searched. Male searches of female prisoners were already prohibited.]

The jurisprudence of this court is clear: equality does not necessarily connote identical treatment and, in fact, different treatment may be called for in certain cases to promote equality. Given the historical, biological, and sociological differences between men and women, equality does not demand that practices which are forbidden where male officers guard female inmates must also be banned where female officers guard male inmates. The reality of the relationship between the sexes is such that the historical trend of violence perpetrated by men against women is not matched by a comparable trend pursuant to which men are the victims and women the aggressors. . . . Viewed in this light, it becomes clear that the effect of cross-gender searching is different and more threatening for women than for men. The different treatment to which the appellant objects thus may not be discrimination at all.

Conway v. Canada (Attorney General) (1993), 83 C.C.C. (3d) 1.

---

often received considerable media attention in Canada. This helps to maintain public awareness of feminist demands, at least within a certain segment of public opinion. But attempts to embarrass governments through public reproaches and protests can backfire, as the NAC seems to have discovered. NAC revenues fell by about 40 per cent between 1993 and 1999, a drop that was largely due to cuts in the federal government's grants to an organization that, in the 1980s, was probably the single most influential women's group in Canada. Today, politicians do not hesitate to suggest that the NAC no longer represents most Canadian women (see Box 13.4).

ACHIEVEMENTS

The achievements of modern feminists can be grouped into three types of change: legislative reform, changes in the process of decision-making, and the material/social conditions of women. Together they add up to a mixed record of successes and failures.

Let us begin with changes to the law. Some of the most celebrated achievements of the women's movement have been on this front. Gender was not one of the proscribed grounds of discrimination in the draft Charter proposed by the Liberal government in 1981. It became part of the Charter after the vigorous representations made by women's groups before the Special Parliamentary Committee on the Constitution. Likewise, the section 28 guarantee of legal equality for men and women was a direct product of intense lobbying by women's groups.[48] And in perhaps the most publicized of court decisions on the Charter, the Supreme Court of Canada struck down the section of the Criminal Code dealing with abortion, a decision that was greeted as a major victory for the women's movement. Several other rulings by Canada's courts have also been generally received as victories by the women's movement. These include: *Blainey* (1986), a decision that opened boy's sports leagues to girls; *Daigle* (1989), in which the Supreme Court ruled that a potential father does not have the right to veto a woman's decision to have an abortion; a 1998 Canadian Human Rights Tribunal decision that found the federal government liable for roughly $5 billion in back pay owed primarily to female public servants under pay equity legislation; and *Ewanchuk* (1999), where the Supreme Court ruled that no defence of implied consent to sexual assault exists under Canadian law.

Other legislative breakthroughs include the maternity leave provisions written into the Canada Labour Code in 1970; the 1983 amendment to the Unemployment Insurance Act that eliminated discrimination against pregnant women; and the pay equity laws passed by Ottawa and the provinces. Human rights codes and commissions to enforce them exist nationally and in all provinces. They have provided opportunities to challenge discriminatory employment and commercial practices in the private sector, practices that the courts have deemed to fall outside the ambit of the Charter.

So have the main legal barriers to sexual equality been eliminated? Not nearly, claim women's groups. They point to inaction or what they believe to be government's inadequate response to such issues as daycare, affirmative action, female poverty, pay equity, and pornography. Today, many feminists argue that a popular backlash has enabled governments to roll back some of the gains made in the past. This may well be true, but it is also true that groups may understate their gains and influence for the possible rea-

---

BOX 13.4   The Fruits of Confrontation?

A group of Liberal cabinet ministers was booed and hissed yesterday by angry members of the National Action Committee on the Status of Women, who chanted a song demanding the government write the group 'one enormous cheque' to support its lobbying efforts on behalf of Canadian feminists.

The NAC lobby session is an annual event on Parliament Hill, where MPs are invited to listen to concerns arising from the group's annual general meeting. In the past, when NAC was at its most influential, the meetings drew dozens of MPs and a horde of media attention.

Though invitations to this year's event were issued to all five official parties, neither the Reform party nor the Tories sent any MPs.

But the group saved its strongest words for the Liberals, in particular Hedy Fry, the Status of Women Minister, who waged a nasty battle last year over a decision to change funding rules for NAC.

Ms Fry said she takes the NAC criticism in stride, but suggested the group consider a softer approach if it wants more MPs to meet with them in future years.

'I think in some cases it may be effective and in some cases it isn't. Many people would like to finish answering their questions ... as opposed to being shouted at,' she said.

Stéphane Dion, the Intergovernmental Affairs Minister, gave as good as he got in terms of criticism. Mr Dion appeared annoyed that none of the NAC questioners spoke French.

'I hope that next time you will have some questions in French if you are going to be representative,' said Mr Dion.

Sheldon Alberts, 'NAC Serenades then Berates MPs',
National Post, 8 June 1999, 1, 8.

son that public crowing about the gains experienced by those they purport to represent may cause their public constituency to doubt whether these groups are still needed.

A second measure of feminism's achievements involves the decision-making structures of the state. Among the striking characteristics of the modern women's movement are its financial and organizational links to government. The 1970 Report of the Royal Commission on the Status of Women was followed by the creation of the Canadian Advisory Council on the Status of Women, now called Status of Women Canada (SWC), and the creation of a women's portfolio in the federal cabinet. Similar advisory councils have been created by all provinces, and some have also established special cabinet positions. Within government departments and agencies it is now common to have special divisions devoted to 'women's issues' or affirmative action. For example, the Public Service Commission of Canada has a Program Development (Affirmative Action) branch that monitors the representation of women, indigenous Canadians, disabled persons, and visible minorities in the federal bureaucracy. The Treasury Board Secretariat has an Affirmative Action Group and an Employment Equity section within its Human Resources Division. As Penney Kome observes, the creation of status of women councils was followed by a 'deluge of equal-opportunity officers, women's directorates, grant officers, labour specialists, and other women's advocates attached to various branches of government.'[49]

Financially, the women's movement is heavily dependent on money provided by government. This dependence operates through two main channels. One is the budget of the Secretary of State for the Status of Women, within Heritage Canada, which has responsibility for SWC. The second channel involves social spending, much of which takes the form of transfers from Ottawa to provincial governments. Much of the money that ultimately reaches the hands of rape crisis centres, women's counselling services, halfway houses for battered women, and the vast network of services geared to

meeting women's needs, as well as women's research and information organizations, is buried in the budget of the Canada Health and Social Transfer to the provinces. Cutbacks in Ottawa's transfers to the provinces, and to social spending generally, squeeze the financial lifeline of grassroots women's groups that depend on public money.

Those on the left of the women's movement have often criticized the organizational and financial ties between women's groups and the state, arguing that such ties have the effect of co-opting feminists into the state. The demands of these groups will perforce be more moderate and their influence strategies less confrontational—and perhaps less effective—than if they resisted the siren call of money and a seat at the table. On the other hand, the independent resources available to voluntary associations are often meagre—the NAC, for example, received only about $30,000 in private donations in 1999, representing about 5 per cent of its budget—and so the temptation to seek and accept state support is strong. Likewise, direct representation on a government body provides an opportunity to be part of the process and to express women's perspectives from inside the state.

In fact, despite the financial dependence of women's groups on government, there is little evidence that this has made them more 'polite' towards the hand that feeds. Based on his examination of the Secretary of State Department's support for voluntary groups since the 1960s, Les Pal concludes that there is no evidence that these groups have been co-opted into an agenda set by the bureaucrats and politicians. On the contrary, he argues, women's groups in particular have not hesitated to criticize and embarrass the governments that have provided them with the means to publicize the alleged failures of government policy.[50] Sylvia Bashevkin's study of the NAC's strong opposition to the Conservative government's free trade initiate confirms this view. Bashevkin argues that the depth of Ottawa's cuts in funding for the NAC was certainly influenced by the NAC's vigorous opposition to free trade, in alliance with other critics of the Conservative government.[51] Reading through the annual reports and other publications of the SWC, one would be hard-pressed to conclude that representation within the state has muted the voice of feminist criticism.

What about the social conditions of women? Has the women's movement managed to improve their material circumstances or change social attitudes towards men and women. Reforming the law and the state is fine, but has it delivered more equality in the daily lives of women?

Here, the record of achievement is mixed. There is no doubt that social attitudes regarding appropriate roles and behaviour for males and females have changed over the last two generations. For example, the vast majority of Canadians believe that a woman could run most businesses as well as a man. Most Canadians claim that the sex of a political party leader does not influence the likelihood of their voting for that party (a tiny minority say that a female leader would make them less inclined to support the party, but a considerably larger minority say that a woman at the helm would make them more likely to support such a party). On such issues as abortion and equality of job opportunities for men and women, there is a little evidence of a significant gender gap.

Alongside the evidence of changed attitudes there are signs that considerable sexism persists. These signs include gender characterizations in commercial advertising and entertainment programming, the child-rearing practices of many, indeed probably most, parents, the unequal division of domestic responsibilities between men and women, and the relative infrequency of women's career choices taking precedence over men's even in this age of two-earner households. The 2001 Canadian census reported that women were twice as likely as men to say that they spent 15 hours or more each week on housework and almost twice as likely as men to say that they spent at least 15 hours per week on unpaid child care.[52] The findings of pollsters need to be weighed against the empirical evidence of inequality.

When one turns to the material conditions of women one is reminded of the French phrase, *plus ça change, plus c'est la même chose*. Despite the fact that there are today more women lawyers, professors, accountants, and even engineers than in the past, the breakthroughs made by middle-class women have not been matched by their less privileged sisters. Consider the following facts:

- About 60 per cent of working women are employed in clerical, sales, and service jobs where the pay tends to be lower. This is almost exactly the same percentage that was employed in these occupations five decades ago.

- The average income of a full-time female worker is not quite three-quarters of what the average male earns. This represents 'progress' when one considers that the figure was under 60 per cent a generation ago. Most of this difference is accounted for by three factors: the segregation of women into low-paying occupations; more women than men having part-time jobs (when both full- and part-time workers are taken into account the average income of female workers falls to about 62 per cent of males); and the greater seniority of male employers.

- Women are more likely to be poor than men. Approximately 60 per cent of those below the poverty lines established by Statistics Canada are women. Over time, poverty has assumed an increasingly feminine aspect. For example, in 1961 only about 15 per cent of low-income families (i.e., families with incomes below the poverty line) were headed by women. Today the share is over one-third, as higher levels of marital breakdown have produced many more female single-parent households. Single-parent families headed by women constitute the most poverty-prone group in Canada, about 60 per cent of them living below the poverty line.

The *Globe and Mail's* 'Report on Business' annually publishes The Top 1000, a survey of the top companies in Canada. It includes a list of the 50 best-paid CEOs. As of 2001, not a single female CEO made the list of the 50 best-paid bosses. In a poll of Canadian CEOs conducted by the *Globe and*

Mail in 1999, respondents were asked to name the best-run corporations in Canada. All of the top 25 were headed by male CEOs. A 2002 study by the consulting firm Catalyst found that 7.4 per cent of all directorships on the boards of Canada's largest corporations were held by women.[53] By whatever measure one cares to use, women are rare at the highest rungs of the business ladder.

The continuing exclusion of women from Canada's corporate elite, at the same time as their participation in the political elite has been increasing, may thwart some of the gains achieved by the women's movement. This, at least, was the conclusion reached by a Norwegian think-tank over a decade ago. It argued that as economies become internationalized, domestic politics matters less and business matters more. Increasingly, decisions with major social implications are taken by the corporate elite, an elite from which women are still excluded.[54] The general opposition of the women's movement to globalization, though it cannot be explained by this factor alone, certainly is influenced by the realization that a relative decline in the power of states and an increase in that of transnational corporations and markets tend to reduce the political clout of women's groups.

Materially, women are still less well off than men. This is a reality that has remained stubbornly unchanged, although attenuated, despite the legal reforms and changed social attitudes that have been produced by the women's movement. Poverty and economic dependence undermine the ability of individuals to control their lives and to grasp the opportunities promised by formal legal and political equality. So far as women are concerned, Canadian democracy remains flawed.

CONCLUSION

Diversity has become one of the central values associated with Canadian democracy. The official motto of the United States, 'E pluribus unum'—from the many, one—might be modified in the case of Canada to read 'E pluribus'. The evolving Canadian ethos concerning diversity does not balance pluralism with a sort of civic obligation to assume a common Canadian identity that supersedes ethnic, religious, and cultural attachments. Some Canadians are dismayed by this, seeing in it a recipe for division, resentment, and preferential treatment, while others believe it to be a model of equality worthy of emulation in democracies throughout the world and a principal difference between Canadian and American society.

The impact of the politics of diversity has been experienced most profoundly in Canada in the area of gender relations. In a little more than a generation the Canadian political, social, and economic scenes have been dramatically transformed in ways that provide women with many more choices and opportunities than existed previously. To a significant degree the feminist movement, in Canada as elsewhere, pioneered the modern discourse of diversity politics. That real democracy cannot be achieved without recognizing the different circumstances experienced by members of different groups and that justice requires that the law recognize these different group experiences in its treatment of individuals are notions that have been championed by the women's movement. Today, these ideas form the basis for political demands of groups that include Aboriginal Canadians, visible minorities, gays and lesbians, and the disabled.

Appendix 1: Selected Women's Organizations in Canada

Date Established	Name
1870	Young Women's Christian Association
1893	National Council of Women of Canada
1897	Federated Women's Institutes of Canada
1897	National Council of Jewish Women
1908	Canadian Nurses' Association
1918	Federation of Women Teachers Association of Canada
1919	Canadian Federation of University Women
1920	Canadian Teachers' Federation
1930	Canadian Federation of Business and Professional Women's Clubs
1939	Canadian Association of Elizabeth Fry Societies
1960	Voice of Women
1967	Fédération des Femmes du Québec
1971	Women for Political Action
1972	National Action Committee on the Status of Women
1972	Canadian Congress for Learning Opportunities for Women
1974	Canadian Abortion Rights Action League
1974	National Association of Women and the Law
1976	Canadian Research Institute for the Advancement of Women
1983	REAL Women (Realistic, Equal, and Active for Life)
1985	Women's Legal Education and Action Fund

Appendix 2: Dates in Women's Progress Towards Legal and Political Equality

1916	Alberta, Saskatchewan, Manitoba give vote to women.
1918	Women given franchise in federal elections.
1921	Agnes Macphail first woman elected to Parliament.
1928	Supreme Court rules women are not 'persons' and cannot be appointed to Senate.
1929	Judicial Committee of the British Privy Council overturns Supreme Court decision.
1931	Cairine Wilson first woman appointed to the Senate.
1940	Quebec gives vote to women.
1947	Married women restricted from holding federal public service jobs.
1955	Restrictions on married women in federal public service removed.
1957	Ellen Fairclough sworn in as first woman federal cabinet minister.
1967	Royal Commission on Status of Women established.
1971	Canada Labour Code amended to allow women 17 weeks' maternity leave.
1973	Supreme Court upholds section of Indian Act depriving Aboriginal women of their rights.
	Supreme Court denies Irene Murdoch right to share in family property.

1977	Canadian Human Rights Act passed, forbidding discrimination on basis of sex.
1981	Canada ratifies UN Convention on the Elimination of all Forms of Discrimination Against Women.
1982	Bertha Wilson becomes the first woman appointed to the Supreme Court of Canada.
1983	Affirmative action programs mandatory in the federal public service.
1984	Twenty-seven women elected to Parliament, six appointed to cabinet.
1985	Section 15 of Charter of Rights and Freedoms comes into effect. Employment Equity legislation passed.
1988	*Morgentaler* decision strikes down Canada's abortion law.
1989	Indian Act amended to remove discrimination against Aboriginal women.
1989	*Andrews* decision introduces the concept of 'substantive equality' in applying section 15 of the Charter.
1989	Audrey McLaughlin chosen to lead the national NDP.
1991	Ontario passes pay equity law that applies to the private sector (repealed in 1995).
1993	Kim Campbell becomes Canada's first female Prime Minister.
1994	Alexa McDonough chosen to lead the national NDP.
2000	Sixty-two women elected to House of Commons, eight appointed to cabinet.
2000	Right Honourable Beverley McLachlin appointed Chief Justice of the Supreme Court of Canada.

CACSW, 'Progress toward Equality for Women in Canada' (Feb. 1987), 15, and author's additions.

NOTES

1. John Porter, *The Vertical Mosaic* (Toronto: University of Toronto Press, 1965).

2. Leslie A. Pal, *Interests of State: The Politics of Language, Multiculturalism, and Feminism in Canada* (Montreal and Kingston: McGill-Queen's University Press, 1993).

3. Ibid., 281.

4. R. Brian Howe and David Johnson, *Restraining Equality: Human Rights Commissions in Canada* (Toronto: University of Toronto Press, 2000), 35.

5. Sylvia Bashevkin, *Toeing the Lines* (Toronto: University of Toronto Press, 1985).

6. See the literature review in Pat Armstrong and Hugh Armstrong, *The Double Ghetto* (Toronto: McClelland & Stewart, 1984), 158–67.

7. Sheila Rowbotham, *Hidden from History* (London: Pluto Press, 1974), 47.

8. Terry Copp, *Anatomy of Poverty* (Toronto: McClelland & Stewart, 1974), 43.

9. The statement was made by Montreal's Chief Inspector of Factories in the late 1800s. Quoted ibid., 49.

10. John Stuart Mill, *On the Subjection of Women* (London: Dent, 1970 [1869]).

11. Nellie McClung, 'Hardy Perennials', in McClung, *In Times Like These* (Toronto: University of Toronto Press, 1972), 56.

12. See the discussion in Penney Kome, *Women of Influence* (Toronto: Doubleday Canada, 1985), ch. 2.

13. Quoted ibid., 32.

14. This was the title of a retrospective article that Macphail wrote in 1949, after having served six terms as an MP for Ontario's South Grey constituency.

15. Quoted in Bashevkin, *Toeing the Lines*, 16.

16. McClung, 'Hardy Perennials', 48.

17. See, for example, Bashevkin, *Toeing the Lines*, 20–3.

18. Catherine L. Cleverdon, *The Woman Suffrage Movement in Canada* (Toronto: University of Toronto Press, 1974), 98, 114, 204.

19. The terms 'hard-core' and 'soft-core' feminism were first used by William O'Neill in *Everyone was Brave: A History of Feminism in America* (New York: Quadrangle, 1971).

20. Deborah Gorhan, 'Flora MacDonald Denison: Canadian Feminist', in Linda Kealey, ed., *A Not Unreasonable Claim: Women and Reform in Canada* (Toronto: Women's Press, 1979), 47–70.

21. Joan Sangster, 'The Role of Women in the Early CCF', in Linda Kealey and Joan Sangster, eds, *Beyond the Vote: Canadian Women and Politics* (Toronto: University of Toronto Press, 1989), 127.

22. Simone de Beauvoir, *The Second Sex*, trans. H.M. Parshley (London: Jonathan Cape, 1970), ch. 2; Germaine Greer, *The Female Eunuch* (Nylesbury, UK: Hazel Watson and Viney, 1970); Betty Friedan, *The Feminine Mystique* (New York, W.W. Norton, 1963), ch. 5; Kate Millet, *Sexual Politics* (Garden City, NY: Doubleday, 1970).

23. A. Richard Allen, 'Social Gospel', in *The Canadian Encyclopedia*, 2nd edn (Edmonton: Hurtig, 1988), vol. 3, 2026.

24. See Richard Allen, *The Social Passion* (Toronto: University of Toronto Press, 1971).

25. Nellie McClung, 'Women and the Church', in McClung, *In Times Like These*, 67–79.

26. Friedan, *The Feminine Mystique*.

27. Ibid., 32.

28. Armstrong and Armstrong, *The Double Ghetto*, 42–3.

29. The ratio of males to females in universities was 5:1 in 1920, 3.1:1 in 1960, and 1.8:1 in 1970. About an equal number of males and females are enrolled in undergraduate programs today.

30. Anne Firor Scott, *Making the Invisible Woman Visible* (Urbana: University of Illinois Press, 1984).

31. See Kealey and Sangster, eds, *Beyond the Vote*.

32. Ibid.

33. Judy Rebick, 'Fighting Racism', *Feminist Action* 6, 2 (June 1992).

34. Barbara Frum, 'Why there are so few women in Ottawa', *Chatelaine* 44 (1971): 33, 110.

35. Bashevkin, *Toeing the Lines*, 110–19.

36. See the summaries of landmark judgements in National Action Committee on the Status of Women, *Women and Legal Action* (Oct. 1984), 8–27.

37. This was true in *Murdoch* (1973), *Canard* (1975), and *Bliss* (1979).

38. Michael Mandel, *The Charter of Rights and the Legalization of Politics in Canada* (Toronto: Wall and Thompson, 1995), 389–99.

39. *Re Casagrande and Hinton Roman Catholic Separate School District* (1987), 38 D.L.R. (4th) 382.

40. Canadian Advisory Council on the Status of Women, *Canadian Charter and Equality Rights for Women: One Step Forward or Two Steps Back?* (Sept. 1989), 19.

41. *Hunter v. Southam* (1984); *R. v. Big M Drug Mart* (1985).

42. *Edwards Books and Art Ltd et al. v. The Queen* (1986), 30 C.C.C. (3d) 385.

43. Quoted in F.L. Morton, Rainer Knopff, and Peter Russell, *Federalism and the Charter* (Ottawa: Carleton University Press, 1989), 483.

44. *Alberta Labour Reference* (1987).

45. *Law Society of British Columbia v. Andrews and Kinersley*, [1989] 1 S.C.R. 143.

46. See the abridged text of the ruling in Morton et al., *Federalism and the Charter*, 582–603.

47. Canadian Advisory Council on the Status of Women, *Every Voice Counts: A Guide to Personal and Political Action* (Ottawa, 1989), 39–58.

48. Penney Kome, *The Taking of Twenty-Eight: Women Challenge the Constitution* (Toronto: The Women's Press, 1983).
49. Kome, *Women of Influence*, 93.
50. Pal, *Interests of State*, ch. 10.
51. Sylvia Bashevkin, 'Free Trade and Canadian Feminism: The Case of the National Action Committee on the Status of Women', *Canadian Public Policy* 15, 4 (Dec. 1989): 363–75.

52. Statistics Canada, 'The Changing Profile of Canada's Labour Force', Catalogue no. 96F0030XIE2001009, 11 Feb. 2003.
53. Cited in Julie Smyth, 'Women Managers up 40%', *National Post*, 12 Feb. 2003, A10.
54. *The Economist*, 'Women Left, Right, and Centre', 23 Mar. 1991.

SUGGESTED READINGS

Yasmeen Abu-Laban and Christina Gabriel, eds, *Selling Diversity: Immigration, Multiculturalism, Employment Equity and Globalization* (Peterborough, Ont.: Broadview Press, 2002). The editors and contributors argue that social justice objectives associated with diversity have been hijacked by a neo-liberal agenda that views the value of diversity through an economic lens.

Neil Bissoondath, *Selling Illusions: The Cult of Multiculturalism in Canada* (Toronto: Penguin, 2002). The author challenges the prevailing belief that official multiculturalism benefits the ethnic, racial, and other minorities that it purports to help.

Raymond Breton and Jeffrey Reitz, *The Illusion of Difference: Realities of Ethnicity in Canada and the United States* (Toronto: C.D. Howe Institute, 1994). This is one of the very few works that actually attempts to test whether the rate of ethnic assimilation is faster in the United States than in Canada.

Alexandra Dobrowolsky, *The Politics of Pragmatism: Women, Representation, and Constitutionalism in Canada* (Toronto: Oxford University Press, 2000). In this work, Dobrowolsky relates the political struggles of the Canadian women's movement to the Meech Lake and Charlottetown accords and examines closely the sexual equality provisions of the Charter.

Linda Trimble and Jane Arscott, *Women and Politics Across Canada* (Peterborough, Ont.: Broadview Press, 2003). The authors examine why women continue to be under-represented in Canadian political life.

Review Exercises

1. In January 2003 Statistics Canada announced that it would be asking Canadians to declare their sexual orientation in a national survey. In its 2001 census, Statistics Canada for the first time asked how many people in common-law relationships were of the same sex. Why do you think Canada's official statistics agency would attempt to collect such information? Do you think the information collected on such matters could make a difference for politics and policy?

2. Ethnic and racial profiling involves the practice of singling out people for different and disadvantageous treatment because of their ethnicity or race. Find two or three cases where this has been alleged to be a systematic practice in Canada. You might start by going to the Web sites of the Canadian Race Relations Foundation <www.crr.ca>, the Canadian Bar Association <www.cba.org>, and the Canadian Civil Liberties Association <www.ccla.org>.

3. How many women hold public office in your community? Make a list of public office-holders on your local city, town, or township council, your mayor, your MP, and your provincial representative. Include MPs and provincial representatives from a couple of adjoining constituencies. You can find all this information with a telephone book and a little bit of resourcefulness.

4. Read the document entitled 'Gender-Based Analysis', found at <www.swc-cfc.gc.ca/publish/gbabro-e.html>, and respond to the following questions:

    (a) Is this an appropriate approach to analyzing and making policy recommendations? Why or why not?
    (b) How influential would this approach be if applied to issues like trade, national security, agriculture, fisheries, and economic growth? Why?
    (c) On what sorts of issues might this approach be most influential? Why?

Symbol of the close ties between Canada and the United States, the Ambassador Bridge joining Windsor and Detroit is North America's busiest border crossing, carrying over 8,000 trucks and about $1 billion in goods per day.

The boundary separating Canadian politics from events in and the influence of the rest of world has always been porous, and never more so than today. In this chapter we examine Canada's place in the world, focusing on the possibilities and limits available to Canada's policy-makers as they navigate a turbulent and fast-changing international scene. Topics include the following:

- ❏ How Canadians view their place in the world.
- ❏ How the world sees Canada and Canadians.
- ❏ The meaning of globalization.
- ❏ Arguments made about the consequences of globalization.
- ❏ Globalization and the intensification Canadian–American relations.
- ❏ The asymmetrical relationship between Canada and the United States.
- ❏ Is more integration with the US the answer?
- ❏ Multilateralism versus the tug of continentalism.
- ❏ Soft power: option or illusion?

CHAPTER FOURTEEN

CANADA IN THE WORLD

'The twentieth century will belong to Canada.' This was the bold prediction of Sir Wilfrid Laurier, Liberal Prime Minister of Canada from 1896 to 1911. Laurier's forecast of greatness for Canada was made against the backdrop of the enormous growth that had occurred in the United States over the previous century, when Canada's southern neighbour went from being a cluster of states hugging the Atlantic seaboard to a continent-wide power with the world's largest economy. In the heady years of the early 1900s, as the nation-building strategy launched by Sir John A. Macdonald in 1879 appeared to be fulfilling its promise and about 200,000 immigrants arrived in Canada each year, Laurier's prediction that something similar would happen in Canada probably appeared to many to be more than the rhetoric often expected from politicians.

One hundred years later it is clear that the twentieth century did not 'belong' to Canada. The friends and foes of the United States would probably agree that it was the American century, for better or worse. By century's end the economic, cultural, and military dominance of the United States was such that, in the eyes of many, comparisons to previous empires understated the sheer scale of America's global influence. The term 'hyperpower' entered the modern lexicon.

Notwithstanding the rise of the United States to its current status as the world's only superpower, some Canadians believe that their country has achieved the greatness predicted by Wilfrid Laurier, though in a form that Canada's first French-Canadian Prime Minister did not foresee. 'For generations', says philosopher Mark Kingwell, 'we have been busy creating, in [the shadow of the United States], a model of citizenship that is inclusive, diverse, open-ended and transnational. It is dedicated to far-reaching social justice and the rule of international law. And we're successfully exporting it around the world . . . by seeing [the UN] for the flawed but necessary agency it is.'[1] Canada is, according to many of its opinion leaders, the cosmopolitan, multicultural, equality-oriented, internationalist face of the future. The Canadian model, as it has come to be thought of by some, is the real achievement of the last century and the one that is most likely to shape the direction of history in the twenty-first century.

Perhaps so, although Canadians might be surprised to learn that when the world's thoughts turn to the future of democracy, the evolving new world order, or the trajectory of world history, few people other than Canadians mention this country as charting the course. John Ralston Saul, one of Canada's most prominent public intellectuals, argues that 'Canada is above all an idea of what a country could be, a place of the imagination . . . it is very much its own invention.'[2] Canada is, he has argued, a successful model of accommodation and flexible ways of thinking about citizenship. But a survey of books written in recent years by leading Western intellectuals on democracy—excluding those written by Canadians—turns up very few references to Canada and certainly no sense that the rest of the world is watching, much less emulating, whatever the Canadian model might involve. Indeed, accustomed as we are to hearing that Canada is loved and admired by the rest of the world and that we are often looked to for wise counsel and assistance on troublesome issues far from our shores, it probably comes as something of a surprise to learn that not only our American neighbours, but other national populations as well, appear to know hardly anything about us (except that we are like the Americans in some ways, without being the Americans).

I still say we're up the creek without a paddle.

But it's still our creek.

Some pundits claim that as the United States flexes its military and economic muscle as the world's new and only hyperpower, Canada's role as an actor on the international stage has become irrelevant. (Roy Peterson, *Vancouver Sun*)

In a public lecture at Carleton University in February 2003,[3] Michael Ignatieff challenged his fellow Canadians to think about the ideas that most Canadians hold about their country and its role in the world. 'Are we what we seem to be?' he asked. 'Are the images that we have of ourselves true in the world?' Most Canadians, prompted by their opinion leaders, subscribe to a view of themselves and their country's place in the firmament of nations that has the following main elements:

- We are a peace-loving people.
- We are respected, listened to, and admired abroad.
- We stand for multilateralism and reliance on the United Nations and its agencies to solve global conflicts.
- We 'hit above our weight' in international affairs.

In addition to this short list of national characteristics, most Canadians probably would agree with the sentiment expressed by 'Joe Canada' in the hugely popular Molson beer commercial, released in 2000, known as 'The Rant'. Canadians stand for tolerance, not assimilation, says Joe, suggesting that the Canadian idea of citizenship is quite dramatically different from that of our southern neighbours. And as definers of the Canadian identity and interpreters of Canada's role in the world such as John Ralston Saul and Mark Kingwell argue, this Canadian idea of citizenship is perhaps our greatest contribution to world history.

For the most part, Canadians feel very good about themselves, their lives, and the state of their country. In the 2002 report of the Pew Global Attitudes Project,[4] involving a cross-national survey of 44 countries, only Guatemalans expressed a higher level of satisfaction with their lives. Canadians expressed slightly higher levels of personal satisfaction than Americans and markedly higher levels than those in the other wealthy industrialized countries surveyed for this study. Moreover, they were far more likely than Americans and the citizens of several other wealthy nations to express satisfaction with the state of their country. When prompted to say whether one or more problems from a list of 10 was a 'very big' problem in their country, Canadians appeared to be remarkably complacent. The leading vote-getter was 'corrupt political leaders', which 32 per cent of Canadians agreed was a 'very big' problem.

Complacency and self-congratulations may be appropriate in some circumstances. They are not, however, particularly useful in regard to understanding Canada's role in the world. The conventional wisdom that most Canadians subscribe to when thinking about themselves and their country is flawed in many important ways. In this chapter we will consider some of the hard realities of Canada's relations with and influence in the world.

GLOBALIZATION'S MEANING AND CONSEQUENCES IN CANADA

The central feature of Canada's economic condition is the degree to which it is dependent on markets outside Canadian borders. This has always been true. From the arrival 500 years ago of European fishermen who trolled the cod-rich waters off the coast of Newfoundland until the middle of the twentieth century, the economic prosperity of the northern reaches of North America depended on the exploitation and export of a succession of natural resources—fish, fur, timber, and wheat—to markets abroad, and on the import of people, capital, and finished goods. From the time Euro-

---

BOX 14.1   'The Unknown North?' Canada's Image Abroad

Parisians are renowned for being arrogant and pedantic but it turns out they have nothing to be snooty about when it comes to their knowledge of Canada.

[A] federal government study of attitudes and knowledge reveals that the City of Lights is in the dark when it comes to Canadians and their country.

In fact, the ignorance of Canada is so widespread that the report says Parisians don't even hold any of the stereotypical images involving Mounties, moose, hockey and Indians.

Conducted for the Department of Canadian Heritage by the Quebec polling firm Leger Marketing, four focus groups were held in Paris in preparation for Expo 2004.

'It is important to note that when we interrogated the participants about their knowledge, several took on an interrogative air not knowing what to answer', said the report.

'A large majority (of participants) had no knowledge on the subject of Canadian society, its geography, economy, technology, the country's history and its role on the world stage.' The report also said some Parisians didn't know why people speak French in Canada, seemingly ignorant of France's role in founding the country: 'Several participants seemed stunned—'uh!!!'—not knowing what to say.'

Jack Aubry, 'Canada a mystery to Parisians'.
Available at: <www.canada.com>. Accessed 5 Mar. 2003.

peans began to be seriously interested in what would become Canada by sending ships, settlers, and goods, the Canadian economy was integrated into greater patterns of trade and shaped by forces beyond its borders.

At some point, however, there developed a hope and even an expectation that Canada would shake off this dependence and become the master of its economic destiny. One sees this already in Sir John A. Macdonald's ambitious National Policy of 1879, the first and only coherent and explicit economic development strategy that Canada had known before the decision to embrace free trade in the late 1980s, and therefore dependence, as the Canadian fate. One sees it also in Sir Wilfrid Laurier's optimistic prediction that the twentieth century would belong to Canada. And one sees it in the rise of economic nationalism in Canada, particularly from the 1950s to the early 1980s, the path of which was marked by a series of policies and institutions designed to limit American influence in the Canadian economy and promote indigenous capital.

Some of these nationalistic hopes still survive, although they have come to appear increasingly atavistic in a world characterized by unprecedented levels of economic interdependence and global communication. Today, the serious debate is not about whether the forces of globalization can be rolled back, but how and in what instances they should be controlled. In Canada the question of globalization is inseparable from that of Canada's relationship to the United States. For Canada, at least, globalization has meant an enormous intensification in economic and other ties to the world's only superpower. Whether, on balance, this is a good thing is certainly one of the leading issues in Canadian public life.

What Is Globalization?

'Globalization', declares Alan Greenspan, chairman of the US Federal Reserve Board and one of the world's most influential economic policy-makers, 'involves the increasing interaction of nation-al economic systems.'[5] This rather spare definition of globalization contains two elements. First, globalization involves something that is in fact centuries, even millennia, old, that is, trade between the economies of different communities, countries, or even civilizations. The Spice Road that snaked from the ports of the eastern Mediterranean across the Middle East and Asia to China 2,000 years ago was an early precursor of the massive flow of goods and services that today knit together the globe. The second element of Greenspan's definition—and the aspect of globalization that usually is thought to distinguish it from international trade in earlier times—is the unprecedented volume and speed of the economic exchanges that are one of the hallmarks of the contemporary global economy. According to Harvard economist Jeffrey Sachs, only about one-quarter of the world's population, accounting for about half of global production, was linked by trade in 1980. He estimates that, two decades later, this had grown to closer to 90 per cent of the world's population, whose economies accounted for all but a tiny fraction of the world's wealth.[6]

Economists point to two chief factors that have driven globalization in recent decades. One is technology. Developments in transportation, telecommunications, and manufacturing technologies have made it profitable to assemble in Mexico appliances designed in Canada or the United States, with parts and component systems from perhaps several different countries, and destined for sale in many different national markets. The global integration of goods production was accompanied by increased transnational flows of investment capital, leading inevitably to a greater integration of financial markets as banks, investment funds, and companies increasingly realized that their activities and opportunities spilled across national borders. Since the end of World War II, policy-makers in the developed countries of the world have generally favoured a more open trading environment that has encouraged this process of globalization. Although the world economy is still far from the level playing field that free trade boosters often talk about, there can be no doubt that protectionist barriers have declined over the last several decades, through bilateral agreements like the **Canada–US Free Trade Agreement**, regional free trade such as that which occurs under NAFTA and in the European Union, and more comprehensive trade liberalization under the aegis of the General Agreement on Tariffs and Trade, which has now become the more formalized and institutionalized World Trade Organization (WTO). National subsidies and protectionism in various guises are still practised to varying degrees by all governments, but the overall trajectory of trade policy in Canada, as elsewhere, has been in the direction of more open markets.

The fact that free or freer trade has become the fashionable norm among the powerful across the developed countries of the world does not mean that doubt has been silenced or dissent squelched. The 1999 Seattle meeting of the WTO, the 2000 meeting of the Organization of American States (OAS) in Windsor, Ontario, and the 2001 G-8 meeting in Genoa were a few of the events accompanied by varying degrees of anti-globalization protest and violence. Protestors in the streets have been complemented by various other forms of anti-globalization that range from intellectual attacks to political parties, social movements, and interest groups for whom the critique of globalization is a central ideological principle, or even *the* central principle. In Canada these forces include many—very likely most—of those who teach in the social sciences, a significant part of the country's media elite, much of the leadership of the labour movement, the

Neither one of them has been elected to anything...

...and yet they blame us for never voting.

From 'the Battle in Seattle' to lesser clashes over globalization, all sides have attempted to wrap themselves in the flag of democracy, claiming to represent the interests of the people. (Roy Peterson, *Vancouver Sun*)

NDP, many religious organizations, environmental groups, and nationalist groups like the Council of Canadians. Their criticisms of globalization receive considerable coverage, from the television screen to the classroom. Indeed, the critique of globalization is probably better known to most Canadians and, for that matter, citizens in other wealthy countries than is its defence.

The Anti-Globalization Indictment

In many ways the anti-globalization movement and the analysis that underpins it represent the latest edge of a tradition whose origins go back to the critique of capitalism developed by Karl Marx in the middle of the nineteenth century. Marx made several claims that sound familiar today. They include the following:

- Market economies necessarily create competitive and mutually exclusive interests, most important-ly between those who control the means of pro-ducing and distributing wealth—the capitalist class—and those who must sell their time, talents, or skills to make a living—the working class.
- As capitalism achieves a higher order of control over the economy and the people's lives, an increasing polarization of class interests occurs and the gap separating the rich from the poor grows.
- The saturation of domestic market opportunities drives capitalists in search of opportunities abroad, and thus other countries and populations are drawn into the cycle of exploitation, of work-ers and resources, upon which advanced capital-ism depends.
- Governments in the capitalist world—and this would include international organizations like the WTO, the International Monetary Fund (IMF), the World Bank, and the G-7—are essentially and unavoidably instruments for the repression of subordinate class interests and the protection of capitalism and capitalists.

With only some minor tweaking this is, of course, pretty much the core of the modern condemna-tion of globalization. Globalization is blamed by its critics for exacerbating the income gap between the affluent and the poor in developed societies, widening the divide between standards of living in the developed and underdeveloped world, under-mining indigenous cultures, weakening the abili-ty of governments everywhere to regulate business in the public interest, and reducing governments' willingness and ability to finance social programs. To this list may be added such additional sins as degradation of ecosystems across the globe, child labour and forced labour in parts of the world, international conflict in regions of the world such as the Gulf War of 1991 and the Iraq War of 2003, and the rise of global terrorism. Some of these claims are more plausible than others. Some are almost certainly false. Almost all of them are diffi-cult to prove with any certainty.

The pros and cons of globalization cannot be sorted here. Nevertheless, because these issues are hotly debated in Canadian politics, and because the broader consequences of globalization are related to its effects in Canada and affect the inter-national system of which Canada is a part, we need to at least consider the evidence for these various claims. Moreover, a fair assessment of globalization's impact on Canada and throughout the world should also be open to the possibility that globalization has been, on balance, a good thing, or at least that the balance sheet is not entirely red.

Let us review the charges made concerning the general consequences of globalization and the specific impacts alleged by some to have been experienced in Canada.

1. *Inequality between the rich and the poor in Canada and the number of people living in poverty have increased due to globalization.*

Contrary to the conventional wisdom purveyed by probably most academics and journalists, and many politicians, these claims are not self-evi-dently true. First of all, the distribution of income in Canada is not more unequal today than it was 30 years ago, at least if one compares the share of national income received by those in the top quintile of all families to that received by those in the bottom quintile. There are, granted, various ways of measuring the distribution of income. By some of these measures it appears that income inequality has increased over time. Other measures, however, tell a different story. And in any case, the causal linkage between globalization and developments in the distribution of income is not as clear as many contend. Income inequality may change or remain the same in response to numerous factors, including government policies, shifting demographic patterns, economic restructuring caused by factors other than globalization, and so on. Globalization may be part of an explanation, but ideology more than analysis often elevates it to the status of *the* primary cause of income inequality.

What about poverty? The argument is often made that globalization has increased the ranks of the marginalized, producing more who are unable to afford a decent standard of living. Child poverty, the phenomenon of the working poor, and an apparent increase in visible destitution—homelessness, begging, 'squeegee kids', etc.—are argued by some to be at least partially due to economic globalization.

There are at least two problems with such claims. The first is the one of wrongly attributed causality. As in the case of the distribution of income, change may be the result of a number of factors that have little or nothing to do with economic globalization. For example, it is demonstrably true and known to all serious students of family policy that the sharp increase over the last generation in the number of single-parent households—usually headed by women—has been a major factor driving the increase in child poverty. As a group, single mothers tend to have lower-than-average incomes. Consequently, their dependent children are at a greatly elevated risk of falling below the poverty line, however that line is defined. This has a lot to do with ideas about marriage, divorce laws, and income supports for single parents, but not much to do with globalization.

The other problem involves the very claim that poverty has increased. The truth of this claim is at least open to dispute. Using Statistics Canada's definition of what constitutes a low income, a smaller share of the population falls below what is often called the 'poverty line' at present than was the case 40 years ago. Moreover, claims about the extent of poverty are often confused with developments in the distribution of income, so that greater inequality in income is assumed—mistakenly—to signify an increase in poverty. Although an undeniable problem in a rich country like Canada, it requires a rather imaginative and contestable definition of poverty to conclude that the scale of poverty has increased.

2. *Economic globalization has increased the income gap between the rich and poor countries of the world.*

There is no doubt that the income gap has been exacerbated in recent decades. This has been due not so much to poor countries becoming even poorer in some absolute sense—although some have reached new lows of destitution, due often to such factors as drought, civil war, bad policies, corrupt regimes, and other factors—but mainly because the rich world has become richer, and thus the gap has widened. But is this due to globalization?

The answer is mixed. Increased trade between such countries as China, Mexico, Malaysia, the Philippines, Vietnam, and the rest of the world has in fact contributed to rising incomes in these countries and the growth of a middle class that, while very small by Western standards, is usually thought to be a crucial ingredient if a society is to acquire democratic institutions. Countries such as Bangladesh, Pakistan, and virtually all of Africa remain desperately poor, but the examples of the countries where living standards have improved suggest that it is not increasing participation in the global economy that causes countries to remain mired in destitution. Some argue that the loan conditions of the IMF and the World Bank and the subsidies that rich countries often provide to domestic industries—especially agriculture and natural resources—which might otherwise be export opportunities for developing countries, are among the reasons for the large and even widening gap between the rich and poor countries of the world. Even assuming that there is some truth to these claims, increasing participation in the world economy has generated higher average standards of living in many countries that, until a couple of decades ago, were miserably poor.

3. *Globalization undermines indigenous cultures, producing broadly homogeneous Western values and lifestyles in societies across the world.*

At one level this claim is obviously—but deceptively—true. Robert Reich, Secretary of Labor during the first several years of Bill Clinton's presidency, many years ago wrote about the new class of highly educated professionals generated by the knowledge-based economy.[7] These people, he observed, are at home almost anywhere in the world. The work they do and the lifestyles they lead are very similar in New York, Toronto, Brussels, or Tokyo. The experience of travelling abroad and switching on CNN International in hotel rooms across the world, seeing American products and corporate logos virtually everywhere, and being able to carry on with one's work and life through an Internet system dominated by Western- and especially American-based sites certainly seems to corroborate the claim that globalization has swamped local cultures in its wake. And at the level of general populations, there can be no doubt that some significant convergence in the music people listen to, the films they watch, the clothing styles they favour, and the food they eat has taken place.

These signs of cultural convergence in the direction of a Western norm are not merely superficial. But at the same time they are probably not nearly as profound or, for that matter, as insidious as critics claim. If one examines social and political institutions from the family to structures of national and local governance, there is little evidence that globalization has eroded differences and pushed different societies and cultures towards a common norm. On the contrary, students of contemporary nationalism and of the upsurge in radical Islam routinely argue that the resurgence of these communities is, in fact, a reaction to cultural homogenization. In other words, economic integration and the cultural consequences that inevitably accompany it may actually generate an affirmation of distinctive cultural identities. This affirmation is partly because national and regional communities—and especially their elites—may be motivated to resist the displacement of their languages, values, and institutions by those of the dominant global culture, but also because the strength of local customs and institutions is often underestimated. As Francis Fukuyama observes, '[I]f you look beneath the surface and ask people in different countries where their loyalties lie, how they regard their families, and how they regard authority, there will be enormous differences. When people examine a culture, they pay too much attention to aspects like the kinds of consumer goods that people buy. That's the most superficial aspect of culture. A culture really consists of deeper moral norms that affect how people live together.'[8] Most young people in the Netherlands speak English; Hollywood films routinely top the box office charts in Europe; American soap operas—significantly edited—are enormously popular in Egypt; and wealthy Saudis often send their sons to be educated at American universities. These are not inconsequential indications of globalization, or rather, of the Americanization of the world. They should not, however, be interpreted as signs that the pillars of local cultures are being washed away by globalization.

4. *Globalization has undermined the resolve and the ability of governments to regulate business in the public interest, to finance social safety needs, and, generally, to act as a counterweight to markets and rampant individualism.*

Despite being widely believed, there is in fact little solid evidence for either of these related claims. Taking the case of Canada as an example, the size of government, as measured by the share of GDP accounted for by the public sector, is about 43 per cent today, compared to about 45 per cent 20 years ago. Public spending on health care, education, and income maintenance programs (public pensions, employment insurance, social assistance, disability payments, etc.) accounts for as great a share of all program expenditures today as it did 20 years ago. While it is true that no new 'big ticket' social spending programs have been added over the last couple of decades, none of the major ones have been eliminated. Overall levels of individual taxation have increased in Canada over this period, as they have in most affluent countries. And despite the privatizations and deregulation that have taken place in some sectors, if the sheer volume of health, consumer, and workplace safety and environmental and rights-based regulation is examined, as well as the number of regulatory bodies, one would be hard-pressed to conclude that the state's regulatory function is in decline. Indeed, many argue that regulation, before direct spending, has become increasingly popular as policy-makers' instrument of choice in dealing with policy problems.

A recent report carried out by the United Nations acknowledges the fact that economic globalization has not produced, across the board, a decline in what the report calls **state capacity**.[9] On the contrary, the UN report concludes that, among developed countries, the state's capacity to maintain social safety nets and pursue such non-market goals as protection of the environment remains solid. The report argues that, notwithstanding what has become the conventional wisdom, 'there is no evidence that globalization weakens the State. On the contrary, increased globalization goes hand in hand with higher [public] expenditure.'[10]

The story is quite different in the case of many developing countries, but the authors of this report do not point the finger of blame at globalization. Rather, they blame 'state capacity deficit' in these countries—ineffective public administration characterized by low levels of professionalism, high levels of unethical conduct, inadequate technology, and weak social policies—for their failure to take advantage of the economic opportunities that globalization offers. In other words, the fundamental problem that besets many developing countries is governance, not economic globalization.

5. *Globalization has rendered the health of developed countries' economies more precarious than in the past.*

The old industrial model, pioneered by Henry Ford, was all about vertical integration. Coal, steel, rubber, and workers would enter the factory at one end, and vehicles would roll off the assembly line at the other. The new post-industrial model spawned by globalization is all about outsourcing. At the extreme, huge companies like communications equipment manufacturer Cisco Systems and computer manufacturer Dell 'exert a sort of postindustrial "Command Control" over [a] vast network of outsourced production',[11] depending on minimal parts inventories to keep costs down. Cisco Systems and Dell are not particularly exceptional, differing from such important companies operating in Canada as Nortel, Bombardier, Chrysler, and Magna only in the extent of their dependence on a complex chain of outsourcing that extends across the world.

The problem with this, argues Barry Lynn, is that it introduces a vulnerability in the economies of rich countries that is far more significant in its potential implications than dependence on foreign sources of oil. Disruption at a crucial link or links in the supply and distribution network of the globalized economy, argues Lynn, could bring entire industries to a screeching halt because the globalized supply chain is more specialized than is often believed. This is particularly true of the flagship industries of the post-industrial economy—electronics and telecommunications. The effects of political upheaval or even natural disaster in a country far from Canada could send shock waves reverberating through Canadian industries.

The validity of Lynn's argument hinges on his claim that, faced with something like a catastrophic earthquake in Taiwan or a new anti-capitalism revolution in China, companies in developed countries like Canada would not be able to adjust their sources of supply quickly enough to avert a sort of meltdown in their production activities. Lynn probably overstates the extent of this dependence and, therefore, of the vulnerability to which globalization exposes the economies of the developed world. Nevertheless, he raises a question that is at least worth considering: 'As our companies continue to scatter industrial capacity to the far corners of the globe, then to trim slack at home until they come to depend on that distant capacity, are we not witnessing the creation of a new strategic commodity like oil, control of which can be exploited to wrangle away our wealth and security?'[12]

Canadians had a glimpse of the scenarios that Lynn argues have become increasingly possible after the terrorist attacks of 11 September 2001. Traffic at all border crossings to the United States ground to a halt, costing businesses on both sides of the border millions of dollars. At the Detroit-Windsor bridge crossing, the busiest transportation link in the world's largest trading partnership, truck traffic was backed up for over 20 kilometres at one point. The crisis brought home to Canadians and their governments just how precarious their economic prosperity has become.

GLOBALIZATION AND CANADA–US RELATIONS

The Chrysler minivan that rolls off the assembly line at Windsor, Ontario, appears to be the very embodiment of what economic globalization is about. Assembled in Canada by a Canadian workforce, the vehicle includes parts and component systems from the United States, Mexico, and China. The plastics and metals in these parts come from an even broader set of countries. Many of these components move across the Canada–US border on the hundreds of trucks whose daily destination is the Windsor minivan

plant. Decisions about the design and marketing of the vehicle are made principally at Daimler-Chrysler headquarters, about an hour's drive away in Michigan. The company that produces the minivan is based in Stuttgart, Germany, but individual and institutional shareholders in DaimerChrysler are spread across Canada, the United States, and Europe.

Globalized production, sourcing, and investment have forced us to rethink what were, until fairly recently, firmly established ideas about what is Canadian. The case of the Chrysler minivan is merely one example—though a particularly important one in terms of its employment and income implications—of the new economic realities that characterize Canadian industry. Products exported from companies operating in Canada routinely include foreign content, and imported products will often include content produced in Canada. Moreover, every Canadian provincial economy, with the exception of PEI, does more business with economies outside of Canada than it does with the rest of Canada. Thus, not only is the old idea of a 'Canadian product' cast in doubt, but the very notion of a Canadian economy seems a bit outdated given the reality of this country's enormous dependence on international or, more accurately, American trade.

The essential fact to keep in mind, however, is that in Canada's case economic globalization has really meant greater integration with and dependence on the economy of the United States. The numbers are quite astounding. The total value of Canada–US trade in merchandise, services, and investment makes this easily the largest bilateral trading relationship in the world (although the Mexico–US relationship is increasing dramatically). Over 85 per cent of Canadian exports go to the United States, accounting for close to 40 per cent of Canada's total GDP. Only a slightly lower share of Canada's substantial import trade comes from the United States, at about three-quarters of total imports. Canada has been the major export market for American goods for over half a century and is today the leading export market for about three-quarters of all state economies. The United States has long been the largest source of foreign investment in Canada, currently accounting for close to two-thirds of all foreign investment, and is the location for about half of all Canadian direct investment abroad.

This bilateral trading relationship has a long history, but in recent years it has achieved an unprecedented level of intimacy. The real value of local transactions between the Canadian and American economies has more than doubled since the FTA took effect in 1989, increasing gradually at first and then more dramatically since NAFTA came into effect (see Figures 14.1 and 14.2). For Canada, more trade with the rest of the world has in fact meant more trade with the United States.

This relationship has never been one of equals and is not more so today than in the past. Revealingly, when the Canadian media were full of stories about the imposition of American duties on Canadian softwood lumber imports in the spring of 2002, there was barely any attention to the issue in the American media. Canada–US trade disputes that lead the national news in Canada are lucky if they receive a mention in the American press, particularly outside border states that might be more immediately affected. The trading relationship is not only huge; it is hugely asymmetrical, affecting Canada's vital interests far more than it does those of the United States (see Table 14.1).

Figure 14.1   The Dependence of Provincial Economics on Trade with the United States, 1989 and 2001

Exports of Goods and Services as a percentage of GDP

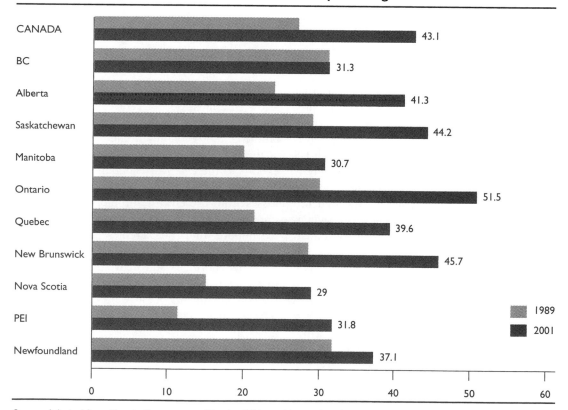

Source: Adapted from Canada, Department of Foreign Affairs and International Trade, *State of Trade 2002*, statistical annex, Table 1A.

Figure 14.2   Total Value of Canada–US Merchandise Trade 1998–2001 (in billions of dollars)

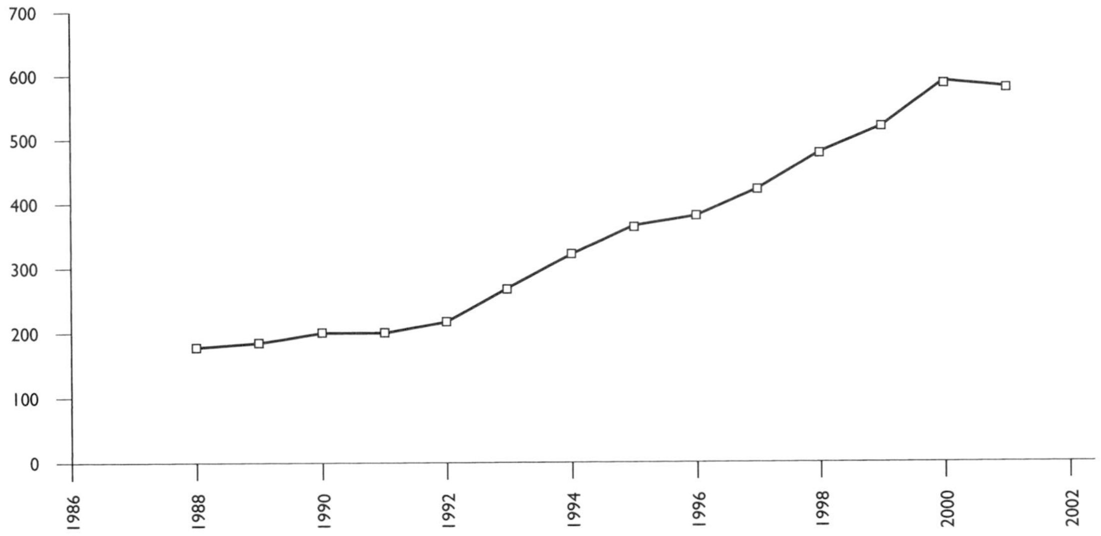

Source: Statistics Canada, Department of Foreign Affairs and International Trade, *State of Trade 2002.*

It would be an overstatement to say that Canada has no leverage in this relationship. After all, Canada—not Saudi Arabia!—is the single largest source of energy imports to the US and is the destination for over half the value of all US automotive exports. The Canadian economy is extremely important, and even strategically important, to the United States. But the influence that this might otherwise give Canadian negotiators in trade disputes with Washington is diluted by Canada's far greater across-the-board dependence on the American economy. To give but two examples, an end to petroleum exports from Alberta to the United States would bring Alberta's economy to its knees and ripple through the rest of the Canadian economy in various ways, but this would represent only a drop of 8 per cent in the total supply of petroleum products consumed in the United States. Likewise, if the American border were to be closed to automobiles, trucks,

and auto parts from Canada, this would represent a loss of almost 30 per cent of total Canadian exports, or about 12 per cent of GDP. The impact on the Ontario economy would be as devastating as the hypothesized loss of Alberta's oil and gas exports to the US. State economies like those of Michigan and Ohio would experience serious losses from the end of automotive trade with Canada, but the total value of American automotive imports from Canada represents a little under 1 per cent of American GDP.

This enormous and unavoidable imbalance in the Canada–US trade relationship was one of the chief arguments put forward in the 1980s by the Canadian advocates of free trade. The federal government's official policy of reducing Canada's reliance on trade and investment with the United States—a policy called the Third Option, adopted in the early 1970s—had proven about as effective as a statute repealing the law of gravity. A decade later, Canada was even more dependent on the American economy as a destination for exports and a source of imports. Canada's major manufacturers, but also important exporters of natural resources such as wood products, oil and gas, and hydroelectricity, recognized that their growth prospects depended on access to the American market. The Canadian Manufacturers' Association (since renamed the Alliance of Canadian Manufacturers and Exporters), which began life a century earlier calling for protectionist tariffs, became a convert to and a politically weighty advocate of a Canada–US free trade agreement. A growing wave of protectionist sentiment in the American Congress during the 1980s seemed to lend urgency to Canadian free traders' case—which was given a major boost by the pro-free trade recommendations of the 1981–5 Royal Commission on the Economic Union and Development Prospects for Canada—that Canada's best economic hope was in tighter formal economic integration with the United States. Even among many of those who were dubious about some of the economic claims made for free trade, the political argument that this would help shield Canadian industries from Congress's protectionist moods was persuasive.

The Canada–US Free Trade Agreement took effect on 1 January 1989. It was followed several years later by the **North American Free Trade Agreement**, bringing Canada, the United States, and Mexico together into a free trade zone that encompasses most industries and forms of investment. Both agreements created an architecture of dispute settlement rules, agencies, and monitoring requirements that have not taken the politics out of trade disputes, but provide administrative forums for their resolution. Experience has demonstrated that these new forums do not replace other methods of making trade policy. The older forums and channels still matter, as does the World Trade Organization. But on the whole it is fair to say that the rules and the dispute settlement mechanisms created under the FTA and NAFTA make it more difficult for the member governments to pursue trade policies that favour their domestic interests. They may still do so, but they run the risk of eventually having to pay the cost of sanctions if their policies are found to be in violation of these agreements.

The asymmetry in the Canada–US economic relationship is not helped, from Canada's point of view, by the fact that Americans—from policymakers to average citizens—often have little awareness of the scale of these relations or, perhaps worse, harbour misconceptions about them. When as wonkish a President as Bill Clinton identified China as the United States' leading trading partner—which he did in a 1993 speech—Canadians should not be surprised if lesser mortals also get things a bit muddled. A 2001 Time/CNN poll found that 64 per cent of those surveyed believed that Mexico, not Canada, had more of an impact on the US economy,[13] despite the fact that the annual

Table 14.1   An Asymmetrical Economic Relationship, 2002

	Canada	United States
1. Trade with the other country as a share of total GDP	35%	5%
2. Investment from the other country as a share of total foreign investment[a]	64% (1st)	8% (6th)
3. Share of total exports going to the other country	85%	23%
4. Share of total imports coming from the other country	73%	19%

[a]These figures are for 2000

Source: CIA Fact Book, www.cia.gov/cia/publications/factbooks/geos/us/html and www.cia.gov/cia/publications/factbook/geos/ca.html, accessed 22 March 2003.

value of Canada–US trade is about 40 per cent greater than trade across the Rio Grande. In that same survey Americans were also much more likely to say that Mexico has a greater impact than Canada on US politics (50 per cent versus 34 per cent) and culture (65 per cent versus 26 per cent). These assessments illustrate Americans' general lack of awareness of Canada's economic importance to the United States.

Ignorance may sometimes be benign. In this case, however, the fact that neither American policy-makers nor American public opinion demonstrates much in the way of awareness of the size and nature of Canadian–American economic relations may be, on balance, a liability for Canada. The long-standing saga of Canadian softwood lumber exports to the United States, which over the years has involved American measures to protect US producers from Canadian competition, illustrates the problem. Leaving aside the thorny and extremely contentious question of whether Canadian softwood lumber exporters are in fact subsidized by timber licence fees that are so low as to effectively undervalue Canadian timber in comparison to that produced in the American market, it is certainly the case that home builders and homebuyers in the US benefit from less expensive Canadian softwood. Moreover, the overall thrust of American trade policy for the last few decades has been towards trade liberalization, a position that all American presidents since Ronald Reagan have defended with some vigour. None of this has made much difference in the face of effective US lumber industry lobbying of Congress and the US Commerce Department to impose sanctions on Canadian imports, a step that was taken in the spring of 2002.

As Allan Gotlieb, the Canadian ambassador to the United States from 1981 to 1989, has observed, part of Canada's problem in its trade relations with the United States is getting the attention of those who matter in Washington.[14] He argues, however, that the answer may not lie in government-financed media blitzes designed to let Americans know how important we are to

them. Nor does he put much stock in Canadian efforts to lobby US interests, such as home builders' associations or Chambers of Commerce, in the hope that they will pressure Congress and administrative officials in ways congruent with Canadian trade interests. 'Like it or not,' Gotlieb says, 'in the US political system a foreign country is just another special interest. And not a very special one at that. It lacks the clout of a domestic special interest because it cannot contribute to political campaigns or deliver votes.' What, if anything, can Canadian policy-makers do to change this rather bleak prognosis?

Gotlieb's answer has two parts. 'First and foremost,' he argues, 'influence must be aimed at the highest level of the US political system, the presidency, the top personal advisors to the President and the key cabinet secretaries.' Gotlieb places special importance on the personal relationship between Prime Minister and President—complemented, ideally, by a good rapport between the Canadian Foreign Minister and the US Secretary of State, a factor that tends to be dismissed as irrelevant or of distinctly minor importance by most political scientists. Gotlieb's own experience in Washington, however, leads him to believe that '[i]f a matter is on the President's personal agenda, there is far better chance of a favourable outcome. If the President is concerned, word goes down to many hundreds of top loyal political appointees.'

Second, Gotlieb argues that tighter formal integration across the Canada–US border would help protect Canadian economic interests from precisely the sort of US domestic political pressures at play in the softwood lumber dispute. 'It is possible', he maintains, 'that a single market or customs union would enhance our interests.' Moreover, Gotlieb notes that Canadian governments may well have more leverage in economic matters than is often believed if they are willing to offer trade-offs on border control, terrorism, and defence issues. To be sure, this is a rather large 'if'. His conclusion extends the logic that led the Canadian government to embrace the free trade option in the 1980s. 'Canada', Gotlieb states, 'should look to a broader and deeper economic and security zone in which the rules of engagement would be less arbitrary, more predictable and provide greater common security.' He advocates a 'grand bargain' with the United States, establishing a North American community of law.[15] This, he believes, is the best hope for overcoming the unavoidable and lopsided asymmetry—both political and economic—in the Canadian-American relationship (see Box 14.2).

THE CANADIAN DILEMMA IN FOREIGN AFFAIRS

The Canadian dilemma boils down to this: Is it possible for Canada to maintain a margin of foreign policy independence when this country has a population about one-tenth that of the United States and an economy about one-eleventh the size of that of its giant neighbour to the south, especially when Canadian economic prosperity is more dependent on its leading trade and investment partner than is the economy of any other rich democracy (see Figure 14.3)? In what circumstances does this margin exist? How large is it? And is economic dependence, on balance, a liability or an opportunity?

These questions have occupied centre stage in debates over Canadian foreign policy since the end of World War II and the emergence of the United States as the unchallenged leader of the Western world. Former Canadian Prime Minister and Nobel Peace Prize winner Lester B. Pearson, undeniably one of the chief architects of Canadian foreign policy in the post-war era, acknowledged in his memoirs that American dominance and Cana-

---

BOX 14.2   Is a 'Grand Bargain' with the US in Canada's Interest?

The most basic question of Canadian foreign policy remains: What can Canada do to better protect its interests in the United States?

If we fail to find an answer, the consequences for Canada could be higher than ever before. For a country generating some 40 per cent of its annual income from exports to a single political destination, much of it requiring just-in-time delivery, and with millions of annual transborder crossings, the disruptions that would follow new terrorist strikes could be intolerable.

For any initiative to succeed, it must meet a number of conditions. It must be bold, it must come from Canada and be espoused at the highest level. It must be comprehensive so as to allow trade-offs and broad constituencies to come into play. It must address the US agenda as well as ours. Incrementalism won't work.

The Canadian political agenda is economic security; for Americans it is homeland security. Therein lie the potential elements of a grand negotiation.

The aim of Canada should be the creation of a North American community of law. It would substitute the rule of law for political discretion, arbitrary and discriminatory action. This may be the only way to establish restraints on unpredictable legislative behaviour which governments are often not in a position to resist. This is particularly true in the United States given the primacy of congressional powers over trade and immigration.

Allan Gotlieb, 'A Grand Bargain with the US',
National Post, 5 Mar. 2003, A16.

da's particular dependence on the United States were among the key hard realities confronting Canadian policy-makers. These realities, Pearson observed, 'brought us anxiety as well as assurance'.

This continues to be the Canadian condition when it comes to the possibilities open to this country in world affairs. The asymmetrical economic relationship between Canada and the United States, overlain by structures of policy integration that operate through the Canada–US Free Trade Agreement and NAFTA—and before these comprehensive trade agreements, through sectoral treaties including the Auto Pact and the Canada–US Defence Production Sharing Agreement—leave Canada with little room to throw its weight around in conflicts with its American neighbour. As demonstrated in the previous sec-

tion of this chapter, Canada's economic prosperity has never been more dependent on the United States than it is today. The policy implications of this can hardly be overstated.

For several decades the response of successive Canadian governments—the Conservative government of Brian Mulroney (1984–93) excluded—has been to search for and support counterweights to American dominance. Chief among these has been the United Nations and multilateralism more generally. **Multilateralism** involves the resolution of international differences and conflicts through structures and processes that represent many states and that give all of them a voice, though not necessarily an equal voice, in decision-making. The United Nations has been the most prominent structure for multilateralism

Being a player on the international stage requires skill and credibility. Individual MPs, like Svend Robinson of the NDP, have occasionally tried to give solo performances—to mixed reviews. (Roy Peterson, Vancouver Sun)

Figure 14.3   Trade Development for G-7 Countries, Export as a Percentage of GDP, 1989 and 2001

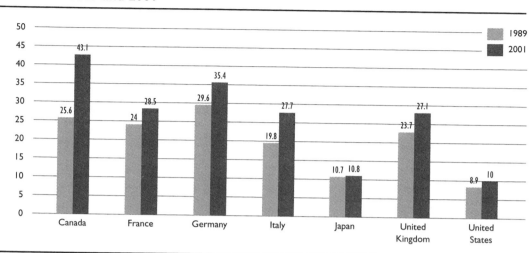

Source: Adapted from Canada, Department of Foreign Affairs and International Trade, *State of Trade 2002*, statistical annex, Table 1B

in the post-World War II era. There are, however, many other international organizations to which Canada belongs, including the North Atlantic Treaty Organization (NATO), the World Bank, the Organization for Economic Co-operation and Development, the World Trade Organization, the Organization of American States, the Commonwealth, and la Francophonie.

Some of these multilateral organizations are dominated by the United States and therefore can hardly be said to serve as counterweights to its might. NATO, for example, has almost never blocked the will or modified the military objectives of American administrations, the 2003 refusal of several of its members to guarantee the alliance's support for Turkey in the event of an attack by Iraq being the chief exception to this rule. Influence in the International Monetary Fund's decision-making is weighted, based on the size of member-state contributions, and the United States is its major contributor. Multilateralism does not, therefore, necessarily dilute American influence. It can, in fact, magnify this influence

by providing greater political legitimacy to American goals through their association with other countries and structures of multilateral decision-making. On the whole, however, multilateralism clearly holds out the possibility of allowing for the representation of interests and points of view that might dilute the dominance of the United States.

'One of the great foreign policy challenges facing Canada', observes Michael Ignatieff, 'is staying independent in an age of [American] empire.'[16] This is a large part of the explanation for multilateralism's attractiveness in the eyes of many Canadians and those who govern them. Multilateralism, when it is not a convenient cover for the ambitions and interests of a single member state, as the Warsaw Pact clearly was for the former Soviet Union or as the IMF and World Bank are alleged to be by critics of America's global economic power, implies that states are willing to accept some limitations on their national sovereignty. Canada's governing elites and opinion leaders, like their counterparts in Europe, 'have a vision of a multilateral world in which . . . sovereignty is not unconditional, but limited and bound by human rights agreements, or multilateral engagements which limit and constrain the sovereignty of states in the name of collective social goods.'[17] Canadian leadership in the creation of the International Criminal Court and in the process, known as the Ottawa Process, that led to the international treaty banning landmines, and Canada's ratification of the Kyoto Protocol on greenhouse gas emissions and support for the United Nations as the proper and necessary forum for the discussion of issues of war and peace and the authorization of the use of force reflect this commitment to multilateralism. It would be an overstatement to say that all Canadians accept this multilateral vision of the world, but recent history suggests that it has broad popular support. The problem for Canada—a problem experienced by many other allies of the United States, though less acutely—is that multilateralism is not embraced as enthusiastically by its major trading partner and sometimes produces outcomes that set Canada seriously at odds with the United States.

One of the great ironies of Canadian politics in recent times is that Canada's greater economic integration with the United States, under the free trade architecture of the FTA and NAFTA, may well have created the political space for Canada to pursue a more independent line in matters of foreign policy than was available before free trade. This is exactly opposite to the prediction of Canadian critics of free trade, who argued that the last shreds of Canadian sovereignty and policy autonomy would be vaporized by the tighter economic embrace produced by the FTA and NAFTA. If, however, one looks at the actual record of Canadian foreign policy over the last decade there are several notable instances of Canada being at loggerheads with the United States over global warming, landmines, an International Criminal Court, and, most importantly, the formal refusal of the Canadian government to join the American-led 'coalition of the willing' in the 2003 invasion of Iraq. In all of these cases it is arguable that the Canadian refusal to side with the Americans and Canadian criticism of the American position did not have serious and enduring consequences beyond a loss of goodwill in Washington towards Canada. While not wanting to diminish the importance of political goodwill in the Can–Am bilateral relationship, this is certainly a more nebulous consequence than being slapped with trade duties by the US Commerce Department or facing the punitive wrath of Congress.

Before free trade Canadian governments had to depend on the so-called 'special relationship' between Canada and the United States as protection against American retaliation if Canadian policy strayed unacceptably far from the line Washington deemed acceptable. It may be that free trade has loosened the leash to some degree, because some of these forms of retaliation are no longer available to Congress and the White House or, if employed, at least can be challenged under the terms of the free trade agreements that now join us at the hip.

There are, however, as there have long been, limits to how far and in what circumstances Canadian foreign policy can depart from that of the United States. In the case of Canada's refusal to support the war on Iraq, this did not damage the security interests and military goals of the United States. The fact that the United Kingdom, Spain, over a dozen other European governments, Japan, Australia, and an assortment of other countries lent their support to this military action made the absence of Canadian support virtually unnoticed in the United States. Indeed, this was only noticed when some American media outlets reported the booing of the American national anthem at a hockey game in Montreal! In the case of the 'war on terrorism', launched after the terrorist attacks of 11 September 2001, the space available for Canada to ignore American preferences has been considerably less. This is because the policy actions taken by the American government involved border security, air travel, and immigration, matters that directly affected Canada. With over $1 billion per day in trade crossing the border between the two countries, and given the enormous number of jobs and investments in Canada that depend on the smooth flow of goods and people across this border, the Canadian government has had little choice but to co-ordinate its policies with those of the American government. This co-ordination, however, has stopped short of Canadian acceptance of the idea of a common security perimeter around Canada and the United States, a concept that would require that Canadian immigration policy be brought into line with American policy.

Over the last decade the dominant paradigm for Canadian foreign policy has become what is known as **soft power**. This is a term first coined by Harvard's Joseph Nye. It involves international influence based on intangible or indirect factors that include culture, values, and a sense of legitimacy ascribed to a nation's international aims. Soft power operates, says Nye, through 'the complex machinery of interdependence, rather than . . . expensive new weapons systems'.[18] Nye has identified Canada, the Netherlands, and the Scandinavian countries as examples of countries whose governments have successfully exercised soft power, 'hitting above their weight' as a former Canadian Minister of Foreign Affairs, Lloyd Axworthy, liked to say.

It is easy to see why the doctrine of soft power would be an attractive one for many Canadians, suggesting as it does that their country can make a difference on the international stage through the values it stands for, its reputation as a good global citizen, and without having to spend much on defence. Canadians see themselves as peacekeepers and internationalists, a self-image that can be maintained without the latest military technology or much in the way of combat-readiness. Indeed, Canada spends less on defence, at about 1 per cent of GDP, than almost any other country in NATO.

Some have argued, however, that this self-image is an illusion. Although Canadians never hear this from those who govern them, by 2003 Canada had fallen to thirty-fourth in the world in terms of countries' contributions to UN peacekeeping. Bangladesh and India were first and sec-

ond, respectively, and the United States was ahead of Canada. Michael Ignatieff argues that the Canadian belief in multilateralism is laudable, but that international influence cannot be sustained by good intentions alone. It requires, he maintains, three national attributes:

- moral authority as a good global citizen;
- military capacity;
- international assistance capability.

Canada still has a good deal of the first attribute, Ignatieff argues, but far too little of the latter two. Indeed, the decline in our international assistance capability, of which peacekeeping is an important part, he blames on the steep decline in Canada's military capacity. Peacekeeping, he notes, is seldom about simply imposing bodies between two belligerents who have laid down their arms and agreed not to fight. It has become an often dangerous task that requires military capability, as was true in the Balkans in the 1990s and in Afghanistan in more recent times.

Moral authority on the international stage, Ignatieff argues, cannot be totally disconnected from a willingness to bear some of the military and economic burdens of defending the values and interests that are important to Canadians. The images that Canadians have long had of themselves as 'honest brokers', 'fixers', peacekeepers, and good global citizens certainly are not false. But Ignatieff raises the important question of whether there is a price that eventually must be paid to sustain the reality of this image. 'The disagreeable reality for those who believe in human rights', he argues, 'is that there are some occasions when war is the only real remedy for regimes that live by terror. This does not mean that the choice is morally unproblematic.'[19] In other words, soft power cannot abandon the occasional need for the older weapons-based variety.

CONCLUSION

As Canadians and their government struggled to come to grips with the world after the terrorist

BOX 14.3   Does the Effectiveness of Soft Power Depend on Military Might?

Canadians tend to argue that you can have ... development assistance or we can have a capable military, but we can't have both. What kind of country are we? Is this a great country? What is the *misérablisme* that says we can't even defend ourselves, we can't project power overseas, and we can't do a decent job at good citizenship? We have to get out of the mindset that says we must choose between the military and development assistance because the reality of the dirty world out there—that I see when I walk out there—is that you cannot help in a dangerous and divided world unless you have military capacity.

And it is not just the capacity to be peacekeepers, it's the capacity to have combat-capable lethality. There is something very curious about the way the military spine that was a part of our central national identity has just slipped away, so that when you make a claim in favour of national defence and military expenditure, you are ultimately regarded as some kind of foaming-at-the-mouth warmonger. It is a very odd thing and literally incomprehensible to my parents' and grandparents' generations, like my uncle who landed in Italy in 1943 and fought to the very gates of Berlin. That is part of the Canadian tradition and it is something of which we should be intensely proud.

Michael Ignatieff, 'Canada in the Age of Terror: Multilateralism Meets a Moment of Truth', *Policy Options* (Feb. 2003).

attacks on New York City and the Pentagon of 11 September 2001, the bombing of Afghanistan, and the American-led invasion of Iraq, it became increasingly evident that the choices facing them were about nothing less than the meaning of democracy, what threatened it, and what sort of world order would best protect it. Although most Canadians supported the war on terrorism launched by the United States after the terrorist attacks, and their government sent troops to Afghanistan and ships to the Persian Gulf in support of removal of the repressive Taliban regime and the Al-Qaeda camps that were allowed to operate in Afghanistan under its protection, Canadian public opinion was deeply divided and more than a little skeptical on the question of attacking Iraq without the authorization of a UN Security Council resolution.

When the American and British governments decided to attack Iraq without the support of most of their traditional allies and in the face of rather overwhelming public opposition in most countries, the Canadian government found itself in a difficult and unenviable position. On the one hand, Canada historically has supported the principles and institutions of multilateralism, particularly the United Nations, and has sought not to appear to be a mere lackey of the US administration. On the other hand, the tug of continentalist realities described in this chapter appears almost unavoidable. The ambiguous position taken by the Chrétien government—unwillingness to give official support to the Anglo-American war effort at the same time as the Prime Minister and some members of his government made cautiously approving noises at various points during the war and after the fall of Saddam Hussein's regime—fairly accurately reflected the ambivalence among Canadians. The government's position satisfied neither the NDP on the left nor the Alliance on the right, but in the successful Liberal tradition of sticking to the middle of the road it seemed to be one that most Canadians could live with.

But the tough questions will not go away. Events since 9/11 have brought home to Canadians and people throughout the world the remarkable lopsidedness of the world's power structure, dominated by the United States, and have forced them to think hard about what this means for Canada and the world. There can be no doubt about whether the United States has become a new imperium, whose power is perhaps unmatched in the history of the world. The only serious question in this regard is whether this is a good or bad thing. Ranged on one side are those, such as Canadians Michael Ignatieff, J.L. Granatstein, Charles Krauthammer, and Mark Steyn, who maintain that a world under the Pax Americana is, on the whole, a good thing or at least the lesser of evils in the contemporary world. On the other side are those Canadians, such as Mark Kingwell, Janice Gross Stein, Gwyn Dyer, and Lloyd Axworthy, who argue that decisions involving war and peace should always be made multilaterally and that the UN is the proper forum and sanctioning body for the use of force against any state.

More than virtually any other country, Canada is caught in a vice on this question. American decisions relating to what has come to be called 'homeland security' have unavoidably affected Canada because of the long border between the two countries and the enormous volume of goods and people crossing that border each day.

Although many Canadian politicians and opinion leaders echoed French President Jacques Chirac's immediate post-9/11 pronouncement that the terrorist attacks were an attack on us all, it soon became clear that most Canadians, and indeed most people outside the United States, did not believe this. Polls taken shortly after the September 2001 terrorist attacks showed that 80 per cent of Canadians believed that the actions and policies of the US were at least partly responsible for the attacks. It also was clear that Canadians did not feel vulnerable in the way that Americans, whose territory was the target of those attacks, did.

This creates a dilemma for Canada. Actions taken in and by the United States in the name of combatting terrorism and eliminating regimes deemed to pose a threat to American security and to a world order that does not endanger American interests carry a cost. That cost involves individual liberties, such as personal privacy and equality rights that may be jeopardized by practices like ethnic profiling. The debate over the issue of national security versus preservation of democratic rights and freedoms has been raging in the US since 11 September 2001. But it also concerns Canada. Likewise, the question of whether the UN is capable of dealing with international threats to human rights and peace, or whether the American globo-cop is a sort of *faute de mieux* way of dealing with these problems, is one that Canadians and others—including Americans—will continue to face for the foreseeable future. Questions about what promotes and what threatens democracy do not stop at Canada's borders. This becomes clear when Canadians ask themselves what sort of world, governed in what way, is most likely to guarantee the values and interests they cherish.

NOTES

1. Mark Kingwell, 'What distinguishes us from the Americans', *National Post*, 5 Mar. 2003, A16.

2. John Ralston Saul, *Reflections on a Siamese Twin: Canada at the End of the Twentieth Century* (Toronto: Penguin, 1997), 171.

3. Published as Michael Ignatieff, 'Canada in the Age of Terror—Multilateralism Meets a Moment of Truth', *Policy Options* (Feb. 2003). Available at: <www.irpp.org>.

4. The Pew Research Center for the People and the Press, 'What the World Thinks in 2002', part of the Pew Global Attitudes Project. Available at: <www.people-press.org>.

5. Alan Greenspan, 'Global Economic Opportunities and Challenges', remarks delivered at Jackson Hole, Wyoming, 25 Aug. 2000. Available at: <http://www.federalreserve.gov/boarddocs/speeches/2000/20000825.htm>.

6. Jeffrey Sachs, 'Nature, Nurture and Growth', *The Economist*, 14 June 1997, 19–22.

7. Robert Reich, *The Work of Nations: Preparing Ourselves for 21st Century Capitalism* (New York: Alfred A. Knopf, 1991).

8. Francis Fukayama, 'Economic Globalization and Culture', available at: <http://www.ml.com/woml/forum/global.htm>.

9. United Nations, Department of Economic and Social Affairs, *World Public Sector Report: Globalization and the State* (New York: UN, 2001).

10. Ibid., ch. 3.

11. Barry Lynn, 'Unmade in America: the True Cost of a Global Assembly Line', *Harper's* (June 2002): 37.

12. Ibid., 41.

13. *Time*, 11 June 2001, 30.

14. Allan Gotlieb, 'Getting attention', *National Post*, 17 May 2002, A17.

15. Allan Gotlieb, 'A grand bargain with the US', *National Post*, 5 Mar. 2003, A16.

16. Ignatieff, 'Canada in the Age of Terror'.

17. Ibid.

18. Joseph Nye, 'The misleading metaphor of decline', *The Atlantic* (Mar. 1990): 86–94.

19. Michael Ignatieff, 'The Burden', *New York Times Magazine*, 5 Jan. 2003. Available at: <http://www.nytimes.com/2003/01/05/magazine/05EMPIRE.html>.

SUGGESTED READINGS

Mark Brawley, *The Politics of Globalization: Gaining Perspective, Assessing Consequences* (Peterborough, Ont.: Broadview Press, 2002). Brawley presents a very accessible introduction to the phenomenon of globalization, including an examination of the evidence for the various claims made about its consequences.

David Cameron and Janice Gross Stein, eds, *Street Protests and Fantasy Parks: Globalization, Culture, and the State* (Vancouver: University of British Columbia Press, 2002). This is one of the many books on offer that are critical of globalization, written by two of Canada's leading academics.

David Carment, Fen Osler Hampson, and Norman Hillmer, eds, *Canada Among Nations 2003: Coping with the American Colossus* (Toronto: Oxford University Press, 2003). The 'Canada Among Nations' series, produced out of The Norman Paterson School of International Affairs at Carleton University, is published annually and includes analyses from leading scholars of Canadian foreign policy and Canada's role in the world. Notable is the ideological range of the contributors, as illustrated in this nineteenth volume in the series that focuses on the Canada–US relationship post-11 September.

Stephen Clarkson, *Uncle Sam and Us: Globalization, Neoconservatism, and the Canadian State* (Toronto: University of Toronto Press, 2002). Clarkson presents a critical examination of the impact of globalization and neo-conservative ideology on the ability of governments in Canada to respond to non-corporate interests and values.

Anthony DePalma, *Here: A Biography of the New American Continent* (New York: Public Affairs, 2001). Written by a journalist for the *Wall Street Journal* who was that paper's correspondent for several years both in Canada and in Mexico, this is an engaging and insightful account of the realities of North American integration.

Review Exercises

1. Canada participates in a large number of international organizations. For each of the following organizations explain what it does, the nature of Canada's participation, and the leading issues faced by the organization in recent years.
    - Organization of American States
    - North Atlantic Treaty Organization
    - World Trade Organization
    - International Criminal Court

2. How dependent is your community on international trade? To find out, identify the five or six leading employers in your area. You can do this by contacting your local Chamber of Commerce or the economic development office of city hall. Contact these companies and ask for information about how much of their goods or services they export, to what countries, and how many people they employ.

3. In March 2003 the Canadian government announced that it would not participate in the US-led war on Iraq. Identify the positions taken by the five political parties represented in the House of Commons, including the two or three main arguments used to support their respective positions. You can find information on this by going to <www.parl.gc.ca>.

THE CONSTITUTION ACT, 1867
(THE BRITISH NORTH AMERICA ACT, 1867)

30 & 31 Victoria, c. 3. (U.K.)
(Consolidated with amendments)
An Act for the Union of Canada, Nova Scotia, and New Brunswick,
and the Government thereof; and for Purposes connected therewith
[29th March 1867.]

Whereas the Provinces of Canada, Nova Scotia, and New Brunswick have expressed their Desire to be federally united into One Dominion under the Crown of the United Kingdom of Great Britain and Ireland, with a Constitution similar in Principle to that of the United Kingdom:

And whereas such a Union would conduce to the Welfare of the Provinces and promote the Interests of the British Empire:

And whereas on the Establishment of the Union by Authority of Parliament it is expedient, not only that the Constitution of the Legislative Authority in the Dominion be provided for, but also that the Nature of the Executive Government therein be declared:

And whereas it is expedient that Provision be made for the eventual Admission into the Union of other Parts of British North America: [1]

I. PRELIMINARY

Short title	1.	This Act may be cited as the *Constitution Act, 1867.* [2]
[Repealed]	2.	Repealed. [3]

II. UNION

Declaration of Union	3.	It shall be lawful for the Queen, by and with the Advice of Her Majesty's Most Honourable Privy Council, to declare by Proclamation that, on and after a Day therein appointed, not being more than Six Months after the passing of this Act, the Provinces of Canada, Nova Scotia, and New Brunswick shall form and be One Dominion under the Name of Canada; and on and after that Day those Three Provinces shall form and be One Dominion under that Name accordingly. [4]
Construction of subsequent Provisions of Act	4.	Unless it is otherwise expressed or implied, the Name Canada shall be taken to mean Canada as constituted under this Act. [5]
Four Provinces	5.	Canada shall be divided into Four Provinces, named Ontario, Quebec, Nova Scotia, and New Brunswick. [6]
Provinces of Ontario and Quebec	6.	The Parts of the Province of Canada (as it exists at the passing of this Act) which formerly constituted respectively the Provinces of Upper Canada and Lower Canada shall be deemed to be severed, and shall form Two separate Provinces. The Part which formerly constituted the Province of Upper Canada shall constitute the Province of Ontario; and the Part which formerly constituted the Province of Lower Canada shall constitute the Province of Quebec.
Provinces of Nova Scotia and New Brunswick	7.	The Provinces of Nova Scotia and New Brunswick shall have the same Limits as at the passing of this Act.

Decennial Census	8. In the general Census of the Population of Canada which is hereby required to be taken in the Year One thousand eight hundred and seventy-one, and in every Tenth Year thereafter, the respective Populations of the Four Provinces shall be distinguished.

III. EXECUTIVE POWER

Declaration of Executive Power in the Queen	9. The Executive Government and Authority of and over Canada is hereby declared to continue and be vested in the Queen.
Application of Provisions referring to Governor General	10. The Provisions of this Act referring to the Governor General extend and apply to the Governor General for the Time being of Canada, or other the Chief Executive Officer or Administrator for the Time being carrying on the Government of Canada on behalf and in the Name of the Queen, by whatever Title he is designated.
Constitution of Privy Council for Canada	11. There shall be a Council to aid and advise in the Government of Canada, to be styled the Queen's Privy Council for Canada; and the Persons who are to be Members of that Council shall be from Time to Time chosen and summoned by the Governor General and sworn in as Privy Councillors, and Members thereof may be from Time to Time removed by the Governor General.
All Powers under Acts to be exercised by Governor General with Advice of Privy Council, or alone	12. All Powers, Authorities, and Functions which under any Act of the Parliament of Great Britain, or of the Parliament of the United Kingdom of Great Britain and Ireland, or of the Legislature of Upper Canada, Lower Canada, Canada, Nova Scotia, or New Brunswick, are at the Union vested in or exerciseable by the respective Governors or Lieutenant Governors of those Provinces, with the Advice, or with the Advice and Consent, of the respective Executive Councils thereof, or in conjunction with those Councils, or with any Number of Members thereof, or by those Governors or Lieutenant Governors individually, shall, as far as the same continue in existence and capable of being exercised after the Union in relation to the Government of Canada, be vested in and exerciseable by the Governor General, with the Advice or with the Advice and Consent of or in conjunction with the Queen's Privy Council for Canada, or any Members thereof, or by the Governor General individually, as the Case requires, subject nevertheless (except with respect to such as exist under Acts of the Parliament of Great Britain or of the Parliament of the United Kingdom of Great Britain and Ireland) to be abolished or altered by the Parliament of Canada. [7]
Application of Provisions referring to Governor General in Council	13. The Provisions of this Act referring to the Governor General in Council shall be construed as referring to the Governor General acting by and with the Advice of the Queen's Privy Council for Canada.
Power to Her Majesty to authorize Governor General to appoint Deputies	14. It shall be lawful for the Queen, if Her Majesty thinks fit, to authorize the Governor General from Time to Time to appoint any Person or any Persons jointly or severally to be his Deputy or Deputies within any Part or Parts of Canada, and in that Capacity to exercise during the Pleasure of the Governor General such of the Powers, Authorities, and Functions of the Governor General as the Governor General deems it necessary or expedient to assign to him or them, subject to any Limitations or Directions expressed or given by the Queen; but the Appointment of such a Deputy or Deputies shall not affect the Exercise by the Governor General himself of any Power, Authority, or Function.
Command of Armed Forces to continue to be vested in the Queen	15. The Command-in-Chief of the Land and Naval Militia, and of all Naval and Military Forces, of and in Canada, is hereby declared to continue and be vested in the Queen.
Seat of Government of Canada	16. Until the Queen otherwise directs, the Seat of Government of Canada shall be Ottawa.

IV. LEGISLATIVE POWER

Constitution of Parliament of Canada

17. There shall be One Parliament for Canada, consisting of the Queen, an Upper House styled the Senate, and the House of Commons.

Privileges, etc., of Houses

18. The privileges, immunities, and powers to be held, enjoyed, and exercised by the Senate and by the House of Commons, and by the members thereof respectively, shall be such as are from time to time defined by Act of the Parliament of Canada, but so that any Act of the Parliament of Canada defining such privileges, immunities, and powers shall not confer any privileges, immunities, or powers exceeding those at the passing of such Act held, enjoyed, and exercised by the Commons House of Parliament of the United Kingdom of Great Britain and Ireland, and by the members thereof. (8)

First Session of the Parliament of Canada

19. The Parliament of Canada shall be called together not later than Six Months after the Union. (9)

[Repealed]

20. Repealed. (10)

THE SENATE

Number of Senators

21. The Senate shall, subject to the Provisions of this Act, consist of One Hundred and five Members, who shall be styled Senators. (11)

Representation of Provinces in Senate

22. In relation to the Constitution of the Senate Canada shall be deemed to consist of *Four* Divisions:

> 1. Ontario;
> 2. Quebec;
> 3. The Maritime Provinces, Nova Scotia and New Brunswick, and Prince Edward Island;
> 4. The Western Provinces of Manitoba, British Columbia, Saskatchewan, and Alberta;

which Four Divisions shall (subject to the Provisions of this Act) be equally represented in the Senate as follows: Ontario by twenty-four senators; Quebec by twenty-four senators; the Maritime Provinces and Prince Edward Island by twenty-four senators, ten thereof representing Nova Scotia, ten thereof representing New Brunswick, and four thereof representing Prince Edward Island; the Western Provinces by twenty-four senators, six thereof representing Manitoba, six thereof representing British Columbia, six thereof representing Saskatchewan, and six thereof representing Alberta; Newfoundland shall be entitled to be represented in the Senate by six members; the Yukon Territory and the Northwest Territories shall be entitled to be represented in the Senate by one member each.

In the Case of Quebec each of the Twenty-four Senators representing that Province shall be appointed for One of the Twenty-four Electoral Divisions of Lower Canada specified in Schedule A. to Chapter One of the Consolidated Statutes of Canada. (12)

Qualifications of Senator

23. The Qualifications of a Senator shall be as follows:

> (1) He shall be of the full age of Thirty Years:
> (2) He shall be either a natural-born Subject of the Queen, or a Subject of the Queen naturalized by an Act of the Parliament of Great Britain, or of the Parliament of the United Kingdom of Great Britain and Ireland, or of the Legislature of One of the Provinces of Upper Canada, Lower Canada, Canada, Nova Scotia, or New Brunswick, before the Union, or of the Parliament of Canada after the Union:

(3) He shall be legally or equitably seised as of Freehold for his own Use and Benefit of Lands or Tenements held in Free and Common Socage, or seised or possessed for his own Use and Benefit of Lands or Tenements held in Franc-alleu or in Roture, within the Province for which he is appointed, of the Value of Four thousand Dollars, over and above all Rents, Dues, Debts, Charges, Mortgages, and Incumbrances due or payable out of or charged on or affecting the same:

(4) His Real and Personal Property shall be together worth Four thousand Dollars over and above his Debts and Liabilities:

(5) He shall be resident in the Province for which he is appointed:

(6) In the Case of Quebec he shall have his Real Property Qualification in the Electoral Division for which he is appointed, or shall be resident in that Division. [13]

Summons of Senator

24. The Governor General shall from Time to Time, in the Queen's Name, by Instrument under the Great Seal of Canada, summon qualified Persons to the Senate; and, subject to the Provisions of this Act, every Person so summoned shall become and be a Member of the Senate and a Senator.

[Repealed]

25. Repealed. [14]

Addition of Senators in certain cases

26. If at any Time on the Recommendation of the Governor General the Queen thinks fit to direct that Four or Eight Members be added to the Senate, the Governor General may by Summons to Four or Eight qualified Persons (as the Case may be), representing equally the Four Divisions of Canada, add to the Senate accordingly. [15]

Reduction of Senate to normal Number

27. In case of such Addition being at any Time made, the Governor General shall not summon any Person to the Senate, except on a further like Direction by the Queen on the like Recommendation, to represent one of the Four Divisions until such Division is represented by Twenty-four Senators and no more. [16]

Maximum Number of Senators

28. The Number of Senators shall not at any Time exceed One Hundred and thirteen. [17]

Tenure of Place in Senate

Retirement upon attaining age of seventy-five years

29. (1) Subject to subsection (2), a Senator shall, subject to the provisions of this Act, hold his place in the Senate for life.
(2) A Senator who is summoned to the Senate after the coming into force of this subsection shall, subject to this Act, hold his place in the Senate until he attains the age of seventy-five years. [18]

Resignation of Place in Senate

30. A Senator may by Writing under his Hand addressed to the Governor General resign his Place in the Senate, and thereupon the same shall be vacant.

Disqualification of Senators

31. The Place of a Senator shall become vacant in any of the following Cases:

(1) If for Two consecutive Sessions of the Parliament he fails to give his Attendance in the Senate:

(2) If he takes an Oath or makes a Declaration or Acknowledgment of Allegiance, Obedience, or Adherence to a Foreign Power, or does an Act whereby he becomes a Subject or Citizen, or entitled to the Rights or Privileges of a Subject or Citizen, of a Foreign Power:

(3) If he is adjudged Bankrupt or Insolvent, or applies for the Benefit of any Law relating to Insolvent Debtors, or becomes a public Defaulter:

(4) If he is attainted of Treason or convicted of Felony or of any infamous Crime:

(5) If he ceases to be qualified in respect of Property or of Residence; provided, that a Senator shall not be deemed to have ceased to be qualified in respect of Residence by reason only of his residing at the Seat of the Government of Canada while holding an Office under that Government requiring his Presence there.

Summons on Vacancy in Senate

32. When a Vacancy happens in the Senate by Resignation, Death, or otherwise, the Governor General shall by Summons to a fit and qualified Person fill the Vacancy.

Questions as to Qualifications and Vacancies in Senate

33. If any Question arises respecting the Qualification of a Senator or a Vacancy in the Senate the same shall be heard and determined by the Senate.

Appointment of Speaker of Senate

34. The Governor General may from Time to Time, by Instrument under the Great Seal of Canada, appoint a Senator to be Speaker of the Senate, and may remove him and appoint another in his Stead. [19]

Quorum of Senate

35. Until the Parliament of Canada otherwise provides, the Presence of at least Fifteen Senators, including the Speaker, shall be necessary to constitute a Meeting of the Senate for the Exercise of its Powers.

Voting in Senate

36. Questions arising in the Senate shall be decided by a Majority of Voices, and the Speaker shall in all Cases have a Vote, and when the Voices are equal the Decision shall be deemed to be in the Negative.

THE HOUSE OF COMMONS

Constitution of House of Commons in Canada

37. The House of Commons shall, subject to the Provisions of this Act, consist of two hundred and ninety-five members of whom ninety-nine shall be elected for Ontario, seventy-five for Quebec, eleven for Nova Scotia, ten for New Brunswick, fourteen for Manitoba, thirty-two for British Columbia, four for Prince Edward Island, twenty-six for Alberta, fourteen for Saskatchewan, seven for Newfoundland, one for the Yukon Territory and two for the Northwest Territories. [20]

Summoning of House of Commons

38. The Governor General shall from Time to Time, in the Queen's Name, by Instrument under the Great Seal of Canada, summon and call together the House of Commons.

Senators not to sit in House of Commons

39. A Senator shall not be capable of being elected or of sitting or voting as a Member of the House of Commons.

Electoral districts of the four Provinces

40. Until the Parliament of Canada otherwise provides, Ontario, Quebec, Nova Scotia, and New Brunswick shall, for the Purposes of the Election of Members to serve in the House of Commons, be divided into Electoral Districts as follows:

1.   Ontario
Ontario shall be divided into the Counties, Ridings of Counties, Cities, Parts of Cities, and Towns enumerated in the First Schedule to this Act, each whereof shall be an Electoral District, each such District as numbered in that Schedule being entitled to return One Member.

2.   Quebec
Quebec shall be divided into Sixty-five Electoral Districts, composed of the Sixty-five Electoral Divisions into which Lower Canada is at the passing of this Act divided under Chapter Two of the Consolidated Statutes of Canada, Chapter Seventy-five of the Consolidated Statutes for Lower Canada, and the Act of the Province of Canada of the Twenty-third Year of the Queen, Chapter One, or any other Act amending the same in force at the Union, so

that each such Electoral Division shall be for the Purposes of this Act an Electoral District entitled to return One Member.

3.   Nova Scotia
Each of the Eighteen Counties of Nova Scotia shall be an Electoral District. The County of Halifax shall be entitled to return Two Members, and each of the other Counties One Member.

4.   New Brunswick
Each of the Fourteen Counties into which New Brunswick is divided, including the City and County of St. John, shall be an Electoral District. The City of St. John shall also be a separate Electoral District. Each of those Fifteen Electoral Districts shall be entitled to return One Member. [21]

Continuance of existing Election Laws until Parliament of Canada otherwise provides

41.   Until the Parliament of Canada otherwise provides, all Laws in force in the several Provinces at the Union relative to the following Matters or any of them, namely, — the Qualifications and Disqualifications of Persons to be elected or to sit or vote as Members of the House of Assembly or Legislative Assembly in the several Provinces, the Voters at Elections of such Members, the Oaths to be taken by Voters, the Returning Officers, their Powers and Duties, the Proceedings at Elections, the Periods during which Elections may be continued, the Trial of controverted Elections, and Proceedings incident thereto, the vacating of Seats of Members, and the Execution of new Writs in case of Seats vacated otherwise than by Dissolution, — shall respectively apply to Elections of Members to serve in the House of Commons for the same several Provinces.

Provided that, until the Parliament of Canada otherwise provides, at any Election for a Member of the House of Commons for the District of Algoma, in addition to Persons qualified by the Law of the Province of Canada to vote, every Male British Subject, aged Twenty-one Years or upwards, being a Householder, shall have a Vote. [22]

[Repealed]

42.   Repealed. [23]

[Repealed]

43.   Repealed. [24]

As to Election of Speaker of House of Commons

44.   The House of Commons on its first assembling after a General Election shall proceed with all practicable Speed to elect One of its Members to be Speaker.

As to filling up Vacancy in Office of Speaker

45.   In case of a Vacancy happening in the Office of Speaker by Death, Resignation, or otherwise, the House of Commons shall with all practicable Speed proceed to elect another of its Members to be Speaker.

Speaker to preside

46.   The Speaker shall preside at all Meetings of the House of Commons.

Provision in case of Absence of Speaker

47.   Until the Parliament of Canada otherwise provides, in case of the Absence for any Reason of the Speaker from the Chair of the House of Commons for a Period of Forty-eight consecutive Hours, the House may elect another of its Members to act as Speaker, and the Member so elected shall during the Continuance of such Absence of the Speaker have and execute all the Powers, Privileges, and Duties of Speaker. [25]

Quorum of House of Commons

48.   The Presence of at least Twenty Members of the House of Commons shall be necessary to constitute a Meeting of the House for the Exercise of its Powers, and for that Purpose the Speaker shall be reckoned as a Member.

Voting in House of Commons

49.   Questions arising in the House of Commons shall be decided by a Majority of Voices other than that of the Speaker, and when the Voices are equal, but not otherwise, the Speaker shall have a Vote.

Duration of House of Commons	**50.** Every House of Commons shall continue for Five Years from the Day of the Return of the Writs for choosing the House (subject to be sooner dissolved by the Governor General), and no longer. [26]

Readjustment of representation in Commons

51. (1) The number of members of the House of Commons and the representation of the provinces therein shall, on the coming into force of this subsection and thereafter on the completion of each decennial census, be readjusted by such authority, in such manner, and from such time as the Parliament of Canada from time to time provides, subject and according to the following rules:

Rules

1. There shall be assigned to each of the provinces a number of members equal to the number obtained by dividing the total population of the provinces by two hundred and seventy-nine and by dividing the population of each province by the quotient so obtained, counting any remainder in excess of 0.50 as one after the said process of division.

2. If the total number of members that would be assigned to a province by the application of rule 1 is less than the total number assigned to that province on the date of coming into force of this subsection, there shall be added to the number of members so assigned such number of members as will result in the province having the same number of members as were assigned on that date. [27]

Yukon Territory, Northwest Territories and Nunavut

(2) The Yukon Territory as bounded and described in the schedule to chapter Y-2 of the Revised Statutes of Canada, 1985, shall be entitled to one member, the Northwest Territories as bounded and described in section 2 of chapter N-27 of the Revised Statutes of Canada, 1985, as amended by section 77 of chapter 28 of the Statutes of Canada, 1993, shall be entitled to one member, and Nunavut as bounded and described in section 3 of chapter 28 of the Statutes of Canada, 1993, shall be entitled to one member. [28]

Constitution of House of Commons

51A. Notwithstanding anything in this Act a province shall always be entitled to a number of members in the House of Commons not less than the number of senators representing such province. [29]

Increase of Number of House of Commons

52. The Number of Members of the House of Commons may be from Time to Time increased by the Parliament of Canada, provided the proportionate Representation of the Provinces prescribed by this Act is not thereby disturbed.

MONEY VOTES; ROYAL ASSENT

Appropriation and Tax Bills

53. Bills for appropriating any Part of the Public Revenue, or for imposing any Tax or Impost, shall originate in the House of Commons.

Recommendation of Money Votes

54. It shall not be lawful for the House of Commons to adopt or pass any Vote, Resolution, Address, or Bill for the Appropriation of any Part of the Public Revenue, or of any Tax or Impost, to any Purpose that has not been first recommended to that House by Message of the Governor General in the Session in which such Vote, Resolution, Address, or Bill is proposed.

Royal Assent to Bills, etc.

55. Where a Bill passed by the Houses of the Parliament is presented to the Governor General for the Queen's Assent, he shall declare, according to his Discretion, but subject to the Provisions of this Act and to Her Majesty's Instructions, either that he assents thereto in the Queen's Name, or that he withholds the Queen's Assent, or that he reserves the Bill for the Signification of the Queen's Pleasure.

Disallowance by Order in Council of Act assented to by Governor General	56. Where the Governor General assents to a Bill in the Queen's Name, he shall by the first convenient Opportunity send an authentic Copy of the Act to One of Her Majesty's Principal Secretaries of State, and if the Queen in Council within Two Years after Receipt thereof by the Secretary of State thinks fit to disallow the Act, such Disallowance (with a Certificate of the Secretary of State of the Day on which the Act was received by him) being signified by the Governor General, by Speech or Message to each of the Houses of the Parliament or by Proclamation, shall annul the Act from and after the Day of such Signification.
Signification of Queen's Pleasure on Bill reserved	57. A Bill reserved for the Signification of the Queen's Pleasure shall not have any Force unless and until, within Two Years from the Day on which it was presented to the Governor General for the Queen's Assent, the Governor General signifies, by Speech or Message to each of the Houses of the Parliament or by Proclamation, that it has received the Assent of the Queen in Council.

An Entry of every such Speech, Message, or Proclamation shall be made in the Journal of each House, and a Duplicate thereof duly attested shall be delivered to the proper Officer to be kept among the Records of Canada.

V.   PROVINCIAL CONSTITUTIONS

EXECUTIVE POWER

Appointment of Lieutenant Governors of Provinces	58. For each Province there shall be an Officer, styled the Lieutenant Governor, appointed by the Governor General in Council by Instrument under the Great Seal of Canada.
Tenure of Office of Lieutenant Governor	59. A Lieutenant Governor shall hold Office during the Pleasure of the Governor General; but any Lieutenant Governor appointed after the Commencement of the First Session of the Parliament of Canada shall not be removeable within Five Years from his Appointment, except for Cause assigned, which shall be communicated to him in Writing within One Month after the Order for his Removal is made, and shall be communicated by Message to the Senate and to the House of Commons within One Week thereafter if the Parliament is then sitting, and if not then within One Week after the Commencement of the next Session of the Parliament.
Salaries of Lieutenant Governors	60. The Salaries of the Lieutenant Governors shall be fixed and provided by the Parliament of Canada. [30]
Oaths, etc., of Lieutenant Governor	61. Every Lieutenant Governor shall, before assuming the Duties of his Office, make and subscribe before the Governor General or some Person authorized by him Oaths of Allegiance and Office similar to those taken by the Governor General.
Application of Provisions referring to Lieutenant Governor	62. The Provisions of this Act referring to the Lieutenant Governor extend and apply to the Lieutenant Governor for the Time being of each Province, or other the Chief Executive Officer or Administrator for the Time being carrying on the Government of the Province, by whatever Title he is designated.
Appointment of Executive Officers for Ontario and Quebec	63. The Executive Council of Ontario and of Quebec shall be composed of such Persons as the Lieutenant Governor from Time to Time thinks fit, and in the first instance of the following Officers, namely, — the Attorney General, the Secretary and Registrar of the Province, the Treasurer of the Province, the Commissioner of Crown Lands, and the Commissioner of Agriculture and Public Works, with in Quebec the Speaker of the Legislative Council and the Solicitor General. [31]

Executive Government of Nova Scotia and New Brunswick	64. The Constitution of the Executive Authority in each of the Provinces of Nova Scotia and New Brunswick shall, subject to the Provisions of this Act, continue as it exists at the Union until altered under the Authority of this Act. (32)
Powers to be exercised by Lieutenant Governor of Ontario or Quebec with Advice, or alone	65. All Powers, Authorities, and Functions which under any Act of the Parliament of Great Britain, or of the Parliament of the United Kingdom of Great Britain and Ireland, or of the Legislature of Upper Canada, Lower Canada, or Canada, were or are before or at the Union vested in or exerciseable by the respective Governors or Lieutenant Governors of those Provinces, with the Advice or with the Advice and Consent of the respective Executive Councils thereof, or in conjunction with those Councils, or with any Number of Members thereof, or by those Governors or Lieutenant Governors individually, shall, as far as the same are capable of being exercised after the Union in relation to the Government of Ontario and Quebec respectively, be vested in and shall or may be exercised by the Lieutenant Governor of Ontario and Quebec respectively, with the Advice or with the Advice and Consent of or in conjunction with the respective Executive Councils, or any Members thereof, or by the Lieutenant Governor individually, as the Case requires, subject nevertheless (except with respect to such as exist under Acts of the Parliament of Great Britain, or of the Parliament of the United Kingdom of Great Britain and Ireland,) to be abolished or altered by the respective Legislatures of Ontario and Quebec. (33)
Application of Provisions referring to Lieutenant Governor in Council	66. The Provisions of this Act referring to the Lieutenant Governor in Council shall be construed as referring to the Lieutenant Governor of the Province acting by and with the Advice of the Executive Council thereof.
Administration in Absence, etc., of Lieutenant Governor	67. The Governor General in Council may from Time to Time appoint an Administrator to execute the Office and Functions of Lieutenant Governor during his Absence, Illness, or other Inability.
Seats of Provincial Governments	68. Unless and until the Executive Government of any Province otherwise directs with respect to that Province, the Seats of Government of the Provinces shall be as follows, namely, — of Ontario, the City of Toronto; of Quebec, the City of Quebec; of Nova Scotia, the City of Halifax; and of New Brunswick, the City of Fredericton.

LEGISLATIVE POWER

1. ONTARIO

Legislature for Ontario	69. There shall be a Legislature for Ontario consisting of the Lieutenant Governor and of One House, styled the Legislative Assembly of Ontario.
Electoral districts	70. The Legislative Assembly of Ontario shall be composed of Eighty-two Members, to be elected to represent the Eighty-two Electoral Districts set forth in the First Schedule to this Act. (34)

2. QUEBEC

Legislature for Quebec	71. There shall be a Legislature for Quebec consisting of the Lieutenant Governor and of Two Houses, styled the Legislative Council of Quebec and the Legislative Assembly of Quebec. (35)
Constitution of Legislative Council	72. The Legislative Council of Quebec shall be composed of Twenty-four Members, to be appointed by the Lieutenant Governor, in the Queen's Name, by Instrument under the Great Seal of Quebec, one being appointed to represent each of the Twenty-four Electoral Divisions of Lower Canada in this Act referred to, and each holding Office for the Term of his Life, unless the Legislature of Quebec otherwise provides under the Provisions of this Act.

Qualification of Legislative Councillors	73. The Qualifications of the Legislative Councillors of Quebec shall be the same as those of the Senators for Quebec.
Resignation, Disqualification, etc.	74. The Place of a Legislative Councillor of Quebec shall become vacant in the Cases, *mutatis mutandis*, in which the Place of Senator becomes vacant.
Vacancies	75. When a Vacancy happens in the Legislative Council of Quebec by Resignation, Death, or otherwise, the Lieutenant Governor, in the Queen's Name, by Instrument under the Great Seal of Quebec, shall appoint a fit and qualified Person to fill the Vacancy.
Questions as to Vacancies, etc.	76. If any Question arises respecting the Qualification of a Legislative Councillor of Quebec, or a Vacancy in the Legislative Council of Quebec, the same shall be heard and determined by the Legislative Council.
Speaker of Legislative Council	77. The Lieutenant Governor may from Time to Time, by Instrument under the Great Seal of Quebec, appoint a Member of the Legislative Council of Quebec to be Speaker thereof, and may remove him and appoint another in his Stead.
Quorum of Legislative Council	78. Until the Legislature of Quebec otherwise provides, the Presence of at least Ten Members of the Legislative Council, including the Speaker, shall be necessary to constitute a Meeting for the Exercise of its Powers.
Voting in Legislative Council	79. Questions arising in the Legislative Council of Quebec shall be decided by a Majority of Voices, and the Speaker shall in all Cases have a Vote, and when the Voices are equal the Decision shall be deemed to be in the Negative.
Constitution of Legislative Assembly of Quebec	80. The Legislative Assembly of Quebec shall be composed of Sixty-five Members, to be elected to represent the Sixty-five Electoral Divisions or Districts of Lower Canada in this Act referred to, subject to Alteration thereof by the Legislature of Quebec: Provided that it shall not be lawful to present to the Lieutenant Governor of Quebec for Assent any Bill for altering the Limits of any of the Electoral Divisions or Districts mentioned in the Second Schedule to this Act, unless the Second and Third Readings of such Bill have been passed in the Legislative Assembly with the Concurrence of the Majority of the Members representing all those Electoral Divisions or Districts, and the Assent shall not be given to such Bill unless an Address has been presented by the Legislative Assembly to the Lieutenant Governor stating that it has been so passed. [36]

3.   ONTARIO AND QUEBEC

[Repealed]	81. Repealed. [37]
Summoning of Legislative Assemblies	82. The Lieutenant Governor of Ontario and of Quebec shall from Time to Time, in the Queen's Name, by Instrument under the Great Seal of the Province, summon and call together the Legislative Assembly of the Province.
Restriction on election of Holders of offices	83. Until the Legislature of Ontario or of Quebec otherwise provides, a Person accepting or holding in Ontario or in Quebec any Office, Commission, or Employment, permanent or temporary, at the Nomination of the Lieutenant Governor, to which an annual Salary, or any Fee, Allowance, Emolument, or Profit of any Kind or Amount whatever from the Province is attached, shall not be eligible as a Member of the Legislative Assembly of the respective Province, nor shall he sit or vote as such; but nothing in this Section shall make ineligible any Person being a Member of the Executive Council of the respective Province, or holding any of the following Offices, that is to say, the Offices of Attorney General, Secretary and Registrar of the Province, Treasurer of the Province, Commissioner of Crown Lands, and Commissioner of Agriculture and Public Works, and in Quebec Solicitor General, or shall disqualify

him to sit or vote in the House for which he is elected, provided he is elected while holding such Office. [38]

Continuance of existing Election Laws

84. Until the legislatures of Ontario and Quebec respectively otherwise provide, all Laws which at the Union are in force in those Provinces respectively, relative to the following Matters, or any of them, namely, — the Qualifications and Disqualifications of Persons to be elected or to sit or vote as Members of the Assembly of Canada, the Qualifications or Disqualifications of Voters, the Oaths to be taken by Voters, the Returning Officers, their Powers and Duties, the Proceedings at Elections, the Periods during which such Elections may be continued, and the Trial of controverted Elections and the Proceedings incident thereto, the vacating of the Seats of Members and the issuing and execution of new Writs in case of Seats vacated otherwise than by Dissolution, — shall respectively apply to Elections of Members to serve in the respective Legislative Assemblies of Ontario and Quebec.

Provided that, until the Legislature of Ontario otherwise provides, at any Election for a Member of the Legislative Assembly of Ontario for the District of Algoma, in addition to Persons qualified by the Law of the Province of Canada to vote, every Male British Subject, aged Twenty-one Years or upwards, being a Householder, shall have a Vote. [39]

Duration of Legislative Assemblies

85. Every Legislative Assembly of Ontario and every Legislative Assembly of Quebec shall continue for Four Years from the Day of the Return of the Writs for choosing the same (subject nevertheless to either the Legislative Assembly of Ontario or the Legislative Assembly of Quebec being sooner dissolved by the Lieutenant Governor of the Province), and no longer. [40]

Yearly Session of Legislature

86. There shall be a Session of the Legislature of Ontario and of that of Quebec once at least in every Year, so that Twelve Months shall not intervene between the last Sitting of the Legislature in each Province in one Session and its first Sitting in the next Session. [41]

Speaker, Quorum, etc.

87. The following Provisions of this Act respecting the House of Commons of Canada shall extend and apply to the Legislative Assemblies of Ontario and Quebec, that is to say, — the Provisions relating to the Election of a Speaker originally and on Vacancies, the Duties of the Speaker, the Absence of the Speaker, the Quorum, and the Mode of voting, as if those Provisions were here re-enacted and made applicable in Terms to each such Legislative Assembly.

4.   NOVA SCOTIA AND NEW BRUNSWICK

Constitutions of Legislatures of Nova Scotia and New Brunswick

88. The Constitution of the Legislature of each of the Provinces of Nova Scotia and New Brunswick shall, subject to the Provisions of this Act, continue as it exists at the Union until altered under the Authority of this Act. [42]

5.   ONTARIO, QUEBEC, AND NOVA SCOTIA

[Repealed]

89. Repealed. [43]

6.   THE FOUR PROVINCES

Application to Legislatures of Provisions respecting Money Votes, etc.

90. The following Provisions of this Act respecting the Parliament of Canada, namely, — the Provisions relating to Appropriation and Tax Bills, the Recommendation of Money Votes, the Assent to Bills, the Disallowance of Acts, and the Signification of Pleasure on Bills reserved, — shall extend and apply to the Legislatures of the several Provinces as if those Provisions were here re-enacted and made applicable in Terms to the respective Provinces and the Legislatures thereof, with the Substitution of the Lieutenant Governor of the Province for

the Governor General, of the Governor General for the Queen and for a Secretary of State, of One Year for Two Years, and of the Province for Canada.

VI. DISTRIBUTION OF LEGISLATIVE POWERS

POWERS OF THE PARLIAMENT

Legislative Authority of Parliament of Canada

91. It shall be lawful for the Queen, by and with the Advice and Consent of the Senate and House of Commons, to make Laws for the Peace, Order, and good Government of Canada, in relation to all Matters not coming within the Classes of Subjects by this Act assigned exclusively to the Legislatures of the Provinces; and for greater Certainty, but not so as to restrict the Generality of the foregoing Terms of this Section, it is hereby declared that (notwithstanding anything in this Act) the exclusive Legislative Authority of the Parliament of Canada extends to all Matters coming within the Classes of Subjects next hereinafter enumerated; that is to say,

1. Repealed. [44]
1A. The Public Debt and Property. [45]
2. The Regulation of Trade and Commerce.
2A. Unemployment insurance. [46]
3. The raising of Money by any Mode or System of Taxation.
4. The borrowing of Money on the Public Credit.
5. Postal Service.
6. The Census and Statistics.
7. Militia, Military and Naval Service, and Defence.
8. The fixing of and providing for the Salaries and Allowances of Civil and other Officers of the Government of Canada.
9. Beacons, Buoys, Lighthouses, and Sable Island.
10. Navigation and Shipping.
11. Quarantine and the Establishment and Maintenance of Marine Hospitals.
12. Sea Coast and Inland Fisheries.
13. Ferries between a Province and any British or Foreign Country or between Two Provinces.
14. Currency and Coinage.
15. Banking, Incorporation of Banks, and the Issue of Paper Money.
16. Savings Banks.
17. Weights and Measures.
18. Bills of Exchange and Promissory Notes.
19. Interest.
20. Legal Tender.
21. Bankruptcy and Insolvency.
22. Patents of Invention and Discovery.
23. Copyrights.
24. Indians, and Lands reserved for the Indians.
25. Naturalization and Aliens.
26. Marriage and Divorce.
27. The Criminal Law, except the Constitution of Courts of Criminal Jurisdiction, but including the Procedure in Criminal Matters.
28. The Establishment, Maintenance, and Management of Penitentiaries.
29. Such Classes of Subjects as are expressly excepted in the Enumeration of the Classes of Subjects by this Act assigned exclusively to the Legislatures of the Provinces.

And any Matter coming within any of the Classes of Subjects enumerated in this Section shall not be deemed to come within the Class of Matters of a local or private Nature comprised in the Enumeration of the Classes of Subjects by this Act assigned exclusively to the Legislatures of the Provinces. [47]

EXCLUSIVE POWERS OF PROVINCIAL LEGISLATURES

Subjects of exclusive Provincial Legislation

92. In each Province the Legislature may exclusively make Laws in relation to Matters coming within the Classes of Subjects next hereinafter enumerated; that is to say,

1. Repealed. [48]
2. Direct Taxation within the Province in order to the raising of a Revenue for Provincial Purposes.
3. The borrowing of Money on the sole Credit of the Province.
4. The Establishment and Tenure of Provincial Offices and the Appointment and Payment of Provincial Officers.
5. The Management and Sale of the Public Lands belonging to the Province and of the Timber and Wood thereon.
6. The Establishment, Maintenance, and Management of Public and Reformatory Prisons in and for the Province.
7. The Establishment, Maintenance, and Management of Hospitals, Asylums, Charities, and Eleemosynary Institutions in and for the Province, other than Marine Hospitals.
8. Municipal Institutions in the Province.
9. Shop, Saloon, Tavern, Auctioneer, and other Licences in order to the raising of a Revenue for Provincial, Local, or Municipal Purposes.
10. Local Works and Undertakings other than such as are of the following Classes:
    (a) Lines of Steam or other Ships, Railways, Canals, Telegraphs, and other Works and Undertakings connecting the Province with any other or others of the Provinces, or extending beyond the Limits of the Province:
    (b) Lines of Steam Ships between the Province and any British or Foreign Country:
    (c) Such Works as, although wholly situate within the Province, are before or after their Execution declared by the Parliament of Canada to be for the general Advantage of Canada or for the Advantage of Two or more of the Provinces.
11. The Incorporation of Companies with Provincial Objects.
12. The Solemnization of Marriage in the Province.
13. Property and Civil Rights in the Province.
14. The Administration of Justice in the Province, including the Constitution, Maintenance, and Organization of Provincial Courts, both of Civil and of Criminal Jurisdiction, and including Procedure in Civil Matters in those Courts.
15. The Imposition of Punishment by Fine, Penalty, or Imprisonment for enforcing any Law of the Province made in relation to any Matter coming within any of the Classes of Subjects enumerated in this Section.
16. Generally all Matters of a merely local or private Nature in the Province.

NON-RENEWABLE NATURAL RESOURCES, FORESTRY RESOURCES AND ELECTRICAL ENERGY

Laws respecting non-renewable natural resources, forestry resources and electrical energy

92A.(1) In each province, the legislature may exclusively make laws in relation to

(a) exploration for non-renewable natural resources in the province;

(b) development, conservation and management of non-renewable natural resources and forestry resources in the province, including laws in relation to the rate of primary production therefrom; and

(c) development, conservation and management of sites and facilities in the province for the generation and production of electrical energy.

Export from provinces of resources

(2) In each province, the legislature may make laws in relation to the export from the province to another part of Canada of the primary production from non-renewable natural resources and forestry resources in the province and the production from facilities in the province for the generation of electrical energy, but such laws may not authorize or provide for discrimination in prices or in supplies exported to another part of Canada.

Authority of Parliament

(3) Nothing in subsection (2) derogates from the authority of Parliament to enact laws in relation to the matters referred to in that subsection and, where such a law of Parliament and a law of a province conflict, the law of Parliament prevails to the extent of the conflict.

Taxation of resources

(4) In each province, the legislature may make laws in relation to the raising of money by any mode or system of taxation in respect of

(a) non-renewable natural resources and forestry resources in the province and the primary production therefrom, and

(b) sites and facilities in the province for the generation of electrical energy and the production therefrom,

whether or not such production is exported in whole or in part from the province, but such laws may not authorize or provide for taxation that differentiates between production exported to another part of Canada and production not exported from the province.

"Primary production"

(5) The expression "primary production" has the meaning assigned by the Sixth Schedule.

Existing powers or rights

(6) Nothing in subsections (1) to (5) derogates from any powers or rights that a legislature or government of a province had immediately before the coming into force of this section. [49]

EDUCATION

Legislation respecting Education

93. In and for each Province the Legislature may exclusively make Laws in relation to Education, subject and according to the following Provisions:

(1) Nothing in any such Law shall prejudicially affect any Right or Privilege with respect to Denominational Schools which any Class of Persons have by Law in the Province at the Union:

(2) All the Powers, Privileges, and Duties at the Union by Law conferred and imposed in Upper Canada on the Separate Schools and School Trustees of the Queen's Roman Catholic Subjects shall be and the same are hereby extended to the Dissentient Schools of the Queen's Protestant and Roman Catholic Subjects in Quebec:

(3) Where in any Province a System of Separate or Dissentient Schools exists by Law at the Union or is thereafter established by the Legislature of the Province, an Appeal shall lie to the Governor General in Council from any Act or Decision of any Provincial Authority affecting any Right or Privilege of the Protestant or Roman Catholic Minority of the Queen's Subjects in relation to Education:

(4) In case any such Provincial Law as from Time to Time seems to the Governor General in Council requisite for the due Execution of the Provisions of this Section is not made, or in case any Decision of the Governor General in Council on any Appeal under this Section is not duly executed by the proper Provincial Authority in that Behalf, then and in every such Case, and as far only as the Circumstances of each Case require, the Parliament of Canada may make remedial Laws for the due Execution of the Provisions of this Section and of any Decision of the Governor General in Council under this Section. (50)

Quebec

93A.   Paragraphs (1) to (4) of section 93 do not apply to Quebec. (50.1)

UNIFORMITY OF LAWS IN ONTARIO, NOVA SCOTIA, AND NEW BRUNSWICK

Legislation for Uniformity of Laws in Three Provinces

94. Notwithstanding anything in this Act, the Parliament of Canada may make Provision for the Uniformity of all or any of the Laws relative to Property and Civil Rights in Ontario, Nova Scotia, and New Brunswick, and of the Procedure of all or any of the Courts in those Three Provinces, and from and after the passing of any Act in that Behalf the Power of the Parliament of Canada to make Laws in relation to any Matter comprised in any such Act shall, notwithstanding anything in this Act, be unrestricted; but any Act of the Parliament of Canada making Provision for such Uniformity shall not have effect in any Province unless and until it is adopted and enacted as Law by the Legislature thereof.

OLD AGE PENSIONS

Legislation respecting old age pensions and supplementary benefits

94A.   The Parliament of Canada may make laws in relation to old age pensions and supplementary benefits, including survivors' and disability benefits irrespective of age, but no such law shall affect the operation of any law present or future of a provincial legislature in relation to any such matter. (51)

AGRICULTURE AND IMMIGRATION

Concurrent Powers of Legislation respecting Agriculture, etc.

95. In each Province the Legislature may make Laws in relation to Agriculture in the Province, and to Immigration into the Province; and it is hereby declared that the Parliament of Canada may from Time to Time make Laws in relation to Agriculture in all or any of the Provinces, and to Immigration into all or any of the Provinces; and any Law of the Legislature of a Province relative to Agriculture or to Immigration shall have effect in and for the Province as long and as far only as it is not repugnant to any Act of the Parliament of Canada.

VII. JUDICATURE

Appointment of Judges

96. The Governor General shall appoint the Judges of the Superior, District, and County Courts in each Province, except those of the Courts of Probate in Nova Scotia and New Brunswick.

Selection of Judges in Ontario, etc.	97. Until the Laws relative to Property and Civil Rights in Ontario, Nova Scotia, and New Brunswick, and the Procedure of the Courts in those Provinces, are made uniform, the Judges of the Courts of those Provinces appointed by the Governor General shall be selected from the respective Bars of those Provinces.
Selection of Judges in Quebec	98. The Judges of the Courts of Quebec shall be selected from the Bar of that Province.
Tenure of office of Judges	99. (1) Subject to subsection two of this section, the Judges of the Superior Courts shall hold office during good behaviour, but shall be removable by the Governor General on Address of the Senate and House of Commons.
Termination at age 75	(2) A Judge of a Superior Court, whether appointed before or after the coming into force of this section, shall cease to hold office upon attaining the age of seventy-five years, or upon the coming into force of this section if at that time he has already attained that age. [52]
Salaries, etc., of Judges	100. The Salaries, Allowances, and Pensions of the Judges of the Superior, District, and County Courts (except the Courts of Probate in Nova Scotia and New Brunswick), and of the Admiralty Courts in Cases where the Judges thereof are for the Time being paid by Salary, shall be fixed and provided by the Parliament of Canada. [53] .
General Court of Appeal, etc.	101. The Parliament of Canada may, notwithstanding anything in this Act, from Time to Time provide for the Constitution, Maintenance, and Organization of a General Court of Appeal for Canada, and for the Establishment of any additional Courts for the better Administration of the Laws of Canada. [54]

VIII. REVENUES; DEBTS; ASSETS; TAXATION

Creation of Consolidated Revenue Fund	102. All Duties and Revenues over which the respective Legislatures of Canada, Nova Scotia, and New Brunswick before and at the Union had and have Power of Appropriation, except such Portions thereof as are by this Act reserved to the respective Legislatures of the Provinces, or are raised by them in accordance with the special Powers conferred on them by this Act, shall form One Consolidated Revenue Fund, to be appropriated for the Public Service of Canada in the Manner and subject to the Charges in this Act provided.
Expenses of Collection, etc.	103. The Consolidated Revenue Fund of Canada shall be permanently charged with the Costs, Charges, and Expenses incident to the Collection, Management, and Receipt thereof, and the same shall form the First Charge thereon, subject to be reviewed and audited in such Manner as shall be ordered by the Governor General in Council until the Parliament otherwise provides.
Interest of Provincial Public Debts	104. The annual Interest of the Public Debts of the several Provinces of Canada, Nova Scotia, and New Brunswick at the Union shall form the Second Charge on the Consolidated Revenue Fund of Canada.
Salary of Governor General	105. Unless altered by the Parliament of Canada, the Salary of the Governor General shall be Ten thousand Pounds Sterling Money of the United Kingdom of Great Britain and Ireland, payable out of the Consolidated Revenue Fund of Canada, and the same shall form the Third Charge thereon. [55]
Appropriation from Time to Time	106. Subject to the several Payments by this Act charged on the Consolidated Revenue Fund of Canada, the same shall be appropriated by the Parliament of Canada for the Public Service.
Transfer of Stocks, etc.	107. All Stocks, Cash, Banker's Balances, and Securities for Money belonging to each Province at the Time of the Union, except as in this Act mentioned, shall be

the Property of Canada, and shall be taken in Reduction of the Amount of the respective Debts of the Provinces at the Union.

Transfer of Property in Schedule

108. The Public Works and Property of each Province, enumerated in the Third Schedule to this Act, shall be the Property of Canada.

Property in Lands, Mines, etc.

109. All Lands, Mines, Minerals, and Royalties belonging to the several Provinces of Canada, Nova Scotia, and New Brunswick at the Union, and all Sums then due or payable for such Lands, Mines, Minerals, or Royalties, shall belong to the several Provinces of Ontario, Quebec, Nova Scotia, and New Brunswick in which the same are situate or arise, subject to any Trusts existing in respect thereof, and to any Interest other than that of the Province in the same. [56]

Assets connected with Provincial Debts

110. All Assets connected with such Portions of the Public Debt of each Province as are assumed by that Province shall belong to that Province.

Canada to be liable for Provincial Debts

111. Canada shall be liable for the Debts and Liabilities of each Province existing at the Union.

Debts of Ontario and Quebec

112. Ontario and Quebec conjointly shall be liable to Canada for the Amount (if any) by which the Debt of the Province of Canada exceeds at the Union Sixty-two million five hundred thousand Dollars, and shall be charged with Interest at the Rate of Five per Centum per Annum thereon.

Assets of Ontario and Quebec

113. The Assets enumerated in the Fourth Schedule to this Act belonging at the Union to the Province of Canada shall be the Property of Ontario and Quebec conjointly.

Debt of Nova Scotia

114. Nova Scotia shall be liable to Canada for the Amount (if any) by which its Public Debt exceeds at the Union Eight million Dollars, and shall be charged with Interest at the Rate of Five per Centum per Annum thereon. [57]

Debt of New Brunswick

115. New Brunswick shall be liable to Canada for the Amount (if any) by which its Public Debt exceeds at the Union Seven million Dollars, and shall be charged with Interest at the Rate of Five per Centum per Annum thereon.

Payment of interest to Nova Scotia and New Brunswick

116. In case the Public Debts of Nova Scotia and New Brunswick do not at the Union amount to Eight million and Seven million Dollars respectively, they shall respectively receive by half-yearly Payments in advance from the Government of Canada Interest at Five per Centum per Annum on the Difference between the actual Amounts of their respective Debts and such stipulated Amounts.

Provincial Public Property

117. The several Provinces shall retain all their respective Public Property not otherwise disposed of in this Act, subject to the Right of Canada to assume any Lands or Public Property required for Fortifications or for the Defence of the Country.

[Repealed]

118. Repealed. [58]

Further Grant to New Brunswick

119. New Brunswick shall receive by half-yearly Payments in advance from Canada for the Period of Ten Years from the Union an additional Allowance of Sixty-three thousand Dollars per Annum; but as long as the Public Debt of that Province remains under Seven million Dollars, a Deduction equal to the Interest at Five per Centum per Annum on such Deficiency shall be made from that Allowance of Sixty-three thousand Dollars. [59]

Form of Payments

120. All Payments to be made under this Act, or in discharge of Liabilities created under any Act of the Provinces of Canada, Nova Scotia, and New Brunswick

respectively, and assumed by Canada, shall, until the Parliament of Canada otherwise directs, be made in such Form and Manner as may from Time to Time be ordered by the Governor General in Council.

Canadian Manufactures, etc.

121. All Articles of the Growth, Produce, or Manufacture of any one of the Provinces shall, from and after the Union, be admitted free into each of the other Provinces.

Continuance of Customs and Excise Laws

122. The Customs and Excise Laws of each Province shall, subject to the Provisions of this Act, continue in force until altered by the Parliament of Canada. [(60)]

Exportation and Importation as between Two Provinces

123. Where Customs Duties are, at the Union, leviable on any Goods, Wares, or Merchandises in any Two Provinces, those Goods, Wares, and Merchandises may, from and after the Union, be imported from one of those Provinces into the other of them on Proof of Payment of the Customs Duty leviable thereon in the Province of Exportation, and on Payment of such further Amount (if any) of Customs Duty as is leviable thereon in the Province of Importation. [(61)]

Lumber Dues in New Brunswick

124. Nothing in this Act shall affect the Right of New Brunswick to levy the Lumber Dues provided in Chapter Fifteen of Title Three of the Revised Statutes of New Brunswick, or in any Act amending that Act before or after the Union, and not increasing the Amount of such Dues; but the Lumber of any of the Provinces other than New Brunswick shall not be subject to such Dues. [(62)]

Exemption of Public Lands, etc.

125. No Lands or Property belonging to Canada or any Province shall be liable to Taxation.

Provincial Consolidated Revenue Fund

126. Such Portions of the Duties and Revenues over which the respective Legislatures of Canada, Nova Scotia, and New Brunswick had before the Union Power of Appropriation as are by this Act reserved to the respective Governments or Legislatures of the Provinces, and all Duties and Revenues raised by them in accordance with the special Powers conferred upon them by this Act, shall in each Province form One Consolidated Revenue Fund to be appropriated for the Public Service of the Province.

IX. MISCELLANEOUS PROVISIONS

GENERAL

[Repealed]

127. Repealed. [(63)]

Oath of Allegiance, etc.

128. Every Member of the Senate or House of Commons of Canada shall before taking his Seat therein take and subscribe before the Governor General or some Person authorized by him, and every Member of a Legislative Council or Legislative Assembly of any Province shall before taking his Seat therein take and subscribe before the Lieutenant Governor of the Province or some Person authorized by him, the Oath of Allegiance contained in the Fifth Schedule to this Act; and every Member of the Senate of Canada and every Member of the Legislative Council of Quebec shall also, before taking his Seat therein, take and subscribe before the Governor General, or some Person authorized by him, the Declaration of Qualification contained in the same Schedule.

Continuance of existing Laws, Courts, Officers, etc.

129. Except as otherwise provided by this Act, all Laws in force in Canada, Nova Scotia, or New Brunswick at the Union, and all Courts of Civil and Criminal Jurisdiction, and all legal Commissions, Powers, and Authorities, and all Officers, Judicial, Administrative, and Ministerial, existing therein at the Union, shall continue in Ontario, Quebec, Nova Scotia, and New Brunswick respectively, as if the Union had not been made; subject nevertheless (except with

respect to such as are enacted by or exist under Acts of the Parliament of Great Britain or of the Parliament of the United Kingdom of Great Britain and Ireland), to be repealed, abolished, or altered by the Parliament of Canada, or by the Legislature of the respective Province, according to the Authority of the Parliament or of that Legislature under this Act. (64)

Transfer of Officers to Canada

130. Until the Parliament of Canada otherwise provides, all Officers of the several Provinces having Duties to discharge in relation to Matters other than those coming within the Classes of Subjects by this Act assigned exclusively to the Legislatures of the Provinces shall be Officers of Canada, and shall continue to discharge the Duties of their respective Offices under the same Liabilities, Responsibilities, and Penalties as if the Union had not been made. (65)

Appointment of new Officers

131. Until the Parliament of Canada otherwise provides, the Governor General in Council may from Time to Time appoint such Officers as the Governor General in Council deems necessary or proper for the effectual Execution of this Act.

Treaty Obligations

132. The Parliament and Government of Canada shall have all Powers necessary or proper for performing the Obligations of Canada or of any Province thereof, as Part of the British Empire, towards Foreign Countries, arising under Treaties between the Empire and such Foreign Countries.

Use of English and French Languages

133. Either the English or the French Language may be used by any Person in the Debates of the Houses of the Parliament of Canada and of the Houses of the Legislature of Quebec; and both those Languages shall be used in the respective Records and Journals of those Houses; and either of those Languages may be used by any Person or in any Pleading or Process in or issuing from any Court of Canada established under this Act, and in or from all or any of the Courts of Quebec.

The Acts of the Parliament of Canada and of the Legislature of Quebec shall be printed and published in both those Languages. (66)

ONTARIO AND QUEBEC

Appointment of Executive Officers for Ontario and Quebec

134. Until the Legislature of Ontario or of Quebec otherwise provides, the Lieutenant Governors of Ontario and Quebec may each appoint under the Great Seal of the Province the following Officers, to hold Office during Pleasure, that is to say, — the Attorney General, the Secretary and Registrar of the Province, the Treasurer of the Province, the Commissioner of Crown Lands, and the Commissioner of Agriculture and Public Works, and in the Case of Quebec the Solicitor General, and may, by Order of the Lieutenant Governor in Council, from Time to Time prescribe the Duties of those Officers, and of the several Departments over which they shall preside or to which they shall belong, and of the Officers and Clerks thereof, and may also appoint other and additional Officers to hold Office during Pleasure, and may from Time to Time prescribe the Duties of those Officers, and of the several Departments over which they shall preside or to which they shall belong, and of the Officers and Clerks thereof. (67)

Powers, Duties, etc. of Executive Officers

135. Until the Legislature of Ontario or Quebec otherwise provides, all Rights, Powers, Duties, Functions, Responsibilities, or Authorities at the passing of this Act vested in or imposed on the Attorney General, Solicitor General, Secretary and Registrar of the Province of Canada, Minister of Finance, Commissioner of Crown Lands, Commissioner of Public Works, and Minister of Agriculture and Receiver General, by any Law, Statute, or Ordinance of Upper Canada, Lower Canada, or Canada, and not repugnant to this Act, shall be vested in or imposed on any Officer to be appointed by the Lieutenant Governor for the Discharge of the same or any of them; and the Commissioner of Agriculture

and Public Works shall perform the Duties and Functions of the Office of Minister of Agriculture at the passing of this Act imposed by the Law of the Province of Canada, as well as those of the Commissioner of Public Works. [68]

Great Seals

136. Until altered by the Lieutenant Governor in Council, the Great Seals of Ontario and Quebec respectively shall be the same, or of the same Design, as those used in the Provinces of Upper Canada and Lower Canada respectively before their Union as the Province of Canada.

Construction of temporary Acts

137. The words "and from thence to the End of the then next ensuing Session of the Legislature," or Words to the same Effect, used in any temporary Act of the Province of Canada not expired before the Union, shall be construed to extend and apply to the next Session of the Parliament of Canada if the Subject Matter of the Act is within the Powers of the same as defined by this Act, or to the next Sessions of the Legislatures of Ontario and Quebec respectively if the Subject Matter of the Act is within the Powers of the same as defined by this Act.

As to Errors in Names

138. From and after the Union the Use of the Words "Upper Canada" instead of "Ontario," or "Lower Canada" instead of "Quebec," in any Deed, Writ, Process, Pleading, Document, Matter, or Thing shall not invalidate the same.

As to issue of Proclamations before Union, to commence after Union

139. Any Proclamation under the Great Seal of the Province of Canada issued before the Union to take effect at a Time which is subsequent to the Union, whether relating to that Province, or to Upper Canada, or to Lower Canada, and the several Matters and Things therein proclaimed, shall be and continue of like Force and Effect as if the Union had not been made. [69]

As to issue of Proclamations after Union

140. Any Proclamation which is authorized by any Act of the Legislature of the Province of Canada to be issued under the Great Seal of the Province of Canada, whether relating to that Province, or to Upper Canada, or to Lower Canada, and which is not issued before the Union, may be issued by the Lieutenant Governor of Ontario or of Quebec, as its Subject Matter requires, under the Great Seal thereof; and from and after the Issue of such Proclamation the same and the several Matters and Things therein proclaimed shall be and continue of the like Force and Effect in Ontario or Quebec as if the Union had not been made. [70]

Penitentiary

141. The Penitentiary of the Province of Canada shall, until the Parliament of Canada otherwise provides, be and continue the Penitentiary of Ontario and of Quebec. [71]

Arbitration respecting Debts, etc.

142. The Division and Adjustment of the Debts, Credits, Liabilities, Properties, and Assets of Upper Canada and Lower Canada shall be referred to the Arbitrament of Three Arbitrators, One chosen by the Government of Ontario, One by the Government of Quebec, and One by the Government of Canada; and the Selection of the Arbitrators shall not be made until the Parliament of Canada and the Legislatures of Ontario and Quebec have met; and the Arbitrator chosen by the Government of Canada shall not be a Resident either in Ontario or in Quebec. [72]

Division of Records

143. The Governor General in Council may from Time to Time order that such and so many of the Records, Books, and Documents of the Province of Canada as he thinks fit shall be appropriated and delivered either to Ontario or to Quebec, and the same shall thenceforth be the Property of that Province; and any Copy thereof or Extract therefrom, duly certified by the Officer having charge of the Original thereof, shall be admitted as Evidence. [73]

Constitution of Townships in Quebec

144. The Lieutenant Governor of Quebec may from Time to Time, by Proclamation under the Great Seal of the Province, to take effect from a Day to be appointed therein, constitute Townships in those Parts of the Province of Quebec in which Townships are not then already constituted, and fix the Metes and Bounds thereof.

X.   INTERCOLONIAL RAILWAY

[Repealed]

145. Repealed. [74]

XI.   ADMISSION OF OTHER COLONIES

Power to admit Newfoundland, etc., into the Union

146. It shall be lawful for the Queen, by and with the Advice of Her Majesty's Most Honourable Privy Council, on Addresses from the Houses of the Parliament of Canada, and from the Houses of the respective Legislatures of the Colonies or Provinces of Newfoundland, Prince Edward Island, and British Columbia, to admit those Colonies or Provinces, or any of them, into the Union, and on Address from the Houses of the Parliament of Canada to admit Rupert's Land and the North-western Territory, or either of them, into the Union, on such Terms and Conditions in each Case as are in the Addresses expressed and as the Queen thinks fit to approve, subject to the Provisions of this Act; and the Provisions of any Order in Council in that Behalf shall have effect as if they had been enacted by the Parliament of the United Kingdom of Great Britain and Ireland. [75]

As to Representation of Newfoundland and Prince Edward Island in Senate

147. In case of the Admission of Newfoundland and Prince Edward Island, or either of them, each shall be entitled to a Representation in the Senate of Canada of Four Members, and (notwithstanding anything in this Act) in case of the Admission of Newfoundland the normal Number of Senators shall be Seventy-six and their maximum Number shall be Eighty-two; but Prince Edward Island when admitted shall be deemed to be comprised in the third of the Three Divisions into which Canada is, in relation to the Constitution of the Senate, divided by this Act, and accordingly, after the Admission of Prince Edward Island, whether Newfoundland is admitted or not, the Representation of Nova Scotia and New Brunswick in the Senate shall, as Vacancies occur, be reduced from Twelve to Ten Members respectively, and the Representation of each of those Provinces shall not be increased at any Time beyond Ten, except under the Provisions of this Act for the Appointment of Three or Six additional Senators under the Direction of the Queen. [76]

ENDNOTES TO APPENDIX A

(1) The enacting clause was repealed by the *Statute Law Revision Act, 1893*, 56-57 Vict., c. 14 (U.K.). It read as follows:

Be it therefore enacted and declared by the Queen's most Excellent Majesty, by and with the Advice and Consent of the Lords Spiritual and Temporal, and Commons, in this present Parliament assembled, and by the Authority of the same, as follows:

(2) As enacted by the *Constitution Act, 1982*, which came into force on April 17, 1982. The section, as originally enacted, read as follows:

1. This Act may be cited as The British North America Act, 1867.

(3) Section 2, repealed by the *Statute Law Revision Act, 1893*, 56-57 Vict., c. 14 (U.K.), read as follows:

2. The Provisions of this Act referring to Her Majesty the Queen extend also to the Heirs and Successors of Her Majesty, Kings and Queens of the United Kingdom of Great Britain and Ireland.

(4) **The first day of July, 1867, was fixed by proclamation dated May 22, 1867.**

(5) **Partially repealed by the *Statute Law Revision Act, 1893*, 56-57 Vict., c. 14 (U.K.). As originally enacted the section read as follows:**

4. The subsequent Provisions of this Act shall, unless it is otherwise expressed or implied, commence and have effect on and after the Union, that is to say, on

and after the Day appointed for the Union taking effect in the Queen's Proclamation; and in the same Provisions, unless it is otherwise expressed or implied, the Name Canada shall be taken to mean Canada as constituted under this Act.

(6) Canada now consists of ten provinces (Ontario, Quebec, Nova Scotia, New Brunswick, Manitoba, British Columbia, Prince Edward Island, Alberta, Saskatchewan and Newfoundland) and two territories (the Yukon Territory and the Northwest Territories).

The first territories added to the Union were Rupert's Land and the North-Western Territory, (subsequently designated the Northwest Territories), which were admitted pursuant to section 146 of the *Constitution Act, 1867* and the *Rupert's Land Act, 1868*, 31-32 Vict., c. 105 (U.K.), by the *Rupert's Land and North-Western Territory Order* of June 23, 1870, effective July 15, 1870. Prior to the admission of those territories the Parliament of Canada enacted *An Act for the temporary Government of Rupert's Land and the North-Western Territory when united with Canada* (32-33 Vict., c. 3), and the *Manitoba Act, 1870*, (33 Vict., c. 3), which provided for the formation of the Province of Manitoba.

British Columbia was admitted into the Union pursuant to section 146 of the *Constitution Act, 1867*, by the *British Columbia Terms of Union*, being Order in Council of May 16, 1871, effective July 20, 1871.

Prince Edward Island was admitted pursuant to section 146 of the *Constitution Act, 1867*, by the *Prince Edward Island Terms of Union*, being Order in Council of June 26, 1873, effective July 1, 1873.

On June 29, 1871, the United Kingdom Parliament enacted the *Constitution Act, 1871* (34-35 Vict., c. 28) authorizing the creation of additional provinces out of territories not included in any province. Pursuant to this statute, the Parliament of Canada enacted the *Alberta Act*, (July 20, 1905, 4-5 Edw. VII, c. 3) and the *Saskatchewan Act*, (July 20, 1905, 4-5 Edw. VII, c. 42), providing for the creation of the provinces of Alberta and Saskatchewan, respectively. Both these Acts came into force on Sept. 1, 1905.

Meanwhile, all remaining British possessions and territories in North America and the islands adjacent thereto, except the colony of Newfoundland and its dependencies, were admitted into the Canadian Confederation by the *Adjacent Territories Order*, dated July 31, 1880.

The Parliament of Canada added portions of the Northwest Territories to the adjoining provinces in 1912 by *The Ontario Boundaries Extension Act*, S.C. 1912, 2 Geo. V, c. 40, *The Quebec Boundaries Extension Act*, 1912, 2 Geo. V, c. 45 and *The Manitoba Boundaries Extension Act, 1912*, 2 Geo. V, c. 32, and further

additions were made to Manitoba by *The Manitoba Boundaries Extension Act, 1930*, 20-21 Geo. V, c. 28.

The Yukon Territory was created out of the Northwest Territories in 1898 by *The Yukon Territory Act*, 61 Vict., c. 6, (Canada).

Newfoundland was added on March 31, 1949, by the *Newfoundland Act*, (U.K.), 12-13 Geo. VI, c. 22, which ratified the Terms of Union of Newfoundland with Canada.

Nunavut was created out of the Northwest Territories in 1999 by the *Nunavut Act*, S.C. 1993, c. 28.

(7) See the note to section 129, *infra*.

(8) Repealed and re-enacted by the *Parliament of Canada Act, 1875*, 38-39 Vict., c. 38 (U.K.). The original section read as follows:

> 18. The Privileges, Immunities, and Powers to be held, enjoyed, and exercised by the Senate and by the House of Commons and by the Members thereof respectively shall be such as are from Time to Time defined by Act of the Parliament of Canada, but so that the same shall never exceed those at the passing of this Act held, enjoyed, and exercised by the Commons House of Parliament of the United Kingdom of Great Britain and Ireland and by the Members thereof.

(9) Spent. The first session of the first Parliament began on November 6, 1867.

(10) Section 20, repealed by the *Constitution Act, 1982*, read as follows:

> 20. There shall be a Session of the Parliament of Canada once at least in every Year, so that Twelve Months shall not intervene between the last Sitting of the Parliament in one Session and its first sitting in the next Session.

Section 20 has been replaced by section 5 of the *Constitution Act, 1982*, which provides that there shall be a sitting of Parliament at least once every twelve months.

(11) As amended by the *Constitution Act, 1915*, 5-6 Geo. V, c. 45 (U.K.) and modified by the *Newfoundland Act*, 12-13 Geo. VI, c. 22 (U.K.), the *Constitution Act (No. 2), 1975*, S.C. 1974-75-76, c. 53, and the *Constitution Act, 1999 (Nunavut)*, S.C. 1998, c. 15, Part 2.

The original section read as follows:

> 21. The Senate shall, subject to the Provisions of this Act, consist of Seventy-two Members, who shall be styled Senators.

The *Manitoba Act, 1870*, added two for Manitoba; the *British Columbia Terms of Union* added three; upon admission of Prince Edward Island four more were provided by section 147 of the *Constitution Act, 1867*; the *Alberta Act* and the *Saskatchewan Act* each added four. The Senate was reconstituted at 96 by the *Constitution Act, 1915*. Six more Senators were added upon union with Newfoundland, and one Senator each was added for the Yukon Territory and the Northwest Territories by the *Constitution Act (No. 2), 1975.* One Senator was added for Nunavut by the *Constitution Act 1999 (Nunavut).*

(12) As amended by the *Constitution Act, 1915,* 5-6 Geo. V, c. 45 (U.K.), the *Newfoundland Act,* 12-13 Geo. VI, c. 22 (U.K.), and the *Constitution Act (No. 2), 1975,* S.C. 1974-75-76, c. 53. The original section read as follows:

> 22. In relation to the Constitution of the Senate, Canada shall be deemed to consist of Three Divisions:
>
> 1. Ontario;
> 2. Quebec;
> 3. The Maritime Provinces, Nova Scotia and New Brunswick;
>
> which Three Divisions shall (subject to the Provisions of this Act) be equally represented in the Senate as follows: Ontario by Twenty-four Senators; Quebec by Twenty-four Senators; and the Maritime Provinces by Twenty-four Senators, Twelve thereof representing Nova Scotia, and Twelve thereof representing New Brunswick.
>
> In the case of Quebec each of the Twenty-four Senators representing that Province shall be appointed for One of the Twenty-four Electoral Divisions of Lower Canada specified in Schedule A. to Chapter One of the Consolidated Statutes of Canada.

(13) Section 44 of the *Constitution Act,* 1999 *(Nunavut),* S.C. 1998, c. 15, Part 2, provided that, for the purposes of that Part, (which added one Senator for Nunavut) the word "Province" in section 23 of the *Constitution Act, 1867,* has the same meaning as is assigned to the word "province" by section 35 of the *Interpretation Act,* R.S.C. 1985, c. I-21, which provides that the term "province" means "a province of Canada, and includes the Yukon Territory, the Northwest Territories and Nunavut."   Section 2 of the *Constitution Act (No. 2),* 1975, S.C. 1974-75-76, c. 53 provided that for the purposes of that Act (which added one Senator each for the Yukon Territory and the Northwest Territories) the term "Province" in section 23 of the *Constitution Act, 1867,* has the same meaning as is assigned to the term "province" by section 28 of the *Interpretation Act,* R.S.C. 1970, c. I-23, which provides that the term "province" means "a province of Canada, and includes the Yukon Territory and the Northwest Territories."

(14) Repealed by the *Statute Law Revision Act, 1893,* 56-57 Vict., c. 14 (U.K.). The section read as follows:

> 25. Such Persons shall be first summoned to the Senate as the Queen by Warrant under Her Majesty's Royal Sign Manual thinks fit to approve, and their Names shall be inserted in the Queen's Proclamation of Union.

(15) As amended by the *Constitution Act, 1915,* 5-6 Geo. V, c. 45 (U.K.). The original section read as follows:

> 26. If at any Time on the Recommendation of the Governor General the Queen thinks fit to direct that Three or Six Members be added to the Senate, the Governor General may by Summons to Three or Six qualified Persons (as the Case may be), representing equally the Three Divisions of Canada, add to the Senate accordingly.

(16) As amended by the *Constitution Act, 1915,* 5-6 Geo. V, c. 45 (U.K.). The original section read as follows:

> 27. In case of such Addition being at any Time made the Governor General shall not summon any Person to the Senate except on a further like Direction by the Queen on the like Recommendation, until each of the Three Divisions of Canada is represented by Twenty-four Senators and no more.

(17) As amended by the *Constitution Act, 1915,* 5-6 Geo. V, c. 45 (U.K.), the *Constitution Act (No. 2), 1975,* S.C. 1974-75-76, c. 53, and the *Constitution Act 1999 (Nunavut),* S.C. 1998, c. 15, Part 2. The original section read as follows:

> 28. The Number of Senators shall not at any Time exceed Seventy-eight.

(18) As enacted by the *Constitution Act, 1965,* S.C., 1965, c. 4, which came into force on June 1, 1965. The original section read as follows:

> 29. A Senator shall, subject to the Provisions of this Act, hold his Place in the Senate for Life.

(19) Provision for exercising the functions of Speaker during his absence is made by Part II of the *Parliament of Canada Act,* R.S.C. 1985, c. P-1 (formerly the *Speaker of the Senate Act,* R.S.C. 1970, c. S-14). Doubts as to the power of Parliament to enact the *Speaker of the Senate Act* were removed by the *Canadian Speaker (Appointment of Deputy) Act,* 1895, 2nd Sess., 59 Vict., c. 3 (U.K.), which was repealed by the *Constitution Act, 1982.*

(20) The figures given here result from the application of section 51, as enacted by the *Constitution Act, 1985 (Representation)* , S.C., 1986, c. 8, Part I, and readjusted pursuant to the *Electoral Boundaries Readjustment Act,* R.S.C. 1985, c. E-3. The original section (which was altered from time to time as the result of the addition of new provinces and changes in population) read as follows:

> 37. The House of Commons shall, subject to the Provisions of this Act, consist of one hundred and eighty-one members, of whom Eighty-two shall be elected for Ontario, Sixty-five for Quebec, Nineteen for Nova Scotia, and Fifteen for New Brunswick.

(21) Spent. The electoral districts are now established by Proclamations issued from time to time under the

Electoral Boundaries Readjustment Act, R.S.C. 1985, c. E-3, as amended for particular districts by Acts of Parliament, for which see the most recent Table of Public Statutes and Responsible Ministers.

(22) Spent. Elections are now provided for by the *Canada Elections Act*, R.S.C. 1985, c. E -2; controverted elections by the *Dominion Controverted Elections Act*, R.S.C. 1985, c. C-39; qualifications and disqualifications of members by the *Parliament of Canada Act*, R.S.C. 1985, c. P-1. The right of citizens to vote and hold office is provided for in section 3 of the *Constitution Act, 1982*.

(23) Repealed by the *Statute Law Revision Act, 1893*, 56-57 Vict., c. 14 (U.K.). The section read as follows:

> 42. For the First Election of Members to serve in the House of Commons the Governor General shall cause Writs to be issued by such Person, in such Form, and addressed to such Returning Officers as he thinks fit.
>
> The Person issuing Writs under this Section shall have the like Powers as are possessed at the Union by the Officers charged with the issuing of Writs for the Election of Members to serve in the respective House of Assembly or Legislative Assembly of the Province of Canada, Nova Scotia, or New Brunswick; and the Returning Officers to whom Writs are directed under this Section shall have the like Powers as are possessed at the Union by the Officers charged with the returning of Writs for the Election of Members to serve in the same respective House of Assembly or Legislative Assembly.

(24) Repealed by the *Statute Law Revision Act, 1893*, 56-57 Vict., c. 14 (U.K.). The section read as follows:

> 43. In case a Vacancy in the Representation in the House of Commons of any Electoral District happens before the Meeting of the Parliament, or after the Meeting of the Parliament before Provision is made by the Parliament in this Behalf, the Provisions of the last foregoing Section of this Act shall extend and apply to the issuing and returning of a Writ in respect of such Vacant District.

(25) Provision for exercising the functions of Speaker during his absence is now made by Part III of the *Parliament of Canada Act*, R.S.C. 1985, c. P-1.

(26) The term of the twelfth Parliament was extended by the *British North America Act, 1916*, 6-7 Geo. V., c. 19 (U.K.), which Act was repealed by the *Statute Law Revision Act, 1927*, 17-18 Geo. V, c. 42 (U.K.). See also subsection 4(1) of the *Constitution Act, 1982*, which provides that no House of Commons shall continue for longer than five years from the date fixed for the return of the writs at a general election of its members, and subsection 4(2) thereof, which provides for continuation of the House of Commons in special circumstances.

(27) As enacted by the *Constitution Act, 1985 (Representation)*, S.C. 1986, c. 8, Part I, which came into force on March 6, 1986 (See SI86-49). The section, as originally enacted, read as follows:

> 51. On the Completion of the Census in the Year One Thousand eight hundred and seventy-one, and of each subsequent decennial Census, the Representation of the Four Provinces shall be readjusted by such Authority, in such Manner, and from such Time, as the Parliament of Canada from Time to Time provides, subject and according to the following Rules:
>
> (1) Quebec shall have the fixed Number of Sixty-five Members:
> (2) There shall be assigned to each of the other Provinces such a Number of Members as will bear the same Proportion to the Number of its Population (ascertained at such Census) as the Number Sixty-five bears to the Number of the Population of Quebec (so ascertained):
> (3) In the Computation of the Number of Members for a Province a fractional Part not exceeding One Half of the whole Number requisite for entitling the Province to a Member shall be disregarded; but a fractional Part exceeding One Half of that Number shall be equivalent to the whole Number:
> (4) On any such Re-adjustment the Number of Members for a Province shall not be reduced unless the Proportion which the Number of the Population of the Province bore to the Number of the aggregate Population of Canada at the then last preceding Re-adjustment of the Number of Members for the Province is ascertained at the then latest Census to be diminished by One Twentieth Part or upwards:
> (5) Such Re-adjustment shall not take effect until the Termination of the then existing Parliament.

The section was amended by the *Statute Law Revision Act, 1893*, 56-57 Vict., c. 14 (U.K.) by repealing the words from "of the census" to "seventy-one and" and the word "subsequent".

By the *British North America Act, 1943*, 6-7 Geo. VI, c. 30 (U.K.), which Act was repealed by the *Constitution Act, 1982*, redistribution of seats following the 1941 census was postponed until the first session of Parliament after the war. The section was re-enacted by the *British North America Act, 1946*, 9-10 Geo. VI, c. 63 (U.K.), which Act was also repealed by the *Constitution Act, 1982*, to read as follows:

> 51. (1) The number of members of the House of Commons shall be two hundred and fifty-five and the representation of the provinces therein shall forthwith

upon the coming into force of this section and there-after on the completion of each decennial census be readjusted by such authority, in such manner, and from such time as the Parliament of Canada from time to time provides, subject and according to the following rules:

(1) Subject as hereinafter provided, there shall be assigned to each of the provinces a number of members computed by dividing the total population of the provinces by two hundred and fifty-four and by dividing the population of each province by the quotient so obtained, disregarding, except as here-inafter in this section provided, the remainder, if any, after the said process of division.

(2) If the total number of members assigned to all the provinces pursuant to rule one is less than two hundred and fifty-four, additional members shall be assigned to the provinces (one to a province) having remainders in the computation under rule one commencing with the province having the largest remainder and continuing with the other provinces in the order of the magnitude of their respective remainders until the total number of members assigned is two hundred and fifty-four.

(3) Notwithstanding anything in this section, if upon completion of a computation under rules one and two, the number of members to be assigned to a province is less than the number of senators representing the said province, rules one and two shall cease to apply in respect of the said province, and there shall be assigned to the said province a number of members equal to the said number of senators.

(4) In the event that rules one and two cease to apply in respect of a province then, for the purpose of computing the number of members to be assigned to the provinces in respect of which rules one and two continue to apply, the total population of the provinces shall be reduced by the number of the population of the province in respect of which rules one and two have ceased to apply and the number two hundred and fifty-four shall be reduced by the number of members assigned to such province pursuant to rule three.

(5) Such readjustment shall not take effect until the termination of the then existing Parliament.

(2) The Yukon Territory as constituted by Chapter forty-one of the Statutes of Canada, 1901, together with any Part of Canada not comprised within a province which may from time to time be included therein by the Parliament of Canada for the purposes of represen-tation in Parliament, shall be entitled to one member.

The section was re-enacted by the *British North America Act, 1952*, S.C. 1952, c. 15, which Act was also repealed by the *Constitution Act, 1982*, as follows:

51. (1) Subject as hereinafter provided, the number of members of the House of Commons shall be two hundred and sixty-three and the representation of the provinces therein shall forthwith upon the coming into force of this section and thereafter on the completion of each decennial census be readjusted by such authority, in such manner, and from such time as the Parliament of Canada from time to time provides, subject and according to the following rules:

1. There shall be assigned to each of the provinces a number of members computed by dividing the total population of the provinces by two hundred and sixty-one and by dividing the population of each province by the quotient so obtained, disre-garding, except as hereinafter in this section provided, the remainder, if any, after the said process of division.

2. If the total number of members assigned to all the provinces pursuant to rule one is less than two hundred and sixty-one, additional members shall be assigned to the provinces (one to a province) having remainders in the computation under rule one commenc-ing with the province having the largest remainder and continuing with the other provinces in the order of the magnitude of their respective remainders until the total number of members assigned is two hun-dred and sixty-one.

3. Notwithstanding anything in this section, if upon completion of a computation under rules one and two the number of members to be assigned to a province is less than the number of senators representing the said province, rules one and two shall cease to apply in respect of the said province, and there shall be assigned to the said province a number of members equal to the said number of senators.

4. In the event that rules one and two cease to apply in respect of a province then, for the purposes of computing the number of mem-bers to be assigned to the provinces in respect of which rules one and two continue to apply, the total population of the provinces shall be reduced by the number of the population of the province in respect of which rules one and two have ceased to apply and the num-ber two hundred and sixty-one shall be reduced by the number of members assigned

to such province pursuant to rule three.

5. On any such readjustment the number of members for any province shall not be reduced by more than fifteen per cent below the representation to which such province was entitled under rules one to four of the subsection at the last preceding readjustment of the representation of that province, and there shall be no reduction in the representation of any province as a result of which that province would have a smaller number of members than any other province that according to the results of the then last decennial census did not have a larger population; but for the purposes of any subsequent readjustment of representation under this section any increase in the number of members of the House of Commons resulting from the application of this rule shall not be included in the divisor mentioned in rules one to four of this subsection.

6. Such readjustment shall not take effect until the termination of the then existing Parliament.

(2) The Yukon Territory as constituted by chapter forty-one of the statutes of Canada, 1901, shall be entitled to one member, and such other part of Canada not comprised within a province as may from time to time be defined by the Parliament of Canada shall be entitled to one member.

Subsection 51(1) was re-enacted by the *Constitution Act, 1974*, S.C. 1974-75-76, c. 13 to read as follows:

51. (1) The number of members of the House of Commons and the representation of the provinces therein shall upon the coming into force of this subsection and thereafter on the completion of each decennial census be readjusted by such authority, in such manner, and from such time as the Parliament of Canada from time to time provides, subject and according to the following Rules:

1. There shall be assigned to Quebec seventy-five members in the readjustment following the completion of the decennial census taken in the year 1971, and thereafter four additional members in each subsequent readjustment.

2. Subject to Rules 5(2) and (3), there shall be assigned to a large province a number of members equal to the number obtained by dividing the population of the large province by the electoral quotient of Quebec.

3. Subject to Rules 5(2) and (3), there shall be assigned to a small province a number of members equal to the number obtained by dividing

(a) the sum of the populations, determined according to the results of the penultimate decennial census, of the provinces (other than Quebec) having populations of less than one and a half million, determined according to the results of that census, by the sum of the numbers of members assigned to those provinces in the readjustment following the completion of that census; and

(b) the population of the small province by the quotient obtained under paragraph (a).

4. Subject to Rules 5(1)(a), (2) and (3), there shall be assigned to an intermediate province a number of members equal to the number obtained

(a) by dividing the sum of the populations of the provinces (other than Quebec) having populations of less than one and a half million by the sum of the number of members assigned to those provinces under any of Rules 3, 5(1)(b), (2) and (3);

(b) by dividing the population of the intermediate province by the quotient obtained under paragraph (a); and

(c) by adding to the number of members assigned to the intermediate province in the readjustment following the completion of the penultimate decennial census one-half of the difference resulting from the subtraction of that number from the quotient obtained under paragraph (b).

5. (1) On any readjustment,

(a) if no province (other than Quebec) has a population of less than one and a half million, Rule 4 shall not be applied and, subject to Rules 5(2) and (3), there shall be assigned to an intermediate province a number of members equal to the number obtained by dividing

(i) the sum of the populations, determined according to the results of the penultimate decennial census, of the provinces, (other than Quebec) having populations of not less than one and a half million and not more than two and a half million, determined according to the results of that census, by the sum of the numbers of members assigned to those provinces in the readjustment following the completion of that census, and

    (ii)   the population of the intermediate province by the quotient obtained under subparagraph (i);

  (b)   if a province (other than Quebec) having a population of

    (i)   less than one and a half million, or

    (ii)   not less than one and a half million and not more than two and a half million

does not have a population greater than its population determined according to the results of the penultimate decennial census, it shall, subject to Rules 5(2) and (3), be assigned the number of members assigned to it in the readjustment following the completion of that census.

(2) On any readjustment,

  (a)   if, under any of Rules 2 to 5(1), the number of members to be assigned to a province (in this paragraph referred to as "the first province") is smaller than the number of members to be assigned to any other province not having a population greater than that of the first province, those Rules shall not be applied to the first province and it shall be assigned a number of members equal to the largest number of members to be assigned to any other province not having a population greater than that of the first province;

  (b)   if, under any of Rules 2 to 5(1)(a), the number of members to be assigned to a province is smaller than the number of members assigned to it in the readjustment following the completion of the penultimate decennial census, those Rules shall not be applied to it and it shall be assigned the latter number of members;

  (c)   if both paragraphs (a) and (b) apply to a province, it shall be assigned a number of members equal to the greater of the numbers produced under those paragraphs.

(3) On any readjustment,

  (a)   if the electoral quotient of a province (in this paragraph referred to as "the first province") obtained by dividing its population by the number of members to be assigned to it under any of Rules 2 to 5(2) is greater than the electoral quotient of Quebec, those Rules shall not be applied to the first province and it shall be assigned a number of members equal to the number obtained by dividing its population by the electoral quotient of Quebec;

  (b)   if, as a result of the application of Rule 6(2)(a), the number of members assigned to a province under paragraph (a) equals the number of members to be assigned to it under any of Rules 2 to 5(2), it shall be assigned that number of members and paragraph (a) shall cease to apply to that province.

6. (1) In these Rules,

"electoral quotient" means, in respect of a province, the quotient obtained by dividing its population, determined according to the results of the then most recent decennial census, by the number of members to be assigned to it under any of Rules 1 to 5(3) in the readjustment following the completion of that census;

"intermediate province" means a province (other than Quebec) having a population greater than its population determined according to the results of the penultimate decennial census but not more than two and a half million and not less than one and a half million;

"large province" means a province (other than Quebec) having a population greater than two and a half million;

"penultimate decennial census" means the decennial census that preceded the then most recent decennial census;

"population" means, except where otherwise specified, the population determined according to the results of the then most recent decennial census;

"small province" means a province (other than Quebec) having a population greater than its population determined according to the results of the penultimate decennial census and less than one and a half million.

(2) For the purposes of these Rules,

  (a)   if any fraction less than one remains upon completion of the final calculation that produces the number of members to be assigned to a province, that number of members shall equal the number so produced disregarding the fraction;

  (b)   if more than one readjustment follows the completion of a decennial census, the most recent of those readjustments shall, upon taking effect, be deemed to be the only readjustment following the completion of that census;

(c)   a readjustment shall not take effect until the termination of the then existing Parliament.

(28)   As enacted by the *Constitution Act, 1999 (Nunavut)* , S.C. 1998, c.15, Part 2. Subsection 51(2) was previously amended by the *Constitution Act (No. 1), 1975*, S.C. 1974-75-76, c. 28, and read as follows:

> (2) The Yukon Territory as bounded as described in the schedule to chapter Y-2 of the Revised Statutes of Canada, 1970, shall be entitled to one member, and the Northwest Territories as bounded and described in section 2 of chapter N-22 of the Revised Statutes of Canada, 1970, shall be entitled to two members.

(29)   As enacted by the *Constitution Act, 1915*, 5-6 Geo. V, c. 45 (U.K.)

(30)   Provided for by the *Salaries Act*, R.S.C. 1985, c. S-3.

(31)   Now provided for in Ontario by the *Executive Council Act*, R.S.O. 1990, c. E.25, and in Quebec by the *Executive Power Act*, R.S.Q. 1977, c. E-18.

(32)   A similar provision was included in each of the instruments admitting British Columbia, Prince Edward Island, and Newfoundland. The Executive Authorities for Manitoba, Alberta and Saskatchewan were established by the statutes creating those provinces. See the notes to section 5, *supra*.

(33)   See the notes to section 129, *infra*.

(34)   Spent. Now covered by the *Representation Act*, R.S.O. 1990, c. R.26.

(35)   The Act respecting the Legislative Council of Quebec, S.Q. 1968, c. 9, provided that the Legislature for Quebec shall consist of the Lieutenant Governor and the National Assembly of Quebec, and repealed the provisions of the *Legislature Act*, R.S.Q. 1964, c. 6, relating to the Legislative Council of Quebec. Now covered by the *Legislature Act*, R.S.Q. 1977, c. L-1. Sections 72 to 79 following are therefore completely spent.

(36)   The Act respecting electoral districts, S.Q. 1970, c. 7, s. 1, provides that this section no longer has effect.

(37)   Repealed by the *Statute Law Revision Act, 1893*, 56-57 Vict. c. 14 (U.K.). The section read as follows:

> 81. The Legislatures of Ontario and Quebec respectively shall be called together not later than Six Months after the Union.

(38)   Probably spent. The subject-matter of this section is now covered in Ontario by the *Legislative Assembly Act*, R.S.O. 1990, c. L.10, and in Quebec by the *National Assembly Act*, R.S.Q. c. A-23.1.

(39)   Probably spent. The subject-matter of this section is now covered in Ontario by the *Election Act*, R.S.O. 1990, c. E.6, and the *Legislative Assembly Act*, R.S.O. 1990, c. L.10, in Quebec by the *Elections Act*, R.S.Q.

c. E-3.3 and the *National Assembly Act*, R.S.Q. c. A-23.1.

(40)   The maximum duration of the Legislative Assemblies of Ontario and Quebec has been changed to five years. See the *Legislative Assembly Act*, R.S.O. 1990, c. L.10, and the *National Assembly Act*, R.S.Q. c. A-23.1, respectively. See also section 4 of the *Constitution Act, 1982*, which provides a maximum duration for a legislative assembly of five years but also authorizes continuation in special circumstances.

(41)   See also section 5 of the *Constitution Act, 1982*, which provides that there shall be a sitting of each legislature at least once every twelve months.

(42)   Partially repealed by the *Statute Law Revision Act, 1893*, 56-57 Vict., c. 14 (U.K.), which deleted the following concluding words of the original enactment:

> and the House of Assembly of New Brunswick existing at the passing of this Act shall, unless sooner dissolved, continue for the Period for which it was elected.

A similar provision was included in each of the instruments admitting British Columbia, Prince Edward Island and Newfoundland. The Legislatures of Manitoba, Alberta and Saskatchewan were established by the statutes creating those provinces. See the footnotes to section 5, *supra*.

See also sections 3 to 5 of the *Constitution Act, 1982*, which prescribe democratic rights applicable to all provinces, and subitem 2(2) of the Schedule to that Act, which sets out the repeal of section 20 of the *Manitoba Act, 1870*. Section 20 of the *Manitoba Act, 1870* has been replaced by section 5 of the *Constitution Act, 1982*.

Section 20 reads as follows:

> 20. There shall be a Session of the Legislature once at least in every year, so that twelve months shall not intervene between the last sitting of the Legislature in one Session and its first sitting in the next Session.

(43)   Repealed by the *Statute Law Revision Act, 1893*, 56-57 Vict. c. 14 (U.K.). The section read as follows:

> 5. Ontario, Quebec, and Nova Scotia.
>
> 89. Each of the Lieutenant Governors of Ontario, Quebec and Nova Scotia shall cause Writs to be issued for the First Election of Members of the Legislative Assembly thereof in such Form and by such Person as he thinks fit, and at such Time and addressed to such Returning Officer as the Governor General directs, and so that the First Election of Member of Assembly for any Electoral District or any Subdivision thereof shall be held at the same Time and at the same Places as the Election for a Member to serve in the House of Commons of Canada for that Electoral District.

(44) Class I was added by the *British North America (No. 2) Act, 1949*, 13 Geo. VI, c. 81 (U.K.). That Act and class I were repealed by the *Constitution Act, 1982*. The matters referred to in class I are provided for in subsection 4(2) and Part V of the *Constitution Act, 1982*. As enacted, class I read as follows:

1. The amendment from time to time of the Constitution of Canada, except as regards matters coming within the classes of subjects by this Act assigned exclusively to the Legislatures of the provinces, or as regards rights or privileges by this or any other Constitutional Act granted or secured to the Legislature or the Government of a province, or to any class of persons with respect to schools or as regards the use of the English or the French language or as regards the requirements that there shall be a session of the Parliament of Canada at least once each year, and that no House of Commons shall continue for more than five years from the day of the return of the Writs for choosing the House: provided, however, that a House of Commons may in time of real or apprehended war, invasion or insurrection be continued by the Parliament of Canada if such continuation is not opposed by the votes of more than one-third of the members of such House.

(45) Re-numbered by the *British North America (No. 2) Act, 1949.*

(46) Added by the *Constitution Act, 1940*, 3-4 Geo. VI, c. 36 (U.K.).

(47) Legislative authority has been conferred on Parliament by other Acts as follows:

1. The *Constitution Act, 1871*, 34-35 Vict., c. 28 (U.K.).

2. The Parliament of Canada may from time to time establish new Provinces in any territories forming for the time being part of the Dominion of Canada, but not included in any Province thereof, and may, at the time of such establishment, make provision for the constitution and administration of any such Province, and for the passing of laws for the peace, order, and good government of such Province, and for its representation in the said Parliament.

3. The Parliament of Canada may from time to time, with the consent of the Legislature of any province of the said Dominion, increase, diminish, or otherwise alter the limits of such Province, upon such terms and conditions as may be agreed to by the said Legislature, and may, with the like consent, make provision respecting the effect and operation of any such increase or diminution or alteration of territory in relation to any Province affected thereby.

4. The Parliament of Canada may from time to time make provision for the administration, peace, order, and good government of any territory not for the time being included in any Province.

5. The following Acts passed by the said Parliament of Canada, and intituled respectively, — "An Act for the temporary government of Rupert's Land and the North Western Territory when united with Canada"; and "An Act to amend and continue the Act thirty-two and thirty-three Victoria, chapter three, and to establish and provide for the government of the Province of Manitoba", shall be and be deemed to have been valid and effectual for all purposes whatsoever from the date at which they respectively received the assent, in the Queen's name, of the Governor General of the said Dominion of Canada.

6. Except as provided by the third section of this Act, it shall not be competent for the Parliament of Canada to alter the provisions of the last-mentioned Act of the said Parliament in so far as it relates to the Province of Manitoba, or of any other Act hereafter establishing new Provinces in the said Dominion, subject always to the right of the Legislature of the Province of Manitoba to alter from time to time the provisions of any law respecting the qualification of electors and members of the Legislative Assembly, and to make laws respecting elections in the said Province.

The *Rupert's Land Act, 1868*, 31-32 Vict., c. 105 (U.K.) (repealed by the *Statute Law Revision Act, 1893*, 56-57 Vict., c. 14 (U.K.)) had previously conferred similar authority in relation to Rupert's Land and the North Western Territory upon admission of those areas.

2. The *Constitution Act, 1886*, 49-50 Vict., c. 35 (U.K.).

1. The Parliament of Canada may from time to time make provision for the representation in the Senate and House of Commons of Canada, or in either of them, of any territories which for the time being form part of the Dominion of Canada, but are not included in any province thereof.

3. The *Statute of Westminster, 1931*, 22 Geo. V, c. 4 (U.K.).

3. It is hereby declared and enacted that the Parliament of a Dominion has full power to make laws having extra-territorial operation.

4. Under section 44 of the *Constitution Act, 1982*, Parliament has exclusive authority to amend the Constitution of Canada in relation to the executive government of Canada or the Senate and House of Commons. Sections 38, 41, 42 and 43 of that Act authorize the Senate and House of Commons to give their approval to certain other constitutional amendments by resolution.

<u>(48)</u> Class I was repealed by the *Constitution Act, 1982.* As enacted, it read as follows:

> 1. The Amendment from Time to Time, notwithstanding anything in this Act, of the Constitution of the Province, except as regards the Office of Lieutenant Governor.

Section 45 of the *Constitution Act, 1982* now authorizes legislatures to make laws amending the constitution of the province. Sections 38, 41, 42 and 43 of that Act authorize legislative assemblies to give their approval by resolution to certain other amendments to the Constitution of Canada.

<u>(49)</u> Added by the *Constitution Act, 1982.*

<u>(50)</u> **An alternative was provided for Manitoba by section 22 of the *Manitoba Act, 1870,* 33 Vict., c. 3 (Canada), (confirmed by the *Constitution Act, 1871*), which reads as follows:**

> 22. In and for the Province, the said Legislature may exclusively make Laws in relation to Education, subject and according to the following provisions:
>
> > (1) Nothing in any such Law shall prejudicially affect any right or privilege with respect to Denominational Schools which any class of persons have by Law or practice in the Province at the Union:
> >
> > (2) An appeal shall lie to the Governor General in Council from any Act or decision of the Legislature of the Province, or of any Provincial Authority, affecting any right or privilege, of the Protestant or Roman Catholic minority of the Queen's subjects in relation to Education:
> >
> > (3) In case any such Provincial Law, as from time to time seems to the Governor General in Council requisite for the due execution of the provisions of this section, is not made, or in case any decision of the Governor General in Council on any appeal under this section is not duly executed by the proper Provincial Authority in that behalf, then, and in every such case, and as far only as the circumstances of each case require, the Parliament of Canada may make remedial Laws for the due execution of the provisions of this section, and of any decision of the Governor General in Council under this section.

An alternative was provided for Alberta by section 17 of the *Alberta Act,* 4-5 Edw. VII, c. 3, 1905 (Canada), which reads as follows:

> 17. Section 93 of the *Constitution Act, 1867,* shall apply to the said province, with the substitution for paragraph (1) of the said section 93 of the following paragraph:
>
> > (1) Nothing in any such law shall prejudicially affect any right or privilege with respect to separate schools which any class of persons have at the date of the passing of this Act, under the terms of chapters 29 and 30 of the Ordinances of the Northwest Territories, passed in the year 1901, or with respect to religious instruction in any public or separate school as provided for in the said ordinances.
>
> 2. In the appropriation by the Legislature or distribution by the Government of the province of any moneys for the support of schools organized and carried on in accordance with the said chapter 29 or any Act passed in amendment thereof, or in substitution therefor, there shall be no discrimination against schools of any class described in the said chapter 29.
>
> 3. Where the expression "by law" is employed in paragraph 3 of the said section 93, it shall be held to mean the law as set out in the said chapters 29 and 30, and where the expression "at the Union" is employed, in the said paragraph 3, it shall be held to mean the date at which this Act comes into force.

An alternative was provided for Saskatchewan by section 17 of the *Saskatchewan Act,* 4-5 Edw. VII, c. 42, 1905 (Canada), which reads as follows:

> 17. Section 93 of the *Constitution Act, 1867,* shall apply to the said province, with the substitution for paragraph (1) of the said section 93, of the following paragraph:
>
> > (1) Nothing in any such law shall prejudicially affect any right or privilege with respect to separate schools which any class of persons have at the date of the passing of this Act, under the terms of chapters 29 and 30 of the Ordinances of the Northwest Territories, passed in the year 1901, or with respect to religious instruction in any public or separate school as proviced for in the said ordinances.
>
> 2. In the appropriation by the Legislature or distribution by the Government of the province of any moneys for the support of schools organized and carried on in accordance with the said chapter 29, or any Act passed in amendment thereof or in substitution therefor, there shall be no discrimination against schools of any class described in the said chapter 29.
>
> 3. Where the expression "by law" is employed in paragraph (3) of the said section 93, it shall be held to mean the law as set out in the said chapters 29 and 30; and where the expression "at the Union" is employed in the said paragraph (3), it shall be held to mean the date at which this Act comes into force.

An alternative was provided for Newfoundland by Term 17 of the Terms of Union of Newfoundland with Canada (confirmed by the *Newfoundland Act,* 12-13 Geo. VI, c. 22 (U.K.)). Term 17 of the Terms of Union of Newfoundland with Canada, set out in the penul-

timate paragraph of this footnote, was amended by the *Constitution Amendment, 1998 (Newfoundland Act)*, (see SI/98-25) and now reads as follows:

17. (1) In lieu of section ninety-three of the *Constitution Act, 1867,* this term shall apply in respect of the Province of Newfoundland.

(2) In and for the Province of Newfoundland, the Legislature shall have exclusive authority to make laws in relation to education, but shall provide for courses in religion that are not specific to a religious denomination.

(3) Religious observances shall be permitted in a school where requested by parents.

Prior to the *Constitution Amendment,* 1998 (*Newfoundland Act*), Term 17 of the Terms of Union of Newfoundland with Canada had been amended by the *Constitution Amendment,* 1997 (*Newfoundland Act*), (see SI/97-55) to read as follows:

17. In lieu of section ninety-three of the *Constitution Act, 1867,* the following shall apply in respect of the Province of Newfoundland:

In and for the Province of Newfoundland, the Legislature shall have exclusive authority to make laws in relation to education but

(a)   except as provided in paragraphs (b) and (c), schools established, maintained and operated with public funds shall be denominational schools, and any class of persons having rights under this Term as it read on January 1, 1995 shall continue to have the right to provide for religious education, activities and observances for the children of that class in those schools, and the group of classes that formed one integrated school system by agreement in 1969 may exercise the same rights under this Term as a single class of persons;

(b)   subject to provincial legislation that is uniformly applicable to all schools specifying conditions for the establishment or continued operation of schools,

(i)   any class of persons referred to in paragraph (a) shall have the right to have a publicly funded denominational school established, maintained and operated especially for that class, and

(ii)   the Legislature may approve the establishment, maintenance and operation of a publicly funded school, whether denominational or non-denominational;

(c)   where a school is established, maintained and operated pursuant to subparagraph (b) (i), the class of persons referred to in that subparagraph shall continue to have the right to provide for religious education, activities and observances and to direct the teaching of aspects of curriculum affecting religious beliefs, student admission policy and the assignment and dismissal of teachers in that school;

(d)   all schools referred to in paragraphs (a) and (b) shall receive their share of public funds in accordance with scales determined on a non-discriminatory basis from time to time by the Legislature; and

(e)   if the classes of persons having rights under this Term so desire, they shall have the right to elect in total not less than two thirds of the members of a school board, and any class so desiring shall have the right to elect the portion of that total that is proportionate to the population of that class in the area under the board's jurisdiction.

Prior to the *Constitution Amendment, 1997 (Newfoundland Act)*, Term 17 of the Terms of Union of Newfoundland with Canada had been amended by the *Constitution Amendment, 1987 (Newfoundland Act)*, (see SI/88-11) to read as follows:

17. (1) In lieu of section ninety-three of the *Constitution Act, 1867,* the following term shall apply in respect of the Province of Newfoundland:

In and for the Province of Newfoundland the Legislature shall have exclusive authority to make laws in relation to education, but the Legislature will not have authority to make laws prejudicially affecting any right or privilege with respect to denominational schools, common (amalgamated) schools, or denominational colleges, that any class or classes of persons have by law in Newfoundland at the date of Union, and out of public funds of the Province of Newfoundland, provided for education,

(a)   all such schools shall receive their share of such funds in accordance with scales determined on a non-discriminatory basis from time to time by the Legislature for all schools then being conducted under authority of the Legislature; and

(b)   all such colleges shall receive their share of any grant from time to time voted for all colleges then being conducted under authority of the Legislature, such grant being distributed on a non-discriminatory basis.

(2) For the purposes of paragraph one of this Term, the Pentecostal Assemblies of Newfoundland have in Newfoundland all the same rights and privileges with respect to denominational schools and denominational colleges as any other class or classes of persons had by law in Newfoundland at the date of Union, and the words "all such schools" in paragraph (a) of paragraph one of this Term and the words "all such colleges" in paragraph (b) of paragraph one of this Term include, respectively, the schools and the colleges of the Pentecostal Assemblies of Newfoundland.

Term 17 of the Terms of Union of Newfoundland with Canada (confirmed by the *Newfoundland Act*, 12-13 Geo. VI, c. 22 (U.K.)), which Term provided an alternative for Newfoundland, originally read as follows:

17. In lieu of section ninety-three of the *Constitution Act, 1867*, the following term shall apply in respect of the Province of Newfoundland:

In and for the Province of Newfoundland the Legislature shall have exclusive authority to make laws in relation to education, but the Legislature will not have authority to make laws prejudicially affecting any right or privilege with respect to denominational schools, common (amalgamated) schools, or denominational colleges, that any class or classes of persons have by law in Newfoundland at the date of Union, and out of public funds of the Province of Newfoundland, provided for education,

(a) all such schools shall receive their share of such funds in accordance with scales determined on a non-discriminatory basis from time to time by the Legislature for all schools then being conducted under authority of the Legislature; and

(b) all such colleges shall receive their share of any grant from time to time voted for all colleges then being conducted under authority of the Legislature, such grant being distributed on a non-discriminatory basis.

See also sections 23, 29 and 59 of the *Constitution Act, 1982*. Section 23 provides for new minority language educational rights and section 59 permits a delay in respect of the coming into force in Quebec of one aspect of those rights. Section 29 provides that nothing in the *Canadian Charter of Rights and Freedoms* abrogates or derogates from any rights or privileges guaranteed by or under the Constitution of Canada in respect of denominational, separate or dissentient schools.

(50.1) Added by the *Constitution Amendment, 1997 (Quebec)*. See SI/97-141.

(51) Added by the *Constitution Act, 1964*, 12-13 Eliz. II, c. 73 (U.K.). As originally enacted by the *British North America Act, 1951*, 14-15 Geo. VI, c. 32 (U.K.), which was repealed by the *Constitution Act, 1982*, section 94A read as follows:

94A. It is hereby declared that the Parliament of Canada may from time to time make laws in relation to old age pensions in Canada, but no law made by the Parliament of Canada in relation to old age pensions shall affect the operation of any law present or future of a Provincial Legislature in relation to old age pensions.

(52) Repealed and re-enacted by the *Constitution Act, 1960*, 9 Eliz. II, c. 2 (U.K.), which came into force on March 1, 1961. The original section read as follows:

99. The Judges of the Superior Courts shall hold Office during good Behaviour, but shall be removable by the Governor General on Address of the Senate and House of Commons.

(53) Now provided for in the *Judges Act*, R.S.C. 1985, c. J-1.

(54) See the *Supreme Court Act*, R.S.C. 1985, c. S-26, the *Federal Court Act*, R.S.C. 1985, c. F-7 and the *Tax Court of Canada Act*, R.S.C. 1985, c. T-2.

(55) Now covered by the *Governor General's Act*, R.S.C. 1985, c. G-9.

(56) Manitoba, Alberta and Saskatchewan were placed in the same position as the original provinces by the *Constitution Act, 1930*, 20-21 Geo. V, c. 26 (U.K.).

These matters were dealt with in respect of British Columbia by the *British Columbia Terms of Union* and also in part by the *Constitution Act, 1930*.

Newfoundland was also placed in the same position by the *Newfoundland Act*, 12-13 Geo. VI, c. 22 (U.K.).

With respect to Prince Edward Island, see the Schedule to the *Prince Edward Island Terms of Union*.

(57) The obligations imposed by this section, sections 115 and 116, and similar obligations under the instruments creating or admitting other provinces, have been carried into legislation of the Parliament of Canada and are now to be found in the *Provincial Subsidies Act*, R.S.C. 1985, c. P-26.

(58) Repealed by the *Statute Law Revision Act, 1950*, 14 Geo. VI, c. 6 (U.K.). As originally enacted the section read as follows:

118. The following Sums shall be paid yearly by Canada to the several Provinces for the Support of their Governments and Legislatures:

	Dollars.
Ontario	Eighty thousand.
Quebec	Seventy thousand.
Nova Scotia	Sixty Thousand.
New Brunswick	Fifty thousand.

Two hundred and sixty thousand;

and an annual Grant in aid of each Province shall be made, equal to Eighty Cents per Head of the Population as ascertained by the Census of One thousand eight hundred and sixty-one, and in the Case of Nova Scotia and New Brunswick, by each subsequent Decennial Census until the Population of each of those two Provinces amounts to Four hundred thousand Souls, at which Rate such Grant shall thereafter remain. Such Grants shall be in full Settlement of all future Demands on Canada, and shall be paid half-yearly in advance to each Province; but the Government of Canada shall deduct from such Grants, as against any Province, all Sums chargeable as Interest on the Public Debt of that Province in excess of the several Amounts stipulated in this Act.

The section was made obsolete by the *Constitution Act, 1907,* **7 Edw. VII, c. 11 (U.K.) which provided:**

1. (1) The following grants shall be made yearly by Canada to every province, which at the commencement of this Act is a province of the Dominion, for its local purposes and the support of its Government and Legislature:

(*a*) A fixed grant

where the population of the province is under one hundred and fifty thousand, of one hundred thousand dollars;

where the population of the province is one hundred and fifty thousand, but does not exceed two hundred thousand, of one hundred and fifty thousand dollars;

where the population of the province is two hundred thousand, but does not exceed four hundred thousand, of one hundred and eighty thousand dollars;

where the population of the province is four hundred thousand, but does not exceed eight hundred thousand, of one hundred and ninety thousand dollars;

where the population of the province is eight hundred thousand, but does not exceed one million five hundred thousand, of two hundred and twenty thousand dollars;

where the population of the province exceeds one million five hundred thousand, of two hundred and forty thousand dollars; and

(*b*) Subject to the special provisions of this Act as to the provinces of British Columbia and Prince Edward Island, a grant at the rate of eighty cents per head of the population of the province up to the number of two million five hundred thousand, and at the rate of sixty cents per head of so much of the population as exceeds that number.

(2) An additional grant of one hundred thousand dollars shall be made yearly to the province of British Columbia for a period of ten years from the commencement of this Act.

(3) The population of a province shall be ascertained from time to time in the case of the provinces of Manitoba, Saskatchewan, and Alberta respectively by the last quinquennial census or statutory estimate of population made under the Acts establishing those provinces or any other Act of the Parliament of Canada making provision for the purpose, and in the case of any other province by the last decennial census for the time being.

(4) The grants payable under this Act shall be paid half-yearly in advance to each province.

(5) The grants payable under this Act shall be substituted for the grants or subsidies (in this Act referred to as existing grants) payable for the like purposes at the commencement of this Act to the several provinces of the Dominion under the provisions of section one hundred and eighteen of the *Constitution Act, 1867,* or of any Order in Council establishing a province, or of any Act of the Parliament of Canada containing directions for the payment of any such grant or subsidy, and those provisions shall cease to have effect.

(6) The Government of Canada shall have the same power of deducting sums charged against a province on account of the interest on public debt in the case of the grant payable under this Act to the province as they have in the case of the existing grant.

(7) Nothing in this Act shall affect the obligation of the Government of Canada to pay to any province any grant which is payable to that province, other than the existing grant for which the grant under this Act is substituted.

(8) In the case of the provinces of British Columbia and Prince Edward Island, the amount paid on account of the grant payable per head of the population to the provinces under this Act shall not at any time be less than the amount of the corresponding grant payable at the commencement of this Act, and if it is found on any decennial census that the population of the province has decreased since the last decennial census, the amount paid on account of the grant shall not be decreased below the amount then payable, notwithstanding the decrease of the population.

See the *Provincial Subsidies Act,* **R.S.C. 1985, c. P-26 and the** *Federal-Provincial Fiscal Arrangements and Federal Post-Secondary Education and Health Contributions Act,* **R.S.C. 1985, c. F-8.**

See also Part III of the *Constitution Act, 1982,* **which sets out commitments by Parliament and the provin-**

cial legislatures respecting equal opportunities, economic development and the provision of essential public services and a commitment by Parliament and the government of Canada to the principle of making equalization payments.

(59) Spent.

(60) Spent. Now covered by the *Customs Act*, R.S.C. 1985, c. 1 (2nd Supp.), the *Customs Tariff*, S.C. 1997, c. 36, the *Excise Act*, R.S.C. 1985, c. E-14 and the *Excise Tax Act*, R.S.C. 1985, c. E-15.

(61) Spent.

(62) These dues were repealed in 1873 by 36 Vict., c. 16 (N.B.). And see *An Act respecting the Export Duties imposed on Lumber*, etc. (1873) 36 Vict., c. 41 (Canada), and section 2 of the *Provincial Subsidies Act*, R.S.C. 1985, c. P-26.

(63) Repealed by the *Statute Law Revision Act, 1893*, 56-57 Vict., c. 14 (U.K.). The section read as follows:

127. If any Person being at the passing of this Act a Member of the Legislative Council of Canada, Nova Scotia, or New Brunswick, to whom a Place in the Senate is offered, does not within Thirty Days thereafter, by Writing under his Hand addressed to the Governor General of the Province of Canada or to the Lieutenant Governor of Nova Scotia or New Brunswick (as the Case may be), accept the same, he shall be deemed to have declined the same; and any Person who, being at the passing of this Act a Member of the Legislative Council of Nova Scotia or New Brunswick, accepts a Place in the Senate shall thereby vacate his Seat in such Legislative Council.

(64) The restriction against altering or repealing laws enacted by or existing under statutes of the United Kingdom was removed by the *Statute of Westminster, 1931*, 22 Geo. V., c. 4 (U.K.) except in respect of certain constitutional documents. Comprehensive procedures for amending enactments forming part of the Constitution of Canada were provided by Part V of the *Constitution Act, 1982*, (U.K.) 1982, c. 11.

(65) Spent.

(66) A similar provision was enacted for Manitoba by section 23 of the *Manitoba Act, 1870*, 33 Vict., c. 3 (Canada), (confirmed by the *Constitution Act, 1871*). Section 23 read as follows:

23. Either the English or the French language may be used by any person in the debates of the Houses of the Legislature, and both these languages shall be used in the respective Records and Journals of those Houses; and either of those languages may be used by any person, or in any Pleading or Process, in or issuing from any Court of Canada established under the British North America Act, 1867, or in or from

all or any of the Courts of the Province. The Acts of the Legislature shall be printed and published in both those languages.

Sections 17 to 19 of the *Constitution Act, 1982* restate the language rights set out in section 133 in respect of Parliament and the courts established under the *Constitution Act, 1867*, and also guarantees those rights in respect of the legislature of New Brunswick and the courts of that province.

Section 16 and sections 20, 21 and 23 of the *Constitution Act, 1982* recognize additional language rights in respect of the English and French languages. Section 22 preserves language rights and privileges of languages other than English and French.

(67) Spent. Now covered in Ontario by the *Executive Council Act*, R.S.O. 1990, c. E.25 and in Quebec by the *Executive Power Act*, R.S.Q. 1977, c. E-18.

(68) Probably spent.

(69) Probably spent.

(70) Probably spent.

(71) Spent. Penitentiaries are now provided for by the *Corrections and Conditional Release Act*, S.C. 1992, c. 20.

(72) Spent. See pages (xi) and (xii) of the Public Accounts, 1902-03.

(73) Probably spent. Two orders were made under this section on January 24, 1868.

(74) Repealed by the *Statute Law Revision Act, 1893*, 56-57 Vict., c. 14, (U.K.). The section read as follows:

X.   Intercolonial Railway

145. Inasmuch as the Provinces of Canada, Nova Scotia, and New Brunswick have joined in a Declaration that the Construction of the Intercolonial Railway is essential to the Consolidation of the Union of British North America, and to the Assent thereto of Nova Scotia and New Brunswick, and have consequently agreed that Provision should be made for its immediate Construction by the Government of Canada; Therefore, in order to give effect to that Agreement, it shall be the Duty of the Government and Parliament of Canada to provide for the Commencement, within Six Months after the Union, of a Railway connecting the River St. Lawrence with the City of Halifax in Nova Scotia, and for the Construction thereof without Intermission, and the Completion thereof with all practicable Speed.

(75) All territories mentioned in this section are now part of Canada. See the notes to section 5, *supra*.

(76) Spent. See the notes to sections 21, 22, 26, 27 and 28, *supra*.

THE FIRST SCHEDULE[77]

Electoral Districts of Ontario

A.   Existing Electoral Divisions

Counties

1.   Prescott.

2.   Glengarry.

3.   Stormont.

4.   Dundas.

5.   Russell.

6.   Carleton.

7.   Prince Edward.

8.   Halton.

9.   Essex.

Ridings of Counties

10.   North Riding of Lanark.

11.   South Riding of Lanark.

12.   North Riding of Leeds and North Riding of Grenville.

13.   South Riding of Leeds.

14.   South Riding of Grenville.

15.   East Riding of Northumberland.

16.   West Riding of Northumberland (excepting therefrom the Township of South Monaghan).

17.   East Riding of Durham.

18.   West Riding of Durham.

19.   North Riding of Ontario.

20.   South Riding of Ontario.

21.   East Riding of York.

22.   West Riding of York.

23.   North Riding of York.

24.   North Riding of Wentworth.

25.   South Riding of Wentworth.

26.   East Riding of Elgin.

27.   West Riding of Elgin.

28.   North Riding of Waterloo.

29.   South Riding of Waterloo.

30.   North Riding of Brant.

31.   South Riding of Brant.

32.   North Riding of Oxford.

33.   South Riding of Oxford.

34.   East Riding of Middlesex.

Cities, Parts of Cities, and Towns

35.   West Toronto.

36.   East Toronto.

37.   Hamilton.

38.   Ottawa.

39.   Kingston.

40.   London.

41.   Town of Brockville, with the Township of Elizabethtown thereto attached.

42.   Town of Niagara, with the Township of Niagara thereto attached.

43.   Town of Cornwall, with the Township of Cornwall thereto attached.

B.   New Electoral Divisions

44.   The Provisional Judicial District of Algoma.

The County of Bruce, divided into Two Ridings, to be called respectively the North and South Ridings:

45.   The North Riding of Bruce to consist of the Townships of Bury, Lindsay, Eastnor, Albermarle, Amable, Arran, Bruce, Elderslie, and Saugeen, and the Village of Southampton.

46.   The South Riding of Bruce to consist of the Townships of Kincardine (including the Village of Kincardine), Greenock, Brant, Huron, Kinloss, Culross, and Carrick.

The County of Huron, divided into Two Ridings, to be called respectively the North and South Ridings:

47.   The North Riding to consist of the Townships of Ashfield, Wawanosh, Turnberry, Howick, Morris, Grey, Colborne, Hullett, including the Village of Clinton, and McKillop.

48.   The South Riding to consist of the Town of Goderich and the Townships of Goderich, Tuckersmith, Stanley, Hay, Usborne, and Stephen.

The County of Middlesex, divided into three Ridings, to be called respectively the North, West, and East Ridings:

49.   The North Riding to consist of the Townships of McGillivray and Biddulph (taken from the County of Huron), and Williams East, Williams West, Adelaide, and Lobo.

50.   The West Riding to consist of the Townships of Delaware, Carradoc, Metcalfe, Mosa and Ekfrid, and the Village of Strathroy.

[The East Riding to consist of the Townships now embraced therein, and be bounded as it is at present.]

51.   The County of Lambton to consist of the Townships of Bosanquet, Warwick, Plympton, Sarnia, Moore, Enniskillen, and Brooke, and the Town of Sarnia.

52. The County of Kent to consist of the Townships of Chatham, Dover, East Tilbury, Romney, Raleigh, and Harwich, and the Town of Chatham.

53. The County of Bothwell to consist of the Townships of Sombra, Dawn, and Euphemia (taken from the County of Lambton), and the Townships of Zone, Camden with the Gore thereof, Orford, and Howard (taken from the County of Kent).

The County of Grey divided into Two Ridings to be called respectively the South and North Ridings:

54. The South Riding to consist of the Townships of Bentinck, Glenelg, Artemesia, Osprey, Normanby, Egremont, Proton, and Melancthon.

55. The North Riding to consist of the Townships of Collingwood, Euphrasia, Holland, Saint-Vincent, Sydenham, Sullivan, Derby, and Keppel, Sarawak and Brooke, and the Town of Owen Sound.

The County of Perth divided into Two Ridings, to be called respectively the South and North Ridings:

56. The North Riding to consist of the Townships of Wallace, Elma, Logan, Ellice, Mornington, and North Easthope, and the Town of Stratford.

57. The South Riding to consist of the Townships of Blanchard, Downie, South Easthope, Fullarton, Hibbert, and the Villages of Mitchell and Ste. Marys.

The County of Wellington divided into Three Ridings to be called respectively North, South and Centre Ridings:

58. The North Riding to consist of the Townships of Amaranth, Arthur, Luther, Minto, Maryborough, Peel, and the Village of Mount Forest.

59. The Centre Riding to consist of the Townships of Garafraxa, Erin, Eramosa, Nichol, and Pilkington, and the Villages of Fergus and Elora.

60. The South Riding to consist of the Town of Guelph, and the Townships of Guelph and Puslinch.

The County of Norfolk, divided into Two Ridings, to be called respectively the South and North Ridings:

61. The South Riding to consist of the Townships of Charlotteville, Houghton, Walsingham, and Woodhouse, and with the Gore thereof.

62. The North Riding to consist of the Townships of Middleton, Townsend, and Windham, and the Town of Simcoe.

63. The County of Haldimand to consist of the Townships of Oneida, Seneca, Cayuga North, Cayuga South, Raynham, Walpole, and Dunn.

64. The County of Monck to consist of the Townships of Canborough and Moulton, and Sherbrooke, and the Village of Dunnville (taken from the County of Haldimand), the Townships of Caister and Gainsborough (taken from the County of Lincoln), and the Townships of Pelham and Wainfleet (taken from the County of Welland).

65. The County of Lincoln to consist of the Townships of Clinton, Grantham, Grimsby, and Louth, and the Town of St. Catherines.

66. The County of Welland to consist of the Townships of Bertie, Crowland, Humberstone, Stamford, Thorold, and Willoughby, and the Villages of Chippewa, Clifton, Fort Erie, Thorold, and Welland.

67. The County of Peel to consist of the Townships of Chinguacousy, Toronto, and the Gore of Toronto, and the Villages of Brampton and Streetsville.

68. The County of Cardwell to consist of the Townships of Albion and Caledon (taken from the County of Peel), and the Townships of Adjala and Mono (taken from the County of Simcoe).

The County of Simcoe, divided into Two Ridings, to be called respectively the South and North Ridings:

69. The South Riding to consist of the Townships of West Gwillimbury, Tecumseth, Innisfil, Essa, Tosorontio, Mulmur, and the Village of Bradford.

70. The North Riding to consist of the Townships of Nottawasaga, Sunnidale, Vespra, Flos, Oro, Medonte, Orillia and Matchedash, Tiny and Tay, Balaklava and Robinson, and the Towns of Barrie and Collingwood.

The County of Victoria, divided into Two Ridings, to be called respectively the South and North Ridings:

71. The South Riding to consist of the Townships of Ops, Mariposa, Emily, Verulam, and the Town of Lindsay.

72. The North Riding to consist of the Townships of Anson, Bexley, Carden, Dalton, Digby, Eldon, Fenelon, Hindon, Laxton, Lutterworth, Macaulay and Draper, Sommerville, and Morrison, Muskoka, Monck and Watt (taken from the County of Simcoe), and any other surveyed Townships lying to the North of the said North Riding.

The County of Peterborough, divided into Two Ridings, to be called respectively the West and East Ridings:

73. The West Riding to consist of the Townships of South Monaghan (taken from the County of Northumberland), North Monaghan, Smith, and Ennismore, and the Town of Peterborough.

74. The East Riding to consist of the Townships of Asphodel, Belmont and Methuen, Douro, Dummer, Galway, Harvey, Minden, Stanhope and Dysart, Otonabee, and Snowden, and the Village of Ashburnham, and any other surveyed Townships lying to the North of the said East Riding.

The County of Hastings, divided into Three Ridings, to be called respectively the West, East, and North Ridings:

75. The West Riding to consist of the Town of Belleville, the Township of Sydney, and the Village of Trenton.

76. The East Riding to consist of the Townships of Thurlow, Tyendinaga, and Hungerford.

77. The North Riding to consist of the Townships of Rawdon, Huntingdon, Madoc, Elzevir, Tudor, Marmora, and Lake, and the Village of Stirling, and any other surveyed Townships lying to the North of the said North Riding.

78. The County of Lennox to consist of the Townships of Richmond, Adolphustown, North Fredericksburg, South Fredericksburg, Ernest Town, and Amherst Island, and the Village of Napanee.

79. The County of Addington to consist of the Townships of Camden, Portland, Sheffield, Hinchinbrooke, Kaladar, Kennebec, Olden, Oso, Anglesea, Barrie, Clarendon, Palmerston, Effingham, Abinger, Miller, Canonto, Denbigh, Loughborough, and Bedford.

80. The County of Frontenac to consist of the Townships of Kingston, Wolfe Island, Pittsburg and Howe Island, and Storrington.

The County of Renfrew, divided into Two Ridings, to be called respectively the South and North Ridings:

81. The South Riding to consist of the Townships of McNab, Bagot, Blithfield, Brougham, Horton, Admaston, Grattan, Matawatchan, Griffith, Lyndoch, Raglan, Radcliffe, Brudenell, Sebastopol, and the Villages of Arnprior and Renfrew.

82. The North Riding to consist of the Townships of Ross, Bromley, Westmeath, Stafford, Pembroke, Wilberforce, Alice, Petawawa, Buchanan, South Algona, North Algona, Fraser, McKay, Wylie, Rolph, Head, Maria, Clara, Haggerty, Sherwood, Burns, and Richards, and any other surveyed Townships lying North-westerly of the said North Riding.

Every Town and incorporated Village existing at the Union, not especially mentioned in this Schedule, is to be taken as Part of the County or Riding within which it is locally situate.

THE SECOND SCHEDULE

Electoral Districts of Quebec specially fixed

Counties of

Pontiac.	Missisquoi.	Compton.
Ottawa.	Brome.	Wolfe and Richmond.
Argenteuil.	Shefford.	Megantic.
Huntingdon.	Stanstead.	Town of Sherbrooke.

THE THIRD SCHEDULE

Provincial Public Works and Property to be the Property of Canada

1. Canals, with Lands and Water Power connected therewith.

2. Public Harbours.

3. Lighthouses and Piers, and Sable Island.

4. Steamboats, Dredges, and public Vessels.

5. Rivers and Lake Improvements.

6. Railways and Railway Stocks, Mortgages, and other Debts due by Railway Companies.

7. Military Roads.

8. Custom Houses, Post Offices, and all other Public Buildings, except such as the Government of Canada appropriate for the Use of the Provincial Legislatures and Governments.

9. Property transferred by the Imperial Government, and known as Ordnance Property.

10. Armouries, Drill Sheds, Military Clothing, and Munitions of War, and Lands set apart for general Public Purposes.

THE FOURTH SCHEDULE

Assets to be the Property of Ontario and Quebec conjointly

Upper Canada Building Fund.

Lunatic Asylums.

Normal School.

Court Houses in Aylmer. Montreal. Kamouraska. (Lower Canada.)

Law Society, Upper Canada.

Montreal Turnpike Trust.

University Permanent Fund.

Royal Institution.

Consolidated Municipal Loan Fund, Upper Canada.

Consolidated Municipal Loan Fund, Lower Canada.

Agricultural Society, Upper Canada.

Lower Canada Legislative Grant.

Quebec Fire Loan.

Temiscouata Advance Account.

Quebec Turnpike Trust.

Education - East.

Building and Jury Fund, Lower Canada.

Municipalities Fund.

Lower Canada Superior Education Income Fund.

THE FIFTH SCHEDULE

Oath of Allegiance

I A.B. do swear, That I will be faithful and bear true Allegiance to Her Majesty Queen Victoria.

Note. The Name of the King or Queen of the United Kingdom of Great Britain and Ireland for the Time being is to be substituted from Time to Time, with proper Terms of Reference thereto.

Declaration of Qualification

I A.B. do declare and testify, That I am by Law duly qualified to be appointed a Member of the Senate of Canada [*or as the Case may be*], and that I am legally or equitably seised as of Freehold for my own Use and Benefit of Lands or Tenements held in Free and Common Socage [*or seised or possessed for my own Use and Benefit of Lands or Tenements held in Franc-alleu or in Roture (as the Case may be*),] in the Province of Nova Scotia [*or as the Case may be*] of the Value of Four thousand Dollars over and above all Rents, Dues, Debts, Mortgages, Charges, and Incumbrances due or payable out of or charged on or affecting the same, and that I have not collusively or colourably obtained a Title to or become possessed of the said Lands and Tenements or any Part thereof for the Purpose of enabling me to become a Member of the Senate of Canada [*or as the Case may be*], and that my Real and Personal Property are together worth Four thousand Dollars over and above my Debts and Liabilities.

THE SIXTH SCHEDULE [78]

Primary Production from Non-Renewable Natural Resources and Forestry Resources

1. For the purposes of section 92A of this Act,

    (*a*) production from a non-renewable natural resource is primary production therefrom if

        (i) it is in the form in which it exists upon its recovery or severance from its natural state, or

        (ii) it is a product resulting from processing or refining the resource, and is not a manufactured product or a product resulting from refining crude oil, refining upgraded heavy crude oil, refining gases or liquids derived from coal or refining a synthetic equivalent of crude oil; and

    (*b*) production from a forestry resource is primary production therefrom if it consists of sawlogs, poles, lumber, wood chips, sawdust or any other primary wood product, or wood pulp, and is not a product manufactured from wood.

ENDNOTES TO SCHEDULES

(77) Spent. *Representation Act*, R.S.O. 1990, c. R.26

(78) As enacted by the *Constitution Act*, 1982

APPENDIX B

CONSTITUTION ACT, 1982 [79]

PART I
CANADIAN CHARTER OF RIGHTS AND FREEDOMS

Whereas Canada is founded upon principles that recognize the supremacy of God and the rule of law:

Rights and freedoms in Canada

1. The *Canadian Charter of Rights and Freedoms* guarantees the rights and freedoms set out in it subject only to such reasonable limits prescribed by law as can be demonstrably justified in a free and democratic society.

Fundamental Freedoms

Fundamental freedoms

2. Everyone has the following fundamental freedoms:

    (*a*) freedom of conscience and religion;
    (*b*) freedom of thought, belief, opinion and expression, including freedom of the press and other media of communication;
    (*c*) freedom of peaceful assembly; and
    (*d*) freedom of association.

Democratic Rights

Democratic rights of citizens

3. Every citizen of Canada has the right to vote in an election of members of the House of Commons or of a legislative assembly and to be qualified for membership therein.

Maximum duration of legislative bodies

4. (1) No House of Commons and no legislative assembly shall continue for longer than five years from the date fixed for the return of the writs of a general election of its members. [80]

Continuation in special circumstances	(2) In time of real or apprehended war, invasion or insurrection, a House of Commons may be continued by Parliament and a legislative assembly may be continued by the legislature beyond five years if such continuation is not opposed by the votes of more than one-third of the members of the House of Commons or the legislative assembly, as the case may be. [81]
Annual sitting of legislative bodies	5. There shall be a sitting of Parliament and of each legislature at least once every twelve months. [82]

Mobility Rights

Mobility of citizens

6.   (1) Every citizen of Canada has the right to enter, remain in and leave Canada.

Rights to move and gain livelihood

(2) Every citizen of Canada and every person who has the status of a permanent resident of Canada has the right

    (a)   to move to and take up residence in any province; and
    (b)   to pursue the gaining of a livelihood in any province.

Limitation

(3) The rights specified in subsection (2) are subject to

    (a)   any laws or practices of general application in force in a province other than those that discriminate among persons primarily on the basis of province of present or previous residence; and
    (b)   any laws providing for reasonable residency requirements as a qualification for the receipt of publicly provided social services.

Affirmative action programs

(4) Subsections (2) and (3) do not preclude any law, program or activity that has as its object the amelioration in a province of conditions of individuals in that province who are socially or economically disadvantaged if the rate of employment in that province is below the rate of employment in Canada.

Legal Rights

Life, liberty and security of person

7.   Everyone has the right to life, liberty and security of the person and the right not to be deprived thereof except in accordance with the principles of fundamental justice.

Search or seizure

8.   Everyone has the right to be secure against unreasonable search or seizure.

Detention or imprisonment

9.   Everyone has the right not to be arbitrarily detained or imprisoned.

Arrest or detention

10.   Everyone has the right on arrest or detention

    (a)   to be informed promptly of the reasons therefor;
    (b)   to retain and instruct counsel without delay and to be informed of that right; and
    (c)   to have the validity of the detention determined by way of *habeas corpus* and to be released if the detention is not lawful.

Proceedings in criminal and penal matters

11.   Any person charged with an offence has the right

    (a)   to be informed without unreasonable delay of the specific offence;
    (b)   to be tried within a reasonable time;
    (c)   not to be compelled to be a witness in proceedings against that person in respect of the offence;
    (d)   to be presumed innocent until proven guilty according to law in a fair and public hearing by an independent and impartial tribunal;
    (e)   not to be denied reasonable bail without just cause;
    (f)   except in the case of an offence under military law tried before a mil-

itary tribunal, to the benefit of trial by jury where the maximum punishment for the offence is imprisonment for five years or a more severe punishment;

(g) not to be found guilty on account of any act or omission unless, at the time of the act or omission, it constituted an offence under Canadian or international law or was criminal according to the general principles of law recognized by the community of nations;

(h) if finally acquitted of the offence, not to be tried for it again and, if finally found guilty and punished for the offence, not to be tried or punished for it again; and

(i) if found guilty of the offence and if the punishment for the offence has been varied between the time of commission and the time of sentencing, to the benefit of the lesser punishment.

Treatment or punishment

12. Everyone has the right not to be subjected to any cruel and unusual treatment or punishment.

Self-crimination

13. A witness who testifies in any proceedings has the right not to have any incriminating evidence so given used to incriminate that witness in any other proceedings, except in a prosecution for perjury or for the giving of contradictory evidence.

Interpreter

14. A party or witness in any proceedings who does not understand or speak the language in which the proceedings are conducted or who is deaf has the right to the assistance of an interpreter.

Equality Rights

Equality before and under law and equal protection and benefit of law

15. (1) Every individual is equal before and under the law and has the right to the equal protection and equal benefit of the law without discrimination and, in particular, without discrimination based on race, national or ethnic origin, colour, religion, sex, age or mental or physical disability.

Affirmative action programs

(2) Subsection (1) does not preclude any law, program or activity that has as its object the amelioration of conditions of disadvantaged individuals or groups including those that are disadvantaged because of race, national or ethnic origin, colour, religion, sex, age or mental or physical disability. [83]

Official Languages of Canada

Official languages of Canada

16. (1) English and French are the official languages of Canada and have equality of status and equal rights and privileges as to their use in all institutions of the Parliament and government of Canada.

Official languages of New Brunswick

(2) English and French are the official languages of New Brunswick and have equality of status and equal rights and privileges as to their use in all institutions of the legislature and government of New Brunswick.

Advancement of status and use

(3) Nothing in this Charter limits the authority of Parliament or a legislature to advance the equality of status or use of English and French.

English and French linguistic communities in New Brunswick

16.1. (1) The English linguistic community and the French linguistic community in New Brunswick have equality of status and equal rights and privileges, including the right to distinct educational institutions and such distinct cultural institutions as are necessary for the preservation and promotion of those communities.

Role of the legislature and government of New Brunswick

(2) The role of the legislature and government of New Brunswick to preserve and promote the status, rights and privileges referred to in subsection (1) is affirmed. [83.1]

Proceedings of Parliament	17. (1) Everyone has the right to use English or French in any debates and other proceedings of Parliament. [84]
Proceedings of New Brunswick legislature	(2) Everyone has the right to use English or French in any debates and other proceedings of the legislature of New Brunswick. [85]
Parliamentary statutes and records	18. (1) The statutes, records and journals of Parliament shall be printed and published in English and French and both language versions are equally authoritative. [86]
New Brunswick statutes and records	(2) The statutes, records and journals of the legislature of New Brunswick shall be printed and published in English and French and both language versions are equally authoritative. [87]
Proceedings in courts established by Parliament	19. (1) Either English or French may be used by any person in, or in any pleading in or process issuing from, any court established by Parliament. [88]
Proceedings in New Brunswick courts	(2) Either English or French may be used by any person in, or in any pleading in or process issuing from, any court of New Brunswick. [89]
Communications by public with federal institutions	20. (1) Any member of the public in Canada has the right to communicate with, and to receive available services from, any head or central office of an institution of the Parliament or government of Canada in English or French, and has the same right with respect to any other office of any such institution where

    (*a*)   there is a significant demand for communications with and services from that office in such language; or

    (*b*)   due to the nature of the office, it is reasonable that communications with and services from that office be available in both English and French.

Communications by public with New Brunswick institutions	(2) Any member of the public in New Brunswick has the right to communicate with, and to receive available services from, any office of an institution of the legislature or government of New Brunswick in English or French.
Continuation of existing constitutional provisions	21. Nothing in sections 16 to 20 abrogates or derogates from any right, privilege or obligation with respect to the English and French languages, or either of them, that exists or is continued by virtue of any other provision of the Constitution of Canada. [90]
Rights and privileges preserved	22. Nothing in sections 16 to 20 abrogates or derogates from any legal or customary right or privilege acquired or enjoyed either before or after the coming into force of this Charter with respect to any language that is not English or French.

Minority Language Educational Rights

Language of instruction	23. (1) Citizens of Canada

    (*a*)   whose first language learned and still understood is that of the English or French linguistic minority population of the province in which they reside, or

    (*b*)   who have received their primary school instruction in Canada in English or French and reside in a province where the language in which they received that instruction is the language of the English or French linguistic minority population of the province,

have the right to have their children receive primary and secondary school instruction in that language in that province. [91]

Continuity of language instruction	(2) Citizens of Canada of whom any child has received or is receiving primary or secondary school instruction in English or French in Canada, have the right to have all their children receive primary and secondary school instruction in the same language.
Application where numbers warrant	(3) The right of citizens of Canada under subsections (1) and (2) to have their children receive primary and secondary school instruction in the language of the English or French linguistic minority population of a province

> (a) applies wherever in the province the number of children of citizens who have such a right is sufficient to warrant the provision to them out of public funds of minority language instruction; and
>
> (b) includes, where the number of those children so warrants, the right to have them receive that instruction in minority language educational facilities provided out of public funds.

Enforcement

Enforcement of guaranteed rigns and freedoms	24. (1) Anyone whose rights or freedoms, as guaranteed by this Charter, have been infringed or denied may apply to a court of competent jurisdiction to obtain such remedy as the court considers appropriate and just in the circumstances.
Exclusion of evidence bringing administration of justice into disrepute	(2) Where, in proceedings under subsection (1), a court concludes that evidence was obtained in a manner that infringed or denied any rights or freedoms guaranteed by this Charter, the evidence shall be excluded if it is established that, having regard to all the circumstances, the admission of it in the proceedings would bring the administration of justice into disrepute.

General

Aboriginal rights and freedoms not affected by Charter	25. The guarantee in this Charter of certain rights and freedoms shall not be construed so as to abrogate or derogate from any aboriginal, treaty or other rights or freedoms that pertain to the aboriginal peoples of Canada including

> (a) any rights or freedoms that have been recognized by the Royal Proclamation of October 7, 1763; and
>
> (b) any rights or freedoms that now exist by way of land claims agreements or may be so acquired. [92]

Other rights and freedoms not affected by Charter	26. The guarantee in this Charter of certain rights and freedoms shall not be construed as denying the existence of any other rights or freedoms that exist in Canada.
Multicultural heritage	27. This Charter shall be interpreted in a manner consistent with the preservation and enhancement of the multicultural heritage of Canadians.
Rights guaranteed equally to both sexes	28. Notwithstanding anything in this Charter, the rights and freedoms referred to in it are guaranteed equally to male and female persons.
Rights respecting certain schools preserved	29. Nothing in this Charter abrogates or derogates from any rights or privileges guaranteed by or under the Constitution of Canada in respect of denominational, separate or dissentient schools. [93]
Application to territories and territorial authorities	30. A reference in this Charter to a Province or to the legislative assembly or legislature of a province shall be deemed to include a reference to the Yukon Territory and the Northwest Territories, or to the appropriate legislative authority thereof, as the case may be.
Legislative powers not extended	31. Nothing in this Charter extends the legislative powers of any body or authority.

Application of Charter

Application of Charter

32. (1) This Charter applies

    (*a*) to the Parliament and government of Canada in respect of all matters within the authority of Parliament including all matters relating to the Yukon Territory and Northwest Territories; and

    (*b*) to the legislature and government of each province in respect of all matters within the authority of the legislature of each province.

Exception

(2) Notwithstanding subsection (1), section 15 shall not have effect until three years after this section comes into force.

Exception where express declaration

33. (1) Parliament or the legislature of a province may expressly declare in an Act of Parliament or of the legislature, as the case may be, that the Act or a provision thereof shall operate notwithstanding a provision included in section 2 or sections 7 to 15 of this Charter.

Operation of exception

(2) An Act or a provision of an Act in respect of which a declaration made under this section is in effect shall have such operation as it would have but for the provision of this Charter referred to in the declaration.

Five year limitation

(3) A declaration made under subsection (1) shall cease to have effect five years after it comes into force or on such earlier date as may be specified in the declaration.

Re-enactment

(4) Parliament or the legislature of a province may re-enact a declaration made under subsection (1).

Five year limitation

(5) Subsection (3) applies in respect of a re-enactment made under subsection (4).

Citation

Citation

34. This Part may be cited as the *Canadian Charter of Rights and Freedoms*.

PART II
RIGHTS OF THE ABORIGINAL PEOPLES OF CANADA

Recognition of existing aboriginal and treaty rights

35. (1) The existing aboriginal and treaty rights of the aboriginal peoples of Canada are hereby recognized and affirmed.

Definition of "aboriginal peoples of Canada"

(2) In this Act, "aboriginal peoples of Canada" includes the Indian, Inuit and Métis peoples of Canada.

Land claims agreements

(3) For greater certainty, in subsection (1) "treaty rights" includes rights that now exist by way of land claims agreements or may be so acquired.

Aboriginal and treaty rights are guaranteed equally to both sexes

(4) Notwithstanding any other provision of this Act, the aboriginal and treaty rights referred to in subsection (1) are guaranteed equally to male and female persons. [94]

Commitment to participation in constitutional conference

35.1 The government of Canada and the provincial governments are committed to the principle that, before any amendment is made to Class 24 of section 91 of the "*Constitution Act, 1867*", to section 25 of this Act or to this Part, (*a*) a constitutional conference that includes in its agenda an item relating to the proposed amendment, composed of the Prime Minister of Canada and the first ministers of the provinces, will be convened by the Prime Minister of Canada; and

(*b*) the Prime Minister of Canada will invite representatives of the aboriginal peoples of Canada to participate in the discussions on that item. [95]

PART III
EQUALIZATION AND REGIONAL DISPARITIES

Commitment to promote equal opportunities

36. (1) Without altering the legislative authority of Parliament or of the provincial legislatures, or the rights of any of them with respect to the exercise of their legislative authority, Parliament and the legislatures, together with the government of Canada and the provincial governments, are committed to

(*a*) promoting equal opportunities for the well-being of Canadians;

(*b*) furthering economic development to reduce disparity in opportunities; and

(*c*) providing essential public services of reasonable quality to all Canadians.

Commitment respecting public services

(2) Parliament and the government of Canada are committed to the principle of making equalization payments to ensure that provincial governments have sufficient revenues to provide reasonably comparable levels of public services at reasonably comparable levels of taxation. [96]

PART IV
CONSTITUTIONAL CONFERENCE

37. [97]

PART IV.I
CONSTITUTIONAL CONFERENCES

37.1 [98]

PART V
PROCEDURE FOR AMENDING CONSTITUTION OF CANADA [99]

General procedure for amending Constitution of Canada

38. (1) An amendment to the Constitution of Canada may be made by proclamation issued by the Governor General under the Great Seal of Canada where so authorized by

(*a*) resolutions of the Senate and House of Commons; and

(*b*) resolutions of the legislative assemblies of at least two-thirds of the provinces that have, in the aggregate, according to the then latest general census, at least fifty per cent of the population of all the provinces.

Majority of members

(2) An amendment made under subsection (1) that derogates from the legislative powers, the proprietary rights or any other rights or privileges of the legislature or government of a province shall require a resolution supported by a majority of the members of each of the Senate, the House of Commons and the legislative assemblies required under subsection (1).

Expression of dissent

(3) An amendment referred to in subsection (2) shall not have effect in a province the legislative assembly of which has expressed its dissent thereto by resolution supported by a majority of its members prior to the issue of the proclamation to which the amendment relates unless that legislative assembly, subsequently, by resolution supported by a majority of its members, revokes its dissent and authorizes the amendment.

Revocation of dissent

(4) A resolution of dissent made for the purposes of subsection (3) may be revoked at any time before or after the issue of the proclamation to which it relates.

Restriction on proclamation

39. (1) A proclamation shall not be issued under subsection 38(1) before the expiration of one year from the adoption of the resolution initiating the amendment procedure thereunder, unless the legislative assembly of each province has previously adopted a resolution of assent or dissent.

Idem

(2) A proclamation shall not be issued under subsection 38(1) after the expiration of three years from the adoption of the resolution initiating the amendment procedure thereunder.

Compensation

40. Where an amendment is made under subsection 38(1) that transfers provincial legislative powers relating to education or other cultural matters from provincial legislatures to Parliament, Canada shall provide reasonable compensation to any province to which the amendment does not apply.

Amendment by unanimous consent

41. An amendment to the Constitution of Canada in relation to the following matters may be made by proclamation issued by the Governor General under the Great Seal of Canada only where authorized by resolutions of the Senate and House of Commons and of the legislative assembly of each province:

(a) the office of the Queen, the Governor General and the Lieutenant Governor of a province;
(b) the right of a province to a number of members in the House of Commons not less than the number of Senators by which the province is entitled to be represented at the time this Part comes into force;
(c) subject to section 43, the use of the English or the French language;
(d) the composition of the Supreme Court of Canada; and
(e) an amendment to this Part.

Amendment by general procedure

42. (1) An amendment to the Constitution of Canada in relation to the following matters may be made only in accordance with subsection 38(1):

(a) the principle of proportionate representation of the provinces in the House of Commons prescribed by the Constitution of Canada;
(b) the powers of the Senate and the method of selecting Senators;
(c) the number of members by which a province is entitled to be represented in the Senate and the residence qualifications of Senators;
(d) subject to paragraph 41(d), the Supreme Court of Canada;
(e) the extension of existing provinces into the territories; and
(f) notwithstanding any other law or practice, the establishment of new provinces.

Exception	(2) Subsections 38(2) to (4) do not apply in respect of amendments in relation to matters referred to in subsection (1).
Amendment of provisions relating to some but not all provinces	43. An amendment to the Constitution of Canada in relation to any provision that applies to one or more, but not all, provinces, including

> (*a*) any alteration to boundaries between provinces, and
> (*b*) any amendment to any provision that relates to the use of the English or the French language within a province,

may be made by proclamation issued by the Governor General under the Great Seal of Canada only where so authorized by resolutions of the Senate and House of Commons and of the legislative assembly of each province to which the amendment applies.

44. Subject to sections 41 and 42, Parliament may exclusively make laws amending the Constitution of Canada in relation to the executive government of Canada or the Senate and House of Commons.

Amendments by Parliament

45. Subject to section 41, the legislature of each province may exclusively make laws amending the constitution of the province.

Amendments by provincial legislatures

46. (1) The procedures for amendment under sections 38, 41, 42 and 43 may be initiated either by the Senate or the House of Commons or by the legislative assembly of a province.

Initiation of amendment procedures

(2) A resolution of assent made for the purposes of this Part may be revoked at any time before the issue of a proclamation authorized by it.

Revocation of authorization

47. (1) An amendment to the Constitution of Canada made by proclamation under section 38, 41, 42 or 43 may be made without a resolution of the Senate authorizing the issue of the proclamation if, within one hundred and eighty days after the adoption by the House of Commons of a resolution authorizing its issue, the Senate has not adopted such a resolution and if, at any time after the expiration of that period, the House of Commons again adopts the resolution.

Amendments without Senate resolution

(2) Any period when Parliament is prorogued or dissolved shall not be counted in computing the one hundred and eighty day period referred to in subsection (1).

Computation of period

48. The Queen's Privy Council for Canada shall advise the Governor General to issue a proclamation under this Part forthwith on the adoption of the resolutions required for an amendment made by proclamation under this Part.

Advice to issue proclamation

49. A constitutional conference composed of the Prime Minister of Canada and the first ministers of the provinces shall be convened by the Prime Minister of Canada within fifteen years after this Part comes into force to review the provisions of this Part.

Constitutional conference

PART VI
AMENDMENT TO THE CONSTITUTION ACT, 1867

50. (100)

51. (101)

PART VII
GENERAL

Primacy of Constitution of Canada

52. (1) The Constitution of Canada is the supreme law of Canada, and any law that is inconsistent with the provisions of the Constitution is, to the extent of the inconsistency, of no force or effect.

Constitution of Canada

(2) The Constitution of Canada includes

    (*a*) the *Canada Act 1982*, including this Act;

    (*b*) the Acts and orders referred to in the schedule; and

    (*c*) any amendment to any Act or order referred to in paragraph (*a*) or (*b*).

Amendments to Constitution of Canada

(3) Amendments to the Constitution of Canada shall be made only in accordance with the authority contained in the Constitution of Canada.

Repeals and new names

53. (1) The enactments referred to in Column I of the schedule are hereby repealed or amended to the extent indicated in Column II thereof and, unless repealed, shall continue as law in Canada under the names set out in Column III thereof.

Consequential amendments

(2) Every enactment, except the *Canada Act 1982*, that refers to an enactment referred to in the schedule by the name in Column I thereof is hereby amended by substituting for that name the corresponding name in Column III thereof, and any British North America Act not referred to in the schedule may be cited as the *Constitution Act* followed by the year and number, if any, of its enactment.

Repeal and consequential amendments

54. Part IV is repealed on the day that is one year after this Part comes into force and this section may be repealed and this Act renumbered, consequentially upon the repeal of Part IV and this section, by proclamation issued by the Governor General under the Great Seal of Canada. [102]

[Repealed]

54.1 [103]

French version of Constitution of Canada

55. A French version of the portions of the Constitution of Canada referred to in the schedule shall be prepared by the Minister of Justice of Canada as expeditiously as possible and, when any portion thereof sufficient to warrant action being taken has been so prepared, it shall be put forward for enactment by proclamation issued by the Governor General under the Great Seal of Canada pursuant to the procedure then applicable to an amendment of the same provisions of the Constitution of Canada.

English and French versions of certain constitutional texts

56. Where any portion of the Constitution of Canada has been or is enacted in English and French or where a French version of any portion of the Constitution is enacted pursuant to section 55, the English and French versions of that portion of the Constitution are equally authoritative.

English and French versions of this Act

57. The English and French versions of this Act are equally authoritative.

Commencement

58. Subject to section 59, this Act shall come into force on a day to be fixed by proclamation issued by the Queen or the Governor General under the Great Seal of Canada. [104]

Commencement of paragraph 23(1)(*a*) in respect of Quebec

59. (1) Paragraph 23(1)(*a*) shall come into force in respect of Quebec on a day to be fixed by proclamation issued by the Queen or the Governor General under the Great Seal of Canada.

Authorization of Quebec

Repeal of this section

(2) A proclamation under subsection (1) shall be issued only where authorized by the legislative assembly or government of Quebec. [105]

(3) This section may be repealed on the day paragraph 23(1)(*a*) comes into force in respect of Quebec and this Act amended and renumbered, consequentially upon the repeal of this section, by proclamation issued by the Queen or the Governor General under the Great Seal of Canada.

Short title and citations   60. This Act may be cited as the *Constitution Act, 1982*, and the Constitution Acts 1867 to 1975 (No. 2) and this Act may be cited together as the *Constitution Acts, 1867 to 1982*.

References   61. A reference to the "*Constitution Acts, 1867 to 1982*" shall be deemed to include a reference to the "*Constitution Amendment Proclamation, 1983*". [(106)]

ENDNOTES TO APPENDIX B

[(79)] Enacted as Schedule B to the *Canada Act 1982*, (U.K.) 1982, c. 11, which came into force on April 17, 1982. The *Canada Act 1982*, other than Schedules A and B thereto, reads as follows:

An Act to give effect to a request by the Senate and House of Commons of Canada

Whereas Canada has requested and consented to the enactment of an Act of the Parliament of the United Kingdom to give effect to the provisions hereinafter set forth and the Senate and the House of Commons of Canada in Parliament assembled have submitted an address to Her Majesty requesting that Her Majesty may graciously be pleased to cause a Bill to be laid before the Parliament of the United Kingdom for that purpose.

Be it therefore enacted by the Queen's Most Excellent Majesty, by and with the advice and consent of the Lords Spiritual and Temporal, and Commons, in this present Parliament assembled, and by the authority of the same, as follows:

1. The *Constitution Act, 1982* set out in Schedule B to this Act is hereby enacted for and shall have the force of law in Canada and shall come into force as provided in that Act.

2. No Act of the Parliament of the United Kingdom passed after the *Constitution Act, 1982* comes into force shall extend to Canada as part of its law.

3. So far as it is not contained in Schedule B, the French version of this Act is set out in Schedule A to this Act and has the same authority in Canada as the English version thereof.

4. This Act may be cited as the *Canada Act 1982*.

[(80)] See section 50 and the footnotes to sections 85 and 88 of the *Constitution Act, 1867*.

[(81)] Replaces part of Class 1 of section 91 of the *Constitution Act, 1867*, which was repealed as set out in subitem 1(3) of the Schedule to this Act.

[(82)] See the footnotes to sections 20, 86 and 88 of the *Constitution Act, 1867*.

[(83)] Subsection 32(2) provides that section 15 shall not have effect until three years after section 32 comes into force.

Section 32 came into force on April 17, 1982; therefore, section 15 had effect on April 17, 1985.

[(83.1)] Section 16.1 was added by the *Constitution Amendment, 1993 (New Brunswick)*. See SI/93-54.

[(84)] See section 133 of the *Constitution Act, 1867*, and the footnote thereto.

[(85)] *Id.*

[(86)] *Id.*

[(87)] *Id.*

[(88)] *Id.*

[(89)] *Id.*

[(90)] See, for example, section 133 of the *Constitution Act, 1867*, and the reference to the *Manitoba Act, 1870*, in the footnote thereto.

[(91)] Paragraph 23(1)(*a*) is not in force in respect of Quebec. See section 59 *infra*.

[(92)] Paragraph 25(*b*) was repealed and re-enacted by the *Constitution Amendment Proclamation, 1983*. See SI/84-102.

Paragraph 25(*b*) as originally enacted read as follows:

"(*b*) any rights or freedoms that may be acquired by the aboriginal peoples of Canada by way of land claims settlement."

(93) See section 93 of the *Constitution Act, 1867*, and the footnote thereto.

(94) Subsections 35(3) and (4) were added by the *Constitution Amendment Proclamation, 1983*. See SI/84-102.

(95) Section 35.1 was added by the *Constitution Amendment Proclamation, 1983*. See SI/84-102.

(96) See the footnotes to sections 114 and 118 of the *Constitution Act, 1867*.

(97) Section 54 provided for the repeal of Part IV one year after Part VII came into force. Part VII came into force on April 17, 1982 thereby repealing Part IV on April 17, 1983.

Part IV, as originally enacted, read as follows:

37. (1) A constitutional conference composed of the Prime Minister of Canada and the first ministers of the provinces shall be convened by the Prime Minister of Canada within one year after this Part comes into force.

(2) The conference convened under subsection (1) shall have included in its agenda an item respecting constitutional matters that directly affect the aboriginal peoples of Canada, including the identification and definition of the rights of those peoples to be included in the Constitution of Canada, and the Prime Minister of Canada shall invite representatives of those peoples to participate in the discussions on that item.

(3) The Prime Minister of Canada shall invite elected representatives of the governments of the Yukon Territory and the Northwest Territories to participate in the discussions on any item on the agenda of the conference convened under subsection (1) that, in the opinion of the Prime Minister, directly affects the Yukon Territory and the Northwest Territories.

(98) Part IV.1, which was added by the *Constitution Amendment Proclamation, 1983* (see SI/84-102), was repealed on April 18, 1987 by section 54.1.

Part IV.1, as originally enacted, read as follows:

37.1 (1) In addition to the conference convened in March 1983, at least two constitutional conferences composed of the Prime Minister of Canada and the first ministers of the provinces shall be convened by the Prime Minister of Canada, the first within three years after April 17, 1982 and the second within five years after that date.

(2) Each conference convened under subsection (1) shall have included in its agenda constitutional matters that directly affect the aboriginal peoples of Canada, and the Prime Minister of Canada shall invite representatives of those peoples to participate in the discussions on those matters.

(3) The Prime Minister of Canada shall invite elected representatives of the governments of the Yukon Territory and the Northwest Territories to participate in the discussions on any item on the agenda of a conference convened under subsection (1) that, in the opinion of the Prime Minister, directly affects the Yukon Territory and the Northwest Territories.

(4) Nothing in this section shall be construed so as to derogate from subsection 35(1).

(99) Prior to the enactment of Part V certain provisions of the Constitution of Canada and the provincial constitutions could be amended pursuant to the *Constitution Act, 1867*. See the footnotes to section 91, Class 1 and section 92, Class 1 thereof, *supra*. Other amendments to the Constitution could only be made by enactment of the Parliament of the United Kingdom.

(100) The amendment is set out in the Consolidation of the *Constitution Act, 1867*, as section 92A thereof.

(101) The amendment is set out in the Consolidation of the *Constitution Act, 1867*, as the Sixth Schedule thereof.

(102) Part VII came into force on April 17, 1982. See SI/82-97.

(103) Section 54.1, which was added by the *Constitution Amendment Proclamation, 1983* (see SI/84-102), provided for the repeal of Part IV.1 and section 54.1 on April 18, 1987.

Section 54.1, as originally enacted, read as follows:

"54.1 Part IV.1 and this section are repealed on April 18, 1987."

(104) The Act, with the exception of paragraph 23(1)(*a*) in respect of Quebec, came into force on April 17, 1982 by proclamation issued by the Queen. See SI/82-97.

(105) No proclamation has been issued under section 59.

(106) Section 61 was added by the *Constitution Amendment Proclamation, 1983*. *See* SI/84-102.

See also section 3 of the *Constitution Act, 1985 (Representation)*, S.C. 1986, c. 8, Part I and the *Constitution Amendment, 1987 (Newfoundland Act)* SI/88-11.

GLOSSARY

Advocacy advertising The purchase of newspaper/magazine space, signs or billboards, or broadcast time to convey a political message.

Affirmative action Measures intended to increase the representation of a targeted group or groups beyond what it would be without special intervention. These measures may include hiring and promotion practices, school admission policies, selection rules for committees, and so on.

Authority A form of power based on the recognition by the person or persons who obey that the person or organization issuing a command or making a rule has the right to do so and should be obeyed.

Bilingual belt A term coined by Richard Joy in *Languages in Conflict*, it refers to the narrow region running from Moncton, New Brunswick, in the east to Sault Ste Marie, Ontario, in the west, in which is found the vast majority of Canada's francophone population and where the rate of francophone assimilation is lower than elsewhere in Canada.

Bill 101 Quebec's Charte de la langue française, the first piece of legislation passed by Quebec's National Assembly, in 1977, after the Parti Québécois came to power. It made French the sole official language in Quebec for purposes of provincial public administration, restricted access to English-language schools, and imposed French-language requirements on business in Quebec. Despite some setbacks in the courts over the years, Quebec's language policy continues to be based on the principles set forth in Bill 101.

Block funding Under this formula, Ottawa's financial contribution to a provincially-administered program or policy field is not geared to the level of provincial spending. The Federal-Provincial Fiscal Arrangements Act of 1977 began this practice of replacing the *shared-cost program* model with block funding. The Canada Health and Social Transfer is the major block funding transfer from Ottawa to the provinces.

Brokerage politics Style of politics that stresses the ability of parties to accommodate diverse interests, a feat that requires flexibility in policy positions and ideological stance. Brokerage politics is often characterized as non-ideological, a characterization that is somewhat misleading because the claim of brokerage-style parties to be non-ideological simply means that they represent the dominant ideology accepted uncritically by most members of society. The Liberal and Conservative parties have been the main practitioners of brokerage politics on Canada's national stage, the Liberal Party being the more successful of the two over the last century.

Calgary Declaration A statement agreed to in 1997 by all of the provincial premiers except Quebec's Lucien Bouchard. It stopped short of endorsing the recognition of Quebec as a distinct society, instead referring to the 'unique character of Quebec society'.

Canada–US Free Trade Agreement A wide-ranging trade agreement between Canada and the United States that has been in effect since January 1989. The FTA reversed the historical pattern of Canadian protectionism that was enshrined in the National Policy of 1878–9 but that had been steadily eroded after World War II. The FTA created an architecture of dispute settlement rules, agencies, and monitoring requirements.

Canadian Bill of Rights Passed by the Canadian Parliament in 1960, it includes many of the same rights and freedoms guaranteed by the Charter. However, the Bill of Rights is a statute and does not have the status of constitutional law.

Canadian content rules Regulations developed and enforced by the Canadian Radio-television and Telecommunications Commission that require television and radio broadcasters and cable companies to ensure that a specified share of their programming satisfies the criteria of Canadian content.

Caucus The elected members of a particular political party in the legislature. When Parliament is sitting, each party's caucus usually will meet at least once per week, during which time matters of policy and political strategy may be discussed.

Central agencies Parts of the bureaucracy whose main or only purpose is to support the decision-making activities of cabinet. The five organizations usually considered to have central agency status are the Privy Council Office, the Prime Minister's Office, the Department of Finance, the Treasury Board Secretariat, and the Intergovernmental Affairs Office within the PCO.

Charter groups (old and new) Until a generation ago it was common in Canada to speak of French and British Canadians as Canada's two founding peoples or 'charter groups'. With the 1982 passage of the Charter of Rights and Freedoms and the explosion of Charter-based litigation, the term 'Charter groups' has come to be associated with rights-seeking organizations representing such groups as women, gays and lesbians, disabled persons, and Aboriginal Canadians. Another reason for the eclipse of the older meaning of the term 'charter groups' is that it is thought by many to ignore the original pre-European inhabitants of what would become Canada.

Cité libre The intellectual revue founded in the 1950s by such prominent Quebecers as Pierre Trudeau and Gérard Pelletier, which was one of the key centres for opposition to the so-called *unholy alliance* of the Church, anglophone capital, and the Union Nationale under Maurice Duplessis.

Class analysis A perspective on politics that insists on the overriding importance of social classes based on their relationship to the means of producing and distributing wealth.

Coercion A form of power based on the use or threat of force (e.g., fines, imprisonment).

Common law In Anglo-American legal systems such as Canada's, the component of the law based on the decisions of courts. Like statute law, passed by legislatures, common law rules are enforceable in the courts.

Communitarianism Those belief systems, like socialism, based on the premise that real human freedom and dignity are only possible in the context of communal relations that allow for the public recognition of group identities and that are based on equal respect for these different group identities.

Concurrent powers Legislative powers, including those relating to agriculture, immigration, and public pensions, that under the written Constitution are shared between Ottawa and the provinces.

Conquest, 1759 The military victory of the British forces led by Wolfe over Montcalm in what was New France, but which subsequently became British territory under the Treaty of Paris of 1763. The Conquest has always been a symbol in French Canada, particularly in Quebec, of subjugation to the English community and the loss of communal autonomy.

Conservatism Historically, an ideology based on the importance of tradition that accepted human inequality and the organization of society into hierarchically arranged groups as part of the natural order of things.

Today, conservatism in Canada and the United States is associated with the defence of private property rights and free trade, individualism, opposition to the welfare state, and, in the case of social conservatives, emphasis on the traditional family, religion, and what are sometimes referred to as 'traditional values'.

Constituencies Also known as ridings, these are the territories represented by members of Parliament. At present there are 301 constituencies—scheduled to become 309 at the next general election, to be held by 2005—the populations of which range from a low of about 30,000 to a high of roughly 200,000 constituents.

Constitution The fundamental law of a political system. In Canada it includes written components—chiefly the Constitution Acts—and unwritten conventions that are more or less established, such as the understanding that the calling of an election is the Prime Minister's prerogative.

Constitutional conventions Practices that emerge over time and are generally accepted as binding rules of the political system, such as the convention that the leader of the political party with the most seats in the House of Commons after an election shall be called upon to try to form a government with majority support in the House. Unlike the written Constitution, conventions are not enforceable in the courts.

Constitutional supremacy Section 52(1) of the Constitution Act, 1982 declares that 'The Constitution of Canada is the supreme law of Canada, and any law that is consistent with the provisions of the Constitution is, to the extent of the inconsistency, of no force or effect.' This means that the laws of all governments and their agencies must conform to the Constitution. Before the Constitution Act, 1982 came into force, Parliament and provincial legislatures were supreme so long as each acted within its own sphere of legislative competence. This was known as parliamentary supremacy.

Co-operative Commonwealth Federation (CCF) Predecessor to the New Democratic Party, the CCF was created in 1932 as an alliance of three main elements: disgruntled farmers, chiefly from western Canada, central Canadian intellectuals, and labour activists. The party first ran candidates in the 1935 federal election. Its founding policy document, the Regina Manifesto, called for extensive state planning and control of the economy, a steeply progressive income tax, and the creation of a welfare state.

Corporate elite Those who control the dominant corporations and investment firms in an economy. John Porter defined the term in *The Vertical Mosaic* (1965) to include the directors of Canada's dominant corporations, a usage that was followed by Wallace Clement and Milan Korac in their later studies of this elite. All of these researchers concluded that the Canadian corporate elite is a largely self-perpetuating group whose exclusive social backgrounds and activities set them apart form the general population.

Corporatism A political structure characterized by the direct participation of organizations representing business and labour in public policy-making.

'Court party' This term, first coined by Canadian political scientist Ted Morton, refers to those interest groups whose preferred venue for pursuing their policy objectives is the courts and whose preferred instrument for challenging laws is the Charter. The 'court party' consists chiefly of groups representing minorities and located primarily on the left of the political spectrum, including feminists, homosexuals, abortion rights advocates, official-language minorities, Aboriginals, and those accused of crimes or in prison.

Cultural hegemony According to Marxists and some elements within contemporary feminism, the values and beliefs of the dominant class or of males, respectively, are accepted as normal and inevitable by society as a whole, despite the fact that they are contrary to the true interests of subordinate classes or females.

Democracy A political system based on the formal equality of all citizens, in which there is a realistic possibility that voters can replace the government, and in which certain basic rights and freedoms are protected.

Dependence The limitations on a country's autonomy that may arise from its economic, cultural, or military ties to another country or countries. During the 1960s and 1970s it was popular on the left of Canadian politics to characterize Canada as a dependent satellite within the orbit of the United States. The ties between these two countries have not weakened since then, but it is now more common to view Canada's dependent condition within the broader framework of economic and cultural globalization.

Distinct society The Meech Lake Accord of 1987 proposed the amendment of the Constitution to recognize Quebec as a distinct society unlike other provincial societies. In both the Meech Lake and Charlottetown (1992) accords the distinct society clause was explicitly linked to the fact that Quebec is the only province in which a majority of the population is francophone and would have required the Quebec government to protect and promote the French language. In 1995 Parliament passed a resolution recognizing Quebec as a distinct society. It does not, however, have the force of constitutional law.

Economic disparities The gap between the prosperity and, consequently, the tax bases of Canada's provinces. For several decades Canadian governments have attempted to narrow the gap in the provinces' abilities to finance social services and other programs by providing equalization payments to the less affluent provinces.

Election Expenses Act, 1974 Before 1974 party and candidate spending on election campaign activities was essentially unregulated and there were no legal requirements that revenues and expenditures be publicly disclosed. The Election Expenses Act places spending limits on registered political parties and their candidates during election campaigns, allows for the reimbursement for part of the expenses of candidates who receive at least 15 per cent of the vote, and requires the public disclosure of all contributions of $100 or more to parties and candidates.

'End of Ideology' A thesis advanced by American sociologist Daniel Bell in the 1960s, which argued that traditional right/left ideological thinking had become irrelevant and outmoded as a consequence of a developing consensus on the desirability of the welfare state, government regulation of business, and political pluralism.

Entitlements What might be called social rights of citizenship, such as public education, pensions, welfare, and various forms of assistance for those in need. It is a concept associated with the welfare state and a redistributive ethic in public life.

Equalization Transfers made by Ottawa to provincial governments whose per capita tax revenues (according to a complex formula negotiated between Ottawa and the provinces) fall below the average of the two most affluent provinces. Equalization is the second largest federal transfer to the provinces, after the Canada Health and Social Transfer.

Estimates Sometimes referred to as the expenditure budget. Every year towards the end of February the government will table its spending estimates for the forthcoming fiscal year (1 April to 31 March) in the House of Commons.

Executive federalism A term often used to describe the relations between the Prime Minister and premiers and cabinet ministers of the two levels of government. The negotiations between them and the agreements they reach have often been undertaken with minimal, if any, input from their legislatures or the public.

False consciousness A Marxist concept describing the inability of subordinate social classes to see where their real interests lie and their acceptance of cultural values and beliefs that justify their exploitation by the dominant class.

Feminism A framework for interpreting and explaining politics and society that sees gender as the fundamental basis of conflict in society and associates politics, in all its forms, with the systemic domination of males over females.

Formal equality One of two different standards, the other being *substantive equality*, that may be applied by the courts to the Charter's equality guarantees. The formal equality standard requires that all individuals be treated the same under the law, regardless of the fact that the life circumstances of members of different groups may be significantly different and may affect the likelihood of their achieving constitutional guarantees of equality.

Fragment theory American historian Louis Hartz developed this theory, which maintains that the ideological development of New World societies such as Canada, settled by European colonization, was strongly determined by the social characteristics and cultural values of their early immigrants. Such societies were fragments of the Old World because their creation coincided with a particular ideological epoch in the Old World from which the founding immigrants came.

Free-rider problem As the number of members in an organization increases, the likelihood that some individuals will believe that they can reap the benefits of the organization's actions without having to contribute to it also increases.

Gender roles One of the fundamental premises of much of contemporary feminism is that male and female genders are socially constructed. As Simone de Beauvoir put it, 'One is not born, but rather becomes, a woman.' This premise provides the intellectual basis for attacks on many of the traditional roles and expectations associated with males and females. A spirited debate exists between those who argue that gender roles are fundamentally socially constructed and those who maintain that biological differences between the sexes provide the basis for many of the important differences in male and female behaviour, aptitudes, and preferences.

Globalization The increasing interdependence of states, economies, and societies throughout the world, a phenomenon characterized by, among other things, dramatically higher levels of international trade and capital mobility than in the past, cultural convergence in terms of consumer tastes between societies, particularly in the developed countries of the world, and the emergence of international institutions for the development and enforcement of economic and human rights standards.

Government The elected individuals and party controlling the state at a particular point in time.

Human rights All the basic rights and freedoms of citizens. Also called 'civil liberties' or 'civil rights', these include political rights, democratic rights, legal rights, economic rights, equality rights. Other human rights can include language rights, social entitlements, and environmental rights.

Ideology A set of interrelated beliefs about how society is organized and how it ought to function.

Influence A form of power that depends on the ability of a person or group of persons to persuade others that it is reasonable and/or in their self-interest to behave in a particular way (e.g., to vote for a particular candidate or party).

Infotainment A hybrid television form that packages news and public affairs reporting in an entertainment format that typically includes a 'celebrity journalist/host', short analysis that emphasizes action, confrontation, and controversy, and relatively little historical and background information. It is sometimes called 'soft news'.

Institutional groups Interest groups characterized by a high degree of organizational sophistication, the distinguishing features of which include organizational continuity, stable membership, extensive knowledge of sectors of government that affect their members and easy access to public officials in these sectors, concrete and immediate objectives, and overall organizational goals that are more important than any specific objective.

Intrastate federalism The representation and accommodation of regional interests within national political institutions such as the Senate. In Canada, federalism has operated mainly through intergovernmental relations. Intrastate federalism, while often argued to be a means of overcoming decentralist tendencies in Canada, has not achieved much success.

Intra vires From the Latin, meaning within its strength, a judicial ruling of intra vires means that a legislature has acted within its constitutional competence.

Iron triangle An American term used to describe the closed system of relations between an interest group and the administrative or regulatory agencies and congressional committees with which the group normally deals.

JPMs Acronym for 'jolts-per-minute', a term coined by Canadian media analyst Morris Wolfe to refer to what he calls The First Law of Commercial Television: 'Thou shalt give them enough jolts per minute or thou shalt lose them.'

Judicial independence The principle according to which judges should be free from any and all interference in their decision-making. It is particularly important that they be free from interference by the government to ensure that the courts are seen to be independent and non-partisan. One of the key protections for judicial independence is the fact that once appointed they cannot be removed from office before retirement age, usually 75, except for serious cause (such as criminal behaviour or serious incompetence).

Judicial restraint The practice of judges deferring to the will of elected governments when their laws and actions are challenged as being unconstitutional. Before the Charter was passed in 1982, it was extremely rare for Canadian courts to declare duly passed laws unconstitutional, unless they were *ultra vires*. Section 1 of the Charter, the reasonable limits clause, provides the courts with the opportunity to defer to elected public officials. However, many critics charge that the tradition of judicial restraint has been replaced by American-style judicial activism.

Legitimacy The acceptance by most people that the rules and institutions comprising the state are fair and should be obeyed. It is closely related to the concept of consent in democracies.

Liberalism Historically, an individualistic ideology associated with freedom of religious choice and practice, free enterprise and free trade, and freedom of expression and association in politics. During the latter half of the twentieth century in Canada and the United States, liberalism came to be associated with support for the welfare state, the protection of minority rights, and the regulation of business.

Libertarianism The belief that individuals should be allowed the largest possible margin of freedom in all realms of life, including those that involve moral choices. Although often thought of as an ideologically conservative stance, libertarians are more likely to align themselves with people and groups thought of as left-leaning on such issues as abortion, homosexual rights, and banning prayer from public schools.

Lobbying Any form of direct or indirect communication with public officials that is intended to influence public policy. Although often associated in the public mind with unfair privilege and corruption, lobbying is not limited to organizations representing the powerful and is not inherently undemocratic.

Loyalism The value system associated with the Loyalists, those who opposed the American Revolution and who migrated north to the British colonies after the defeat of the British in the American War of Independence. Their ideological beliefs have been the subject of much debate, but there is a consensus that they brought

to Canada a loyalty to the British Crown and to that which was deemed 'British' and a rejection of the developing American identity.

Maîtres chez nous The Quebec Liberal Party's 1962 election campaign slogan, meaning 'masters in our own house'. It captured the new spirit of Quebec nationalism that emerged during the period of the Quiet Revolution.

Manufacturing consent Phrase originally used by Walter Lippmann to refer to government's use of propagandistic techniques to cultivate popular acceptance of its rule. It is also the title of a 1988 book by Noam Chomsky and Edward Herman, in which they argue that the privately owned and oligopolistic media system in the United States—and, according to like-minded critics, in Canada as well—fosters popular consent for a social system that operates mainly in the interests of a privileged minority.

Marxism A framework for interpreting and explaining politics and society that sees class divisions as the fundamental basis of conflict in society and associates politics with a pervasive pattern of domination by those who own and control the means of creating and distributing wealth over those who do not.

Materialism Stresses economic security, material well-being, and acquisition; consequently, incomes and employment are of greater concern than human rights or the environment, for example.

Maternal feminism Also called social feminism, this describes the early women's movement from the late 1800s to the early twentieth century. Maternal feminism accepted the assumption that the biological differences between men and women provided the basis for their different social roles, women being by nature more caring about life and the conditions that nurture it. They fought for legal and political reforms that they expected would improve the conditions of women and their families. The temperance movement was clearly allied to maternal feminism, for the simple reason that alcohol was widely seen as one of the chief threats to the security of women and their families.

Ministerial responsibility The obligation of a cabinet minister to explain and defend in the legislature—and, ultimately, to be responsible for—the policies and actions of his or her department.

Minority government A situation where no single political party controls a majority of seats in the House of Commons. In such circumstances the party with the largest number of seats will require the support of at least some members of one or more other parties in order to win votes in the House of Commons and govern. The most recent minority government in Canada was the short-lived Joe Clark Conservative government of 1979, which lost a budget vote less than a year after taking office. Before that, the Trudeau Liberals governed from 1972 to 1974 with a minority by acquiescing to the NDP on some issues and then regained a majority in the 1974 election. Majority government, when one party controls most of the seats in the House, is more common in Canada.

Mobility of capital   Producers and investors enjoy a wide, but not absolute, freedom to shift their operations or investments between sectors of the economy and from one national economy to another. This mobility of capital is a major reason why governments must be concerned with business confidence and will often be reluctant to take measures that, while politically popular, may offend important business interests.

Multiculturalism   A value system based on the premise that ethnic and cultural identities and traditions are important to human happiness and dignity and that public policy ought to recognize, support, and promote the retention of these identities and traditions. In Canada an official policy of multiculturalism has existed since 1971. The Charter of Rights and Freedoms acknowledges the 'multicultural heritage of Canadians' and the Multiculturalism Act, 1988 commits the Canadian government to a policy of promoting multiculturalism. This is done largely through the Department of Canadian Heritage.

Multilateralism   An approach to the resolution of problems that relies on collective decision-making through international organizations such as the UN, the International Criminal Court, NATO, and the WTO. It is based on an assumption that member states should be willing to give up some national sovereignty and accept the decisions of multilateral organizations to which they belong.

Nation   A group of people who share a sense of being a community based on religion, language, ethnicity, a shared history, or some combination of these. See also Box 1.4.

National Action Committee on the Status of Women   An umbrella organization that represents roughly 700 women's organizations across Canada. During the 1980s the NAC was generally viewed by the media and government as the major organizational voice for the women's movement, and most of the group's revenue came from the federal government. In recent years, however, the NAC has experienced a loss of status in the eyes of policy-makers, many of whom accuse it of being out of touch with the mainstream concerns of women, and government financial support for the organization has fallen dramatically.

National Energy Policy (1981)   Nationalist economic policy that limited the price that could be charged in Canada for oil and gas from Canadian sources and provided preferential tax treatment for Canadian-owned companies investing in the petroleum sector. It was viewed by Alberta as a thinly disguised subsidy that their province—Canada's leading petroleum producer—was made to pay to the petroleum-consuming populations and industries of central Canada. The NEP was opposed by multinational petroleum companies and the American government as discriminating against foreign investors.

National Policy (1878-9)   The Conservative Party's election platform in 1878, this nation-building strategy began to be implemented in 1879. Its three components included a significant increase in protective tariffs to promote manufacturing in Ontario and Quebec, construction of a transcontinental railroad, and encouragement of western settlement to expand the market for the manufactured products of central Canada and to protect this territory from American encroachment.

National standards   Rules established by the federal government that apply to areas of provincial jurisdiction, particularly health care and social assistance. For example, the Canada Health Act, 1984 prohibits extra-billing by doctors and imposes financial penalties on provinces that allow the practice. The enforcement of national standards depends primarily on the fact that Ottawa transfers money to the provinces to pay for certain social programs.

Neo-institutionalism   A perspective on policy-making that emphasizes the impact of formal and informal structures and rules on political outcomes. The roots of this perspective lie in economics, organization theory, and a reaction to society-centred approaches to understanding politics and policy.

News management   The practice of organizing press conferences, photo opportunities, and other planned events in ways that accommodate the media's need for images and information that are available by newspaper/broadcaster deadlines and in a form likely to be attractive to readers or viewers.

North American Free Trade Agreement   A treaty signed by Canada, Mexico, and the United States, under which most duties on goods and services traded between these economies are eliminated and the treatment of each country's investors is, with some limited exceptions, the same as that of domestic investors. Critics claimed that NAFTA would produce a huge exodus of manufacturing jobs to lower-wage Mexico, but employment has grown in both Canada and the US since the agreement came into effect in 1993.

Notwithstanding clause Section 33 of the Charter of Rights and Freedoms, which states that either Parliament or a provincial legislature may expressly declare that a law shall operate even if it contravenes the fundamental freedoms (s. 2), legal rights (ss. 7-14), or equality rights (s. 15) in the Charter. This clause has been invoked rarely, most controversially by the Quebec government in 1989.

Oakes **test** Established by the Supreme Court of Canada, this is a test that the courts apply in determining whether a law or government action that contravenes a right or freedom guaranteed by the Charter is nevertheless constitutional under the 'reasonable limits' section of the Charter (s. 1). To be considered 'reasonable', a limitation must be based on an important public policy goal and must be proportionate to the importance of this goal.

Ottawa mandarins 'Mandarins', the term given to high officials in the ancient Chinese empire, was applied to the coterie of top officials, particularly deputy ministers and the governor of the Bank of Canada, who dominated federal policy-making during the period of the 1940s to the 1960s.

Paid access opportunities Fundraising events, i.e., dinners and cocktail parties, where, for a donation that can range up to several thousand dollars, donors receive the opportunity to meet and exchange views with party leaders or cabinet ministers.

Paramountcy In areas of *concurrent powers*, where both Ottawa and the provinces have the constitutional authority to pass laws, the Constitution specifies which government's laws will be paramount (i.e., take precedence) in the event of a conflict. Ottawa, for example, has paramountcy in the areas of agriculture and immigration, and the provinces have paramountcy in public pensions.

Parliamentary supremacy This means that Parliament's authority is superior to that of all other institutions of government. In concrete terms this means that the courts will not second-guess the right of the legislature to pass any law, on any subject, as long as it does not involve a matter that, under the Constitution, is properly legislated on by another level of government. Parliamentary supremacy was effectively replaced by *constitutional supremacy* as a result of the Constitution Act, 1982.

Party discipline The practice of MPs belonging to the same party voting as a unified bloc in the way directed by their leader. This practice is based on a combination of reasons, the foremost being the understanding that the government is required to resign if it loses an important vote in the House of Commons. The Prime Minister and other party leaders control various levers that can be used to maintain party discipline, including expulsion of a member from party caucus, withholding promotion or other rewards from an MP, or refusing to allow him or her to run as the party's candidate in the next election.

Patronage The awarding of favours, such as contracts, jobs, or public spending in a community, in exchange for political support. This was the central preoccupation of Canadian politics during the first several decades after Confederation. It continues to be an important practice in Canada and other democracies, although when the exchange of support for government largesse is too obvious this is seen by many to border on corruption.

Peace, order, and good government (POGG) The preamble to section 91 of the Constitution Act, 1867 includes this clause, which has been interpreted by some as a general grant of legislative power to the federal government. Over time, however, court rulings reduced POGG to an emergency power that can only provide the constitutional basis for federal actions in special circumstances. In a 1977 decision, the Supreme Court indicated that it would not be quick to question Parliament's judgement that special circumstances, warranting legislation under the authority of POGG, exist.

Personal is political The slogan of the modern feminist movement that emerged in the 1960s, 'the personal is political' expresses the feminist view that the roots of gender inequality are found in structured male-female relations throughout society and that therefore the achievement of equality for women requires that attitudes and practices in the home, school, workplace, media, and elsewhere must be changed.

Persons **case, 1929** In this decision of the Judicial Committee of the Privy Council, the JCPC overturned a Supreme Court of Canada ruling that women were not considered persons for purposes of holding certain public offices.

Pluralism An explanation of politics that sees organized interests as the central fact of political life and explains politics chiefly in terms of the activities of groups.

Policy community The constellation of state and societal actors active in a particular policy field.

Policy network The nature of relations among the actors in a *policy community*.

Political faction A group of citizens whose goals and behaviour are contrary to those of other groups or to the interests of the community as a whole.

Political identities An identity is a state of mind, a sense of belonging to a community that is defined by its language, ethnic origins, religion, regional location, gender, or some other social or cultural characteristics. Identities become political when those who share them make demands on the state or when the state recognizes a group identity as a reason for treating a group's members in a special way.

Politics The activity by which rival claims are settled by public authorities. See Box 1.1.

Populism A vision of politics based on the premise that the general population should have as many opportunities as possible to participate directly in political decision-making and that those elected to govern ought to view themselves as delegates of the people and therefore obliged to reflect their preferences. Populists favour recall votes to remove unfaithful public officials, plebiscites and referendums, short terms of office and term limits for public officials, and citizen initiatives to force action on an issue or policy proposal. They oppose party discipline.

Post-materialism Emphasizes human needs for belonging, self-esteem, and personal fulfillment; consequently, high value is placed on quality-of-life issues such as the environment, group equality, and human rights.

Poverty lines Statistics Canada has established what it calls 'low-income cut-offs' that are routinely referred to by journalists, politicians, academics, and others as 'poverty lines'. These cut-offs or poverty lines represent a relative measure of low income, currently defined to mean that more than 56.2 per cent of income (20 percentage points above the national average) is spent on food, clothing, and shelter. This method of measuring need was changed in late May 2003 when Statistics Canada and Human Resources Development Canada introduced a 'market basket measure' that would have the effect of fewer people being considered as living below the poverty line.

Power The ability to influence what happens. It may assume various forms, including coercion, influence (persuasion), and authority.

Prime ministerial government The argument made in recent years by commentators such as Jeffrey Simpson and Donald Savoie that the concentration of power in the hands of the Prime Minister and his advisers has reached unprecedented levels and that both Parliament and cabinet have been relegated to the margins of the policy-making process. While both Simpson and Savoie suggest that the development of prime ministerial government was partly due to the leadership style of Liberal Prime Minister Jean Chrétien, they argue that there are more fundamental and enduring factors that have contributed to this concentration of power.

Privy Council Essentially the cabinet, under the leadership of the Prime Minister. Formally, however, anyone who has ever been a member of cabinet retains the title of privy councillor, but only those who are members of the government of the day exercise the constitutional and legal powers associated with the Privy Council.

Propaganda The promotion of a particular ideology or view on public policy by the public media dissemination of selected information and/or misinformation. Although propaganda is commonly understood to be a tool used by non-democratic governments to mislead and deceive the populace, powerful economic interests and governments in democratic societies are able to use the media system for what are essentially propagandistic purposes.

Proportional representation Under this system, variants of which exist in many European countries, the number of seats that a party receives in the legislature is based roughly on the share of the popular vote cast for that party.

Protest parties Political parties that have arisen out of dissatisfaction with the operation of brokerage politics in Canada and what has been seen, particularly in western Canada, as the inability of the Liberal and Conservative parties to represent certain regional interests. The Reform Party (now Canadian Alliance), created in 1987, is the most recent of these parties. Others have included the Progressives, Social Credit, the Western Canada Concept, and the early Co-operative Commonwealth Federation.

Province-building The phenomenon of powerful provincial governments creating large and competent bureaucracies and using the various constitutional, legal, taxation, and public opinion levers available to them in order to increase their control over activities and interests within their provincial borders and, in consequence, vis-à-vis Ottawa. Province-building is most often associated with Alberta in the 1970s and Quebec during the 1960s and 1970s, but is observed more generally in several provinces at various points in time.

Purchasing power parities (PPPS) A measure of average real purchasing power that takes into account both average nominal incomes and what a standardized currency unit can purchase in a country. Although average nominal incomes are much higher in many countries than in Canada, if PPPS are used to measure standardized purchasing power Canadians are among the most affluent people in the world.

Quality of life (QOL) This concept may refer to the level of satisfaction with life that members of a society experience, their material well-being, their level of health, the state of their environment, the level of equality between groups, or some combination of these. The United Nations annually ranks countries according to its 'human development index', which combines various factors, including literacy, infant mortality, average life expectancy, average income, and average years of formal education. This UN index is accepted by some as a measure of QOL.

Québécois de souche Quebecers, and more specifically francophone Quebecers, whose roots in the province go back many generations. The term is used to distinguish what in English might be called old-stock Quebecers from more recent arrivals whose first language usually is not French and whose cultural heritage is not French Canadian. A similar term is '*Québécois pur laine*' (pure wool Quebecers). This distinction between old-stock Quebecers and others is objected to by some as being fundamentally discriminatory, but others maintain that the attachment of immigrants to the French language and Quebec's distinctive culture has often been weak.

Quiet Revolution The early 1960s in Quebec when the provincial Liberal government of Jean Lesage reorganized and developed the Quebec state to take control of important institutions such as education and the economy. During the Lesage years (1960–6) the conservative traditional nationalism was swept away by a more aggressive Quebec nationalism that turned to the Quebec state as the chief instrument for the modernization of Quebec society and the advancement of francophone interests.

Rattrapage French for 'catching up', this was one of the key goals of the anti-establishment challenge to the conservative ideology and elites that dominated Quebec during the 1940s and 1950s. *Rattrapage* involved bringing Quebec's society, economy, and government up to the level of development that existed in the rest of Canada, a goal that required a larger and more interventionist provincial government

Reasonable limits Section 1 of the Charter of Rights and Freedoms states that the rights and freedoms guaranteed by the Charter are subject to 'such reasonable limits prescribed by law as can be demonstrably justified in a free and democratic society'. See also *Oakes test*.

Receptive bilinguals People who are capable of responding to French communication but do not themselves initiate conversations in French, consume French-language media, or seek out opportunities to live in their acquired second language.

Red Toryism The belief system associated with Canadian conservatives who believe that government has a responsibility to act as an agent for the collective good and that this responsibility goes far beyond maintaining law and order. Red Tories have supported the creation of public enterprises to achieve a range of cultural and economic goals and are generally supportive of Canadian nationalism.

Reform Party Founded in 1987 under the slogan 'The West wants in', it became the Canadian Alliance Party in 2000. The Reform Party emerged out of the feelings of alienation that peaked in western Canada during the 1980s, triggered by the Conservative government's 1987 decision to award a major defence contract to Quebec instead of Manitoba and the widespread view that whether the Liberal or Conservative Party was in power federally, western interests would continue to be sacrificed to those of central Canada.

Regionalism A political identity based on a shared sense of place. It may be linked to a variety of cultural, economic, institutional, and historical factors that tend to distinguish the inhabitants of one region of a country from those of other regions.

Repertory of stereotypes A term coined by Walter Lippmann, it refers to the media's tendency to fit current news to a limited number of stereotypes that make news stories more easily understandable for audiences/readers, but that also sacrifice nuance and even distort the news by squeezing it into a familiar package.

Representative bureaucracy The practice of hiring and promotion so that the composition of the bureaucracy reflects in fair proportion the representation of demographic characteristics in society. In Canada, the concept and practice of representative bureaucracy were first applied to increase the share of francophones in the public service. Since the 1980s it has been expanded to include women, Aboriginal people, visible minorities, and disabled persons.

Representative democracy A form of democracy in which citizens delegate law-making authority to elected representatives, holding them responsible for their actions through periodic elections.

Responsible government The constitutional principle according to which the Prime Minister and cabinet require the support of a majority of members in the House of Commons in order to govern. If the government can no longer maintain majority support in the House, in other words, if it loses the confidence of the House, it is compelled by constitutional convention to resign.

Revanche des berceaux French for 'revenge of the cradles', a term that referred to the high birth rate that enabled French Canada to maintain its numerical strength vis-à-vis English Canada from Confederation until the 1960s. Since then the birth rate in predominantly francophone Quebec has fallen to one of the lowest provincial rates in Canada. This, combined with non-francophone immigration to Canada and the assimilation of francophones outside Quebec, has contributed to a gradual decline in the francophone share of Canada's population.

Revenue budget A taxation budget presented from time to time in Parliament, announcing changes to the taxation system. Whereas the expenditure budget (*estimates*) is tied to a regular cycle of decision-making, a new revenue budget may be tabled at any time as, in the government's view, conditions require.

Revolution and counter-revolution American sociologist Seymour Martin Lipset argues in *Revolution and Counter-Revolution* (1960) that the political histories and ideological development of the United States and Canada have been significantly marked by the American Revolution of 1776. The political values, symbols, and institutions of the United States have been based on the liberal ideas of the Revolution while, historically, those in Canada have been based on a rejection of what the Revolution stood for.

Right, left, and centre Labels that signify a range of ideological beliefs from collectivist (left) at one end of the spectrum to individualistic (right) at the other, with those in the middle ground (centre) embracing elements from both extremes.

Royal Commission on Bilingualism and Biculturalism This federal Royal Commission was created in 1963 in response to the new assertive nationalism of the Quiet Revolution. The B&B Commission recommended numerous reforms aimed at protecting the rights of the francophone minority outside Quebec and transforming the federal government into a more bilingual institution. The Official Languages Act, 1969, embodied some of the recommendations made by the B&B Commission.

Rule of law A vital principle of democratic government, it means that the actions of governments and their agents must be based on the authority of law and that all persons, the governed and those who govern, are subject to the same laws.

Separation of powers A constitutional principle, supported by s. 24 of the Charter, that guarantees the special role of the judiciary, without interference from the legislature or the executive, to interpret what the law and the Constitution mean when disputes arise.

Sexism Term coined during the 1960s as a label for behaviour that treats males and females unequally for no other reason than the fact of being male or female.

Shared-cost programs Provincially administered programs, such as those in the field of health care, to which Ottawa contributes money earmarked for a particular program. During the 1960s and 1970s it was common for Ottawa's contribution to be determined by how much a province spent on such a program. Since the late 1970s successive federal governments have abandoned this model in favour of *block funding*.

Single-member, simple-plurality electoral system An electoral system under which each member of the legislature is elected to represent a particular *constituency*, receiving this right when he or she receives more votes than any other single candidate in the election held in that constituency. It is not necessary to receive a majority of the votes cast in a constituency and most successful candidates do not.

Socialism An ideology based on the principle of equality of condition. Historically, socialists led the fight for a greater state role in managing the economy, better working conditions and rights for workers, and the egalitarian and redistributive policies associated with the welfare state. Modern socialists, or social democrats, often temper their advocacy of an egalitarian society with an acceptance of capitalism and the inequalities that inevitably are generated by a market economy.

Socio-economic mobility The ability of individuals, families, and groups to move from one social or economic position to another. Where socio-economic mobility is high, movement up and down the social ladder is relatively common and the barriers to entry into high-paying occupations, prestigious status groups, or powerful elites are relatively low.

Soft power Term coined by American scholar Joseph Nye to describe forms of international influence based on culture, values, and the perceived legitimacy of a nation's international aims, rather than on armaments, sanctions, and coercion. Soft power is associated with *multilateralism* and support for international structures of governance and problem resolution such as the UN and the International Criminal Court.

Sovereignty-association A term generally understood to mean that a politically sovereign (independent) Quebec would continue to be linked to Canada through some sort of commercial union, free trade agreement, and shared currency. Sovereignty-association was the option proposed to Quebecers in the 1980 referendum.

Split-run publications American magazines, such as *Time* and *Sports Illustrated*, that published a Canadian edition at low cost by importing the American version via satellite, adding some pages of Canadian content, and thereby qualifying for the same advertising rates that apply to Canadian-based magazines.

State The structures through which public authority is exercised, including the legislature, bureaucracy, courts, police, armed forces, and other publicly owned or controlled institutions, such as schools and hospitals. See Box 1.2.

State capacity A term used in a 2002 UN report on globalization to refer to a state's ability to maintain social safety nets and pursue non-market goals such as protection of the environment and promotion of equality. This report suggested that a 'deficit' in state capacity, resulting from low levels of training and professionalism, inadequate technology, and corruption, impedes the ability of many developing countries to take advantage of economic opportunities presented by globalization.

Substantive equality An approach to the interpretation of equality rights and s. 15 of the Charter premised on the idea that individuals may experience advantages or disadvantages as a result of belonging to a particular group and that their equality rights claims should be judged against the reality of these group-based inequalities in society. This approach rejects the concept of *formal equality* that treating all individuals identically under the law can guarantee equality.

Suffragists Advocates of the right to vote for women. Many of the early suffragists supported female enfranchisement on the grounds that women voters would inject a morally uplifting element into politics. Nellie McClung was Canada's best-known suffragist.

Survivance, la. French for 'survival'. *La survivance* captures the conservative character of traditional French-Canadian nationalism, focused as it was on preserving the religious and linguistic heritage of French Canada in the face of assimilationist pressures.

Systemic discrimination Discrimination without conscious individual intent. Systemic discrimination inheres in traditions, customary practices, rules, laws, and institutions that have the effect of placing the members of one or more ascriptive groups at a disadvantage compared to other groups.

'The higher, the fewer' Canadian political scientist Sylvia Bashevkin's characterization of the fact that, although female participation levels in politics are about the same as men's for activities like voting and campaigning, the proportion of women tends to decrease as the political activity becomes more demanding, such as holding office in a political party or being a candidate for public office.

Totalitarianism A system of government that suppresses all dissent in the name of some supreme goal.

Two-nations theory Canada, viewed from this perspective, is fundamentally a partnership between two ethnolinguistic communities or nations, one French-speaking and the other English-speaking. This premise underlies such constitutional proposals as a Quebec right of veto over constitutional reform and recognition of Quebec as a distinct society. Although the two-nations theory continues to enjoy popularity among French-Canadian nationalists and some English-Canadian intellectuals, it appears to have much less public support in English-speaking Canada.

Tyranny of the majority Alexis de Tocqueville used this term in *Democracy in America* (1835) to refer to the danger that majoritarian democracy might oppress the rights of minorities.

Ultra vires From the Latin, meaning beyond its strength; a judicial ruling of ultra vires means that a legislative act is beyond or outside the constitutional power or authority of that legislature.

Unholy alliance The term that critics sometimes applied to the three pillars of the conservative Quebec establishment during the 1940s and 1950s: the Catholic Church, anglophone capital, and the Union Nationale under the leadership of *le chef*, Maurice Duplessis.

Universal Declaration of Human Rights A declaration passed by the United Nations in 1948 that provides the basis for various international covenants to which Canada is a signatory, such as the International Covenant on Civil and Political Rights and the International Covenant on Economic, Social and Cultural Rights.

Vertical mosaic The title of a 1965 book by Canadian sociologist John Porter in which he argued that Canadian society was characterized by a vertical mosaic of patterned inequality between different ethnic and religious groups. See also *corporate elite.*

Welfare gap The difference between total welfare income (social assistance benefits, child tax benefits, and federal and provincial sales tax credits) and the low-income cut-offs established by Statistics Canada. See Figure 3.5.

Western alienation A belief held by many in western Canada, but particularly in Alberta and British Columbia, that Ottawa and the mainstream political parties are by and large insensitive to the interests and preferences of western Canadians. The roots of this sentiment go back to the high tariff policies and freight rates of the federal government from the late nineteenth century.

Regional parties of protest such as the Progressives after World War I and the *Reform Party*, predecessor to today's Canadian Alliance, have emerged from this sense of regional grievance.

Women's liberation This term came into widespread use during the 1960s to refer to the struggle for equal rights for women. Feminist intellectuals such as Betty Friedan, Germaine Greer, and Gloria Steinem were among the leaders of the women's liberation movement. The character and demands of the movement were to some degree influenced by the black civil rights movement in the United States, feminist leaders drawing parallels between the systematic oppression and subordination of blacks and what they argued was the rather similar treatment of women.

INDEX

Note: *Italic page number indicates Figure.*

CKKD

OCT 0 2 2003
MAR 0 9 2004
APR 4 2004
DEC 1 0 2004
JAN 1 0 2005
DEC 2 1 2005

BRODART   Cat. No. 23 233   Printed in U.S.A